RAS MALA

RAS MALA;

OR,

HINDOO ANNALS

OF THE

PROVINCE OF GOOZERAT,

IN

WESTERN INDIA.

BY THE LATE

ALEXANDER KINLOCH FORBES

GYAN

Published by

Gyan Publishing House
5, Ansari Road
Daryaganj, New Delhi-110002
Phone: 011-47034999, 9811692060
E-mail: books@gyanbooks.com

Distribution Network
gyanbooks.com
India, USA, Canada, UK, Australia, France

ISBN: 978-81-212-7103-5 (PB)
First Published, 1856

2nd Impression 2024

Printed at: Gyan Press, Delhi.

RAS MALA
Author: ALEXANDER KINLOCH FORBES

SKETCH MAP OF GOOZERAT AND SORETH.

RÂS MÂLÂ;

रास माला

OR,

HINDOO ANNALS

OF THE

PROVINCE OF GOOZERAT,

IN

WESTERN INDIA.

BY THE LATE

ALEXANDER KINLOCH FORBES,

Of the Honorable East India Company's Civil Service.

NEW EDITION.

WITH AN INTRODUCTION BY MAJOR J. W. WATSON, B.S.C.,

AND A

MEMOIR OF THE AUTHOR BY A. K. NAIRNE, ESQ., B.C.S.

LONDON:
RICHARDSON AND CO., 13, PALL MALL.
1878.

INTRODUCTION.

SINCE the Râs Mâlâ was first published, in 1856, there has been an increasing demand for a fresh edition, and it is to satisfy this demand that the present reprint has been put through the press.

Though professing to be a mere collection of legends, or garland of chronicles, the Râs Mâlâ is in fact the first and most important epitome of the history of Goozerat hitherto made. It is the work of a profound and accurate scholar, pervaded by a thorough and intelligent sympathy with the people whose historical phases and domestic life he has in this work so vividly depicted. And though the Author in his original Preface modestly disclaimed for his book all pretensions to a scientific character, the work is in truth eminently scientific, and shows us Goozerat under each of the great dynasties which have swayed her destinies; and whether under the Wullubhee kings, the Châvaḍâs or Châlookyas of Unhilwârâ, the renowned Sultans of Goozerat, or the even more famous house of Timur the lame; whether he describes Goozerat under the Guikowâr or the Guelphs, we find his pictures not only true but pleasing, not only accurate but interesting.

When, too, we consider the vastness of the field of time comprehended in this single volume, stretching as it does from the days of the half-fabulous monarchs of Wullubhee to the middle of the nineteenth century after Christ, it must be conceded that Mr. Forbes has most ably acquitted himself of his interesting task, and it is impossible to say what a debt of gratitude is due from all Goozerat officials to the Author of the Râs Mâlâ. He has brought home to us no less Sidh Râj, "the Lion of Victory," and the politic Koomâr Pâl, than Ahmed Shah, or the gallant Mahmood Begurra—the one the founder of that proud city on the banks of the Sâbhermutee, which the Mohummedan historians loved to call the "ornament of cities," and the other the conqueror alike of Gurh, Girnâr, and Powan-gurh Châmpâner; while, at the same time, he has shown us the Emperor Akbar and Dâmâjee Guikowâr, and described the first advent of the British power.

It is easiest to picture what the official mind would be without him, by referring to the obsolete opinions held on most important questions of tenure, &c., as shown in the old Revenue Selections; though indeed we also find there that the lucid intellect of Elphinstone had already thrown much light upon the subject, and had prevented grievous injustice being done to large classes of landed proprietors. Still, even now it is most instructive to read any of the Government selections relating to Goozerat after a careful study of Râs Mâlâ.

When, too, it is borne in mind that, excepting the Râs Mâlâ, there is no other work which affords any check to the mass of error that may be found in most of the Government Selections relating to Goozerat, and when we also remember that not only are these Selections liberally quoted by parties in any ordinary dispute, but often accepted by Government itself, as works laying down dicta from which there can be no appeal, it is easy to picture the benefit conferred by the Râs Mâlâ on Government officials of every class.

To give an example of some of these errors I will quote from one of the best Selections,—I refer to that containing Colonel Walker's reports on the province of Kâteewâr,—and from that select one of the most interesting reports, viz., that on Soreth.

At paragraph 32 Colonel Walker speaks of Sher Khân Bâbi, a scion of one of the noblest Mohummedan families in the province, whose father and grandfather before him had governed large districts, as "a soldier of fortune."

Lower down, in paragraph 37, we find the following astounding statement, viz., "Sher Khân did not long survive his establishment "in Soreth. He was succeeded by his son Salâbat Khân, who "shortly afterwards retired to Goozerat, and left his son Bahâdoor

"Khân at Joonâgadh in possession of the Government." The reader will probably be surprised to hear that Sher Khân long survived his establishment in Soreth; that so far from his being succeeded by his son Salâbat Khân, Salâbat Khân was his (Sher Khân's) father, and that Bahâdoor Khân so far from being his grandson, was Sher Khân himself, Bahâdoor Khân being the style assumed by Sher Khân after becoming independent at Joonâgurh.

And so again in paragraph 49:—"Salâbat Khân bequeathed to his "sons Dillut Khân and Zemân Khân, who were junior to Bahâdoor "Khân, the district of Bântwâ." The truth being that Bântwâ never belonged to Salâbat Khân, and that Diler Khân and Sher Zamân Khân (not Dillut Khân and Zemân Khân) succeeded their father in his jâgir of Goghâ, but were thence expelled by Sohrâb Khân, who afterwards, through the influence of Burhân-ool-Moolk at the court of Delhi, obtained not only the jâgirdari of Goghâ from the Bâbis, but also the Naib-Foujdâri of Soreth; and it was when exercising these latter functions that he granted Bântwâ in jâgir to Diler Khân and Sher Zamân Khân, as he saw the imprudence of alienating this influential family.

Now the Râs Mâlâ is almost always accurate, and even where possibly better versions of historical facts may be offered than those accepted by Mr. Forbes, it will invariably be found that he had the best authority then available for his statements. The researches of Dr. Bühler[1] show that the four kings of the name of Sheelâditya, mentioned at page 16 of the Râs Mâlâ, may be increased to five. Dr. Bühler gives the date of this fifth monarch as St. 441 of the at present unknown era, and this prolongation of the rule of the Wullubhee line may perhaps eventually show that the Mlechh destroyers of this renowned city were some of the earlier Musalmân invaders; even though the name of another king be not discovered, and added to those of the eighteen of the line at present known.

With regard to the Solunkhee kings of Unhilwârâ, Dr. Bühler's researches have (see his "eleven land grants of the Chaulukyas of

[1] Indian Antiquary, part lxiii., for January, 1877.

"Unhilwâd") shown us cause to believe that the story of Mool Râj's arrival at Sâmunt Singh's court, as given by Mr. Forbes, on the authority of the Prubundh Chintâmunee, is a fabrication cf the chroniclers and bards, and that in reality Mool Râj conquered the Sarasvatimandal by force of arms. He gives good reasons why we should consider the Kuleeân, where Mool Râj's father ruled, was, as stated by the chroniclers, in the Kânouj dominions, and that it is not the Kuleeân near Bombay, as supposed by Mr. Forbes (Râs Mâlâ) and by Mr. Elphinstone. He modifies the date ascribed by Mr. Forbes to Bheem Dev I., and adds a new monarch, Treehoowun Pâl (S. 1299), as a twelfth sovereign. Dr. Bühler further shows that the dismemberment of the Unhilwârâ kingdom and the establishment of an independent principality by Luwun Prusâd, the Wâghelâ chieftain of Dholkâ, took place during the reign of Bheem Dev II. Luwun Prusâd was succeeded by his son Veer Dhuwul, and Dr. Bühler shows that Veesul Dev, Veer Dhuwul's successor, displaced Treehoowun Pâl on the throne of Unhilwârâ, probably by force of arms. It would seem from local tradition in Goozerat that Veesul Dev made Dubhoee his capital previous to the conquest of Unhilwârâ Puttun, and it is probable that any inscriptions found at Dubhoee may elucidate this point. The Waghelâs, who derived their name from the township of Wâghel, in North Goozerat (now under Râdhanpoor), were the most renowned branch of the Solunkhees in Goozerat, and a local poem celebrating the nine branches of the Solunkhees commences, "The greatest branch is that of Wâghel; "consider them most excellent Solunkhees."

Dr. Bühler, at page 5 of his pamphlet on the Chalookyas of Unhilwârâ, points out that the reason of the information given in the Râs Mâlâ being scanty is that Somesvara's "Kirtikaumudi," Râjasekhara's "Prabandh Kosha," and Harshagani's "Vastoopâlacharitra" were not available when Mr. Forbes wrote.

There are of course inaccuracies in dates in cases where legends are faithfully copied, for all legends are notoriously untrustworthy in such matters. A curious instance occurs in the account of the Gohil clan, where Rânjee Gohil, the father, is represented as expelled from

Rânpoor by Mahmood Begurrâ while Mokherâjee, Gohil, the son, is slain in battle fighting with the Emperor Mohummed Toghluk, their respective dates being, Mahmood Begurrâ A.D. 1459 to 1511, and Mohummed Togluk A.D. 1323 to 1351; but I can also bear witness that the original legend contains precisely this anachronism.

Though the rule of the imperial viceroys under the house of Timur is but briefly noticed, it could hardly be expected that so long a period could be introduced in a single volume, nevertheless the concluding days of the imperial rule and the gradual assumption of the paramount sway by, first the Mahrattas and then the British, is graphically described.

Imbued as he was with a thorough admiration for the Râjpoot races, we can hardly expect Mr. Forbes to be quite fair to the Mahrattas; but it is only just to say that his predecessors, Colonel Walker and others, are equally, if not more prejudiced against them; and even so late as 1842, I find so high an authority as Sir G. Le Grand Jacob speaking in an official report of "the customary Mahratta process of deglutition." It is, however, but fair to the Mahrattas to point out that when they entered Goozerat they were hailed as deliverers from the Mogul yoke, and to show that the decay of the imperial power was caused more by the general disaffection of the Hindoo chieftains, the impatience of the predatory tribes, whose license of plunder had been sternly checked, and the efforts towards independence of the imperial servants, than it ever was by the Mahratta incursions, which, without connivance, would have been impossible.

The Mahrattas, indeed, in Goozerat almost immediately aimed at territorial acquisition, and the establishment of Peelâjee Guikowâr at Songurh was speedily followed by a secret treaty with Râjpeepla for an unobstructed passage through his territory, and an unhindered crossing of the Nerbudda at Bâbâ Piârah's ford. Owing to this connivance with the Guikowâr, the chieftain of Râjpeepla was afterwards enabled to reconquer his ancient capital of Nândod and absorb the whole of the Nândod Sarkâr. It was owing to the Mahrattas that Eedur was able to expel its Mohummedan garrison, and that the tributary Sarkâr of Nowânugger, in the peninsula, which had been made Khâlsâ by

Aurangzeb, was able again to resume its tributary relations. By Mahratta sufferance the Thâkoris were undisturbed in their jâgirs of Pahlunpoor and Devee (Deesa), and, but for Mahratta moderation, neither would Sher Khân Bâbi and his descendants have been allowed to absorb the imperial district of Soreth, nor would many other of the local chieftains of the peninsula have been able to enlarge their petty holdings into extensive principalities by wholesale absorption of the imperial domain.

One of the reasons why this absorption was so easy was this : in latter times, as the imperial hold on the province grew more slack, it was customary to farm out the villages for a fixed sum (jamâ), and, as in the case of the peninsula, the farmers were almost invariably the local landholders, nothing was easier than to retain a hold over the villages so farmed when the power of collecting the jamâ was gone. In almost every case the Mahrattas were very moderate in their demands, and, indeed, until the time of Shivrâm Gârdee and Bâbâjee Âppâjee, the latter of whom was strengthened by the countenance of the English, not only were the amounts of tribute levied in the peninsula enforced with the greatest irregularity, but the actual sums taken were insignificant in amount; and if we are to believe the Târikh-i-Soreth, so late as A.D. 1803-4 Bâbâjee himself had to refund two-thirds of the amount of tribute levied, owing to the pressure exerted by the armies of the Joonâgurh Dewân.

Mr. Forbes notices that the Moolukgeeree circuits of the Mahrattas were merely copied from their Mogul predecessors, from whose official nomenclature not only the term Moolukgeeree, but also most of the official titles and technical revenue terms, etc., in Goozerat are borrowed.

Nor is it merely in historical detail that Mr. Forbes's volumes are instructive. About one fourth of the volume is devoted to an account of the customs of the different classes of natives; their religious services, marriages, funerals are specially dealt with, together with their ideas regarding Bhoots, and other popular beliefs, and a very able and elaborate account of the Râjpoot land tenures under the Mohummedans, the Mahrattas, and the British is also furnished.

Not only has the general scheme of the government of this important province and the history of the governing dynasties been accurately and faithfully pourtrayed, but together with this we have histories of the principal Râjpoot houses, who then, as now, were among the principal nobles of the empire; and we are thus enabled to form a more thorough conception of the times depicted, as we read of the subject from the view both of the rulers and the governed.

There are but few other books of reference about Goozerat, and none of them of so encyclopædic a character. Bird's "Goozerat" contains, amongst certain historical speculations of the author, a translation of the smallest and least important portion of the "Mirât-i-Ahmadi," and that translation contains several errors. Brigg's "Ferishtâ" gives the same period as Bird, also with a few errors. Colonel Tod alone, in his "Western India," deals with the Unhilwârâ kings and more recent times, while Forbes' "Oriental Memoirs," and a few others, complete the list.

These works, however, instructive and valuable though they are in many respects, are so much more limited in their scope than the Râs Mâlâ that they fail to give us what this work does, viz., a complete sketch of the history of the province from the earliest times to the present day. All government officials will, I am sure, willingly acknowledge what they owe to this valuable book, and not only will they, as well as others, gladly hail its reprint, but I feel sure that government will in its turn be better served accordingly as its servants study the contents.[1]

JOHN W. WATSON.

BÂLÂCHERI, KÂTHIÂWÂR,
November 8th, 1877.

[1] It has been thought well to retain in this Introduction the same form in the spelling of Indian names which has been used by the Author.

PREFACE.

To ancient India—a subject attractive to the historian and the scholar—much attention has been directed; the more humble task of investigating its mediæval story has been comparatively little attempted. If, however, the days of Asoka and of Chundragoopt afford a nobler field of enquiry, it should not, on that account, be forgotten that the times which are less remote are more practically connected with existing Hindoostan. Modern India, moreover, affords a safe basis from which to stretch forward to immediately preceding times, while as long as these shall continue to be covered with darkness, it is but a hazardous task to grasp at the light, however splendid, which shines beyond them. The stranger who is for any length of time resident in the land of the Hindoos can hardly fail to notice customs and usages of that people which are evidently relics of a state of society not long gone by—visions, as it were, of a noble vessel, whose phantom-like outline, if only by an illusion such as that which produces the Fata Morgana, exhibits, in exalted reflection, these existing things. The very remains of Moslem power themselves are most strongly impressed with the character of the race whose rule was supplanted by that of the crescent, and from even these we might have gathered the fact that many a splendid metropolis must have adorned the plains of Aryaverta before the avalanche of Mohummedan invasion fell from the western mountains upon the land. We have, however, more definite traces of these glories of bygone days, and can picture to ourselves, at least in outline, the gorgeous Kanouj, the mysterious Yogeeneepoor, the almost fabulous metropolis of Bhoj. Nor did the cities which we have mentioned exist alone. The monarchs of Kuleeân extended their sway over a territory more ample still than that which owned the supremacy of either, and equal, at least, to the Purmâr, the Chohân, or the Râthor was the Solunkhee of Unhilpoor.

It is to the story of the city of Wun Râj, and of the Hindoo principalities and chieftainships which sprang up amidst its ruins, and which have, many of them, continued in existence to the present day, that the reader's attention is in the present work invited. I am well aware that my subject—not only Indian, but also local, as it is—is likely to be one of but little general interest, nor am I blind to many of my own deficiencies in its treatment. Eight years' residence in Goozerat, and much association, public and private, with its varied people, from the banks of the Taptee to those of the Bunâs, may, however, have given me some advantages.

While at the outset disclaiming, on my own part, all pretensions to Oriental learning, I have, nevertheless, to mention that I have received from Hindoo scholars assistance which, though it detract from the merit of the compiler, will not be thought to lessen the value of the compilation.

To the late Peerchundjee Bhundâree, a native of Marwar and a Jain by religion, who, though a member of the commercial class, which is usually indifferent to literature, was a proficient in both the classical and the popular lore of his nation, I am obliged, first, for the gift of a copy of the Prubundh Chintâmunee, and, secondly, for indispensable assistance in translating it.

To Dulputrâm Dâyâ, a Brahmin, and a native of Wudwân, on the frontier of Soreth, I am still more widely indebted.

I had not been very long in Goozerat when, in the course of my public employment, a paper was placed before me which bore the characteristic signatures of two bards.[1] My curiosity was excited; I made enquiries, and sought the

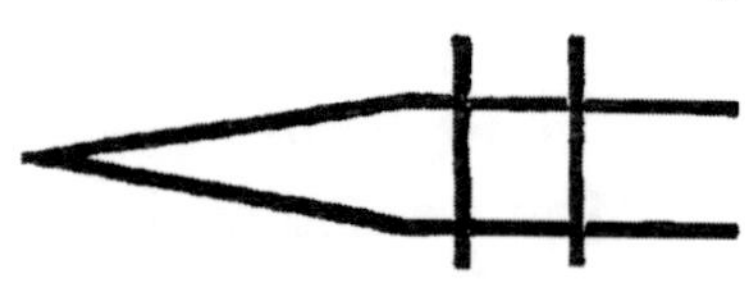

acquaintance of such of the class as were within my reach. Of the

[1] This paper will be found translated in the note in book iii. chap. vi.

treasures of the bardic repertoire I thus obtained a glimpse which stimulated instead of satisfying me. I soon felt that native assistance was absolutely necessary both to enable me to overcome the scruples of those who possessed the legendary hoard in which I desired to participate, and also to furnish me with some knowledge of the bardic dialect, which was required as a means of unlocking the casket in which the treasure was contained. Good fortune brought early to my notice the name of the Kuveshwur, or poet,—for with that title Dulputrâm is invested by the suffrage of his countrymen,—and I secured his services in A.D. 1848. From that period my valuable coadjutor has been almost constantly by my side. It was some time before our efforts met with any success, although I furnished him with the means of making the tour of a considerable portion of Goozerat, with the view of collecting chronicles and traditions, and of copying inscriptions. It might, perhaps, amuse, but would certainly weary, the reader were I to describe the numerous obstacles which we found opposed to us, by ignorance, jealousy, and avarice. Sufficient notion of these will be conveyed when I mention the facts that I was sometimes believed to be employed in searching for concealed treasure, that at other times my object was supposed to be that of detecting flaws in the titles to lands with the view of their assumption by government, and that it was frequently hinted to me that the proper return for permission to extract from a bardic record would be the presentation *of a village* to the family of the recorder. Subsequently, however, my official duties brought me into personal contact with the chiefs of the Wâghela, Jhâlâ, and Gohil clans, and I soon discovered that a hint from one of these traditionally-honored feudal lords was far more influential than any intreaties which I could use, or any advantages which I could offer. As Political Agent in the Myhee Kântâ, I found these facilities extended not only to the clans of that province, but also to the Guikowâr territories (from the authorities of which I had received at least one previous rebuff), and through the kindness of Bâbâ Sahib, the worthy lieutenant of the Baroda government at Puttun, I secured a copy of the Dwyâshrây, and other valuable materials from the very centre of interest—the site of Unhilpoor.

My researches, pursued, as they necessarily were, in the hours of relaxation from tolerably heavy official duties, were not confined to the Jain and the bardic chronicles ; I availed myself also of every opportunity of observing Hindoo popular customs, more especially such as were alluded to in the writings and traditions which I collected ; I procured copies of inscriptions on temples, wells, and tombstones, and I examined every remnant of Hindoo architecture which I found myself able to visit. In this last department of enquiry much assistance was furnished me by Premchund Sulât, the able architect of the new Jain temple at Ahmedabad, and by two very intelligent persons of the carpenter caste—the late Turbhowundâs, and Bhoodhur Dâyârâm.

Meanwhile the Goozerat Vernacular Society sprung up, and the Kuveshwur, who was well prepared for the purpose, won prizes for two essays,—on popular superstitions in Goozerat, and on Hindoo castes—of both of which I have made much use in the Fourth Book of the present work.

My return for a limited period to England, and the valuable permission of the Honorable the Court of Directors of the East India Company to my inspecting the records, have enabled me to complete my labours. The result is now placed before the public, in the hope that, unworthy as it is, it may still be of use to the local officer, and may interest some few even of my countrymen at home in the fortunes of their fellow-subjects—*the Hindoos in Goozerat.*

In imitation of the titles of some of the legends from which it is derived, I have called my compilation " Râs Mâlâ," or " A Garland of Chronicles."[1]

[1] As the present work is wholly popular, and advances no pretensions to a scientific character, I have used the common form in spelling names which are in daily use, and I have, in other cases, adopted the mode of spelling which experience has shown me to be most readily accepted by the general reader. Thus, for the correct *Khumbâyut,* I use *Cambay,* a word which has established itself in English literature ; and for the classical *Anhilpur* I substitute the popular *Unhilpoor,* which is to be pronounced according to the usual sound of the vowels in English. I have, however, taken the liberty of accenting one letter, the long *â,* as in Râs Mâlâ. Wherever it occurs it should be pronounced as the *a* in *Mario.* May I trouble the reader so far as to add, that the *ye* in *Jye Singh, Shutroonjye,* &c., should be pronounced as the *y* in *why, by,* &c., or as the *igh* in *high.*

MEMOIR OF THE AUTHOR.

"A LIFE UNBLAMABLE AND JUST."

IT is thought that the admirers of the Râs Mâlâ will be glad to know something of the life of the author.

Alexander Kinloch Forbes was born in London, in July, 1821, and educated at a school at Finchley. He was then articled to an architect, but having in 1840 received an appointment to the Bombay Civil Service from Sir Charles Forbes, he went to the College at Haileybury. He left this in 1842, and arrived in Bombay in November, 1843.

He spent the first two years and a half of his service as Assistant Collector in Ahmednugger and Khandeish, and in November, 1846, went to Ahmedabad as Assistant Judge. From this time till he went home, in March, 1854, he served continuously in Goozerat, not in the judicial department only, but also in the appointments of First Assistant Collector at Ahmedabad and Political Agent in the Myhee Kântâ. During his furlough he worked up all the materials he had got together during these years into the Râs Mâlâ, which was published in 1856.

He returned to India at the end of 1856, and went to Surat as Acting Judge, and in 1858 served in the same capacity in Khandeish. But, as was to be expected, he found the Mahratta country tame and uninteresting after Goozerat, which he appreciated so highly, and on the Political Agency of Kâteewâr falling vacant, he applied for it, at the same time expressing his willingness to spend the rest of his service in that appointment. It was then much less thought of and not so well paid as now; so that this offer showed how little he had of the ordinary ambition of getting on in the service. The appointment, however, was not given to him, but in September, 1859, when he was about to leave his acting appointment in Khandeish for a lower one, he unexpectedly received from Lord Elphinstone an order to go immediately to Kâteewâr and take temporarily, and with special powers, the appointment which had been refused him shortly before. The circumstances of the province had in the meantime changed, and the occasion was pressing, as the Wâghars in Okamandal were in a state of rebellion, requiring the despatch of a military force from Bombay to coerce them, and it was feared that the disturbances might extend to the rest of Kâteewâr. Mr. Forbes, therefore, made no objection, but went at very short notice; and by March, 1860, the Wâghars were subdued, and his special work done. A permanent vacancy could not be made for him in Kâteewâr, and he therefore returned to Surat as Acting Judge. But his proceedings in Kâteewâr, and his reports on the settlement and government of the province, were highly approved both by the Bombay government and the home authorities, and in March, 1861, Sir George Clerk gave him the acting appointment of Secretary to Government. In December of the same year there was a vacancy in the Sudder Adawlut, and Sir George Clerk wrote that he felt bound to offer it to him, sorry as he should be to lose him from the secretariat. The work of the latter, however, was not nearly so much to Mr. Forbes's taste as judicial business, and he therefore accepted the appointment in the Sudder Court, which in August, 1862, made him a Judge of the Bombay High Court, and in this he remained till his death. The only other office he held was the honorary one of Vice-Chancellor of the University, which Sir Bartle Frere gave him in December, 1864. He died at Poona on August 31st, 1865, after a short illness, having shortly before completed his forty-fourth year.

Mr. Forbes's administrative capacity is proved by the name he made in each department in which he served, and by the value set on his services by governors of such great though various ability as Lord Elphinstone, Sir George Clerk and Sir Bartle Frere. Of his learning and literary skill the Râs Mâlâ is the most lasting record.

Though it was from the first highly appreciated by those who were inclined to studies of the sort, and favourably received by some English papers, yet it must be remembered that twenty years ago the kind of research which it shows was far less fashionable than now, when every district has its own historian of one sort or another. And so it has come to pass, as Dr. Wilson with his usual acuteness predicted at the time of Mr. Forbes's death, that the Râs Mâlâ is more highly valued as time goes on, because the very multiplication of works of this sort has proved how difficult it is to reach the standard of its excellence. Sir Henry Lawrence, whose acquaintance Mr. Forbes had made at Mount Aboo in 1853, and whom he regarded with the greatest reverence and affection, compared it favourably with the work which had long been looked on as the first of the sort, and the letter which he wrote on this occasion is worth giving entire:—

"*Neemuch, Jan.* 30, 1857.

"My dear Forbes,—Best thanks for your kind invitation to Surat, but my face, I am sorry to say, is turned towards Lucknow, where I am off post-haste. I should have been glad to have met you again. I have been much interested in and edified by your book, which is a vast improvement on Tod. I wish I could have talked over Goozerat with you. I took a ride round it last month. With kind regards to Mrs. Forbes,

"Yours very sincerely,

"H. M. LAWRENCE."

It must seem particularly surprising to those who know by experience the difficulty of getting together any local history in this country that Mr. Forbes, in a little over seven years from first going to Goozerat and beginning to study its language, should have collected such stores of information, and become so thoroughly acquainted with everything connected with the province. Mr. Dalpaliâm Dâyabhai, who was engaged by Mr. Forbes in 1848 as a Goozerathi pundit, has given an account of his mode of study. He had before that begun to collect manuscripts and to take copies of them, and at first used to read Goozerathi poetry with Mr. Dalpaliâm for two hours a day. He soon became deeply interested in the subject, and for the purpose of collecting and translating Goozerathi works, he, with the assistance of some other gentlemen, founded the Goozerat Vernacular Society, in connection with which a library, newspaper, and school were soon afterwards established at Ahmedabad. Mr. Forbes himself translated an essay on Evil Spirits (Bhût Nibandh), which was written in Goozerathi for the Vernacular Society. When he went to the Myhee Kântâ in 1852 he used to have letters of invitation written to any Bhâts Chârans or Brahman poets whom he heard of as likely to give him information or tell him legends, and he kept by him a stock of shawls, turbans, &c., as presents to these bards. He was in constant correspondence with the chief of the Swâmi Narâyan sect at Ahmedabad and other intelligent natives, and by all these means he gained an influence in Goozerat which enabled him to see and hear much which is generally closely guarded from Europeans. But this knowledge and confidence were not gained by the adoption of native customs or prejudices, or by the profession of any extravagant admiration for native manners and character. On the contrary, no man ever guarded more carefully the character of a Christian and a gentleman, or was more successful in proving to natives the true effects and superiority of European culture.

Both before and after the publication of the Râs Mâlâ Mr. Forbes contributed to the "Bombay Quarterly Review." The best articles are one on Indian Architecture, in April, 1857, and one on Oude, in October, 1858. The first of these shows the deep feeling he had for art in all its branches, and his great knowledge of architecture in particular. The end of it is worth quoting :—

"The purpose of a building comes not within the domain of an "architect; his duty lies rather in the proper expression of that "purpose. When therefore our readers contemplate a Hindoo temple, "let them, if they would do justice to the architect, forbear to upbraid "him with the want of all godlike characteristics in the being to "whose worship his talents are perforce devoted : let them rather "admire the honesty and the skill with which he works out in "massive structure or in rock-hewn cave those ideas of fear and "gloom with which his religion associates divinity; and let them "picture to themselves the far happier effects no doubt destined to "be realized at some future time by that patient fidelity and that "untiring zeal when at length worthily consecrated to a religion not "of gloom and fear but of light and love."

An article on the Rewa Kantâ in April, 1856, believed but not ascertained to be Mr. Forbes's, deals with great skill and clearness with the relations that should exist between the British Government and native chiefs of whatever rank, and while many of the proposals there made have since been carried out, the remainder, which have not yet got beyond the stage of discussion, are in full accordance with principles then disputed but since acknowledged. While insisting on making the British power really supreme in all cases, Mr. Forbes protested most strongly against the then fashionable policy of depressing the chiefs and landlords in favour of the ryots. In the article on Oude he showed how hopeless the British connection with that country had been from the time of the earliest treaty down to the annexation. In one on Sir John Malcolm's Life, in July, 1857, he showed a fine discrimination (quite wanting in Malcolm's biographer) in the deep admiration he felt for "the patriarchal ruler, "the friend, the father, the tutelar saint of Central India," and the indifference with which he contemplated "the formal and cere-"monious Governor of Bombay." His last contribution to literature was a learned paper on Pattan Somnâth, in the "Journal of the Bombay Branch of the Royal Asiatic Society" for 1864.

Mr. Forbes was a constant and appreciative student of Shakspeare, and in the habit of quoting him very freely. He was a true lover of art, and a good draughtsman, and his illustrations in the first edition of the Râs Mâlâ showed how well he had used his time in the architect's office. One of the pleasures to which he looked forward for a great part of his life was a tour through Normandy, to visit the cathedrals; but this he never attained, and after his long furlough the only visit he paid to Europe was one on three months' leave the year before his death.

Enough has been said to show that Mr. Forbes's acquirements and services were a good deal more than those of the ordinary Indian judge with a literary turn, and it only remains to say something about his private character and disposition. He married early, and had a large family, and being domestic in his tastes and studious in his habits, he cared very little for general society. His health was never very strong, and his qualities were not of the showy or popular sort, and altogether he was never one of the very well known men of the Presidency. But he was thoroughly appreciated by all who had the good fortune to know him, and his acquantance was sought by many on account of his acquirements. Undoubtedly modesty and simplicity were the leading features of his character, and his manners were so gentle and pleasing, and he was so utterly unchanged by high position, that even up to the end of his life young men or his inferiors had no difficulty in opening their minds to him. So little did he care to assert himself that he would often, until appealed to, sit silent while others were mangling the very subjects with which he was best acquainted. The same feeling made him refuse the office of Vice-President of the Asiatic Society of Bombay, which was pressed on him soon after he was settled there. Yet there was no reserve about him when in congenial society, and in conversation and argument he was thoroughly able to hold his own.

It is quite in accordance with the rest of his character that while he made no great profession of religion he was evidently and essentially a religious man, and showed in his life and conversation that he understood the great principles of Christianity which he practised in their most attractive form. Everything in the shape of Positivism and Materialism was repugnant to the whole bent of his mind and thoughts ; not that he had any idea of denouncing these tenets as irreligious or contrary to revelation, but because his mind, at once reverent and imaginative, was affected more by the evidence of things not seen than by the mere accidents of the material world. Thus when he had read enough of Buckle's "History of Civilization," (which was for a time hailed by its admirers as a new Gospel), to see what its purport was, he sent it back to the friend who lent it him with the quotation—

> "There are more things in heaven and earth, Horatio,
> Than are dreamt of in *our* philosophy."

His stand-point being wholly different from and antagonistic to that of the materialists, there was naturally no chance of his conclusions agreeing with theirs. With all his stores of learning no one was more ready than Mr. Forbes to urge that—

> "Knowledge is earthly of the mind,
> But wisdom heavenly of the soul."

This sketch may be properly concluded and summed up by extracts from two notices of Mr. Forbes which appeared soon after his death. A writer in the "Bombay Saturday Review," which, like the other English and Goozerathi newspapers of this presidency, gave memoirs of his life, described him as, "Simply the Christian gentleman: all "else, abilities, accomplishments, position, opportunities, were but "the accidents of that. . . . At the time of his death it may be said of "him that he was unequalled for the individual affection entertained "for him by his friends of all classes."

"And Sir Bartle Frere, at the first convocation of the Bombay "University after his death, said: "It was not his intellectual ability, "great as that was, nor his learning and accomplishments, though we "know them to have been profound and varied, but it was his innate "English love of justice, which with such singular modesty was "his great characteristic, which gave him such a hold on the sympathy "of all with whom he came in contact, and which was the true secret "of his power."

Many still in India can testify that there was no exaggeration in this eulogy. He had shortly before his death founded in Bombay the Goozerathi Vernacular Society, with the same objects as that which he had founded at Ahmedabad early in life, and this after his death was called the Forbes Goozerathi Sabha. It is to be regretted that a considerable sum of money collected for a memorial of him was spent on nothing better than the endowment of a useless scholarship; but the Râs Mâlâ remains as a monument, not of learning only, but of love for all that is beautiful, and sympathy for all that is human.

CONTENTS.

BOOK I.

BOOK II.

CONTENTS.

BOOK III.

BOOK IV., OR CONCLUSION.

BOOK I.

RÂS MÂLÂ.

CHAPTER I.

NATURAL BOUNDARIES OF GOOZERAT — SHUTROONJYE — WULLUBHEEPOOR.

THE province of Goozerat, in Western India, is composed of two portions—the one of these is continental, the other is peninsular and projects into the Arabian Sea nearly opposite the coast of Oman, and below that of Mekran and Sindh. Hindoos usually assume the river Nerbudda to be the southern boundary of the continental portion, or Goozerat proper. The language of the province is, however, spoken much further to the south—as far even as Damaun, or St. John's, about half-way between the mouth of the river and Bombay. Stretching northwards from the banks of the Nerbudda, a range of hills connecting the Vindhya with the Arawullee mountains forms the eastern and northern barrier of Goozerat, and separates it from Malwa, Mewar, and Marwar. The Gulf of Kutch and a salt, and sometimes partially inundated, desert called the Runn are the boundaries of the province on the north-west and west; the Arabian Sea and the Gulf of Cambay wash its southern and south-western shores. The least protected part of this frontier line, and that by which Goozerat has usually been invaded, is on the north-west, where a sandy plain intervenes between the desert and the foot of Mount Aboo.

The mountains which bound Goozerat on the north and east, and which project numerous branches into the nearest parts of the province, are steep, craggy, and difficult of access. The shoulders of the hills and the valleys which intervene between the spurs are covered with forest. From the dark shadow of these woods numerous streams emerge, whose lofty banks are indented by long, deep, and intricate ravines, and overgrown with almost impenetrable underwood. As the plains are approached, and the forest disappears the rivers widen and become less wild in their character; they unite at length in one or other of the three great arteries—the Sâbhermutee, the Myhee, and the Nerbudda, and eventually discharge their waters into the Gulf of

Cambay. Nearly the whole of the south-west portion of Goozerat, a tract of country sixty miles deep, extending from the Runn of Kutch to the banks of the Nerbudda, along the frontier of the peninsula and the northern and eastern shores of the Gulf of Cambay, is an open and alluvial plain; much of this fertile tract, and especially that part of it which lies between the Sâbhermutee and the Myhee, is covered with noble groves of trees, many of them, the mango and others, bearing fruit and exhibiting foliage of the most brilliant colour—"it may vie," says the historian of the Mahrattas, "for hundreds of miles with the finest parks of the nobles of England." The hill country also, though some of it is neglected, exhibits great fertility wherever it is cultivated. The fields are well taken care of, and covered with fine crops; mangoes and other planted trees are even here unusually numerous, and, as the surface is undulating and the wood and mountains often in sight, "no part of India," as Mr. Elphinstone remarks, "presents a richer or more agreeable prospect."

About twenty miles from the extremity of the lesser Runn of Kutch in a south-easterly direction, commences a large lake of brackish water which stretches towards the head of the Gulf of Cambay, and forms a boundary between Goozerat proper and the peninsula of Soreth or Kâteewar. It is probable that in former days the separation was even more complete, and that Soreth was in fact an Island.[1]

There is on the western shore of the Gulf of Cambay, a few miles to the north of Bhownugger, a range of granite hills, which, lying in a country level as an unruffled lake, seems like a cluster of islands floating on the waves. From the summit of one of these rugged peaks which overhangs the village of Chumârdee may be beheld a scene surpassed by few in India in the variety and interest of its historical and legendary association.

Surrounded by apparently wave-hollowed cavities which countenance the traditional belief that the rocks of Chumârdee were once washed by the waters of the ocean, the spectator beholds stretched before him on the north and east, and extending beyond the horizon, a vast and level plain of black soil, covered annually with crops of wheat or cotton (except where, as it approaches the high tides of the gulf, it wears a salt and desolate fringe), and broken only by the streams which vainly struggle to force their way eastwards along its surface. There may be observed, sluggishly creeping along its winding

[1] For information on this subject see Major Fulljames's paper in the Journal of the Bombay Branch of the Royal Asiatic Society, vol. v., page 109. See also Elphinstone's India, vol. i., page 558. Edit. 1841.

bed in the heats of summer, or in the rains furiously tearing its way towards the ocean, the river which washed the walls of the magnificent Wullubhee. There too may be traced the salt-water creek called "the Bhownugger" or "*the former*" river which of old bore seawards the argosies of the still mysterious race of Kunuksen, and which, though ridden now by poor and scanty sails, exhibits some vestiges of its former greatness as it rushes by the town from whence it derives its names, and passing the port of Gogo, precipitates itself with headlong fury into the channel that separates from the main land of Soreth the curious and interesting islet of Peerum. In this plain, a few miles to the north of Chumârdee, lie the modern town of Wulleh (now a chieftainship of the Rajpoot Gohils) and the remains of the ancient City of Wullubheepoor, and further on, as if to continue the historical interest of the scene, a tall minaret shows the town of Loleeyânah, where for many years the lieutenants of the Mohummedan emperors collected the revenues of the province, while close beside the fallen mosque the vulgar Mahratta has built his snug temple and placed upon its front the following badly spelt and rudely engraved inscription :—

"Shree Shiva's foot-impress with assiduity Dâmâjee Guikowâr continually worships. Sumwut 1794. (A.D. 1738)."

On turning to the south, the spectator standing on the hill of Chumârdee, would, however, behold an outline, diversified by mountain ranges; a few miles inland and somewhat to the south of Peerum rise the Khokurâ hills; nearer and more to the west, a rocky range encircles the "Lion city" Seehore, and still westwards, in the distance, the noble form of the sacred mountain Shutroonjye, crowned with a rocky upper hill, covered with palatial edifices, rears itself above the towers and minarets of Pâleetânâ.

The holy mountain of Shutroonjye, sacred to Âdeenâth,[1] the first of the twenty-four hierophants of the Jains, rises to the height of

[1] Corresponding with the four yoogs or ages of the Hindoos are the six Ârâs of the Jains. In the third Ârâ lived Nâbhee Raja, descended of Ikshwâkoo Raja, of the race of Kusyup, the Sage. He had a wife, Muroo Devee, and their son was Rishub Dev, or Âdeenâth, the first Teerthunker or Pontiff of the Jains. Before the time of Rishub Dev no rain fell upon the earth, no fire existed, nor any thorny tree; there was neither learning nor skilled occupation in the world. All these were introduced by Rishub Dev, who taught men the three Kurums,—*Ushee Kurum*, or the science of war and government; *Mâshee Kurum*, or the science of literature; and *Kâshee Kurum*, or the science of cultivation. From this time men adopted regular occupations. The last of the Teerthunkers, Muhâveer Swâmee, became incorporated with the Divine essence, in the year before Vikrum 470 (B. C. 526); three years, eight months, and two weeks after which commenced the fifth Ârâ, which is to last twenty-one thousand years.

nearly two thousand feet above the plains. The pilgrim approaching it passes to the base of the mountain, through the town of Pâleetânâ, and along a road on either side of which rows of burr-trees afford him a cloister-like shelter from the heat of the sun. After a toilsome ascent of from two to three miles upon the shoulder of the mountain, over a path marked on either side by frequent resting places, supplied with wells and pools of water, and adorned with small temples, whose altars are impressed with the holy feet of the hierarchs, he at length arrives in sight of the island-like upper hill, formed of rocks of very beautiful color, upon which stand the shrines of his religion. It consists of two peaks, divided by a valley which has been partially filled in, and covered with temples, terraces, and gardens. The whole is surrounded by a fortified wall, supplied in places with embrasures for cannon, and this enclosure is divided into smaller castles, many of the temples themselves forming independent fortifications. On the southern summit are the mediæval temples, founded by Koomâr Pâl and Veemul Shâ, with a pool sacred to a local goddess named Khodeeâr, near which is a gigantic image of the Jain Pontiff, Rishub Dev, with the sacred bull at his feet, hewn out of the living rock. On the northern elevation the largest and most ancient temple is that, the erection of which is attributed to a fabulous prince named Sumpriti Raja. The old erections upon Shutroonjye are, however, few; and frequent restoration has caused them to be with difficulty discernible from the modern fanes around them, but of those of later date the name is legion. There is hardly a city in India, through its length and breadth, from the river of Sindh to the sacred Ganges, from Heemâla's diadem of ice peaks, to the throne of his virgin daughter, Roodra's destined bride, that has not supplied, at one time or other, contributions of wealth to the edifices which crown the hill of Pâleetânâ; street after street, and square after square, extend these shrines of the Jain faith, with their stately enclosures, half palace, half fortress, raised, in marble magnificence, upon the lonely and majestic mountain, and like the mansions of another world, far removed in upper air from the ordinary tread of mortals. In the dark recesses of each temple one image or more of Âdeenâth, of Ujeet, or of some other of the Teerthunkers is seated, whose alabaster features, wearing an expression of listless repose, are rendered dimly visible by the faint light shed from silver lamps; incense perfumes the air, and barefooted, with noiseless tread, upon the polished floors, the female votaries, glittering in scarlet and gold, move round and round in circles, chanting forth their monotonous, but not unmelodious, hymns. Shutroonjye indeed might fitly represent one of the fancied hills of eastern romance, the inhabitants of which have been instantaneously changed into marble, but which fay hands are ever employed upon, burning perfumes, and keeping all clean and brilliant, while fay voices haunt the air in these voluptuous praises of the Devs.

Westwards from the summit of the hill of Pâleetânâ may be beheld, on a clear day, the mount sacred to Nemeenâth,—the noble Girnâr: northwards the hills around Seehore hardly intercept the view of the fallen city of Wullubhee; close at the foot of Âdeenâth's mountain, the minarets of Pâleetânâ, glittering in the sun through the dense foliage, form a foreground to the view; and the eye insensibly following the silver river Shutroonj, in its meandering eastern course, rests awhile upon the beautiful and temple-crowned rock of Tulâjâ, and beyond it roams to where the ancient Gopnâth and Mudhoomâwutee are washed by the rippling sea.

Shutroonjye is one of the most ancient and most sacred shrines of the Jain religion. It is described as the first of places of pilgrimage, the bridal hall of those who would marry everlasting rest: like our own sacred Iona,[1] it is not destined to be destroyed even at the end of the world. Many and long are the tales that are told of fabled kings from every part of the land of the Hindoos, who by austerities and religious services, rendered valuable by their performance on this sacred ground, have freed themselves from the intolerable load of their sins, and attained the blessing of liberation. But it would test all the patience even of a votary of the Teerthunkers, to thread this labyrinth of wonders, nor shall we attempt to tell our readers of Kupurddee Yuksh, of Kundoo Raja, and his patron Umbeekâ, of Sumoodra Veejye the Yâduv, or of the temples which Soondur, the beautiful King of Kuleeân, and his incomparable consort, raised upon the sacred hill.

To some traditions, however, which are of more general interest we may here allude, premising that they are derived from the Muhâtmâ, or sacred chronicle, of the mountain, which purports to have been abridged from a former work on the same subject, by

[1] "That so many crowned heads from different nations should prefer this (Iona) "as the place of their interment is said to have been owing to an ancient "prophecy :—

> "'Seven years before the end of the world
> "A deluge shall drown the nations :
> "The sea at one tide shall cover Ireland,
> "And the green-headed Islay, but Columba's Isle
> "Shall swim above the flood.'"

Graham's Antiquities of Iona.

Shree Dhuneshwur Sooree in the renowned city of Wullubhee, at the order of "Soorâshtra's lord, Sheelâditya.".

Bhurut Raja, the son of Rishub Dev, ruled in Ayoddhya. He led an army northwards from Shutroonjye, and engaged in battle with a barbarian raja of great power. In the first struggle Bhurut was defeated, in a subsequent one he was successful. The barbarian sovereign fled on his defeat to the river Indus, "as a child in distress flies to his mother."

Bhurut was, however, stayed by the rainy season, but at its close his minister Sookhen took a fort north of the Indus, between the sea and the mountains. Somyushâ, son of Bâhoobulee Raja, the younger brother of Bhurut, built the temple of Rishub Dev, and Bhurut himself gave up for the services of the place of pilgrimage the revenues of Soorâshtra, which from that day received the title of Dev-desh, or the Holy Land.[1] Shuktee Singh, Bhurut's relative, then presided in Soreth, and with the assistance of the army of that sovereign, led by Sookhen, expelled the demons from Girnâr, and founded temples, lofty as Mount Meroo, to Âdeenâth and Urisht Nemee. The temples on Shutroonjye were afterwards destroyed by barbarians, and for a long time desolation reigned in the holy mountain.

At the time when Vikrum arose to free the earth from debt, a poor Shrâwuk, or layman of the Jain faith, named Bhâwud, and his wife Bhâwulâ, dwelt in Kâmpilyapoor. Having hospitably entertained two holy men who visited their house, they became the possessors of a mare of wonderful qualities. Bhâwud, after this beginning, soon arrived at eminence as a breeder of horses, and having made valuable additions to the stud of King Vickrumâditya, he received from that sovereign the gift of Mudhoomâwutee (or Mhowa) in Soreth. In that town, a son, named Jâwud, was born to him, who succeeding his father at his death, managed his city like a second god of wisdom. In a bad time an army of "Moodguls"[2] swept over the land like a tide of the sea violently driven up. The Moodguls carried off cows, grain, property of all kinds, children, women of all classes, men also, from Soreth, Lâth, Kutch, and other countries, and retired to their own country, "Moodgul." Jâwud, among other captives of all castes, was carried off thither; but even there the merchant acquired wealth; he preserved his religion as in the land of virtue, and erected a Jain temple. Holy men visiting it, and being well received by

[1] The word *Dev* means generally a dweller in one of the upper worlds. For a more detailed explanation, the reader must be referred to the Conclusion.

[2] So in the original. In the Goozeratee translation, "*Mooguls.*"

Jâwud, recited the praises of Shutroonjye, and predicted that he was destined to effect its restoration. They informed him that the tutelary Devs of the sacred mountain had become destroyers of life and consumers of flesh and liquor; that an apostate, named Kuwud Yuksh, put to death all those of the Jain religion who ventured thither; that the land was desolate for leagues around Shutroonjye; and that Rishub Dev was without a worshipper. Following their directions, Jâwud propitiated the goddess Chukreshwuree, and offered gifts to the unclean Devs. They pointed out to him the place where the image of Rishub Dev lay concealed,—at the city of Tuksh Sheela, namely, where Raja Jugutmâl ruled. Jâwud with great exertion obtained the images from the king. With the Raja's assistance, he organized a caravan, in which he, with many of his caste fellows, set off escorting the images towards Shutroonjye. After many hardships, Jâwud and his companions succeeded in making their way to Mudhoomâwutee in Soreth, and they were so fortunate as to find in the harbour a fleet of vessels which Jâwud had formerly despatched to Bhot and Cheen, and which had that moment returned laden with gold and other costly freight. At the same moment, also, the great sage Shree Vâyur Swâmee arrived at Mudhoomâwutee, bringing with him Kuwud Yuksh, whom he had reconverted, and who followed him, attended by a numerous train of Devs and Yukshes. Jâwud and the holy Vâyur Swâmee, with their ally Kuwud, repaired with all speed to Shutroonjye, where they were horrified at the sight of corpses and blood defiling the mountain, and whitened bones scattered over it. Having cleansed the hill until it was as pure as their own hearts, the pilgrim band, placing the images before them, on the fortunate day pointed out by Shree Vâyur Swâmee, ascended the mountain with much music and festive display. They were, however, unsuccessful in repeated endeavours to restore the place of pilgrimage, which were always frustrated by the malevolent opposition of the demons. Jâwud at last died broken-hearted in the one hundred and eighth year after Vikrum (A.D. 52,) and his continual failures gave rise to the proverb still common in the country in reference to a work which never arrives at completion,—"It is a Jâwud Bhâwud affair."[1]

Several years subsequent to the death of Jâwud, the Boudhists converted the kings of Soorâshtra to their faith, and took possession of Shutroonjye and all the other holy places. At last Dhuneshwur

[1] The Scottish adage is similar, "Like Saint Mungo's work, it will never be finished."

Sooree arose, who brought over to the Jain religion Sheelâditya, King of Wullubheepoor, and expelling the Boudhists from the country, recovered the places of pilgrimage and erected many temples.

The date which the Muhâtmâ assigns to this latter transaction is the year of Vikrum four hundred and seventy-seven (A. D. 421). Reserving, however, the question of the probable time of Sheelâditya, we proceed with further Jain legends regarding the conversion of that sovereign from the Boudhist faith, and the destruction of himself and his kingdom by barbarian invaders.[1]

In the great city named Kaira, in Goojur-land, there lived, says the

[1] It may be as well to remark in this place, that the Sougut, or Boudh, and the Urhut, or Jain, were two of the heretical schools opposed to the religion of the Veds and to the Brahminical class. The Boudhs of Hindustan were annihilated in the furious contest waged against them by the followers of the orthodox Hindoo religion. The Jains even escaped with difficulty, though they have survived the terrors of the storm, and may now defy its force. "The Souguts," says Professor Wilson, (As: Res. xvi. art. Religious Sects of the Hindus), "are identified even by Mâdhuv Âchârya with the Boudhs, but there seems to have been some, although probably not any very essential difference: the chief tenet of this class, according to Ânund Geeree, was their adopting the doctrine taught by Soogut Moonee, that tenderness towards animated nature comprehends all moral and devotional duty, a tenet which is, in a great measure, common to both the Boudh and Jain schisms." At Wullubhee the Boudhs and Souguts appear to form one body, and the opposition is between them and the Jains, and not between these heretical sects and the orthodox Hindoos.

It is probable that the sect called Souras, who worshipped the Sun as the creator and cause of the world, and a few of whom, chiefly Brahmins, still exist as a sect, were at this time numerous in the peninsula of Soorâshtra. Ânund Geeree enumerates divisions of this class, which are now, it is believed, unknown. "He distinguishes them," says Professor Wilson, "into the following six classes :—

"Those who adored the rising sun, regarding it as especially the type of Brahmâ, or the creative power. Those who worshipped the meridian sun as Eshwur, the destructive and regenerative faculty; and those who reverenced the setting sun, as the prototype of Vishnoo, or the attribute of preservation.

"The fourth class comprehended the advocates of the Treemoortee, who addressed their devotions to the sun in all the preceding states, as the comprehensive type of these three divine attributes.

"The object of the fifth form is not quite clearly stated, but it appears to have been the adoration of the sun as a positive and material body, and the marks on his surface, as his hair, beard, &c. The members of this class so far correspond with the Souras of the present day, as to refrain from food until they had seen the sun.

"The sixth class of Souras in opposition to the preceding, deemed it unnecessary to address their devotions to the visible and material sun: they provided a mental luminary, on which they meditated, and to which their adoration was offered: they stamped circular orbs on their foreheads, arms, and breasts with hot irons; a practice uniformly condemned by Shunker Âchârya, as contrary to the laws of the Veds, and the respect due to Brahminical flesh and blood."

legend, a Brahmin who had read the Veds through, named Devâditya. He had a daughter, Soobhugâ, who was left a widow in her childhood. At morning, noon, and eventide she offered every day sacrificial grass, flowers, and water, in honor of the Sun. Astonished at the beauty of the virgin widow, the Sun-God, assuming the form of a mortal, visited earth to enjoy her embraces. She became pregnant. Her parents, enraged at the disgrace which they supposed Soobhugâ had entailed upon them, drove her from home. She fled, attended by an attached servant, to the city of Wullubhee, where in due time she was delivered of twin children. Eight years passed over the splendid infants as if in a moment. The boy then began to sit at the feet of the instructors; but, associating with other children, the lesson which earliest and most vividly impressed itself upon his mind was that he was "without a father." Distressed at the jeers of his companions, he began to complain to Soobhugâ—"How, mother! "have not I a father, that such a speech is used?" "I know not," she answered, "why do you give me pain by your enquiries?" The boy sorrowfully turned away, but from that time forth his only desire was to possess himself of poison or other means of avoiding his shame by self-destruction.

One day the Sun-God, Nârâyun, appeared to him in his grief, and addressing him kindly by the title of "child," promised him protection, and armed him with some pebbles which should enable him to slay his enemies. By the fame of these weapons of the Sun the boy became renowned under the name of Sheelâditya.[1] The King of Wullubhee, resenting the death of one of his subjects who had been slain by Sheelâditya, himself perished under the heaven-given missiles, and the son of Soobhugâ became the lord, as he was already the luminary, of Soorâshtra. Borne by a horse, the gift of Nârâyun, like a sky-traveller moving wherever he would, by his exploits conquering a circle of territory, for a long time he continued to rule.

Once on a time certain teachers of the Boudhist doctrines, fierce with the pride of learning, approached the throne of Sheelâditya. "These white-robed ones," said they, "if they can subdue us in dis-"putation, let them remain, otherwise expel them the country." The King, agreeing to this demand, held a court of four kinds,[2] himself presiding therein, and decreed that whichever party should be worsted in the discussion should quit the dominions of Wullubhee. By the

[1] Which means "Stone of the Sun."

[2] A court that is composed of *Sâdhoos* and *Sâdhwees*, or male and female ascetics of the Jain faith, and of *Shrâwuks* and *Shrâweekâs*, or persons male and female who have not entered any religious order.

fiat of destiny the Boudhists proved victorious, and the Swetâmburs[1] retired to foreign countries, hoping to renew the contest at a future time. Then Sheelâditya Raja worshipped the Boudhists, but he still continued to serve with his former zeal the great Rishub Dev of Shutroonjye.

Sheelâditya had given his twin-sister to the Raja of Bhrigoopoor (Broach), to whom she bore a son, in qualities and splendor resembling a Dev. Some time afterwards, having lost her husband, she took the ascetic vow at a good place of pilgrimage, in the presence of a good religious teacher. Her son also, at the age of eight years, took the vow. To people of good character and wisdom they began, as occasion offered, to unfold the doctrines of their religion. One day Mull, inflamed with zeal, began to enquire of his mother, the Sâdhwee, whether the fortunes of their co-religionists had always been as lowly as he then beheld them. She, with tears in her eyes, made answer :—"Son! how shall a sinner such as I am make "reply? The illustrious white-robed company was formerly numerous "in every town; but Veer Soorendra, the famous teacher, having left "the world, the other religionists enthralled the lord of earth, Sheelâditya, your uncle. The holy place of pilgrimage, Shutroonjye, "which is the renowned giver of liberation, in the absence of "Swetâmburs affords a residence to Bhoot-like[2] Boudhists. The "Swetâmburs live in foreign countries, their pride humbled, their "splendor lost." Mull, having been born in a family of the warrior caste, not forgetting his feud, sought for the opportunity of conquering. By austerities and assiduous worship he won the favor of the the Goddess of Eloquence, who, to enable him to subdue the Boudhists, as Vishnoo's eagle subdues a snake, presented him with a book named Nye Chukra. Taking this weapon, Mull, resembling in beauty the Pânduv Urjoon when he bore the arms of Shiva, coming to Wullubhee, the ornament of Soorâshtra presented himself before Sheelâditya. "The Boudhists have falsely enthralled the world, O "King! To them have I, Mull, the son of your sister, arisen as an "antagonist." Having caused the court to be arranged as before, the King sat to hear the disputants. Mull, armed with the strength of the goddess, speedily struck consternation into the Boudhists, who trembled at the fierce blaze into which the expiring spark of the Swetâmbur faith had burst forth. They determined to leave the field to their opponent rather than to suffer the ignominy of a more public

[1] "Men of the white robe," the Jains.

[2] A Bhoot is the ghost of a deceased man; see, however, for explanation of the word, the Conclusion.

defeat. "Well done," said they, "to him who escapes the sight of "the destruction of his country, or the extinction of his race, or the "rape of his wife, or the calamity of his friends." The heretics thus defeated, having been expelled the country at the order of the King, and the Jain teachers recalled, in consequence of Mull's having defeated the Boudhists, the learned men, with the Sovereign's permission, gave him the title of *Sooree.* With the aid of his uncle, Sheelâditya, knowing the immeasurable greatness of Shree Shutroonjye, the sovereign of places of pilgrimage, he effected its restoration. Shree Mull Sooree, having established his reputation, was soon after entrusted by the Convocation with the charge of the place of pilgrimage at Cambay or Stumbh Teerth, which had been planted by Shree Ubhye Dev Sooree. With Shrenik and other Shrâwuks he caused his soul to be enrolled.

At this time a trader named Kâkoo left his native town of Pâlee in Marwar, and, carrying his property with him on his head, travelled to Wullubhee. He lived with some herdsmen in a collection of huts at the city gate, and on account of his extreme misery became known as "Runk," or "poverty stricken." Becoming, however, possessed of a pad of "Krishn Chitruk,"[1] and other articles containing magical properties, Kâkoo, the Runk, soon set fire to his thatched hut, and, entering the city, erected a large mansion near one of the other gates, where he took up his residence. His property daily increasing, he began to count his wealth by tens of millions; but so great was his avarice, that he refrained from spending money in any place, either for the benefit of holy men, or in pilgrimages, or in acts of compassion; on the contrary, he exhibited his wealth to the world in the disguise of "fate," and took advantage of it to wrest their substance from his poorer neighbours. One day Runk's daughter was observed by the daughter of the Raja wearing a magnificent gold comb adorned with jewels; this the Princess became anxious to obtain, and on her father's refusing to give it up, Sheelâditya caused it to be taken away by force. Upon this quarrel Runk retired to a barbarian country, and offered the King thereof ten millions of gold to destroy Wullubhee. The monarch agreeing, set forth on the expedition, but Runk had made no present to the umbrella holder; in the royal tent,

[1] "Many years ago a girl who lived near Nether Witton (in Northumberland), as she was returning from milking with her pail on her head, saw the fairies playing in the fields, and though she pointed them out to her companions they could not see them. The reason, it seemed, was that her *weise*, or pad, for bearing the pail on her head, was composed of four-leaved clover, which gives the power of seeing fairies."—*Keightley's Fairy Mythology.*

therefore, at night time, when the lord of earth was betwixt sleeping and waking, some person, in pursuance of a plan previously arranged, began to speak as follows,—"In our lord's council there is no wise "man, else how should this horse-lord, the great Indra of the world, "set forth—by the advice of a man of unknown family and character, "a trader, no one knows whether good or bad, Runk by name—on "an expedition against the sun's child, Sheelâditya." Hearing this speech, which resembled wholesome medicine, the king advanced no further the next day. Then Runk, perceiving the real state of the case, in a fright, giving gold, satisfied that servant's desire of gold; thereupon, the day after, in the morning, the servant thus spoke in the king's presence: "With or without consideration a start has been "made—this great king, lion-like, has taken one step—now, there- "fore, to proceed is the honorable course. When a lion can, even "in sport, destroy elephants, why should he stoop to be called deer- "lord or deer-slayer? There is no honor in either term. Our "sovereign's exploits are endless. Who shall stand before him?" Pleased with this speech, the barbarian lord, filling heaven and earth with the sound of the kettle-drum, proceeded in his advance.

At that time, in Wullubhee, the images of Shree Chundra Prubh, Shree Wurddhumân Dev, and others, knowing the impending calamity, made their way to Shiv Puttun (Prubhâs), Shreemâl Poor, and other cities; Shree Mull Wâdee also, the great sage, retired to Punchâsur with his followers.[1] The barbarian army drew near to the town, and Runk, the disgraceful cause of the ruin of his country, having treacherously taught them to defile the fountain of the sun with the blood of cows, the sacred horse, which was the foundation of Sheelâditya's fortunes, deserted him, springing up, like Vishnoo's eagle, into the sky. Thus rendered helpless, Sheelâditya was slain, and the barbarians, as if in sport, destroyed Wullubheepoor.

The oral Hindoo tradition relating to the fall of the city of Wullubhee is very different from the account given in these Jain legends, and is probably altogether destitute of historical foundation. It bears to the story of the cities of the plain, and of the death of Lot's

[1] "Excessere omnes adytis arisque relictis
"Dî, quibus imperium hoc steterat."—*Virgil, Æneid II.*, 351-2.

"The ancient nations had a custom of loading with chains the statues of their "gods, when the state was menaced with danger, in order to prevent their flight. "Among the Phenicians, the idol Melkarth was almost constantly chained.—*Vide Anthon's Classical Dictionary, p.* 601.

"Let us depart hence, said the invisible guardian of the Jewish temple, when "the provocations of that infatuated race were about to receive their punishment." —*Heber's Sermons in England*, p. 60, *quoting Josephus, Bell. Judaic.*, *IV.* 5.

wife, a resemblance so close, that we find difficulty in supposing it to be other than a faint and far-transmitted echo of that wonderful tale. A circulation of intelligence scarcely to be credited, and not easily to be accounted for, has, we know, existed among Asiatic nations both of the earliest and of the most modern times, and the state in which the once proud Wullubhee has lain for centuries would not unnaturally lead the Hindoo, who ever delights in bringing home the marvellous, to fix upon it as the scene of so terrible an act of vengeance of that Almighty "who turneth a fruitful land into saltness for the wickedness "of them that dwell therein."

"Dhoondulee Mull, the sage," says the tradition, "came with a "single disciple to Wullubheepoor. The holy man made his residence "at the foot of the hill called Eeshâlwo, near Chumârdee, a spot "which was at that time in the very outskirts of Wullubhee. The "disciple went into the city to seek alms, but received none; he then "cut wood in the jungle, which he took into the city and sold, and "thus procuring money, purchased flour. No one however would "make it into bread for him, until at last a potter's wife performed "this service. After several days had passed on in this manner, the "hair on the disciple's head began to be worn away, from his con-"tinually carrying loads. The sage asked the reason, and received "for answer, 'Mighty sovereign! in this city there is no one who gives "alms. I am therefore compelled to cut wood and sell it, and a "potter's wife makes bread for me—in this labor my hair is worn "away.' The holy man said, 'I will myself go to-day to beg.' He "did so, but with the exception of the potter's wife no one gave alms. "The saint became very angry; he sent his disciple to tell the potter, "—'Take your family with you and leave the city. This very day "it shall be overwhelmed.' The potter and his wife quitted Wullub-"hee, taking their son with them. The sage had cautioned the "woman that she should not turn to look back, but when she had "reached the sea shore, near where the town of Bhownugger now "stands, she disobeyed the order, and, turning back, looked toward "Wullubhee. She was immediately changed into a stone image, "which is to this day worshipped in that place, under the name of "the Roowâpooree Mother. Meanwhile the saint having taken into "his hands an earthen vessel, reversed it, pronouncing the words,— "'City! be thou overthrown, and thy wealth turned into dust.' In "that moment Wullubhee was destroyed."

A jungle of peeloo trees,[1] of considerable extent, lies on the western

[1] "There is," says Sir Alexander Burnes, in his travels into Bokhara, vol. iii., p. 122, "a shrub called 'peeloo,' (Salvadora Persica,) which is to be found in this

and northern sides of the modern town of Wulleh. It is traversed in every direction by roads, and includes the principal part of the remains of Wullubheepoor which is exposed to view. Numerous excavations have been made within this jungle by the people of the town in search of materials for building; they exhibit what are apparently foundation-walls, frequently four-and-a-half feet wide, constructed of large burnt bricks and earth. The trenches assume occasionally the form of mines, and are carried down in some places to water, which is found to be saline. Similar traces of brickwork walls are discoverable, it is said, in most places within a distance of three or four miles from the town of Wulleh. The bricks measure frequently sixteen inches in length, ten in width, and three in depth.

A river called the Ghelo, or "insane," from its violent movements during the rainy months, runs round the outside of the peeloo jungle, and as it frequently alters its course, it has been an active agent in laying bare to view the remains of Wullubhee; in this task it has been assisted, to a considerable extent, by occasional streams formed, for the time being, by an accumulation of water in the rains struggling in this level plain to find for itself a means of escape.

To the north of the town the site of a reservoir, which bears the name of Ghorârdumun, is pointed out, and to the south-west is a large flat space, covered in the cold months with a rich clothing of green wheat, which is called the Rutun-tank, and the surrounding mound of which may still in some places be traced.

Within the space occupied by the peeloo trees, and on all sides of Wulleh, are to be found numerous emblems of Shiva and of the bull, his attendant, formed of granite, and considerable in point of size. These, where they rest upon brickwork, are found at nearly the actual ground level, a fact which (as they must have stood upon the floors of temples) would seem to indicate that the town had not been submerged. The Phallic emblems are themselves mostly entire, but the bulls, which accompany them, have in no case escaped mutilation. Of the latter, the most remarkable is a large granite figure, wanting

"neighbourhood, (the desert that lies between the Chenab and the Indus,) and in all "tracts of saline soil that border on the Indus and Punjab rivers. It produces a "red and white berry, which has but a poor flavour; the taste of its seed resembles "water-cresses: this is the season of the fruit (June), and it was exposed for sale "in the bazaars of Mooltan. I observed this shrub in the greatest abundance in "the Delta and lower parts of Sinde; and, as I am satisfied that it is only to be "found in the particular soil described, I believe we recognise it in Arrian's Indian "History. 'The leaves resemble those of the laurel; they grow *chiefly* in places "where the tide flows among them, and where they are again left dry at low water. "Their flower is white, and in shape like a violet, but much excelling it in sweet-"ness.'"

the head, and split across the body, which lies near a large Ling,[1] called Butheshwur Muhâ Dev. Every one of the emblems which has been discovered has a name assigned to it by the Bramins, as Wyejnâth, Rutuneshwur, Eeshwureeo Muhâ Dev, and others. The bulls are well executed, and, unlike modern figures of Nundee, are placed in the true position of a sitting animal.

According to Colonel Tod, Kunuksen, a prince of the race of the sun, abandoned his native kingdom of Koshul—that kingdom of which Ayoodhya was the capital and Rama the monarch—in A.D. 144 or 145, and established himself on the site of Veirât, the celebrated abode of the sons of Pândoo during their exile, and which is supposed to have occupied the position of the modern town of Dholka. He wrested dominion from a prince of the Purmâr race, and founded Wurnugger. Four centuries afterwards his descendant Veejye founded Veejâpoor, and Vidurba, since called Seehore, and the same race founded also the renowned city of Wullubhee and Gujnee, near the modern Cambay, which was involved in the fall of Wullubhee.[2]

In another place the same author states, that Kunuksen, having migrated to Soorâshtra, fixed his residence at Dhânk, anciently called Moongee Puttun, and that on the conquest of the region called Bâlkhetur, (still known as "the Bhâl,") his race assumed the title of Bâlla Rajpoots. On the fall of Wullubhee, part of the inhabitants fled to Balli, a Jain town on the borders of Mewar and Marwar, others to Sandera and Nadole in the latter province.[3]

The Jain writers, whose description we have quoted, place the fall of Wullubhee in the year of Vikrum 375 (A.D. 319). In that year, however, an era, called the "Wullubhee era," commenced,[4] and it is probable that the date of the fall of the city has been confounded by these writers with the date of the commencement of the era called by its name. The Shutroonjye Muhâtmâ gives the year of Vikrum 477 (A.D. 421) for the accession of a king named Sheelâditya, who restored temples on the mountain. As many as four kings of the name of Sheelâditya are, however, mentioned in different lists of the

[1] "Ling" is the name of the Phallic emblem. The lings at Wulleh are similar to those which are found in modern temples, but very much larger. They are granite monolithes, commencing in a square pedestal about two feet high, which passes into a cylinder about three feet in height and eight in circumference, rounded at the top. Some of them ascend from the square into an octagon, and thence into the cylinder.

[2] *Vide* Annals of Rajasthan, vol. i., pp. 83 and 215 to 218.

[3] *Vide* Western India, pp. 51, 148, 268, 352. Rajasthan, vol. i., p. 217.

[4] *Vide* Tod's Western India, p. 506 Inscription from Billâwul.

Wullubhee sovereigns, derived from inscriptions on copper plates.[1]

Of these princes eighteen are mentioned, the first two of whom bore the title of senâputee, or military chief, and are conjectured to have been vassals of the Purmârs of Oojein.[2] The remaining princes used the sovereign title "Muhâ Râjâ." They were also called "Shree Bhuttârk," or illustrious warrior, and appear to have been (the large majority of them) "great worshippers of Muheshwur," or followers of Shiva, the figure of the sacred bull, his attendant Nundee, appearing both upon their seals and banners, and the emblems of the god forming, as we have seen, one of the most striking features in the remains of their long-fallen capital. The dates which have been derived (conjecturally) from these inscriptions range from A.D. 144 to A.D. 559. The latest of these would, however, appear to be too early for the true date of the fall of Wullubhee. We are told in a Chinese account of India that "Under the Tang dynasty, in the years Woo teh (A.D. 618 "to 627), there were great troubles in India: the king (Sheelâditya?) "fought great battles. The Chinese Buddhist priest, Hiuan thsang, "who writes his travels, arrived in India at this period and had "audience of Sheelâditya."[3]

"The country of Wullubhee," as is remarked in the narrative quoted by M. Jacquet,[4] "a country so named north of Larica, has more than "six thousand leagues (li) of circumference. The capital city of that "country has more than thirty leagues of circumference. The pro- "ductions of the sun, the conditions of the temperature, the manners "and the physical character of the inhabitants, are the same as in the "country of Malwa. The number of the inhabitants is considerable; "the families are opulent; indeed, they number there more than a "hundred houses possessing a fortune of a hundred lakhs; immense "treasures come from the most remote countries to accumulate them- "selves in this kingdom. One finds there more than a hundred "*Kialan* (Buddhist monasteries); the clergy there are more than six "thousand in number; they study for the most part the section of "the Scriptures called *the perfect measure*, which belongs to the little "*yâna*. There are some hundreds of temples consecrated to Devs; "the heretics are there in great number. Buddha, during the time

[1] *Vide* Journ. Asiat. Soc. (Bengal), iv. 477; ditto, vii. 966; Journ. Asiat. Soc. (Bombay), iii. 213, &c. &c.

[2] More probably, we should say, of the Solunkhees of Kuleeân.

[3] *Vide* Journal of the Royal Asiatic Society, vol. vi. p. 351, et seq.

[4] In his note on Wullubhee in the Journ. Asiatic Soc. (Bengal), vol. v. p. 685, from "The Narrative of a Chinese Buddhist priest who visited Transoxiana, Bac- "tria, and India in the year 632 of our era and the following years." The names have been substituted according to M. Jacquet's suggestions.

"that he was in the world of men, has often visited this country; the "king *Asoka*, too, has raised pillars beside all the trees under which "Buddha had rested himself, to cause them to be recognised. The "reigning dynasty is of the race of the Kshutriyas; the old king was "the nephew of Sheelâditya, king of the country of Malwa; he who "now rules is son-in-law of Sheelâditya, king of the country of Canouj; "he is named Drouv-Bhatta." This Drouv-Bhatta, M. Jacquet considers to be Drouv Sen II., the eleventh prince of the dynasty of Wullubhee. The reign of Sheelâditya IV., the last sovereign of the line, in whose time the destruction of the city occurred, would thus (allowing twenty years for each reign) be brought down to as late a time as about A.D. 770. Mr. Wathen, however, conjecturally fixes it more than two centuries earlier.

The barbarian invaders of Wullubhee are supposed by the annalist of Rajasthan to have been Scythians. Mr. Wathen suggests that they were Bactro-Indians, of which race many coins have been found in Soreth; and Mr. Elphinstone thinks they may have been Persians under Nousheerwân the Great. Were it not mentioned that the invaders were Mlechh, or tribes that were not Hindoos, we might have supposed that the Solunkhees of Kuleeân in the Dekkan had destroyed Wullubhee in the attempt to recover their supremacy in Soreth. So much uncertainty, however, exists in regard to the time of the fall of Wullubhee, that any speculations in regard to its destroyers can be raised upon but an insecure foundation. The next dynasty which we hear of in this part of India is that of the Chowras of Unhilpoor, a capital said to have been founded in A.D. 746. The accounts which we shall now have to present would seem to indicate that the foundation of the Chowra capital succeeded not very distantly the fall of Wullubheepoor.

CHAP. II.

JYE SHEKER THE CHOWRA, PRINCE OF PUNCHÂSUR.

WE now proceed, following Shree Mull Sooree and the other fugitives, whom we have beheld escaping thither from Wullubhee to Punchâsur, near the Runn of Kutch. Our guide is the "Rutun Mâlâ," or garland of jewels, a work composed in verse by a Brahmin named Krishnâjee, to celebrate the praises of the great lion-king of Goozerat.

"Great is the fame of the Solunkhee race," exclaims the poet; "it "is a race of Devs; Sidh Râj is the light thereof." It is the aid of his patron, the Goddess of Eloquence alone, which can enable him to recount, worthily, the praises of his hero, though the compositions of former poets have smoothed the road he has to travel, and the pearls which he is proceeding to string have been already pierced by their diamond-like ingenuity. But Krishnâjee would have been no true bard had he been dissatisfied with his own performances, and his self-laudation is conveyed in language which proves that, however liberal in estimating the works of others, he was by no means insensible to the value of his own.

"As a man who has bathed in the ocean, has performed all pil-"grimages,[1] as a man who has tasted ambrosia requires no longer any "other food, as a man who possesses the philosopher's stone is the "owner of all wealth, so that man has read all books who has studied "Rutun Mâlâ. He whose research is infinite, but who has not read "Rutun Mâlâ, is like a marble reservoir which is destitute of water, "or a splendid temple which wants a spire."

We are sorry to have to add, that of this inestimable garland, which originally contained one hundred and eight jewels, only eight remain.

The scene is Kuleeân, where Raja Bhoowur, the Solunkhee, rules, and the time is the year of Vikrum 752, or A.D. 696. The king is surrounded by his sixteen military nobles, whom he retains always about his person. They are faithful men; lovers of the king's prosperity; blenching not in fight; resolute as pillars of the sky. Their names are contained in the verse,—

"Chund, Dwund, Bhut, Veyd, Veer,
"Singh, Sindhoo, Geeree, Dheer,
"Sâmut, Dheemut, Dhunwee, Putoo,
"Bheem, Muhâruthee, Meer."

Of these, Meer is the principal, and he is never sent abroad on service. The others are despatched to conquer on all sides, south, north, west, east. Of the surrounding princes, the Goozerat Raja alone remains unvanquished. He is of the Chowra race; his name Jye Sheker; that of his consort Roop Soonduree. Punchâsur is his royal seat. Strong, handsome, and wise; his treasures are inexhaustible, and his army cannot be counted. Of his very existence, however, Bhoowur is kept in ignorance by his chieftains, and fondly reposes in the belief that the whole world is under his control.

[1] Because the sacred rivers, which are the scenes of pilgrimage, flow into the ocean.

The capital city, Kuleeân, is filled with the spoils of conquered foes, with camels, horses, cars, and elephants. Jewellers, cloth-makers, chariot-builders, makers of ornamental vessels reside there, and the walls of the houses are covered with colored pictures. Physicians and professors of the mechanical arts abound, as well as those of music, and schools are provided for public education. It is for the sole purpose of comparing the capital city of Ceylon with Kuleeân that the sun remains half the year in the north and half in the south.

Among other virtues, King Bhoowur is personally ambitious of all kinds of wisdom, and he is besides a great patron of literature, and especially, as becomes a wise Hindoo sovereign, of grammar and prosody. His encouragement of learned men is so great, that all cleverness travels towards his palace as certainly as all the waters of the rainy season travel seawards.

One day the king is seated in a garden as beautiful as Shiva's paradise, adorned with exquisite flowers and fruit-trees, where he regales himself with song and the dance. Prince Kurun, the heir apparent, sits beside him royally apparelled, and Chund and others of the nobles adorn the assembly. There sit there also a number of learned men and poets, each outshining the other in wit and wisdom; but superior to all is the poet king Kâm Râj, the sovereign's friend, who shines among the wise as Bhoowur himself among the warriors. At this time a foreign poet approaching King Bhoowur, presents, as his offering, a string of verses in his praise. The king, delighted with the skill therein displayed, calls upon the poets who surround him to compose an answer, but this no one has the courage to attempt. Bhoowur presents the stranger with a magnificent dress of honor, and enquires of him what is his name, and what that of the country in which he has remained concealed so many years. The poet replies that his name is Shunkur. "I come," says he, "from Goojur-"land, the fairest portion of the earth, a land full of fertility, splendid "with water, grass, and trees, where money is plentiful, and where "men are generous. There is Punchâsur, the residence of Ocean's "daughter,[1] which equals the city of the gods so completely, that no "one dwelling there has any desire for Paradise. The Chowra Raja "rules there, who is the pinnacle of all warrior races, and who by his "exploits, having raised a mountain of fame, has been hailed by the "poets as Jye Sheker.[2] His chief queen is the incomparable Roop "Soonduree, whose brother is the wise and valiant Soor Pâl. Jye

[1] Suruswutee, the Goddess of Eloquence.
[2] Which name means the "Fame-pinnacle."

"Sheker and Soorpâl united could tear the King of Heaven from his "throne, but little need have they of that, for their own royal "Goozerat is the essence of the universe. There Suruswutee dwells "for ever incarnate; it is there I have acquired this skill, and thence "I have come forth to conquer the world." King Bhoowur, hearing this praise of Goozerat, claps his hand on his moustache in defiance. The poet Kâm Râj starts up, and challenges Shunkur to contend with him in verse, but is signally defeated by the latter, who scornfully reminds him that Shiva (Shunkur) is notoriously the conqueror of the God of Love (Kâm.)

Bhoowur Raja, not well pleased with this termination of the day's amusements, returns to his palace. In the evening he summons his chieftains, and desires to hear more of Goozerat. The assembled warriors attempt to impose upon him with a story of their having defeated Jye Sheker, and taken Punchâsur, which they had, however, refrained from destroying, on its prince's submission. The Raja, however, disbelieves this tale, and eventually compels Chund to tell the truth. He learns from him that the nobles of Kuleeân, on their way southwards from Urbood Geeree, or Mount Aboo, had met with Soorpâl, in command of his brother-in-law's troops, and that finding it a dangerous matter to contend with him, they had avoided an engagement, and passed on by a circuitous route to Soreth. The Raja immediately gives orders for the preparation of an army, which is soon in array and marching to attack Jye Sheker. Bad omens meet them as they advance, but the king's orders being peremptory, the chieftains do not permit a halt.

Shunkur, the poet, has in the meantime returned home, and made his prince acquainted with what has happened. Jye Sheker, who is of a warlike temper, is delighted at the prospect of the strife, and commences to distribute bracelets, earrings, and other ornaments among his chieftains.

King Bhoowur's force continues to advance. The horsemen and elephants are numerous; there are four thousand war chariots, troops bearing missile weapons, and foot soldiers without number. The villages on their route are deserted by the inhabitants immediately the approach of the army is perceived; such as resist are stormed and plundered. Where the invaders pass, watered lands become dry, and dry lands are moistened. At each halting place the troops practice athletic games, and exercise themselves in missile and hand-to-hand weapons. Having reached their enemy's country, they take and plunder a frontier town, and at last pitch their camp six miles from Punchâsur, from which position they plunder the country round, carrying off men and women as prisoners.

Jye Sheker, when he hears of these proceedings, is inflamed with anger from head to foot. He writes a letter to Meer, the chief of the invaders, upbraiding him with his oppression of the poor, so unworthy of a warrior, and comparing him to a dog which when it has been struck with a stone, bites the stone instead of fronting the striker. Meer replies by summoning him to make submission to King Bhoowur, taking grass in his mouth, and denounces war as the alternative, a challenge which Jye Sheker has no sooner received than he calls his "brothers" and other warriors together, and prepares for battle on the morrow.

Soorpâl, who has not been present when Meer's answer is received, determines, unknown to his prince, on surprising the camp of the invaders during the night, at the head of his own partisans. Circumstances favor his intention, and he finds the enemy wholly unprepared; some are absent plundering the neighbouring villages, some eating and drinking, some asleep, some enjoying music and the dance. Soorpâl's followers bursting in upon them, sword in hand, find no more labour in destroying them than the grass-cutter does in cutting grass. Chund is cut down by Soorpâl himself, and Dwund severely wounded; their army is scattered as a crowd of deer among whom a lion has rushed, and flies with the greatest precipitation. Dwund dies of his wounds in the retreat. Veyd, the kinsman of the Purmâr Raja, broken hearted at his disgrace, casts off his military attire, and in the dress of a monk takes the road to Benares. Meer, the chief leader, knowing that his face has been blackened, halts his flying army at eight days' march distance from the capital of his sovereign. King Bhoowur, hearing of this defeat, repairs to Meer's encampment, and addresses himself to re-encourage the fugitive troops, reminding them that retreat is sometimes only the prelude to victory, and that a weapon does not strike its hardest blows until it has been swung backwards. Bhoowur having succeeded in reinspiriting the army and its leaders, holds a council of war, in which an immediate advance upon Goozerat, led by the king in person, is determined upon. They meet good omens on their way, and the air resounds with their instruments of music—the war-horn, the tabor, and the terrible drum.

On their approach, Jye Sheker shuts himself up in Punchâsur, which is closely invested by King Bhoowur. An attack by Meer is met and repulsed by Soorpâl. The Prince of Punchâsur having assembled his warriors, recommends those who "love their lives" to retire, but the unanimous answer is, that they are Rajpoots, of good descent, and that all are ready to die with him; that should any one disgrace himself by deserting in such an emergency, the crows would disdain to eat his flesh, and he would remain for ten millions of the days of Brahma in hell. After fifty-two days spent in unsuccessful attacks, King Bhoowur calls Meer into council, and the latter advises that an attempt should be made to corrupt the fidelity of Soorpâl. A letter, written with the milk of a shrub, is then despatched to that chieftain, who, on applying saffron to it, ascertains its contents. The offers of King Bhoowur are, however, indignantly rejected by Soorpâl, who, in answer, declares himself to be as inseparable from Jye Sheker as water which has been once mingled with it is from milk. "O! full of folly," he exclaims, "I am well born, how of seducing "me do you entertain hope. Were the three worlds' royalty offered, "none but a bastard would receive it."

As night comes on, the kings, each in his own army, cause verses from the Muhâbhârut to be recited,—that great poem which increases the zeal of the warrior, while it supplies him with science. The chieftains of Goozerat, when they hear the wonderful exploits of Bheem, become full of fire. They ask, "When will the night pass "away; when will the morning come—the time of battle?"

"As a lonely wife longs for her husband's coming,
"So they restlessly await the morning till it arrives;
"From the lessons of the Muhâbhârut they have learned
"That the battle-slain win Upsuras to wife.
"Joyful then they long to obtain the residence of the gods,
"Abandoning this home of dust and worthlessness.
"At Jye Sheker's call, when the morning rises,
"The splendid warriors all prepare;
"From the field, victorious, they have no hope to return—
"To fight, to die, to wed the Heavenly damsels, is all their desire.
"Such stedfastness of the heroes perceiving,
"For marriage prepare the divine brides—
"What time the warriors don their armour,
"The Upsurâs deck themselves in gay apparel—
"What time the warriors grasp their weapons,
"The Virgins of Paradise wave the marriage garland with their hands;
"What time the warriors shake their horses reins,
"The celestial damsels urge their chariots to speed."

Roop Soonduree, from the inmost hall, hears the terrible sound of commencing battle—she sends for her lord, and entreats him not to venture into the field unless the omens are propitious, but Jye Sheker replies, that when a bride is to be married, or a foe driven from the gates, there is no omen but the name of Shree Krishn. The opposing armies meet as clouds dashed together by the violence of the storm; their weapons gleam like lightning; the earth resounds with their tread as with the rumbling of thunder; war music sounds, making even the timid valorous; arrows and missiles fall in showers, as rain from the monsoon clouds; with the bill, the mace, the trident, they struggle; elephant strives with elephant, horse with horse, chariot lord with chariot lord. The corpses of the dead float in rivers of blood; the warriors laugh as the terrible roar of battle increases in loudness. The minstrels encourage the less eager—"Well done, sons "of the warriors," they cry, "in this battle-pilgrimage, never again to "be met with, acquire world-wide fame, win paradise, extort homage "from gods and men, in this world and the other be immortal."

The shout of battle rising to the skies attracts the attention of the divinities; they ask whether the fight has begun again in the field of the Kooroos.[1] The Upsuras dance, the heavenly minstrels strike their lyres, the deities and the snakes of hell tremble. Shiva hovers over the spot, stringing his never-to-be-completed chaplet of human skulls; witches and ghosts surround him, and the terrible Flesh-eaters and Fates, with their cups of blood, are attracted to the scene like vultures.

Soorpâl, with his accustomed valour, drives back that part of the attacking force which is led by the chieftain Bhut; but King Bhoowur, in person, rallies the fugitives, threatening them with death, and Bhut himself plunges desperately into the thick of the enemy, slaying numbers of them, until he falls pierced with a shower of arrows, and at last mortally wounded by the hand of Soorpâl. The headlong valour of Bhut, however, gains its purpose, for his followers succeed in repulsing the troops of Jye Sheker and establishing themselves under the west side of the fort, in which a breach is soon effected.

Jye Sheker finds that the number of his warriors has been frightfully reduced in this sanguinary engagement, and now, deprived of all hope of victory, he sends for Soorpâl and entreats him to preserve the seed of his race by conveying to some place of safety his pregnant sister Roop Soonduree. Soorpâl at first refuses, but the prince adjures him by his love to obey his directions—"for my advantage let it be "done at once," he says, "there is none of my race to make funeral "offerings, the progenitors will obtain no respect, no liberation will

[1] The battle field of the Kooroos and Pânduvs in the epic poem, the Muhâ Bhârut.

"the sonless find, O! brother; the seed of my race will be destroyed, "the enemy will rule without a thorn." Thus urged, Soorpâl retires from the fort, taking his sister with him; but, Roop Soonduree, when at last she discovers the cause of their flight, refuses to continue it, and declares her resolution of burning with the body of her lord. She is, however, dissuaded from this intention by the same argument, regarding the extinction of the race, which had prevailed with Soorpâl himself. Her brother leaves her in the forest, with the intention of returning to die with the prince Jye Sheker.[1]

Meanwhile, King Bhoowur, perceiving that the fort cannot be defended longer, sends an embassy to Jye Sheker, proposing to leave him in possession of the throne of Goozerat on his making submission in the usual form, and appearing to touch the feet of his conqueror, with his hands bound behind him, holding grass in his mouth. Jye Sheker answers, that life would have no pleasure for him after such submission, that Paradise will be good exchange for Goojurland, and that he, the last of the Chowra race, will at least leave behind him its honor. Bhoowur, enraged, immediately prepares to complete his conquest. The few followers that remained to Jye Sheker soon fall, oppressed by superior numbers. The prince himself makes a most desperate resistance, mowing down his enemies like grass; at last, however, he is slain, and over his body the enemy enters Punchâsur. The keepers of the gates, and the guards at the court, resist to the death; but, after a tremendous struggle, Bhoowur forces his way to the palace. He is there opposed by a furious band of female attendants, armed with the bars of the doors or whatever other weapon offers, and his troops are driven by these beyond the gates of the city. The damsels have now gained their object, which is to secure the corpse of their master, and they soon erect a funeral pile of scented wood, interspersed with cocoa-nuts, upon which they consume themselves along with the body of Jye Sheker. Four queens also ascend the pile, with many slaves and damsels. Townspeople too, many of them, love enthralled, follow their prince to the gate of the King of Heaven. At last Bhoowur, forcing his way back with his

1 "And I the rather wean me from despair,
"For love of Edward's offspring in my womb.
"This is it that makes me bridle passion
"And bear with mildness my misfortune's cross;
"Ay, ay, for this I draw in many a tear,
"And stop the rising of blood-sucking sighs,
"Lest with my sighs or tears I blast or drown
"King Edward's fruit, true heir to the English crown."
Third Part of King Henry VI. Act IV., scene 4.

army, causes the burning to cease, and takes upon himself to celebrate duly the funeral rites of the Chowra prince, whom he praises as an honor to those who gave him birth—a true warrior. Over the place where the pile stood he builds a temple of Shiva, who is there enthroned under the title of "the Goojur Lord." The day that Jye Sheker finds his death, the sun is obscured, the four points of the compass wear a terrible aspect, the earth trembles, the river's water becomes muddy, the wind blows hot, the fires of the sacrificial pits emit a dense smoke, stars fall from the heavens; men, seeing these portents, lament that a hero has perished.

King Bhoowur, having received the submission of the lords of Kutch and Soreth, and perceiving the beauty of Goozerat, is desirous of living there; but his councillors remind him that Soorpâl lives to be a thorn in his side, and he is therefore content with fixing the tribute to be paid by the surrounding princes, and appointing a minister to represent him in Goozerat.

Soorpâl, returning from placing his sister in safety, finds Jye Sheker already slain. His first impulse is to rush into the fight and follow him in death; but on reflection he considers, "if I die fighting, then "Bhoowur's kingdom will be without a thorn; what was to happen "has happened; now, for the future, counsel must be taken. If "fortune shall grant a son to my sister, I will again recover the "royalty of Goozerat; without my aid that task cannot be effected." He sets off to seek his sister; but being unsuccessful in his attempts at discovering her, or, as some say, being ashamed to present himself before her, he takes up his residence in the forests about the mountain of Girnâr to await better times.

Roop Soonduree herself, after Soorpâl's departure, is discovered by a Bheel woman, who, perceiving her to be a lady of rank, addresses her respectfully,—"remain in the forest with me, O sister! flowers, "leaves, fruits good for food may be had in the mountains, safe "shelter shall you find there." The queen accedes to her entreaties and remains her guest until the time of her delivery arrives, and she gives birth to a son. It is in the spring season, on the fifteenth day of the delightful month of Wyeshâk, at the time of the sun's appearing, that this sun of the land rises; he who is destined to be full of exploits, the protector of cows and Brahmins. Clear that morn rises the orb of day, clear is the sky, clear the river's stream, the Brahmins' sacrificial pit emits no smoke, men know that a hero has been born.

When the boy is six years old, a Jain monk, passing through the forest, beholds a cradle swinging from the branches of a tree, the infant reposing in which seems like a dweller in the courts of the King of Heaven. Astonished, the holy man makes enquiry, and, discovering the mother to be a queen, a king's wife, he brings her with due respect to the city. He informs the mourning lady of the death of Jye Sheker, and, re-assuring her, promises to protect her infant. Born in the forest the child receives from the ascetic the name of Wun Râj, "the Forest King;" but the secret of his birth is soon known to Soorpâl, who from his forest lair keeps the minister of King Bhoowur in continual alarm. Thither he secretly brings the son of his sister, and under his protection Wun Râj resides until his fourteenth year, rising, like a young lion, ever in valor, strength, and prudence, and meditating in his heart the recovery of his father's throne.

CHAP. III.

WUN RÂJ AND HIS SUCCESSORS—THE CHOWRA DYNASTY OF UNHILPOOR.

THE Jain accounts, and those which are still traditionally related in Goozerat, of the rise of Wun Râj agree with that given in the Rutun Mâlâ. The Châpotkut or Chowra tribe, to which the prince of Punchâsur belonged, is supposed to have had its origin in the countries west of the Indus. It belongs neither to the solar nor to the lunar race, and is confined to Western India. The predecessors of Jye Sheker or Jus Râj Chowra are said to have been princes of Dev and Puttun Somnâth, two sea-ports on the coast of Soreth. They may have been vassals of the Kings of Wullubhee, and have retreated on the destruction of that city to the less exposed situation of Punchâsur, the Jains and other subjects of Wullubhee who have been already spoken of availing themselves of their protection. The name of Punchâsur is still preserved in a small town belonging to the Nowâb of Rhâdunpoor, on the edge of the lesser Runn of Kutch. The village of Chundoor, a few miles north of Punchâsur, is the place assigned for Wun Râj's birth; and another small town, named after him Wunod, is pointed out as the spot at which he resided in his childhood. There is a temple there dedicated to Wunâvee mother, his family goddess, and a well, called Wen, said to have been constructed by his order. This part of Goozerat is still known by the name of Wudeeâr,[1] which is that given to it by the Jain chroniclers. It is a flat and poorly-cultivated country, partaking of the character of the Runn in its immediate neighbourhood, and studded with small villages, easily discerned from a distance by the clumps of trees which are entirely confined to their vicinity. At Rântoj and Sunkheshur, which are near Punchâsur, there still remain temples of the Jain religion, which, though they have been more than once re-erected, have probably occupied those sites from a very early date, and at Vishroda and other places in the neighbourhood vestiges of ancient towns similar to those which are found about Wulleh may still be discerned.

The Jain monk, who was the means of the preservation of Wun Râj, was named Sheelgun Sooree. The young prince is said to have spent his earlier years in the convent to which the Sooree was attached, and stories, such as those which are told of Cyrus in old, or of Guiderius and Arviragus, or of Norval, in modern literature, are related of the unusual spirit of the royal child, which belied his apparent origin. When old enough to endure the hardships of the outlaw's life he joined his uncle Soorpâl in many a foray, in which he distinguished himself by his personal valor as well as encouraged his followers by his bold assumption of royal state, and by his partitioning among them, as if already in his gift, the honors and offices of his still-to-be-recovered kingdom. Shree Devee, the wife of a trader who had hospitably entertained him, was promised the honor of anointing him at his coronation. Jâmb or Châmpâ, a merchant, distinguished by his gallantry and warlike skill, the future founder of Châmpâner, was already designated as the King's minister, and for Unhil, another of his followers, to whose local knowledge he was indebted, was reserved the honor of giving his name to the royal city. Many years, however, passed away in these wanderings; the accession of new friends was counterbalanced by the loss of his brave and faithful kinsman Soorpâl, and the Forest King, though abandoning none of his pretensions, seemed likely to acquire practically no more permanent title of royalty than that for which he was indebted to the misfortunes of his birth. His constancy, however, at last obtained its reward. King Bhoowur had assigned the revenues of Goozerat as the portion of his daughter, Milan Devee, and the Chowra chieftain was appointed by that princess's council of management to the office of "Selbhrut" or spear-bearer, receiving probably, like chiefs of more modern times, emoluments designed as much to secure his forbearance

[1] *Vide* Hamilton's Gazeteer, Art. Werrear. "Beecharjer," there, is a mistake for Becherâjee or Boucherâjee, the temple, &c., of the Devee so named.

as to purchase his protection. For neither purpose, however, were they effectual. The delegates from Kuleeân having remained six months in the country, and collected a large sum of money and numbers of the valuable horses for which Soreth has ever been famed, were on their return homewards, when they were attacked, plundered, and slain by Wun Râj. For some time after this exploit he appears to have found it necessary to retire to different parts of the country, where forests or mountains afforded him shelter from the vengeance of the Kuleeân monarch; but the spoils which he had acquired enabled him shortly afterwards to carry out his long-meditated project, by commencing the erection of the new capital of Unhilpoor or Unhilwârâ.

"In the year 802 (A.D. 746)," says a bardic verse, "a city was "founded to last for ever; on Muhâ wud 7th, on the day of strength "Saturday, at three in the afternoon Wun Raja's order was proclaimed. "The Jain monks skilled in astrology having been consulted, after "studying the city's horoscope, made known that in the year twelve "hundred and ninety-seven Unhilpoor would be desolate." How this prophecy was fulfilled in the bloody and destructive days of Allah-ood-Deen, "The Murderous," will be seen in the sequel of our story.

Having celebrated his enthronization, at which Shree Devee assisted, and having installed Jâmb as his minister, Wun Râj next directed his attention to his old protector, Sheelgun Sooree, under whose care his mother, Roop Soonduree, still remained, consoled for her widowed state and fallen fortunes by the practice of the rites expected from a zealous follower of the Jain religion. The old Queen and her spiritual preceptor, with the idol which they served, were brought to Unhilpoor, where a temple was erected which received the object of their worship, under the title of Punchâsura Pârusnâth. An image of Wun Râj himself (which is still preserved) in the attitude of a worshipper, covered, however, by the scarlet umbrella, denoting his royal state, was also placed in the temple; and in the protection thus given to the religion of the Shrâwuks, the Jain chronicler had doubtless some foundation for his boast that "the throne of Goozerat from the time "of Wun Râj even the Jains established, though from hate this truth "is not received." What religion Wun Raja himself adhered to cannot be decisively ascertained. He is described as "a lover of Devs," and is praised for his conquests over that God of Love who claims even the great Muhâ Dev[1] as his sometime slave. There are

[1] Muhâ Dev is the common name of Shiva. The group called "Oomâ Mu-"heshwur" represents this deity and his consort Pârwutee. Gunesh, the God of Wisdom, is the son of the latter.

still to be found at Puttun images of Oomâ Muheshwur and of Gunesh, which bear inscriptions asserting that they were installed by Wun Râj in the year of the foundation of Unhilwârâ. Probably the first Chowra prince was, as some of his successors appear to have been, sufficiently liberal in his religious opinions; and though himself a follower of Shiva, he may have been prompted by gratitude and filial affection, as well as by policy, to encourage the professors of the religion of the Teerthunkers.

Wun Raja was born in A.D. 696, and reigned sixty years in Unhilwârâ. He died in 806, and was succeeded on the throne by his son, Yog Râj.[1]

Of the son of Wun Râj little has been handed down, but that little would seem to declare him to have been a prince worthy of more fortunate times. He steadily increased his dominion and its resources; he was skilled in martial exercises, "an archer equal to the lord of the Devs." He was also what may appear more extraordinary, skilful in literature. A work written by Yog Raja, of the nature of which, however, we are not informed, is stated to have been in existence in the time of his chroniclers. It related, perhaps, to the annals of the Châpotkut clan, or more probably was devoted to the praises of Oomâ's lord, or to the divine lover[2] of Râdhâ, celebrated in so many a verse.

One incident alone is preserved by the chroniclers of Goozerat, of the times when Yog Raja reigned in Unhilwârâ. Certain foreign ships having arrived at the sea port of Puttun in Soreth, laden with valuable merchandise, though neither the port from which they departed nor the country to which they were destined is known, the traders were, contrary to the express prohibitions of the king, attacked and plundered by the heir to the throne, Prince Kshem Râj. This violation of the laws of hospitality appears to have been most bitterly regretted by the king, who blamed Kshem Râj and his two brothers, who had shared

[1] According to the author of Rutun Mâlâ, Wun Râj was born in A.D. 696. Wilford, quoting from the Ayeen i Akberi, says that he built Nerwala in 746, at the age of fifty, and must therefore have been born in 696. The Prubundh Chintâmunee states that Wun Râj reigned sixty years, from 746 to 806. This would make him 110 years old at the time of his death. Colonel Tod places the beginning of his reign in 746, and says he ruled fifty years and lived sixty. But he could not have founded Unhilpoor at the age of ten, nor would the date of his death, according to this account, agree with that given by the other authorities. Probably the date assigned to Wun Râj's birth is incorrect. As to the long reigns of the Balhara princes, see, however, Tod's Western India and the remarks of the Arabian travellers.

[2] Shree Krishn, an Uvutâr or incarnation of Vishnoo.

in his expedition, declaring that they had undone all that he had striven for during his life. "When in distant countries," said he, "the "men of wisdom have weighed the actions of princes, then the sove-"reigns of Goozerat have been despised as ruling over a kingdom of "thieves. That fault of our ancestors I had hoped to have made "dim, that I too might have been received into the line of kings. "This avarice of yours has brightened it anew. It is thus written in "the rules of policy—'Disobeying the injunction of a king, destroy-"ing the livelihood of a Brahmin, departing from the bed of a wife, "these three are wounds inflicted without a weapon.'" Yog Raja[1] lived to a great age, and at the close of a reign of five and thirty years "ascended the funeral pile."

Of the immediate successors of Yog Râj still less has been handed down. His son, Kshem Râj, though passionate in his temper, and on that account probably unfortunate in those he employed, and separated from his own kinsmen, still added to the extent and wealth of his kingdom. He died in A.D. 866, after a reign of five and twenty years.

Shree Bhooyud, the son of Kshem Râj, reigned till A.D. 895. His reign was prosperous and peaceful, "no enemy opposing him."

Shree Vair Singh, "the lion of his enemies," had a more troubled reign than his father, Bhooyud. He encountered the barbarians, but with success—"contending in war, he never suffered defeat." He was assisted by a minister "of great wisdom." We have been unable to discover any clue to the foreign war here mentioned.

Rutunâditya, the Reshadut of the Mohammedan Historians, succeeded his father Vair Singh, in the year A.D. 920.

"The sun he seemed of the earth, his splendor was measureless, "he took affliction from the world, famous was he for strength, coura-"geous, adhering to his pledge; neither thieves, cheats, libertines, "nor liars did he permit to remain in the land." He died A.D. 935, and was succeeded by his son, Sâmunt Singh, the last prince of the direct line of Wun Râj, and of the house of the Chowras.

[1] A Mohammedan invasion is stated to have occurred in the reign of Khoman of Cheetore, a contemporary of Yog Râj, when among other chiefs, of names afterwards well known in Goozerat, the following came to aid the Gehlote prince,—from Mangrol, the Mucwahana; from Taragur, (q. Taringa), the Rewur; from Puttun, the royal Chawura; from Sirohee, the Deora; the Jâdoo from Joonagurh; the Jhala from Pâtree; from Choteeala (Choteyla), the Balla; from Perumgurh, the Gohil. Our authorities, however, make no mention of Yog Raja's having been engaged against the Mussulman, nor does it appear that the clans, whose leaders are mentioned, were, with the exception of the Yadoos and Balas of Soorashtra, settled at so early a period in Goozerat.

It was in the reigns of Kshem Râj and Bhooyud, that the Arabian travellers, according to M. Renaudot, visited India; and in the scanty annals of these reigns, their remarks, supposed, as they have been, to refer to the descendants of Wun Râj, deserve a place, however difficult may be the task of applying them. The first traveller states as follows:—

"Both the Indians and Chinese agree, that there are four great or "principal kings in the world; they allow the King of the Arabs to "be the first, and to be, without dispute, the most powerful of kings, "the most wealthy and the most excellent every way; because he is "the prince and head of a great religion, and because no other sur-"passes him in greatness or power."

"The Emperor of China reckons himself next after the King of "the Arabs, and after him the King of the Greeks; and lastly, the "*Balhara*, King of *Moharmi al Adan*, or of *those who have their* "*ears bored*. This *Balhara* is the most illustrious prince in all the "Indies; and all the other kings there, though each is master and "independent in his kingdom, acknowledge in him this prerogative "and pre-eminence. When he sends ambassadors to them, they re-"ceive them with extraordinary honors, because of the respect they "bear him. This king makes magnificent presents, after the manner "of the Arabs; and has horses and elephants in very great number, "and great treasures in money. He has of those pieces of silver, "called Thartarian Drams, which weigh half-a-dram more than the "Arabesque Dram. They are coined with the die of the prince, and "bear the year of his reign from the last of the reign of his prede-"cessor. They compute not their years from the æra of Mohammed, "as do the Arabs, but only by the years of their kings. Most of "these princes have lived a long time, and many of them have "reigned above fifty years; and those of the country believe that the "length of their lives, and of their reigns, is granted to them in re-"compense for their kindness to the Arabs. In truth, there are no "princes more heartily affectionate to the Arabs, and their subjects "profess the same friendship for us."

"*Balhara* is an appellative common to all these kings, as was "*Cosroes* and some others, and is not a proper name. The country "which owes obedience to this prince begins on the coast of the "province called *Kamkam*, and reaches by land to the confines of "China. He is surrounded by the dominions of many kings who "are at war with him, and yet he never marches against them. One "of these kings is the King of *Haraz*, who has very numerous forces, "and is stronger in horse than all the other princes of the Indies;

"but is an enemy to the Arabs, though he, at the same time, confesses their king to be the greatest of kings; nor is there a prince in the Indies who has a greater aversion to Mohammedism. His dominions are upon a promontory, where are much riches, many camels, and other cattle. The inhabitants here traffic with silver they wash for, and they say there are mines of the same on the continent. There is no talk of robbers in this country no more than in the rest of the Indies.

"On one side of this kingdom lies that of Tafek, which is not of very great extent; this king has the finest white women in all the Indies, but he is subject to the kings about him, his army being small. He has a great affection for the Arabs as well as the Balhara.

"These kingdoms border upon the lands of a king called *Rahmi*, who is at war with the King of Haraz and with the Balhara also. This prince is not much considered either for his birth or the antiquity of his kingdom, but his forces are more numerous than those of the Balhara, and even than those of the Kings of Haraz and Tafek. They say that when he takes the field he appears at the head of fifty thousand elephants, and that he commonly marches in the winter season, because the elephants not being able to bear with thirst, he can move at no other time. They say, also, that in his army there are commonly from ten to fifteen thousand tents. In this same country they make cotton garments in so extraordinary a manner, that nowhere else are the like to be seen. These garments are for the most part round, and wove to that degree of fineness that they may be drawn through a ring of a middling size.

"Shells are current in this country, and serve for small money, notwithstanding that they have gold and silver, wood-aloes and sable-skins, of which they make the furniture of saddles and housings. In this same country is the famous *karkandan* or unicorn. * * *

"After this kingdom there is another, which is an inland state, distant from the coast, called *Kashbin*. The inhabitants are white, and bore their ears; they have camels, and their country is a desert and full of mountains.

"Farther on upon the coast there is a small kingdom, called *Hitrange*, which is very poor; but it has a bay, where the sea throws up great lumps of ambergreese. They have, also, elephants' teeth and pepper, but the inhabitants eat it green, because of the smallness of the quantity they gather."

It is difficult to recognize in the term "Balhara"[1] anything which

[1] The term Balhara has been variously supposed to be a corruption of Balca Raee (Prince of Bal, or the Sun,) Balhiraee (for Wullubhee Râj, King of Wullub-

applies to the early Chowra sovereigns of Unhilwârâ, nor does the description of the Balhara kingdom, beginning on the coast of Kamkam, and reaching by land to the confines of China, present much more that is tangible. The traveller's assertion of the supremacy of the Balhara appears to be a more qualified one than it has been considered. Each king, it is said, though acknowledging the Balhara's pre-eminence, "is master and independent in his kingdom;" and again, in another place, "the several states of the Indies are not "subject to one and the same king, but each province has its own "king; nevertheless the Balhara is, in the Indies, as king of kings." The King of Haraz bears so far a resemblance to the Yâduv ruler of Soreth, the Râ, whose regal seat was the old fort on the hill near Girnâr, that he is described as possessing dominions situated upon a promontory, and as maintaining a superiority to his neighbours in the number of his cavalry. We can discover no clue to the account of the Kings of Tafek or Kashbin, nor to that of the Rahmi. Colonel Tod concludes Kashbin to be Kutch Bhooj, but this latter province can hardly be identified with "an inland state, distant from the "coast." The same author conjectures that Hitrunje refers to Shutroonjye. Renaudot's own remark upon the general subject is one which is still applicable. "It is well known," he says, "that the "names of these countries as they stand with us, have been for the "most part corrupted; and that they are hard to be expressed in "Arabian characters: it were then almost to no purpose to enter upon "a number of conjectures, which at the best must be very doubtful."

Some notices of customs which occur in this traveller would, however, appear well adapted to the probable state of society among the Hindoos in Goozerat at this period. The account of ordeals by fire and water we shall hereafter extract, and, in addition, we may refer to the custom, reported to be universal, of burning the bodies of the dead, to that of the voluntary self-sacrifice of wives on the funeral pile of their husbands, to the description of Ascetics, naked or covered only with a leopard's skin, standing for periods of great length with their faces exposed to the heat of the sun. "In all these king-"doms," says the traveller, "the sovereign power resides in the royal "family, and never departs from it; and those of this family succeed "each other. In like manner there are families of learned men, of "physicians, and of all the artificers concerned in architecture, and "none of these ever mix with a family of a profession different from

hee,) Bhuttarkah (Cherishing Sun, a royal title,) or to be a titular distinction locally derived from the district called the Bhal. *Vide* Jour. Roy. As. Soc., vol. xii., p. 7, and the references there quoted.

"their own." Polygamy, the common use of rice, the practice of taking answers from idols, that of total ablutions before eating, and others, are also mentioned. "The Indian dominions," it is said, "furnish a great number of soldiers who are not paid by the king, but "when they are rendezvoused for war, take the field entirely at their "own expense, and are no charge to the king."

Aboo Zeid al Hassan, the second traveller, adds "it is a customary "thing for a man and woman of the Indian blood to desire those of "their family to throw them into the fire, or drown them, when they "are grown old or perceive themselves to sink under the weight of "years, firmly believing they are to return in other bodies. The "Indians," he says, "have devotees and doctors known by the name "of Brahmins. They have poets also who compose verses stuffed "with flattery in praise of their kings. Astrologers they have, philo-"sophers, soothsayers, and men who observe the flight of birds, and "others who pretend to the calculation of nativities, particularly at "Kanuge, a great city in the kingdom of Goraz."[1] He notices the peculiarities of the rainy season—"these rains are the life of the "Indians; were they to fail they would be reduced to the deepest "want." Add the following description of the Ascetics, "Bicars," as Aboo Zeid terms them, a name which Colonel Tod conjectures to be a mistake for "Fakeers," but which may more easily be traced to "Bheekâree," "beggar," a common name for these vagrants:—

"In the Indies there are certain men called *Bicar* who go all their "lifetime naked, and suffer their hair to grow till it hides their bodies. "They suffer also their nails to grow so that they become pointed "and sharp as swords, nor do they ever cut them, but leave them to "break and fall off as it happens, and this they observe as a religious "duty. Each of them has a string about his neck whereto hangs an "earthen porringer; and when they are pressed by hunger they stop

[1] "The large majority of Asiatics are so infatuated in favor of judicial astrology, "that, according to their phraseology, no circumstance can happen below, which is "not written above. In every enterprise they consult their astrologers; when two "armies have completed every preparation for battle, no consideration can induce "the generals to commence the engagement until the sahet be performed—that is, "until the propitious moment for attack be ascertained. In like manner, no com-"manding officer is nominated, no marriage takes place, and no journey is under-"taken, without consulting these seers. Their advice is considered absolutely "necessary even on the most trifling occasions, as the proposed purchase of a slave, "or the first wearing of new clothes. This silly superstition is so general an an-"noyance, and attended with such important and disagreeable consequences, that I "am astonished it has continued so long: the astrologer is necessarily made ac-"quainted with every transaction, public and private, with every project, common "and extraordinary."—*Bernier, translated by Irving Brock.*

"at the door of some Indian house, and those within immediately "and joyfully bring out rice to them, believing there is great merit in "so doing; while they eat out of the porringer and withdraw, never "returning to make the same request if not by necessity urged "thereto." Again, "one part of their devotion consists in building "of kans or inns upon the highways for the accommodation of "travellers; where also they set up dealers, of whom the passengers "may purchase what they may happen to want." In another place, "there are certain Indians who never eat two out of the same dish, "or upon the same table; and would deem it a very great sin if they "should. Were they a hundred in number they must each have a "separate dish, without the least communication with the rest. Their "kings, and persons of high quality, have fresh tables made for them "every day, together with little dishes and plates wove of the cocoa-"nut leaf, in which they eat what is prepared for their subsistence; "and their meal over, they throw the table, the dishes, and plates "into the water, together with the fragments they have left. Thus at "every meal they have a new service.

"The kings of the Indies wear ear-rings of precious stones set in "gold. They wear also collars of great price, adorned with precious "stones of divers colours, but especially green and red; yet pearls are "what they most esteem, and their value surpasses that of all other "jewels; they, at present, hoard them up in their treasures with their "most precious things. The grandees of the court, the great officers "and captains, wear the like jewels on their collars; they dress in a "half vest, and carry a parasol of peacock's feathers to shade them "from the sun, and are surrounded by those of their train."

CHAP. IV.

MOOL RÂJ SOLUNKHEE.

SÂMUNT SINGH is no favorite of the chroniclers; he is described as a prince of no reputation, who had no consideration for what he spoke either night or day, who was possessed of neither discretion nor firmness, knew no distinction between good and bad—between hostile and friendly, and who was continually changing his mind. Little, however, is recorded of his short reign of seven years, except the fact of his being son-less, and the circumstances which led to the establishment of the Solunkhee family on the throne of Unhilwârâ.

Three youths, named Râj, Beej, and Dunduk, sons of Bhoowunâditya, who was fourth in descent from King Bhoowur of Kuleeân, visited the court of Sâmunt Singh on their return from a pilgrimage to the shrine of Somnâth. Probably, religion was not their only object in quitting home, and they appear to have come forth, as has always been the practice of the younger brothers of a Rajpoot royal house, to seek that fortune in foreign lands which the jealousy, attendant upon their contiguity to the throne, denied to them at home. The eldest of the three brothers is described by the author of Rutun Mâlâ as fair in complexion, of middling stature, and very handsome. It is added, "He was observant of religion, the continual worshipper "of Shiva; but he suffered affliction on account of his wives, nor was "he more happy in regard to the other gifts of fortune." Distinguished by his birth and by the qualities of a good warrior, Prince Râj obtained from the King of Unhilwârâ the hand of his own sister, Leelâ Devee. This princess became pregnant by him, and died in labour; but a male child was taken alive from her womb, who, from the fact of his having been born under the constellation so entitled, received the name of *Mool* Râj. He was adopted by Sâmunt Singh, and distinguished himself at an early age, "exhibiting the splendour of a rising "sun," extending the territories of his uncle, and rendering himself dear to all. The subsequent acts of Mool Râj, however, justify the character given of him by the author of Rutun Mâlâ, who asserts him to have been treacherous, unmerciful, and intent upon self-aggrandisement. "He was handsome in person, though dark in his "complexion; a slave to the deity of love; he held money in a firm "grasp, concealing it below the earth; in war he was unskilled, but if "opposed to an enemy he destroyed him, inspiring confidence by his "deceitfulness." When he was arrived at mature age, Sâmunt Singh, in a fit of drunkenness, caused the ceremony of his inauguration to be performed; but no sooner had the king recovered his senses, than he revoked his abdication of the throne. "From that time," says the Jain annalist, "the valuelessness of the gift made by a Chowra became "proverbial." Mool Râj, however, having once tasted the delights of royal power, was little likely to resign them. Collecting troops, he attacked and slew his uncle, and seated himself firmly on the throne upon which he had been placed in a too dangerous sport. "There "are seven things without gratitude," observes, upon this, the author of the Koomâr Pâl Churittra, "a daughter's husband, a scorpion, a "tiger, wine, a fool, *a sister's son*, and a king. Each is incapable of "estimating benefits." To ensure to himself a thornless rule, Mool Râj, as is asserted by a Brahminical authority, put to death, besides, "the whole of his mother's race,"—a murderous act, the guilt of which was not, as will be seen in the sequel, unfelt by himself, however it may have been extenuated by his chronicler, who endeavours to make light of the fate of the sufferers, stigmatizing them as "sinners, "proud, drinkers of liquor, oppressors of the people, despisers of "Devs and Brahmins."[1]

The demise of the direct line of the Chowras rendered Goozerat an object for the ambition of more than one of the surrounding princes, and the political craftiness of Mool Râj was soon employed in protecting his newly acquired throne from numerous enemies. On the north, the king of the hundred thousand villages, otherwise described as the Rajâ of Nâgor, or of Sâmbhur—the country afterwards known as Ujmeer—was his first assailant. Almost simultaneously Goozerat was invaded by Bârp, the general of Teilip, the sovereign of Telingânâ.[2] Mool Râj retired under this double pressure from Unhilwârâ, and, following his usual wily system, or, as his chroniclers assert, persuaded by his ministers—who recommended him to restrain his valour by the example of the ram, retiring that he may strike the harder, or of the tiger, angrily crouching that he may spring with more deadly effect—he established himself in the fort of Kunt Kot, within the remote and unassailable frontier of Kutch, in the hope that the necessities of the season might compel the Raja of Ujmeer to retire. That prince, however, held his ground during the monsoon, and when the Nowrâttra[3] arrived was prepared to assume the offensive. Mool Râj then collected his chieftains, and having, by inducements, of which there is no intelligible record, procured the withdrawal of the troops of Ujmeer, he attacked the army of

[1] "A sceptre, snatch'd with an unruly hand,
"Must be as boisterously maintain'd, as gain'd;
"And he that stands upon a slippery place
"Makes nice of no vile hold to stay him up."
King John, Act III., scene 4.

[2] In an account of the Châlookya, or Solunkhee dynasty of Kuleeân, by Mr. Walter Elliot, (*vide* Journal of the Royal Asiatic Society, vol. iv., p. 1), mention is made of a king named "*Teilapa Deva,*" who reigned from Saka, 895 to 919 (or A.D. 974 to 998), and who was, therefore, a contemporary of Mool Râj, and, doubtless, the Teilip here alluded to. The same "Teilapa Deva" is, however, mentioned as having slain "*the brave Munja,*" a king of Malwa, of whom hereafter. The northern limit of the kingdom of Kuleeân is stated, by Mr. Elliot, to have been the river Nerbudda.

[3] The festival of nine nights: *vide* Conclusion.

Bârp, slew that general, and dispersed his followers with great slaughter.[1]

Mool Râj, thus relieved of his foes, commenced the erection of several religious buildings at Unhilwârâ, and of that more famous shrine of Muhâ Dev, which he did not live to complete, the Roodra Mâlâ of Sidhpoor. Shiva, it is related, was so won by the assiduities of his royal votary, that he gave him the kingdom of Soreth, containing one of the most memorable of all the temples of the god—that of Somnâth. The story of the acquisition of Soreth is, however, related in detail by the celebrated Hemâchârya in his Dwyâshray, from which we now proceed to offer an extract :—

"Mool Râj," says the Jain teacher, "was the benefactor of the "world ; he was generous-minded—full of all good qualities. All "kings worshipped him as they worshipped the sun, all subjects "who abandoned their own country found a happy residence under "his protection ; so that he won the title of 'enthraller of the uni-"'verse.' Of his enemies, the half he slew, the other half he forced "to beg alms, like out-casts, without the walls of his city. Their "wives, who, like frogs in a well,[2] had never beheld anything "more remote than the entrance to their dwellings, were seized "by Bheels as they wandered in the forests, and sold in the towns as "slaves."

Once on a time Somnâth Muhâ Dev appeared to Mool Râj in a dream, desiring him to destroy Grâh Ripoo,[3] and other Dytes (or demons), who laid waste the sacred place of pilgrimage at Prubhâs, and assuring him that "by my splendor you shall have victory."

The next morning, as soon as the "crown-wearing princes who were "present, according to custom," withdrew from the royal chamber,

[1] It is this event, perhaps, which the traditions of the Chohâns of Nadole allude to in the following verse :—

"In S. 1039 (A.D. 983), at the farther gate of the city of Putton, Lâkhun "Row, the Chohan, collected the commercial duties. He took tribute from the "lord of Mewar, and performed whatever he had a mind to."—*Tod's Rajasthan*, *II.*, 446.

[2] "to dive, like buckets, in concealed wells."—*King John, Act V., scene* 2.

[3] Grâh Ripoo appears to be a title or epithet, rather than a name. A commentator on the Dwyâshrây makes its meaning to be "enemy (*ripoo*) of water-animals "(*Grâh*)." It may mean "seizer of enemies." One of the princes of Ujmeer, from having defeated a Mohammedan king, was called "Sultan Graha," the sultan-seizer. (*Vide* Tod's Rajasthan, II., 447, 451.) Prubhâs, called also Shiv Putton, Someshwur Puttun, Puttun Somnâth, is the port on the coast of Soreth, within the confines of which stood the celebrated temple of Shiva, which was attacked by Mahmood of Ghuznee.

the Solunkhee Raja consulted with his ministers, Jumbuk and Jehul, the Prince of Kherâloo, "as to the mode in which he should obey "the commands of Muhâ Dev." "Grâh Ripoo," he said, "was made "of consequence by myself; but if born in an inauspicious time, he "has become shameless, destroying the performers of pilgrimage, "should I not slay him, though entrusted with authority by myself?" Jehul answers by enumerating the misdeeds of Grâh Ripoo:—

"This shepherd is very tyrannical; ruling in Soorâshtra, on a "throne until his time shining with the splendor derived from the rule "of Shree Krishn, he slays the pilgrims that travel towards Prubhâs, and "strews the highway with their flesh and bones. He lives as fearless "as Râwun, at Wâmunsthulee, a city over which waved the splen-"did banners of Hunoomân and Gurood;[1] and he permits thieves to "dwell in other places of sacred recollections; he despises Brahmins, "and plunders people passing along the road; therefore he is like an "arrow, causing pain in the hearts of the religious. He is young and "lusty, and full of desire; therefore, slaying his enemies, he carries "off their wives by force to his own female apartments. This bar-"barian hunts upon mount Girnâr, and slays the deer at Prubhâs. "He eats the flesh of cows, and drinks spirituous liquor, and in battle "he feeds the Bhoots, the Pisâchs, and all their crew, with the blood "of his enemies. This lord of the west, Grâh Ripoo, has caused "many rajas of the south and the north to fly, leaving their chariots; "now, therefore, he regards no one, but looks lofty as he walks as if "he meditated the conquest of Heaven. Grâh Ripoo is huge in per-"son like Yuma, the King of Hades, and like Yuma, too, in temper, "he seems disposed to devour the whole earth, or to seize upon "Paradise. The men of skill in his kingdom, from associating with "such an evil one, employ their science in constructing all sorts of "weapons from which it is impossible to escape, in matters discrimi-"nating religious and irreligious practice they do not exercise them-"selves. He is strong in military force, so that all rajas are compelled to "bend to him. He is very wealthy; he seized the Raja of Sindh and "compelled him to pay, as a fine, elephants and horses, and he has "subdued many other sovereigns. I believe that the King of Hades, "himself, were he to make war upon him, would have no means of "escape but submission to paying tribute. He destroys great forts

[1] Gurood is the eagle of Vishnoo, represented sometimes as a crowned prince borne through the air upon wings. Hunoomân is the monkey (or aboriginal) king who joined Vishnoo when, incarnate under the form of Râm, he conquered Râwun, the giant king of Ceylon. Bhoots and Pisâchs are part of the goblin crew which follows Shiva.

"and safe places among the mountains; he can pass and repass the "ocean too, therefore people have no single means of escaping. It "is as when destiny, enraged with the world, leaves no means of "escape. The earth suffers pain from the load of his sins. The "raja who can punish murderers, and neglects to do so, is a murderer "himself; therefore, if you do not destroy him, his sin will be yours, "O! King. Shiva has given the order to you because you can des- "troy him. Assemble your army and expel him, lest his strength day "by day increase, until, at last, he become too strong to be subdued "even by yourself."

Mool Râj, when he had heard the advice of Jehul to this effect, made a sign to Jumbuk, the minister, sage as the counsellor of the gods, who, thus invited, spake as follows:

"Wâmunsthulee,[1] where Grâh Ripoo makes his residence, is under "the shadow of the great Girnâr, and, besides, the roaring of the "ocean may be heard therefrom. It is strengthened by another castle, "still more nearly protected both by sea and mountain. Grâh Ripoo "is one who closes his eyes not even in the night time; to conquer "him without large resources is as impossible as it is to cut down a "huge tree with a grass-cutter's sickle. An army could not encamp "within many miles of his city, and even were this accomplished, he "would surround it and prevent the possibility of your rendering any "assistance. Kutch, too, is within easy reach of Soreth, and Lâkhâ, "the lord thereof, the son of Phoolâ, a great raja, and unconquered "by any, is as inseparable from Grâh Ripoo as if they were the sons "of the same mother. There are many other rajas, too, assisting "these confederates,—barbarians that cause terror to the universe. "O! king, it is well known that an enemy, who is aided by moun- "tain, forest, or ocean, is hard to conquer. This Grâh Ripoo num- "bers all three as his supporters. Entrust this expedition to no other, "then, but in person set forth and win the victory. Though un- "tameable by others, these warriors of shepherd race will tremble "the moment they hear of your advance against them, and their "wives will at once commence the widow's song of lamentation."

Mool Râj, incited by these warlike counsels, which added fuel to the fiery zeal for battle already burning in his bosom, rose from his throne, brilliant as a flower just expanded into full bloom by the heat of the day-bringer's rays, and clenching his hands like one already

[1] Wâmunsthulee is the modern Buntullee, near Joonagurh. Colonel Walker, in his report on the Soreth district, has the following: "The ancient residence of the "Rajahs of Soreth was first at Buntullee."

engaged in combat, strode forth from the council chamber, followed by the leaders of his warriors.

The season of cold had arrived, an abundant crop covered the earth; the water of the tanks and of the rivers became clear, the sky was cleared of clouds, the lotus was in full bloom, its hue reminding the poet of the shining lips of the lovely. The lingering drops of rain fell in pearls upon the coasts of Soreth.[1] The swan, rising from the Himalayan lake, its retreat during the season of rains, returned to the Ganges and the other rivers. The cultivators' wives, guarding the ripening rice-crop in the plains, made the country joyous with their songs. In the temples of the Devs the Brahmins read the Veds and the Book of Doorgâ,—setting up the water-jar, fasting and keeping a solitary watch, they passed the nine nights; then feasting on the tenth day, they anointed the head of the raja with water from the consecrated jar. High festival was held to the lord of Paradise, and flags flaunted over the temples. The memories of Wâmun and Bulee Raja[2] filled the earth with joy, while from his lengthened meditation, stretched on the sea of Milk, the great Vishnoo arose.

At the gate of Mool Râj the drum sounded and the royal drum rolled. The conch-shell spoke a good omen; the noise of many musical instruments proclaimed even to the dwellers in Paradise that the king prepared to lead forth his warriors. The princes that followed the banner of Unhilwârâ poured in with their followers, eager to advance upon Soreth. The king sat upon his throne; beside him they formed upon the ground with pearls the crosses[3] that betoken success and happiness; singers sang songs, standing on either side; the servants waved fans over his head. Astrologers, full of science from their cradle, calculated the auspicious time. The household priest performed the worship of horse and elephant; the king bent

[1] "Some say when it rains the oysters rise up to the surface, and that, gaping, "the drops of water they catch turn to pearls."—Renaudot, p. 97.

[2] Vishnoo assumed the form of the dwarf Wâmun to prevent Bulee Raja from obtaining the dominion of the three worlds. See, however, account of "Bulev day" in the Conclusion.

[3] A cross thus shaped is a common sign of rejoicing among Hindoos. It is called "Swusteek," and is the usual female signature. It is also the sign of Soopârswa the seventh Teerthunker of the Jains. *Vide* Asiat. Researches IX., p. 306. "This cross, denominated "in a MS. of the fifteenth century the 'Fylfot,' was in use at a "very remote period, as a mystic symbol amongst religious de- "votees in India and China, whence it appears to have been in- "troduced, probably in the sixth century, into Europe. 'It occurs,' says Mr. Waller, "'on very early Christian remains, and is found on the girdle of a priest of the

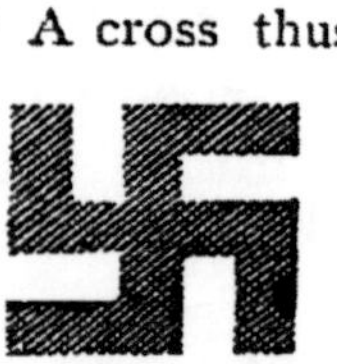

his head before them. At length the rod-bearers advanced; the soldiers grasping their arms stood in lines about the doors. Again the instruments of music sounded. As the king rose from his cushion, the priest, stepping forward, placed the royal mark (teeluk) upon his forehead, pronouncing the words "auspicious, auspicious." Mool Râj and his chieftains made presents, as they set forth, to Brahmins and to Bards, the recorders of fame. Mounting, the king made obeisance to his patron deity; he rode upon an elephant, black and huge as a mountain, overshadowed by clouds; the horses neighed as he set forth; all hailed the omen of success: from the palace to the city-gate the whole way was sprinkled with reddened water; the astrologers blessed the king, crying, "May you be victorious,—"may your enemy depart to the south, to the city of Yuma!" As the cavalcade went on, great was the throng in the city; women crowded the streets, dressed in scarlet clothes and glittering with ornaments; in the press many a flower garland was broken, many a necklace of pearls scattered; as the procession passed through the market-place the people strewed fruit and flowers before the raja on the way; the women of the city abandoned their housework, and left their children crying; they hastened to behold the cavalcade; for many a mile as it passed along, the villagers thronged from far to behold their sovereign, for as Indra among gods, so among men shone Mool Râj in beauty, qualities, and power.

Hearing that the King of Unhilwârâ approached with a large force, Grâh Ripoo assembled his army. The kings that adhered to him, whether allies or tributaries, joined his standard; many forest Bheels were with him; the sons of his wives, Neelee and others, who dwelt on the banks of the Bhâdur river, famous in Soreth, came arrayed in iron armour. He was joined also by his friend Lâkhâ, the Raja of Kutch, who, though his death in the war was predicted by the astrologers, desired to win his way through the battle-field to Paradise. "Lâkhâ cries shame to him whose youthful deeds no one has wit-"nessed. The days of my life are counted; how shall I know their "span?" Sindhoo Raja, also, whose kingdom was on the banks of the ocean, brought up an army, and with it occupied a position in the south.

On the side of Mool Râj fought the Raja of Sheelprusth, a skilful bowman; a raja of Marwar, followed by men wearing long locks

'date A.D. 1077.' On brasses it is a common ornament anterior to the accession of Richard II." *Vide* Monumental Brasses and Slabs, by Rev. Charles Boutel, M.A., Oxford. Parker, 1847. Footnote to page 28.

upon their unshorn heads; a raja from the land of Benares; the Prince of Shreemâl and his paramount lord, the Purmâr Raja of mount Aboo and the north; the Raja Gungâmah, the brother of the Prince of Unhilwârâ, was also there, but the Solunkhee's cousins, the sons of Bheej and Dunduk, refused to follow the head of their line.

Mool Raja's force was drawn up in serried phalanxes, while the warriors of Aboo, being pre-eminent in valor, fought separate from the main body of the army, lining the banks of the river Jumboomâlee, where their prince, after slaying many warriors, won "a banner of victory" from the enemy. The soldiers of Goozerat displayed great valor and skill in weapons, and the demons, their enemies, though they were covered with defensive armour and carried ponderous shields, and though roaring like thunder-clouds they discharged a storm of arrows, were at last seized with a panic and fled, leaving in the conqueror's hands their leader, who had been struck from his elephant by the hand of Mool Râj.

Lâkhâ, the Prince of Kutch, at this time sought a parley and offered ransom for his friend, which was, however, refused by the King of Unhilwârâ. He then rushed fiercely upon Mool Râj; but that prince was filled with strength derived from the divinity he served, and Lâkhâ, in this unequal contest, fell, pierced by the Solunkhee spear. Treading down the Jhâreja prince, Mool Râj set his foot upon his throat. The mother of Lâkhâ beholding the corpse of her son, his long moustache stirred by the wind, heaped her curses upon his destroyer. "By the spider poison may his race perish."[1]

Râ Lâkhâ appears, however, to have had other causes for hostility to Mool Râj in addition to that of his alliance with the Prince of Soreth. It is said that Râj Solunkhee, on becoming a widower, proceeded on a pilgrimage towards Vishnoo's temple at Dwârkâ, and that on his return he visited the court of Lâkhâ Phoolânee and espoused that prince's sister, Râyâjee, by whom he had a son named Râkhâeech. The evil destiny attributed to him by the chronicler followed him,

[1] That is to say "*Lootâ*," the leprosy, a disease which was supposed by the Hindoos to be inflicted as the punishment of an offence against the sun. In the Prubundh Chintâmunee, a poet named Bân, at the court of Bhoj Raja, of Malwa, is represented as having been struck with leprosy, from which he recovered by making submission to the sun. This deity was, we know, much worshipped of old in Soreth. A similar notion among the Persians is mentioned by Herodotus (Clio). "If any of the citizens have a leprosy or scrofulous disease, he is not per-"mitted to stay within the city nor to converse with other Persians, having, as "they believe, drawn this punishment upon himself by some offence committed "against the sun." The Jews, in like manner, accounted leprosy to be an especial visitation on account of especial sins.

however, in this second matrimonial connection. In an untoward dispute regarding precedence, Râj Solunkhee, with many of his Rajpoot followers, was slain by Lâkhâ, and the Jhâreja princess, Râyâjee, became a Sutee. Beej Solunkhee, the uncle of Mool Râj, urged his nephew to take revenge on account of this feud ; and Mool Râj himself appears to have been incited against Lâkhâ by political reasons also, the Râ maintaining at his court Râkhâeech, the younger son of Râj, with the view of opposing him to his brother.

The honor of slaying Lâkhâ in single combat has not been allowed to Mool Râj without a contest. Perhaps, like the Duke of Clarence, slain by Buchan and his knights at Beaugé, the Prince of the Jhârejas, fell under the strokes of more than one of the warriors who assailed him. The Raja of Marwar, who is mentioned by Hemâchârya, by name Seeyojee Râthor, the ancestor of the royal houses of Jodhpoor and Eedur, had visited Unhilwârâ and contracted a marriage with the daughter of Mool Râj, and being thus present at the engagement, it was by his hand, as the bards of his race assert, that the Phoolânee fell.

"The very powerful raja took a vow of pilgrimage—the son of "Set[1]—with his army. Mool Râj sent a cocoa-nut. Help me to-"day, O! Lord of Kanouj. 'I am going on pilgrimage to Gomtee "—betrothal must be talked of afterwards. When, having com-"pleted my pilgrimage, I commence my return home, I will then "listen to your proposals.' At Puttun, Seeyo married at Mool Râj's "bridal-hall. The Jhâreja's fort the Râthor destroyed. In the "heart of the enemy he rankled like an arrow. When did the "Kumdhuj[2] and the Yâduv quarrel? But it was the Solunkhee "that he assisted. In fight Seeyo slew Lâkhâ. Ages shall wear "away, but this tale shall survive."

Mool Râj, rejoining his army, paid his adoration at the holy Prubhâs, worshipping the sacred Someshwur. He then returned home, his army laden with spoils, and followed by a train of elephants taken from the enemy.

Sometime after his return to Unhilwârâ, a son, named Châmoond, was born to Mool Râj. The prince displayed unusual intellectual tastes, even from his childhood, but of his frequent visits to the Roodra Mâlâ those delighted him the most which enabled him to listen to the story of the Muhâbhârut recited in the assembly of sages.

[1] Set Râthor was Seeyojee's father. Sending a cocoa-nut is the form of making proposals of marriage. *Vide* Conclusion.

[2] That is, the Râthor.

One day the prince, entering the royal presence-chamber and making his obeisance, had seated himself when ambassadors from kings of remote countries were ushered in, bearing the gifts by which their sovereigns sought to propitiate the favor of the King of Unhilwârâ. Chariots from Ung were presented, red jewels from the sea-shore, and gold from Wumwâs. The Raja of Devgeeree offered a yearly tribute, he of Kollâpoor laid jewels at the feet of Mool Râj. The Kashmeer prince presented the celebrated musk of his country, he of Kooroo land an umbrella of many colors, the Sovereign of Punchâl sent cows and slaves. Last of all came the ambassador from Lâth, the country of the south, presenting from his master, Dwârup, an elephant so ill-favored, that the astrologers at once pronounced it to be "an incarnation of death." The "bad omen" produced by this present struck the courtiers with consternation, and the insult offered by King Dwârup so roused the anger of Châmoond, the heir-apparent, that he could with difficulty be restrained by Mool Râj from immediately setting forth to resent it. The astrological conjunction, however, being adverse, Mool Râj refused to set forth, and contented himself with ordering that the ambassadors from Lâth, with their ill-boding presents, should be contemptuously expelled. As soon, however, as the fortunate time arrived, Mool Râj and the prince advanced with an army to punish the insolence of Dwârup. They reached the banks of the Nerbudda, the boundary of their kingdom, advancing with such rapidity that the women bathing in the river received no alarm until they saw the warriors descending from the lofty banks into the stream. The army passed through the towns of Sooryâpoor and Bhrigoo Kucha[1] (Broach), and arrived at the country of Dwârup, celebrated at that time for ill-favored women, whose clumsy waists, and complexions, dingy as if from continual proximity to the cooking fire, provoked the laughter of the chiefs of Goozerat. The Raja of Lâth, though supported by the kings of the islands, was an easy conquest. He was attacked and slain by Prince Châmoond with the van of the Goozerat army, supported only by small detachments from the troops commanded by Mool Râj. Châmoond having thus fleshed his maiden sword, was received with delight by his father, and the army soon retraced its steps to Unhilwârâ.

The career of Mool Râj had now reached its limit. Lord of the kingdom of Unhilwârâ, in right of his mother, he had pushed forward its frontier in every direction; Kutch had been subdued by him; the

[1] Bhrigoo Kucha appears to be the nearest approach to the "Barygaza" of the Greeks of any Hindoo name under which Broach is known.

holy land of Soreth obeyed his commands; the inhabitants of the Dekkan had beheld his standards flying victoriously beyond the Nerbudda and the range of Injâdree; his supremacy was acknowledged by the Purmâr prince, who ruled in the impregnable towers of Uchulgurh on the summit of the sacred Aboo; and under his leading the chivalrous errants of Marwar and northern India followed, for the first time, the banners of Goojur Râshtra. His domestic life had also been prosperous, and he possessed that blessing so invaluable to a Hindoo, and which the most illustrious of the future sovereigns of Unhilpoor were not destined to obtain—a son worthy to be his successor.

At the close of his reign, however, Mool Râj is represented as wandering about painfully from one place of pilgrimage to another, full of remorse for the slaughter of his mother's kindred, and eager only to obtain, at whatever price, the means of expiation. Tired of his wanderings, full of sin and calamity, of great age, ignorant and a lover of repose, his thoughts at last reverted to Sidhpoor, where we have already beheld him winning the favor of Muhâ Dev, by commencing the erection of a temple in his honor.

The small but translucent river Suruswutee runs westwards towards the Runn of Kutch, from the celebrated shrine of Kotheshwur Muhâ Dev, in the marble hills of Ârâsoor. For a short distance, however, as it passes the town of Sidhpoor, the virgin river makes a bend towards the east, and though sacred at all times, its course is at this point esteemed more peculiarly holy, as pursued so far towards the face of the rising sun.

The picturesque town of Sidhpoor stands on the steep northern bank of the Suruswutee, exhibiting towards the river numerous modern houses, the residences of Borahs and other wealthy traders, which, half European as they are in form, with balustered terraces, and windows fenced with Venetian screens, contrast not unpleasingly with the frequent spire-covered Hindoo shrines of the sacred town. Here and there patches of garden intervene, with plantain and other fruit-bearing trees, among which the statelier mango is not wanting; and above all still protrudes the grim and giant-like skeleton of the old Roodra Mâlâ, with its flight of steps, extending to a considerable distance along the edge of the river. On the level southern bank is a striking foreground of convents used by the Shaivite devotees, the handsomest of which was constructed by Ahilya Bye, the widow of Holkar, and in the remote distance the mountains stretching towards Ârâsoor and Aboo, complete the view:—

Sidhpoor is a place of unusual sanctity.

"Of all places of pilgrimage the greatest is Shreesthul, as great "sages of old have declared. It is the giver of all wealth; he who "but beholds it attains liberation. At Gyâ, Paradise is three leagues "distant; at Pruyâg, a league-and-a-half; at Shreesthul, a cubit "only; there where Suruswustee travels eastwards."

To this holy place of pilgrimage the worn out king retired to purify himself for the approach of death. But personal austerities alone he had been taught were not sufficient. "Fasting, vows, bathing, pil-"grimages, and penances, when ratified by Brahmins, are fruitful—"not otherwise. The deities ratify what Brahmins pronounce; by "their words, as if by water, unclean men are cleansed." Mool Râj prepared therefore for the reception of holy Brahmins with their families, whom he brought by his entreaties from the mountains of the north or from good places of pilgrimage near founts of water, or in the forest. The sons of the sages, well skilled in the Veds, married, youthful, worthy to be served, agreed to repair to the banks of the virgin river. One hundred and five came from where the Yumoona mingles with the Ganges,[1] a hundred readers of the Sâm Ved came from Chyuwun Âshrum, two hundred from Kunyâcoobj, one hundred, bright as the sun, from Benares, two hundred and seventy-two from Kooroo Kshetra, one hundred from Gungâdwâr, one hundred from Naimeech Ârunya. A further hundred and thirty-two the king sent for from Kooroo Kshetra. The smoke of their sacrifices ascended in clouds into the sky.

The king having been informed of their arrival, prostrated himself before them, and received their benediction. Then joining his hands, he said, "By your kindness I have at last obtained some ad-"vantage from having been born. My hope will now be realized; "therefore, O Brahmins! receive my kingdom, my wealth, my ele-"phants, my horses, whatever may be your desire, in kindness to "me. I am humble, your servant, full of grief." They answered: "O great king! we are not capable of conducting the affairs of a "kingdom; why, then, should we receive it to its destruction. Pur-"shoorâm, the son of Jumudugnee, twenty-one times gave the land to "us, taking it by force from the Kshutrees." The king said: "I "will protect you, O great Brahmins; do you remain in your aus-"terities free from care." The Brahmins said: "Learned men "have declared, that they who live near a king suffer calamity; kings "are boastful, deceitful, full of their own objects; still, if you are

[1] The Jumna and the Ganges unite under the walls of Allahabad, at the sacred spot known by Hindoos as Pruyâg.

" desirous of giving, give us this great and heart pleasing Shreesthul, " O king of kings! where we may remain in pleasure. The gold " and silver, the jewels, which you proposed to give to Brahmins, lay " out in adorning the town. The raja, joyful at the attainment of his wishes, washed the feet of the Brahmins, and presented them with earrings and bracelets. He gave to them Shreesthulpoor, with cows, and chariots hung with garlands of gold, and jewels, and other gifts.

Mool Râj gave also the beautiful and wealthy city of Singhpoor (Seehore) to ten Brahmins, with many other presents. To other Brahmins he gave also many smaller villages in the neighbourhood of Sidhpoor and Seehore. A company of six priests for a long time refused his gifts, even after they had been accepted by their friends. With these, however, the entreaties of the king at last prevailed, and they accepted the gift of the town of Cambay with twelve villages.

" Stumbh Teerth first he gave, among men Khumbât called, to " six of these that delight in the moon-leaf,[1] together with sixty " horses." Having made these gifts, Mool Râj called his sons and sons' sons, and recommended the Brahmins to their protection. He then committed the kingdom to his son Châmoond, and retiring to Sidhpoor, spent the remainder of his life there in a palace which he had built, called Rumeeyâshrum, or " the house of delights." At length he passed to Nârâyunpoor to the presence of Lukshmee's lord.

" Him, the fire-god, with his tresses of smoke worshipped; by " worship only was he enthralled. What of another warrior's story? " The sun's disk he divided."

Mool Râj reigned fifty-five years, from A.D. 942 to 997.

[1] It used to be the practice among Hindoos at the time of sacrifice, to cause each person who proposed to officiate, to take into his mouth a portion of the " Som-wullee," or moon-plant, which, it was supposed, no one but a true Brahmin could retain.—See p. 61.

The following list of the successors of Mool Râj is from a copper-plate inscription, dated Sumwut 1266 (or A.D. 1210,) found a few years ago in a treasure room at Ahmedabad, and since presented by the author of the present work to the Royal Asiatic Society of London.

I. He who was splendid in the line of kings, the very valiant, the great king of kings, the supreme lord, the illustrious Mool Râj Dev.

II. The successor to his throne, the very valiant, the great king of kings, the supreme lord, the illustrious Châmoond Râj Dev.

III. The successor to his throne, the very valiant, the great king of kings, the supreme lord, the illustrious Doorlubh Râj Dev.

IV. The successor to his throne, the very valiant, the great king of kings, the supreme lord, the illustrious Bheem Dev.

V. The successor to his throne, the very valiant, the great king of kings, the supreme lord, who was without a competitor in fight in Heaven, Earth, or Hell, the illustrious Kurun Dev.

VI. The successor to his throne, the very valiant, the great king of kings, the supreme lord, the conqueror of Wurwurk the lord of Oojein, the emperor of Siddhs (demi-gods,) the illustrious Jye Singh Dev.

VII. The successor to his throne, the very valiant, the great king of kings, the supreme lord, of great splendor, Vishnoo-like in his exploits, who conquered with his army * * * *, the illustrious Koomâr Pâl Dev.

VIII. The successor to his throne, the very valiant, the great king of kings, the supreme lord, a stainless incarnation in the Iron Age, who gained from the great a title, the illustrious Ujye Pâl Dev.

IX. The successor to his throne, the very valiant, the great king of kings, the supreme lord, in fight unconquerable as Nâgârjoon, the illustrious Mool Râj Dev.

X. The successor to his throne, the very valiant, the great king of kings, the supreme lord, a second Siddh Râj Dev, or an incarnation of Nârâyun, the illustrious Bheem Dev, rules auspiciously, &c. &c. &c.

CHAP. V.

CHÂMOOND—WULLUBH—DOORLUBH—THE FALL OF SOMNÂTH.

THE writers of Hindoo historical legends (whether these be derived from Jain or Brahminical sources, or contained in the compositions of the bards, who were the "recorders of fame" of the Rajpoot races) are apt to preserve a constant and sullen silence in regard to all circumstances, no matter how notorious or how widely influential in their results, which seem to them to derogate from the reputation of their heroes. Over the career of a guilty, unwise, or unfortunate sovereign, the Hindoo annalist draws a black curtain, upon which is recorded, with more than Venetian brevity, the facts that a prince was born, and died. There can be few more striking instances of this peculiarity than that which is furnished by the Jain monk of Wudwân, the author of the chronicle called "Prubundh Chintâmunee," in his record of the reign of Châmoond, the successor of Mool Râj. It was in his time that the sun of the Rajpoots began to decline before the Moslem crescent, that a strange and furious invader burst upon the plains of India, that ancient dynasties were shaken, ancient gods—the eternal Muhâ Kâl himself—confounded with the dust; and yet, in such times as these, the powerful sovereign of Unhilwârâ, a chief actor in the troubled scene, is dismissed with words as unsuggestive and few as those which shortly afterwards were engraved upon the monumental slabs of the peaceful abbots who repose within the quiet cloisters of Westminster:—

"From the year of Vikrum one thousand and fifty-three, (A.D. 997,) Châmoond Râj reigned thirteen years."

A fragment of the Rutun Mâlâ paints the personal character of Raja Châmoond, but supplies little further information, though it is in one respect important, as furnishing a Hindoo allusion to the presence of the Mohammedan in Goozerat during this king's reign. It is as follows:—

"The son of Mool Râj was Châmoond Râj; he was attenuated "in person and yellow in his complexion; very fond of eating and "drinking, and of handsome dress. He cultivated good trees in his "garden; he built wells and tanks; leaving many tasks unfinished, "he went to the gate of Yuma. He was better than his father; *he* "*had no enemy but the Yuwun;* "in the kingdom his memory was "long respected."

The short account of Châmoond's reign, which is found in the Dwyâshrây, though it is very remarkable for the faults of omission which we have already noticed, and though some of the statements made in it are probably attempts to cover the truth by a version of facts more in consonance with the feelings of the writer and those he addresses, is nevertheless valuable as affording, perhaps, the true solution of many difficulties in the history of the first Mohummedan invasion of India.

After the death of his father, Châmoond Râj, it is said, managed the affairs of the kingdom of Unhilwârâ in a good manner; increasing his treasures, his army, and his fame. He was defective in no point; and he preserved the landgift which had been bequeathed to him by Mool Râj. A son, named Wullubh Râj, was born to Châmoond; he, too, became skilled in royal science, and fit to fill the throne. He was condescending and brave, and the king, therefore, was very much delighted in heart, while the enemies of the throne, who had looked forward with expectation to living in quiet after Châmoond's decease, abandoned that hope.

"Wullubh Râj," says Krishnâjee, the Brahmin, "was of dwarfish "stature, but in mind able; abandoning wickedness. He was ruddy "in complexion; on his body freckles were very prevalent; he never

" broke his word, though very ambitious of rule ; leaving his schemes " unfinished, he departed quitting the body."

Châmoond Râj, continues Hemâchârya, had another son, named Doorlubh Râj. He, too, became so full of exploits, that from fear of him no *Usoor*[1] dare raise his head. When the astrologers examined this prince's horoscope, they pronounced with confidence that he would be celebrated for great achievements ; that he would conquer his enemies ; encourage the practice of wisdom, and become a king of kings. This Doorlubh Râj and his elder brother Wullubh Râj pursued their studies together, and bore great affection to each other, setting their father before them as an example. Afterwards Châmoond Râj had a third son, named Nâg Râj.

Once on a time, Châmoond Râj, inflamed by the passion of love, injured his own sister Châcheenee Devee. To expiate this sin, he placed Wullubh Râj on the throne, and proceeded on a pilgrimage to Benares. As he went, the Raja of Malwa took from him the umbrella, horse-hair fans, and other royal ensigns. Then Châmoond, having completed his pilgrimage, returned to Unhilwârâ, and urged Wullubh, by his filial affection, to punish the author of this insult. Wullubh Râj, thereupon assembling an army, advanced upon Malwa, but on the road, as fortune had so decreed, he was attacked with the disease called *seetulâ* (i.e. small-pox,) which no physician was able to cure. Then Wullubh Râj, dismissing the hope of battle, began to pray to the supreme lord, and to perform religious rites. He died there, and the army in great grief returned to Unhilwârâ.[2] Châmoond, heart-broken at the loss of his eldest son, caused Doorlubh Râj to be placed on the throne, and then retired, as a penitent, to Shookul Teerth, near Broach, on the banks of the Nerbudda, the place celebrated for the repentance of the famous Chundra Goopt and his wicked minister Chânukya ;[3] and in that retreat he died.

[1] Barbarian, one not a Hindoo.

[2] It is stated in the annals of Jesulmer, that Rawul Bachera, one of the opponents of Mahmood of Ghuznee, in his invasion of India, married in A.D. 1010, the daughter of Wullubh, sen. Solunkhee Raja of Puttun. *Vide* Tod's Rajasthan ii., 240, and foot notes.

[3] " It is said that it was the wicked *Chânacya* who caused the eight royal " brothers (of Chandra-Gupta) to be murdered ; and it is added, that *Chânacya*, " after his paroxysm of revengeful rage was over, was exceedingly troubled in his " mind, and so much stung with remorse for his crime, and the effusion of human " blood, which took place in consequence of it, that he withdrew to the *Sucla-* " *Tìrtha*, a famous place of worship near the sea, on the bank of the *Narmadâ*, and " seven coss to the west of *Baroche*. to get himself purified. There, having gone " through a most severe course of religious austerities and expiatory ceremonies, he

After that event Doorlubh Râj managed the affairs of the kingdom in a good manner, bravely conquering the Usoors, building temples, and performing many religious actions. He constructed the reservoir, called the Doorlubh Surowur at Unhilwârâ. Shree Jineshwur Sooree gave instruction to Doorlubh Raja; therefore being informed of the rudiments of the Jain religion, he travelled in the good road of pity for living things. His sister chose Muhendra, the Raja of Marwar, for her husband, when she beheld him seated in the Swuyumbur Mundup.[1] Doorlubh Raja himself was the choice of Muhendra Raja's sister Doorlubh Devee, whose selection of him drew upon him the enmity of many other rajas, and at the same time her younger sister was espoused by Nâg Râj, the youngest son of Châmoond.

Afterwards, Doorlubh's younger brother, Nâg Râj, had a son, named Bheem. Mortals owe three debts; which are paid by chastity and the cultivation of wisdom, by performance of fire sacrifice, and by begetting a son. When, therefore, Bheem was born, Doorlubh and Nâg Râj, on account of the debt to the progenitors (Peetrees) having been discharged, joyfully held high festival in the court. At the time of the prince's birth a voice from the sky proclaimed his future greatness.

When Bheem grew up, Doorlubh, desiring to retire to a place of pilgrimage, that he might perform penances for the happiness of his soul, pressed that prince to relieve him of the burden of royalty. Bheem at first refused, but Doorlubh and Nâj Râj continuing to entreat him, he at length allowed his enthronization to be performed. At that time a rain of flowers fell from the sky. Afterwards Doorlubh and Nâg Râj departed to Paradise.

The following character of Doorlubh Râj from the Rutun Mâlâ will be useful in our subsequent enquiries. "Doorlubh was lofty in "stature and fair in complexion; he was much addicted to asceticism;

"was directed to sail upon the river in a boat with white sails, which, if they turned "black, would be to him a sure sign of the remission of his sins; the blackness of "which would attach itself to the sails. It happened so, and he joyfully sent the "boat adrift, with his sins, into the sea.

"This ceremony, or another very similar to it, (for the expense of a boat would "be too great), is performed to this day at the *Sucla-Tirtha;* but, instead of a "boat they use a common earthen pot, in which they light a lamp, and send it "adrift with the accumulated load of their sins. * * *

"It seems that *Chandra-Gupta*, after he was firmly seated on his imperial throne, "accompanied *Chânacya* to the *Sucla-Tirtha*, in order to get himself purified also." *Vide* Wilford's Essay on the Kings of Magadha. Asiat. Res. ix., page 96.

[1] The hall in which a princess publicly selected her husband from among her assembled suitors.

"the worshipper of the husband of Heemâlâ's daughter; he was not "easily incited by anger, being enlightened by knowledge; he loved "the society of ascetics, bathing, gifts, and the banks of the Ganges; "warlike ambition from his birth abandoning."

The same story which is told by Hemâchârya of Châmoond Raja is repeated by the author of the Prubundh Chintâmunee, in reference to Doorlubh Râj, who is stated to have proceeded on a pilgrimage to Benares, after having resigned the throne to Bheem Dev, and to have been obstructed in his passage through Malwa by Moonj Raja, who then ruled there, and who compelled him to lay aside the ensigns of royalty. Doorlubh, it is said, proceeded on his pilgrimage in the attire of a monk, and died at Benares, having, however, caused Bheem Dev to become acquainted with the insulting conduct of the raja of Malwa. From that time, it is added, there arose a root of enmity between the lord of Goozerat and the Malwa king.

It is mentioned in the Bhoj Churittra, that Doorlubh Râj visited Moonj, by whom he was advised to resume the throne, which advice was subsequently resented by Bheem.[1] Such a resignation of royal state appears to have been a common practice in ancient times, the Rajpoot princes esteeming a death in the holy land of Gyâ as the safe passage to beatitude, for which at a later period they substituted a raid against the enemies of their faith, when the followers of Islam made war upon their religion. It does not, however, so easily appear how Doorlubh could have been considered competent to resume the throne. A prince having once abandoned the government should, according to Rajpoot practice, never again enter the capital. He is virtually dead; he cannot be a subject, and he is no longer king; he drops his former name, and assumes one suited to the future ascetic. To render the act more impressive, an effigy of the abdicated king is made, and on the twelfth day following his resignation, (being the usual period of mourning,) it is committed to the flames of the funeral pyre. The hair and moustache of his successor are removed, and the women's apartments resound with wailings and lamentations for the dead.[2]

The character of Bheem Raja is given, evidently *con amore*, by the bard Krishnâjee, and though we propose turning aside to the oft-told tale of Somnâth, as related by the Mohammedan historians, before proceeding with the Hindoo traditions of the reign of Bheem, we prefer quoting Krishnâjee's fragment in this place, as it may tend to

[1] *Vide* Tod's Western India, page 170-1.
[2] *Vide* Tod's Rajasthan, i. 277; ii. 460, 495.

elucidate the part which his hero played in the resistance opposed to the fierce iconoclast of Ghuznee.

"Doorlubh's successor was Bheem Dev; splendid as the Dev's "Dev; skilled in the practice of war; seizing the bow. He was "strong and tall in person; his body covered with hair; his face was "somewhat swarthy, but goodly to behold. He was high spirited, "fond of martial deeds; not he afraid, the Mlech challenging."

It was about the time when Canute the Great, having defeated the Danes in England, was employing himself in decorating the old minster at Winchester "with such magnificence as confounded the "minds of strangers at the sight of the gold and silver and the "splendor of the jewels," that another sovereign, as successful a soldier, and as enthusiastic a lover of architectural display, undertook, in the far east, an enterprise in which he sought to perpetuate his name by the destruction of an idolatrous shrine, perhaps more splendid than that Christian temple which the politic western sovereign was engaged in founding. Eleven expeditions against the Hindoo enemies of Islam had, for a time, satisfied the avarice and satiated the zeal of the Sultan of Ghuznee; but the faith of the idolaters was unbroken, and from the ancient oracle of Muhâ Kâl the response still went forth which asserted that the victories of the crescent were but permitted scourges by which an inattentive people was to be compelled to the more assiduous worship of the great Someshwur. At this time, therefore, the champion of the faith once more called up his energy, and determined on a final effort which should transmit his name to posterity among the greatest scourges of idolatry, if not the greatest promoters of Islam.

Mahmood left Ghuznee on his expedition against Somnâth in September, A.D. 1024; his numerous army was accompanied by crowds of volunteers, the flower of the youth of Toorkistan. In a month they had reached Mooltan, and prepared themselves for the arduous task of crossing the wide desert which still intervened between them and the plains of India. This barrier was successfully surmounted. The town of Ujmeer quickly fell into their hands,[1] and, without heeding the fortress which crowned the adjacent hill,

[1] The Rajpoot traditions relate that Mahmood was repulsed from Ujmeer by the Chohân prince, Beer Beelun Dev, or Dhurumguj, who lost his life in the action, T. R. ii. 447, 451; (but, afterwards), "Mahmood attacked Ujmeer, which was "abandoned, and the country around given up to devastation and plunder. The "citadel, Gurh Beetli, however, held out, and Mahmood was foiled, wounded, and "obliged to retreat by Nadole, another Chohan possession which he sacked, and then proceeded to Nehrwalla, &c." *Id.* 448.

they continued their march, skirting the base of the Arâwul mountains, until, the stupendous Aboo looming in their rear, they had passed into the plains of Goozerat, and beheld, stretched before them, the city of Unhilwârâ. Completely surprised, his feudal vassals unassembled, his own thoughts perhaps occupied rather with the trees in his garden, or with the reservoirs which he was constructing, than with preparations for the day of battle, Châmoond Raja was totally without the means of maintaining, against such an enemy, the widely extended defences of his capital. He fled, and the army of Islam entered without opposition.

It was against the gods, however, and not the kings of the Hindoos, that Mahmood now made war; and, the city of Wun Râj left behind, his banners were soon rapidly advancing towards Somnâth.

The small port and bay of Verâwul lie on the south-western coast of Soorâshtra, in a country exceedingly rich, thickly wooded, and in high cultivation. Upon a projection of land, forming the southern extremity of this little bay, which, with its bold and graceful curvature, and its golden sands kept in perpetual agitation by the surf, has been pronounced to be unrivalled in India, stands the city of Dev Puttun or Prubhâs. Its massive walls of uncemented stones, pierced by double gates and defended by numerous rectangular towers, enclose a square possessing a circumference of nearly two miles; a ditch twenty-five feet broad, and about as deep as it is wide, faced with masonry, and capable of being inundated at pleasure, surrounds the whole. Its general plan, the mutilated images which here and there protrude, and the architectural ornaments which appear on numerous mosques or private houses still, in language that cannot be mistaken, proclaim the Hindoo origin of the city of Somnâth through all the innovations of its conquerors. The celebrated shrine of Muhâ Kâl occupies a lofty and projecting rock in the south-western corner of the city, and close to the walls whose base is washed by the ocean. Its original design, and the gorgeous style of its architecture, may still be traced in the complete ruin which it now presents. For a considerable distance around the temple, the whole space is occupied by portions of columns, sculptured stones, and other fragments of the original building, and the wonderful solidity of its structure was, within a few years, visibly attested by a battery of heavy ordnance, mounted upon its roof, to defend from the pirates, who formerly infested this coast, the neighbouring port of Verâwul.

Such is the present state of the far-famed shrine of Someshwur Muhâ Dev; but to behold it as it met the eye of the army of Islam, we must recal its lofty spire rising far above the blue horizon of its ocean background, the tawny banner of Shiva fluttering from its summit, the porticoes and pyramid-like dome, the courts and columned isles that surrounded them, and the numerous subordinate shrines which, as satellites, heightened the splendor of this chosen dwelling of the "Lord of the Moon"—all now levelled with the earth, or built into the walls of mosques, ruined in their turn, or into the humble dwellings of mortals.[1]

Notwithstanding the rapidity of his approach, and though the country which he had passed through had been undefended, Mahmood found a host of men in arms ready to risk their lives for the protection of Somnâth, and the punishment of the invaders. Making a signal for a herald to approach, they proclaimed defiance, and vaunted that the mighty Someshwur had drawn the Mohammedans thither to blast them in a moment, and avenge the insults of the gods of India. Next morning the green banner of the prophet was unfurled, and the Mohammedan troops, advancing to the walls, commenced the attack. The battlements were in a short time cleared by the archers, and the Hindoos, astonished and dispirited at the unexpected fury of the assault, leaving the ramparts, crowded into the sacred precincts, and prostrating themselves in tears before the symbol of their god, implored his aid. The assailants, seizing this opportunity, applied their scaling ladders, and mounted the walls amidst shouts of "Allah Akbar;" but the Rajpoots, as easily excited as dispirited, rallied in defence, and, before the sun went down, the soldiers of Mahmood, unable to retain their footing, and wearied with fatigue, fell back on all sides, and retired.

Next morning the action was renewed; but the assailants as fast as they scaled the walls were hurled down headlong by the besieged, and the labours of the second day proved to the Mohammedans even more unsuccessful than those of the first.

On the third day the princes of the neighbourhood, who had assembled to rescue the temple, presented themselves in order of battle within sight of the camp of Mahmood. The Sultan, determined to prevent this attempt to raise the siege, ordered a force to keep the garrison in check, and himself advanced to give the enemy battle. The contest raged with great fury, and victory was already doubtful, when Wullubh Sen, the heir-apparent, and his chivalrous nephew, the young Bheem Dev, arriving with a strong

[1] This description of Somnâth is from Tod's "Western India," and Kittoe's "Notes on a journey to Girnar;" Journal of the Bengal Branch of the Asiatic Society, vol. vii., p. 865.

reinforcement, inspired their countrymen with fresh courage. Mahmood, at this moment, perceiving his troops to waver, leaped from his horse, and, prostrating himself on the ground, implored the assistance of Allah ; then mounting, and taking by the hand a valiant Circassian leader by way of encouragement, he advanced on the Rajpoot lines, cheering his troops with such energy that, ashamed to abandon a king with whom they had so often fought and bled, they with one accord rushed forwards. This furious charge was not to be withstood ; the Mohammedans broke through the enemy, and five thousand Hindoos lay dead at their feet. The rout now became general—the garrison of Somnâth, beholding the royal banner of Unhilwârâ cast to the ground, abandoned the defence of the place, and issuing out at a gate towards the sea to the number of four thousand, made their escape, though not without considerable loss.

Having now placed guards round the walls and at the gates, the victorious Sultan of Ghuznee, accompanied by his sons and a few of his nobles, entered the shrine of Someshwur. He beheld a superb edifice of hewn stone, its lofty roof supported by pillars curiously carved and set with precious stones. In the adytum, to which no external light penetrated, and which was illuminated only by a lamp suspended from the centre by a golden chain, appeared the symbol of Someshwur—a stone cylinder which rose nine feet in height above the floor of the temple, and penetrated six feet in depth below it. Two fragments of this object of idolatrous worship were, at the king's order, broken off, that one might be thrown at the threshold of the public mosque, and the other at the court gate of his own palace at Ghuznee. Other fragments were reserved to grace the holy cities of Mecca and Medina. While Mahmood was thus employed, a crowd of Brahmins, petitioning his attendants, offered an enormous ransom if the king would desist from further mutilation. Mahmood hesitated, and his courtiers hastened to offer the advice which they knew would be acceptable ; but after a moment's pause, the Sultan exclaimed that he would be known by posterity not as "the idol-seller," but as "*the destroyer.*" The work of spoliation then continued, and was rewarded by the discovery, in the vaults below the adytum, of untold treasures.

Having secured the wealth of Somnâth, Mahmood prepared to follow the brave prince, Bheem Dev, who, as the Mohammedan historians confess, had, in his unsuccessful attempt to raise the siege, cut off above three thousand of the faithful, and who, after the taking of Dev Puttun, had thrown himself into a fort called Gundaba, at the distance of forty leagues from the despoiled shrine. The Sultan on arriving at this fort found it apparently impracticable of approach, from its being surrounded on all sides by water, which was only in one place fordable. Mahmood, however, having ordered public prayers, and having cast his fortune on the Koran,[1] availed himself of the low state of the tide to enter the water with his troops, and, reaching in safety the opposite side, immediately commenced the attack. Bheem Dev fled at the approach of the Mohammedans, and the assailants obtaining easy possession, made dreadful havoc among the defenders of the fort. The women and children were made captive, and the spoils of Gundaba added to the treasures of Mahmood.

The Sultan, thus victorious, returned to Unhilwâra, where it is probable that he passed the rainy season. He found the soil of that place so fertile, the air so pure and salubrious, and the country so well cultivated and pleasant, that it is said he proposed to take up his residence there for some years, and to make it his capital, conferring the government of Ghuznee upon his son, the Prince Musaood. His imagination was dazzled with stories which he had heard of the jewels of Ceylon and the mines of Pegoo, and, as he was almost childishly fond of amassing precious stones, he is said to have seriously intended to fit out a fleet for the conquest of those regions, but the more sedate counsel of his officers diverted him from his scheme, and, yielding to their advice, he consented to return to his native kingdom.

It was probably these misfortunes of his country, rather than the reported incestuous connection with his sister, which induced the pleasure-loving Châmoond Raja to resign the sceptre of his race. However this may be, his name no longer appears, and when the attention of Mahmood and his counsellors was turned to the discovery of an eligible person to be invested with authority as the Sultan's tributary in Goozerat, the choice appears to have lain between the two brothers Wullubh and Doorlubh Sen. The heir-apparent, it was represented, was very wise and learned, all the Brahmins having great reliance in his wisdom. He had been, it was urged, already invested with power in a particular district, and was so upright and trustworthy, that having once taken upon himself the payment of tribute he would, without fail, remit the annual payments to Ghuznee. Others contended that the government should be conferred upon Doorlubh Sen, who had been employed in studying

1 "The Mohammedans use the Koran as school-boys sometimes apply to the Sortes Virgilii."—Col. Briggs's Note.

philosophy and in mortifying the flesh; but their opponents stigmatized him as an evil-disposed person, who had fallen under the displeasure of God, and whose seclusion from the world came not of his own choice, but had been adopted with the view of saving his life, after his brothers had several times confined him for attempts upon the throne. To these arguments the Sultan replied, that had the heir-apparent presented himself to request the government he might have consented to grant it, but that he would not confer so large a territory on one who had neither done a service nor even paid a courtesy. Doorlubh Sen, "the anchorite," was therefore selected, and having been invested with the government of Goozerat, bound himself to the payment of a tribute—equivalent to that of Kabool and Khorasân. He petitioned the Sultan, however, to leave him some troops for his protection, asserting that Wullubh Sen would undoubtedly attack him before his authority could be thoroughly established. This consideration prevailed with the Sultan to form a design for reducing Wullubh Sen before he left the country, and that prince was in a short time seized and brought as a prisoner to Mahmood.

The Sultan having now passed upwards of a year in Goozerat began to think of directing his steps homewards, and at the request of Doorlubh Sen he determined to carry the heir-apparent with him to Ghuznee. The route by which he had advanced was, however, occupied by the unconquered Bheem Dev, and his ally Veesul Dev, the Raja of Ujmeer. The Moslem force was by this time reduced by the casualties of war and climate, and the Sultan, instead of risking a further encounter, determined to attempt a new route by the sands to the east of Sindh. Here also he encountered deserts in his march, wherein his army suffered greatly from want of water, and his numerous cavalry found themselves destitute of forage; for three days and nights the army was misled by a Hindoo guide, in a sandy desert; many of the soldiers died raving mad from the intolerable heat and thirst, and the guide, submitted to the torture, is said to have confessed himself to be a priest of Somnâth, who, to revenge the injuries done to the temple, had thus endeavoured to accomplish the ruin of the Moslem army. The king ordered his execution, and, it being towards evening, fell prostrate before God, imploring a speedy deliverance. A meteor, says the Mohammedan historian, was immediately seen in the north, towards which direction he shaped his course, and before morning found himself on the border of a lake or pool of water.

The conquerors of Somnâth at length reached Mooltan, and from thence returned to Ghuznee.

The account of Mahmood's expedition to Somnâth is from Brigg's Ferishta, the Ayeen-i-Akbery, Bird's Mirat Ahmadi, Elphinstone's India, &c.

Raja Châmoond (or as he is there called, Jamund) is expressly named by the authors of the Ayeen-i-Akbery, and Mirat Ahmadi, as the prince who ruled at Unhilwârâ when Mahmood of Ghuznee took possession of it. The Hindoo legends, as we have seen, make no mention of Mahmood's invasion, but they represent Châmoond to have survived his son, Wullubh Sen. There can, we think, be little danger in assuming Wullubh Sen and his brother, Doorlubh Sen, to be the two "Dabishleems" spoken of by the Mohammedan historians, and Bhram Dev can be no other than Bheem Dev. There is some difficulty in assigning their different parts to the two brothers, Wullubh and Doorlubh. All the accounts agree in making the short reign of Wullubh Sen to have immediately followed that of Châmoond. It would seem to be proved, by the copper-plate inscription, quoted in the note at page 49, which, in giving a list of the Kings of Unhilwârâ from Mool Râj I. to Bheem Dev II., makes no mention of Wullubh Sen's having reigned at all, that Doorlubh Sen was the prince who maintained himself on the throne. Supposing Châmoond to have resigned in favor of his heir-apparent, Wullubh Sen, and this latter to have appeared with Bheem Dev in arms against Mahmood, and at no time to have tendered his submission, all which is probable in itself, and, we think, fairly inferrible from the Mohammedan accounts, taken in connection with the few facts handed down in the Hindoo legends, Mahmood would then naturally have selected Doorlubh Sen as the more fitted person for his tributary government. Doorlubh would, no doubt, have had a party in his favor, as against his brother, even among their own countrymen, but supposing the heir-apparent to have been the prince selected byMahmood, it seems difficult to account for his nervous apprehension of being supplanted by his brother in what the majority must have acknowledged to have been no more than his rights. Besides, it appears to us, that the Mohammedan historians, in the whole story, point to a departure from the strict line of succession in the selection of "Dabishleem, the Anchorite." In this view we are compelled to reject the story of the revolution which reversed the destinies of the parties, and consigned the anchorite to a dungeon which he had himself prepared, although, as Mr. Elphinstone has remarked, "it is by no means improbable in itself, and is too true a picture of the "hypocritical humanity of a Hindoo priest in power, to have been invented by a "Mahometan author."

The fact mentioned to the honor of Wullubh Râj, by the author of Rutun Mâlâ, his fidelity to his word, is the very point urged by Mahmood's advisers in favor of the candidate who was rejected.

There is a still greater difficulty in regard to the dates, which we will state, though we can offer no solution:—It was in A.D. 1024-5, according to the Mohammedan accounts, that Mahmood effected his conquests in Goozerat, but the Hindoo authors place the accession of Wullubh Sen (who reigned six months) and of Doorlubh Sen in A.D. 1010, and that of Bheem Dev in A.D. 1022.

CHAPTER VI.

BHEEM DEV I.

THE transactions of the reign of Bheem Dev I. (A.D. 1022—72) are given in outline by the author of Dwyâshrây, an authority, who though by no means free from the usual Hindoo vice of suppressing whatever is not altogether favourable to his own party, is still of value from his contiguity to the period of which he treats, and from the suggestiveness of his accounts and the means which they afford for the arrangement of materials drawn from different sources.

"Bheem Dev," says Hemâchârya, "ruled in a good manner, and "refused pardon to the crime of incontinency. He apprehended "thieves cleverly, and punished them, so that the offences of depre- "dation diminished in his reign. He preserved life very exceedingly, "so that even the wolf in the forest was restrained from taking life. "Some kings who had fled from fear of their enemies took shelter "with Bheem; some kings took service under his standard, thence "he acquired the title of Raja of Rajas. The Kings of Poondra and "Undra sent him presents, his fame spread into Mugudh also; "poets celebrated his exploits in verses composed in the Mâgudhee "and other languages, from which his fame was so spread abroad "that the inhabitants of distant countries knew him as if by sight.

"Once on a time it was told to Bheem, by his spies, that the "Sindh Raja and the Raja of Chedee[1] alone on the earth despised "his fame, and that they caused books to be composed in his "dispraise. The Sindh Raja, it was said, also used threats in regard "to Bheem. The strength of this prince was only equalled by the "ambition of his projects. He had subdued the Raja of Shivshân, "with many other lords of fortresses and princes of islands. Bheem, "when he heard these things, sending for his ministers, began to "consult them upon the matter. Soon he collected an army and "set forth. In the Punjâb, which was contiguous to Sindh, five "rivers flowed together, the volume of which rolled like a sea. It "was owing to the strength of these floods, resembling a strong "fortress, that the Sindh Raja slept in peace, having conquered his

[1] *Chedee* has been conjectured to be the modern Chundail in Gondwana. It was the country of Shishoopâl, the enemy of Shree Krishn.

" enemies. The army of Bheem, breaking down hills, with great " stones thereof began to build a bridge which, as it proceeded " towards completion, forced the waters of the stream to divide and " take another channel, as milk boils over when placed upon the " fire. Trees, both green and dry, and earth, as well as stones, were " used in the construction of the bridge. When Bheem beheld the " work approaching completion he was pleased, and, to make all " happy, he caused sugar and other luxuries to be distributed among " his troops. Then, crossing the bridge, he advanced with his army " into Sindh, the raja of which country, whose name was Hummook, " coming to oppose him in fight, a contest ensued. The moon-" descended Bheem fought valiantly, and, taking many prisoners, " subjected to himself the Raja of Sindh.

" Bheem Dev next went against Chedee, subduing the rajas " through whose territory he passed. Kurun, the Raja of Chedee, " when he heard that Bheem was approaching, collected an army of " hill-men and barbarians, but as he had heard of the fame of " Bheem, and felt that he was not to be conquered, he was un-" willing to engage him and sought rather to come to an agreement. " Meanwhile his horsemen and foot soldiers advanced prepared for " the fight, and the royal drum and other warlike instruments were " sounded. A servant of Bheem Dev's, named Dâmodhur, was at " this time sent to the camp of the Raja of Chedee to offer him " peace on his consenting to pay tribute. Dâmodhur represented " that his master had subdued many princes, the Raja of Dushârnuv, " the Raja of Kâshee, and others; also that the Raja of Gujbundh, " by name Bhudr Bhut, had come from a distant country to signify " submission; that Tunteek, the Raja of Teling, had thrown away " his arms and paid obeisance; that the Raja of Uyodhya, who " never before paid tribute to any one, had given up to Bheem the " treasures which he had taken from the King of Gord. Kurun " Raja, after some demur, agreed to follow the example of the great " princes he had been told of and make submission to Bheem, and " Dâmodhur was sent back to the King of Unhilwârâ bearing " presents from the Chedee prince, consisting of gold, elephants, a " horse as swift as the wind, and other valuables, and, in addition, a " gold litter which Kurun had taken from Bhoj, the Raja of Malwa. " With these offerings the successful ambassador returned to " Bheem Dev, who, assenting to the terms that had been proposed, " caused them to be confirmed by his ministers, and then marched " back in triumph to Unhilwârâ. There he was joyfully received by " the people, who had dressed themselves in holiday attire and "adorned their city as on a festive day; for Bheem was a favourite "of his subjects, because, in his reign, they suffered no calamity, "being not only protected from secret depredators, but also from "the open enemies that might have brought the horrors of fire and "plunder to their towns."

Such is the account given by Hemâchârya. He is borne out by other authorities in the connection which he asserts between the fortunes of Bheem and those of the celebrated Bhoj, the Raja of Malwa, and of a more eastern prince, named Kurun, and his allusion to wars in the Punjâb and Sindh may have reference to the contest carried on in his time between the Hindoos and the followers of Modood, the Sultan of Ghuznee, for the expulsion of the Mohammedan from "the land of virtue;" though, in this latter struggle, it has been elsewhere asserted that Bheem Dev took no share, but, on the contrary, by his refusal to do so drew upon himself the arms of the confederated Rajpoot princes. We now turn to the relations of these events afforded by other authorities.

The Purmâr King of Malwa, Shree Singhbhut, being at the time sonless, adopted a foundling, to whom, from the fact of his having discovered him in a thicket of Moonj grass, he gave the name of Moonj. Singhbhut afterwards had a son named Seedhul. At the close of his life Singhbhut announced to Moonj his intention of making him his successor, and, at the same time, informed him of the facts which attended his birth and adoption, urging him to live in affection with his brother Seedhul.

Moonj having succeeded to the throne, with the aid of his wise minister, Roodrâditya, increased his territories, but exhibited a cruel spirit, putting to death his wife who had been cognizant of the last instructions of Singhbhut and the secret of his birth, and expelling from Malwa Seedhul the legitimate heir to the throne. This prince appears to have given Moonj provocation by turbulence of spirit and by refusing obedience. He retired for a time to Goozerat and lived at Kâsahrud (probably Kâsindra Pâlaree, about fourteen miles from Ahmedabad), where he founded a village. Seedhul, however, subsequently returned to Malwa, and was favourably received by Moonj, who assigned to him an allotment of territory; but this agreement did not long continue, and Moonj subsequently seized upon Seedhul and imprisoned him, putting out his eyes.

The celebrated Bhoj was the son of Seedhul. He became in his youth skilful in martial exercises as well as learned in the Shâstras, but the astrologers drew upon him the anger of Moonj Raja by a too flattering horoscope, which predicted as follows:—

"For fifty years and five, for six months and three days Bhoj Raja "shall enjoy the Dekkan with Goud."

The king, fearing that the accession of Bhoj should exclude his own son from the throne, determined to put him to death. Those who were employed for this purpose, however, failed in its execution, being won over by the beauty and virtues of Bhoj. When the king demanded of them an account of their commission, they intimated to him that it had been completed, placing at the same time in his hands a paper with which they had been charged by Bhoj. It ran thus:—

"King Mândhâtâ, the ornament of the Golden Age, has perished; "where is he who bridged the mighty ocean—the destroyer of the "ten-handed Râwun? Yoodishteer also, and other great princes "have all of them set, but not with any one of them has the earth "passed away. I suppose with you it will pass."

Moonj on reading this verse was struck with remorse, and wept many tears, reproaching himself with the slaughter of the boy. He was then informed that the life of Bhoj had not been sacrificed, and, delighted with the intelligence, he sent for the young prince and caused him to be installed as "Yoov Râj," or heir-apparent. Moonj, according to tradition, signalized his penitence by performing a pilgrimage to the country lying on the east of the lesser Runn of Kutch, which is called by the Brahmins Dhurum Arunya, where he founded a town which is still called Moonjpoor.

The king now prepared for an expedition against Teilip Dev, Raja of Telingânâ.[1] He was in vain dissuaded by his minister, Roodrâditya, who reminded him of former disasters sustained in similar attempts, and repeated to him an old prophecy, which predicted destruction to the King of Malwa who should pass the Godâvery. His remonstrances being disregarded, Roodrâditya, full of melancholy presentiments, retired from his employments, and soon after entered the funeral fire. Moonj Raja obstinately sought his fate, and having engaged the army of Teilip Dev, was defeated and made prisoner. He might even then have effected his escape by means arranged by his minister, but having confided the secret to Mrinâlwutee, the sister of Teilip Dev, with whom he had formed a connection while in confinement, he was betrayed by her. Moonj was now subjected to the most ignominious treatment, and at last carried

[1] See foot-note at page 38.

to the place where the lowest criminals were executed, and there beheaded, his head being set upon a stake near the palace of Teilip Raja to be destroyed by carrion birds.

Moonj Raja is said to have written a geographical description of the world, which was afterwards corrected and improved by Raja Bhoj.[1] His patronage of literature seems to have been the most conspicuous point in his character, as is evidenced by the remarks made on his death:—"When Moonj, the accumulation of good "qualities, perished, wealth departed to the presence of Shree "Krishn, (the husband of Lukshmee the goddess of wealth), valour "to the house of Shree Veer, but Suruswutee (the goddess of litera-"ture) was left without support."

Moonj was succeeded by Shree Bhoj Raja, who was a contemporary of the Solunkhee Bheem Dev I. of Unhilwârâ. In Bhoj the chroniclers have met with a king who entirely filled their interested outline of the duties of a sovereign. He is represented to have continually reflected upon the facts that fortune is unstable, and life as transitory as a wave, and to have practically deduced from these meditations the necessity of giving to all comers. Beggars, players, Brahmins, thieves, who had penetrated into his palace for the purpose of robbing him, were the equally welcome recipients of the generosity of Shree Bhoj. The ministers who sought to restrain his profusion were dismissed, and Bhoj delighted himself with the idea that he had surpassed Bulee Raja, Kurun, or Vikrumâditya, and had given such gifts as before had been given by none. His extravagance, however, seems to have been its own cure, for having met with a poet who as fast as he was recompensed for one brilliant euloge composed another of still exceeding sublimity, Bhoj Raja was at length forced to allow himself fairly conquered; and, as his last resource for maintaining an equality with his too devoted admirer, was compelled to enjoin upon him *silence.*

Bheem Dev appears to have sent ambassadors, called *Sândhee Vigraheek*, or makers of war and peace, to seek the alliance of Bhoj, but the negotiation had no better effect than the exchange between the rival sovereigns of verses more highly seasoned than courteous, and though Bhoj might have been supposed to have been more fitted for such a contest than the active warrior of Unhilwârâ, Bheem Dev must be admitted on the whole to have maintained a decided advantage.

[1] *Vide* Asiat. Res. ix., p. 176.

Once on a time, a scarcity having arisen in Malwa, Bhoj Raja prepared to invade Goozerat, but he was diverted from his purpose by Bheem Dev's ambassador, Dâmur (the Dâmodhur we suppose of Hemâchârya), who contrived to resuscitate the ancient feud with Teilip, Raja of Telingânâ, and this prince, preparing to invade Malwa, Bhoj was glad to make peace with Bheem Dev on his own terms. Freed from anxiety on these points, Bhoj Raja employed himself in founding or restoring the city of *Dhârâ Nugger*, since commonly known as Dhâr.

Subsequently, when Bheem Dev was employed in an expedition against Sindh (probably that to which allusion has already been made), Bhoj Raja seized the opportunity to attack Goozerat. His forces were led by an adventurer named Koolchunder, who had promised to fulfil the prophecy recorded in his sovereign's horoscope by making him master of the Dekkan and Goud. Koolchunder penetrated to Unhilpoor in the absence of its sovereign, and, having sacked the city, sowed shell-money at the gate of the palace, and at that where the gong was sounded, and extorted a *jye-puttra* or deed of victory, with which he returned to Malwa. Bhoj received him with honor, but blamed him for sowing shell-money among the ruins instead of salt, adding that he had produced an omen which portended that the treasures of Malwa should at a future time be carried to Goozerat. The prediction was, as we shall see, fulfilled in the time of Yushowurm, a descendant of Bhoj.

Bheem Dev is said to have paid a secret visit to the court of Bhoj, disguising himself as one of the suite of the ambassador Dâmur, but no result appears to have followed the adventure. At another time Bhoj, while worshipping at the temple of the goddess of his race, near the gate of the city of Dhâr, was nearly surprised and made prisoner by a party of Goozerat horse who had ventured so far into his territory. The two princes appear, indeed, to have been hostilely opposed to each other throughout their reigns.

One of the most superb of the marble shrines of the Jain religion which adorn the "Dailwârâ," or region of temples on the table-land of Mount Aboo, is that which, as its inscription shows, was erected in A.D. 1032, by Veemul Shâ. As tradition asserts, the ground was formerly occupied by shrines of Shiva and Vishnoo, but the Shâ giving this the preference to any other site upon Mount Aboo, and calling in the aid of Lukshmee to gain a triumph for his faith, offered to cover with silver coin as much ground as he required for the sacred edifice which he contemplated erecting. His offer was accepted; and the orthodox divinities were now for the first time on this their sacred ground supplanted by Adeenâth. The prince who then held the towers of Uchuleshwur was Dhundoo Râj Purmâr, descended through Kânhur Dev from the warrior who had issued from the pit of fire. The capital of Dhundoo Râj was Chundrâ-wutee-poor, the ruins of which still remain. His ancestors, as we have seen, acknowledged the supremacy of the kings of Unhilwârâ, but Dhundoo Râj, as is stated in the inscription, had quitted the service of King Bheem Dev, and allied himself with Bhoj. The Sovereign of Goozerat had thereupon sent Veemul Shâ to exercise the office of his *Dundputee* or vice-gerent at Aboo, and it was while he was thus employed that the Goddess Umbâ Bhuwânee appeared to the Shâ in the night time, and ordered him to erect a temple to the Yoogâdee Nâth.

It was the same Veemul Shâ who also erected the temples at Koombhâreea on the hill of Arâsoor near the celebrated shine of Umbâ Bhuwânee. They are similar in construction and in magnificence to the temple of Dailwârâ, with which they are supposed to be connected by a subterranean passage. The traditions relating to them will hereafter be narrated.

At this time a raja named Kurun reigned in Dâhul-land, the modern Tipera, and over the sacred city of Kâshee, or Benares. He was the son of Queen Demut, distinguished for her religious observances, who lost her life in giving him birth. Being born under a good star, this king extended his territory towards all four points of the compass. One hundred and thirty-six kings worshipped the lotus feet of Kurun.

Envious of the fame of the lord of Oojein, Kurun prepared to attack Bhoj, and in that view arranged an interview with Bheem Dev at a frontier village, and procured from him a promise that he would make a diversion by attacking Malwa from the west. Bhoj Raja, assailed by the two kings and unable from indisposition to take the field against them, contented himself with occupying by his troops the mountain passes leading into his country. Dâmur was at this time employed by his sovereign as his representative in the camp of Raja Kurun. Bheem Dev having dispatched a messenger to Dâmur for intelligence, the ambassador taught him a verse which he repeated on his return to the King of Goozerat:—

"The fruit on the mango tree is fully ripened, the stalk has become "loosened, with much wind the bough shakes, the end I know not."[1]

[1] See the Bhow's note before the battle of Paniput. As. Res. iii., 155. "The cup is now full to the brim and cannot hold another drop."

When Bheem Dev heard this verse he determined upon remaining inactive.

Bhoj Raja finding that he must journey to another world, performed the religious duties suitable to that state, and dividing the management of his kingdom among his servants, gave them orders to place him in his funeral car, with his hands extended beyond it to denote that he carried nothing with him. He then attained Paradise.

Having been informed of the death of Bhoj, Kurun Raja advanced upon Dhâr, which he destroyed, taking possession of the royal treasury. Dâmur, on the part of Bheem Dev, now laid claim to a share of the spoils, and it was arranged that the revenues of the temples of Malwa should be the property of the King of Goozerat.

The attention of the successors of Sultan Mahmood was for many years occupied with intestine feuds, which prevented their active interference with the affairs of India; and thirteen years after his death, his grandson, the Sultan Modood, being then upon the throne, the Hindoos found an opportunity of making a grand effort to shake off the yoke which oppressed them. In the year A.D. 1043, according to Ferishta, the Raja of Delhi, in conjunction with other Hindoo sovereigns, retook Hânsee, Tâhnesur, and their dependencies from the governors to whom Modood had entrusted them. From thence the Rajpoots marched towards the fort of Nuggurkot, which, after a siege of four months, the garrison, distressed for provisions and despairing of succour, was compelled to surrender. The God of Nuggurkot was induced to grace with his presence the recovered shrine, and so great was the enthusiasm encited by this triumph of their religion, that thousands of pilgrims hurried thither from all parts of Hindoostan to present their offerings of gold and silver and jewels, and to restore to its pristine splendor the temple of the fort of Bheem.

This success gave such confidence to the Rajpoot chiefs, that though before this time, as the Moslem historian asserts, they, like foxes, durst hardly creep out of their holes for fear of the Mohammedan arms, yet now they put on the aspect of lions, and openly set their masters at defiance. Three rajas, with ten thousand horse and an innumerable army of foot, invested Lahore. For seven months the Mohammedans exerted themselves to the utmost, defending, street by street, the ruined town, until at last, finding themselves on the point of being overpowered, they bound themselves by an oath to victory or martyrdom, and sallying out in order compelled their enemies to retire.

It was Veesul Dev, the Chohân King of Ujmeer, who, according to Hindoo authorities, headed this confederacy. The King of Unhilwârâ was, it is said, invited with the other princes of the land to join in this last united stand for the religion and liberties of the Hindoos, but though in former days, when the destroyer of Somnâth was at the threshold, Bheem Dev had combined with the Lord of Sâmbhur against the common enemy, the ancient jealousies between their houses prevented him from following where the Chohân sovereign led, and the forces of Goozerat were inactive, while Veesul Dev led his troops from triumph to triumph, and won for himself the right of inscribing on his monumental pillar the proud boast, that he had made "the Land of Virtue" once more what its name implied by the extermination of the barbarians.[1]

The conduct of Bheem Dev involved his kingdom in a war with the successful confederates, which, together with other incidents in the story of the sovereign of Ujmeer, forms the subject of one of the sixty-nine books of the poem of the Bhârot Chund, which we now propose to introduce to our readers.

"The sages," says the Rajpoot bard, "produced at Aboo, from "the fire-pit, a man to whom they entrusted royalty. Of his race "sprung a great and religious king, named Bâlun.[2] His son was "Veesul Dev. It was Friday, the first day of the month, the light "half of the month, the month Wyeshâk, when Veesul mounted the "throne. The thirty-six races assembled—the regenerate ones and "the bards; Veesul was presented with the royal umbrella; he "received the mark of sovereignty on his forehead; the Brahmins "repeated Veds and verses of power.

"When the umbrella was placed over the head of Veesul, the "Brahmins prepared the pit of fire sacrifice, placing therein five "arrows. The smoke issued—the flame burst forth; the Brahmins "repeating charms, performed his enthronement, giving him their "blessing; the assembly cried, 'Be victorious, be victorious! "Veesul, earth-protector!'

"Veesul enjoyed as happy a state as that of Indra; he restored "justice and fame. In Ujmeer-nugger dwelling—his enemies sub-

[1] *Vide* As. Res. vii., p. 180.

[2] This is the Beer Beelum Dev of Colonel Tod, who defended the Gurh Beetli, or hill-fortress of Ujmeer, against Mahmood of Guznee. On the pillar of Feeroz Shah (*vide* As. Res. vii., p. 180) his name is written "Vella Deva," or Vel Dev, the V and B being synonymous. Thus Veesul Dev is commonly called Beesul Dev.

" duing—Veesul reigned a pure reign. Many mighty cities he took ; " in his reign the world seemed to be covered by one umbrella.

" He adorned the city as if it had been adorned by the architect " of the gods. Abandoning irreligion, he caused religion to flourish ; " sinful deeds he sought not to perform. He exacted only his " rights—without right he indulged not his avarice ; the four castes " were subservient to the Chohân ; the thirty-six races served him.[1] " Veesul Raja, the religious, was resplendent as a Dev upon the earth.

" Once on a time, Veesul the king hunted deer in the forest. " Seeing a place well adapted for the purpose, the desire of con- " structing a tank arose in his mind. He examined the good place, " where the streams flowed from the mountains, where the forest was " good. He sent for his principal minister : 'Cause a reservoir to " be made here ; such as that of Pooshkur.' Having given this " order, he returned home ; joy without limit arose in his mind. " Upon a throne he sat like Yoodishteer, the son of Dhurum, did " Veesul, the Indra of the world of men. Over his head an um- " brella, on each side horse-hair fans waving, he was very beautiful " to the sight,—like Ushweenee Koomâr. The thirty-six races then " assembled—the Putâsurs, the Toonwurs valiant. The king called " them into his presence ; he presented them with betel-nut. The " minstrels in their verses celebrated his praise ; the king, smiling, " bent his head ; the assembly shone like a constellation ; the Chohân " in the midst like a moon. With compliments he dismissed them " all. As they retired, the bards pronounced a blessing. When a " watch of the night had passed, the raja retired within the palace. " Camphor, sandal, musk, and other perfumes scented the place. " It was redolent of precious essences which had been strewed upon " it. An apartment well colored, fit to inspire pleasure, received the " raja. He sent for actors, for singers, and other amusements. He " enjoyed the society of the Purmâr's daughter, the favorite queen, " who in beauty and youth resembled an Upsura, who was dear to " him as his life, whom he forgot not for one moment. No other " fair one did he ever look upon."

The Purmar queen gave birth to a son named Sârung Dev, who was sent, on attaining a sufficient age, under the care of the Kâyuth Keerpâl, to the town of Sâmbhur, the favorite of Sâkumbhuree Devee, which was assigned for his residence. A suitable bride was soon provided for him—" The daughter of Râwur Dev Râj, Gouree

[1] The *four castes* are the Brahmins, Kshutrees, Vaishyas, and Shoodras. The thirty-six races are the Rajpoot tribes. *Vide* Conclusion.

" by name, shone by the side of Sârung Dev, as Rutee beside " Kâm."[1]

Under these happy auspices the reign of Veesul commenced; but his prosperity was afterwards more clouded, and the chronicler represents him as driven from his throne, apparently owing to the jealousy created in the minds of his other wives and their kindred by his exclusive preference of the "daughter of the Purmâr." By the aid of Shiva, however, Veesul regained his power, which he seems thereafter to have used in so tyrannical a manner, particularly by giving himself up to an unbridled lust, that his subjects, in despair, threatened to retire in a body from the country.

" The inhabitants of the city thronged together to the house of the " minister. 'Calamity falls upon all, both men and women—we will " not remain here—we will depart in anger.' The minister soothed " the enraged people, and, in conjunction with the council of their " head men and the wives of the raja, approached Veesul. 'To " protect the land,' said they, 'a prince should travel about it. On " the earth there are many rajas; a great sovereign should attack " and subdue their cities and territories to destroy such thorns.' " The raja understood the object of what they had said: 'The flame " which has been excited in me singes you. Well, I will do what " you have urged; I will send for Keerpâl, and to whatever coun-" tries you may think fit to go, I will mount and accompany you.' " He gave the order to all the ministers and sent for Keerpâl. " From Sâmbhur he came to the city of Ujmeer. On his arrival " he touched the feet of the king; he placed a sword before him " as an offering. The hilt and the scabbard were studded with " jewels. The raja bound it on his loins; the skilful in vaticina-" tion pronounced the omen to be good. The raja said, 'As this " omen has been granted to me, I will draw my sword in all the " nine divisions of the earth, the whole world I will subdue; I " will make tributary rajas, be they as firm as Meroo. Hear, O! " Keerpâl, my speech. Providing treasure, prepare to accompany " me—at the Veesul Surowur pitch our tents.' To the ten direc-" tions he sent summonses: 'Let all come and meet me at Ujmeer.' " Muhunsee Pureehâr came and joined his standard, the chief of " Mundowur touched his feet, all the Gahilots came, crowning the " assembly. Râm Gour, the Toonwur, Pâwâ's lord, Muhesh the " lord of Mewar, the Mohil of Doonâpoor[2] came with his followers,

[1] The Cupid and Psyche of the Hindoos.

[2] The Mohils are a branch of the Chohâns descended from Manik Race.—Tod's Rajasthan, ii., 445. *Vide* this passage *idem*, ii., 448.

" the Buloch too brought his infantry, the King of Sindh flying, went " to Sindh, the King of Bhutner sent presents, the chiefs of the " country as far as Mooltan hastened to join him. The order went " to Jesulmer, all the great Bhoomeeâs were submissive; the Yâduv, " the Wâghela, the Moree, the great Goojur, responded to his call. " From Unturved came the Koorumbh. All the Mairs submissively " touched his feet. Jeyt Singh, obeying the order, set forth; the " chief of Tuchitpoor he brought with him. Many Purmârs mounted; " the Dors came to follow him; the Chundails, the Dâheemas, " worshipped him. Shaking his sword, he made all the Bhoomeeâs " submissive. No Solunkhee came to pay obeisance, they stood " aloof, sternly grasping the sword. Perceiving this, Jeytshee, the " Golwâl, spoke: 'Leaving a force at Ujmeer to protect our homes " and city, let us advance—the Châlook cannot escape.' Stage by " stage advanced the warriors, by the way of the mountains the " raja advanced to strike his first blow at the Solunkhee. Many " forts he levelled with the earth. He took Jhâlor and destroyed " its castle; to the mountains and the forest the enemy retreated. " Ascending Aboo, he beheld Uchuleshwur; Wâgur he subdued; " in Soreth, the land of Girnâr, he found tribute and salutations—he " found no battle.

" In Goozerat, land of the seventy towns, was the Châlook Row, " Bâlook the warrior. Hearing the news, Bâlook mounted and " came, he worshipped Shiva and Doorgâ, his spear he took upon " his shoulder. With him he had thirty thousand horsemen, seventy " elephants streaming with honey; at a league's distance he made a " halt. The Chohân heard the noise—heard the noise, did Veesul " the King, of the Châlook Row's advance. Calling for a charger, " he mounted; he caused the royal drum to sound; setting his " army in array, he moved onward; the sound of his approach " reached the camp of the enemy. With seventy thousand soldiers " he came on; it seemed as if the crickets in some rainy season " raised their humming noise; shields glanced, spears glittered; the " warrior was full of joy, the coward full of sorrow. Destroying the " lands of Châlook, on rolled the army as a rolling tide of the ocean; " cities, towns, and villages, all that came in their way, they plun- " dered.

" The Châlook heard the news. Angrily at once he started up, " as when a flame starts up without smoke. Bâlook Râee, the " Châlook warrior, calling for water, laved his body; he drank a " handful of water which had washed the feet of Vishnoo. Huree " he placed on his throat. 'To-day I go forth to conquer or to "meet fate. If I fly, may dishonour fall on my race. In all this land "is there no warrior, that this Veesul has advanced without being de- "barred by weapons?'

"Shreekunt, the bard, was sent to the enemy; he met Veesul-Dev "Chohân; raising his hands he pronounced a benediction; he in- "formed him of the movements of Bâlook Râee. 'When it is with "kings that you should have to do, why have you to do with sub- "jects? You have done ill injuring them, no Hindoo prince would "thus act; cease to molest the subjects and return home—to Ujmeer "depart and there reign. The Bâlook Raja has said, 'I am of the "Bruhm race, it is my occupation to carry on war, to fly were great "grief to me, but the day of my death is a day of holiday. The "chiefs that are around me are of noble race. We will never retreat "from before you; turn back, then, and abandon war—let us not "meet on the field of battle." ' When the Chohân received this "message he at once gave orders for sounding the royal drum. "Armour they placed on horses and on elephants, the warriors as- "sumed their armour. The two armies approached within sight of "each other—they seemed like billows of the ocean bending their "crests. The Chohân formed a phalanx. 'Let us see whether the "Bâlook Râee is an Ubheemânya,[1] that he may break it. What "destiny has determined will come to pass.'

"The two armies met; the warriors called to their friends: "'Brother, brother, strike, strike!' They fought and wounded each "other. The Châlook's army gave back; the Bâlook Râee came to "their assistance. He shook the phalanx. The Pureehâr and Gahi- "lot turned their backs, the Pureehâr fled to the position of the "Toonwur; the phalanx was broken and collapsed. At that time "the Khundhâr and Buloch advanced against Bâlook boldly, nothing "regarding. The warriors' surcoats were stained red, as if they "played together at the Hoolee;[2] they were bathed in gore. The "elephants, streaming with blood, showed as brilliantly as pulâsh[3] "trees covered with scarlet flowers in the spring. Bâlook and "Veesul, the king of men, perceived each other. It was as if the "moon grew dim from being opposed to the sun. The Châlook rode "on horseback, the Chohân was seated on an elephant; the two

[1] A phalanx of a peculiar form, called "Chukravyooh," is described in the Muhâbhârut, as having been formed by the Kouruv army. Ubheemânya, the son of Urjoon, broke through six ranks of it, and was slain in front of the seventh.

[2] The Hindoo Saturnalia, in the course of which the revellers sprinkle each other with red water.

[3] The "pulâsh" is a tree which bears red blossoms—the "Butea frondosa."

"rajas fought a terrible fight, they crossed weapons with each other, "when to the teeth of the elephant Bâlook urged on his steed. "Night at last separated the warriors; returning each to his own tent, "they bestowed attention on the wounded.

"The next morning the ministers of the Châlook came together. "Without the knowledge of their sovereign they sent a message to "the Chohân. Pâwâ's lord hearing this went to the raja. Keerpâl "was sent for. The Châlook's ministers came to meet them. "'Whatever property you may demand we will place it at your feet.' "The King replied: 'Listen, I will leave a post here, in a month's "time I will build a city—assent to this and bring your offering.' "Thus were the terms arranged. The Chohân gained the field—the "Châlook was wounded. Veesul returned home again when he had "founded Veesulnugger."[1]

The bard having carried Veesul back to Ujmeer, relates how that raja, returning to the course from which he had been reclaimed for a time, at last suffered the penalty of his vices, by the curse of a female devotee whose chastity he had violated, and, losing his human form, became an "Usoor" or "Dânuv," an "eater of the flesh of men." The common belief, however, was that he had perished by the bite of a snake. The Purmâr Rânee burned herself with the corpse of her lord.

The first act of Sârung Dev, Veesul's successor, was to place his wife, who was then pregnant, in security at Rintumbor, the inaccessible fortress which was the seat of her own family. He next turned his attention to the destruction of the Dânuv, who had taken up his abode at Ujmeer, and, in his fury and voracity, had rendered the place a desert; but he not only was unsuccessful in this, but himself fell a victim to the monster.

Âno, the son of Sârung Dev and Gouree, was more successful. He adopted, however, an opposite course to that pursued by his father, and instead of attempting to oppose the Dânuv in arms, he submitted himself to him and entreated his protection. The demon was pleased with his humility, and having promised that Âno's race, from father to son, should reign in Ujmeer, he rose into the sky and proceeded to Nigumbodh, on the Jumna, where he remained performing penances for three hundred and eighty years, until the time that Unung Pâl

[1] Colonel Tod, Western India, p. 172, mentions that one stipulation of this treaty was that the Châlook should give a daughter in marriage to Veesul Dev. He also mentions, quoting the Hamir Rasa, a work relating the exploits of a Chohân prince of that name, that Veesul Dev took Prince Kurun, son of Raja Bheem, prisoner.

Toonwur founded Delhi. From the fragments of his body, as Chund relates, sprung the Sâmunts or Paladins of Prutheerâj (of whom hereafter), and the poet claims for himself an origin from the tongue of the Dânuv. Âno was succeeded by his son, Jesingh Dev, whose son and successor, Ânund Dev, was the father of Someshwur, the opponent of Bheem Dev II., and father of Prutheerâj.

Bheem Dev I. married Oodayâmutee, by whom he had a son named Kurun. This queen caused to be constructed at Unhilwârâ a well, which alone of all the monuments of the race of Wun Raja still exists, though in a ruined state. It is known as the Rânee's well. Bheem Dev had also two other sons, named Mool Râj and Kshem Râj, both of whom were, it would appear, born before Kurun. The name of Mool Râj's mother has not been handed down, that of the mother of Kshem Râj was Bukoolâ Devee, who was probably a concubine and of low origin. The author of Prubundh Chintâmunee calls her a courtezan, and says she was purchased as a slave by Bheem Dev. Kshem Râj is sometimes described as Hureepâl Dev, a name which he probably acquired as a worshipper of Vishnoo after his retirement into the position of an ascetic.

The same Âchârya tells the following story of the prince Mool Râj, which is curious as giving us a glance at the revenue arrangements of the period of Bheem Dev I., and also proving to us that the cultivator of Goozerat was then in character much what he is now in regard to his stubbornness when assailed with demands, as well as his sensibility to kindness. "Once on a time, in a year when the rains had failed "in Goozerat, the householders (Koutoombeeks) of the grâms, or "small villages, of Dundâhee and Vishopuk, were unable to supply "to the king his usual share of the produce. A minister (muntree, "the mehta of modern days,) who was sent to make enquiry, brought "all the people whom he found possessed of property to the capital, "and presented them to Bheem. One morning the prince Mool Râj, "who was celebrated for his truthfulness and fidelity to his promises, "was walking about in that place attended by a servant of the king's. "When he perceived all these persons, alarmed, talking among them-"selves, having informed himself of their case through the attendant "who was with him, he compassionated them with tears in his eyes. "Soon after, having pleased the king much by his skill in horseman-"ship, he was commanded to ask a boon. Mool Râj begged that the "householders might have their rent remitted to them. The king, "with tears of joy in his eyes, both granted what he had asked and "pressed him to seek a further boon for himself.

"The people, on being released from confinement, came to touch

" his feet. Some of them remained to attend him continually; the " rest, returning home, spread his praises far and wide.

" Shortly afterwards, that merciful spirit of his gained Mool Râj " admission to the delights of Paradise. The king and his court, as " well as the people who had been released at his intercession, were " immersed in the ocean of grief for his loss. By slow degrees the " learned, by the power of the wisdom they taught, depressed the " trunk of this elephant-like sorrow. The next year the husbandmen, " delighted with an abundant fall of rain, having obtained a plentiful " crop of all kinds of grain, came to present to the king his share " both for the past and the present year. Bheem Dev refused to " receive the arrears, but at the solicitation of the husbandmen, agreed " at last to nominate, in conjunction with themselves, a jury who " should arrange the matter to mutual satisfaction. The assessors " decreed that the royal share of the produce for both years should " be placed in the king's hands for the erection of a temple, called " the Treepooroosh Prâsâd, for the happiness of Prince Mool Râj."

At the close of his reign, as the author of Dwyâshrây records, Bheem Dev, following the example of Mool Râj, the first of the Solunkhees and others of his ancestors, proposed to retire to perform penances for the attainment of Paradise, leaving his throne to Kshem Râj, his eldest son. Kshem Râj, however, refused the proffered dignity, and said, " I will not separate myself from you, but will accompany you to your place of retirement." After some discussion, Bheem Dev and Kshem Râj jointly placed Kurun on the throne, and retired, and not long afterwards Bheem became an inhabitant of Swerga.

Afflicted at his separation from his father, Kshem Râj withdrew to a pure place, called Moondeekeshwur, on the banks of the Suruswutee, no great distance from the village of Dudheesthul or Deyṭhulee, which village Kurun Raja granted to the Prince Dev Prusâd, the son of Kshem Râj, that he might attend upon his father in his religious seclusion.

CHAPTER VII.

RAJA KURUN SOLUNKHEE—REGENCY OF MYENUL DEVEE—SIDH RÂJ.

GOOZERAT, during the reign of Raja Kurun, (A.D. 1072 to 1094,) enjoyed an exemption from foreign wars. It is said that that prince continued the tributary expeditions, which his predecessors had already set on foot, into countries which owned his supremacy, but no mention is made of his having been engaged in a contest with any of the surrounding potentates. Kurun appears, however, to have availed himself of the opportunity which was thus afforded him for consolidating the strength of his kingdom by reducing the wild and inaccessible parts of the country, called the "Mewâs."

It is commonly believed that Goozerat was occupied from a remote period by rude tribes, the descendants of whom still exist, who bore a general resemblance to each other, but of the nature of whose religion or government little has been even traditionally handed down. According to Bishop Heber, they were unquestionably the original inhabitants of central and western India, and were driven to their fastnesses and desperate and miserable way of life by the invasion of those tribes, wherever they may have come from, who profess the Brahminical religion. "This, the Rajpoots themselves virtually allow "by admitting, in their traditional history, that most of their principal "cities and fortresses were founded by such and such Bheel chiefs, "and conquered from them by the children of the sun." One branch of them sprung, as the bards relate, from an ancestor named Bheel or Kaiyo, who was produced from the body of Venoo, a descendant of Ootânpât, who died under the curse of a sage. Kaiyo enjoyed the royalty of the forests around Aboo, and left a son, named Ujânbâhoo, who ruled over the same territory, and was very powerful. From him came Goho, whose occupation was that of a ferryman, and at whose house Râm rested when he first left Uyodhya. From Goho descended all the Bheels, who are, however, subdivided into ten branches.

The tribe of Kaiyos are spoken of in the Muhâbhârut as resident in Goozerat. When the Pânduvs took refuge with Vyerât Raja at Mutsyunugger or Vyerâtpoor, which is believed to have occupied the site of the present town of Dholka, they found there a queen of the Kaiyo race, named Soodeeshnâ, whose brother, Keechuk Kaiyo, was slain by Bheem Sen for an attempt upon the chastity of Droupudee. This Kaiyo is represented as having lately returned conquering with his tribe in all the wars, and as having wasted the Treegurtt country belonging to Raja Dooryodhun, or his friend Sooshurmâ.

A similar fabulous descent is given to the Koolees from Youwunâshwa, the father of Mândhâtâ Raja. Their ancestor, Koolee, was brought up by a sage in the forest, and always led a jungle life, whence it happened, as the bard says, that his descendants, though in the towns they are of little importance, are *lions in the jungle*. The Koolees lived for a long time on the sea-shore, in the neighbourhood of the Indus, but they were removed to the country about the Null by the Goddess Hinglâz, and brought with them the earth-nut called "beerd," which even in famine does not fail. They were called at this time Mairs, as well as Koolees, and Sonung Mair was their leader. He left twelve sons, each of whom became the head of a clan. Nurwân, the eldest, established himself at Null Bowlee, where Hinglâz Devee took up her residence in a temple erected to her honor. This building has disappeared, but its situation is still pointed out on an island in the Null, the ford to which is now called Hinglâz Âra.[1] The second son, Dhun Mair, or Dhând, founded Dhundhooka, which was long held by his descendants, and became so powerful as to assume the title of raja. "Fifteen thousand were "his foot-soldiers, eighteen thousand were his horsemen, eight "elephants shook their heads at the castle of Dhând." The other brothers had each a village. In these times, says the bard, there was not so great a population in Goozerat, but there was much forest, and the Bheels and Koolees lived in security. They were doubtless then, as now, hereditary and professional plunderers, "soldiers of the "night," as they describe themselves. Raja Kurun Solunkhee is the first ruler of Goozerat on record who devoted his attention to putting a curb upon these wild tribes,—a task which has engaged the solicitude, more or less, of all his successors down to the present time.

The predatory tribes have always had some of their principal haunts in the country which stretches from the eastern side of the lesser Runn of Kutch to the river Sâbhermutee. Kurun Raja is said to have attacked a Bheel chieftain, named Âshâ, who lived at Âshâpullee, now Âshâwul, near the city of Ahmedabad, and led an innumerable force of bowmen. The Bheel was defeated and slain by Kurun, who, in consequence of a good omen which had occurred to him, built in the same place a temple to a Devee, called Kochuruv, a name which is still preserved in that of a locality on the banks of the river immediately contiguous to Ahmedabad. Merootoong (the author of Prubundh Chintâmunee) goes on to say, that the king founded in the same place a temple to Jyeuntee Devee, the two temples of Kuruneshwur and Kurun Meroo Prâsâd, to his patron god, and a reservoir, called Kurun Sâgur, or the sea of Kurun, and also that he built a town, called Kurunâwutee, and made it his residence.

The situation of Kurunâwutee[2] cannot be decisively ascertained,

[1] Jour. Bom. Br. Roy. As. Soc., vol. v., p. 113.
[2] The probability is that Kurun's city stood on the site of that of his Moslem

but there can be no doubt as to the proper position to be assigned to the magnificent reservoir, the Kurun Sâgur. Near the town of Modheyra, not many miles to the south of Unhilwârâ Puttun, is a village still called "Kunsâgur," in the lands of which are the remains of an immense reservoir known in the surrounding villages as "the "ten miles tank," and which local tradition still attributes to "the "father of Sidh Râj, the Goodman Kun." The design was worthy of a monarch, and may be clearly traced, though but little now remains of the structure itself. The river Roopeyn, flowing down from the hills beyond Kherâloo, was here arrested in its course towards the Runn, and compelled to relinquish its natural outlet and to empty its waters into the sea of Kurun. Nor could the execution have been unequal to the design, for century after century passed on, the dynasty of Wun Raja was forgotten, the Moslem had conquered, ruled, and fallen in his turn, the locust-like Mahratta cloud was already dissipating beneath the booming thunder of the western cannon, and yet, in the chains forged by Kurun Solunkhee, Roopeyn still was bound; these fetters broke at last, and the ocean of the king became in a moment an uncared for waste.[1]

The town of Modheyra is situated on a low hill or mound formed of the debris of brick buildings, and rising out of a level plain. The character of the country near it, and the presence of salt water creeks carried up from the Runn, suggest the probability of its having at a former time stood very near the edge of the sea, which once covered that tract. It is known in Jain legends as Modherpoor, or Modhbunk Puttun, and it gave its name to the caste of Brahmins called Modh. A very handsome Hindoo temple stands in the immediate vicinity of the town, which (as the erections mentioned by Meroo-

successor, Shah Ahmed. The names of Kochuruv and Âshâwul point to this site, and there can be no question that an old Hindoo city existed in the position now occupied by Ahmedabad. Mohammedan story associates the names of Âshâ Bheel and Âshâwul with Shah Ahmed, adapting probably the older tradition relating to Raja Kurun. Ahmedabad is mentioned under the name of "Shree-Nugger" in modern Hindoo and Jain writings and inscriptions. Thus the situation of the well called "Dâdâ Huree's," near Ahmedabad, which was built by Bâee Hureer, a lady of the household of Mahmood Begurra in A.D. 1500, is described in the inscription on it as "in Hureerpoor, on the north-east of *Shree Nugger*." We shall see the name of Shree Nugger occurring in the annals of the reign of Sidh Râj. Shree Nugger, it is true, may be only an epithet—it means "the illustrious city."

[1] This occurred in A.D. 1814. The year before there had been a famine, and in that year the fall of rain was so heavy that the Roopeyn, becoming for the time a large stream, broke through the embankment.

toong may be looked for in the neighbourhood of Kurun Sâgur as well as in that of Âshâwul) we may surmise to be either the Kurun-eshwur or Kurun Meroo Prâsâd. This temple will be more fully described hereafter; but we may in this place notice that it corresponds exactly in style with two small shrines still remaining of those which adorned the "ocean of Kurun," and that the finish everywhere visible in its execution, indicates that it was erected at a time when resources were plentiful, and when an external enemy was not apprehended.

A superb temple to Nemeenâth which stands upon Rewutâchul or Girnâr, is also attributed to Raja Kurun, and called after him the Kurun Veehâr.

Kurun Raja appears to have been for a long time denied the blessing of a son to succeed him; towards the close of his reign, however, a romantic incident made him the father of a young prince, who was destined to raise to its culminating point the glory of Unhilwârâ. One day, soon after the king had mounted the throne, an usher came to him and informed him that a portrait painter who had travelled in many countries stood at the door seeking permission to appear in his presence. At the raja's order the painter was introduced into the court, and, having made obeisance, sat down and said, "O! king, your fame has travelled into many countries, there-" fore many people think of you, and are desirous of seeing you, " I, too, for a long time have been so desirous." Then the painter submitted to the king a roll of pictures. Therein Lukshmee was represented dancing before a raja, and beside her there was a maiden portrayed much more beautiful than Lukshmee. The raja, when he saw the picture, praised the maiden's beauty exceedingly, and asked of what race she was. The painter replied, "there is in the Dekkan " a city named Chundrâpoor, the king thereof is Jye Keshee;[1] this " maiden is his daughter, the princess Myenul Devee. She is in the " bloom of youth. Many princes desired to wed her, but she " assented to no one. Her relations told her that the flower of her " age was passing away, and that she should consent to receive a " husband. Then the maiden began to worship Gouree in order to " obtain a bridegroom full of great qualities.[2] The Boudhist Jutees, " too, that shave the hair of their heads and their beards, having " painted portraits of many royal princes, exhibited them to her. " Afterwards some unskilled painter who had come to Chundrâpoor,

[1] Jye Keshee is described in another place as the son of Shoobkeshee, King of Kurnât-land, who perished in a forest conflagration.

[2] See account of the festival of Gouree in the Conclusion.

"exhibited to the princess the portrait of your highness. She, when "she saw it, was delighted in heart, and announced to her mother, "that she had chosen you for her bridegroom. When she sees birds "flying from the north, she asks them if they are come from Raja "Kurun. She refuses to eat or drink, and because her desire of "marrying you is not speedily gratified, she is pining away. For this "reason the maiden has sent me privately to your presence, and Jye "Keshee Raja also has authorized my coming." Having thus spoken, the painter presented gold, jewels, and other gifts with which he had been entrusted by Jye Keshee. Kurun Raja received them, and great eagerness for marrying the maiden arose in his mind.

The princess was soon conducted to Unhilwârâ Puttun and married to Kurun Raja, who, according to his engagement, received her with great honor, and placed her in the position of chief queen. Myenul Devee, however, instead of being possessed of the charms the description of which had so much captivated the king, appeared to him to be singularly ill-favored, and though he kept his word by allowing the ceremony of espousal to be performed, he refused to consummate the marriage, and "even with his eyes wholly regarded her not." This resolution of her husband's was the cause of great affliction to Myenul Devee, who prepared to destroy herself by fire, with her attendants, and bring down the gilt of murder upon the head of Kurun. His mother, Oodayâmutee, too, who could not endure the sight of her daughter-in-law's sufferings, threatened to accompany her in her death. The king's subjects also loudly expressed their sense of his cruelty, and complained of his impolicy in refusing to strengthen his throne by the prospect of a successor to its honors. Kurun, however, remained unmoved, and would, perhaps, have been contented to try to the utmost the patience of his people, as well as the fortitude of his mother and his bride, had he not been deceived by a stratagem, such as that by which Tamar practised upon Judah, or Mariana (as the poet represents) compelled the reluctant love of Angelo.

The king, having fallen in love with the very beautiful actress, Numoonjâlâ, had arranged with her a secret assignation. A minister of the name of Moonjâl, becoming cognizant of the fact, contrived to substitute Myenul Devee in her place. Kurun fell into the snare, and the queen became pregnant by him, having secured from the hand of her husband his signet ring as a token which could not be disclaimed. No sooner had the king, however, gratified his wishes, than he repented that he had indulged them, and having consulted the Brahmins, prepared to undergo a terrible penance in the embrace of seven images of heated brass. The minister then explained to him the stratagem by which he had been deceived. Thus Myenul Devee became the mother of the illustrious Sidh Râj Jye Singh Dev, who, as local tradition relates, first saw the light at Pâhlunpoor.

Sidh Râj was yet a child when his father Kurun, fixing his thoughts on Vishnoo, went to Indrapoor. During his minority there appears to have been a struggle between rival factions for the possession of royal power. Dev Prusâd, the son of Kshem Râj, Kurun's brother, when he heard of that king's death, prepared a funeral pile on the banks of the Suruswutee, and burned himself alive. He left a son, Treebhoowun Pâl, who was a close attendant upon the person of the young prince, and, in after times, when Sidh Râj went forth subduing the whole earth as far as the ocean, Treebhoowun Pâl placed himself before his sovereign in the battle. The reins of government were first held by Mudun Pâl, the brother of Kurun's mother, Oodayâmutee; but this prince, behaving in a tyrannical manner and having, in particular, oppressed and extorted a large sum of money from a celebrated and popular physician of the court, named Leelâ, a combination was formed against him, and the minister Sâmtoo, having obtained possession of the person of the young prince by a stratagem, and conveyed him to his own house, caused Mudun Pâl to be put to death by the hands of his soldiers.

Power now passed into the hands of the young sovereign's mother, Myenul Devee, who was assisted by the ministers Sâmtoo and Moonjâl, and by another named Oodâ, who appear to have been all of them Wâneeos in caste, and Jains in religion. It was during the regency of Myenul Devee that the two reservoirs which received names from her—the Meenul Sur, or Mon Sur, at Veerumgâm, and the Mulâv, or Meenul-tulâv, at Dholka, were constructed.

On the east of the latter tank, was a courtezan's house, which, as it interfered with the symmetry of her design, the Rânee proposed to purchase for a large sum of money. The owner, however, declined to part with it, remarking that her name would be rendered as famous by the refusal as that of the queen would be by the construction of the reservoir. Myenul Devee was too upright to employ force, and her conduct in the matter, though it produced an irregularity in the tank, which is still apparent, procured for her government a reputation which is preserved in the local proverb, "Would you see justice, visit "the Mulâv." Her ministers also vied with the queen in erecting costly works of architecture, of which the chronicler mentions a Jain convent, called Ooden Veehâr, at Kurunâwutee, and the temples of "*Shree Moonjâl's Lord*," and "*Sâmtoo's Foundation*," probably in the same city.

Before she left her own country Myenul Devee, doubtless at the persuasion of the priests of Shiva, had bound herself by a vow that she would procure the remission of the duties levied at a place called Bâhoolod (now Bhâlod), a ford of the Nerbudda river, a little above Shookulteerth, upon the pilgrims proceeding to the Shrine of Someshwur. In a former birth, as her spiritual preceptors informed her, she had been a Brahminee, and had arrived at Bâhoolod with the view of performing pilgrimage at Dev Puttun, but being unable to pay the duties demanded of her, she had been refused permission to advance further, and in grief on that account had produced her death by abstaining from all food. The opportunity having now arrived for the accomplishment of her vow, Myenul Devee carried the young Sidh Râj with her to Bâhoolod, where they had the opportunity of observing personally the inconveniences to which the pilgrims were exposed. The jury of five, to whom the collection of the tax was entrusted, were summoned to produce their accounts, and though the amount realized was found to be an immense sum, Sidh Râj, placing water in his mother's hand as a kol,[1] and declaring the act to be a religious gift on her part, remitted the levy. Myenul Devee then worshipped Someshwur with great splendour, presenting an elephant, a gold figure called a "toolâ pooroosh,"[2] holding a set of scales, and other great gifts.

While the young sovereign of Goozerat was thus employed, Yushowurmân, the king of Malwa, invaded the northern part of his dominions. The minister, Sâmtoo, who held the deputed power of Sidh Râj, at Unhilwârâ, being either without the means of repelling this invasion, or without the energy to employ them, induced Yushowurmân to retire by paying him a sum of money, but the young king, on his return to the capital, was much enraged at what had happened, and from that time forward set his heart upon the reduction of Malwa.

It was while preparing for this expedition that Sidh Râj commenced the construction of the Suhusra Ling tank at Unhilwârâ,[3]

[1] The ceremony called Choollook or Kol, which is performed by pouring water into the hand of a party to whom a promise is made, as an earnest that the engagement is irrevocable, is still used in Goozerat. Sometimes the water being discarded, the maker of a promise merely places his hand in the hand of the other party.

[2] Or perhaps Myenul Devee gave her weight in gold to the shrine: this was an usual practice.

[3] This reservoir appears to have been in existence in the reign of Akber. "Beiram Khan, his minister," it is said, "proceeded to Goozerat, in order to "embark for Mecca, and reached the suburbs of Puttun, (Unhilwârâ,) then

so celebrated in tradition and tale. The excavation made for this reservoir is still pointed out at Puttun, but of the fabric itself nothing remains. It was one of the circular, or rather multilateral tanks, of which several examples, more or less perfect, are to be met with in Goozerat, and its name, (which may be rendered "the reservoir of the thousand temples of Shiva,") was probably derived from numerous shrines of Muhâ Dev encircling it, similar to those which still remain around the Meenul-sur of Veerumgâm. The following story, in connection with this reservoir, is still a popular subject of recitation and song :—

TALE OF JUSMÂ THE ODUN.

Once on a time, a countryman from Malwa came to Sidh Râj, and praised the beauty of Jusmâ, the Odun. The raja sought to possess her, and made many attempts to do so which were unsuccessful. At length, when he was commencing the Suhusra Ling tank, at Puttun, he sent his sister's son, Doodhmul the Chowra, to bring a number of Ods[1] and Oduns from Malwa. Doodhmul set out to fetch them, and arrived at their village, and said that Sidh Râj, the Solunkhee, had a large tank to excavate and wanted the assistance of a number of Ods and Oduns. Jusmâ thereupon collected a number of her caste-fellows, and with her husband came to Puttun. Sidh Râj gave orders that the other Ods should be accommodated outside the town, but that Jusmâ should be brought into the palace. Jusmâ refused, saying, "Rânees sleep in palaces, "it is fitter for the Odun to lie upon the ground."

When the digging of the tank commenced, the raja in person sat looking on; he became very much enamoured of Jusmâ. He said to her, "Jusmâ, do not lift such heavy loads of earth, you will "injure yourself." She said there was no fear of that. He told her to take care of her child and let the other Oduns lift the earth. She said, "I have hung him to the branch of a tamarind tree, as I come "and go I swing his cradle."

When the excavation was completed, the raja paid all the Ods, but said that Jusmâ should remain and he would pay her by and bye. Meanwhile he gave the Ods leave to retire; Jusmâ, however,

"governed by Moosy Khan Lody. During his stay there he went to visit a spot "called Sahasnuk, so called from the thousand temples erected in its vicinity." Briggs's Feristah II., p. 203. The same nobleman is the reputed founder of the Khan Surowur at Puttun.

1 The Ods are a low caste, whose occupation is that of excavating tanks.

secretly went with them. When he became aware of this, the raja mounted and pursued them as far as Modheyra, slaying some of the Ods. Jusmâ upon this plunged a dagger into her belly, and as she died, cursed Sidh Râj, and said that his tank should never contain water.

The raja, returning to Puttun, found the tank dried up. He asked the minister what ought to be done that water might remain in the tank. The Prudhân, after consulting the astrologers, said that if a man's life were sacrificed, the curse would be removed. At that time the Dhers (or out-castes) were compelled to live at a distance from the towns; they wore untwisted cotton round their heads and a stag's horn, as a mark, hanging from their waists, so that people might be able to avoid touching them. The raja commanded that a Dher, named Mâyo, should be beheaded in the tank, that the water might remain. Mâyo died, singing the praises of Vishnoo, and the water after that began to remain in the tank. At the time of his death Mâyo had begged, as a reward for his sacrifice, that the Dhers should not in future be compelled to live at a distance from the towns, nor to wear a distinctive dress. The raja assented, and these privileges were afterwards permitted to the Dhers for the sake of Mâyo.

After this Jye Singh prepared to go quickly to Oojein, collecting his army from village to village. He advanced stage by stage, subjecting the rajas whose towns he passed on the road, and compelling them to accompany him; he caused the tops of many high places to be lowered, in order that his army might find a more level road. Some Bheel chieftains, with their followers, attended the king, who astonished Sidh Râj with their feats of activity—"In his army they seemed as the followers of Hunoomân, "in attendance upon Râm." At last the king of Goozerat encamped on the banks of the river Seepra; the tents were pitched, the horses secured in order, and all details arranged. Then there was festival held in the tent of Jye Singh—the dancers danced before him.

Sidh Râj made war in Malwa, it is said, for twelve years, with great renown, but after many ineffectual attempts to obtain possession of the capital city, Dhârâ Nugger, he began to be disheartened, and consulted Moonjâl Muntree, who accompanied him, on the propriety of returning to his dominions. That minister, however, obtained from a deserter intelligence which led to the hope that an attack on the southern gateway of the fort might be made with success. Sidh Râj headed the assault in person. The favorite elephant upon which he rode, after incredible exertion, broke down two of the three gates, though fastened with iron chains, but won this success with its life. The king of Goozerat, having thus effected an entrance, soon became master of the fort, and his triumph being completed by the capture of Yushowurmân, who had behaved gallantly in the defence, his standard was raised in the city of Bhoj, as four hundred years afterwards the banners of his Moslem successor were planted upon the battlements of Mandoo.[1]

As he returned homewards, Sidh Râj attacked and drove from their fortresses the chieftains who plundered pilgrims travelling along the road, thus making the country "fearless."

It was when Sidh Râj made his triumphal entry into Unhilwârâ, after his conquest of Malwa, Yushowurmân placed a flag of victory (Yushputâkâ) on the royal elephant, that the king's notice was first attracted to the future author of the Dwyâshrây, Hemchunder the Âchârya, who as first of the priests of the Jain religion, proclaimed among the white-robed train the glory of the hero of Goojur Râshtra :—

"O! Kamdooghâ, sprinkle the land. O! sea, make a swusteek of "pearls. O! moon, shine in full splendour. O! elephants, sup-"porting the eight regions of heaven, wave garlands of good leaves "of the tree of desire—conquering the earth, Sidh Râj comes."[2]

[1] The following Pedigree of the Kings of Malwa is from an inscription translated by Mr. L. Wilkinson, in the Journal of the Asiatic Society (Bengal Branch), v. p. 380, and from the other authorities quoted :—

I. Raja Bhoj Dev.
II. Oodayâdit.
III. Nurwurm, died St. 1190 (A.D. 1134), v. Ins: from Oojein, translated by Colebrooke, Trans. R. A. S. I. 232.
IV. Yushowurm.
V. Ujye-wurm, "by the favor of this raja, the learned and accomplished "Prince Shree Hurischundra Dev received dominion:" who from his capital of Neelâgeeree made gifts to Brahmins in St. 1235 (A.D. 1179), v. Journ. Ben. A. S. vii. 736.
VI. Vindhya-wurm, "who directed his ambition to the reduction of the "country of Goozerat."
VII. Umooshyâyun.
VIII. Soobhut-wurm, or Sohud. "The angered prowess of this conqueror, like "the fiery rays of the sun, which exercised its thundering rage in the "city of Puttun, in (or cities of) Goozerat, is witnessed to the present "day in the forest conflagrations that still prevail in the country."
IX. Urjoon Raja. "This prince when still a child put Jye Singh Raja to "flight, even in child's play." In the fort of Mandoo, on the 10th Phalgoon Shukla Sumwut, 1267 (A.D. 1210), he grants a village to his family priest "in commemoration of his accession."

[2] "Kâmdooghâ" is the cow of paradise. The word *swusteek* has been explained already (*vide* p. 42, and note). The allusion is to the usual decoration of houses at times of rejoicing, viz., purifying with cow-dung, painting swusteeks on

The excitement and joy of his triumphal return over, the king was called upon to preside in a court which was to determine the merits of a new treatise on grammar, composed by Hemâchârya, to silence the opponents who attributed his skill to the assistance he had derived from Brahminical learning. The decision was given in the Âchârjee's favor, and his work was, at the order of the sovereign, placed upon the head of one of the royal elephants, and, with the white umbrella extended over it, the hair fans and other emblems of imperial state, was conveyed to the treasury of the palace. The "evil disposed," however, remarked that the work contained no eulogy of the king's ancestors. Sidh Râj was displeased on hearing this remark, but, the next morning, when the grammar was re-examined, Hemâchârya was duly prepared to remedy the deficiency, and burst forth into eloquent verse in the praise of the solunkhee sovereigns. Soon afterwards he still further repaired his omission by the composition of the Dwyâshrây.

Sidh Râj next turned his attention to the state of the Treepooroosh Prâsâd, the funeral shrine of the Prince Mool Râj, and the other royal temples, providing the means of maintaining them, and the "income of the Devs," on so extravagant a scale as to call forth prophetic remonstrances from Yushowurmân who here appeared playing the part of Crœsus to this Cyrus of India. "Malwa is a "territory producing hundreds of thousands of treasure, yet it has "been absorbed by Goozerat, as if a sea were drowned in a jar of "water. The reason is that Malwa was formerly given to Muhâ "Kâl Dev,[1] and became the property of the god. We enjoyed it, "but, from that splendour, we have now descended as the sun "descends beneath the horizon. The kings of your race, too, not "being able to furnish so much religious income, will diminish each "Dev's possessions, until calamity cut you off from the very root."

The temple of Roodra Muhâ Kâl, at Shreesthul, which had been established by Mool Raja, had fallen into disrepair, and the demons, or "Râkshuses,"[2] had been emboldened to annoy the Brahmins so

the wall with vermilion, or forming them with jewels or grains upon a table, and hanging garlands at the door.

[1] Bhoowur Raja, of whom mention has been made as the enemy of Jye Sheker, the father of Wunrâj, is reported to have been restored to the use of his limbs at the shrine of Muhâ Kâl, at Oojein; and, in gratitude for the cure, to have given up to Muhâ Dev the whole of Malwa with the metropolis, assigning the protection of it to Purmâr Rajpoots.

[2] In the Dwyâshrây, the leader of these "Râkshuses" is called Burbur, or Burburuk, a name which, under the form of Wurwurk, is mentioned in the

that the smoke of the sacrificial fire no longer rose to the heavens. Sidh Râj, expelling the enemies of the Brahmins, employed his most skilful architect in the completion of the edifice. Then, having consulted the astrologers, and being warned that the arrival of a foreign conqueror would be fatal to this new shrine as it had been to the temple of Dev Puttun, Sidh Râj caused images of "horse lords" and other great kings to be made, and, installing them in the temple, placed near them a representation of himself in the attitude of supplication, with an inscription praying that even if the land was laid waste this temple might not be destroyed. Meanwhile the "victorious" pendant of Muhâ Dev was planted on the summit of the Roodra Mâlâ, and the king, as an act of grace, gave permission that flags should be raised also upon the Jain temples, which before had been forbidden. It was at this time that the town of Shreesthul, in commemoration of its royal restorer, assumed the name of Sidhpoor. The Jains add, that the king caused to be built also, in the same place, a temple to Muhâ Veer Swâmee, and that he worshipped the "congregation" there.

Sidh Râj soon after returned to Malwa, and spent the rainy season in that country. While there, he received the agreeable intelligence that the Suhusra Ling tank was completed and filled with water. On his arrival in Goozerat, at the close of the rains, he took up his residence at Shree Nugger, "a great city." Observing many flags on the temples of that city, he made inquiries of the Brahmins, who detailed to him the different shrines of their faith that there existed, as well as those of the Jain religion. Sidh Râj angrily exclaimed: "In Goojur-land I have forbidden the flag to Jain temples, how is "it, then, that in your city this order is disregarded?" The council who managed the temple of Shree Rishub Dev thereupon brought forth their copper-plates and other records to prove, in the royal court, the antiquity of their privileges. This point was, at the close of the proceedings, admitted even by the Brahmins, upon which the "high-minded" sovereign granted permission that the flags should be raised on the Jain temples at the end of a year from that day.

Among the Senâputees, or generals of the army of Sidh Râj, was a celebrated Purmâr chieftain, named Jugut Dev, whose existence is alluded to by the monk of Wudwân but merely with the remarks that he was "thrice valiant," or possessed of strength, talent, and

inscription alluded to, in the note at p. 50, as that of the King of Malwa. The allusion may, therefore, be to the invasion, by Yushowurm, which excited the anger of Sidh Raj.

wealth; that he was much admired by Sidh Râj, and that he at length quitted that king's service for the court of Purmurddee Raja, of whose principal queen he was the bracelet-bound brother.

The tale which is now introduced to the reader, and which has for its hero this valiant chieftain, is more than usually barren of historical fact, but presents some spirited pictures of Rajpoot life, and may serve as a not unfavourable specimen of the romances which are a source of delight to every true son of the Kshutrees.

CHAPTER VIII.

THE TALE OF JUG DEV PURMÂR.

IN the land of Malwa, in the city of Dhârâ, Oodayâdit ruled. He had two Ranées, one of the Wâghela clan, the other of the Solunkhee. The Wâghelee had a son, Prince Rindhuwul.[1] She was the favorite; the Solunkhunee was held in less estimation. The latter had a son, Jug Dev; he was somewhat swarthy in complexion, but handsome. Rindhuwul was the elder son, and the heir apparent; there was a difference of two years in the age of the brothers. When Jug Dev reached the age of twelve years, the raja asked Mudâr, one of his household, "Has the Solunkhee lady a son or not?" Mudâr answered, "The Solunkhee lady has a son, Jug Dev, but he never "comes to the palace." The raja said, "In the world there is "nothing greater than a son." So saying, he sent to call Jug Dev. Then Jug Dev came to the palace; his coat was of coarse cloth; on his head was a turban, that might have been bought for two shillings;

[1] Colonel Tod, (Rajasthan ii., 242,) quoting the Annals of Jesulmur, has the following:—

"Raedhuwul Püar, son (or descendant) of Udyadit of Dhâr, had three "daughters, one of whom he betrothed to Jeipâl (Ujye Pâl) Solunkhi, son of Sid "Râj, another to Beeji Râj Bhatti, and the third to the Rana of Cheetore."

Sidh Râj, however, left no son; Ujye Pâl, who succeeded him eventually, was his relation, but not his descendant. *Vide* pedigree of Malwa kings in the note at page 87.

The Jug Dev of the time of Sidh Râj might have been the son of Oodayâdit, the successor of Bhoj. The present tale is, however, a pure romance.

his ears and hands were unadorned. In this state he appeared, and made his obeisance. The raja pressed him to his bosom, seated him near himself, and seeing his dress, said, "Son! how is it you "wear such clothes?" Jug Dev replied, "My austerities have been "few; born in the house of a mighty prince, still in that great king's "land of Malwa, I hardly obtain a pound of salt and water. To "my mother one village you have assigned. This is a subsistence "for her, and the business of its rule is in her hands. Tunsoo-Gâm[1] "is a great name, but the produce of it is little. Meat and drink, "clothing, men-servants' and maid-servants' subsistence, cars and "oxen—these, all of them, are supplied by the produce of a single "village. My own clothes are beyond the produce." The raja, when he heard this, said to the treasurer, "Give him four shillings a "day." Jug Dev said, "Mighty prince! the present you have given "me I have accepted, but the illustrious Mâojee[2] is very affectionate "to me, therefore I shall not obtain it. Well, whatever has been "written will come to pass!" Then the raja, demanding a bag of money from the treasurer, gave it into his hand, and said, "Son, buy "clothes, live comfortably." Then he gave Jug Dev permission to retire. Jug Dev, taking leave, detailed to his mother what had happened, and gave her the purse. Some follower of the Wâghelee's, who heard and saw what occurred, went and told his mistress. "To-day "the raja shewed great kindness to Jug Dev; he granted him four "shillings a day, and presented him with a purse." When she heard that, the flame of anger sprung from her foot up to her head. Sending an eunuch, she called the raja thither—she paid him obeisance. The raja seated himself on a cushion. The Wâghelee, with reddened eyes, addressed him: "What is this you have been "giving to the Doohâgun's son to-day?" The raja said, "The "Solunkhunee is the Doohâgun,[3] but her son is first. Rindhuwul "is the Teelâyut heir-apparent, but Jug Dev pleases my eye; he will "be a good Rajpoot." Then said the Wâghelee, "He is swarthy "in complexion; his fortune, too, is written in black letters. Why "do you praise him; send for the purse back again." The raja replied, "That I have presented to him; another time I will consult "you before I give."

[1] The name means "three good villages."

[2] Meaning the Wâghelee Rânee, Mâ (mother) is respectfully rendered Mâjee, Mâojee.

[3] *Soohâgun* is the title of the favorite, and *Doohâgun* of the less esteemed wife. Compare the passage in Deuteronomy xxi., 15 to 17. Teelâyut is the head of the house, who bears the mark of royalty (the teeluk) on his forehead.

At that time the Raja of Mândoogurh, whose service Oodayâdit performed, sent a letter commanding his speedy attendance. The raja quickly went off upon that business. Both princes remained at home. Jug Dev's associates were good; he admitted visitors affably, he gave good advice, his manner of living was good, his temper was pleasing, therefore people spoke well of him in the world, and his fame increased. Rindhuwul dwelt in the palace, but Jug Dev in his own house. In this way two years passed away. At that time the lord of Gord-land, a raja of the Gord clan, by name Gumbheer, hearing of the reputation of Jug Dev, sent a cocoa-nut for him to Dhârâ-nugger, with an elephant and nine horses, the cocoa-nut mounted in silver and gold, a family priest to present the cocoa-nut, and a minister. They arrived at Dhâr; everybody talked about the Gord raja's cocoa-nut having arrived. They were welcomed, a place was given them to lodge in, and fodder for their cattle provided. The family priest, the eunuch, and the minister together said, "Bring "forward the cocoa-nut." The Gord priest answered, "My raja "has ordered me to cause Prince Jug Dev to take it. Do you, "therefore, place him on the cushion; I will make the royal mark "on his forehead, and present the cocoa-nut." After this conversation the party separated. The Wâghelee was held in much awe: they went and told her, "The cocoa-nut is Jug Dev's." Then the Wâghelee, in a rage, exclaimed, "O, destiny! do you give the "cocoa-nut to this black-leprosied one of ours. The cocoa-nut "befits my son—explain this to the comers, and cause the cocoa-"nut to be given to Rindhuwul. I will do them service."[1] The priest said to Mutoowee, the Gord priest, presenting him at the same time with a sum of money, "Jug Dev is the son of the "Doohâgun; he does not get as much food as he could eat; Rind-"huwul is the heir-apparent; his mother is the chief queen; give "the cocoa-nut to him." Afterwards the cocoa-nut was given to the good Prince Rindhuwul; he was marked with the royal mark, the great drum sounded, thirty-two musical instruments were played." The priest then said, "For once, shew me Jug Dev." Letting the Wâghelee know, they brought Jug Dev. The priest Mutoowee saw him; he shook his head when he beheld how handsome Jug Dev was, and how clever he seemed, and splendid in appearance. However, he said, "What is written must come to pass." He asked leave to retire: they presented him with a dress of honor, and dismissed him. He returned to his own country, and told the story

[1] This expression means, in plain English, "I will give them a bribe."

to Raja Gumbheer as follows:—"We gave the cocoa-nut to Rind-"huwul. The heir-apparent is Rindhuwul, but the handsome is Jug "Dev. He has no good clothes, but he is like the rays of the sun "in splendour. However, no one is strong against what is written." The raja said, "You have made a great mistake; but what has been "given cannot be made ungiven, nor have I another daughter." So saying, he sent for an astrologer; caused the letter, announcing the day of marriage, to be written, and sent it to Dhâr. He gave a separate letter to the minister, in which was written, "Bring Prince "Jug Dev with you; if you do not, the matter cannot be arranged." The messenger, taking the letter, went to Dhâr; he presented it to the minister, who read it, and gave it to the Rânee. The Wâghelee said, "Take away the black fellow." They prepared the cavalcade, and caused it to be told to Jug Dev:—"Prince! prepare to go in "the marriage band." Jug Dev said, "How shall I prepare without "jewels or clothes fit to be seen? besides, I cannot travel as a foot-"man." The ministers went and told the Wâghelee. She sent him from the treasury handsome clothes, bracelets, a pearl necklace, a collar, a gold chain. She said, too, "Take a good horse from the "stables; there are many servants, some of them must go." Afterwards the cavalcade of about twenty thousand men set off. On their way they halted at Took Todâ; a raja, named Râj, ruled there, who was of the Dâk Chowra race. His son Beerj was regent, Raja Râj being blind, though he saw with the eyes of his intellect. That raja had a daughter, by name Veermutee, who was a virgin, and marriageable. Her father was looking out for a good connection for her, but could not discover a suitable bridegroom. There the marriage party arrived. Raja Râj said, "In this cavalcade is Jug "Dev; he is a very good Rajpoot, and worthy of rule; with him "cause the young lady to walk the rounds."[1] Prince Beerj assented to what he said; he went to the stranger's camp to pay his respects. When he reached the camp, he said, "Having accepted my hos-"pitality, proceed in the morning." With urgency he compelled them to accept his invitation. Afterwards, returning into the fort, he made enquiries of the astrologer, and ascertained that the fortunate hour fell the next day at even-time, when cattle return into the villages from grazing. The necessary preparations were made. Next day the lady Veermutee was anointed with tumeric; Gunesh was installed. At three in the afternoon they assembled for the feast: all eat together. By the time they

[1] Circumambulation of a sacrificial pit is the most important part of the marriage ceremonial; for a description of which, see Conclusion.

had washed their hands and risen from the feast the auspicious time came round. Then the prince Beerj said to the priest and minister, "I am going to give my sister to prince Jug Dev;" he presented the cocoa-nut, with four horses to him, and said, "Passing "the garland-ornamented door, grace the bridal-hall." The Dhâr minister knew that a good thing had happened. Passing the garland, the bridegroom graced the hall. It became morning—an elephant, five-and-twenty horses, nine maid-servants were presented. The guests requested leave to depart; as they were bound to a particular day, the Chowree Vermutee was left at her own home. They said, "As we return we will take her with us." The cavalcade proceeded, and arrived in the Gord territories. The news of Jug Dev's marriage was known. Raja Gumbheer, scrutinising Jug Dev's appearance, was very much annoyed at finding him married; but the written matter alters not. The Gord chief celebrated the marriage of his daughter—he presented double presents; horses he gave, elephants, eleven maid-servants. He dismissed the bridegroom's friends. The cavalcade returned to Todâ; placing the Chowree in a chariot, they took her with them; they returned home. The Wâghelee became aware that Jug Dev was married; she was much annoyed in mind. She began to say, "Ah! this swarthy fellow; a raja gives him his "daughter, gives her without seeing him!" They performed the ceremony of going out to meet the new comers; the Gord lady and the Chowree paid obeisance to their mother-in-law; the worship of the Devs was performed. A month afterwards the Gord and the Chowra chieftains sent and took away their daughters to their family homes. Jug Dev sent back the marriage presents he had received with the Chowree, retaining only the dresses and jewels. He said, "I will not keep them here now."

Jug Dev attained his fifteenth year, then Raja Oodayâdit returned from the duty he had been employed upon. He was in high spirits. Prince Rindhuwul went out to meet him: he paid his obeisance to the raja, also to the leading men of the city. The whole court met and saluted each other, but Jug Dev did not make his appearance. The raja was in high spirits; he took his seat on a cushion in the court. He said to the attendants, "Prince Jug Dev, where is he?" They said, "He must be with the Solunkhee lady." An eunuch was sent to call him; then Jug Dev came dressed in coarse clothes. He made his obeisance. The raja pressed him to his bosom, grasped him by his hand, seated him very near himself, and said to him, "My boy, "are these the clothes you wear?" The prince, joining the palms of his hands, said, "Sire! when you set out you allotted a sum for my "daily expenses. Without her order I did not get the money. As "is one's food, so is the state of one's body—that you are aware of. "With the produce of one village, besides the expenses of servants, "how can clothes for me be procured?" Then the raja presented to him his own amulets, necklace of pearls, waistband, collar, arm-chains, turban ornament, also his shield, dagger, and sword, and a dagger with a hilt mounted with jewels. Jug Dev received them with an obeisance; but joining his hands, he made a petition:—"Sire! "I have obtained that which you have honored me with, but Wâg-"helee Mâjee has a great affection for me, so that when you go to "her palace she will seek to have the whole back again. I will not "give back again what I have once received, even though yourself "order it." The raja said, "The Wâghelee may say so; but, son, "I like you better than Rindhuwul, and what I give you is my own. "In my suite there is a fine horse, which I give you; take it, and in "the evening come to the court." Thus saying, he dismissed him. Jug Dev took the horse with him, causing it to be led before. Going to the Solunkhunee, he made obeisance. Seeing the unusual handsomeness of his appearance, she said, "Son, if he remain with the "Wâghelee, have you any confidence?"

The chief of the eunuchs running, said to the Wâghelee, "To-day "the raja presented to Jug Dev every thing he had upon him; the "best horse in his suite, too, he gave him." Hearing this, her heart was inflamed with anger. She caused it to be said, "Sire! grace the "refreshment room, the meal is ready; the Wâghelee has not washed "her mouth; first having seen the king and having worshipped the "auspicious time, she will split the dâtun."[1] The raja hearing this, came quickly to her apartments in the morning. The Rânee Wâghelee paid obeisance; a carpet was spread and a cushion set. The raja seated himself. The Wâghelee said, "I wave myself as an "offering to your handsomeness. You are looking stout, and there-"fore you have abandoned the fancy for ornament; but, O! Lord "of Earth, without jewels you do not look splendid." The raja said, "Jewels I had, plenty of them beside me; but I saw Prince Jug "Dev unadorned, so I presented all the jewels to him." Hearing this, the Rânee said, "In this black fellow what craft is there! Of

[1] The *dâtun* is a piece of stick used to clean the teeth. It is afterwards split and employed as a tongue-scraper. In Africa the same custom would appear to prevail. "Before breakfast Addizetta was employed above an hour in cleaning "and polishing her teeth, by rubbing them with the fibrous roots of a certain shrub "or tree, which are much esteemed and generally used for the purpose in her own "country, as well as in the more interior parts."—*Lander's Journal*, iii. 217.

"jewels he has a double share; besides, I sent him new ones from "the treasury. Then he gave them to Todâ Chowra. But, Sire! "you have done this without reflection. Sire! to my son you have "never once given a present. Send for the jewels again, and give "them to Rindhuwul." The raja said, "A poor man even does not "take back again what he has given; I am a lord of the land. "Rindhuwul and Jug Dev are alike to me. I cannot ask or take "these things back again." The Rânee Wâghelee said, "The dagger, "the sword, and the principal horse are the heir-apparent's. When "you have sent for these back again, then I will split the dâtun." The raja considered that the obstinacy of a woman was difficult to be overcome, according to the proverb—

I.

"The store of the poor regard not
"When their obstinacy is excited, these four,—
"A child, a beggar, a king,
"A petted woman.

II.

"As cold as ice, but burning forests;
"Where water was, strewing stones;
"That an angry woman can do
"Which destiny cannot accomplish.

III.

"A king punishes his subjects;
"A woman punishes all the world;
"A sage's mind she will upset;—
"A woman's wit is boundless."

Then the raja sending the chief of the eunuchs, caused him to say, "Son! I will give you another very good sword, but send back "the one I gave you if you respect my peace. Son! do not be "obstinate in this matter." Thus he made petition to the prince. Then Jug Dev, in a pet, gave back the sword, considering that bickering would only procure for him the title of a bad son. Afterwards, passionately, he exclaimed, "I am a Rajpoot's son: I will go "somewhere or other and earn my bannock:—

I.

"A stone article, a good man
"Are not sold by weight;
"The further they go from home
"The more valuable they become.

II.

" A lion does not wait till the moon is good,
" He waits not for money or supplies.
" Quickness only is good;
" Where speed, there success.

III.

" If wealth be not acquired in youth
" By travel in foreign lands,
" Thrown away is that season
" In the life of a man.

IV.

" If a good man be a stay-at-home,
" Three losses he will sustain;
" His clothes will wear out, his debts increase,
" His name remain unknown.

" Therefore, good mother, if you give the order, I will go somewhere " to seek my fortune." Then his mother said, " Son, you are young; " whither would you go? To travel alone in foreign lands is a very " dangerous matter." Jug Dev answered, " Mother! God will prosper " me; I will get service somewhere. God has preserved the honor " of the sons of good nobles before this, He will preserve mine too. " Mother, from your splendor I shall obtain fortune." His mother reflected—

" In his own business calm,
" In another's business strong;
" Him God will protect,
" Interposing his arm."

She said, too, " Do what will give you ease." Then Jug Dev took from the stables a good horse, and opening the treasury took out thence two bags of gold coins; he took arms, too—a bow, a quiver full of arrows—and having slung the latter on his shoulder, he made obeisance to his mother. Angrily he mounted his horse, and quickly made his way to Took Todâ. He halted at a garden outside the town: his horse, tied to a tree, stood champing the bit; he himself spread a thin cloth among the shrubs and sat down. His shield he laid on the ground beside him. He determined to go into the city when it became evening. At that time the Chowree Veermutee, seated in a litter, came thither by chance with her attendant damsels. It was three or four years since the pair had been married. A carpet having been spread, the lady sat down in a pavilion in that garden, as there was a little rain falling at the time. An eunuch was seated at the door to keep it. Then the lady ordered her damsels—"Go, "and gather some fruit." A damsel went out to gather fruit; she saw the horseman and his horse, which was worth four or five hundred pounds, with rich furniture for the yellow saddle. Then the damsel quietly surveyed the young chief. She thought, "He looks like the "lady's bridegroom; I am sure it is the prince by the ridge of his "nose and the redness of his eyes." She ran and told her mistress: "Lady, happiness to you; nineteen to one, here is the noble prince!" The Chowree said, "I may not look at the face of a man; but you "are a discreet person, therefore go again and bring correct intelli-"gence." The damsel went back and looked again, and returned, saying, "Lady, a hundred thousand to one it is the prince." Then the lady said, "See, you are a person of understanding, you are very "wise, so it is enough." Afterwards, cautiously peeping from behind the screen of the flower-trees, she found that it was indeed the prince himself. Then the Chowree, going quickly, paying obeisance, said—

"At home I was starting the crows,[1]
"Came my husband that minute;
"Half my bracelet clung to my arm,
"Half only was broken off.

"A soft couch, a cool mansion,
"My husband's presence grant me!
"My hope, the desire of my heart,
"Destiny has fulfilled."

The Chowree said, "Auspicious hour! auspicious time! well rose "the sun this day on which I have met your illustrious highness; "but where are your attendants? Alone, in the garden, as if for "secrecy, you are seated. What is the meaning of this?" Then the prince spoke to the Chowree, telling his story from the beginning, and concluding thus:—"I am come forth in the hope of attaining "service, you must not make the matter known." However, in the meantime the damsel, quickly running, had gone to the palace and said, "Good news! The royal son-in-law has come." They began at once to prepare the procession of welcome; the damsel received a present for her good news. Prince Beerj ran off on foot, he came and found Jug Dev. The Chowree returned to the palace. Prince Beerj brought Jug Dev with him thither. He made obeisance to Raja Râj. He remained there five days, and then asked permission

[1] It is a superstition that if a woman, whose husband is absent, succeed quickly in starting the crows which have alighted on the ground, this is a sign that her husband will soon return. The broken bracelet is the sign of widowhood.

to proceed. Then Raja Râj said, "This palace is your own. We "have only one will between us. Highness! remain even here." Then Jug Dev said, "Do not press this subject. For once I will go "alone into a foreign land. I must put my destiny to the test." They strove much with each other; at last Jug Dev was forced to say "yes." When it became night, however, Jug Dev explained his intentions to the Chowree, and began to take leave of her. She said, "I will continue doing the prince's service—your handmaid will "wait upon you." Jug Dev said, "Are you wise, and do you make "such a proposal? In a foreign land a wife is as a fetter on the "legs. I must go alone. I will send for you very soon." Then the Chowree, throwing her arms round him, said, "Can the shadow of "the body be separated from the body? If the shadow can be "separated from the body, then you may order me to remain here." Jug Dev argued with her much, but the Chowree would not be persuaded. With great constancy, she prepared to go with him. They saddled two horses. They took with them many ornaments, mounted with precious stones of great value. The Chowree covered herself with a veil; when Jug Dev mounted his horse she was already prepared. Two bags of gold coins were put in their horses' grain bags. Their intended departure was soon known; at that time Prince Beerj came up with three hundred horsemen to see them off. The Chowree embraced her father and mother; running, she embraced her chief attendants. Then the mother-in-law, giving Jug Dev a silver coin and a cocoa-nut, made the royal mark on his forehead. She commended her daughter, the Chowree, to Jug Dev's protection. Making obeisance, receiving benediction, taking leave of Raja Râj, they set forth. They went a few miles from the city. The escort said to him, "Your Highness! if you are proceeding homewards, "this is your road." Jug Dev then announced his intention,—"I "am going to Puttun, to take service with Sidh Row Jesingh Dev, "the Solunkhee." He enquired the direct road. One of the horsemen said, "The direct road to Toduree, which is the next village, "is twenty miles; and if you go by the safe road, avoiding the hills, "it is thirty miles." Then Jug Dev said, "Why should you leave "the direct road? Have you an ill-will at the horses?" The leader of the Rajpoots said, "The direct road is infested by a tiger "and a tigress, the villages have been rendered desolate by them; "the male is like a Dev; rajas and nobles have gone against him "with great and small drums, but no one has been able to subdue "him or the tigress. From fear of them, no quadruped attains its "full growth. The road has been stopped up for the last nine years,

" and the grass has grown tall. The pathway is broken up, therefore " go round by the longer road to Toduree; that road is a safe one." Hearing this, Jug Dev, taking leave of Beerj, after saluting him, went on by the direct road. Beerj remonstrated very much, but without effect; Jug Dev said, " Why should one go round about from fear " of this fool and his wife?" The two together fearlessly pushed on their horses. Then Jug Dev said to the Chowree, " Do you keep your " eye upon the grass on the left hand as we go." Thus they went on for six kos; then the Chowree said, " Royal prince! the tigress is in " front." Jug Dev drew an arrow, and, laying it upon his bow, said, " Tigress, you are a female, do not come against me, get out of the " road and couch on the right or on the left." When she heard the word female, the tigress, raising her tail, depressing her head to the ground, sprang towards him. At that moment he let fly the arrow; it struck her on the forehead, and, passing through, came out, and fell ten paces on the other side. Then the tigress sprang up into the air and fell dead. When they had gone on a distance of a hundred paces, they saw the tiger sitting. Jug Dev then, drawing another arrow from his quiver, said to him, " Go to the right hand or to the " left, or else I will send you to keep company with your foolish " female." Then the tiger, lashing himself with his tail, bending his head to the ground, sprang forwards; at him, too, Jug Dev shot an arrow; it passed through his brain, and, coming out, fell twenty paces off. The tiger, in like manner, sprang up into the air, and fell dead. Jug Dev said, " Why should I have slain the poor animals? " I have been guilty of murder." The Chowree said, " Your high- " ness! this is royal sport!" Thus conversing, they came to the tank outside the village of Toduree; there were many sacred fig-trees there; the water was ruffled into little waves. At that place they dismounted beneath a spreading tree, and divested themselves of their arms; they drew water, cool as that of the Ganges, and watered their horses. The Chowree was employed in washing her mouth. In the meantime Beerj had returned and reported to Raja Râj: " Jug " Dev has taken the direct road." Then Râj was angry, and said, " Take two hundred and fifty-five horsemen with you, armed with " bows and arrows; where you find them, commit them to the funeral " pile, or if they be alive, bring the news." Receiving this order, the horsemen started; as they went on cautiously and fearfully, they found the tigers lying dead by the road side; but they saw neither horse nor man. They supposed the objects of their search must be resting at some place where there was water, and that they were not in any danger. The horsemen, who had been dispersed to make search, now all of them came together again, and "Râm! Râm!"[1] passed between them. They congratulated each other on having accomplished a task which they expected would have cost their lives. Taking the two arrows with them, pleased, and without fear, they hastened on; when they arrived at the tank they found Jug Dev there. The Chowree recognized them as they came up, saying, "These are "some of our Rajpoots." The horsemen went up and made obeisance; they said to Jug Dev, "Prince royal! you have done a great "piece of religion for both the world and the cows. These were "like servants of the angel of death, neither king nor noble could kill "them. Who but you, prince! could mitigate the calamity of the "world!" Jug Dev, however, did not think much of the matter. He gave the Rajpoots leave; they went and related the story of the tigers having been slain. Raja Râj, and the brother-in-law, Beerj, hearing the news, were very much delighted. When the day went down, Jug Dev and the Chowree entered the city and made a meal; paying a few pence to a man, they got their horses rubbed down. They remained there two nights and a day, and spent a few shillings for their food. In this way, travelling by stages, they arrived at Puttun. There is a sacred fig-tree on the bank of the Suhusra Ling tank which Sidh Râj built; they dismounted from their horses beneath it, and fastened the animals there. They procured good water, and took care of their horses. The horses stood champing their bits. They took out something to drink, and made themselves ready. At that time Jug Dev said to the Chowree, "Do you remain here with the horses. I will go into "the city and hire a house, and come back and take my little queen "into the city; it would not look well for both of us to be wandering "about." The Chowree said, "Go, then, I will remain here." Then Jug Dev, putting on dagger and sword, went into the city to search for a house to hire. Hear what happened after that!

Now, the master of Sidh Râj's principal province, Doongur-shee, was also the Castellan of Puttun. He had a son, the lord Lâl, who was very haughty and in the prime of his youth; on account of the Castellanship of Puttun and the extent of the province there was truly no lack of haughtiness, so that he disdained to tread the earth. There were five hundred houses of courtezans in Puttun; among the mistresses of them was a courtezan, named Jâmotee, who possessed great wealth, and had many sons and daughters. The sons,[2] too,

[1] The name "*Râm*" of one of the incarnations of Vishnoo: a common salutation among Hindoos.

[2] The sons of these persons generally remain with their mothers, and act as musicians (Gundhurvs) and attendants on the dancing women.

were very wealthy. Once on a time, the castellan's son came to that Jâmotee's house to gamble; he said to her, "O! Jâmotee, if I could find "a very beautiful and good caste woman I would keep her, and make "you a present." Jâmotee said, "Very good, I will find one, and "pay my respects." Then Jâmotee gave notice to her daughters, and they too began to inquire for a beautiful woman. Many days passed on in this way. The day that Jug Dev and his bride arrived at Puttun, one of the girls, at noon-tide, taking a water vessel, came to the Suhusra Ling tank to draw water. The Chowree, raising the veil from off her face, seeing no man near, threw off the veil. She sat looking at the sheet of water and the buildings of the tank. The damsel, too, recollecting Jâmotee's order, was looking about her. She saw the Chowree, who seemed to her like one of the virgins of Paradise, bright as the lightning of heaven. The girl was pleased when she saw the Chowree; she took up her water-vessel and approached her, and, saluting her, said, "Lady! whence have you "come, and where is the rider of that horse gone?" The Chowree replied, "Who are you that enquire?" The girl said, "I am a principal servant of the palace of Sidh Râj Jesingh." The Chowree said, "As for me, I am married to the son of Oodayâdit Raja, the "Purmâr." The girl said, "Has your husband an elder brother?" "Yes; his elder brother is Rindhuwul," she said. Again the damsel asked, "Lady, what is his highness' name?" The Chowree replied, "Silly one! can one mention one's husband's name?"[1] The damsel said, "One should take one's husband's name, or the illustrious world-creator's. However, you are the mistress of the "country, do as seems good to you." Then the Chowree said, "The "prince's name is Jug Dev." Again the damsel enquired, "Where "is your own family residence?" The Chowree said, "At Todâ; "I am Raja Râj's daughter, and Beerj's sister." Then the damsel said, "Now the prince has gone into the city, you keep a good look "out after the horses, I suppose." The Chowree said, "No one "dare cast an eye upon the horse of that black antelope of the "herd." The damsel said again, "How is it that the son of a great "raja should have come forth alone?" The Chowree said, "He "left home in a passion with his step-mother;" and she related the whole story. The damsel, having heard the tale to the end, having made salutation, filled her water vessel, and proceeded home. She said to the courtezan, Jâmotee, "If you wish to pay your respects to "the young lord, there is a woman seated with two horses at the

[1] This is generally forbidden to Hindoo women.

"tank, such a one as I have seen in the country—the very person "you were describing. She told me her caste, the names of her "father-in-law and husband, and where her home was." Then Jâmotee dressed the girl in clothes of great value, and put upon her Goozeratee jewels. She also caused to be prepared a very beautiful chariot, and took her seat therein. The servants closed the scarlet screens of the car. Jâmotee caused other girls to dress themselves in beautiful ornaments. She took twenty or thirty chariots with her, several servants accoutred and armed; also an eunuch of great wealth to precede her on horseback. In this fashion she proceeded to where the Chowree was seated. Having arrived at that place, she caused the tent walls to be set up. Then Jâmotee descended. The girl who had been talking to the Chowree came and made obeisance to her. Jâmotee said, "Bride! rise, that I may embrace you. I am "your father-in-law's sister. This principal maid told me of your "arrival, and I immediately caused my chariot to be prepared. I "am come with the king's permission. When my nephew, Jug Dev, "was married at Todâ I was not able to come, but I know Rindhu-"wul very well. Where is my nephew, Jug Dev—where has he "gone? You had better wait in my house; you are my daughter; "you are married into a family of importance; this is not a fit place "for you to be sitting in." The Chowree, seeing the splendid appearance she made, became confused, and suffered herself to be deceived. She considered that the Prince Jug Dev had never mentioned to her any connectionship between him and Sidh Râj Jesingh, but that a raja might very probably be a raja's connection. Thus believing, and taking another look at the stranger's dress and ornaments, she saluted her and embraced her. Jâmotee gave her her benediction, and invited her to sit in the chariot, saying, that she would leave a servant to bring her nephew to the court when he returned to that place. She called also to a servant, desiring him to take care of the horses. The Chowree took the purses into her own possession, and ascended the chariot, which drove on. Jâmotee brought her to her own house. The house was a large one, with a gate leading into the courtyard. They drove in, and then stopped the chariot. Jâmotee alighted, and so did the Chowree. The procession of welcome came forth from the house; women, dressed handsomely and adorned with jewels, advanced to meet the Chowree, and saluted her. Some of them touched her feet—some preceded her, exclaiming, "Prosper, prosper." Thus they escorted her into the interior. The house was four stories high, and very handsome; it was plastered all round; on all sides were fastened hangings, upon which pictures were wrought in gold and silver; in the windows pierced lattice work was fixed. The servants spread a very handsome carpet; upon it they placed cushions, bolsters, and pillows for the cheek, covered with gold brocade. They caused the Chowree to seat herself; she retained, however, the two purses beside her. They brought her warm water. Jâmotee said to a damsel, "Go and inform "his Majesty that the Purmâr Queen's nephew, Prince Jug Dev, has "arrived here, and that he will soon pay his respects. Inform the "raja that he should receive him with great respect, and say that the "Chowree, his wife, is at my palace." The damsel, when she heard this, made obeisance, and withdrew. Half-an-hour after she returned, and said, "His Majesty is very much pleased, and has given orders "that Jug Dev shall first visit him, and afterwards wait upon you." At this time refreshment was served. Jâmotee said, "Bride, get ready to dine." The Chowree said, "I have taken the puteevrut "vow.[1] When the prince has dined I will think of dining. The "prince has not arrived yet." Then a girl came and said, "Your "nephew, Jug Dev, has paid his respects to his majesty, and "embraced him; he is seated near the king,—dishes have arrived "from the royal kitchen." Jâmotee said, "Hasten and forbid Jug "Dev's dining with the king,—petition the king, and bring Jug Dev "with you. To-day aunt and nephew must dine together; dinner "is ready here." Jâmotee continued: "My nephew, Jug Dev, has "not arrived; how can I sit down to eat before he has eaten; when "I hear of his having dined, I will think of dining." In the meantime the girl who had gone, returned, and said, "Madam, the prince "is dining with the king; both chiefs are seated at a large dish; I "saw them before I came away; but your nephew is now preparing "to come hither. How dark he is in complexion!" Jâmotee said, "This is a distinguishing mark of my father's house; my brother "Oodayâdit is swarthy also, but I have never seen any so handsome "as those of my own family." Thus they conversed. Jâmotee then called for handsome dishes; she gave a plate to the Chowree, and said, "Bride! take some food." The Chowree eat a little, and the maids removed the plate. They resumed their conversation. When three o'clock in the afternoon arrived, the Chowree said, "How is it that the prince has not come to pay his respects to "his father's sister?" Jâmotee answered, "Run, girl! and bring "my nephew Jug Dev." Again she entered into conversation with

[1] That is, to consider her husband as "a Dev," and to fast until after she had waited upon him.

the young lady, but the talk seemed to the Chowree to be without flavor in the absence of Jug Dev. The girl came back again in about half-an-hour, and said, "The king is conversing with him, and will "not allow him to rise; he says, that after nine o'clock Jug Dev will "come to sleep in this mansion, and that he will then meet his "aunt." Hearing this, Jâmotee was angry with the girl, and said, "Petition his majesty, and say to him, that it is many years since I "have met Jug Dev, and that he will have plenty of leisure for talk- "ing to the king in the morning, but that now he must be allowed "to visit me." The girl came back again after another half-hour, and said, that the raja had given the same answer as before. Jâmotee sent notice to the lord Lâl, "To-day I salute you! come directly nine "o'clock arrives; I have a woman in my hands, whom, if you please, "you may make your mistress; if not, I will keep her with me." Then Lâl began to take opium, very strong, with mixed spices in it; he took also intoxicating potions made of hemp and sugar; he put on a handsome dress and ornaments, and applied perfumes to his body, and ointment of musk. He came reeling about, and supporting himself with a spear: in his hand was a "duck"[1] full of strong liquor. The damsel, when she saw him, ran and said, "Bride! I "claim a present for good news; the prince has arrived." The Chowree fancied he had really come. At that minute the young lord Lâl came to the door of the mansion, which was as far off as one could see. When he entered, the girl closed the door behind him, and, applying the chain, went away. The Chowree saw that it was not her husband: she suspected treachery, but considered with herself that she must be cautious, as she could not be so strong as a man, and he inflamed with liquor. She called to mind the proverb, that with the deceitful one must use deceit, and determined to be wary, as under such difficult circumstances she had to defend her chastity. Thus considering, she rose and said, "Prince! come and sit on the "couch." He answered, "Chowree, do you sit." Seeing how beautiful she was, the Golo[2] was pleased: the Chowree, too, shot arrow-like glances at him, which pierced his breast. The Golo began to be as ductile as water, and the Chowree led him on to tell her the truth. "Jâmotee," she said, "has done well for me." Lâl said, "O, "Chowree! I had told her that if I could find a good caste,

[1] A vessel so called, resembling a duck in form.

[2] It appears that Lâl, though the son of an office holding high dignities, was of the caste called Golo or Khuwâs, who are either slaves or descendants of them, though sometimes appointed to the most important situations.

"beautiful, clever, young woman, I would keep her as a mistress; you "are just what I wanted. I will do whatever you desire." The Chowree then knew that it was a courtezan that had thus deceived her exceedingly, bringing her and him together by force. Seeing the "duck" and cup which Lâl had brought with him, and reflecting that he was already excited with liquor, she took the "duck" and cup from his hand, and filling the cup full, extended it towards him, saying, "Prince! take a cup from my hand." Then Lâl answered, "This is very strong, and I have already drunk much. Do you give me "another cup, then? No, no, we must talk together." The Chowree said, "What matters talking, do not push back my hand the first "time I offer it you; receive what I present; I am urgent you should "do this." When she said so much, he took the cup and emptied it, and then, with trembling hand, filling it again, offered it to the Chowree. She, drawing her veil over her, poured the liquor out on her bodice. She filled again, and seeing that the Golo had reclined his person, but was not yet fully intoxicated, she gave him the cup again. While in the act of drinking he fell along the couch, clenching his teeth. The Chowree knew then that he was so much intoxicated as to be helpless. She immediately got up, and taking his own sword, cut his throat; then she took the coverlet off the couch and rolled him up in it. Beneath the window was the king's road: she threw the bundle into it. It became midnight, and the watchmen arrived on their rounds; they saw the bundle lying before them, and supposed that some thieves had broken into a merchant's house, and being alarmed by them, had thrown down the bundle, and made off. They fancied they would get praise from the castellan, so they lifted up the bundle, which they found very heavy. They said to each other, "Let us not open it now; at sunrise the owner will come "for his property and to trace the footmarks of the thieves, therefore "let us put the bundle as it is at the castellan's guard-house; in the "morning we will tell him." Now all this time the Chowree sat in the upper room prepared to defend her life as resolutely as she might.

Now as to Jug Dev: At five in the afternoon, having hired a house and made his arrangements, he went to the tank where he had left his bride and the horses. He saw there the track of cars and horses, and understood that some one had deceived the Chowree, and carried her off. He went to the court to tell what happened. At the stable yard, in front of the court, the master of the horse was seated. Jug Dev arriving there, that officer thought within himself, "This is a worthy chief." He rose and embraced him, and asked

"Whence are you come?" Jug Dev said, "I come in the hope of "getting a loaf of bread here. I am a Purmâr Rajpoot." The master of the horse said, "If you can overlook these horses we may "live together, and you shall have pay and your food." Jug Dev's heart and thoughts were not there; but he thought the officer might introduce him, and when he promised to bring him into the king's presence, he remained with him, though much distressed in mind. However,

> "One moment lessening, one moment increasing,
> "Now a half-moon, now a crescent,
> "Destiny has not given to the moon
> "All days alike."

He considered, "It is bad, but what can be done." When evening came he fed the horses. The master of the horse brought dishes for dinner from his own house; but Jug Dev had no appetite; still he pretended to eat before the officer, and returned the dish. All night he tumbled and tossed upon his bed. At last the day broke. The castellan, Doongurshee, came to the guard-house. The watchmen, paying obeisance, showed him the bundle, saying that they had it from thieves, who had run away during the night. The castellan was pleased at the capture; he said, "Open the bundle and see "what is in it." The servants quickly began to do so; when they came to the third fold they saw blood. They all started, and hastening to open the bundle, they found that a man had been killed and rolled up in it. Then Doongurshee recognized the corpse, and said, "Ah! that is surely Lâlro! how dear was he to my heart! he is just "as he was—drest in his ornaments." The castellan beat his breast, "and said to his servants, Run, get news, truly this is your young lord "Lâl's face." They said, "He is sleeping at home." They sent to inquire of his eunuch, who said that he had gone to the courtezan, Jâmotee's house, at nine o'clock at night. Thither the men ran and enquired of the courtezan. She said he was safely asleep in the upper room. They told her to wake and call him. The maid then went and called, "Wake the prince, Chowree, and send him here." Then the Chowree angrily said, "Wretched prostitute! the mo-"ment that father of yours came I killed him, tied him in a bundle, "and threw him into the road. Have you dared to play off such a trick "upon the daughter of a Chowra! Wretch! when the prince, my "husband, comes to know of it, you will suffer. Other women may "act like courtezans and have friends; but, may Nârâyun destroy "your house? was it into my presence that you dared to send a

"Golo, a Golo fit to sit outside my door! was it upon me that you "dared cause him to cast an eye!" Hearing this, the courtezan felt ready to expire. The servants running, told the castellan, "Some Chowree Rajpootnee has killed the young lord." Then the castellan, taking two hundred men with him, went to Jâmotee, the courtezan's house, and ascended to the upper floor. The door of the room where the Chowree was, was closed firmly; but in the back wall there was a window large enough to admit one man at a time. Placing a ladder, one of the servants ascended, and looked into the room. The Chowree struck him with her sword—his head fell into the room, and his trunk outside; in the same way she slew five or six men; but no one was able to kill her. They all began to tremble. The story got abroad, and it became known to Sidh Râj Jesingh that a trick had been played off upon a Chowree Rajpootnee, and that the castellan's son, and four or five others, had been slain by her; also that she defended herself, shut up in an upper room. The king said, "Run quickly, and give "orders that no one interfere with her until I come; I will be there "immediately." Sidh Râj, calling for his horse, mounted; the master of the horse and Jug Dev making obeisance. The raja was surprised when he saw Jug Dev, and thought within himself, "That is a good looking chief; but I never saw him before." Jug Dev rode before the raja, who kept looking at him all the way to Jâmotee's house. The soldiers made way among the crowd. The king ascended, followed by the master of the horse and Jug Dev. Then Jye Singh said, "Daughter Chowree! tell me where is your family residence, "where your father-in-law, and who is it you are married to?" The Chowree looked and knew that it was some great chieftain; she said, "Sire! I am the daughter of a Chowra, Beerj's sister, married to the "younger son of Oodayâdit Purmâr, lord of Dhâr." Then the raja said, "Daughter Chowree! why have you slain my men?" She answered angrily, "Sire! this wretch brought me here to deceive me, "and then a Golo came to violate my chastity; therefore, sire! I "killed him. I am a Rajpoot's daughter; I will kill many more "before I fall. I will fight till I die. God will do as he pleases. "The prince, my husband, too, is in the city." At that moment Jug Dev, stepping forward in front of the raja, said, "Chowree! open "the door. You have suffered much calamity." Then the Chowree, recognizing Jug Dev's voice, opened the door, and threw herself into his arms. The raja knew that this must be Jug Dev. Then Jye Singh said to the Chowree, "You are my adopted daughter." He called to his attendants, and said, "Bring a chariot and ten maidens, "and take these to a handsome house." Then Doongurshee, the castellan, came up and petitioned,—"Mighty sovereign! prosperity "to you! What order are you giving in regard to the spoiler of my "house?" The king said, "This daughter Chowree did but protect her "chastity. When a Golo seeks to make a harlot of the wife or "daughter of a Rajpoot, he is sure to meet with punishment. Was it "for a bad purpose that I entrusted the city to your care?" Then he ordered that the fool should be dismissed from the castellanship, and forbidden the royal presence. Soon after he confiscated his property, and punished him, turning him out of the country, and giving his house up to be plundered. Thus he made the castellan an example to others. Afterwards Sidh Râj arrested the courtezans, and cut off the noses of the whole of them, shaving their heads, and setting them upon Seetulâ's steed,[1] and thus parading them round the city, he expelled them, and gave up their houses to be plundered.

Placing the Chowree in a car, with ten damsels to wait upon her, the king established her in a handsome mansion. Jye Singh himself conducted her thither, he presented to her also an old eunuch for a steward, and stored her house with provisions for a year, and furniture in proportion to the establishment. He gave her, too, a strong doorkeeper, and whatever else was necessary for her suite, and again declared that he had adopted her for his daughter. Then, taking Jug Dev with him, he went to the court. There he seated himself and began to make various enquiries of Jug Dev. The raja was exceedingly pleased with Jug Dev; he caused him to dine with him. When nine o'clock arrived, he presented a dress of honor with bracelets, a pearl necklace, a collar, a turban ornament of jewels, and dismissed him. Jug Dev went home, and embraced the Chowree. He gave her his pearl necklace, and said to her, "You have got us quickly "introduced to the king, otherwise there would have been a delay of "ten or twenty days. We must have sent our respects by some third "party." Thus they talked over the occurrences of the day, till it became night.

The Chowree, having taken the puteevrut vow, had eaten nothing, therefore she rose at three in the morning and began to prepare breakfast, and set water to boil. When all was ready she awakened Prince Jug Dev; he said, "Why so quick to-day?" The Chowree represented that the raja would send for him; "He has been talking "with you, so he will not be without you for a minute all day. You "know the vow I have taken, I am fasting from yesterday; do you "therefore, bathe, and I will then eat." Jug Dev said she was right;

[1] Seetulâ is the goddess of the small pox, and is supposed to ride upon a donkey.

he rose and bathed, and the two breakfasted together. At that time an usher came, bringing a horse with him, and began to call out at the door. Jug Dev, taking leave of his wife, came to the door, and, mounting the horse, rode to the court. The raja, rising, received him with respect. They talked together of old stories. The king enquired, "Will you take service with me?" Jug Dev answered, "It was to earn a loaf of bread that I came out from home." The raja said, "WIll you take a grant of land (puttâ), or will you be paid "at a fixed rate?" Jug Dev said, "Your Majesty, I prefer receiving "fixed pay; I will serve for a thousand crowns a day. Place me in "whatever post there is most danger; if I refuse I am no Rajpoot." The king said, "Very good;" then, calling the treasurer, he gave orders: "Pay daily to Jug Dev two thousand crowns from the "treasury, sixty thousand crowns a month—do not let there be any "difficulty about this payment." Again the king gave Jug Dev a dress of honor, and having caused a deed to be written, and affixed his seal to it, he presented it to him.

When he had dismissed him, the great chiefs of Puttun began to grumble among themselves, saying, "Why has the king taken this "fellow into his service?" They began to say also, "As the sun "rises he gives to a single man two thousand crowns! How will "this one alone defeat an army of eighty thousand horsemen?" The raja, however, continued to be very much pleased with Jug Dev; he used to place him beside or opposite to himself, and never gave him leave without making him a present. Things went on in this way for a year. At the end of that time a son was born to Jug Dev, whom he named Jug Dhuwul; and, three years afterwards, another son was born, whom he named Beej Dhuwul. The young princes were very much petted by the king, who was fond of giving presents to children and simple people who made odd remarks in their simplicity. That king spent also a thousand a day in virtuous gifts. How shall the bard not record this, for, "The spiritual preceptor's name, and the "benefactor's, to remember, is one of the six vows"?

The elder prince had attained the age of five years and the younger that of two years. At that time the month of Bhâdrapud came round. The nights were darkened with clouds, the rain fell from the sky, the frogs croaked, the pea-fowl screamed, the shrill cry of the sparrow-hawk was heard, and the flashes of lightning were seen,—such was the night in Bhâdrapud, making the coward's heart tremble. On such a night as this, a noise reached the king's ear: it was like the sound of four women singing joyful songs in the eastern direction, and of four other women lamenting at a short distance from them.

The king called to the guard, and asked who was awake. Jug Dev made answer—"Your majesty! have you any command?" The raja said, "Jug Dev, have you not gone home?" The prince said, "How "could I go without being dismissed?" The king said, "Well, then, "go home now." Jug Dev said, "Your majesty! what order have "you for the guard; when I have executed it I will go home." The king enquired, "What noises are those that we hear?" Jug Dev said, "There are some women singing songs, and there are others "making lamentation." The king said, "Bring me intelligence who "is singing and who lamenting. In the morning let me hear about "the matter." Jug Dev, paying obeisance, putting his shield on his head, taking his sword in his hand, went out alone. The king thought within himself—"Bhâdrapud nights are dangerous, let us see whether "he goes or not." Thus considering, wrapping a dark dress round him, Sidh Râj followed Jug Dev. Several chiefs were on guard there: the king calling to them, asked what chief was there. Each gave his name. Then Sidh Râj said, "The king desires you to bring news of "the women, some of whom are singing and others lamenting, in the "eastern direction." One of the chiefs said, "Let him send the man "who receives two thousand daily, and presents also. Has he been "drawing his pay all this time for nothing?" The king heard this. Some chiefs, however, said—"We will bring the king intelligence." Then, as they lay in their pallets, they said one to another, "My lord, "get up, get up!" However, after making a noise with their arms, and causing their shields to clash, they fell asleep again.

Meanwhile, Jug Dev went on towards the east, to where the singing appeared to be—Sidh Râj following him. Jug Dev arrived at the gate of the city; the door-keeper opened the wicket and let him out. Sidh Râj said, "I am the chief's henchman, let me go out "too." He, too, passed out. Jug Dev advanced to where the women were lamenting, and said to them, "Who are you? Are you "mortals, or wives of Devs, or are you Bhootnees, or Pretnees, or "Siddhs, or Sheekoturs?[1] Why are you lamenting with so much "grief at this midnight time? Tell me what calamity it is that you "suffer." They said, "Approach, son Jug Dev! wherefore are you "come here?" He said, "I am come to enquire the cause of your "making lamentation." They said again, "We are the Fates of "Puttun. The stroke of ten to-morrow morning is the time of "Sidh Râj Jesingh's death. It is on that account we are lamenting. "Who will perform service, worship, presentation of gifts or "sacrifices? We must needs lament." The king heard what they

[1] Various female goblins.

said from where he stood in concealment. Jug Dev said, "But "who is it that is singing?" The Fates said, "Go and enquire of "themselves." Jug Dev went, and paying obeisance, said, "You sing songs of good news. Who is your king, and what "pleases you that you are thus singing?" They said, "We are the "Fates of Delhi. We are come for Sidh Râj Jesingh: see, there is "the chariot. That is why we sing." Jug Dev said, "When will "he meet his death?" The Fates said, "In the morning, at the "time when he prepares for worship, and putting on the dress of "yellow silk, stands on the platform, we will strike him so that he "shall leave the body." Then Jug Dev said, "In these times there "is no king such as Sidh Row: by what religious observance, gift, "or vow, or by what other means can he escape and be released "from calamity?" They said, "There is but one way of escape "for him; if any chief who is equal to the king will cut off his "head and give it us, then Sidh Row Jesingh's life will be pro-"longed." Jug Dev said, "Will my head avail, that receiving it you "may prolong Sidh Row's life and royalty? If so, I am ready." The Fates assented. "If you make an offering of your own life, Sidh Row "will escape." Then Jug Dev said, "Give me leave for a few "moments; I will make the matter known to my wife, and, having "obtained her assent, will return." The Fates laughed scornfully: "No wife would consent to her husband's dying; but go and ask "and return speedily." Jug Dev turned himself homewards. Sidh Row said within himself, "Let me see whether he will return or not, "and what the Chowree will say." He followed him. Jug Dev, returning, entered his house and ascended into the upper room; he embraced the Chowree. Sidh Row Jesingh heard the conversation between the husband and wife. They sat together as usual. Jug Dev said, "Chowree! there is a matter of this kind." The Chowree, joining the palms of her hands, said, "What orders has my lord?" Then Jug Dev told her the whole story from the beginning, and said, "I am come to ask your permission." The Chowree said, "A day of prosperity, a night prosperous! It was for such a day "that we were enjoying our livelihood. Give it them: it is for the "life that subsistence, grants, and lands are given. You have de-"termined well; such is the duty of a Rajpoot. If Sidh Row live "and reign, all is well; if not, what use would life be! But, my "prince, I have one petition. Why should I survive; for six hours' "existence, why should I undergo so much calamity?[1] I will offer

[1] She meant to convey that she would burn with her husband's corpse in any event.

"my life with yours." Jug Dev said, "But the children, what will "become of them?" The Chowree said, "Let them be offerings "at the same time." Then Jug Dev said, "If it be so, let us not "delay." Jug Dev took the elder child by the hand and descended; the Chowree followed him. Sidh Row Jesingh was filled with astonishment, He said, "Well done! Rajpoot, and well done! Raj-"pootnee." The four went on in front, the king following them to see what would happen. Jug Dev and the Chowree approached the Fates. They said, "Jug Dev, is your head ready to be offered?" He said, "For my head how many years will you grant Sidh Row?" They said, "He shall reign twelve years." Again Jug Dev asked—"The lives of the Chowree and the boys are of equal value with "mine; for the four grant Sidh Row forty-eight years; I will offer "the four lives." The Fates said, "So be it." The Chowree first presented her first-born son. Jug Dev, drawing his sword, cut off the child's head, and prepared to offer the second boy. Then the Fates restrained him: "Jug Dev, we have granted you the forty-eight "years, and your wife and children." They sprinkled ambrosia upon the corpse of the elder child, and the boy rose alive. The Fates laughed and said, "Yours and your wife's faithfulness we have "seen to be great." Placing their hands[1] on the childrens' heads, they gave them to the Chowree. They said, "Jug Dev, for your "fidelity we have granted Sidh Row forty-eight years of royalty." They dismissed him. Jug Dev and the Chowree made obeisance, and, taking the two children, returned home. The king perceiving the fidelity of Jug Dev, and the Chowree's devotion to her husband, was very much delighted. He returned to his palace and lay down. As he lay he reflected in his mind: "Well done! Jug Dev, you have "procured for me forty-eight years of royalty." Sleep did not close his eyes. After four in the morning, the usher, having come, called Jug Dev. He arose and bathed, and worshipped the Supreme Lord, and taking the Divine name, made a mark on his forehead. At break of day he came to the king. Sidh Row was seated in the court when Jug Dev entered. Rising from his royal cushion, he embraced him; placing a second cushion beside him, he with urgency compelled him to be seated thereon. He sent for the chiefs whom he had commanded to bring intelligence, and enquired of them what news they had procured during the night. They said, "There were four Mows[2] in two carts; in the one cart they had had

[1] Spiritual preceptors still impose hands upon their disciples, as of old it is said was done by Devs and other supernal beings.

[2] A Mow is a person who has left home and become vagrant, in consequence of a famine or other distress.

" a son born to them and were singing, in the other they had lost a " son and were lamenting." Sidh Râj, hearing the chieftains' story, laughed contemptuously and said, " You are chieftains worth a " hundred thousand; great pillars you are; if you cannot bring " intelligence, who can bring it!" Then, turning to Jug Dev, he said, " Do you relate the occurrences of the night." Jug Dev said, " It must be as the chieftains have related." The king said again, " Do you tell the whole, even as it happened; I have heard all." Jug Dev said, " If I had seen any thing, I could relate it—I do not " know how to make up a tale." Then, having proved Jug Dev's generosity, and witnessed his fortitude, Sidh Râj Jesingh said— " O! chieftains, brothers, nobles, listen to the tale. The first watch " this morning was the hour appointed for my death; but now, for " forty-eight years, I enjoy royalty at the gift of Jug Dev. His two " sons, his own, and his consort's heads for me he offered to the " Fates; the elder child's head was actually offered. Beholding the " valor and fidelity of this noble, and the devotedness of his wife, " the Fates gave the whole back again, and presented my life also. " This day forth I reign at the gift of Prince Jug Dev. You are " telling falsehoods, thinking to obtain some advantage; but I saw " this thing with my eyes, and heard it with my ears. You grumble " at the pay given to him; but if I were to pay him a hundred " thousand every day, or ten millions even, I could not get such a " Rajpoot as he is." After thus saying, he gave to Jug Dev the cocoa-nut of his elder daughter, and with it two thousand villages. For their personal expenses also he gave five hundred villages. He presented Jug Dev with bracelets, a pearl necklace, a turban ornament, and numerous jewels, and dismissed him. Jug Dev returning home, told what had happened to the Chowree. She said, " You are a lord, in your female apartments there should be " two or four, you have done well, the connection is a great one." Then Jug Dev, discovering an auspicious day, completed the marriage. People looked upon Sidh Râj and Jug Dev as equals. Thus enjoying happiness, they passed two or three years.

In Bhoojnugger, where Raja Phool reigned, his son Lâkhâ had a son Phool, who had two daughters. Once on a time he considered that his daughters were old enough to be married, and therefore determined to find them bridegrooms. Calling his minister, he asked his advice as to sending the cocoa-nut to Sidh Râj Jesingh. The Jhârejee's cocoa-nut accordingly arrived at Puttun. Sidh Row, preparing the marriage cavalcade, took Jug Dev and other great chieftains with him, and setting out, reached Bhoojnugger. They were received with great joy, and brought into the city. Raja Phool had already been informed of Jug Dev's pedigree; the minister also refreshed his memory on the subject, saying, "He is a great Rajpoot, "a warrior, and a man of fortitude,—give the younger princess to "him." Her name was Phool Mutee: Jug Dev received the cocoa-nut for her: Sidh Row, the Solunkhee, and Jug Dev, the Purmâr, married the two Jhârejees at the house of Raja Phool. After receiving the usual presents, they were given leave, and returned to Puttun; they lived in comfort many days. At that time the usual embassy from her father's house came to take the Chowree to visit her parents; she, having obtained Jug Dev's permission, carrying the boys with her, went to her father's house.[1]

The remainder of the tale of Jug Dev is rather marvellous than interesting. The bard relates in detail how his hero laid Sidh Râj under further obligations, by fighting with and conquering a Kâl Bheiruv (or demon), who had fallen in love with his Jhârejee queen. We are also informed of the manner in which Jug Dev surpassed his master in a contest of generosity, by giving his head to Châmoondâ mother, when that Devee appeared at the court in the disguise of a bard's wife begging alms. It appears that Sidh Râj was after this angry with Jug Dev, because he had "put him beneath his feet and "diminished his fame in the world;" and that it was in consequence of that anger that he advanced against Dhâr. Jug Dev, upon becoming informed of this intention of the king's, determined to quit his service, for as the proverb has it,—

"Where there is a Purmâr there is Dhâr,
"And where there is Dhâr there is a Purmâr.
"Without Dhâr the Purmâr is nothing,
"So without the Purmâr is Dhâr."

Jug Dev, therefore, returning home, took counsel with the Jhârejee. "The king has conceived enmity against us; there is no advantage "in remaining here any longer; we will not remain, though the king "entreat us; we have tried our fortune." The Rânee said, "Your "fame has been spread abroad royally, and you have attained great "honor. Do you now proceed home, and embrace your father and "mother. I, too, will pay my respects to my father-in-law and "mother-in-law. Your relations will say, 'the prince has struck out "'a name;' therefore let us examine the omens and set out." Then

[1] It is necessary to remark, in regard to the historical value of this story, that a bard would not dare to take so great a liberty with any Rajpoot house, as to assert that a marriage had occurred, if it had not really taken place. By such presumption he would draw upon himself the anger of all concerned.

Jug Dev sent for the astrologer, and ascertaining the auspicious hour, caused his tents to be pitched outside the city. Meanwhile the Chowree too arrived, and embraced her husband; they enjoyed great happiness. Jug Dev told her the whole story, and she quickly made ready to proceed. They placed all their treasure on camels, and taking with them their elephants, horses, chariots, litters, cattle, men-servants and maid-servants,—their whole household,—they set off. When the whole had arrived outside the city, Jug Dev, mounting his horse, went to the king's presence. Sidh Râj, rising, said, "Be "seated here," but Jug Dev replied, "Your majesty, I have served a "long time; you must now give me leave." The raja was very importunate with him to remain, but Jug Dev would not consent. The ministers and officers added their persuasions, but Jug Dev continued to demand permission to retire. At last, making obeisance to the king and to the company, he retired. Sidh Row's daughter embraced her parents, her brothers, and maidens, and she too withdrew. Jug Dev set out from Puttun at the head of five thousand horse; before him went eight thousand armed men. Travelling stage by stage they reached Took Todâ. Messengers brought the news to the Chowrâ Raja; they demanded a present for the news. Prince Beerj made them presents; he caused the royal drum and instruments of music to sound. The city was adorned, and the prince went out in great pomp to meet them; he embraced the whole company, distributing pearls. Jug Dev remained there a month. The people had heard of the events of Puttun, but the Chowree related the whole story again from beginning to end. The whole were pleased.

After a month Jug Dev took leave and proceeded to Dhâr. The news had reached that place, but they nevertheless sent messengers to announce their approach. The raja was very much delighted: he presented to the messengers jewels, armlets, and pearls. Two special messengers made the announcement to the Solunkhee lady. The procession of welcome was prepared; the city was adorned; Oodayâdit Raja, with litters, horses, and elephants, went out to bring them in. Jug Dev touched his father's feet; he embraced his brothers, his nephews, the chiefs, the nobles, the rajpoots, the ministers, and monied-men—every one of them; he caused his two sons to touch his father's feet. The raja was very much delighted. Many bards sung the fame of Jug Dev. Thus they entered the city, receiving salutations from all sides, attended by a great retinue, with armed men, and elephants covered with armor. Jug Dev touched the feet of his mother, the Solunkhee lady; he bowed himself to the ground. His mother, laying her hands on his head, and then placing them on her own, took his sorrows upon her.[1] The three brides touched her feet. The Solunkhunee was overjoyed that she had seen her son and his wives: she said, "I am fortunate in this "world that I have heard of such deeds of my son with my ears, and "seen them with my eyes." The children sat in their grandmother's lap. Then the raja, being pleased, said, "O son! you have illumined "the thirty-five branches of the Purmârs. O son! there has been "none like you, nor will there be. You have saved Sidh Râj and "preserved his life, and taken the Bheiruv. You have fought with "the king, too, and abased his pride. Well done the Solunkhunee, "that she gave birth to you,—that she bare such a son in the world. "Your name has become immortal."

After this the Wâghelee lady, touching the raja's feet, began to salute Jug Dev. He, taking her by the hand, said, "Mâjee! my fame "is yours—I belong to your lap." Thus the good man forces good out of evil;—

"Think not of the faults of others,
"Though numerous as the thorns of the acacia,
"Says the dark-one; think of their virtues,—
"That the tree has no thorns in its shadow."

Thus reflecting, he touched the Wâghelee's feet and embraced Rindhuwul; the brides, too, paid their respects to them both.

Soon after, Raja Oodâyadit suffered from disease so violently, that he felt he could not survive. He sent for all the nobles, and for Jug Dev and Rindhuwul. Before them all he said, "I give the kingly "mark to Jug Dev, and entrust him with the royal authority." To Rindhuwul he assigned a hundred villages, urging him much to be obedient to Jug Dev; he also recommended Rindhuwul to Jug Dev's protection. Having thus seated Jug Dev on the throne, the raja went to Dev-lok. The Wâghelee and Solunkhunee became sutees. Raja Jug Dev ruled.

It was at the age of fifteen that he left home, and he served Sidh Râj eighteen years. After mounting the throne he reigned fifty-two years; he lived to the age of eighty-five. At last he placed Prince Jug Dhuwul on the throne, and himself went to Dev-lok. The Chowra, the Solunkhee, and the Jhâreja ladies with great joy became sutees, and accompanied their lord to paradise.

Thus, concludes the bard, have I related the good tale. This

[1] See account of the ceremony called "*Nyoonchun*," in the chapter on marriage ceremonies, in the Conclusion.

story of Jug Dev's listening to, truth, absence of anger, valor, firmness, exploits, wisdom, generosity will spring up abundantly. In this world, when Rows and Rânâs[1] hear the story, their want of courage, their meanness and little-mindedness will be dispelled; they will never fall into calamity. Considering this matter, readers will peruse, poets will recite, chieftains will listen. They will receive such joy as those who dwell in the City of Immortality.

Such is the tale of the illustrious Jug Dev Purmâr,—the full of valor.

CHAPTER IX.

RÂ KHENGÂR.

THE author of Prubundh Chintâmunee mentions that Sidh Râj sent an army against an Aheer Rânâ, or shepherd king, named Nowghun, which laid siege to Wurddhumân, now Wudwân, and other towns, but sustained many repulses. Sidh Râj at length set forth in person, and through the treachery of the Rânâ's sister's son, seized that prince, and put him to death. His queen gave vent to her deep grief, lamenting that she had not offered her life a sacrifice in company with Khengâr. "Broken down is Wudwân," she cried; "that king is dead; my father's race exists no longer; desolate is "my life; let Bhogâwo now enjoy me."

There is here a confusion between the names of Nowghun and Khengâr, which are usually applied to two different persons, father and son, chiefs of the Yâdoo race, ruling at Girnâr or Joonagurh in Soreth, of whom the latter was the opponent slain by Sidh Râj, and the husband of the princess who died at Wudwân.

Râ Khengâr's father, Râ Nowghun, says a bard, compelled the Raja of Oometa, on the banks of the Myhee, to give him his daughter as a token of submission. Hunsrâj, the Myheero, her brother, however, declared that it was cowardly in his father to have given the lady, and that some day or other he would slay Nowghun. This he threatened publicly; and Nowghun, in return, swore that he would slay Hunsrâj, the Myheero. Nor was this the only feud that

[1] Royal titles.

Nowghun involved himself in on account of this Rânee, for when her bridal procession was on its way to Joonagurh, and had arrived at Bhoowero, near Jusdun, the Raja of Bhoowero, on being told that the bride was Nowghun's, laughed, and said, that if his fort had only been finished, he would have kept her for himself. Râ Nowghun, when he was told of this, swore that he would break down the fort, and put the raja to death.

Once on a time, Sidh Râj, the Solunkhee, encountered Nowghun in Punchâl land, the border country on the Soreth side of the Null, and Sidh Râj having disarmed him, Nowghun was obliged to take grass in his mouth, and make submission. Then Nowghun took an oath that he would break down the gate of Puttun.

At the same time, Sidh Râj's household bard composed a song in ridicule of Nowghun, which made the Râ so angry, that he swore again that he would split the bard's cheeks.

Râ Nowghun, however, fell sick, and his death approached without having been able to perform either of the oaths which he had sworn. He therefore called his four sons around him, and told them that whoever of them would accomplish the four labors he had vowed to perform, should sit upon his throne. The eldest, Râeedhun, undertook to destroy the fort of Bhoowero: the Râ gave him four districts, and his descendants from the clan called Râeezâdahs. Sher Singh, the second son, promised, in addition, that he would slay Hunsrâj, the Myheero; he also received a few villages, and was the ancestor of the Survaiyas. The third son, Chundra Singh, wore a bracelet of Umbâjeés, having dedicated himself to that goddess; he agreed, beyond what his brothers had said, to break down a gate of Puttun, but declined the task of splitting the bard's cheeks, because that would be a disgraceful act; he also received a few villages, and was the ancestor of the Choodâsumâs. Khengâr, who was the youngest of all the sons, alone undertook to perform the four tasks; Râ Nowghun therefore placed him on the throne of Joonagurh in his own lifetime, and soon after died.

Râ Khengâr, in his first warlike expedition, destroyed the fort of Bhoowero, and killed the raja; next he slew Hunsrâj, the Myheero; afterwards, when Sidh Râj was gone to Malwa, Khengâr, leading an army to Puttun, broke down the eastern gate. On his way back he carried off the betrothed bride of Sidh Râj, Rânik Devee, the daughter of the Devra Rajpoot of Kâlree, and married her. When he had performed these exploits, the household bard extolled his fame. Khengâr filled his mouth with diamonds and pearls till the bystanders cried out, "his cheeks are split, his cheeks are split." That was the only way, Khengâr said, of splitting a bard's cheeks; it could not be done with a dagger.

Afterwards, Sidh Râj brought an army to the country of Joonagurh, and fought against it for twelve years without success. At length Râ Khengâr sister's sons, Dehul and Veehul, being angry with Khengâr, went over to Sidh Râj, to whom they pointed out a subterraneous passage, by which he introduced his army into the fort. Sidh Râj slew Khengâr, and carried off Rânik Devee to Wudwân, where she became a sutee. He cut off the noses of Dehul and Veehul, and expelled them.

Rânik Devee, when she was seized by Sidh Râj, was not aware that her husband had been slain, but thought that he was a prisoner. On their arrival at Wudwân, Sidh Râj told her that he had killed her husband, and sought to induce her to marry him.[1] She, however, refused to enter his female apartments, and threatened to curse him, "sut" having come upon her,[2] if he did not give up the body of her husband. Sidh Râj was terrified, and caused the corpse to be given to her; he asked also what expiation he could make for his offence. Rânik Devee said, "Build me a temple in this place, and your "throne shall stand firm, but as you have slain my children, I lay "this curse upon you,—you shall die without a son to succeed you." She then followed her husband through the flames.[3]

The people of Soreth are still much attached to the memory of the old Râs of Joonagurh, and a proverb is common among them, which

[1] Sidh Râj might have urged with the English Richard,—

> "He that bereft thee, lady, of thy husband,
> "Did it to help thee to a better husband."
> "I did kill King Henry;—
> "But 'twas thy beauty that provoked me.
> " . . . 'twas I that stabb'd young Edward :—
> "But 'twas thy heavenly face that set me on."

[2] For explanation of the expression, "Sut having come upon her," see the account of Sutees in the Conclusion.

[3] We find it stated in the Annals of Mewar, that Asil, the son of Bappa, of Cheetore, by a daughter of the Purmâr Prince of Kalibao, near Dwarka, obtained possessions in Soreth, and founded a race called the Asil-Gehlotes. His son Beejy Pal, it is said, was slain in an attempt to wrest Cambay from Singram Dabee. One of Beejy Pal's wives died a violent death, and was prematurely delivered of a boy, named Setoo, and as in such cases the Hindoos suppose the spirit of the deceased to become one of the Bhoots, called Choodels, the tribe that descended from Setoo were known as the Choodels. Beej, the twelfth from Asil, obtained Sonul from his maternal uncle, Khengâr, Prince of Girnâr, but was slain by Jye Singh Dev.

says, that "the mould in which Soreth land and Râ Khengâr were "formed has been broken, and the workman who made them is no "more."

The city of the Râs is approached from the south-west by a road which passes for some miles through a picturesque and highly-cultivated country, enriched with groves of mangoes, tamarinds, and other luxuriant trees. In front is seen a range of granite hills, richly clothed with underwood, which, extending north and west, occupies an extreme extent of about twelve miles. A large opening in nearly the centre of the range, called the "Portal of Doorgâ," discloses a beautiful valley, its vista filled by the sacred mount of Nemeenâth, the royal Girnâr, which, joined to the lower range by two connecting spurs, raises far above it its bold black granite bluffs and tapering peaks, half concealed in mist and clouds.

At the entrance of this valley is situated the ancient city of Joonagurh, its low walls nearly hidden by the dense jungle around it. In the north-eastern angle, throwing its darkening shadow over "the "streak of gold," the river Sonâ Rekhâ that glides beneath its bastions, rises the old Rajpoot citadel, the Oopurkot, the residence of Râ Khengâr and his ill-fortuned bride. This citadel is still a noble specimen of eastern fortification. Venerable from its age, and romantic from its position, its deeply excavated fosse, its numerous and massive towers, its crenellated parapets, telling of strength and asserting dignity, would, without fail, impress the beholder, were his imagination unexcited by their association with the mysterious glories of the Yâdoo race—the still shadowy line of Shree Krishn.

From the gate of the city of Khengâr, following the river Sonâ Rekhâ towards its source, a pathway, worn by the foot of many a pilgrim, leads to the summit of Girnâr. At the foot of the mountain, the stranger passes by those venerable rocks, which are hallowed by the name of the just and benevolent Asokâ; thence, by a winding and rugged ascent of about a mile, he reaches the point where the western spur or shoulder of the mountain terminates at the foot of the scarp. For the rest of the ascent the sacred mountain rises, an immense bare, black and isolated granite rock, presenting all the gigantic masses peculiar to its formation; on the summit of which, occupying a small ledge or table land, surrounded by a fort, whose wall is erected on the very verge of the scarp, stand the temples of the Jain Teerthunkurs. From the plateau occupied by the temples, a gradual ascent, amidst patches of korunder and wild fig, leads to the point of Girnâr, where stands the shrine of Umbâvee Mâtâ. The mountain has six distinct peaks, separated by deep ravines, the highest of which is dedicated to Goruknâth, and that most remote to Kâleekâ. She it is whose rites are performed by the hideous, and, if report speak true, the cannibal Aghoree, from her patronage of whom she derives the name of the Aghoreshwuree mother. From the plains but four of these peaks are distinctly visible; and at the distance of a few miles these, though majestic individually when observed from the shrine of Goruknâth, gradually merge into the general mass which appears to form the cone of "the Girnâr." No detailed description need here be attempted of the architecture of the temples that rest upon the plateau of the mount of Nemeenâth. Sufficient to mention that, commanding as the sectaries do, by whom they have been erected and maintained, much of the wealth of India, they have here, as at Shutroonjye, omitted nothing which could render these monuments of their faith of surpassing magnificence.[1]

The following version of the story of Rânik Devee was obtained from one of those itinerant musicians, called Toorees, who, standing to the class of Dhers in the same relation which the more famous bards, the Bhâts and Châruns, bear to Hindoos of better caste, roam about the country subsisting upon the alms of their clients, and delighting them in return with the wild and rude tales, half prose and half verse, which they chant to the accompaniment of a species of guitar called the Sâringee:—

In Sindh land is the country of Pâwur, of which Ror Pâwur was raja. A daughter was born to him under the "Mool" constellation. The astrologer said to Raja Ror, that whoever married a girl born in such a time as this princess would lose his throne. The raja was very sorry when he heard this, so he sent his daughter away into the forest, where a potter, named Hurmuteeo, found her and brought her up. She was so very beautiful that the Lâkhâ Phoolânee sent an embassy to demand her in marriage. The potter said he must ask his caste-fellows before he gave away his daughter. Lâkhâ threatened him with violence; and the potter, therefore, fled, and went to Mujeywuree, in Soreth, where he lived with his family.

Once on a time, four household bards of Sidh Râj Jesingh, King of Puttun, named Lâlâ Bhât, Bhungud Bhât, Chunch Bhât, and Dubul Bhât, travelling in foreign countries, arrived at Mujeywuree, where they saw the beautiful daughter of the potter, Hurmuteeo. Wherever she moved she left the impress of her feet in rose colour on the ground. The Bhâts considered that the damsel would adorn

[1] This description is from Tod's Western India, and Kittoe's Notes on Girnâr, Journ. Ben. Ass. Soc., vii., 865.

the court of Sidh Râj, and that if they went to Puttun with the good news they would be sure to receive gifts from the king: so they came to Puttun, where Sidh Râj received them with great respect. He had sixteen Ranees, and he caused the Bhâts to dine with him one day at each of their houses. As they rose from dinner each day, the Bhâts looked at each other and shook their heads. Sidh Râj enquired the reason of this. The Bhâts said, "We have seen your "sixteen Ranees, but no one of them has all the requisites of a "Pudmeenee."[1] The raja said, "You are my household bards, do "you, therefore, travel into foreign countries and search for one who "is a complete Pudmeenee, and, when you have found her, bring "the proposals and fix the day of marriage." The Bhâts went off and searched in many countries without finding a complete Pudmeenee; at last they determined to return to Mujeywuree, in Soreth. Since they had visited it for the first time, the potter, Hurmuteeo, thinking within himself that, as Sidh Râj's Bhâts had seen the maiden, some difficulty would probably arise, had kept her in a concealed chamber underground. The Bhâts, when they arrived, said to him, "Betroth your daughter to the Puttun Raja." The potter said, "I have no daughter." But the Bhâts made answer that they had seen her, and that if he did not perform the ceremony of betrothal Sidh Râj would never let him live in peace. "Besides," they said, "what fortune is this of yours, that you, a potter, should "be Sidh Râj's father-in-law!" Thus, between threatening and making promises, they prevailed upon the potter to make the bethrothal. They further fixed the bridal day for two or three months after, and went away to Puttun, where they told the raja the whole story. Sidh Râj said he would not marry a potter's daughter, for then his house would be disgraced. The Bhâts answered,—

> "As a mango-tree at one man's door
> "Drops its fruit within another's garden,
> "So God has caused to be done with Devuree—
> "She is not of the blood of the Potter."

Hearing this, and also their praises of her beauty, the raja was pleased, and began to prepare for the marriage. He made a bridal-pavilion, and caused Gunesh to be installed.

At the time all this happened the Râ of Joonagurh was the Choodâsumâ Râ Khengâr, whose sister had married a kinsman of

[1] The Hindoos say there are five classes of women—Pudmeenee Husteenee, Cheetrunee, and Shunkheenee, of which the first is the most perfect.

Sidh Râj, but was living at Joonagurh with her two sons, Dehul and Veehul. Dehul said to his uncle one day, "I am going to Mujey-"wuree to see it; the village has been newly founded in our country." Thus taking leave he went with Veehul to Mujeywuree. Hearing the whole story about the potter's daughter, they returned to Joonagurh, and related it to Râ Khengâr. "In our districts," they said, "is a potter's daughter who is very beautiful, and fit to adorn a royal "court. Sidh Râj's household bards have been to see her, and have "fixed the day of her marriage with Sidh Râj. If the Puttun Raja "take such a maiden out of our country, what reputation will remain "to us?". The Choodâsumâ said to Dehul, "Take my sword, and "go and bring the damsel to my court." Dehul took the sword, and went and told the potter that he must marry his daughter to Râ Khengâr's sword.[1] The potter said that the maiden had been betrothed to the Raja of Puttun, and that the bridal procession would come from thence in a few days. If he married his daughter to Râ Khengâr, Sidh Râj would undoubtedly slay him, he said. Dehul replied, "I take her away by force, so no harm will happen to you." The potter said, "The Puttun Raja will dig up Girnâr "from the roots, and cast its stones in all directions. Do you, "therefore, forbear to interfere with a maiden who is betrothed "to Sidh Râj.

"Know Jesingh Dev
"By whom Dhâr Nugger was shaken.
"Wealth that is known to be his,
"Khengâr should not lay hand on."

Dehul sneeringly replied,—

"Fifty-two thousand has he stabled,
"Of horses, at Gurh Girnâr;
"Why should fear the lord of Soreth,
"He of the complete army, Khengâr!"

So it was, at last, that Dehul carried off the maid by force to Râ Khengâr. Rânik Devee, descending from her chariot at Joonagurh, began to enter the outer door; she struck her foot by chance against a stone, and blood sprung forth. She sighed, and said, "My friend! "this is a very bad omen—some calamity will result from this matter."

[1] This is not an unusual practice: *vide* account of Marriage Ceremonies in the Conclusion.

"As she entered the first door
"She stumbled and struck her foot.
"Ah! will widowhood come to Rânik Devee,
"Or ruin to Soreth-land?"[1]

Râ Khengâr married her, the ceremony being performed with royal splendour. The Râ feasted the city of Girnâr for three days. It happened that a hundred Wâghurees[2] of Puttun, who had come to sell earthern vessels, had made a halt outside the northern gate. They were invited together with the rest. The Wâghurees enquired, "What rejoicing is there at the raja's house that we are invited?" The servant answered,—

"The white elephant of Soreth-land,
"By caste a Purmâr,
"The daughter of Raja Rolree,
"Has married Râ Khengâr."

"On this account for the last three days the raja feasts the town, "including the Dhers. He has sent to invite you also to the feast. "Come, therefore." The Wâghurees considered that this maiden, having been betrothed to their sovereign, had been forcibly married to Râ Khengâr, and that they, as well as Sidh Râj, being called Solunkhees, it would not be right for them to attend the marriage feast of a damsel betrothed to a Solunkhee[3] who had been carried off. They determined rather that they would go quickly to Puttun, and make the matter known there. Thus considering, hungry and thirsty, they set forth, and travelled until they arrived in Puttun Wârâ, at the town of Wâghel. Then they laid nets to catch game. In the meantime Sidh Râj's four household bards, who were on a journey, came up on horseback, and the wild bull (roz) that was in the net made its escape. The Wâghurees said, "Sire! we have come night "and day from Joonagurh, and to-day is our seventh fast. Why did "you drive away our roz?" The Bhâts enquired how it happened that they had fasted seven days. They said that Râ Khengâr had taken away by force their raja's betrothed bride. The Bhâts, hearing this, were much discomposed; they mounted at once, and going to Puttun, told Sidh Râj,—

[1] "Brother, I like not this;
"For many men that stumble at the threshold
"Are well foretold that danger lurks within."
Third part King Henry VI., Act IV., scene 7.

[2] The Wâghuree is a person of very low caste, whose employment is that of snaring game, &c.

[3] The narrator called himself a Solunkhee.

"We are without master, without home,
"We are called poor Bhâts,
"We searched for and found Rânik Devee,
"Her Khengâr has snatched from us."

Sidh Râj then called to his assistance his familiar spirit, Bâburo Bhoot, and told him to prepare to accompany him, as he was going to Joonagurh to fight with Râ Khengâr. The king set forth and marched to Wâghel, where he was joined by Bâburo, who had collected five thousand two hundred bhoots. At Sidh Râj's order the bhoots constructed a tank there in one night.[1] From Wâghel the army marched to Moonjpoor, and thence to Junjoowârâ, where they found Dhândo, the head man of the shepherds, dwelling with his tribe in a collection of huts. They built there the fort and a tank. Thence they went on to Veerumgaum, where they built the Monsur tank; thence to Wudwân, where they built the fort; thence to Syelâ, where they built the fort and tank. After some days' march they arrived in the Joonagurh country, where they carried on war for twelve years, without being able to force their way up to Râ Khengâr's palace in Joonagurh. Minul Rânee, who was with her son at this time, practised various enchantments, but without success. At length it happened that Râ Khengâr became jealous of his nephew, Dehul, and accused him of too great intimacy with Rânik Devee. His mother informed Dehul of this fact, who said,—

"I have not killed his horses,
"I have not seen his treasures,
"I have not enjoyed Rânik Devee,
"Why then should Khengâr blame me?"

[1] In Goozerat every ancient reservoir or religious edifice is referred, according to the religion of the person, to either Sidh Râj (under his popular name of Sudderâjee Jesung) or Sultan Mahmood Begurra, in either case assisted by bhoots or other denizens of the spirit world. So it is with other popular heroes in other countries:—

"In both France and England, old military erections whose origin is forgotten "have been vulgarly attributed to Cæsar, as the most renowned soldier whose ex-"ploits make part of the primitive history of the country. Thus the Tower of "London is commonly said to have been built by that great conqueror. 'This is "the way,' says the Queen of the unfortunate Richard II. in Shakspeare,

"'To Julius Cæsar's ill-erected tower.'

"The Bell Tower in the lower ward of Windsor Castle is also called 'Cæsar's "Tower;' although the sturdiest believer in historical romances cannot venture to "assign its origin to the Roman conqueror. In France, in like manner, every "thing possessing any extraordinary character used to be ascribed, by the credulity "of former generations, either to the fairies, the devil, or Cæsar."—*History of Paris.*

His mother said, "You brought her who was betrothed to your "father's relation, and gave her to your mother's brother, but he, forgetting your services, is ungratefully angry with you, so you should "not remain in this city." Afterwards Râ Khengâr himself told him to depart. Dehul, upon this, took his brother Veehul with him, and fled in the night. When they came to the gate of the fort they found Doodo and Humeer, two Rajpoots, on guard, who asked them whither they were going. They said that the prince expected bullocks laden with opium from Malwa, and that they were going to meet them, and would return at midnight, at which time the doors must be opened to them without delay. Then the brothers went out, and came to Sidh Râj, and said to him, "Sire! we knew not that you were our "kinsman, and on that account we brought Rânik Devee to our "maternal uncle, but he now accuses us unjustly, so we are come to "you. If you will accompany us we will slay Râ Khengâr, and "restore Rânik Devee to you." Then, concealing seven score of soldiers in bullocks' panniers, they drove them into the fort, causing Doodo and Humeer to open the gates to them, and slaying them immediately. They pressed on to Râ Khengâr's palace, and sounded the horn. Then Khengâr came to fight—

"They broke the gate and began to plunder,
"They plundered Gurh Girnâr,
"Doodo and Humeer they slew,
"And marred the beauty of Soreth."

At this time, after many had fallen on both sides, Râ Khengâr himself was slain.

Then Dehul, taking Sidh Râj with him, went to Rânik Devee's palace, and said to her, "Aunt, we two brothers and our uncle, "Khengâr, are come—so open the door to us." She did so. Rânik Devee had two sons, Mânero, who was eleven years old, and Dyegucho, who was five years of age. Sidh Râj took the latter from her, and slew him. When he attempted to seize Mânero, the boy escaped from him, and hid himself, weeping, behind his mother. She said,—

"Mânero! weep not,
"Make not red your eyes—
"To your race it were dishonor,
"Dying, recollect not your mother."

Sidh Râj then gave orders that the boy should not be slain there. "If Rânik Devee will not enter Puttun, I will then slay him." The boy, in truth, was at last slain, but it is not known where.

Rânik Devee was brought out of the fort. At that time she saw Râ Khengâr's war-horse, and, sorrowing, said,—

" O ! swift steed,
" Has your bosom not burst?
" Râ Khengâr is dead,
" Will you now visit Goozerat ?"

Next she saw an elk that had belonged to Râ Khengâr; she said,—

" O ! elk-lion bethink you,
" Once you were free,
" But when Khengâr died
" You lost your freedom for aye."

She heard a pea-fowl crying, and said to it,—

" Why cry you, pea-fowl,[1]
" In the caves of Girnâr ?
" Our hearts are broken—
" Our protector is gone."

Rânik Devee came to where the corpse of Khengâr was lying—she addressed it thus,—

" Rise, lord ! collect your army,
" Take your sword, Khengâr :
" This canopied lord is overshading
" The old fort Joonagurh."

As she descended into the valley she took leave of her favorites, the reservoir of water, the garden, and its chumpa trees. She looked up to the mountain, and said,—

" Lofty hill, Girnâr,
" With the clouds that talkest,
" Fall now to the earth,
" For Râ Khengâr has fallen."

When she had gone on some miles she turned back, and, seeing the mountain from another side, thought that it was moving to escort them; she cried,—

" Return, murderous Girnâr,
" Why should you escort your foes,
" Khengâr Râ is dead,
" Why fell you not with him."

[1] The cry of the pea-fowl is supposed to call lovers together.

When she had gone very far, and the mountain had almost disappeared below the horizon, she fancied it was falling, and said,—

"Sink not my support!
"Your stones who shall upraise?
"Though the raiser has departed,
"They that survive will pay you homage."

Dehul and Veehul had beforehand arranged with Sidh Râj that, when he had slain Râ Khengâr, he should give the throne of Joonagurh to Dehul. As he set out homewards, therefore, they reminded him of his promise. Sidh Râj, at first, said, "Take it;" but, afterwards, he reflected, that, as the two brothers had behaved treacherously to their mother's brother, they would some day rebel and oppose him, so he slew them both.

When the train arrived at Puttunwârâ, Sidh Râj strove to console Rânik Devee, and pointed out to her several good places; she said,—

"Burned be Puttun land,
"Where animalculæ die of thirst.
"Best is the land of Soreth,
"Where the forest-beast drinks his fill."

At length they arrived under the walls of Puttun, and made a halt there. The raja caused the inhabitants of the city to be feasted outside, and they all poured forth, dressed in holiday attire. Rânik Devee would take no pleasure in the sight, but said,—

"Burned be Puttun land,
"Where short scarfs cover the women.
"Best is the land of Soreth,
"Where the woman's robe is rich and full."

A Goozerat woman said to her, "You have the great Sidh Râj for "your husband." She said, "My husband! I left him in such a "state as this,—

"His moustache stirred by the wind,
"His teeth glittering in the rays of the sun.
"My husband! O short-scarfed one!
"I have seen my husband thus."

The woman asked her how she could refrain from tears. She said,—

"With drops from my eyelids,
"What need I should fill a well?
"Thinking of my Mânero's death,
"Rivers of tears course through my body."

Thus Rânik Devee refused to be consoled in any manner. Sidh Râj treated her very respectfully, and asked her where it would be her pleasure to reside. She said she would go to Wudwân. Sidh Râj himself escorted her thither. She then informed him that she had determined upon becoming a "sutee." He was afraid to deny her request. A pile was prepared on the banks of the river Bhogâwo, and Rânik Devee took her seat thereon. Sidh Râj, as a last resource, said to her that, if she were a true sutee, the pile would ignite without fire. Rânik Devee knelt down, and prayed to the sun. She rose again, and said,—

"Farewell Wudwân, city good,
"Beneath whose walls Bhogâwo flows!
"Me, Râ Khengâr only enjoyed;
"Enjoy me now, husband Bhogâwo."[1]

The wind blew so hot at this time that the pile was thereby ignited.

"Well blew the heated wind,
"By which the sands were scorched,
"As Sidh Râj stood by Bhogâwo
"To behold the truth of the Sorethyanee."

At this time Sidh Râj threw his own scarf over Rânik Devee; she cast it back to him out of the fire, and said, "If you would become "my husband in another life, you must now burn with me." Sidh Râj declined.

Where Rânik Devee burned, Sidh Raj erected a funeral temple. All Soreth land submitted to him; but it was the palace of Râ Khengâr, upon Girnâr, which received the marks of the sutee's hands for Rânik Devee.

The town of Wurddhumânpoor, or Wudwân, now the capital of a branch of the Jhâlâ Rajpoots, is situated in a level, cotton-growing country, within, but not far removed from, the frontier line of Soreth. Tradition assigns to it a very ancient date, and affirms its priority to the capital of Wun Râj :—

"Wulleh and Wudwân!
"Puttun city was afterwards founded."

[1] It is worthy of remark, that this expression, found in a ballad orally handed down to the present day through the Toorees, is also to be met with in the Prubundh Chintâmunee, a Sanscrit chronicle, composed in A.D. 1305, and since shut up in a Jain monastery, far out of the reach of wandering out-caste bards. *Vide* p. 118.

The northern branch of the river Bhogâwo passes beneath the bastions of the town, and, without being able to force its way to the sea, or even, except in the rainy season, to unite with the southern branch that flows by Limree, it loses itself in the salt flats about the embouchure of the Sâbhermutee. A few rectangular towers, with their connecting curtains, are the only remains of the ancient fort of Wudwân; but the modern town has extended itself much around them, and the funeral temple of Rânik Devee, which must have formerly stood in the neighbourhood of the stream of Bhogâwo, is now enclosed within the walls. Of this shrine the spire, which is much ornamented, and nearly resembles in its style the temple of Modheyra, alone remains. The domed ante-chamber has entirely perished. A mutilated image of Khengâr's unhappy bride still, however, occupies the adytum; and, on days of festival, arrayed in marriage attire, with the crown, the bridal-veil, and royal jewels, shares in the worship paid at other shrines in its vicinity which commemorate the virtuous devotion of wives of the house of Wudwân, who, with the princes of the Jhâlâ race, have here passed through the flames to Paradise.

CHAPTER X.

SIDH RÂJ.

AFTER the death of Râ Khengâr, Sidh Râj committed the affairs of Soreth to a military officer, named Sujjun, a descendant of Jâmb or Champâ, the companion of Wun Râj. This minister, as Merootoong relates, devoted the royal revenue for three years to the re-edification of the temple of Nemeenâth, upon Girnâr; and, on Sidh Râj's calling him to account, assigned reasons so satisfactory to the king, that he was continued in his office, and entrusted particularly with the holy places of Shutroonjye and Oojâyunt. The king himself soon after visited both these sacred mountains on his return from a pilgrimage to Shree Someshwur at Dev Puttun, and made a grant of twelve villages for the worship of Rishub Dev, though envious Brahmins strove to dissuade him.

Religious controversies appear to have been carried on in the reign of Sidh Râj, not only between the followers of the Brahminical religion and those of the Jain faith, but also, and more particularly, between rival sectaries of the latter persuasion, the Digumburs and Swetâmburs, so called, the former, from their living in a state of nudity, clothed only with the atmosphere that surrounded them—the latter, from the use of white vestments. Koomood Chunder, a learned man of the former sect, who, it is said, had conquered his opponent in eighty-four religious contests, came from Kurnât-land to acquire for himself additional fame by the spiritual conquest of Goozerat. Sidh Râj, recognising him as the spiritual preceptor of his mother's father, received him with respect, and Myenul Devee herself at first warmly espoused his cause. Koomood Chunder was opposed, on the part of the Swetâmburs, by Dev Sooree, a learned monk of Kurunâwutee, and also by Hemâchârya. On the day fixed for the contest, Sidh Râj, having taken his seat upon the royal cushion, surrounded by the courtiers who were learned in religious differences, the challenger, Koomood Chunder, made his appearance, borne in a litter with a white umbrella held over him, preceded by a banner and attended by musicians. Dev Soree and Hemâchârya also presented themselves, and sat down on the same cushion, opposite to their opponent. A statement of the opinions held by the disputants had been written down on a previous day, and was now read before the court as follows :—

"Koomood Chunder contends that the Kewulee, who is possessed "of holy knowledge, and is on the way to attain Kyewulya, or eternal "emancipation, should not eat; that the man who wears clothes "cannot attain liberation; that females cannot attain liberation. Dev "Sooree contends that the Kewulee may eat; that the man who wears "clothes, and also the woman, may attain liberation.

Koomood Chunder was already half defeated; the announcement of his opinions having been wisely availed of by his opponents to deprive him of the assistance of the queen mother. Myenul Devee, interesting herself on behalf of her countryman, had given instructions to those about her to facilitate his victory; but Hemâchârya, hearing of this, sought an interview with her, and explained to her that the Digumbur's object was to deny the possibility of virtuous actions being performed by women, which notion the Swetâmbur would resolutely confute. The queen, thus informed, ceased to assist the Digumbur—"*a man ignorant of human character.*"

The opposing doctors commenced their discourses by laudations of the sovereign and of the Châlookya race. They then argued for their respective tenets. Koomood Chunder's speech was short, and delivered in broken language, "like a pigeon's;" but Dev Sooree's eloquence was like the terrible wind, which, at the destruction of the world, will agitate the waves of the ocean. The monk of Kurnât-land was soon obliged to admit that Dev Âchârya had conquered him: he was immediately expelled the city, as a defeated disputant, by the door of bad omen.[1] Sidh Râj, on the other hand, celebrating the praises of the Swetâmbur champion, himself took him by the hand, and conducted him publicly to worship at the temple of Muhâ Veer, with the emblems of royalty, musical instruments, and the warlike conch-shell sounding the note of victory. The king also conferred upon the Sooree the village of Châlâ, and eleven others between the towns of Poorântej and Dehgâm, though the holy man for a long time refused to accept the gift.

The Jains at this period seem to have found it politic to express liberal sentiments in regard to other religions, though the contentions in their own body where somewhat bitter. Sidh Râj, it is said, invited the professors of different religions from all countries, and enquired of them which was the best deity, which the best scripture or "receptacle of wisdom," and which the best practical faith; but as each authority praised his own tenets and dispraised those held by others, the king's mind remained in a state of uncertainty,—"rocked, "as it were, on a swinging bed,"—until at last he procured a more satisfactory answer from Hemâchârya. This monk related to the king the story of a man who having taken a potion, administered to him as an "enthralling" charm by his wife, was metamorphosed into a bullock, but recovered his natural shape by accidentally grazing on some medicinal herbs to which Doorgâ had given the power of conferring manhood. "As these leaves of medicinal virtue," said Hemâchârya, "though their nature was unknown to the bullock that "eat them, produced a happy result, so in this iron age men prac-"tising various religious services, though ignorant of their nature, "may attain liberation. This is certain." Sidh Râj, being perhaps anxious to procure authority for a toleration which he practised on political grounds, expressed great satisfaction with this answer.

There can be little doubt that from the foundation of Unhilwârâ to its destruction, the religions of Shiva and of the Jain Teerthunkurs existed there together, sometimes the one and sometimes the other gaining the predominance. His pilgrimages to the shrine of Someshwur and his restoration of the temple at Shreesthul, prove that Sidh Râj professed the orthodox faith, but none of the traditions

[1] Such doors were elsewhere known. "Plutarch," says Jeremy Taylor, "rarely "well compares curious and inquisitive ears to the execrable gates of cities, out of "which only malefactors, and hangmen, and tragedies pass – nothing that is chaste "or holy."

which relate to him speak of any zealous attachment to his religion. On the contrary, the author of the Prubundh Chintâmunee relates a story, which is not worth here introducing, for the purpose of proving "that Sidh Râj from that day forth believed in the power of virtuous "actions performed in former existence," a cardinal doctrine of Hindooism upon which we must therefore conclude the king to have, at one time at least, held heretical opinions.

The gift of the town of Singhpoor, or Seehore, to Owdich Brahmins by Mool Râj Solunkhee, has already been noticed. This grant was renewed by Sidh Râj, who gave the Brahmins at the same time one hundred villages in Bâlâk-land, or the Bhâl. After some time, however, the Brahmins, finding Seehore and its vicinity to be "a terror-causing country," from the number of wild beasts that then infested it, as until very lately they have continued to do, requested Sidh Râj to allow them to live in Goozerat. The king, granting their request, assigned to them the village of Âshâmbeelee, on the banks of the Sâbhermutee, and remitted in their favour the transit duties on the grain which they removed from Seehore.

The Jain writers mention that the court of Sidh Râj was on one occasion visited by ministers of the barbarians, who after being terrified by a magical display, in which demon ambassadors from Vibheeshun, Raja of Lunkâ, appeared to acknowledge the royal ornament of the Solunkhee race as an incarnation of Râm, and consequently as the master of their lord, were dignified with suitable presents. We are also told, in the annals of Jesulmer, that Lanja Beejiraee, the prince of that country, had, previous to his elevation to the throne, espoused a daughter of Sidh Râj, the Solunkhee; and that during the nuptial ceremonies, as the mother of the bride marked the bridegroom's forehead with the royal mark, she exclaimed, "My "son! do thou become the portal of the north—the barrier between "us and the king, whose power is becoming strong."

The only date given in regard to these occurrences is that of the accession of Doosuj, Lanja Beejiraee's father, which is stated to have occurred in Sumwut 1100, or A.D. 1044, fifty years before the accession of Sidh Râj. As Beejiraee is said to have been born when his father was "in his old age," a synchronism may be admitted.

Though the Mohammedans did not attempt any invasion of Goozerat during the reign of Sidh Râj, their power was sufficiently near at hand to admit of an embassy having reached his court, as well as to account for the anxiety expressed by the Queen of Unhilwârâ to erect the Bhâttee state of Jesulmer into a barrier against them on the north. We are told by Ferishta, that in the time of Sultan

Musaood III., who reigned from A.D. 1098 to 1118, Hajib Toghan-tugeen, an officer of his government and Governor of Lahore, proceeded in command of an army across the Ganges, and carried his conquests further than any Mohammedan had hitherto done, except the great Mahmood, plundering many rich cities and temples of their wealth, with which he returned in triumph to Lahore. That city had now become in some measure the capital of the empire, since the royal house of Ghuznee, deprived of most of its territory both in Iran and Tooran, had there taken up its residence. In A.D. 1118, Lahore was held by Mohammed Bhyleem, who having been placed in that charge by Sultan Arslan, held out on the death of that prince against his brother Beiram, by whom he was, however, reduced. The Sultan having reinstated him in his government, and returned to Ghuznee, Mohammed Bhyleem strengthened the fort of Nagore, in the province of Sewalik, from whence, with any army of mercenaries, he committed great devastations in the territories of the other Indian princes. His success caused him to aspire to the throne, but the Sultan Beiram meeting him in battle at Mooltan the rebellion was quelled.

Several anecdotes are given by Merootoong connected with visits paid by Sidh Râj to Malwa subsequent to its reduction by his arms. On one occasion the king is said to have left his principal carriage, which was of too cumbersome a description for the mountain road he had to traverse, at a village named Wârâhee. On his return he found that the head-men of the village not having been able to agree upon any single person who should undertake so great a responsibility as that of preserving the royal carriage, had taken it to pieces, that each might keep a part in safety. Sidh Râj, however, resented the loss of his chariot only by giving the head-men the nickname of the Booches, or simpletons, of Wârâhee, which they long retained.

On another occasion, Sidh Râj, returning from Malwa, made a halt at the village of Oonjâ, near Unhilwârâ Puttun. Merootoong mentions that the head of the village bore the title of the king's uncle, a circumstance which may be connected with the local tradition, still preserved, that Myenul Devee was sheltered before her marriage by Heemâlo, the head-man of Oonjâ. This village is still, as it was in the time of Sidh Râj, one of the most prosperous in Goozerat; it is also the head-quarters of the important cultivating caste of Kuruwâ Koonbees. Sidh Râj, in the disguise of a pilgrim from Muhârâshtra to the shrine of Somnâth, mingled with the villagers assembled in their town-hall at night time, and was fortunate enough to hear warm praises bestowed upon his good qualities, his attachment to learning, his kind treatment of his servants, and the vigour with which he protected his dominions. One only fault the worthy cultivators of Oonjâ had to find with their sovereign,—" It is " our misfortune that the king has no son to succeed him." The next morning the heads of the village presented themselves at the royal tent for the purpose of making their obeisance; but the king delaying his appearance, the Putels, notwithstanding the remonstrances of the officers of the court, seated themselves in a familiar manner upon the softest couches, not respecting even the cushion of royalty. Sidh Râj, however, was gifted with more bonhommie than a Rajpoot of rank usually possesses, or permits himself to evince, and the conversation of the evening before was not likely to have rendered him more than usually observant of punctilio. The head-men, therefore, were allowed to retain their position, notwithstanding the amazement of the chamberlains at so astounding a violation of decorum.

At another time a force of Bheels, " against whom no one could " fight," obstructed the king's return from Malwa, until he was relieved of their opposition by the minister Sâmtoo, who, bringing an army against them from Goozerat, opened a passage for his sovereign.

Our materials desert us, and we therefore here take leave of the great Hindoo sovereign of Goozerat with the valedictory stanzas of his chroniclers,—

" Long live the fame of Jesul Raja, chief among the warlike " sovereigns of the three Loks, who, destroying the name of king, overshadowed the world with one imperial umbrella!"

" Great were the palaces, great the reservoirs, great the temples, " great the resorts of pilgrims that Sidh Râj caused to be constructed. " No other has formed their equals.

" Ambitious of victory, he could not endure a rival greater by so much as a vowel, therefore that Dhărâ-nâth destroyed the Dhârâ-nâth.[1]

" O! Suruswutee, O! Ganges, abandon the pride of your adorn" ments. O! Rewâ, O! Yumoonâ, lay aside your swiftness and " your fruitless meanderings. The blood of enemies slain by the " sword of the illustrious Sidh Râj has formed a new river. She is " the maiden whom ocean now loves."

As to the personal appearance of Sidh Râj, Krishnâjee gives the following information,—" He was fair in person, spare, but well " formed, his arms as far as the wrists were dark." Of his character

[1] *Dhărâ-nâth* means lord of earth; *Dhârâ-nath*, lord of the city of Dhâr in Malwa.

Merootoong tells us that he was "the receptacle of all good qualities, "as great in kind actions as he was in war; the tree of desire to his "servants."

"His generous hand was spread to all;
"To friends a cloud of vernal rain;
"A lion on the battling plain."

The same author, however, accuses him of lustful excess, and Hindoo tradition records with execration his intrigues with women of the sacred Brahmin caste. His indifference upon religious subjects has been already noticed. He appears to have been good humoured, and fond of unbending in his private life; and stories are told of his disguised nocturnal ramblings, and of his incognito visits to the theatre, or to the domestic entertainment. The marked feature in his character was his ambition of fame, proved not only by the war-like achievements through which he strove to win it, but also by his love of the bard, and solicitude for the preservation of his line; or, if that were impossible, of its memory. "Of a son," says the Brahmin chronicler, "he was very desirous; very desirous of a great "poet; but his hopes were unfulfilled. He caused, however, to be "written the annals of his race." It was this same anxiety to escape oblivion that induced Sidh Râj to strew with so liberal a hand over Soreth and Goojur Râshtra the sumptuous edifices and reservoirs, whose ruins, still remaining, excite the wonder of the rustic and the admiration of the student of ancient history.[1]

Whatever the defects of his character may have been, it cannot be doubted that Sidh Râj is, on the whole, entitled to rank high among Hindoo monarchs as a brave, vigorous, and enterprising sovereign, and that he is rightly described by his chroniclers as "the ornament of Goojur-land, the light of the "Châlookya race." The extent of his kingdom may be fixed with probability in its general features, though not with certainty, or in detail. Goozerat proper, the territory to which he succeeded as the heir of Wun Râj, was held with a firm hand, and surrounded with a girdle of fortresses of no mean extent or power. Uchulgurh and Chundrâwutee, held by his Purmâr vassals, were the outworks of Unhilwârâ on the north, Modheyra and Junjoowârâ on the west, Châmpâner and Dubhoee on the east, with other strongholds, exhibited his banner, and contained his garrisons; but the fertile country which they embraced within their arms was but the lair of the victorious lion. We cannot suppose the

[1] See Lord Bacon's remark,—"Surely a man shall see the noblest works, and "foundations have proceeded, from childless men, which have sought to express "images of their minds, where those of their bodies have failed."

dominions which were held by Mool Râj or Bheem Dev I. to have been in any material point contracted during the sway of Jye Singh. His frontier must therefore be pushed forwards on the north, beyond Aboo, to the neighbourhood of Jhâlor; it must include Kutch. Soreth and Malwa, we have seen, owned his sway, and on the south his dominions extended deep into the Dekkan, where, as Merootoong relates, he excited the alarm of the King of Kollâpoor.[1] The bard Chund alluded to his wars against the monarchs of Canouj, when "he washed his blade in the Ganges;" to an alliance also between the princes of Mewar and Ujmeer, to check his aim at universal conquest. An inscription in the far-famed Cheetore speaks of him as "one whose fame was encased in the riches of victory, and whose "deeds were sounded over the curtain of the earth;" while the historian of those countries bears witness to the fact that his name and exploits are recorded in the poetic annals of every state of Rajpootana.

Sidh Râj reigned forty-nine years, from A.D. 1094 to 1143.

CHAPTER XI.

KOOMÂR PÂL.

SIDH RÂJ leaving no son, the throne passed to the line of Kshem Râj, who was the son of Bheem Dev, by Bukoolâ Devee, and half-brother to Raja Kurun Solunkhee. Treebhoowun Pâl, the son of Dev Prusâd, and grandson of Kshem Râj, left three sons and two daughters. The sons were Myhee Pâl, Keerttee Pâl, and Koomâr Pâl; the daughters, Premul and Dewul. Premul married Kâhn Dev, a general of Jye Singh's army, and her sister was espoused by the King of Kashmeer.

The learned in the science of Chiromancy, says Merootoong, had informed Sidh Râj that Koomâr Pâl was destined to be his successor. "As he was of low origin," however, Sidh Râj refused to acknowledge him in this capacity, and continually sought opportunity

[1] The Seelhâras, or Muhâ Munduleshwurs of Kollâpoor, where among the chief hereditary feudatories of the Solunkhees of Kuleeân. *Vide* Journal of the Royal Asiatic Society, vol. iv. pp. 4, 33; and Transactions of the Bombay Literary Society, vol. iii. p. 394.

to put him to death. Koomâr Pâl fled, and adopting the dress of an ascetic, wandered for several years in foreign countries. Returning to Unhilwârâ, he took up his residence there in the Jain convent of Shree Âdeenâth. At a time when Sidh Râj was celebrating the commemorative funeral ceremonies of his father Kurun, all the ascetics were brought together, in order that the king might exhibit his faith by washing their feet one by one. As he passed his hand over the foot of Koomâr Pâl, "which was as smooth as a lotus," Sidh Râj perceived clearly, by the upright lines and other Chiromantic marks, that "this is one who is destined to royalty." By the expression of the king's face, Koomâr Pâl perceived that he was recognised: he changed his dress, and fled immediately to his native village of Deythulee, the same which Kurun Raja had granted to his ancestor, Dev Prusâd. There he was concealed from the soldiers who were sent in pursuit of him, by a potter named Âling, who placed him in the furnace used in his trade. Koomâr Pâl, seizing an opportunity, escaped from thence, but his pursuers were close at his heels, and he would have been taken had he not again found shelter with a cultivator, who was employed in scaring the crows from the crop of grain standing in his field, and who hid him in a heap of thorny bushes collected for the purpose of fencing the field. The king's soldiers tracing the prince's footsteps to the spot, examined the field, probing even the heap of thorns in which he lay concealed with the point of a spear. Failing, however, to discover the object of their search, they here gave up the pursuit and returned home. Next day the cultivator took Koomâr Pâl out of his place of concealment, and the prince resumed his flight. As he sat under the shade of a tree to rest, after having proceeded some distance, he perceived a rat, which brought out from its hole, one by one, twenty pieces of silver. The animal having produced the whole of its store, began to replace it in the same manner in its depository. Koomâr Pâl then advanced and took what remained of the money, and thus miraculously provided, continued his journey. As he went on, he found a wâneeo's wife on her way, with her carriages and attendants, from her husband's to her father's house, who had halted by the wayside for refreshment. Koomâr Pâl having travelled for three days without food, and being oppressed with hunger, asked permission to join the domestics in their repast, which was courteously granted to him.

After travelling over much country, the prince at last arrived at Stumbh-Teerth or Cambay, and proceeded to the house of Oodâyun Mehtâ to ask for food. Hearing that the minister was at the Jain convent, Koomâr Pâl went thither and found Oodâyun in company with Hemâchârya. No sooner had the monk beheld the prince, than he pronounced him to be the destined king of the whole land. Koomâr Pâl, thinking only of his present poverty and danger, declared such a prediction to be incredible, but Hemâchârya renewed his assurances, and the prince vowed that if the prophecy were fulfilled he would become a follower of the Jain religion. Supplied with money and necessaries by Oodâyun Muntree, Koomâr Pâl proceeded to Malwa, and, visiting the temple of Kudungeshwur, was astonished at finding inscribed on a tablet there the following verse :—

"When there shall have been fulfilled one thousand, one hundred, and ninety-"nine years, then will arise Koomâr Raja, who shall resemble thee, O! "Vikrum."

While in Malwa, the prince received intelligence that Sidh Raj had attained another world. He determined on returning to Goozerat, but being again without the means of subsistence, he fell into many difficulties on the road, before he succeeded in reaching Unhilwârâ.

Having satisfied his hunger, with the alms supplied to him by the charity of a confectioner, Koomâr Pâl made his way to the house of his sister's husband, Kâhn Dev. Before his death Sidh Râj had called to him the ministers and officers of his court, of whom Kâhn Dev was one of the principal, and, causing them to lay their hands on his neck, compelled them to swear that they would never place Koomâr Pâl upon the throne. While, however, the ceremony was in progress the great monarch expired. Whether he had taken the oath or not, Kâhn Dev no sooner heard of Koomâr Pâl's arrival, than coming forth out of his palace, he received him with great respect, and, giving him precedence, conducted him within. The next morning, arming some of his attendents, he took Koomâr Pâl with him to the palace. To determine who should be the king's successor, Kâhn Dev placed on the cushion of the great Sidh Râj, first one prince and then another, probably Myhee Pâl and Keerttee Pâl, the brothers of Koomâr Pâl. The first was quickly rejected; the effeminacy of his dress exciting general disapprobation. The second prince being seated, was asked by the assembled nobles how he would govern the eighteen regions left by Jye Singh; but his reply,—"according to your counsel and instructions," sounded tame in the ears of chiefs accustomed to obey the vigorous voice of Sidh Râj. He was rejected, and Koomâr Pâl, seated on the throne, was called upon to answer the same enquiry. Starting to his feet, his eyes filled with martial fire, that prince half unsheathed his sword.

The royal hall rang with acclamations, and Kâhn Dev, with the other nobles of Goozerat, prostrating themselves before the throne of Koomâr Pâl, while the conch-shell and the bugle sounded, acknowledged him as the fit successor of the "victorious lion."

Koomâr Pâl ascended the throne in the fiftieth year of his age, in A.D. 1143, and reigned thirty-one years. His mature age, and the experience he had gained during his wanderings in foreign lands, produced a division between him and some of the old royal servants, who were thereupon dismissed from their employments. They combined together to revenge themselves by putting him to death, and had placed assassins at one of the city gates, which he was expected to enter during the night; but "owing to the good actions that he "had performed in former birth," the attempt was disclosed to him in sufficient time to allow of his defeating it, by choosing a different route from the one anticipated. Koomâr Pâl now caused the conspirators to be put to death. Soon after, Kâhn Dev, who had placed him on the throne, presuming upon his services and connection, as the husband of his sister, began to speak disrespectfully of the origin and former condition of Koomâr Pâl. The king remonstrating, received a haughty answer, and after a time, finding Kâhn Dev determined to continue disobedient, he caused him to be put to death. The example was a salutary one, and, from that day, all the chieftains feared to disobey the order of the king, for, "as it is wrong to touch "a lamp with the finger, under the idea that 'It was I who first set "it up; it will not burn me though I treat it with disrespect;' so is "it with a monarch."

Koomâr Pâl now conferred the office of principal minister upon Wâgbhut Dev, the son of his most ancient supporter Oodâyun Muntree; he recompensed also the potter, Âling, and others who had shielded him during his adversity. Wâhud, another son of Oodâyun's, however, who had been a principal favorite of Sidh Râj, refusing to obey Koomâr Pâl, fled to take service with the King of Nâgor, Âno, or as Meerootoong styles him, Ânâk, the grandson of Veesul Dev Chohân. By the persuasions of Wâhud, Âno was induced to attempt an invasion of Goozerat, and, with that view, approached the frontier with a large army, hoping to find many of the chieftains of the country his supporters. The Solunkhee sovereign assembled an army to oppose the enemy, and having, as he supposed, secured his own borders from any enterprise of the disaffected, or, in the language of the chronicler, "made the boundary land clear "of thorns," he engaged Âno. Battle was hardly joined, however, when the effects of Wâhud's intrigues were rendered apparent by the desertion of a large number of the Goozerat chieftains. Koomâr Pâl, seeing the whole of his army in confusion, ordered the driver of his elephant to single out the lord of Nâgor, who was rendered conspicuous by the royal umbrella, and to give him an opportunity of personally engaging his rival. The elephant driver accordingly strove to force his way through the army to where the Nâgor King was fighting; but the young lord, Wâhud, rushed between the two sovereigns, and was stepping from his own elephant on to the head of that which bore Koomâr Pâl, with the view of slaying the raja, when the driver, with his goad, forcing the elephant back, he fell in the midst, and was seized by the foot soldiers who surrounded the king. Koomâr Pâl then quickly advancing towards Âno, shouting defiance as he went, discharged an arrow from his bow, which struck the King of Nâgor in the face, and hurled him to the ground. The Goozerat troops pressed on, shouting "Victory!" and the rout of their enemies was soon completed.

The following is the account given by the author of Dwyâshrây, of the wars with which the reign of Koomâr Pâl opened:—

The raja of the country of a hundred thousand villages, whose name was Ânn, when he heard of the death of Jye Sing, though he had been the servant of that monarch, now thought the time was come for making himself known; the government of Goozerat being newly formed, and Koomâr Pâl being a feeble monarch, as he was willing to suppose. Ânn began to make friends of Wullâl, the King of Oojein, and of the rajas of the country on the west of Goozerat, holding out threats to them as well as promises. Koomâr Pâl's spies made known to him that Ânn Raja was advancing upon the western frontier of Goozerat, with an army, among whose chieftains were several leaders "skilled in foreign languages," and that he had been already joined by the Raja of Kunthâgâm (Kuntkote?) and by Châhud, a general of the Unhilwârâ army. The King of Oojein was well informed, they said, of the state of Goozerat, by traders who had been in the habit of passing to and fro between the countries; he had also concerted measures with Wullâl, the King of Malwa, who had prepared to attack Goozerat on the east, as soon as Ânn Raja should have made an advance. Koomâr Pâl was much enraged when he heard this news.

Koomâr Pâl was joined by several rajas, by Koolees also, very celebrated horsemen, and by forest tribes, who assembled from all sides. The people of Kutch, his tributaries, ranged themselves under his banners; with them came men of Sindh also. As the king advanced towards Aboo, he was then joined by mountaineers, dressed in the skins of deer. The Purmâr Raja of Aboo, Vikrum Singh by name, who led the men of Jâlundhur-land, (Jhâlor,) followed Koomâr Pâl, esteeming that raja as his lord. Ânn Raja hearing of Koomâr Pâl's arrival, contrary to the advice of his ministers, prepared to give battle, but before his arrangements were completed the music of war was heard, and the Goozerat army appeared emerging from beneath the shadow of the mountains, the sun streaming full upon the white umbrella that was borne above the king. The soldiers of Ânn Raja shot arrows at the army of Koomâr Pâl; the King of Nagor himself seized his bow; but, though led by canopied lords, the army of the north gave way before the men of Goozerat. Ânn Raja, in person, then rushed on, and was confronted by Koomâr Pâl. "As you were so brave a warrior," said the heir of Sidh Râj, "how is it that you bent the head before the victorious lion? That "act proved your wisdom truly. Now, if I conquer you not, I shall "tarnish the fame of Jye Singh." The two sovereigns fought; the armies, too, joined in close encounter. Âhud led the men of Goozerat; the Marwarees followed their Muntree Gowind Râj. At last an iron shaft struck down Ânn, he fell upon the earth. His chieftains then submitted to the behests of Koomâr Pâl.

The King of Goozerat having struck Ânn such a blow, remained for several days upon the field of battle. Ânn Raja sent horses and elephants as a present to Koomâr Pâl; he proposed to give him a daughter in marriage. The king complained that Ânn had committed an offence to which pardon might well be refused, in having slain wounded men as they lay on the field; he accepted, however, the proposals of the vanquished prince, and returned to Unhilpoor.

Soon afterwards the priest of Ânn Raja's family brought to the city of Wun Raj, the Princess Julhunâ, his master's daughter, who was solemnly married to Koomâr Pâl. These festivities were scarce completed when news was brought that Veejye and Krishn, the two chieftains (Sâmunts) who had been despatched by the king to oppose Wullâl, while he in person advanced against Âno Raja, had gone over to the King of Oojein, and that that monarch was already in the territory of Goozerat and advancing upon Unhilpoor. Koomâr Pâl prepared to win fame by conquering Wullâl, as Jye Singh had won it by subduing Yushowurm. He assembled his troops and went against the King of Malwa, who was defeated and struck from his elephant in the fight.

This notice of the chronicler is confirmed by an inscription in the temple of Tej Pâl upon Mount Aboo, which records that the Purmâr chief of Uchuleshwur and Chundrâwutee, by name Yushodhuwul, "Knowing that the Châlookya Koomâr Pâl Râj was come to make "war, fled immediately to Wullâl, the Lord of Malwa." From a second inscription upon a copper plate in the Jain library at Nadole, which bears date A.D. 1157, we learn that the great minister, Châhud Dev, was in that year the adviser of the king of kings, the illustrious Koomâr Pâl Dev, who then sat upon the throne of Shreemunt Unhil, and who is further described as "the ornament of the line of kings, "a great warrior, who by the strength of his arm conquered the "Sâkumbhuree Raja in the place of strife." There is some confusion in regard to the minister here alluded to. Meerootoong tells us that Châhud Dev was half-brother of Oodâyun Muntree. The author of Dwyâshrây says that Châhud joined Âno Raja; but Meerootoong only mentions that Wâhud, the son of Oodâyun, did so. This latter chieftain, we shall find, subsequently returned to his duty, and was employed by Koomâr Pâl, as it is evident that Châhud may have been before the year in which the inscription is dated, supposing him to have been in the first instance a rebel to his sovereign.

The inscription to which allusion has been made in the account of the reign of Sidh Râj, which is to be found in the temple, called Lakhun's Mundeer, at Cheetore, and bears date A. D. 1151,[1] thus speaks of Koomâr Pâl, the Solunkhee: "What was he like, who by "the strength of his invincible mind crushed all his foes; whose com-"mands the other sovereigns of the earth placed on their foreheads; "who compelled the lord of Sâkumbhuree to bow at his feet; who in "person carried his arms to Sewaluc, making the mountain lords bow "before him, even in the city of Salpoora?"

Sometime after these occurrences, Meerootoong informs us, the Solunkhee sovereign was seated in his court, giving audience, when some bards (Mâgudhs) were admitted, who sang the praises of Mulikâ Urjoon, a king of the Konkun, to whom they gave the title of "Father of Kings."[2] Koomâr Pâl was very much disconcerted at this occurrence, and set himself to discover a chieftain whom he might send to destroy this Mulikâ Urjoon, "who falsely prided himself as a "four-limbed sovereign." A warrior, named Âmbud, or Âmrâ Bhut, a son of Oodâyun Muntree's, undertook the task, and having obtained the command of an army, proceeded without halting to the Konkun. Âmbud passed with considerable difficulty a river called Kulâveenee, and encamped on the opposite bank, where he was

[1] In Tod's Western India, the date is given "S. 1207 (A.D. 1141)" by mistake.
[2] In regard to the Muhâ Munduleshwurs of Kollâpoor, see note at page 138.

attacked and quickly routed by Mulikâ Urjoon. The defeated general returned home and encamped near the capital, wearing black clothes, covered by a black umbrella, and dwelling in a black tent. Koomâr Pâl, perceiving this sombre display, enquired what force it was that was thus encamped. He was informed that it was Âmbud, the general, who, having been defeated in the Konkun, had thus returned. The king strove to console Âmbud in his humiliation, and, treating him with kindness and attention, despatched him with another army, reinforced by strong chieftains, to conquer Mulikâ Urjoon.

Âmbud, arriving at the river Kulâveenee a second time, constructed a bridge or causeway, by which he cautiously passed over his army, and thus gained the opportunity of becoming the assailant. The troops of Goozerat were successful in this second encounter, and Mulikâ Urjoon himself fell by the sword of Âmbud. His capital, also, was taken and plundered, and Âmbud, causing the authority of the Solunkhee king to be proclaimed in that country, returned to Unhilwârâ. In full assembly, he paid obeisance at the feet of his lord, Koomâr Pâl, presenting the head of Mulikâ Urjoon, the king of the Konkun, with gold, jewels, vessels of the precious metals, pearls, elephants, coined money, and other trophies. The king received him graciously, and conferred upon him the great provincial sovereign, or Munduleshwur, Mulikâ Urjoon's title of "Father of Kings."

The Âchârya Hemchunder fills for the future so conspicuous a place in the history of Koomâr Pâl—the king being, it is said, "attracted by his speech, as a wave, full of delight, is by the brilliancy of the moon"—that it may be, therefore, advisable to give in this place the account of his origin, which is furnished by the monk of Wudwân. His parents, whose names were Châchig and Pâheenee, belonged to the Modh Wâneeo caste, and resided at Dhundhooka "in Urddhâshtum-land," the southern border country of Soreth and Goozerat. The father professed the orthodox Hindoo faith, the mother was "as it were a Devee of the Jain religion." Their son received at his birth the name of Chung Dev. When he had attained the age of eight years, Devchunder Âchârya, travelling in that part of the country, came to Dundhooka. Châchig being at this time from home, his wife was persuaded by the Âchârya, who had been much struck by the appearance of Chung Dev, to entrust her son to his care, in order that he might receive the initiatory rite as a Jain ascetic. The Âchârya accordingly carried off the boy to his convent at Kurunâwutee. When Châchig returned from foreign parts, and heard what had happened to Chung Dev, he was much distressed, and vowed that he would eat no food until he had seen his son. Having ascertained the spiritual teacher's name and place of residence, he set off to Kurunâwutee. When he arrived there he went to Dev Chunder to demand his son. Chung Dev was at the house of Oodâyun Muntree, who took upon himself the task of reconciling Châchig to the step which his son wished to take, and as he succeeded therein, Chung Dev took the initiatory vow, and assumed the name of Hemchunder. He soon became famous, and having at an early age made himself acquainted with all the learning of the Hindoos, as well as of the Jains, he received from the Gooroo the title of Sooree.

Hemchunder was the author of the Ubheedhân Chintâmunee, the Hymns to Jin Dev (a commentary on which bears date A.D. 1292), "a pure Yog Shâstra, containing the story of the sixty-three Jain "heroes (Shulâkâ pooroosh), with the praise of the twenty passion-"less ones (vitrâg)," the Dwyâshrây, and other works.

While Koomâr Pâl was with his army in Malwa, the monk Hemchunder came to him to seek his protection on account of an outrage which had been committed by the Shaivite ascetics, on the occasion of the rejoicings[1] at his mother's funeral. "One's own royalty," was the reflection of Hemâchârya, "or the subjection of the king to one's "self, these are the only roads towards effecting an object." The Âchârya was introduced to the king by Oodâyun Muntree; and Koomâr Pâl, recollecting the predictions and promises of Cambay, received him with great favor, and admitted him to a familiar intercourse. The Brahmins about the king were alarmed at the influence Hemchunder was gaining over him, and brought several charges against him, of which the most serious appears to have been, that he refused to worship the Sun. Hemchunder, who was of a politic character, and, for a long time at least, disposed to seek toleration for his own religion, rather than to attack that of his opponents, made an answer which satisfied the king of his faith in the great deity of the Kshutrees :—"This splendid mansion of light I ever retain in my "heart; at the time of whose setting I abandon food."[2] In accordance with the same line of policy, he strengthened his recommendations by quoting the Hindoo as well as the Jain scriptures in their support, and when on one occasion Koomâr Pâl consulted him as to the selection of some object on which he should expend money as a religious action, the Âchârya advised him to restore the temple of

[1] The devotee, whether male or female, is buried with expressions not of sorrow but of joy. See account of funerals in Conclusion.

[2] See note, p. 9, on the sect called Souras.

Someshwur at Dev Puttun, which was endangered "by the strength of "the ocean waves."

This restoration is mentioned by the author of Dwyâshrây, and is also commemorated in an inscription, found by the annalist of Rajpootana, in the temple of Bhudra Kâlee, at Dev Puttun, but which originally belonged to the shrine of Someshwur. It is dated Wullubhee Sumwut 850 (which is equivalent to Vikrum Sumwut 1225, or A.D. 1169), and contains the following narrative:—

"Bhow Vreehusputee, a Brahmin of Canouj, left Benares on pil-"grimage; he reached Uwuntee and Dhârânugger, then ruled by Jye "Singh Dev. The Purmâr prince and all his family elected him their "gooroo, and the prince called him brother.

"Sidh Râj Jye Singh was universal lord when he went to heaven; "Koomâr Pâl succeeded to his throne; Bhow Vreehusputee became "the chief of his advisers. Koomâr Pâl was the tree of desire of "the three worlds. He gave his seal, his wealth, and all, under the "command of Vreehusputee; and said, 'Go and repair the fallen "'temples of Dev Puttun.' Bhow Vreehusputee made them re-"semble Kyelâs; he invited the lord of the world to see his work. "When he saw, he dwelt on the praise of the gooroo, as he said, "'My heart is rejoiced; to you and your sons I give the chief place "'in my kingdom.'"

When the foundations of the temple of Someshwur had been laid, the council to whom the direction of the work had been assigned sent "good-news letters" to Koomâr Pâl. The king, showing the letters to Hemchunder Sooree, enquired how it might be brought about that no obstacle should occur to the completion of the work. The Sooree advised the king, that for this purpose he should take a vow to abstain either from connection with women or from the use of animal food, until the flag should be raised on the summit of the temple. The king assenting, placed water on the image of Muhâ Dev, and vowed that he would eat no animal food. Two years afterwards, the spire having been completed, Koomâr Pâl prepared to set the finial upon the temple, and to hoist the banner: he then asked the Âchârya to release him from his vow. Hemchunder said, "Behold! "in the virtue of this abstinence you are fit to appear before Muhâ "Dev. When your pilgrimage thither shall have been accomplished, "it will be time to throw off that vow." The king was advised by the Brahmins to put Hemchunder to the test, by proposing that he should accompany the royal cortège in its pilgrimage to the temple of the lord of the moon, whose divinity, it was asserted, the Sooree did not acknowledge. Koomâr Pâl acted upon this advice; when Hemchunder, immediately assenting, exclaimed, "What need of pressing "the hungry man to partake of food; pilgrimage is the life of the "ascetic; what need is there of an order from the king!" It was arranged that the monk should travel slowly and on foot, visiting as he went the holy places of Shutroonjye and Girnâr, and that he should join Koomâr Pâl at Dev Puttun. The king making a progress, attended by the whole of his retinue, arrived within sight of the city of Someshwur. Shree Vreehusputee, who was charged with the superintendence of the work, had advanced to this point to escort the monarch to the place prepared for his reception. Hemchunder also joined the cortège: and Koomâr Pâl, with great joy, and amidst the pomp and music of his regal state, entering the city, ascended the steps of the temple of Someshwur, and prostrated himself before the god. Hemchunder also, supported by Vreehusputee, stood at the threshold of the temple, and exclaimed:—"In the splendour of this "shrine, Muhâ Dev, who dwells in Kyelâs, is surely present." Then entering, and worshipping the sacred *ling* in the prescribed forms, he said, "Thou existest, whatever be thy place, whatever be thy time, "whatever be thy name, of whatsoever nature thou art. Thou art he "in whom is no guilty act, no guiltiness consequent upon the act,— "one only God! Praise be to thee! He who has destroyed the "affections, which are the seeds that produce the bud of existence, be "he Brumhâ, be he Vishnoo, be he Shiva, to him be praise!" As he uttered these prayers, the king, with all his courtiers, stood gazing upon him in astonishment. Then Shree Hemâchârya fell flat on the ground, adoring Shiva in the "staff-prostration." The king, under Vreehusputee's direction, worshipped with great faith in the colonnades of the temple, presenting his weight in gold and a gift of elephants, and waving camphor in the *ârâtreek.*[1] The royal suite were then dismissed, and Koomâr Pâl and Hemâchârya entered alone the adytum of the temple, closing the door behind them.

Koomâr Pâl addressed Hemâchârya. "Among so many religions, "I am anxiously desirous to establish one religion which may be "assented to with certainty. There is no Dev like Someshwur; there "is no king like myself; there is no ascetic like you. My wealth of "fortune has thus brought the whole three together. Do you, there-"fore, in the presence of this great Dev, point out to me, with true "speech, the divinity who is the giver of liberation." Hemâchârya replied, "We have no need now of the matters that are contained in "the Poorâns. I will bring the illustrious Someshwur in corporeal

[1] *Vide* account of the ceremonial of Hindoo worship in the Conclusion.

"presence hither, that you may hear the truth from his own mouth." He continued: "Without doubt, in this place the Dev is concealed. "We two, devoting ourselves immoveably to worship in the manner "which the spiritual preceptor has pointed out, may cause the Dev to "present himself. I will profoundly meditate; do you, from this "wood of aloes, raise incense, ceasing not until the three-eyed god, "appearing, restrains you." They laboured both of them thus, the smoke of the incense filling the adytum, darkening the light of the lamps which were arranged around the door and the niches on the three sides. Suddenly a light beamed forth, brilliant as the light of the sun. The king started up, dazzled by this effulgence; he shaded his eyes with his hands, and strove to recover the power of seeing. At that moment he beheld, occupying the basin in which the sacred symbol was set, the form of an ascetic, whose hair was matted on his head, of a beauty incomparable, bright as fine gold, the sight of whom mortal weakness could not endure. The king ascertained, by the touch of his hand, that this was, without doubt, the Dev, corporeally present. Prostrating himself, with great devotion, he thus addressed the god: "Lord of the world! thus worshipping you, my "eyes have attained their object; in kindness, therefore, giving some "command, cause my ears also to fulfil their desire." The face of the Dev shone as the morning after the night of bewilderment; from his mouth issued the following divine words:—"O! king, this monk "is an incarnation of all the gods; he is without deceit; to him it "is given to behold the Divinity as a pearl in his hand; he is acquainted with the past, the present, and the future. The path "which he shall show you, that understand to be, without doubt, the "road to liberation." Thus speaking, the Dev became invisible. While the king lamented his disappearance, the monk, Hemchunder, exhaled his breath, and relaxed his meditative position. Koomâr Pâl then, remembering what the Isht Dev had told him, abandoning the pride of royalty, bending his head before the spiritual teacher, praising him, besought him to tell what was fit to be done. In that same place Hemâchârya administered to him a vow to abstain from animal food and fermented liquor to the end of his life.

The Brahmin, Vreehusputee, as both chroniclers and inscription relate, was left in charge of the shrine of Someshwur; but, in after days, when the influence of Hemâchârya had become fully established, he was deprived for a time of his situation, for "dispraising the Jain religion;" and only restored thereto on his making the most humble submission to the Âchârya, and procuring his intercession with Koomâr Pâl.

The king and the monk returned to Unhilpoor. There Hemâchârya instructed Koomâr Pâl in the purity which proceeded from the mouth of Jin Dev, and caused him to become great among the followers of Urhunt. Under the Âchârya's directions, the king forbad the destruction of life for a period of fourteen years in the eighteen countries of Goozerat, in which his order was obeyed. The Brahmins who offered living sacrifices in their rites, says the author of Dwyâshrây, were forbidden to continue the practice, and thus began to present offerings of grain. The king's order was obeyed in Pullee land also, and the ascetics who used deer-skins for their covering found it impossible to procure any. The people of Punchâl, also, who had been great destroyers of life, being subjects of Koomâr Pâl, were compelled to refrain. The trade of those who sold flesh was put a stop to, and three years' income allowed to them in compensation. The people of the countries about Benares, however, continued to sacrifice life.

One day it was reported to Koomâr Pâl, that the Khus Raja of Kedâr, though he plundered the pilgrims by his exactions, had nevertheless allowed the temple of Kedâr's lord, Muhâ Dev, to fall into disrepair, so that it was becoming a ruin. The king, blaming the Khus Raja, caused his own minister to repair the temple. At another time Muhâ Dev, appearing to the king in a dream, informed him that he was pleased with his service, and had resolved to reside at Unhilpoor. The king thereupon built, in that city, the temple of Koomâr Pâl's lord, Muhâ Dev. He erected also at Unhilpoor a temple of Pârusnâth, named the Koomâr Veehâr, and placed therein images. At Dev Puttun he built another temple of the Jain religion, so splendid as to attract thither crowds of pilgrims.

Koomâr Pâl now assented to the twelve vows of the Jain religion. At the time of taking the third vow, the purport of which was that he would receive nothing which was not acquired by exertions of his own, the Âchârya instructed him that it was a great sin to receive into the royal treasury the property of those who died without male heirs. The king, abandoning that source of revenue, caused his people to proclaim that he had, by that act, rendered himself greater than Rughoo, Nuhoosh, or Bhurut—the kings of the golden age.[1]

[1] "It is your wish," says Aureng-Zebe to his father, in a letter recorded by Bernier, "that I should adhere rigidly to the old custom, and declare myself heir "to every person who dies in my service. We have been accustomed, as soon as "an omrah, or rich merchant, has ceased to breathe—nay, sometimes before the "vital spark has fled—to place seals on his coffers, to imprison and beat the ser- "vants or officers of his household, until they made a full disclosure of the whole

After these occurrences, Koomâr Pâl having collected an army at Wudwân for the purpose of chastising a chief of Soreth, whose name was Sumurshee, or Sâoosur, gave the command of it to Oodâyun Muntree. That minister, however, sustained a defeat, and was himself mortally wounded. He left to his sons, Wâg But, Wâhud, and Âmrâ Bhut, the completion of vows which he had made to erect temples at Broach and Shutroonjye. The latter task was accomplished by Wâhud, in A.D. 1155, who built near Shutroonjye the town called after himself—Wâhudpoor. Âmrâ Bhut took upon himself the construction of the temple at Broach, in which he was ultimately successful, though for a time obstructed by a sudden overflow of the river Nerbudda, which flows beneath the walls of that city. About the same time, the king himself constructed a new temple on the site of the convent, where he had been received by Oodâyun Mehta and Hemâchârya, at Cambay.

The last warlike expedition of the reign of Koomâr Pâl appears to have been one directed against the country of the hundred thousand towns. Oodâyun's son Wâhud, who had before this time, as we have seen, returned to his allegiance, was selected, on account of his knowledge of the country, to command the army. He took and destroyed a fort called Bâburânugger, and proclaimed the supremacy of Koomâr Pâl in that country. On his return he received the thanks of his sovereign, who, however, blamed him for the profuse expenditure which had accompanied his expedition. One of the inscriptions on the pillar at Delhi, called the Lât of Feeroz Shah, which is dated A.D. 1146, mentions the name of the sovereign who reigned at that date in Sâkumbhuree to have been Vigraha Râj. Another name, that of Veesul Dev, is also found on this monument; and the translators are in doubt as to whether Vigraha Râj and Veesul Dev are the names of the same person or of different princes, a point which they pronounce it "impossible to determine from the tenor of the "inscription, without further information."[1] None of the names of the successors of Veesul Dev, the Chohân, as they are given by Chund, the Bhârot, can be certainly identified with the names found upon the monument. Âno, the grandson of Veesul Dev, we have seen opposed to Koomâr Pâl, and the prince here alluded to must be

"property, even of the most inconsiderable jewel. This practice is advantageous, "no doubt; but can we deny its injustice and cruelty; and should we not be "rightly served if every omrah acted as Neiknam Khan; and if, like the Hindoo "merchant's widow, every woman concealed her wealth?" These two stories are given in another place by Bernier.

[1] *Vide* As. Res. vii., p. 180.

either his son Jesingh Dev, or his grandson Âno, or Ânund Dev, both which names, as well as the name Vigraha Râj, express a meaning, and may be merely epithets.[1] There is an anecdote told in the Prubundh Chintâmunee which is curious for the light it throws upon the disputed point, already referred to, in regard to the interpretation of the inscription on the Lât of Feeroz Shah. At another time, says the chronicler, an ambassador from the king of the country of one hundred thousand towns came to the court of Koomâr Pâl. That king enquired after the prosperity of the King of Sâmbhur. "His "name is Vishwul (holder of the universe)," said the ambassador, "what doubt is there of his being always prosperous!" Kupurddee Muntree, a poet of great learning, and a favorite of Koomâr Pâl's, at this time stood beside that monarch. He said,—"The roots "'*shul*' and '*shwul*' mean '*quickly going*.' Thus he is Vishwul, who "flies away quickly like a bird (*Vi*)." The minister, after this, returning home, made known the disrespect with which his master's title had been received; whereupon that raja, consulting the learned, assumed the name of Vigraha Raja. Next year the same minister making his appearance on behalf of Vigraha Raja, in the presence of Koomâr Pâl, Kupurddee explained that name to mean "noseless "Shiva and Brumh" (*vi* without, *gro* nose, *hur* Shiv, *aj* Brumh). Afterwards that king, afraid of Kupurddee's making a jest of his name, assumed the title of Kuvee Bândhuv (poet's brother).

Koomâr Pâl, having on a subsequent occasion encamped near a temple outside the walls of Unhilwârâ, with the view of leading a caravan to perform pilgrimage at Shutroonjye, was alarmed by the intelligence that Kurun Raja of Dâhul land was advancing against him. The king took counsel with Wâg Bhut and Hemâchârya, the latter of whom pledged himself that good news would shortly arrive. Soon afterwards further messengers brought intelligence that Kurun Raja, while travelling at night on his elephant, having fallen asleep, had been caught (Absalom-like) by the branch of a sacred fig-tree, under which the animal had passed too hastily, and that he had thus been strangled. Koomâr Pâl, relieved of his fears of invasion, was then enabled to proceed with his pilgrimage. He arrived at Dhundhooka, and erected there a temple, called the "cradle-Veehâr," over the place of Hemâchârya's birth. Thence he proceeded to Shutroonjye, where he expended a large sum of money, under the direction

[1] Jesingh or Jyesingh means "victorious lion." Ânund means "joy." Vigraha, "war."

of Shree Wâg Bhut, in forming a new road of approach to the sacred mountain.

At the court of Unhilwârâ, at this time, was Ânâk, or Urnorâj, a scion of the valiant race of the Solunkhees, and son of the sister of Koomâr Pâl's mother, who, in recompense of the services rendered by him to his sovereign, received a chieftainship (Sâmuntpud), and with it the town of Vyâghrapullee, or Wâghel (the tiger's city), at which place his descendants remained for many years. One day the king lay on his couch in an upper room of the palace, at the door of which the Sâmunt, Ânâk, kept guard, when he perceived that some one entered the apartment. He called, "Who is there?" Ânâk, stopping the intruder, whom he discovered to be a servant of his own, took him outside to enquire his message. The servant claimed largesse for the news that a son had been born to his master. Ânâk, dismissing him, returned to his post, "his lotus face blooming with "the brilliancy of the sun of that good intelligence." The king enquired what had happened. Ânâk said, "Sire! a son has been born to you." On his saying so, the king, after consideration, spoke as follows,— "As the keepers of the gates did not stop the servant who came to "announce this birth, I am satisfied that the child will be a king in "Goozerat of great virtue; but since the messenger descended from "this place when he told you of a son's having been born, he will rule "in some other city, not in this one, and in a mansion (or 'in "Dhuwul-gruh')." The son whose birth was attended by these circumstances was named Luwun Prusâd, and his descendants subsequently appear in the history of Goozerat as the Wâghela dynasty.

Koomâr Pâl Raja having now completed the thirtieth year of his reign, the curse which the great Sutee, the mother of Lâkho Râj, king of Kutch, had pronounced against the race of Mool Râj, began to work, and the king found himself afflicted with the pains of leprosy. At the same time Hemchunder, who had attained the age of eighty-four years, knowing that his end approached, performed the "last "worship," and commenced a total abstinence from food, that he might anticipate the mandate of Yuma. The king expressing deep affliction on this account, Hemchunder said, "You have yourself but six "months more of life allotted to you; you have no son; do you too, "therefore, perform the works that remain to be performed." Thus, instructing his royal pupil, Hemchunder died. The king, with a mind bowed down by grief, performed the funeral rites of the great Âchârya. With the ashes of the pile, knowing them to be of incomparable purity, Koomâr Pâl and his chieftains made marks upon their foreheads. For many days the lamentation continued; and the king, abandoning all care for mundane affairs, was engrossed thenceforth in deep and devout meditation, until at length, his life escaping by a door of the body, he passed to Paradise.

Such is the account given by the monk of Wudwân, but oral tradition, whether of the Brahmins or of the Jains, delights in assigning more romantic circumstances to the death of the great Hemchunder.

Koomâr Pâl Raja, says the tradition of the Brahminical faith, had wedded a Seesodunee Rânee, a daughter of the house of Mewâr. At the time that the sword went for her the Seesodunee heard that the raja had a vow that his wives should receive initiation into the Jain religion, at Hemâchârya's convent, before entering the palace. The Rânee, therefore, refused to go to Puttun, until satisfied that she would not be called upon to go to the Âchârya's convent. Upon this Koomâr Pâl's household bard, Jye Dev by name, became security to the queen, who then consented to go to Unhilpoor. Several days after her arrival, Hemâchârya said to the raja, "The Seesodunee Rânee "has never come to visit me." Koomâr Pâl told her that she must go; but she refused. The Rânee fell ill, and the bard's wives went to see her. Hearing her story, they disguised her as one of themselves, and brought her privately home to their house. At night the bards dug a hole in the wall of the city, and took the Rânee out by it to carry her home. When Koomâr Pâl Raja became aware of what had happened, he mounted and set off in pursuit with two thousand horse. At the distance of fifteen miles from the fort of Eedur he came up with the fugitives. The bard said to the Rânee, "If you can "but enter Eedur, you are safe. I have two hundred horse with me; "as long as a man of us remains alive no one shall lay hand on you." So saying, he turned upon his pursuers; but the Rânee's courage failed her, and she slew herself in her carriage. The fight going on, and the pursuers forcing their way to the carriage, the maids cried out, "Why struggle any more, the Rânee is dead?" Koomâr Pâl and the force that had accompanied him then returned home.

The bard, Jye Dev, felt that he had lost his character, and determined to die. He retired to Sidhpoor, and sent from thence letters sprinkled with red water to all his caste, by which he told them, "The "honor of our caste has been taken away; so let those who are ready "to burn themselves with me prepare." A heap of sugar-canes was made, and those who intended to burn themselves with their wives took two canes from the heap; those who would burn alone took one each. They prepared funeral piles, both "cheetâs" and "jumors."[1]

[1] "Cheetâ" is a pile for one corpse; "jumor," for more than one.

The first jumor was on the banks of the Suruswutee, at Sidhpoor; the next was an arrows flight nearer to Puttun; the last jumor was near the entrance to that city. Upon each jumor sixteen Bhâts with their wives perished. A sister's son of Jye Dev's was at Kanouj. A letter had been sent to him, but his mother, having no other son, kept it from him. However, the bard's family priest having laden bullocks with the ashes of the jumors, set out for the purpose of casting them into the Ganges. Jye Dev's nephew, who was an officer of the Raja of Kanouj, demanded transit duty from the priest, supposing that he carried merchandise. The priest explained what his load was, and, on the bard's making enquiries, related to him all that had happened. The bard, collecting his family, brought them to Puttun; and he and they perished upon a number of jumors. One of the men's wives had been very lately delivered of a son—she gave the child to the priest and burned herself with her husband; and there are to this day, living in the Puttun district, bards who trace their descent from that child.

It was in consequence of hearing this story that Shunkur Âchârya came to Unhilpoor Puttun, where there had been, before this, much hatred between the Brahmins and the Jain monks. The latter were, by this time, a hundred thousand in number. One day, as Koomâr Pâl Raja was passing along the market in a litter, he met a disciple of Hemâchârya's, and said to him, "Mighty sovereign! what day of "the month is this?" The day was, in fact, the last day of the dark half of the month, but the monk said, by mistake, that it was the last day of the moon-light half. Some Brahmins who overheard what had passed laughed, and ridiculing the monk, said, "What does "this shaven fellow know—to-day is the last day of the dark half of "the month." Koomâr Pâl hearing this, when he reached home, sent for Hemâchârya and the chief of the Brahmins. Meanwhile Hemâchârya's disciple went home to his convent, and was very much ashamed, and very sorrowful. The Âchârya asked what had happened, and, when he was informed, told the monk not to be concerned about the matter. By this time the raja's messenger had arrived, and Hemâchârya accompanied him back to the palace. Koomâr Pâl asked what the day of the month was. The Brahmin answered that it was the thirtieth; but Hemchunder declared it was the fifteenth.[1] The Brahmins said, "Let the evening decide. If it "be the fifteenth we shall see the full moon, and then all we Brahmins

[1] It should be observed on this story that it is sometimes very difficult, in consequence of the extra months and extra days of the month, to know what the day of the Hindoo month really is.

" will banish ourselves from this kingdom; but if the moon fail to " rise, then let the Jain monks be expelled." Hemâchârya agreed to this proposal and returned home. He had a familiar Devee whom he called to his assistance, and by her contrivance an illusion was produced so that all thought the moon really had risen in the east. It was now pronounced that the Brahmins had been defeated, and that they must leave the kingdom.

At this conjuncture Shunkur Swâmee,[1] who had been attracted to Unhilpoor by the matter of the bards, made his appearance at Sidhpoor; and the Brahmins, knowing that they would have to leave the kingdom next morning, sent for him during the night, and brought him to Puttun. In the morning, Koomâr Pâl Raja called for the Brahmins, and commanded them to leave the kingdom. Shunkur Swâmee stepped forward, and said, " What need of expelling any " from the kingdom; at nine o'clock, the ocean, quitting its boun- " daries, will swallow up the whole country." The raja upon this, sending for Hemâchârya, asked him whether the deluge predicted by the recluse would happen. Hemâchârya denied that it would, and asserted the Jain doctrine, that the world never had been created and never would be destroyed. Shunkur Swâmee said, " Set a water- " clock, and let us see what will happen." The three seated themselves beside the clock. When nine o'clock came, they ascended into an upper story of the palace, and looking out at the western window, saw the sea waves rapidly advancing. On and on came the billows, until they had submerged the habitations of the city. The king and the two Âchâryas went up higher and higher, but the water still continued to rise upon them. At last they reached the seventh and uppermost story, and, looking down, found that the whole city, the highest trees and tallest spires, were under water, and that nothing was visible on all sides but surging waves. Koomâr Pâl, in great terror, turned to Shunkur Swâmee, and asked him if there were no means of escape. He said, " A boat will come from the west, which " will pass close to this window. Whoever jumps quickly into it will " escape." The three girded their loins, and prepared to get quickly into the boat. Soon a boat appeared in the distance; it drew nearer and nearer. Then Shunkur Swâmee seized the king by the hand, saying, that they should assist each other into the boat. It approached the window, and the king attempted to jump in, but the Swâmee dragged him back. Hemâchârya jumped from the window. The ocean and the boat, however, were alike illusions, and he fell on

[1] Not, as the narrator says, the first Shunkur Âchârya, but a successor to his name and authority.

the pavement below, and was crushed to death. A massacre of the monk's followers ensued, and Koomâr Pâl became a disciple of Shunkur Swâmee.

The Brahmin Âchârya occupies a distinguished place also in the Jain tradition, which we now proceed to give, and which was procured from no less an authority than the Shree Pooj, or patriarch, of the Pooneemeeo branch of that sect at Puttun, named Oomed Chundjee, or Oomed Prubh Sooree.

A Dundeeo Jogee,[1] says the Sooree, came from the Karnatic to attempt to conquer Hemâchârya by a display of his learning. He lived some time in this city (Unhilwârâ Puttun), and tried many ways of effecting his object, but all without success. Hemâchârya had two principal disciples, Râmchund and Bâlchund; the latter of whom he liked little. Raja Koomâr Pâl was at this time employed in erecting a temple of Pârusnâth under Hemâchârya's directions. Bâlchund conceived the design of throwing obstacles in the way of the completion of this edifice. Hemâchârya had fixed the auspicious hour for enthroning the image of Pârusnâth, and employed Bâlchund to give notice of its arrival. He treacherously pointed out a wrong time, and the result was, that the temple caught fire, and was almost entirely destroyed. Hemâchârya, when he heard of this calamity, being now a very old man, was much shaken in his intellect. Koomâr Pâl came to him, and requested his advice as to rebuilding the temple. The spiritual teacher said, "Why rebuild now? within six months "the periods of life allotted to you and to me will have come to an "end." The raja was astonished, and laid aside his design.

Soon after, Râmchund being absent from some cause, Hemâchârya sent Bâlchund to a Shrâwuk's house to get him some food. As Bâlchund returned with his food, he met the Dundeeo Jogee, who asked him why he looked so sorrowful, and said that he knew his master was not kind to him, but that if Bâlchund liked, he would give him an enthralling charm. He accordingly stirred with his finger the milk that Bâlchund carried, and thus conveyed into it poison which he had concealed under the nail. The disciple returning, presented the milk to Hemâchârya, who drank it, and died. The temple never was finished, and after Hemâchârya's death, the Dundeeo began to do injury to religion.

[1] This is a disrespectful way of indicating a Brahmin ascetic (in fact, Shunkur Swâmee) as "a Jogee with a staff."

CHAPTER XII.

UJYE PÂL—BÂL MOOL RÂJ—BHEEM DEV II.

In the year S. 1230 (A.D. 1174), says Merootoong Âchârya, Ujye Dev mounted the throne. Krishnâjee carries us one step further: he says,—

> " On Sidh Râj's seat Koomâr Pâl
> " Sat for thirty-one years.
> " To him again no son was born,
> " His brother's son became the lord.
> " His name was Ujye Pâl,
> " For three years he held the throne."

The author of Dwyâshrây completes the chain by informing us that Ujye Pâl or Ujye Dev was the son of Myhee Pâl, the brother of the deceased monarch.

The successor of Koomâr Pâl commenced his reign by waging furious war upon the religious edifices constructed by the Jain-converted monarch. The chroniclers, who were of that creed, represent Ujye Dev as an insane and parricidal atheist, but even tradition has handed down no such complaint upon the part of the followers of the orthodox religion. It may therefore be suspected that the rage of the new sovereign was connected, in some degree, with a reaction against the too puritanical authorities of the faith of the Teerthunkers. Ujye Pâl himself, however, it must be admitted, displayed a fierce, ungovernable, and vindictive character. One of his first acts was that of inducing the Muntree Kupurddee, the favorite of Koomâr Pâl, to accept the office of his premier or Prudhân; but his object in so doing was, probably, that of securing the gratification of his hatred, for the Muntree had hardly assumed the duties of his office, when an accusation of attempting to make himself equal to the king was brought against him, and he was put to death by immersion in a vessel of boiling oil. Râmchunder, another Jain leader, and "the "author of an hundred compositions," was the next victim; he was submitted to the torture, and, to escape from his sufferings, bit off his tongue, and died.

After this, says Merootoong, the chieftains, unable to endure the greatness of Âmrâ Bhut, "the father of kings," found an opportunity for carrying him to pay obeisance to the new sovereign. In his case too it appears to have been the profession of the Jain religion which drew down the anger of Ujye Dev. He boldly announced, "I re-"spect Vitrâg, he who is devoid of passion, as a Dev; Hemchunder, "the great sage, as a spiritual adviser; Koomâr Pâl, as a king." Ujye Dev furiously denounced him as a traitor. Âmrâ Bhut, however, a soldier of reputation, was not to become the prey of the tyrant without a struggle. Having worshipped the image of Jineshwur, he armed his followers, and rushing forth from his house, attacked the royal palace, and swept away the external defences of it, as a storm sweeps away a heap of chaff. "As he washed away, in the pilgrimage "of the edge of the sword, the sin of associating with that wicked "man, the Upsuras, who had come to behold his wondrous deeds, "exclaiming, 'He is mine! he is mine!' the warlike son of Oodâyun "passed to Dev Lok." The people lamented his fall, mourning him and saying, "Other warriors may arise, but the son of Oodâyun "having gone to Paradise, learned men have ceased to exist on the "earth."

The career of Ujye Dev was, however, as short as it was turbulent and blood-stained. "In three years, three months, three half months, "or three days, the reward of great virtue, or of great vice, is obtained "even in this world:"—so say the Poorâns. And so it happened, that after he had reigned three years, a "doorkeeper," named Wyejul Dev, plunged his dagger into the heart of Ujye Pâl. "The worms "devoured the sinner who had broken down religious buildings. "Shuddering at the near approach of hell, he vanished from sight."

Ujye Pâl was succeeded by Mool Râj II., or Bâl[1] Mool Râj, who ascended the throne in A.D. 1177, and reigned two years. The little which is recorded of him by Merootoong may be given entire,—"His mother, named Nyekee Devee, the daughter of Purmurdee "Raja, taking in her lap the child king, maintained a struggle at a "hill, named Gâdurârgurh. By the aid of rain, called down out of "its season by her virtue, she defeated the barbarian raja."

Mool Râj II. was the son of Ujye Pâl. "After whom (Koomâr "Pâl), says an inscription[2] in the temple of Uchuleshwur upon Mount "Aboo, Ujye Pâl reigned, whose son was Mool Raja: his younger "brother,[3] the illustrious Bheem, supports the burden of the earth."

[1] Bâl, means "child."

[2] *Vide* As. Res. xvi., p. 288.

[3] Mr. Wilson in his translation of the inscription has a note here to this effect,—"Such is the usual meaning of the original term, *Anujanmâ*; as it, however, implies "merely 'born after,' it may possibly signify son, a sense which there are some "reasons for preferring." Bheem Dev II. seems to have been in the vigour of

The barbarian to whom the Monk of Wudwân alludes, was the Mohummedan, who, after a pause of a century and a half since the time of Mahmood of Ghuznee, again appeared upon the territories of Unhilwârâ. In the year A.D. 1178, as Ferishta records, Mohammed Shahâboodeen Ghoree marched from Ghuznee to Oochâ and Mooltan, and from thence continued his route through the sandy desert to Goozerat. "The Prince Bheem Dev (a lineal descendant from "Brahm Dev of Goozerat, who opposed Mahmood Ghuzneevy), "advanced with an army to resist the Mohummedans, and defeated "them with great slaughter. They suffered many hardships in their "retreat before they reached Ghuznee." The "illustrious Bheem" had not yet assumed the sovereignty, but acted as the loyal, as well as gallant, lieutenant of his sister-in-law and her royal child.

Ujye Pâl's younger brother, Bheem Dev II., called also "Bholo," the arrogant, or insane, ascended the throne in A.D. 1179, and reigned thirty-six years. Merootoongy mentions that during his reign Shree Sohud Dev, the King of Malwa, advanced to the frontier of Goozerat, with the view of laying the country waste, but that he retired on receiving the following threatening message from Bheem,—"The "Raja Mârtund, who gives splendour to the lineage of the sun, is "brilliant only in the east; when the same sun approaches the west "his splendour finds extinction." Afterwards, says the Jain chronicler, Sohud's son, Urjoon Dev, laid Goozerat waste. These notices are fully confirmed by an inscription of Urjoon Raja of Malwa,[1] which is dated A.D. 1210, and records that Soobhutwurm (or Sohud), the father of that prince, "exercised the thundering rage of his angered "prowess on the cities of Goozerat;" and that Urjoon Raja himself, while yet a minor, "put Jye Singh Raja" (no doubt an allusion to the Sovereign of Unhilwârâ, the successor of the conqueror of Malwa) "to flight even in child's play." Another inscription, which has already been alluded to, contains a grant by Bheem Dev II., the successor of Mool Râj II., dated A.D. 1210, and describes that sovereign as "a second Sidh Râj Dev, an incarnation of Nârâyun."[2]

Though the Goozeratee chroniclers contain little information regarding the reign of Bheem Dev II., the blank is fortunately supplied by the Mohummedan historians, and also by the annalist of the rival

age when Mool Râj II. died still a minor. The interpretation which makes him brother to *Ujye Pâl* would, therefore, appear to be preferable. Mr. Wilson's intention is more fully expressed in a subsequent paragraph, in which he speaks of "Bhima, *the younger brother of Mula*, the son of Ujaypala."

[1] *Vide* Jour. Ben. As. Soc., v. 380. See also Note at page 87.

[2] See Note at p. 50.

kingdom of the Chohâns of Sâmbhur, the Bhârot Chund, in whose wild but picturesque epic no inferior place is filled by the gallant Solunkhee, the madman of Unhilwârâ. To these authorities, therefore, we now have recourse.

When Unung Pâl Raja was ruling in Delhi, as Chund Bhârot relates, the Kumdhuj, or Râthor, chief Veejye Pâl, prepared to attack him. Someshwur, son of Ânund Dev, then ruled in Sâmbhur. Hearing that the Kumdhuj and the Tooâr were about to engage, he considered that it was the duty of a Kshutree, under such circumstances, to cease from sitting at home. "I will increase," said he, "the fame of the "house of Âno, or attain Kyelâs, or the throne of Indra." He sounded the royal drum, and advanced to succour Delhi. Somesh and Unung Pâl set off in company to meet the Kumdhuj, the white umbrellas borne above them. They engaged Veejye Pâl, who was wounded by Someshwur, and took to flight. Someshwur acquired great fame in Delhi from defeating the powerful Kumdhuj. Unung Pâl gave him his daughter in marriage, and having formed a strict alliance with him, dismissed him with great honor. Somesh returned home to Ujmeer sounding the instruments of victory.

Unung Pâl, it appears, had no son. Of his two daughters, one, named Kumulâ-Devee, was married to Someshwur, of Ujmeer; the other, named Roop Soonduree, to Jye Chund Râthor, king of Kanouj, who was the son of Veejye Pâl, by the daughter of Unung Pâl's father's sister. By the Tooâr princess, Someshwur had the celebrated Prutheerâj, who united the thrones of Ujmeer and Delhi, and after a romantic struggle, fell before the Mohammedan. "In Kanouj, "Ghuznee, and Unhilpoor," says Chund, "the angel of death began "to shout the day that Prutheerâj was born." Prutheerâj had a sister named Preethâ, who was married by her father Somesh to Sumur Singh, the Râwur of Cheetor.

In these times, Raja Bholo Bheem Dev was the ornament of Unhilpoor, in Goojur-land. He was like the deep ocean in power; he led an invincible four-limbed army; the three Loks sought the protection of the Châlook Râee; many fort-lords served him; he possessed ships that sailed to Sindh; his military posts were in the land of Dhârâ. Umur Singh Shewuro, the Jain monk, was a servant of Bheem Dev, he who, by the compelling charm, drew to him men, women, and Devs. Among the Yâduvs of Parkur, and the Shodâs, he burned all the houses of the Brahmins, and expelled them from the country. He wandered in Malwa, in Pullee-land also, and in the land of Aboo.

Jeytshee Purmâr at this time ruled at Aboo. He had a son named Sulukh, and a daughter Eechenee Koomâree, who was very beautiful, and praised by every one. Bheem Dev formed the desire of marrying her; he listened to every one that spoke of Aboo, or of the daughter of the Purmâr, whether the speech were false or true; his dreams were full of visions of Eechenee. He sent Umur Singh to Aboo to demand the hand of the Purmâr princess; but she was already betrothed to the son of the Chohân. The ambassador of Bheem Dev was so informed; he answered, "O! mountain lord, Bholo Veer, the Châlook, "having heard of Eechenee, forgets her not; he demands that you "betroth her to him; if you give her to the Chohân he will cast you from "the battlements of Aboo-gurh; for him to contend with the Purmâr, "is, as it were, for Urjoon to make war with the wretched." Jeytshee heard the Prudhân with respect; he entertained him for five days honorably, considering with his ministers what answer should be given. At last the son of Jeyt arose, grasping his sword; "If my land were sought," he said, "I would give it; but Bholo Bheem has adopted the Jain "religion, he is full of treacheries, of charms of compelling, and fasci- "nating, and enthralling. It is by the aid of these he has seized "upon so much territory; he knows not a northern foe." Jeytshee also spoke,—"In the land of Muroo there are nine millions of good "warriors; eighteen royal seats belong to Aboo-gurh. The lord of the "Sâmunts will be my ally. Can none of these protect me? Then "he who covered Pureeksheet in his mother's womb, who saved the "children from the burning jungle, who succoured his parents and "slew his uncle, who sheltered Vruj from the rain, raising the moun- "tain Gowurdhun, that Gokul Dev, Shree Krishn, will protect me.[1] "It is well to maintain my royalty, or else to die." With this answer he dismissed the ministers of Bheem.

To five of his kinsmen Jeytshee entrusted Aboo. He said to his son, "Let us seek assistance from the Chohân." Writing a letter with his own hand, he sent to hasten the marriage of Eechenee with the son of Someshwur,—"Sulukh's sister, Jeyt's daughter, Bholo "Bheem demands—'Leave Aboo desolate,' he says, 'or give me "Eechenee in marriage.' Shall the jackal, then, take the lion's share? "He plunders my property; my herdsmen daily vent their complaints; "my subjects are impoverished." The Purmâr was well received by the Chohân. Prutheerâj, sending to Delhi, made known that he was about to go with Sulukh to fight against Bheem. The son of Somesh set forth—he prepared to accompany Sulukh Purmâr home.

[1] For all these and many other exploits of Krishn, see "Prem Sâgur," of which a translation has been published by Professor Eastwick (Madden, Leadenhall-street, 1851).

When Bholo Bheem heard of these occurrences, it was as if some one had struck him on the face. He sent for his ministers, and bade them instantly prepare; he caused the drums of war to sound. "Who is this "that lays hold on the sleeping lion; who is this that seeks to take "the jewel from the head of the earth-supporting serpent; who is this "that thrusts his hand into the bosom of the angel of death; that "wishes to protect the Châlook's fugitive?" As he thus spoke, Bholo Bheem trembled with warlike rage. From Puttun he sent orders in all directions—to Kutch, and to Soreth. Clouds of dust darkened the horizon; a vast army assembled from all sides; there came the Lord of Girnâr; Lohâno the Kutâree also; Veer Dev (or Veer Dhuwulung) the Wâghela; Râm Purmâr; the Lord of Perumbh; Râning the Jhâlâ; Shodâ Sârung Dev; Gung the Dâbhee; Umur Singh Shewuro was there; Châchig also, the Jain Muntreshwur. Bholo Bheem arrived at Aboo, and pitched his tents; he surrounded the fort on all sides. The armies of the Purmâr and the Châlook joined battle; for many days the contest raged; Sulukh and Jeyt at length gave back; but fighting as they retired, they reddened the earth with blood. Bheem pressed on; he beheld Uchuleshwur; the Purmârs fled to Muroo-land, they left the fort to the Châlook; he ascended triumphantly to the summit of Aboo.

At this time a common enemy, whose presence might have stanched these feuds among the Rajpoot princes, hung like a thunder-cloud above their heads. "This land," said Shahabood-deen, the Ghoree, "is the property neither of Hindoo nor of Mlechh, but of him who "can hold it with the sword." Bheem Dev, however, well deserving his title of Bholo, or madman, refused to listen to the dictates of prudence, though some were not wanting, even among his own chieftains, whose advice, had it been adopted, might have obviated, or at least delayed, the approaching fall of India. The Gohil chief of Perumbh urged that the war should cease. "The Purmâr has com"mitted no offence," said he; "if he will restore the slender-waisted "one, it is enough; let us consider to effect this object." "At times "of fighting," said Râning the Jhâlâ, "matters which relate to war "alone should be considered; other disputes are out of place. Let "us take heed lest an enmity with the Shah should arise." Veer Dev, the Wâghela, said, "We should come to an understanding with the "Chohân, and unite against the Sultan. In fight, destroying him, we "shall obtain much territory and great fame." "What you have said "is true," whispered Umur Singh Shewuro; "but it will not be "agreeable to Bheem." The raja himself was determined to follow up his feud at all costs. "If a Rajpoot," said he, "once brook an "insult, he is worthy of every reproach; he incurs the guilt of a thou-"sand sins; he falls into hell, and who shall lift him up. A Rajpoot "must seek release from transmigration with his sword, destiny has so "ordered it. The Purmâr and the Chohân are called great warriors "among the Hindoos; when I have stripped the Chohân of all his "possessions, I will then go against the Ghoree." The Bholo Râj, swearing a mighty oath, ordered the drums to sound.

Then the Chohân was attacked on both sides; the Lord of Sâmbhur seemed like a drum between the Ghoree and the Goojur. Against his Hindoo enemies he appealed to Bhuwânee: "O! Doorgâ, the "Jain religion has seized all things, do you seize these treacherous "ones. No one respects the honor of kings; the truthfulness of "Sâmunts has been destroyed; where the speech of the Veds was, "where the Shuktee's book,[1] there the Jain talks treacherously. O! "Châmoondâ, grasping a mighty sword, protect me; O! Kâlee, with "a countenance like that of the angel of death at the time of the con-"flagration of the world, destroy these Jains—destroy them, thou who "art the conqueror of sins, the protector of gods, the terrifier of "demons. Be victorious, be victorious!" Chund, the Bhârot, himself led a night attack upon the Goozerat troops, and by the aid of Doorgâ obtained great success, though that night the Châlook's army stood like a fort of iron, though elephants went the rounds, and the Jhâlâs mounted guard, who had defeated the Jhârejas, and had plundered Kutch and Punchâl. In the confusion of the night Bheem's troops slew each other; and though the king himself rushed into the fight, and when his elephant was slain and his sword broken, still fought desperately, armed only with a dagger, he was at last obliged to retreat, having suffered a heavy loss.

A force was now left to watch the movements of Bheem, and the main body of the Chohân army advanced against the Sultan, whom also they defeated.

Bheem Dev had an uncle, Sârung Dev, who, at his death, left seven sons,—Pertâp Singh, Uree Singh, Gokuldâs, Gowind, Huree Singh, Shyâm, and Bhugwân. They were brave warriors, and had slain Rân (or Râning), the most powerful of the Jhâlâs. For some reason, which is unexplained, the sons of Sârung Dev had gone into outlawry against their cousin, Bheem Raja, and lived in the hills of Soreth, plundering the Yâduv's country. They became at length so formidable, that Bheem was compelled to advance against them in

[1] The Book of Doorgâ; see account of the Festival of Nine Nights in the Conclusion.

person. He encamped on the bank of a river, and his elephant was bathing in it, when it was put to death, and the driver also slain by Pertâp Singh and Uree Singh. This insult stung Bheem, never very tolerant of such, to the quick, and he declared, that though he had previously purposed merely to seize them, he would now esteem it no fault to put them to death. When the brothers were made aware of this threat, they thought it was high time to quit Goozerat, and accordingly fled for shelter to the young Prutheerâj, who gave them grants of villages (puttâs) and other presents, and treated them with great respect. Once on a time, however, when the son of Someshwur was seated on his throne among his Sâmunts, shining as the new moon surrounded by stars, Pertâp Singh Solunkhee and his brothers paid obeisance to Prutheerâj. The Muhâ Bhârut was the theme of conversation, and warlike deeds of the Chohâns were recited. Pertâp Singh, as the tale was told, put his hand on his moustache. Kun, the Chohân, the uncle of Prutheerâj, saw it; he fired at the supposed insult. Drawing out his sword, the devourer of many a life, he cut Pertâp Singh through the body. The Solunkhee fell dead. Uree Singh and his brothers, enraged, sought revenge; the followers of the Solunkhees also forced their way into the hall. The Prince Prutheerâj rising, retired within the palace. The fight now raged as furiously as a forest conflagration; the Solunkhees fell upon Kun like moths rushing to the flame of a lamp. For an hour the sword moved, and the tooth of Yuma[1] plied its trade. The brothers of Pertâp, following each other, pierced the mansion of the sun. The brother of Somesh, raging like Fate, slew the seven brothers of Bheem, and was victorious. His rage was appeased.

Prutheerâj, when he heard of the matter, was angry with Kun. "Why did you act thus," he said; "all will say that the Chohân "called the Châlook to his house and slew him." For three days the shops were closed in the city of Ujmeer. "Alas! alas!" sounded everywhere—a river of blood flowed in the public street. "Well done, "the Châlook!" sang Chund, the giver of fame; "well done to his "father and mother; not even in thought did he attempt flight."

The story was wafted to a distance as perfume by the wind. Châlook Bheem heard that the Chohân had slain the sons of Sârung; he was inflamed with grief and anger. He wrote to the Chohân, demanding an opportunity for revenge; the Chohân agreed to accept the challenge. Bheem proposed to his officers to advance at once upon Ujmeer; but Veer, the Prudhân, counselled him to remain until the

[1] A curved dagger, called Yum-dunt, Jumdud, or Jumbeea.

rainy season should close. Bheem assented, determining to attack the Chohân in the season of cold. Time passed away, and the rage of the Châlook abated.

From this point the Bhârot loses sight of Goozerat, while he describes how Prutheerâj mounted the throne of Delhi on the retirement of Unung Pâl to Bhudreek-âshrum; how the young hero more than once defeated the Ghoree Shah; how he carried off Shushee Vrittâ, princess of Devgeeree, and affianced bride of Jyechund of Kanouj, having defeated that powerful monarch; and how he performed many other exploits worthy of a Rajpoot Rolando. At length, however, he returns to Bheem, and his many causes of quarrel with the Chohân sovereigns; and from henceforth, for a time, it is purposed to follow the bard more closely than before, in order that as much as possible of the style of the Rajpoot epic may be conveyed to the reader.

The Goojur-land Châlook, Bheem-like, Bheem the very strong, no one could press upon his limits, great was his fame. Someshwur of Sâmbhur in his heart rankled; Prutheerâj, the Lord of Delhi, was as a fire within him. Collecting his ministers, he asked their advice; he prepared a four-limbed army.[1] "Now will I take his land, the enemy "crushing; I will make a rule under one umbrella." For Rânik Dev, the Jhâlâ prince, sent the Châlook sovereign; his mind he opened to him, greatly excited, very hot, and as if heated with fire. The good warriors all he summoned together. "Let us quickly prepare to start; "as the young elephant blows the dust from off the ground, so let us "destroy the Chohân's country; as the Bheel treats the mouse's nest, "so let us treat the land of Sâmbhur." He summoned Kunuk, the prince; he summoned Rânik Râj; Chourâsim Jesingh, Veer Dhuwulung Dev he sent for; he sent for Sârung Mukwâna. Rankling with the ancient feud, the Châlook spoke with his mouth. "The "Bheels and Kâtees in the field are very valorous; victory and fame "without doubt we shall obtain. Let us, warrior-like, take our revenge. "Words of war are pleasing to my heart; valour obtains liberation in "a moment; liberation which, with much pain of body, the ascetic "attains, dwelling in bee-haunted caves, with penances sad in summer, "winter, and rains." Bheem set his warriors in motion. "We will "fight with the Chohân as Râhoo fights with Chundra.[2] Abandon-"ing the hope of life, let us fight, then shall we obtain land; he who

[1] A four-limbed army consists of cavalry, infantry, elephants, and chariots.

[2] Hindoos suppose eclipses of the moon to be occasioned by the conflicts which Chundra, the Moon-God, has to sustain against his implacable enemy, the demon Râhoo.

"regards life as the unbroken grain which a Sutee scatters on all sides "without fear, he it is who obtains land." From hither and thither the army collected, as a river fed by dependant streams. Elephants many were with the warriors; horses, too, that seemed as if they flew on wings. The noise of the elephants was as the roaring of waters, or of the clouds of the monsoon driven together by the winds. The good warriors seemed full of joy, smiling as at sunset smiles the ocean; they had no thought of property or home; their thought was always of Brumh. They were eager to fight in company with their sovereign, as a wife is eager to burn in company with her lord. From all sides the terrible army increased, as clouds rise from the horizon. The umbrella shaded the head of Bheem—he thirsted to drink of the stream of war. Bheels of terrible form composed his van; black as *kâjul*[1] they passed along, bearing bows in their hands. Behind them came a line of elephants, with whose roar the forests and mountains re-echoed; their bells sounded, their necklaces rang; they seemed like mountains in motion. As they went, they broke down trees; their tusks glittered like a line of cranes; the earth shook beneath them. Foot soldiers, armed with shields, followed them, forming battalions. Beholding the warriors, men doubted whether ocean had not overflowed its banks. Heaven, earth, and hell trembled—such was the pride of the army.

When the troops arrived in Someshwur's territories, the inhabitants left their houses and fled; the country was plundered. Hearing the cry of his subjects, Som mounted his horse, ready as a Sutee to attend her lord. Prutheerâj, the very angry, he caused to remain at Delhi; Sâmunts he took with him,—Prusung the Keechee Row, Jâm the Yâduv, Dev Râj, Bhân Bhâttee the slayer of enemies, Oodeeg Bâhoo, Bhulee Bhudra; Kyemâs, too, accompanied Som. Bathing, presenting gifts, muttering his beads in prayer to the Isht Dev, his eyes wide open, his face expanded with joy, as a lotus by the light of morning, Som prepared to lead an army without end in number. Kun Chohân was with him, Jesingh Dev, immovable in battle as a mountain. The earth shook, the serpent was distressed with the weight of his burden; the Châlook approached; the Sâmbhur Raja heard the news; he caused the great instruments of war to sound. Seeing Som's army, the heart of the enemy became lame.

The armies joined battle,—Som, desirous of fight, and Bheem, that never turned back in war. The shields of the soldiers, swung from side to side, seemed like the new tobacco leaves shaken by the wind.

[1] *Kâjul* is the lamp-black with which women stain their eyelids.

Kun commenced the fight; the drums sounded; swords began to rattle; a terrible pestilence arose; for three hours arrows and other missiles rained upon Kun; at last, turning their steps backwards, Bheem's force fled; such strength did Kun exhibit, his sword flashing like lightning. Very proud ones he seized, and dashed to the ground, as the wind dashes trees; many steeds he made riderless; appeasing the hunger of the angel of death, he thinned the army of Bheem. The Fates came thither; their drums began to rattle; they danced, and, cup in hand, were joyful; the flesh-eaters were satisfied with food.

Someshwur Chohân and Bheem fought a terrible fight; the earth was struck with fear; it seemed as if mountain strove with mountain; corpse fell upon corpse, a river of blood flowed; the earth was drenched with it as if with rain. Excited with the wine of war, the warriors fought with well watered weapons. Life mingled with life; not an Upsura remained without a bridegroom; many on both sides were wounded, yet no one left the field or fled. On the right of his friends, Yâdoo Jâm raged as if to destroy the world; against him came Khengâr, like a flame of fire on the earth; in the mud of honor they were both entangled; they fought like two bulls in rage. The elephants that were struck down by them seemed black mountains, from which flowed rivulets of gore. The gods and demons, and the snakes of hell, seeing them, were delighted. From the heavens descended a rain of flowers.

On the left the strong Bhuleebhudra fought, seated on a white elephant; his horses, too, were white; great was the noise of bells and bell-necklaces.

Someshwur himself rushed on; he beheld the Lord of Goozerat with such eyes as Moochkoond's were when he was awakened from sleep.[1] Arrows flew between the two sovereigns, as charms fly in a

[1] After Krishn had slain Kuns, Jurâsindh, the father-in-law of that king, made many ineffectual attempts to drive the incarnate god from Muthoora. At length he brought with him Kâl Yumun, who compelled Krishn to fly, and pursued him to his retreat on the mountain of Girnâr, in Soreth. In that place Moochkoond Raja was sleeping, who, fatigued with unparalleled exertions in favor of the sages, had procured from them the promise that he should slumber undisturbed, or at least that a flame of fire from his eyes should destroy any person who dared to awaken him. Krishn arriving at the place, spread a cloth over Moochkoond as he lay, and Kâl Yumun coming thither, and supposing the sleeper to be his enemy, struck him with his foot, and snatched the cloth from off him. Moochkoond awoke, and Kâl perished. Krishn after this promised Moochkoond that he should be reborn once more, and serve him in an eminent manner, and should then attain to emancipation from the world. See this story in the 52nd chapter of the Prem Sâgur. It is com-

contest between Vreehusputee and Shookra. Two protectors of regions were the kings; two canopied lords; two shielded men; before them both sounded the royal drums; both were of many titles; both the boundaries of Hindoos; both warriors' sons. The field of battle seemed like a dark and stormy night in the rains when a conflagration rages in the mountains. The noise of the music woke Muhâ Dev from his meditative abstraction; he began to clap his hands and dance, and to string a necklace of heads; Nârd, too, was delighted. The Upsurâs, seated in their cars in the sky, strove with each other; the Yukshes and Gundhurvs looked on in amaze at the strange sight, supposing that the time of the destruction of the world drew near. The soldiers who fell in this battle-pilgrimage passed to Vyekoonth. Someshwur Chohân, the warrior, fell in this field, hacked to pieces. His Sâmunts knew that he had certainly fallen, valiantly fighting, his body covered with blood. Many of them passed with him to emancipation from terrestrial things. The field had been one equal to that of the Bhârut. Somesh went to the lord of the moon (Som); his body returned to its elements. The Châlook stayed his hand. "Victory! victory!" sounded upon earth. "Alas! "alas!" among the Devs, for Someshwur winning liberation had forestalled them.

Raja Prutheerâj heard of the battle; he recalled the remains of his army. For the sake of his father he presented sixteen lump offerings;[1] for twelve days and nights he lay on the earth; he swallowed food but once in the day; he avoided the society of his wives. Many gifts he presented to Brahmins, greater than any has ever given in all his life, or ever will give. Eight thousand cows he presented, with rich housings, with gilded horns and hoofs, each cow adorned with heavy ornaments of gold. The remainder of the sixteen gifts also he presented. He determined on taking revenge for his father. He vowed a vow that he would wear no turban. "Killing the Châlook Bheem, I will take my father from his entrails;" so he said again and again. "Shame to him who does not revenge

monly believed in Goozerat that Nurshee Mehta, the poet of Joonagurh, was the promised incarnation of Moochkoond. Nurshee was a Wurnuggur Nâgur Brahmin, and was the first of that powerful caste who deserted the worship of Muhâ Dev for that of Shree Krishn, on which account he suffered much persecution. He is said to have lived about five hundred years ago, and his compositions are still among the most popular in the language of his native country.

[1] For explanation of this and many previous allusions, we must refer our readers to the Conclusion.

"his father." The raja's eyes were red with rage; he was very angry.[1] He prepared an army to execute his purpose of revenge, but determined first to take his seat on the throne, and then to go to the war. Prutheerâj called for Brahmins skilled in the usages of kings, religious, capable of performing sacrifices and other ceremonies; like Brumh, knowing how to destroy sin, scient of the past, the present, and the future. These commenced to perform, in a splendid manner, expiatory ceremonies for Somesh; they offered sacrifice. The king presented gifts that should ensure success in warring in another's country; he offered a thousand silver coins, a thousand gold coins, with great respect. In the prescribed manner, at Nigumbodh, where Yoodishteer received initiatory rites, Prutheerâj's royal unction was performed. The women sung their solemn hymns,—they, whose eyes were like the deer's, around whose necks were garlands of flowers, whose faces were round as the moon, whose throats were slender as the koil's.[2] The cry of "Conquer! conquer! Prutheerâj," sounded. It seemed as if Indra were assuming the throne of the celestial city. The dress of Eechenee was tied in a knot with his; they shone like the King of Heaven and his spouse. Four kinds of wealth were given to the Sâmunts—money, elephants, cars, horses. The courtiers offered the king presents. Kun Chohân gave an elephant; he made the first royal mark upon the head of Prutheerâj; Neerdur Râthor made the second; afterwards the other warriors. White horse-hair fans waved over the head of Prutheerâj, as the rays of the sun shining behind the moon—Prutheerâj, the mighty warrior, who captured, and released the sultan. A golden staff supported the white umbrella which shaded the raja's head. With sacrifices the evil influences of the unpropitious constellations were averted; the subjects made their obeisance; great joy reigned.

In the heart of Prutheerâj, Bheem continually rankled; his rage was like fire, not to be extinguished but by the death of his foe. "Bheem slew Someshwur! Huree! Huree!"[3] Thus with his mouth he kept muttering among his warriors. He suffered great pain. The Purmâr remonstrated with him. "Do not sorrow for your father; "he whose body is cut to pieces by the edge of the sword increases "his fame, and goes to Soor Lok. This is the true religion of a

[1] "Besides, I met Lord Bigot, and Lord Salisbury,
"With eyes as red as new-enkindled fire."
King John, Act IV., scene 2.

[2] The koil is the black or Indian cuckoo (Cuculus).

[3] Huree is a name of Vishnoo, as Hur is of Shiva.

"Kshutree." Said Sindh Purmâr: "Hear my words! make desolate "Goojur-land; Somesh dwelling in Paradise will be pleased. What "of the Châlook—even the sultan's land trembles at your name." Prutheerâj said: "Having bathed, I have offered lump offerings; "I swore an oath that I would be revenged for my father; when I "make Bheem prisoner, I will demand Somesh from him; I will "give pleasure to Yogeenees, Veers, and Vyetâls." Prutheerâj slept. At sunrise the warriors assembled; the raja called for Kun Chohân; when he came, the assembly rose, joining the palms of their hands, for Kun bore the title of "lord of men." Night and day wearing his eyes bandaged, his body like a thunderbolt, he resembled a chained tiger. Jâm the Yâduv came; Bhulee Bhudra; Koorumbh Dev, whom many rajas served; Chund Poondeer came; Ututhye Chohân, like the Pânduv Bheem; Lunguree Râee, in time of battle a fire; Gowind Row Gahilot came, the conqueror of other's territory; great and small, all the Sâmunts came, and seated themselves in the royal court. Chund, the Wurdye, also came, whom kind Doorgâ Devee assists. Prutheerâj thus addressed them all: "To take revenge "for Somesh, let us prepare an army, and fight with the Goojur, king "of men; let us dig up the Châlook from the roots. Bheem has "filled his measure till it brims over, that in fight he has conquered "Someshwur. Let us destroy the Châlook race, even from the "wombs of women. In whatever place he has a terrible forest "retreat, let us dig it up. If I do not so, then the Brahmin has not "given me the name of Prutheerâj."[1] The Sâmunts, all of them, assented to what he said; they sent for the astrologer-king. "When "the conjunction of the stars is good we will advance, so that our "work may be successful." The sage came and examined the signs. "If you set forth immediately, you will, without doubt, have victory." Jugjyotee, the astrologer, encouraged the raja, saying, "The con- "junction is most favorable; you will gain the victory, and secure "your revenge; the heavenly mansions are well situated; at this "time you may effect whatever you have it in your heart to accom- "plish. The fatal sign stands opposed to the enemy,—were he a "Dev even, he would perish." The Chohân raja was pleased with what Jugjyotee said,—"You shall bind Bheem and conquer Goozerat. "This I swear. If, in such a season as this, the task cannot be ac- "complished, I will henceforth abandon the teaching of the stars."

The Chohân summoned his troops; at the appointed hour the drum sounded. He led his troops outside the city; at a place where

[1] Which means "king of earth."

large trees were—where the ground was powerful—he encamped. Devs and Dytes shouted victory! When it became morning, troops arrived at Sâmbhur from all sides; they encamped about the Chohân. War music roared; the five kinds of instruments sounded. With his army Prutheerâj advanced to destroy the houses of Goozerat. The spies of Bheem conveyed to him the intelligence, that the warlike Chohân advanced with sixty-four thousand warriors, his army rolling onwards as the billows of the ocean roll. They told also of the Chohân's vow, and how that Kun and Gowind Râee had sworn, placing water on the head of Muhâ Dev. "Let us, therefore, O raja! "make preparations for meeting him with the sword." Bheem was very angry; the muscles of his frame quivered, his eyes became red, he called for all the royal ministers, and bade them prepare for war. From province to province the order travelled; many rajahs mounted and came; two thousand men, mounted on blood horses, armed with bows and arrows, with hand-tubes and fireball-tubes; from Kutch, three thousand strong men, their horses covered with armour; one thousand and five hundred from Soreth; from Kâkârej came Kolees, such as never missed their mark; from Jhâlâwar came the Jhâlâ, who turned not back in fight, ever desirous of war; Moochkoond, the Kâwâ chief, mounted, of whose mounting hearing the whole country was wont to fly; from Kâteewar came the Kâtee Prince, whose enemies, neither night nor day, find any rest; the troops of other districts, small and large (who could count them?), assembled—the whole array of the land of Goojur. The Sâmbhur spy informed Prutheerâj that the army of the Châlook got ready, roaring as roars the ocean. "He has a hundred thousand soldiers, a number not to "be estimated; of elephants a thousand. I have seen this with my "eyes." Prutheerâj said, "If Bheem will meet me in battle, I will "destroy them as fire in the hot season, with the wind's aid, consumes "a forest. I will then call myself Prutheerâj, when I shall have "ripped up the belly of Bheem, and taken from it my father."

Evening came on; they pitched their tents on the ground on which they stood; food was supplied to them; they lay down, some near, some further off. Kyemâs lay near the raja, armed with a sword. Sleep subdued them, as religious meditation is subdued by fascinating bewilderment. Kun, also, was near the raja; Jeyt and Sulukh, the chiefs of Aboo; Poondeer and Dâheem; Châmoond; Raja Humeer; Sârung, the valiant Koorumbh; Puhâr, the Toonwur; Lohâno; Lunguree Raja. When one watch of the night remained, they determined to follow the chase. The Sâmunts were sad; they said, "No living thing is moving here—our work will not be successful."

At this moment they heard the cry of an animal. "Listen," said Kun, "this creature prophesies what is about to happen; to-morrow "morning there will be a mighty battle." All the Sâmunts were astonished; they wondered how the battle should take place in the morning. Kun said, "The omen that preceded the death of "Someshwur has happened to Bheem. If the raja make use of this "omen, even the angel of death could not withstand him." As they thus conversed the sun arose, the warriors paid obeisance to Nârâyun; as the lotus does, so did they receive pleasure from beholding the sun. Another good omen here occurred, and soon a third. The Sâmunts said, "To-day there will certainly be a battle, within an "hour there will be a terrible fight." Prutheerâj said, "It is need-"less to look for omens—the day of battle is the day of pleasure to "the warrior. The soul of a man we see not, whether he be alive "or dead; fame, too, comes and goes; so Destiny has ordained. "They who are defeated may claim to be as Dooryodhun, they who "conquer as the Pânduvs; therefore think not of omens. We will "give up not a needle's point of ground, we will make a fight such "as the Bhârut. There is no end to omens—they come and go;—let "us advance!" At the raja's order the Sâmunts raised their war-cry here and there. The instruments of war sounded; cymbals, drums, curved horns, some near, some far off; the bells and the necklaces of elephants sounded; horses neighed; the army put itself in motion. Stage by stage they advanced to destroy the land of Puttun, to fall upon the enemy as meteors fall upon the earth. Sixty-four thousand were they in number; the serpent began to be weary of his burden. Prutheerâj used the horse-hair fans; he gave the royal umbrella to Kun, his kinsman; making Kun the marshal, he committed to him the van; next came Prutheerâj in person; Neerdur followed him; then came the Purmâr. As the astrologer rolling up the scroll does not again unroll it, so, advancing stage by stage, they left the love of life behind them. On went the Chohân warrior, whose hands are like the hands of a Dev, who is terrible to his foe.

In the territory of Bheem Dev fear arose; from the jungle and the lesser villages, as coveys of game birds, the people began to fly away; the dust that arose obscured the road. On moved the army like a river's flood; the horses, slowly moving, seemed like cranes, or, urged to speed, leaped like deer; spears, swords, javelin-heads glittered in the sun. Prutheerâj sent forward Chund that he might demand an opportunity of revenge from the Châlook. To the capital of Goozerat went Chund; a net and a ladder he took with him—a spade, a lamp, and an elephant's goad; in his hand he carried a trident. To the court of the Châlook he went; people crowded together to see the wonder. Chund came to Bholo Bheem; he announced that the Sâmbhur Raja had arrived. "O! Bhât," said Bheem, tell us quickly "what mean you by these strange signs." Chund replied, "It is the "order of Prutheerâj that you are to be seized with this net if you "take the water, or with this ladder if you fly into the air; with this "spade you are to be dug up if you seek the lower regions of the "earth; with this lamp your course is to be followed if you attempt "to escape through the darkness. This goad is to bring Bheem into "subjection; this trident to slay him. Wheresoever the sun shines, "should you seek to escape, Prutheerâj will pursue you." Bheem replied, "I will slay him who threatens; I, Bheem, the terrible in "fight, whom many men fear. Be not haughty, but be modest, and "reflect on what was done before." Chund said, "If a mouse at any "time conquered a cat, if a vulture ever danced on the head of the "sacred swan, if a deer ever equalled in fight a lion, if a frog ever "attained fame fighting with a snake—all this has been by some "unaccountable freak of fortune. Do not let it be attempted to "repeat such things frequently. Can a lamp be compared to the fire "that consumes the forests which clothe the mountains?" Bheem said, "The sons of Bhâts may fight with words, as demons fight with "abuse, or brothers, sharing their inheritance, with fists; but this "feud of Someshwur must be fought out to the death. Tell the "Sambhur Raja that a coward might tremble at his threats."

Chund, hearing this answer, rose somewhat confused; his eyes were red with rage. He returned quickly to Prutheerâj, and, with the view of encouraging him, told him all that had occurred. Said the Bhât, "Bholo Bheem told me, 'You are doing what a frog does "'when it treads upon the tail of a snake that is reposing, and "'wakens it.' The Goojur Lord-of-men advances with a four-limbed "army. I saw the troops as I came along. What I spoke the king "did not attend to. I showed him the lamp, the net, the spade. "He asked what hidden matter was there; why Kyemâs, who is "skilled as a minister, was not sent with me; or Châmoond Rây, or "Kun, the clever; why the Lord of Sâmbhur came not himself. "'Many times have I fought,' said Bheem, procuring victory for "'Goozerat. Do not suppose me to be such as the rajas you have "conquered. I have slain a thousand such as the king of Sâmbhur.' "When I heard this I announced to Bheem that the Chohân "advanced with a four-limbed army."

Prutheerâj called Neerdur Raja to him; he took him by the hand and said, "Among all these warriors you are the chief; you are of

" ancient race, and valorous as were your ancestors. Though a Dev " or an angel fought with you, you could subdue him: you exhibit " strength in war such as belonged to the sons of Pândoo. Retain " no love for this earth; think of heaven, and with your Sâmunts fight " with one mind." Neerdur answered, " Our Sâmunts are capable of " destroying the enemy like grass. Remember, O! Prutheerâj! you " are of Dânuv race; it is through your splendour that your warriors " are strong. Kun, in youth, middle age, or old age, has been a " delighter in war; the army against which he fights is broken to " pieces;—he of the great titles, the incarnation of Bheeshm, whom " the world calls lord of men." Prutheerâj, when he heard these words, took from his neck a necklace of pearls of immense value, which he presented to Neerdur. On the raja's neck it seemed like the sun encircled by Gungâ. The great warrior, Neerdur Râthor, caused the drum to sound. As the Veers assemble to fight at the sound of the drum, so assembled the army. He shone among his warriors as Droh among the stars. To Kun, Prutheerâj presented his royal horse; with great urgency he caused him to mount. Said Kun, "O! forest-king, shame to me that I have not yet slain " Someshwur's enemy, nor yet made a way of escape for this soul-" swan from out my body." Prutheerâj answered, "Once on a time " Soogreev's strength failed to protect his wife; once on a time " Dooryodhun was not able to protect Kurun; once on a time Shree " Râm himself lost Seeta from the forest; once on a time the " Pânduvs could not prevent the removal of Droupudee's garments. " O! Kun, do not be distressed about such things. I worship you " as my Isht Dev. Seeing the fire of your eyes, the enemy will fear, " as fears a serpent when he beholds the eyes of a peacock." While he thus paid respect to Neerdur and Kun, Prutheerâj was informed of the approach of Bheem with a large army. Hearing that the valiant warrior had arrived near Puttun to take revenge for his father, Bheem raged as a snake that has been trodden on, or as a lion rudely woken out of sleep, or as a conflagration lit by a spark in the hot weather. Calling for all his warriors he announced what he had heard; they, hearing of the matter, seemed like ascetics who had abandoned the world. The two armies arrived within sight of each other; balls began to fly from the tubes; fire arrows flew into the air. On both sides horsemen pressed forward—they engaged with the sword. The Châlook had so arranged his force that his enemy could not break through it to reach the city; nor could the array of the Chohân be broken. The fight began; some were struck down by maces, others cleft by the sword; " Kill! kill!" was the cry; some struggled like wrestlers; arrows piercing the bodies of some, found their way out. Shiva and Kâlee rejoiced; she drank the blood of the slain; her consort strung a necklace of skulls; vultures tore human flesh instead of offal; the road to Swerga was crowded with travellers as the public street of a city; the warriors plundered, "liberation" paying off their debts. The sword of Kun was flashing as lightning from the thunder cloud. On one side Kun Chohân, on the other Sârung Mukwâna—both of them valiant—fought like lions. They brandished broad [1] swords each of them. Sârung paid his debts; Kun attained glory. The Mukwâna fell in the field amidst the warriors that roared like elephants. Sârung's lands were widowed when the Mukwâna Raja fell. The warriors of the forest-king shouted; the enemy were struck with fear; warlike men attained in a moment the place which, with painful labour, the devotee attains; loving their wealth as little as their shadow, they rushed into the fight; abandoning evil disposition, they made the sword to rage; they seized upon each other; all they sought was "liberation;" life they regarded as a dream. "Let us die to-night, who knows what may "happen to-morrow." The battle raged like fire fed by the wind. The warriors knew that their fame would increase; that the cage of the body, which is broken by the edge of the sword, does not again imprison the swan—the soul; that when the swan has escaped from it, the cage is of no further value. Still raged the fight; on men's heads swords kept striking; much armour was cleft through—many a saddle; cowards cried "Alas! alas!" when they received wounds; their cries were drowned in the note of the drum. Prutheerâj, crying "Well done! well done!" encouraged his warriors. The Sâbhermutee river, which rolls through Goojur-land, was flooded to each bank with blood; elephants, horses, and men floated upon its streams. Again the war-music sounded; for half-an-hour the fight was at the thickest; arrows sung through the air like bees; many of the Chohân's warriors were slain; many ranks of the Châlook's army fell like elephants on the field. Thus Prutheerâj took revenge for his father. Fates, holding cups in their hands, muttered charms; flesh-eaters satisfied their hunger; the warriors' bodies seemed like a forest of scarlet-flowering trees. Prutheerâj angrily put his horse in motion; at the clatter of its hoofs the earth shook; the line of the enemy began to waver as quiver the leaves of the sacred fig-tree; arrows flew so thick in the air that a bird could find no passage; the battle raged dreadfully. The warriors, striking each other, seemed smiths

[1] Kurwâls; paddle-shaped swords.

hammering at anvils; the Sâmunts who died in this battle were they who truly lived. At length the Châlook's army, abandoning the road to heaven, took to flight. Devs and demons cried, "Well done! to "the Kshutree, that cleaving the sun's disk, obtains the heaven of "Indra." Horses cried; swords clashed; soldiers, giving the raja's oath, encouraged each other. When Wâmun advanced three steps he subdued one world; but the warriors, advancing a single step, conquered the three worlds. They danced as if Roodra sported with the Veers. As the Châlook's army was broken, the army of the Chohân grew stronger; firmly fixed, it was as the north star, though many a warrior fell wounded. Blows rained upon them as they rain upon a gong, but the line stood firm. The Chohân was exclaiming, "To-day I will fulfil my hopes, I will make a widow of the land of "Goozerat." To Bheem he cried, "You shall not escape; I will "send you to where Som is seated in Swerga." Kun, following him, encouraged his sovereign. The Sâmbhur Raja struck at Bheem; where the string of regeneration lay, there descended the sword. Devs in the heavens cried "Victory! victory!" Bheem Dev fell. As the shout arose, Shumbhoo opened his eyes. Upsuras pressed forward to behold the sight: flowers descended from the skies upon the conquering Prutheerâj, while Bheem Dev, seated in a celestial chariot, took the road to the city of the Soors.

The five kinds of music sounded joyfully; Châruns and Bhâts sang the praises of Prutheerâj; his anger was appeased; he caused the wounded to be lifted up. Thus Prutheerâj took revenge for his father.

The shades of evening darkened; in the same spot the warriors passed the night. Six Sâmunts had been terribly wounded—their hurts were attended to. In the morning the lotuses began to expand; the moon and stars paled at the appearing of the sun; the temple's doors were opened; thieves, chukors,[1] vicious women hid themselves; conch-shells sounded in the places of worship; travellers pursued their journey; on all the trees the birds warbled. The Sâmunts touched the feet of Prutheerâj. "Many of our warriors are gone to Dev Lok; "Bheem Raja has been slain; the fame of the Lord of Earth has been "increased; the burden has been removed from the land; fifteen hun-"dred horses have been destroyed; five hundred elephants, five thou-"sand soldiers." Chund sang the praises of Prutheerâj and the chieftains:—"This life is like a dream; all that is visible is fated to be "destroyed; but honor to the valiant Sâmunt who is faithful to his "lord; who in a bad age takes the good path to the upper worlds."

[1] The chukor is a fairy bird, said to subsist on the moonbeams.

The king caused a deed of victory to be inscribed; he returned to Delhi; at sunrise he entered the city among his soldiers. Thus Prutheerâj took revenge for his father.

Such is the tale of the Bhârot Chund! More sober history, however, informs us that Bheem Dev II. survived the fall of Prutheerâj the Chohân, and after his death crossed swords, almost as unhappily as himself, with his vanquisher the Mohummedan.

It was eight years after his disastrous attempt upon Goozerat (A.D. 1186), that Mohammed Shahab-ood-deen Ghoree made himself master of Lahore by a stratagem, and obtaining possession of the persons of Sultan Khoosrow Mullik and his family, sent them prisoners to Joorjistân. These princes were some time after put to death, and the dynasty of Mahmood becoming wholly extinct the empire passed from the house of Ghuznee to that of Ghor.[1]

The time had now arrived when the storm, of which the two invasions of Goozerat had been but warning blasts, was to break upon the heads of the Rajpoot princes of India. A long period had intervened since the capture of Somnâth proved the power of the Mohummedan, but, wholly untaught even by stern experience, his destined victims had neglected to erect against him any barrier, and had, in reality, prepared the way for his approach by fratricidal contests. Goozerat and Malwa, Delhi, Sâmbhur, and Kanouj, were alike weakened by intestine struggles, and poisoned against each other by mutual victories and defeats, whose only permanent result was the rendering impossible any true-hearted union.

The first attack was nobly sustained by Prutheerâj, the Chohân

[1] Lanja Beejiraee of Jesulmer, married, as we have seen, the daughter of the great Sidh Râj, Jye Singh. By the princess of Unhilwârâ he had a son named Bhoj Dev, who, on the death of his father, succeeded to the throne at Lodurva, upon which he was for some time maintained by a guard of five hundred Solunkhee Rajpoots, against the attempts made by his uncle Jesul to supplant him. "At this time," say the annals of Jesulmer, "The prince of Unhilwârâ was often engaged with the "king's troops from Tatta. Jesul, in pursuance of his plan, determined to coalesce "with the king (of Tatta) and cause an attack on Unhilwârâ, by which alone he "could hope for the departure of the Solunkhee body-guard. Jesul, with his chief "kin, escorted by two hundred horse, marched to the Punjnud, where he saw the "King of Ghor, who had just overcome the King of Tatta, and placed his own garrison there, and he accompanied him to Arore, the ancient capital of Sinde. "There he unfolded his views, and having sworn allegiance to the king, he obtained "a force to dispossess his nephew of his territory. Lodurva was encompassed and "Bhoj Dev slain in its defence. In two days the inhabitants were to carry off their "effects, and on the third the troops of Ghor were permitted the license of plunder. "Lodurva was sacked, and Kureem Khan departed for Bukkur with the spoils."

(A.D. 1191), who, supported by Châmoond Râj, the viceroy of Delhi, engaged Mohammed Ghoree, at Tirowree, between Tahnesur and Kurnâl, and completely defeated him. Two years afterwards (A.D. 1193), the game was again played, but fortune this time changed hands. The armies met on the banks of the Suruswutee, and after a prolonged contest the Rajpoots, worn out by the skilful tactics of the enemy, were, as the sun went down, charged by twelve thousand of the choicest cavaliers of Islâm, who, covered with steel armour, and led by Mohammed in person, carried death and destruction through the Hindoo ranks. Châmoond was slain, and the prodigious army of the Chohân, "once shaken, like a great building, tottered to its fall, "and was lost in its own ruins." The gallant Prutheerâj himself was taken in the pursuit, and murdered in cold blood. Mohammed Ghoree, in person, advanced to Ujmeer, where he perpetrated a cruel massacre, and thence turned his face homewards, "destroying and "plundering the countries in his retreat towards Ghuznee." He left behind him, as his representative in India, Mullik Kootb-ood-deen, who soon took the fortress of Meerut and the royal city of Yogeenee-poor, and who in after days mounting the throne there on the death of his master, gave rise to the proverb, that "The empire of Delhi was founded by a slave."

Next year (A.D. 1194), Mohammed Ghoree, returning to India, defeated Jye Chunder on the banks of the Jumna, and took Kanouj and Benâres, "where, having broken the idols in above one thousand "temples, he purified and consecrated the latter to the worship of the "true God." The Râthor sovereign himself met a death congenial to the Hindoo, being drowned in the sacred stream. The gorgeous Kanouj ceased henceforth to be a Hindoo city, but not many years after the banner of the Râthor was again displayed by the grandsons of the unfortunate monarch, and transferred by them from the banks of the Ganges to the gloomy deserts of "the land of death," where, firmly planted at last in the citadel of the Jodhpoor, it has witnessed in safety the fall of the empire of Kootb-ood-deen.

Goozerat was next to bear the brunt of the Mohummedan attack. "In A.D. 1194, Kootb-ood-deen led his army to Nehrwala (Unhilwârâ), "the capital of the province of Goozerat, where, having defeated "Bheem Dev, he took ample revenge for the overthrow formerly sus-"tained by his master. He remained some time plundering that rich "country, but was recalled by orders from Ghuznee, and commanded "to repair instantly to Delhi."

In another place, the same Mohummedan historian states that Kootb-ood-deen found, encamped under the walls of Unhilwârâ,

Jeewun Ray, the general of Bheem Dev, who fled at his approach; but on being closely pursued, drew up his army, and fought till he lost his life, when his army resumed its flight. "Bheem Dev," he continues, "hearing of this defeat, fled from his dominions."

No permanent occupation of Goozerat resulted, however, from the victory of Kootb-ood-Deen; and though Bheem Dev had been defeated and driven from his capital, his power was not yet broken. Two years after, or in A.D. 1196, as the historian relates, "News "arrived that the Raja of Nâgor and many other Hindoo Rajas had "entered into alliance with the Mairs, a race of people in that "country, and together with the Raja of Nehrwala, had formed a "design to wrest Ajmeer from the Mohummedans. The army of "Kootb-ood-deen being dispersed over his provinces, he was forced to "march in person against these confederates with the few troops "present in Delhi, in order to prevent, if possible, the junction of the "forces of Nehrwala; but he was defeated. After havingbeen frequently "dismounted in action, and having received six wounds, he still "fought with his wonted courage, till, being forced at length by "his attendants off the field, he was carried in a litter to Ajmeer.

"The Mairs, rejoicing at this victory, now formed a junction with "the forces of Goozerat, and sat down before Ajmeer. Intelligence "of this event coming to the ears of the king, he sent a strong rein-"forcement from Ghuznee to the relief of Kootb-ood-deen. Ajmeer "held out till the arrival of the succours, and the enemy raised the "siege. Kootb-ood-deen, having recovered from his wounds, pursued "the besieging army to Nehrwala, taking in his way the forts of Baly "and Nadole. He then received advices that Walin and Darabarz, "in alliance with the Raja of Nehrwala, were encamped near the fort "of Abooghur, in the province of Sirohy, to defend the passes into "Goozerat. Kootb-ood-deen, notwithstanding the difficulties of the "road and the disadvantages of ground, attacked them; and on this "occasion above fifty thousand of the enemy are said to have fallen "on the field, besides twenty thousand who were taken prisoners. "Vast spoils also fell into the hands of the victors. Having given "his army some rest, Kootb-ood-deen pursued his route into Goo-"zerat, ravaged that country without further opposition, and took the "city of Nehrwala, where he left an officer with a strong garrison. He "now returned to Delhi by the way of Ajmeer, and sent a large "quantity of jewels and gold, and also many slaves, to the king at "Ghizny."

Dhârâwursh and Prulhâdun Dev, here mentioned by Ferishta, were the Purmâr feudatories of Unhilwârâ, who possessed Chundrâwutee and Aboo. They were the sons of Yushodhuwul, already mentioned as the contemporary of Koomâr Pâl; and the inscription above quoted describes the younger brother Prulhâdun as "the able protec-"tor of the Raja of Shree Goorjur-desh, the great enemy of the "Dunooj," meaning the Mohummedan invader. Another inscription upon Mount Aboo speaks of Prulhâdun Dev as being at the time Yoov Raja, or heir apparent, Som Singh, the son of Dhârâwursh, being then unborn.

Mohammed Ghoree was murdered in A.D. 1205, from which time until his own death, which occurred five years afterwards, Kootb-ood-deen Eibuk reigned as sovereign in Delhi. There is little else to record of the reign of Bheem Dev II. He died in A.D. 1215, and was the last prince of the direct line of Mool Râj. The Mohummedan garrison planted in Unhilwârâ by Kootb-ood-deen was probably either withdrawn or gradually annihilated, for we find no further mention of its existence; and fifty years after the death of Bheem Dev, as Ferishta records, the then sovereign of Delhi, Gheias-ood-deen Bulbun, was advised by his council to undertake an expedition against the kingdoms of Goozerat and Malwa, "which had been "annexed to the empire by Kootb-ood-deen, *but had since shaken off* "*the Mohummedan yoke.*" To this measure, however, his fears of the Moghul Tartars on the north of his dominions deprived Gheias-ood-deen of the power of assenting.

It was not, indeed, until the close of the thirteenth century that Unhilwârâ finally succumbed to the Moslem sword, then wielded by the furious hand of Allah-ood-deen, whose patronymic of Khiljy is familiar to every peasant of Goozerat, under the substituted form of "Khoonee," or "the murderer."

CHAPTER XIII.

RETROSPECTIVE VIEW OF THE KINGDOM OF UNHILPOOR.

THE point which has how been reached—that of the death of Bheem Dev II.—is a convenient one from whence to review the story of Unhilwârâ. Long afterwards, and even subsequently to the final overthrow of the kingdom of Sidh Râj and Koomâr Pâl, Goozerât continues to present a picture of anarchy. The work of Moslem conquest still proceeds; and minor aggressions, at once the causes and effects of weakness in the central power, add to the confusion. A gleam of prosperity still gilds occasionally the towers and temples of the city of Wun Râj, but it is henceforth the halo of the setting sun; the heart still feebly beats, but the extremities are now becoming cold,—

"And vast confusion waits,
"As doth a raven on a sick fallen-beast,
"The imminent decay of wrested pomp."

The writers from whose compositions we have derived the account which has been given, require, in the first place, some notice. Of Krishnâjee, the Brahmin, author of Rutun Mâlâ, nothing is known. He wrote subsequently to the death of Bheem Dev II., but probably not long after that event, and his work was founded upon the labours of preceding authors:—

"As a man churns curds, and extracts the clarified butter, throwing "the butter-milk away;—

"As a man squeezes sugar cane, and extracts the juice without pre-"serving anything else;—

"As a man extracts gold from dust, and throws the dust aside;—

"As a man separates grain from the husk, or takes oil from "sesamum;—

"So examining all books, good compositions and true,

"This book, Rutun Mâlâ by name, the writer has composed."

The Dwyâshray appears to have been commenced by the celebrated Hemâchârya, who died in the end of the reign of Koomâr Pâl, before A.D. 1174. It was continued by a Jain monk, named Leshâjye Tiluk Gunee, at Prulhâdun Puttun (probably Palhunpoor), and was completed "on the day of the Deewâlee, in the year of Vikrum, 1312," or A.D. 1256. Lukshmee Tiluk Kuvee, as the monk records, made a "teeka," or commentary on the work, and corrected it. Leshâjye himself deduces his spiritual pedigree from "Shree Wurdhumân "Âchârya, who travelled about Goozerat in the reign of Shree Doorlubh "Râj," and from whom he was ninth in descent. The Dwyâshray is so called, because the author proposed to himself two objects—to teach the construction of the Sanscrit language, and to narrate the story of the race of Sidh Râj. This double task he attempts in verses, which, though written consecutively, must be read alternately.

The Prubundh Chintâmunee dates a little later. It was completed at Wurdhumânpoor (the modern Wudwân), on the last day of the bright half of the month of Wyeshâk, in the year of Vikrum, 1361, or A.D. 1305. The author was Merootoong Âchârya, a monk of the Jain convent, at Wudwân. A similar work, of the same name, or perhaps the commencement of the present work, was, however, written, as Merootoong himself records, by Shree Goonchundar Âchârya. "The mind of the Pundit," says the author in his prelude, "is not "satisfied with hearing so much of ancient stories. I, therefore, in "my book, the Prubundh Chintâmunee, detail the stories of great "kings of recent times;" he adds, in another place, "though with "little wisdom yet with industry."

These works have been our principle guides, but they have been illustrated and corroborated by monumental inscriptions, by copper-plate deeds, by the relations of Mohummedan historians, by the poems of Chund Bhârot, and by bardic and oral tradition.

There is, as might be expected, much similarity of character in the works of the Jain monks of Pahlunpoor and Wudwân. With them, of course, civil affairs are entirely subordinate to ecclesiastical transactions; but, in regard to the latter, as well as the former, they rather content themselves with anecdotes than attempt a connected relation. The outline which they afford is wholly defective, but not, it may be asserted, untrue; for, in almost every case where a comparison is practicable, their statements or allusions are verified or explained by independent authority; and greater research, it is therefore fair to assume, would add still more of corroboration. Were it possible to discover what portion of the Dwyâshray was the composition of Hemchunder himself, and how much of this portion has been transmitted without alteration by Leshâjye and Lukshmee Tiluk, we should have, in regard to two of the principal reigns, the remarks of a contemporary writer. This is, however, manifestly impossible; and we must be content to receive these Jain accounts simply as the recorded tradition of the times in which they were written. Regarded even from this point of view, they are by no means destitute of value. They connect and explain other materials, nay, often supply hints which lead to their discovery; and though their assertions, in regard to particular facts, may be fully believed only in as far as corroborated, it would be wholly unreasonable to refuse credence to the general information which they afford in regard to customs, manners, institutions, tones of thought and feeling, as existing in the times at which they were written; nor will, we suppose, any one to under-estimate their value, who reflects how little is known of the mediæval India of the centuries preceding the Mohummedan conquest, and how important the relics of that period are towards a right understanding of the Hindoo nation in the present time.

Of the poems of Chund the Bhârot, far more picturesque and interesting as they are, it is necessary to speak with somewhat greater reservation. Chund is the first in fame of the bardic chroniclers, and his poems are distinguished by all the vices, as well as by all the rugged merits of the class. It is not as a sober narrator that he must be regarded, but as the bard of the Chohâns, if not excited with "the "red draught," at least drunk with the wine of war and clannish rivalry. The text is so corrupt as to be sometimes well nigh unintelligible, and even where the sense is clear, the difficulty of distinguishing the original composition under the varnishes with which it has been overlaid is immense,—so great indeed as to produce, at times, an almost scepticism in regard to the genuineness of the whole work. Bheem Dev II., as we have seen, fell, according to Chund's account, by the hand of Prutherâj Chohân, while in truth he survived that prince for many years. On other occasions the family names of clans in Goozerat are mentioned in connection with events which, according to all other authorities, occurred centuries before the founders of these races lived. Anachronisms, such as the first mentioned, might be accounted for, without prejudice to the genuineness of the work, by supposing the anxiety of Chund to extol the achievements of his king and his hero: of some of those of the second class it might be said, in defence, that the tribes alluded to existed in the time of Chund, though not at the period to which he refers. But what is to be urged when, to take an example, the achievements of "the Gohil from Perumbh" are celebrated by Chund, and it is found that no Gohil occupied Perumbh until nearly a century after the poet's time? We fear it must be admitted that all is not the work of Chund which passes under his name; and this fact once discovered, it becomes at least very difficult to separate what is genuine from what is spurious, or to refer the latter to any specific period.

In the picture of Unhilwârâ which we receive from the hands of these painters, the prominent figure is, undoubtedly, the sovereign. He is supported by the white-robed priests of the Jain religion, or by the Brahminical wearers of the badge of regeneration; beside him stand warriors of Rajpoot race in ringed tunics, such as defended from the Saxon bill the knights of the bastard William, or, equally gallant in the field, and wiser far in council, the Wâneea Muntreshwurs, already in profession puritans of peace, but not yet drained enough of their fiery Kshutree blood. At the edge of the warlike circle, themselves half warriors, stand the minstrels and the bards; and further off, fierce only in words, a group of peaceful cultivators, with their offerings of the fruits of the earth, behind whom, trusted perforce, and yet feared, their indispensable guards and yet their plunderers, are ranged the bowmen, "black as kâjul," the wild aborigines of the ravine and of the hill.

The sovereign himself is a stately figure; the scarlet umbrella of royalty is borne above him; the pictured sun glitters in gold behind his head; his necklaces are of voluptuous pearls, and his bracelets of sparkling diamonds; yet his is no effeminate form; the spear and the brand suit well his massive arms; his eye is red with the fire of battle; the shrill sound of the war-shell is as familiar to his ears as the deep rolling of the palatial drum; he is a "shielded man," as well as an anointed chief; "a Kshutree's son," no less than the offspring of a queen.

For the portraits of the fair we must turn to another canvas. There we behold her in the "swuyumbur mundup" choosing her favored knight, or in the marriage-hall shining beside him as the Goddess of Love beside her lord. An honored mother, we again behold her guiding the realm of her youthful son, or in his manhood aiding him with her counsel, and winning him to works of mercy and of religion; or again, alas! we view her in another mood, with strangely frenzied eye, supporting in her lap the lifeless form of her lord, while the shriek of the dissonant horn, and the still harsher scream of superstitious madness afflict the ear, while the funeral flame springs fiercely upwards, and the thick black smoky pall is spread above, as if to hide the horrid sight from heaven.

In the annals of a Hindoo society, the subject of land tenures must always be one of fundamental interest. Our authorities, however, were not likely to have made a direct statement upon a matter with which they, no doubt, supposed the whole world to be familiar. We gather, incidentally, that the king had a share in the produce; at times he is represented as taking this share directly from the cultivators, through agents of his, called "muntrees." At other times, we are told that the lords of the villages receive a share of the crop from the cultivators, and that the king receives his share from the lords. The country was divided into villages, called "grâms;" the villagers were householders—Koutombeeks (Koonbees), or husbandmen (Kârshuks); the village head-men were Puttkeels (Putels). The cultivators are exhibited to us employed as in the present day. While the crop is rising, they fence their fields with temporary hedges of thorns;

when it is more advanced, they are active in scaring the birds from it. The cultivators' wives, as at present, watching the rice-crops on the fields, make the country joyous with their songs. A failure of rain produces a default in payment of the king's share, and incarceration of the cultivator is resorted to, to enforce payment. The defaulter resists with obstinacy, and upon principle, and yet moans and seeks commiseration like a helpless child. Much trouble and annoyance to both parties is the result, and the matter is finally settled by a court of reference—a state of things, it may be remarked, exactly parallel to that existing at this day in parts of the country subject to native rule.

Alienations of land were made by the sovereign principally in favor of religious personages or places of worship. Several instances of this kind are recorded; as, for example, the grants of Sidhpoor and Seehore to the Brahmins, or of Châlâ to the Jains. These alienations are frequently called "grâs"—a word, perhaps, exclusively appropriated at the time to religious grants. When Mool Râj builds the Treepooroosh Prâsâd, a temple of Muhâ Dev, at Unhilwârâ, he assigns "grâs" to the ascetic, its custodian; and when Wâg Bhut, the son of Oodâyun, in the reign of Koomâr Pâl, erects at Wâhudpoor, near Pâleetânâ, the Jain temple called "Treebhoowun Pâl "Vehâr" after the father of the king, the subsistence which he assigns in land "for the Dev's people," is also called "grâs." "From "neglecting to give grâs," says Mâgh Pundit, in the court of Bhoj, speaking of a Brahmin's poverty, "the sun of the householder sets." The deed itself was called "shâsun."

Grants of land were also made to members of the royal family—as those of Deythulee and Wâghel. It is said, too, of Koomâr Pâl, "At that time the Solunkhee king, Emperor of the Generous, gave to "Âling, the potter, the grant, in writing, of seven hundred villages. "The potter being ashamed of his descent, his family to this day "retain the name of Sugurâ." Nothing of this grant is, however, traceable. It is remarkable that, unless the case of Wâghel be considered one, there is no instance of a permanent alienation of land for hereditary military service. The fortresses in Goozerat proper are represented as held by the king's garrisons, without the intervention of a baronial vassal; and of all the Rajpoot houses, whose chiefs subsequently appear as large landholders and kinglets in the country, not any one is asserted, even by their own annalists, to have held under grant of the Kings of Unhilwârâ, with the single exception of the Jhâlâs, who claim to have received their lands from Kurun II., the very last prince of the race. "Crown-bearing princes," however, we have seen at the court of Mool Râj; and Munduleshwurs, or lords of provinces, are elsewhere mentioned. Kâhn Dev, the husband of Ḳoomâr Pâl's sister, is so described; and when Oodâyun Muntree marches against Sâoosur, of Soreth, he, it is said, arrives at Wudwân, and there collects "all the Munduleshwurs." These, it would seem, were chiefs of the country; there are other Munduleek Rajas mentioned, whose territories, though subject to the sovereigns of Unhilwârâ, were not included in Goozerat. Such were the lords of Aboo and Girnâr; Mullikâ Urjoon, the Prince of the Konkun, and others.

The Sâmunts, or military officers, probably received their pay from the treasury, and ranked, as did in after times the officers of the imperial Moghul government of Delhi, according to the number of men they commanded. Sidh Râj, it is said, presented to one of his household "the Sâmuntship of one hundred horse;" and, when Koomâr Pâl went against Âno Raja, it is mentioned that "there were in the "army leaders of twenties and thirties called Muhâ-Bhuts, and of "thousands called Bhut-Râjs." The greater officers were "Chutra-"Putees," and "Nobut-possessors;" that is to say, they were allowed to use the insignia of the umbrella and the drums. It is remarkable that so many of the officers possessing high rank, and holding independent commands, are represented to have been Wâneeâs; such were Jâmb, the companion of Wun Râj; and Sujjun, his descendant; Moonjâl, the servant of Jye Singh; Oodâyun and his sons, and others. Among those who served occasionally, and were, perhaps, regarded as auxiliaries rather than as vassals, were chiefs from foreign lands—the Princes of Kuleeân, the Râthor Seeyojee. "Rajpoots and foot soldiers" are spoken of, as if the former were invariably cavalry. The great aim of the kings appears to have been to protect their own subjects from injury by foreign invasion or internal disturbance, and to extend their dominions by rendering the surrounding states tributary; to imitate, in fact, the example of the model-king, Vikrumâditya, "who, overrunning a cir-"cle of territory in all directions, made the Râj Munduls his servants."[1] These military expeditions were called by the expressive name of "Veejye Yâtrâ"—"victory-pilgrimages." At times, indeed, wars arose from some more immediate cause; as when a religious crusade was preached against Grâh Ripoo, or when the provocation given by Yushowurm drew upon him the anger of Sidh Râj; but the object to which hostilities were directed appears to have been still the same; and the victor, satisfied that his enemy had "taken grass in his

[1] Prubundh Chintâmunee.

mouth," and agreed to pay tribute, did not proceed to a permanent occupation of his territory. A country once overrun, future invasions of it seem to have partaken very largely of the character of those expeditions which were at last known by the name of "Moolukgeeree." Conquest meant the acquisition of a right to share in the yearly land revenue—a constantly recurring claim, which, as it was enforced against the cultivators at home by duress of their persons, so was it against foreign princes by military inroads upon their territories. Such appears to have been the case as early as the time when Jye Sheker was subjected to the inroads of King Bhoowur; or when, to facilitate the collection of his dues by the officers deputed for that purpose, Wun Râj, the young prince of the country, was appointed his "Selbhrut" by the King of Kuleeân. The tradition that Goozerat belonged, as a tributary province, to the sovereigns south of the Godâvery, continued apparently during the entire sway of the Chowra dynasty, and as late as the invasion by Bârp, the general of Teilip Raja, in the reign of the first of the Solunkhee kings. Subsequently Kutch, Soreth, the northern Konkun, Malwa, Jhâlor, and other countries were overrun by the descendants of Wun Râj, in numerous expeditions, though not, it would appear, permanently occupied. Though Grâh Ripoo was subdued by Mool Râj, and Lâkhâ slain by him, yet the Jhâreja and Yâdoo dynasties were by no means extinguished; though Yushowurm was vanquished, and Dhâr taken by Jye Singh, yet Urjoon Dev, of Malwa, not many years after, ravaged Goozerat; and though the banners of Unhilwârâ were displayed victoriously in "the country of a hundred thousand towns," yet the kings of Ujmeer continued to be dangerous rivals of the house of Wun Râj, until that latest time when Chohâns and Solunkhees alike fell before the Mohummedan invader.

At the courts of their more powerful neighbours, the kings of Unhilwârâ were represented by accredited diplomatic agents called "Sândhee-Vigraheek," or makers of peace and war, whose duty it was to keep them informed of foreign affairs—a task performed also in another manner by persons called "Sthân Pooroosh," men of the country, or spies, who were probably unrecognised by their employers.

In addition to the land revenue, the kings of Unhilwârâ levied transit duties, "dan," upon goods conveyed through the country; and they also exacted from religious pilgrims a tax called "kur." Of the affairs of navigation and commerce little is said. Ships are, however, mentioned, sea-traders and pirates; and merchants, "vyuvuhâree," are spoken of, apparently possessed of great wealth, for it is said that the trader who had amassed the sum of money which entitled him to that distinction was allowed to raise upon his house "the ten million banner." In the reign of Yog Râj, a foreign king's ships, laden with horses, elephants, and other cargo, are driven into the port of Someshwur Puttun. In Sidh Râj's time, sea-traders, "Sânyâtreek," import madder, concealing their gold among the bales from fear of pirates. The kings of Unhilwârâ held maritime possessions in the northern Konkun, as well as in Goozerat itself and the peninsular. Their ports of Stumbhteerth and Bhrigoopoor are well known as Cambay and Broach; Sooryâpoor may be Surat, and Gundaba is probably Gundevee. Beyt, Dwârka, Dev Puttun, Mhowa, Gopnâth, and others, studded the coast of Soorâshtra.

The two prevalent religions, the Jain and the Brahminical, were continually opposed to each other, and gained in turns the mastery. The former was powerful in the reign of the first sovereign, probably owing, in a great degree, to its protection of the youth of the king, and to the influence of the queen-mother, who was a convert to its doctrines. Wun Râj and his successors, however, professed the faith of Shiva, until the days when Sidh Râj listened to, and Koomâr Pâl adopted, the doctrines of Urhunt. From that period until the times at which we are arrived, with the short interval of the reign of Ujye Pâl, the Jain religion held the ascendancy, and numbered the sovereign among its professors. Their controversies, though bitter in the extreme, appear to have been conducted with much state and order, and the sovereign, being a Hindoo, sat himself as president of the religious synod, Sidh Râj, as we have seen, Shaivite, or more probably "liberal," as he was, being nevertheless the judge between branches of the heretical sect.

Of the places to which pilgrimages were made, the most celebrated were the great shrines of Shiva and Vishnoo, at Somnâth and Dwârka. The temples of Umbâjee at Ârâsoor, and of Kâleekâ at Châmpâner, were also in existence, and the same deity, under the name of Hinglâz, possessed a celebrated shrine at Null Bowlee; but of the local goddesses, now so numerous, no mention occurs. The Jain "teerths," or sacred places of Shutroonjye and Girnâr, have been alluded to. Shunkheshwur, on the borders of the Runn of Kutch, was probably coeval with these, and had been restored in the time of Merootoong Âchârya, who mentions it under the name of Shunkhpoor. Jain teerths existed also at Cambay and Kâvee, on opposite banks of the Myhee, and at Gundhâr on the Dhâdur. Mount Aboo received a Jain temple in the reign of Bheem Dev I., and Koomâr Pâl installed Shree Ujeetnâth upon the not-far-distant hill of Târingâ.

The sacred rivers were numerous, from virgin Suruswutee's bright but slender stream to the mighty flood of the much adored Nerbudda. The Taptee, the Myhee, the Sâbhermutee, and many streams of lesser note, were studded with holy places, and celebrated in sacred Muhâtmâs.

Of domestic affairs we are permitted but an occasional glimpse. The king's slumbers are broken in the morning by the sound of the royal drum and conch-shell. He rises, and goes forth to exercise his horse. His palace is in a citadel, called the Râj Pâtheekâ, which contains also the other royal buildings. It is ornamented with "keerttee sthumbhs," triumphal pillars. A gate, called "the clock-door" (ghutheekâ), opens into the city, and fronting it, in the main street, is the "treepolya," or barrier of three doors. In the day-time the king gives audience; mace-bearers keep the door of the court, and admit or reject visitors; the Yoov Raja, or heir-apparent, is beside the monarch, and the Munduleshwurs and Sâmunts surround him. The Muntree Râj, or Prudhân, is also there with his companions, sagely counselling economy, and ever ready in the production of written authority and precedent not to be disregarded. Business despatched, the Pundits, or men of learning, are called in, with their dreary literature, and pompous splitting of grammatical hairs; or, perhaps—more welcome guest—a wandering bard or "portrait painter" is introduced, with old world stories of Râm and of Vibheeshun, or with tales of fresher fragrance, pointing out a cynosure for every imagination in the beauty of some foreign fair; nor is the courtezan excluded, she of the smart saying, famed for the much-valued cleverness which is gained in "the world,"—who, when the learned fail, is ever ready to cut the Gordian knot of solemn question with the sharp blade of her repartee, for—

"The sight of foreign lands; the possession of a Pundit for a "friend; *a courtezan;* access to the royal court; patient study of the "Shâstras;—the roots of cleverness are these five."

The king appears in public, mounted on an elephant, or borne in the litter called "sookhâsun." On great days the shops, which line the streets through which he passes, are adorned. In the evening, after worship and waving of lamps before the idol, he retires to an upper chamber, called "chundra shâlâ," where his repast is served. It includes, we may be sure, animal food and wine, for we have beheld Sâmunt Singh in his fatal fit of intoxication, and have seen the virtuous abstinence from flesh practised by Koomâr Pâl, as a convert to the faith of the Teerthunkers. The meal finished, his body is anointed with sandal; he uses betel-nut, and reclines upon a swinging bed, which is suspended from the ceiling by chains; his scarlet robe is thrown over the couch and its pillow; sentinels are placed, and a night-lamp burns beside him. The duties of the king are, however, by no means finished; he must rise from his couch to perform the "Veerchuryâ." He goes forth, sword in hand, alone, or attended by a single servant, who carries drinking water, and thus traverses the silent streets of his city, or passing the gates, extends his ramble beyond its walls to some spot frequented only by the filthy birds of night, the Yogeenee and the Dâkin, female sprites, whom he compels to reply to his questions and to inform him of future events. Of the nocturnal rambles of Sidh Râj, it is said by the author of the Dwyâshray, "From what he "saw at night he would send for people in the day-time, and say to "one, 'you suffer from such and such an uneasiness,' or to another, "'you have such and such a ground of rejoicing,' so that people "thought that he knew the very hearts of men, and must be an incar-"nation of a Dev." Not seldom, however, the disguised prince meets with less sorry entertainment than is to be derived from the company of witches and goblins, or even from the contemplation of the private joys or sorrows of his people. The brilliant lights in the mansion of a wealthy merchant attract him, perhaps, to a more festive scene, where, though unknown, he is entertained; or he is drawn by the sound of music and by laughter to where, in the ante-chamber to some temple of Shiva, the actors are delighting a crowd by their extempore wit. The great Jye Singh is exhibited to us, on one occasion, attending in disguise a dramatic representation (nâtuk) at the Kurun Meroo Prâsâd, where he becomes familiar with a Wâneeo, who, in his unrestrained delight at the performance, leans upon the shoulder of the king, and receives supplies of betel-nut from the hand which brought down the pride of Khengâr and Yushowurm. The next morning, called into the presence-chamber, the poor trader is alarmed at beholding, in the occupant of the throne, his last night's companion of the theatre, but a ready speech of compliment provokes the sovereign's smile, and he is dismissed with honor. These exhibitions appear to have been attended with considerable expense, and to have been placed within the means of wealthy persons only. On another occasion, the same monarch beholding a nâtuk given "at Shiva's temple" by a merchant, is described as revolving in his mind the probable amount which his unwitting host might be compelled to contribute towards furnishing forth an army against Malwa.

Neither Merootoong nor the author of the Dwyâshray furnishes us with any account of the architecture, either private or public, of the times to which his work refers. The following description of the capital itself is, however, to be found in the Koomâr Pâl Churittra. "Unhilpoor was twelve coss in circuit, within which were many temples and colleges; eighty-four squares; eighty-four market-places, "with mints for gold and silver coin. Each class had its separate "quarter, as had each description of merchandise—elephants' teeth, "silks, purples, diamonds, pearls, &c. &c.—each had its separate "square. There was one market-place for money-changers; one for "perfumes and unguents; one for physicians; one for artizans; one "for goldsmiths and another for silversmiths; there were distinct "quarters for navigators, for bards, and for genealogists. The "eighteen 'wurun' inhabited the city; all were happy together. The "palace groaned with a multitude of separate buildings—for the "armory, for elephants, for horses and chariots, for the public "accountants and officers of state. Each kind of goods had its "separate custom-house, where the duties of export, import, and sale "were collected—as for spices, fruits, drugs, camphors, metals, and "everything costly of home or foreign growth. It is a place of universal commerce. The daily amount of duties is one lakh of "tunkhas. If you ask for water they give you milk. There are many "Jain temples, and on the banks of a lake is a shrine to Sehesling "Muhâ Dev. The population delights to saunter amidst the groves "of chumpâs, palms, rose-apples, sandal-trees, mangoes, &c., with "every variegated creeper, and fountains whose waters are *umrut*. "Here discussions take place on the Veds, carrying instruction to the "listener. There is no want of Jain priests, or of merchants true to "their word, and skilled in commerce; and there are many schools "for teaching grammar. Unhilwârâ is a sea of human beings. If "you can measure the waters of the ocean, then you may attempt to "count the number of souls. The army is numerous, nor is there any "lack of bell-bearing elephants."[1]

Of all this splendour, it is melancholy to relate, hardly a vestige remains. The relics of Unhilwârâ lie in a flat country within and around the walls of the modern city of Puttun; but, like those of Wullubheepoor, they are discovered only by excavation. Chiselled marble, however, instead of Babylonish brick, forms the debris of the capital of Wun Râj. It was brought probably, in part at least, from the hills of Ârâsoor, whose blue outline may be beheld on the horizon of this scene of sandy desolation. A portion still remains of the well which was constructed by the Queen of Bheem Dev I., and the site of the splendid reservoir of Sidh Râj is indicated at a distance by an octa-

[1] *Vide* Tod's Western India, pp. 156—158.

gonal Moslem tomb, which now occupies a mound in its centre. With the rest, six centuries and the fury of the Mohummedans have done their work. That "which Cambyses or time hath spared," moreover, "avarice now consumeth," and the poor cold ashes of Unhilwârâ are sold for a pitiful gain by her vulgar Mahratta lords, ignorant as they are alike of her glory and of their own dishonor.

Of the domestic edifices of the purely Hindoo times we can form but a general idea, founded upon a view of the structures employed by succeeding generations. The palace of the prince has passed away as completely as the cottage of the peasant, but of the splendors of public architecture we have the palpable evidence of existing remains; and we may with little effort and with complete certainty picture to ourselves, in their perfect state, the wells, the tanks, the triumphal arches, the temples and the fortresses of the sovereigns of Unhilpoor.

Of these relics, the most interesting, perhaps, are the sister fortreses of Dubhoee and Junjoowârâ. They are very similar in construction, as well as in extent; but the latter may be selected for description, both as being more regular in plan, and as having, from its unexposed position, suffered less of injury.

Junjoowârâ forms an exact square, of which each side measures in length about eight hundred yards. The walls which enclose this space are of solid mason-work, and rise about fifty feet in height.[1] In the centre of each side is a large gateway, the platform above which is supported by rows of brackets projected beyond each other until they nearly meet at the top, and forming a substitute for an arch. In the thickness of the wall these bracketted doorways are six times repeated, and upon them is laid a flat stone roof, a construction which was long employed, even after the time when the arch, with its facility for vaulted ceilings, had been introduced by the Mohummedans. At each corner of the fortress is a tower, square in general plan, but broken into the peculiar form in which the Hindoo architect delights; four rectangular bastions intervene between each corner tower and central gateway. The walls are throughout ornamented with sculp-

[1] The following opinion, extracted from an article upon the defence of Sebastopol, in the number of the "United States Journal" for November, 1855, which has been attributed to Sir John Burgoyne, may aid the reader in estimating the value, in their own day, of the fortifications of Junjoowârâ:

"One of the principal ingredients in defensive works is an obstacle to the "approach of the assailants, and the best obstacle is a wall or vertical face to be "surmounted. If this exceeds thirty feet in height it becomes very formidable "indeed; an escalade (which, while the wall is entire, is the only resource) is the "most desperate of military undertakings, and never succeeds but by absolute sur-"prise, or from very great weakness on the side of the defenders."

tured horizontal bands repeated at intervals, and are completed by semi-circular "kângras" or battlements, screening the platformed way along which the warders passed. The gateways themselves are covered with a profusion of sculptured ornament, which the art of photography alone can adequately represent. Within the walls, immediately opposite to, and not far removed from the southern gateway, is a circular or multilateral reservoir, about three hundred yards in diameter, the "ghât," or flight of descending steps, surrounding which is broken at regular intervals by paved roadways, enabling cattle and wheeled carriages to approach the waters of the tank. Each roadway is ornamented with two pavilions, terminating in pyramidal roofs. Beside the tank is a "bowlee," or well, of the peculiar character which we shall presently describe. Of this fortress the four gateways, in different stages of decay, still remain, and the wall which connects two of these with a corner bastion is tolerably perfect. The square space thus indicated, forming about a fourth part of the area of the fortress in its original state, has been re-enclosed by a wall of very inferior character, strengthened with circular bastions, and pierced by arched gateways. This portion is occupied by a modern town belonging to Koolee chieftains; but the buildings which were enclosed within the original circumvallation have wholly perished, and given place to a rank jungle. We must not omit to state that in numerous parts of the ancient work is found the inscription "Muhun Shree Oodul," supposed to indicate that Oodâyun Muntree was the minister employed in the direction of the work.

Dubhoee is, as we have said, very similar, both in form and extent, to Junjeewârâ. It is less regular in form, two of its sides meeting in a sharp angle and exceeding the others in length. The shorter sides extend about eight hundred and the longer about one thousand yards. The walls are somewhat lower than, and three of the gates not quite so magnificent as, those of Junjoowârâ; but this inferiority is redeemed by the fourth, called the Gate of Diamonds, which is more elaborate in design, and far superior in size. One of the corner towers of Dubhoee exhibits much singularity of plan. The walls of the tower slope inwards. Another remarkable feature in this fortification is the colonnade, which follows (on the inside) the line of the walls, and supports a platform several feet in breadth, thus forming a lengthened covered portico, which must have afforded invaluable shelter for a Hindoo garrison.[1] A reservoir of irregular shape is also contained within the encincture of Dubhoee.

[1] The author of "Oriental Memoirs" compares this colonnade to the porticoes in front of the barracks at Pompeii. *Vide* vol. ii, p. 325, orig. edit.

The fortresses we have described, it is necessary to recollect, were but frontier military positions, probably as far surpassed in splendor as in extent by Dholka and other towns of the second class, while these in turn were outshone by the marble-adorned metropolis of Unhilpoor.

Of the temples which still remain, we may mention first the Roodra Mâlâ of Sidhpoor. It was a very large edifice of the usual form, and apparently three stories in height. The mundup, or ante-chamber, was square externally; but the columns were so arranged as to admit of an easy transition into the octagonal form within. In the centre of three sides projected two storied porticoes, called "roop-chorees;" and on the fourth was the adytum, a most massive structure, rising tower-like to the extreme height of the central building, and then mounting beyond it into a "shikur," or spire. Two of the roop-chorees, deprived of their pyramidal roofs, and otherwise in a mutilated state, and part of the frontispiece to the adytum, remain.

On either side stood a "keerttee-stumbh," or triumphal pillar, one of which exists in a nearly perfect state. It consists of two richly adorned columns supporting an entablature and sculptured pediment. Brackets, formed of the heads of marine monsters, project from the columns at about two-thirds of their height. From the brackets springs a delicately fretted arch called "torun," or garland, which is in the centre, touched, as it were but at a tangent, by the architrave. This frontispiece, which is about thirty-five feet in height, is covered, from the ground to the apex, with the most elaborate sculpture.

The principal shrine which we have described, and which fronted the Suruswutee, stood in the centre of an extensive court. Three large gate-houses, opposite to the three porticoes of the temple, gave access to the outside; that in the front opening upon a terrace and flight of descending steps, which were continued for a considerable distance along the banks of the sacred stream. The enclosing wall of the courtyard was formed by numerous lesser shrines, each surmounted by a spire, three of which, occupying the central position in rear of the adytum, still remain, and have been converted into a Mohummedan mosque.

The temple at Modheyra affords us an example of a shrine of somewhat different character. It rose to the height of one story only, and consisted of an adytum, a closed mundup attached to it, and an open mundup separated from the rest of the edifice. The spire has fallen, and the domes are no longer in existence; but the remainder of the building is nearly complete, although indentations are visible upon some of the columns, such as might have been made in wood by sharp weapons, to which the Mohummedans point as marks of the swords of the Islamite saints. The extreme length is about one hundred and fifty feet, and the breadth fifty. On either side of the temple, and before it, are the remains of triumphal arches similar to those of Sidhpoor.

A flight of steps, commencing at the keerttee stumbh, in front of the temple, descends between handsome piers to a "koond," or reservoir. The koond covers an area nearly four times as large as that of the temple itself.

The monotonous appearance of the steps is relieved by small niched shrines placed chequer-wise, and by larger shrines, terminating in spires, which rise in the centre of three of the sides. Around the koond may be traced the remains of other structures; but their exact character it is now impossible to determine. The detached open mundup of the temple is now known under the name of "Seeta's Choree,"[1] or marriage hall, and the reservoir (now called the Râm Koond) is a celebrated place of pilgrimage for Vaishnavite ascetics.

At Wâghel is a temple similar in style to those which have been described, but of smaller dimensions. It consists of a single open mundup, one story in height, with pyramidal roof, three porticoes, and an adytum surmounted by a spire.

Reservoirs, such as that at Modheyra, are to be met with at Seehore, and other places. They were probably always attached, like the Râm Koond, to an adjacent temple; but the shrines have, for the most part, perished. A curious combination of four small koonds, which, with a circular well in the centre, form a Greek cross, is to be found at Lothesur, not far from Modheyra.

The usual form of tank was the multilateral, or almost circular, of which we have seen an instance at Junjoowârâ. Similar reservoirs occur at Moonjpoor, Syelâ, and many other places; some of them attaining a diameter of nearly seven hundred yards. The Suhusra Ling, at Unhilpoor, was probably of this class; and, judging from what is still traceable, of the largest dimensions. It was surrounded by numerous small shrines, and it is not incredible that these

[1] There is a similar detached porch in front of the temple at Barolli. *Vide* Fergusson's Hand Book of Architecture, vol. i., p. 112; and Tod's Annals of Rajasthan, vol. ii., p. 712.—The porch of Barolli is also called a marriage-hall, and tradition assigns it to the Rajpootnee bride of a Prince of the Hoons.

approximated to the number of one thousand. Near Gogo, in the peninsular, are the remains of a rectangular, or nearly square, reservoir, which is attributed to Sidh Râj, and called "the Soneyreea "tank." Of the two celebrated reservoirs which are believed to have been constructed during the regency of Myenul Devee, the mother of Jye Singh—a period prolific in splendid works of architecture—the Mulâv, namely at Dholka, and the Monsur at Veerumgâm, the latter requires a particular description. It is irregular in shape, and is popularly considered to have been constructed in imitation of the form of the conch-shell—the Hindoo war-trumpet. The usual "ghât," or flight of steps, surrounds the whole; in this instance ornamented by a multitude of small spire-covered shrines (many now wanting), which are supposed to have equalled in number the days of the year, and which in reality were more than three hundred. The shrines on one side of the tank are furnished with a pedestal for an image; those on the other side with a circular "julâdhâr," or basin. It is supposed that the former were consecrated to Shree Krishn, and the latter to Muhâ Dev. The water, collected from the surrounding country, passes first of all into a deep octagonal koond, where it leaves the sediment which it has collected. The koond is faced with stone, and ornamented on each side with a niche containing a figure sculptured in bold relief. Thence the water passes by a channel, lined with masonry, into the tunnel through which it enters the tank. The tunnel is divided into three cylinders, and upon the terrace which covers it is placed a large pavilion with pyramidal roof. This building has been restored in Mahratta times, and, one side of it having been built up, has been dedicated as a temple to Mâtâ Boucherâjee. The surrounding ghât is, in several places, interrupted by roadways, which descend to the water's edge. On either hand of one of these is a larger temple, formed of a mundup with a double adytum and spire; and in the corresponding position, on the other side of the tank, is a flat-roofed colonnade.

Of the wells of this period, there remain, in different parts of the country, examples of two kinds. Some are large circular wells of ordinary construction, but containing galleried apartments; others are more properly described as "wâvs" or "bowlees." The wâv (in Sanscrit, wâpeekâ) is a large edifice, of a picturesque and stately, as well as peculiar, character. Above the level of the ground, a row of four or five open pavilions, at regular distances from each other, usually square on the exterior, but sometimes, in the larger examples, passing into the octagonal form within, is alone visible; the roofs are supported on columns, and are, in the structure of the Hindoo times, pyramidal in form. The entrance to the wâv is by one of the end pavilions; thence a flight of steps descends to a landing immediately under the second dome, which is now seen to be supported by two rows of columns, one over the other. A second flight of steps continues the descent to a similar landing under the third pavilion, where the screen is found to be three columns in height. In this manner the descent continues stage by stage, the number of the columns increasing at each pavilion, until the level of the water is at last reached. The last flight of steps frequently conducts to an octagonal structure, in this position necessarily several stories high, and containing a gallery at each story. It is covered by the terminating dome, and is the most adorned portion of the wâv. The structure, which is sometimes eighty yards in length, invariably terminates in a circular well.

The most interesting relic of this nature is the wâv, called "the "Rânee's," at Unhilpoor, of which, however, but little has been preserved. Others are to be found in many parts of Goozerat and Soreth, in various stages of preservation. There is one remarkable one, of uncertain date, but probably, from its architecture, as old as the days when the dynasty of Sidh Râj ruled, near the city of Ahmedabad. It is called "Mâtâ Bhuwânee's," and is popularly attributed to the five Pânduvs. We have mentioned a wâv within the fortress of Junjoowârâ; there are Hindoo wâvs also at Wudwân, both within and without the walls, and in other places too numerous to mention.

The reservoirs, both wells and tanks, which we have described, were constructed, with the same general objects, "for the thirst-"suffering mortals from the four points of the heavens, for animals "and for birds, that eighty-four lakhs of living creatures" might enjoy them. They are to be found commonly in localities which suffer much from drought—in Puttun-wârâ for example, stigmatized by Rânik Devee as the place where animalculæ die for want of water; or in positions where much traffic occurs—at the gates of cities or at cross roads. They were works of religious merit also; for it is said, "than the virtue of building the wall of a city, greater "by ten thousand times is the virtue of constructing a place of "water;" they were offered as "Krishn-gifts;" they were dedicated to Doorgâ, "she who is named Koonduleenee, who is in form as a "well;" or to Wuroon, the god of water, "the witness of virtuous "actions."[1] They were built, to cite another authority, "for the

[1] This title is given to Wuroon because gifts are made, and other "virtuous

"uplifting from Nuruk (hell) of one hundred and one ancestors; for "the increase of hereditary fame; for the increase of sons and sons' "sons; for the enjoyment of Swerga (Paradise) during as long a "period as the sun and moon shall endure." The wâvs, like the koonds, were usually, if not universally, attached to temples; the tanks were consecrated by the symbols of Muhâ Dev himself which encircled them; their waters were sacred, presented already in offering to Shiva. The King of Benares, we are told by Merootoong, after enquiring of the Sândhee Vigraheek of Sidh Râj "the fashion "of the temples, wells, and other water reservoirs of Unhilpoor," made it a subject of reproach, that "the water of the Suhusra Ling "tank was Shiv-Nirmâlya,[1] and unfit for use." The ambassador asked in reply, "Whence, then, do the people of Benares procure "water?" and, receiving for answer that it was from the Ganges, rejoined, that if dedication to Shiva were a fault, it was one surely attaching equally to the sacred river which flowed from the forehead of the god. That these reservoirs were not intended for irrigation would, we think, sufficiently appear from their construction, and from the positions in which we find them, did we possess no knowledge but such as might be thence gathered of the purposes of their founders.

Such, then, are some of the relics of the kings of Unhilpoor. Their greatest and most enduring monument is, however, to be found in the fact, that surpassing the boast of Augustus, they found their country a waste, and left it a land flowing with milk and honey. The contrast is striking; but the general result cannot be doubted, however difficult may be the task of tracing the steps which intervened. At the time when the Chowra dynasty, under Wun Râj, first established itself at Unhilwârâ, the country of Goozerat was destitute of any other inhabitants than the wild aboriginal tribes. Wullubhee had fallen, perhaps not long before, and Cambay, Broach, and other cities on the coast retained somewhat of their prosperity. Inland, even as far northwards as the borders of the salt-lake which separated Soreth from Goojur-râshtra, the hum of peopled cities might have been heard,—

"Wulleh and Wudwân,
"Puttun city was afterwards founded."

"actions" performed, by the side of a river or at the edge of a tank or other water. In the ceremony called *Choollook*, or *Kol*, persons present a handful of water as the sign of the ratification of a gift. *Vide* p. 84, and note.

[1] Anything offered to Shiva is so called; and may not be taken again by the offerer, or devoted to a secular purpose.

But from Umbâ Bhuwânee to the embouchure of the Sâbhermutee river, from the hills which form the barrier of Malwo to the flats about the Runn of Kutch (except where Shunkhpoor, Punchâsur, and, perhaps, a few small towns in their vicinity, sheltered on the edge of the desert, a remnant from the city of Kunuk Sen), the dominion of the beasts of prey was disputed only by men who were little less the children of the forest than themselves.[1] In the reign of the last of the Solunkhee princes, on the contrary, we behold the same tract of country united under one strong government, studded with wealthy townships, adorned with populous cities, fenced with strong fortresses. The temple lifts its emulous spire above the dark foliage of the grove, out-topped as yet but by the rattling palm; shrine-bordered tanks and galleried wells, right royally devised, are seen in spots moistened of old only by the showers of the monsoon; and strings of camels laden with merchandise, or cavalcades of pilgrims furnished with rich offerings, hardly disturb—so familiar has their appearance now become—the antelope herds which formerly roamed alone over the tenantless plains.

The tale of Unhilwârâ's grandeur has been told; there remains now that of her decay and desolation; yet shall we perceive that her glorious morning shines no less brightly in contrast with the fitful, stormy day by which it is succeeded, than first it shone when chasing away the sable clouds of the preceding night. This fact, at least, we cannot fail to recognise—though beholding Ahmed, like Wun Râj, the founder of a new and brilliant dynasty; though observing his grandson, Mahmood, while he inscribes upon the rolls of fame a title almost as glorious as that of the Lion of Unhilpoor; though viewing the banners of Goozerat, borne by these and other princes victoriously abroad—that never was she for one hour unwounded by domestic strife, from that day on which the sceptre was struck from the hand of Bheem Dev II., to the long-distant period when Rajpoot, Moslem, and Mahratta at length agreed to sheathe their swords, and to repose for the just arbitrement of their quarrels on the power, the wisdom, and the faith of the "sea-dwelling stranger."

[1] There are faint traditions, it is true, of the residence of *Brahmins* at Kaira and Wurnugger.

CHAPTER XIV.

THE WÂGHELAS.—TEJ PÂL AND WUSTOO PÂL.—MOUNT ABOO.—THE PURMÂRS OF CHUNDRÂWUTEE.

LUWUN PRUSÂD, the son of the Sâmunt Ânâk Solunkhee, and of whose birth mention has been made in the history of the reign of Koomâr Pâl, is described by Merootoong as "the minister of Shree Bheem." He possessed Wâghel, and probably also Dhuwulgruh, or Dholka, a town which remained in the hands of his descendants until a late period. Luwun Prusâd married Mudun Râgnee, and had by her a son, Veer Dhuwul—the Veer Wâghela, or Veer Dhuwulung, of Chund Bhârot. The names of Veer Dhuwul, and of his father and grandfather, are mentioned in the inscription on the temple, erected by Tej Pâl, upon Mount Aboo, dated A.D. 1231; and in a second inscription in the same shrine, Veer Dhuwul is described under the titles of Muhâ Munduleshwur and Rânâ.

Merootoong relates that Mudun Râgnee left the house of her husband, taking the child Veer Dhuwul with her, and went to live with Dev Raja Puttkeel, the husband of her deceased sister; but that Veer Dhuwul, on attaining years of discretion, returned to the house of his father. The names of several of his cousins, as Sângun, Châmoond, and Raja, are mentioned as "possessors of countries and towns;" and of Veer Dhuwul it is said that he received a considerable territory from his father, to which he made additions by conquest. "The twice-born Châhud Sucheev" was his minister; and the brothers, Tej Pâl and Wustoo Pâl, were also employed by him.

It is probable that after the death of Bheem, Veer Dhuwul Wâghela was the most powerful of the chieftains of Goozerat, if, indeed, he did not possess the royal rank which was certainly possessed by his successors. The few circumstances of a political character mentioned by Merootoong as having occurred during the time of Veer Dhuwul, would, however, convey the impression that a powerful central authority was wanting. Wustoo Pâl, it is said, having quarrelled with a merchant named "Said," perhaps a Mohummedan trader, at Stumbhteerth, or Cambay, Said sent to Broach for a chieftain named Shunkh to protect him from the minister. Wustoo Pâl, on his side, called in the aid of Loon Pâl, a Golo, who attacked

Shunkh, and killed him, but received wounds in the action, of which in a few days he died. The minister, it is said, erected over the spot where he fell the temple of "Loon Pâl's Lord."

On another occasion, "the gooroo, of the Mlechh Sultan, whose "name was Mâlee Munmukh," having come to Goozerat while proceeding on a pilgrimage, though to what shrine is not mentioned, the brothers, Tej Pâl and Wustoo Pâl protected him from Veer Dhuwul and his father, who meditated his seizure—an act which won for them the future goodwill of the sultan.

"A contest for five villages" is mentioned, in which the combatants were on the one side Luwun Prusâd and Veer Dhuwul, and on the other, Shobun Dev, the father of Jyetul Devee, Veer Dhuwul's Queen. The Wâghelas were ultimately successful, but not before the young prince had been many times struck down in his father's presence.

On the death of Veer Dhuwul, one hundred and eighty-two servants having perished in the flames, Tej Pâl was obliged to interpose with a military force to prevent further sacrifices. The ministers placed Veesul Dev on the throne. Of this prince, nothing has been handed down; but he has been usually considered as the first of the Wâghela dynasty of Goozerat.

It is a curious fact, and one which strongly brings out to view the passive vitality of their institutions, that after each succeeding storm has swept over the land, while the clouds are as yet undispersed, and the re-appearing sun discloses little but fissures which have been rent by tempestuous torrents, the Hindoos are observed at once, without an effort, and as it were instinctively, proceeding in "the old ways," apparently as little sensible of sorrow for the past as they are of apprehension for the future. Mahmood, of Ghuznee, had hardly accomplished his disastrous homeward retreat, leaving behind him Unhilwârâ despoiled, and Somnâth a heap of ruins, when the sound of the hammer and the chisel was heard upon Ârâsoor and Aboo, and stately fanes began to arise at Koombhâreea and Dailwârâ, in which an elaboration almost incredible, and a finish worthy the hand of a Cellini, seem to express the founder's steadfast refusal to believe in Mlechh invaders, or iconoclastic destroyers, as other than the horrid phantoms of a disturbing dream. And now, as the second Bheem closes his troubled career—as the sun of Unhilwârâ sinks with him never again to rise in unclouded brightness, while the crescent, perhaps, still waves over the capital, while the roar of battle has not well died away, and the cry of alarm and pain still resounds through the land—at Aboo and Shutroonjye the work is again resumed, and shrines, surpassing even the magnificence of former days, arise as dwelling-places for those silent, ever-brooding, unmoved Teerthunkers.

Wustoo Pâl and Tej Pâl, the ministers of Veer Dhuwul Wâghela, but more widely known as the founders of the most magnificent of the temples of Dailwârâ, were Prâgwât, or Porwâl Wâneeas of the Jain religion, descended from ancestors who had, for several generations, resided at Unhilwârâ. They were brought to Veer Dhuwul's notice by his former minister, Châhud Dev, and appear to have enjoyed his confidence to an unusual extent, though the terms in which this fact is noticed are curiously illustrative of the state of society and of the relations that existed between a sovereign and those he employed. The principles of their policy are thus described by Merootoong :—"That minister is clever, who, without placing his "hand on any one's head, can increase the treasury; without putting "any one to death, protect the country; without war, augment its territories." The same author relates that when Veer Dhuwul entrusted Tej Pâl with the management of his affairs, he caused to be written upon a paper, which he presented to the minister, the following promise :—"Even if I be angry with you, rely upon it I will "restore to you as much property as you are now possessed of;" and the inscription in the temple which they founded records that, "Veer Dhuwul, the Choulookya, the practiser of what was right, by "the advice of the two ministers, refused to listen to the voice of "spies, even though they spoke. The two brothers, also, increased "the kingdom of their master. Troops of horses and of elephants "they fastened near his palace. The king, with happiness, enjoyed "his possessions. The two ministers seemed to be his arms reaching "down to his knees."[1]

Mount Aboo is said to be most easily accessible from the direction of Seerohee and Jhâlor. On the Goozerat side the ascent which possesses the greatest interest is that from the village of Girwur; it is, however, impracticable except to foot-men. The traveller from the shrine of Umbâ Bhuwânee passes, for a long distance, through romantic highland scenery, his lonely pathway usually the bed of a mountain torrent. "All is grand in this region,—lovely and wild, as "if it were destined by nature to be the haunt of her favorite progeny, "where human passions should never intrude to disturb the harmony "of the scene. The sky is cloudless; the notes of cuckoos are

[1] The Chiromantic books assert that men with long arms are prosperous.

" heard responding to each other from amidst the deep foliage, while " the jungle-fowl are crowing their matinals in the groves of bamboo " which shelter them; and groups of grey partridge, nestled in the " trees, vie with the ring-doves in expressions of delight, as the sun " clears the alpine cliffs and darts his fervent rays among them. " Others of the feathered tribe, not belonging to the plains, are " flying about, while the woodpecker's note is heard reverberating " from the hard surface on which he plies the power of his bill. " Fruits and flowers of various kinds and colors invite the inhabitants " of the forest, whether quadruped or feathered, and the industrious " bee here may sip the sweetest of sweets from jasmine, white or " yellow, climbing the giant foliage, from câmbeer or cânoa, whose " clustering purple and white flowers resemble the lilac, or from the " almond-scented oleander which covers the banks of the stream on " whose margin abundantly flourishes the *ricinus*, or the willow." No human form appears to disturb the charm of this enchanting solitude, except, perhaps, the grave figure of some Rajpoot cavalier, a pilgrim to Umbâjee, with shield hanging at his back, and spear swaying on his shoulder, fills the vista of a long and narrow gorge, in which a handful of stout hearts might stand against a host,—or a group of quiet grain-carriers, with piled-up sacks and grazing cattle, occupies some lovely wild spot in the heart of the defile, where the crystal stream expands into a little turf-bordered pool. By-and-bye the hills slope away into a level valley, which, though more or less sandy, exhibits many fertile spots, producing abundant crops of grain, with little villages here and there, and rivulets flowing from the mountains that in the distance raise, in front and rear, their gigantic forms. Majestic Aboo, shrouded in its cloak of mist, now engrosses every thought; its varying outline filling the imagination with a thousand suggestive forms, until a near view is at last obtained of its precipitous face,—its dark recesses lined with forest and underwood, and streaked with many a silver stream,—its diverging shoulders pushed majestically forwards in their garb of sable, variegated, as the sun rises towards his meridian, with tints of brightest gold.

Over one of these spurs a path may be seen from the village of Girwur, winding like a thread upon the mountain's side, now rising and again sinking almost to its former level. Through a thick and tangled forest it pursues its lengthened ascent to a small spot of level ground, below an almost perpendicular scarp, where, amidst a grove of magnificent foliage, is embowered the shrine of Wushisht Moonee. The traveller, who desires protection from the heat of the sun, rests here in a little garden filled with the strongly-perfumed flowering shrubs that are natives of the mountain, among which the yellow kewura is conspicuous; and sight and smell thus regaled, his sense of hearing is not less pleasingly entertained with the melodious murmuring of the waters, which, pouring forth through a cow's mouth sculptured in the rock, are received into an excavated basin beneath it.

The temple of the Moonee is a small and unimportant edifice, sufficient to contain a black marble figure of the sage who, from the fire-fountain of Uchuleshwur, called the ancestors of the Rajpoot tribes. The deep-rolling royal drum at morning, mid-day, and evening, sounds before Wushisht, and contributes not a little to the effect of the gorgeous scenery, which is filled with its sonorous tones. There is also a brass figure here of the martial hero of Aboogurh, "the "terror of the Dunooj," Dhârâwursh the Purmâr, who is represented in the act of supplication to the sage, the creator of his race.

From the shrine of Wushisht Moonee the ascent is continued by a long flight of steps cut in the living rock, which conduct at length to the level of the plains of Aboo. Arrived at this spot, the traveller may well fancy himself to have reached a new world—an island floating in the air. The table-land upon which he now stands is walled on all sides by abrupt and lofty cliffs, similar to those which he has ascended; it possesses an area of several miles; contains villages and hamlets; is ornamented by a lake and by more than one rivulet of water, and wears a coronet of mountain peaks, of which the highest is that called, from a little shrine that occupies it, "The "Saint's Pinnacle," and the most remarkable, that which is crowned by "the fortress that cannot be shaken," the renowned Uchulgurh.

The country between the shrine of Wushisht and Dailwârâ is thus pleasingly described by the annalist of Rajpootana.[1] "This excursion "revealed to me by far the most interesting portion of the table-land "of Aboo. There is more of cultivation, the inhabitants are more "numerous, the streams and foliage more abundant; here and there "a verdant carpet decked the ground, while some new wonder, "natural or artificial, appeared at every step. The kamérie, as usual "unseen, uttered its welcome note, and the strong clear voice of the "blackbird issued from a dark coppice, whence stole a limpid brook. "Every patch where corn could grow was diligently tilled, and in "this short space I passed four of the twelve hamlets of Aboo. "These were in harmony with the scene; the habitations neat and "comfortable, circular in form like wigwams, and coated with clay,

[1] See, for the extracts here made, Colonel Tod's Travels in Western India, chaps. v. and vi.

"washed with a light ochre colour. On the margin of each running "brook was the *aret*, or Egyptian wheel for irrigation, and, as the "water lies close to the surface, the excavations were not required to "be deep. The boundaries of these arable fields, chiefly of the "prickly *thoor*, or cactus, were clustered with the white dog-rose, "here called *khooja*, with which was intermingled the kind called "*seoti* (sacred to Seo or Siva), much cultivated in the gardens of "India. The pomegranate was literally growing out of a knoll of "granite, where there was scarcely any soil beyond the decomposed "surface of the rock. The apricot or nectarine appeared occasion-"ally, covered with fruit, but being yet quite green, it seems pro-"bable that it will never ripen. They also brought grapes, which, "from their size, I should have deemed cultivated. These, as well "as the citron, which I did not see, but which they pointed out in a "deep valley, are claimed amongst the indigenous products of Aboo. "The mango was abundant, and a rich and elegant parasite, with a "beautiful pendant blue and white flower, resembling the *lobelia*, "found root in its moss-covered branches. This parasite is called "*ambatri* (from *amba*, mango,) by the mountaineers, with whom it "appeared to be an especial favourite, as I observed that, whenever "it grew within reach, it was plucked and 'wreath'd in their dark "'locks' and their turbans. The trees generally, from their extreme "humidity, are covered with a vesture of grass and moss, and at "Uchulgurh the lofty *cajoor*, or date tree, was coated to the upper-"most branch. It is from this deposit that the parasites spring. Of "flowers there was a profusion; amongst them were the *chaméli* or "jasmine, and all the varieties of the balsam, as common as thistles. "The golden *chumpa*, the largest of the flowering trees, rarely met "with in the plains, and which, like the aloe, is said to flower but "once in a century, was seen at every hundred yards, laden with "blossoms and filling the air with perfume. In short, it was—

'A blending of all beauties, streams and dells,
'Fruit, foliage, crag, wood, cornfield, mountain, vine,
'And chiefless castles, breathing stern farewells
'From gray, but leafy walls, where Ruin greenly dwells.'"

The Nukhee-tulâv is a picturesque lake studded with foliage-covered islands, from among which frequent palm-trees lift their swaying heads, and surrounded by rocks wooded to the margin. When Colonel Tod saw it, "the water-fowls skimmed its surface, un-"heeding and unheeded by man; for on this sacred hill neither the "fowler's gun nor fisher's net is known; 'thou shalt not kill,' being the "supreme command, and the penalty of disobedience, death." The lake of Aboo has, however, since that time been gradually surrounded by European residences; a barrack for convalescent soldiers has been erected in its vicinity, and a Christian church disputes with the shrines of Âdeenâth and Uchuleshwur the possession of the sacred hill.

Near the Nukhee-tulâv, a broad and well constructed footway affords easy access to Mount Aboo from the village of Unâdurâ at its foot, and the neighbouring cantonment of Deesa.

Dailwârâ, or the region of temples, is near the Nukhee-tulâv. It contains other shrines besides the two principal ones founded by Tej Pâl and Veemul Shâ, but these are both the most ancient and the most magnificent. The temple of Veemul Shâ was founded, as we have seen, in A.D. 1031, before which time no Jain edifice appears to have existed on the sacred mountain. Anything more than the most general description of these celebrated shrines is unnecessary in this place.[1] They are not remarkable for size or for their external appearance, but internally they are finished with all that elaborate elegance which is usually supposed to belong only to the art of the goldsmith. The principal feature in each is the usual octagonal dome, forming a vestibule to the adytum, wherein the objects of worship are enshrined, and around which is a columned peristyle, roofed with numerous domes. The whole edifice is of white marble, and the sculptured ornaments with which every part of the surface is covered, are so finely chisselled, as to suggest the idea that they have been moulded of wax, the semi-transparent edges almost realizing, by their hardly perceptible thickness, the mathematician's definition of a line. The pendant which hangs from the centre of the dome of the temple of Tej Pâl is particularly remarkable, and rivets the attention of every visitor. As Colonel Tod justly remarks, "the delineation of "it defies the pen, and would tax to the utmost the pencil of the "most patient artist;" and he is secure in asserting, that no ornament of the most florid style of gothic architecture can be compared with it in richness. "It appears like a cluster of the half-disclosed lotus, "whose cups are so thin, so transparent, and so accurately wrought, "that it fixes the eye in admiration."[2] The sculpture of these temples

[1] They are described in Fergusson's Handbook of Architecture, vol. i., p. 69, et seq., and illustrations of them given. See also "Picturesque Illustrations of Ancient Architecture in Hindoostan," by the same author.

[2] "No time and no pains," says Mr. Fergusson, speaking of the temple of Tej Pâl and Wustoo Pâl, "would ever have enabled me to transfer to paper the lace-"like delicacy of the fairy forms into which the patient chisel of the Hindu has "carved the white marble of which it is composed." *Vide* Picturesque Illustrations

does not, however, confine itself to the representation of inanimate natural objects, it exercises itself also upon the scenes of domestic life, the labors of navigation and commerce, and the struggles of the battle-field; and it may be safely asserted that the student of antiquities, who should devote sufficient attention to these bas-reliefs, would be amply repaid by a large increase of knowledge regarding many interesting points in the manner and customs of mediæval India.

Colonel Tod ascended to the summit of the saint's pinnacle, the loftiest of the peaks of Aboo, where, before his time, European foot had never trod. "Although presenting internally scarcely any sensible "elevation above the crest of the mountain, as we approached "through the plains of Marwar, it towers full seven hundred feet "above the level of its plateau. A strong chilling wind blew from "the south, to avoid whose influence the cautious mountaineers, "coiling themselves in their black blankets, lay prostrate on the "ground, sheltered behind a projecting rock. The picture was "equally grand and novel; masses of cloud floated under our feet, "through which the sun occasionally darted a ray, as if to prevent "our being dazzled with too much glory. A small circular platform, "having a low parapet wall on the outer side, crowned the giddy "height. On one side was a cavern, about twenty feet square, "within which is a block of granite, bearing the impress of the feet "of Data Brigu, an incarnation of Vishnoo—the grand object of the "pilgrim's attainment; and in another corner are the pudoocâ, or "footsteps, of Râmâ Nund, the great apostle of the Seeta ascetics. "In this gloomy abode dwells a disciple of the order, who rings a "bell on the approach of a stranger, continuing the uproar until an "offering induces silence. The staffs of pilgrims were heaped in "piles around the footsteps of the saint, as memorials of their suc-"cessful intrepidity. Caves innumerable were seen in various parts "of the mountain, indicative of a Troglodyte population in former "ages; and there were many curious orbicular holes, which could "only be compared to cannon-shot. I patiently awaited the termi-"nation of the struggle between the powers of light and darkness, in "conversation with the recluse. He told me, that during the rainy

"of Ancient Architecture in Hindoostan." In his later work, the same author has the following in reference to the Hindoo pendant:—"Its forms, too, generally "have a lightness and elegance never even imagined in Gothic art; it hangs from "the centre of a dome more like a lustre of crystal drops than a solid mass of "marble or of stone."

" season, when the atmosphere is cleared of all impurities, the citadel " of Jodhpoor and the desert plain, as far as Balotra on the Loony, " were visible. It was some time before I could test this assertion, " though, during occasional outbreaks of the sun, we discerned the " rich valley, termed Bheetril, extending to Seerohee; and nearly " twenty miles to the east, the far-famed shrines of Umbâ Bhuwânee, " amongst the cloud-capped peaks of the Ârâwullee. At length, " however, Soorya burst forth in all his majesty, and chasing away " the sable masses, the eye swept over the desert, until vision was " lost in the blending of the dark blue vault with the dusky arid soil. " All that was required to form the sublime was at hand; and silence " confirmed the charm. If the eye, diverted from the vast abyss " beneath, turned but half a circle to the right, it rested on the " remains of the castle of the Purmârs, whose dusky walls refused to " reflect the sunbeams; while the slender palmyra, as if in mockery " of their decay, fluttered its ensign-like leaves amidst the ruined " courts of a race who once deemed their sway eternal. A little " further to the right rose the clustering domes of Dailwârâ, backed " by noble woods, and buttressed on all sides by fantastic pinnacles, " shooting like needles from the crest of the plateau, on whose " surface were seen meandering several rills pursuing their devious " course over the precipitous faces of the mountain. All was contrast— " the blue sky and sandy plain, the marble fanes and humble wig- " wam, the stately woods and rugged rocks."

Descending from the Saint's Pinnacle, the next objects of interest are the fire-fountain and the shrine of Uchuleshwur, one of the most renowned in the fabulous annals of the Hindoos. "The Ugnee- " koond is about nine hundred feet long by two hundred and forty " in breadth, excavated in the solid rock, and lined with solid " masonry of immensely large bricks. An insulated mass of rock " has been left in the centre of the koond, on which are the ruins of " a shrine to Mâtâ, the universal mother. On the crest of the " northern face of the koond is a group of small temples dedicated " to the Pândoo brothers, but, like the former, a mass of ruins. On " the western side is the shrine of Uchuleshwur, the tutelary divinity " of Aboo. There is nothing striking as to magnitude, and still less " as to decoration, in this; but it possesses a massive simplicity, " which guarantees its antiquity. It occupies the centre of a quad- " rangle, surrounded by smaller fanes, alike primitive in form, and " built of blocks of blue slate. * * * On the same side as this " temple, and on the very verge of the Ugnee-koond, is the mauso- " leum of Rao Maun, of Seerohee, who fell a victim to poison while "in one of the Jain temples. His body was burned near the shrine "of his patron deity, when five queens accompanied him to Yum "Lok. * * * * On the east side of the fire-fountain the remains "of a temple, sacred to the founder of his race, the first of the "Purmârs, strewed the ground. The statue, however, of Adeepâl "is firm upon its pedestal, and intact—a type of ancient days, of "antique costume, and early realities. It is of white marble, about "five feet in height, and represents Adeepâl in the act of slaying, "with an arrow, Bhyns Âsoor, a buffalo-headed monster of Titanian "brood, who used to drink, during the night, the sacred waters of the "fire-fountain, to guard which the Purmâr was created. * * * * I "quitted the Ugnee-koond for Uchulgurh, whose ruined towers were "buried in the dense masses of cloud that surrounded us. Having "completed the ascent, I entered this once regal abode through the "Hunoomân portal, which is composed of two noble towers built "with huge blocks of granite, black with the rude blasts of some "thousand winters. The towers had been connected at top by a "guard room, and the gate served as the entrance to the lower fort, "whose dilapidated walls were discoverable up the irregular ascent. "Another portal conducted to the inner fortress. The first object "that strikes the view on passing the latter gate is the Jain temple to "Pârusnâth, erected at the sole expense of a banker of Mandoo, and "at present under repair. The upper fortress is attributed to Rânâ "Koombho, who, when driven from Mewar, raised the banner of the "sun on the long-abandoned battlements of the Purmârs; but he "merely repaired this, the donjon of Uchulgurh, which, with the "inferior works, is of the most remote antiquity. A small lake in the "keep is called Sawun-Bhadoon, and well merits the names of the "two chief months of the monsoon, for in the middle of June it is "yet full of water. On the most elevated knoll, to the east, are the "remains of an alarum-tower of the Purmârs. From this point the "eye, occasionally piercing the swift-scudding clouds, had glimpses "of the ruined altars and palaces of the brave race, who, on the spot "whence I surveyed them, had fought and bled in their defence."

Before bidding a final adieu to the towers of Uchulgurh and to the interesting Aboo, it will be well to say a few words of the Purmâr family, who were, for many years, their sovereigns. Their capital was the fortified city of Chundrâwutee, the ruins of which may still be seen in a country thickly covered with jungle, on the banks of the Bunâs, about twelve miles from the foot of Aboo, and little more than the same distance from the shrines of Umbâ Bhuwânee and

Târingâ. The city itself is now overgrown with rank vegetation; its reservoirs and wells are choked up; its temples are destroyed; and its remains daily despoiled of their marble materials. Judging from the fragments which are strewn over an extensive plain, it must have been considerable in point of size; and its pretensions to great refinement and riches may be admitted from the beautiful remains of its marble edifices, of which twenty were discovered when the spot was first visited by Europeans. The house of Chundrâwutee possessed also Prulhâdun Puttun, or Pahlunpoor, a town which was founded by the warlike Prulhâdun Dev, the brother of Dhârâwursh.

The first of the Purmârs who are mentioned are Shree Dhoomrâj, and his successors Dhundhook, Dhroov, and Bhut—"heroes invincible by the elephant crowd of their enemies." From them descended Râm Dev, the father of Yusho Dhuwul, who reigned at Aboo during the time when Koomâr Pâl was its paramount sovereign. The sons of Yusho Dhuwul were the celebrated brothers, Dhârâwursh and Prulhâdun Dev; of whom the former left a son, Shree Som Singh Dev, who became his successor, and who is mentioned as "Muhâ Munduleshwur," in A.D. 1231, when Bheem Dev II. was Muhâ Râj Adheerâj, in Unhilwârâ. Som Singh again had a son, named Krishn Râj Dev.

The Purmârs, however, gave way, apparently during the reign of the son of Dhârâwursh, to the Chohâns of Nadole, one of whom, named Loond, or Loonig, is stated in the inscription on the temple of Veemul Shâ (dated A.D. 1222), to have slain the Munduleek, and acquired the sovereignty of Aboo: Loonig's son was Tej Singh, who, with his son Kânhur Dev and his grandson Sâmunt Singh, are mentioned in an inscription on the temple of Wushisht (dated A.D. 1338), in which Kânhur Dev is styled Prince of Chundrâwutee. The annals of the Deora Rajpoots, a branch of the Chohâns of Nadole, state that "Rao Loombho" conquered Aboo and Chundrâwutee, and transferred to himself the sovereignty of the Purmârs, in a battle fought at the village of Baraillee, "where Merhutungi, son of Aggun Sen, fell, with seven hundred of his kindred." The final struggle, according to this authority, took place in A.D. 1303, and gave Chundrâwutee to the Deora Chohâns; Aboo having been conquered by them seven years before. "Between these periods, however, the Chohâns had been gradually reducing the inferior fiefs of the Purmârs, each conquest giving birth to a new branch; and many of these being made without the aid of their suzerain, their descendants, such as the chiefs of Madar and Girwur, are disposed to pay but a scanty obedience to his representative."

Another of the Aboo inscriptions specifies Sârung Dev as sovereign of Unhilwârâ in A.D. 1294, and Veesul Dev as governor, under him, of eighteen hundred munduls; having his residence at Chundrâwutee. This Veesul Dev may have been merely the officer of the King of Unhilwârâ, temporarily holding the government of the district. We may suppose that on the irruption of the Chohâns, Sârung Dev occupied the disputed territory of his vassals with his own troops. There is, however, still another statement which is not so easily reconciled with what has been mentioned above. A second Loondh Dev, as is recorded on a slab in the temple of Uchuleshwur (dated A.D. 1321), who was descended from the Chohâns of Sâmbhur, and the names of whose ancestors are entirely different from those of the former Loond, or Loonig, "acquired the district of Chundrâwutee, "and the pleasant mountain Urbood," and placed statues of himself and of his queen in the presence of Uchuleshwur.

From this digression we return, for a short time, to the story of the Wâghelas. Of Veesul Dev, the son of Veer Dhuwul, as has been already remarked, there is little known. Bardic tradition relates that a famine occurred during his reign, which he was instrumental in alleviating; and it is said that he founded, or rather repaired, the town of Veesulnugger, and the fortress of Durbhâwutee, or Dubhoee.[1]

An inscription in the temple of Somnâth, at Dev Puttun, dated A.D. 1264, supplies us with the name of a prince to whom are attributed all the titles of a paramount sovereign—"Purumeshwur "Bhuttârk, Shree Châlook Chukruwurtee, Muhâ Râj Adheerâj "Shreemud Urjoon Dev." The heraldic bards of the Wâghela family state, from their traditional rolls, that Urjoon Dev was the successor of Veesul Dev; but mention nothing relating to the occurrences of his reign. He ruled, it appears, at Unhilwârâ, and followed the religion of Shiva. Of the "numerous princes" who obeyed him, there are mentioned Rânik Shree Someshwur Dev; perhaps the Purmâr Prince of Chundrâwutee; and the Chowra chiefs—Pâlook Dev, Râm Dev, Bheem Singh, and others. His minister was Shree Mull Dev, and he had other officers of the Mohummedan faith, as Hoormuz of Belacool, and Khoja Ibrahim, son of the Nakhoda Noor-ood-deen Feeroz; but nothing is said of the offices which they filled further than is suggested by the title "Nakhoda;" nor is

[1] See, for a tradition in which the name of Veesul Dev, King of Puttun, is connected with Dubhoee, Forbes' Oriental Memoirs, vol. ii., pp. 335–337, original edition.

their appearance in Goozerat, as royal officers under a Hindoo sovereign, at all accounted for.

Following Urjoon Dev, the bards of the Wâghelas place Luwun Raja, a prince who is not mentioned by other authorities, and of whom they themselves have no information to give; and next to him, Sârung Dev, who appears in the Aboo inscriptions as sovereign of Unhilwârâ, in A.D. 1294, having under him Veesul Dev, already mentioned as Munduleshwur of Chundrâwutee. The successor of Sârung Dev was Kurun Wâghela, known by the surname of "Ghelo," or "insane," the last of the Hindoo princes of Unhilpoor.

CHAPTER XV.

RAJA KURUN WÂGHELA.

THE closing scenes of the drama of Unhilwârâ were now to be played. In the year A.D. 1296, Allah-ood-deen Khiljy having murdered him who was not only his sovereign, but also his benefactor and his uncle, stepped over the old man's corpse to the throne of Delhi, and causing the public prayer to be read in his name, commenced a reign of cruelty and bloodshed, in which he was destined to acquire wealth and power such as were unequalled by any prince who sat before him on the throne of Hindoostan, and to surpass by far the almost fabulous riches accumulated in the ten campaigns of Mahmood of Ghuznee. "It being the will of God," says the author of the Meerât Ahmudee, "that the faith and laws of the Prophet should be made known, the "sovereignty and power of the tribes already noticed came to an end, "and were transferred to the supporters of our pure religion and illus-"trious law, in order that the light of the exalted faith might shine "resplendent as the sun amidst that dark region of infidelity; and "we, by publishing the words of truth and obeying the commandments "of that religion, forbidding us to do evil, might turn away the people "from the terrible desert of error, and lead them on the high road of "salvation."

In the commencement of the year A.D. 1297, Aluf Khân, the brother of the sultan, Allah-ood-deen, and Noosrut Khân, his prime minister, were sent with an army to effect the reconquest of Goozerat. Laying waste the country, they again occupied with a Mohummedan garrison the city of Wun Râj, its sovereign, Raja Kurun Wâghela, flying before them to take refuge with the Mahratta prince, Râm Dev, Raja of Devgurh, in the Dekkan. No motive, in addition to the lust of dominion, was required to attract the Moslem invaders, but the Hindoo bards, who delight in assigning a domestic occurrence as the cause of any great political event, have on the present occasion recorded the following story :—" Kurun Ghelaro," say they, " had two ministers, Mâdhuv and Keshuv. They were Nâgur Brahmins, and it was by them " that the Mâdhuv well, which still exists at Wudwân, was constructed. " The raja took away from her husband Mâdhuv's wife, who was a *pud-* " *meenee*,[1] and he slew Keshuv. On the death of his brother, Mâdhuv " went to Delhi, to Allah-ood-deen, and brought in the Mohummedans. " At this period the gates of the cities and towns in Goozerat were " kept shut in the day time ; cattle grazed within the city walls ; people " tied a fold of their turbans under their chins that they might be " ready for flight. In the year A.D. 1300, the Toorks entered Goo- " zerat. Mâdhuv presented Allah-ood-deen with three hundred and " sixty horses, and procured for himself the office of civil minister of " the country. Aluf Khân was the military governor. He com- " manded a lakh of horsemen, fifteen hundred elephants, twenty " thousand foot soldiers, and there were with him forty-five officers " who were entitled to use kettle-drums. He took Goozerat from the " Wâghelas."

Kurun Raja, in his precipitate retreat, had been compelled to abandon his wives, children, elephants, baggage and treasure, all which fell into the hands of the conquerors. Among the Rânees thus made captives by the enemies of their race and religion was Kowlâ Devee, " who, for her beauty, wit, and accomplishments, was the " flower of India." She was carried to the harem of the sultan, and became the cause of further miseries to her country and her family. Aluf Khân and the vizier proceeded to plunder Cambay, which, being a wealthy town and full of merchants, yielded an immense booty to the conquerors. Here Noosrut Khân seized by force a handsome slave belonging to a merchant at Cambay, who, afterwards attracting the attention of the sovereign, rose to great eminence under the title of Mullik Kâfoor. The Mohummedans also took care to repeat their periodical achievement of " destroying the idol of Somnâth, which " had been again set up after the time of Mahmood of Ghuznee."

There is no further mention of the affairs of Goozerat until the year A.D. 1304, about which time, it is said, Aluf Khân was again appointed to the government of that country, and sent thither with a large army.

[1] *Vide* foot-note, p. 123.

He built at Unhilwârâ, says the author of Meerât Ahmudee, "The "Friday mosque, of white marble, which remains at the present time, "and the pillars of which are so numerous that one often makes a "mistake in counting them. They also relate that it was once an "idol temple converted to a mosque; but it is, in short, a wonderful "and noble building, which was then in the centre of the city, though "now distant from the part inhabited."

In A.D. 1306, Kâfoor, the former slave of Cambay, who had been purchased for a thousand deenars, but now the favorite of the sovereign and the envy of the nobles, was invested with the title of Mullik Naib, and placed in command of an army, led by many officers of renown, and destined "to subdue the countries of the south of India." Among other provincial officers, Aluf Khân, governor of Goozerat, was instructed to co-operate in the meditated conquest of the Dekkan. It was at this time that Kowlâ Devee, now the favorite sultana of Allah-ood-deen, becoming acquainted with the intended expedition, sought the royal presence and solicited a boon from her imperial slave. Before she was taken prisoner, she informed him, she had borne two daughters to her Rajpoot husband. One of them, the eldest, she had heard had since died, but the other, whose name was Dewul Rânee, and who was only four years old when she was torn from her mother's embrace, was still alive. She therefore begged that it would please the sultan to give such orders to his generals as should ensure their obtaining possession of Dewul Rânee, and sending her to Delhi.

Mullik Naib Kâfoor received accordingly the royal mandate, and having encamped at Sultânpoor, sent orders to the unhappy Kurun Raja, in his retreat in Bâglânâ, to deliver up the Princess Dewul, or prepare to withstand the power of the imperial arms. The time, however, had not yet quite arrived when the Rajpoot was accustomed, in bitterness of heart, to surrender his beloved daughter to what he felt to be a pollution worse than death, and to console his miserable necessity with the sad proverb, "When the skies rain fire, the father "must shield himself with his child." The clansman of Bheem Dev, the rightful successor of the lion-hearted Sidh Râj, retained, amidst all his misfortunes, a sense of the dignity of his race, and "could by "no means be brought to agree to this demand." Finding that his threats were of no avail with the unfortunate Prince of Unhilwârâ, thus standing like a wounded lion at bay, Kâfoor, the imperial deputy, continued his march, contenting himself with directing that Aluf Khân, with the troops of Goozerat, should endeavour to accomplish the desired object by leading his army through the mountains of Bâglânâ.

Aluf Khân was, however, here opposed by Kurun Raja, whose desperate valour, during a period of two months, in which several actions were fought, defeated him in every attempt to force a passage. While the last of the kings of Unhilwârâ thus maintained an heroic, but almost hopeless struggle, he received solicitations for the hand of Dewul Rânee from another prince, who, though of Mahratta race, and in happier days no equal match for a daughter of the Châlookya blood, still hoped, in this hour of stern necessity, to win the reluctant consent of Kurun. Shunkul Dev, the Prince of Devgurh,[1] had long aspired to the hand of Dewul Rânee; and now his own brother Bheem approached Kurun with presents, offered the aid of Devgurh, and urged that, as the princess was the assigned cause of the war, the leader of the Mohummedans, ascertaining her to be already under the protection of a husband, would despair of obtaining his end, and retire to Hindoostan. Kurun relied much on the young prince's offer of aid—it was as a straw cast to a drowning man; he felt, too, that a Hindoo, though of inferior lineage, was a less bitter alternative than the despised and detested Mlechh, and, consenting to the proposal, he reluctantly promised the hand of his daughter to Shunkul Dev.

But it was too late; and Kurun was destined to drink the cup of humiliation even to the dregs. Aluf Khân, hearing of the proposed marriage, was much concerned lest the sultan should impute the result to his neglect, and resolved, at all hazards, to secure the princess before her departure. He knew the power which Kowlâ Devee wielded, and was apprehensive that his own life hung on his success. He laid the case before his officers, urged that they were equally involved with himself, and engaged their unanimous support. A system of operations was carefully matured; the mountain passes were simultaneously entered; the retreat of Kurun Raja was discovered and broken up; his adherents were dispersed, and he himself was compelled to fly to Devgurh, leaving elephants, tents, and equipage on the field. Aluf Khân pursued him through the defiles of the mountains, and at last arrived within a single march of the fortress of Devgurh. He had entirely lost the track of the fugitives; he was in deep despair, and seemed as if he had thrown his last die and found the chance against him. But accident gave him the success which energy and well-laid schemes had failed of securing.

While the Mohummedan leader halted for two days to refresh his troops among the mountains, a party of his soldiers, three hundred in

[1] For an account of the "*Devagiri Yâdavas*," to which race Shunkul Dev belonged, *vide* Journal of the Royal Asiatic Society, vol. iv., p. 26.

number, set off to explore the wonders of Ellora. As they traversed the defiles that lead to those celebrated caves, they came suddenly upon a body of Mahratta horse, bearing the banner of Devgurh. It was the retinue of Bheem Dev, who conveyed his brother's long-sought bride towards her destined home. The Mohummedans, though few in number, were too far advanced to possess the opportunity of retreat; they stood on the defensive, and prepared to receive the enemy. Bheem Dev, solicitous for his charge, would gladly have avoided an encounter, but the foe was before him, the road to Devgurh was in their possession, and he saw no resource but that of battle. The two parties instantly engaged; at the first onset some of the Hindoos fled, and an arrow piercing the horse of Dewul Rânee, she fell to the ground. A desperate struggle ensued; the swords of Seerohee and the scymitars of Arabia, alike reddened with blood, crossed over the prostrate form of the daughter of Kurun; and a misdirected blow might soon have saved the honor of her race at the expense of her life, had not the alarm of her female slaves induced them to discover to the Mohummedans the name and rank of her whom they had long so vainly sought, and at last so strangely found.

The Princess of Unhilwârâ was conveyed with respect and care to the camp of Aluf Khân, and that commander, well aware how acceptable the prize would be to his sovereign, over whom the lady's mother exercised an influence so supreme, determined upon prosecuting his military operations no further, and returning to Goozerat, proceeded thence with his fair young charge to Delhi, where he placed her in the arms of the sultana. She had scarcely arrived at the seat of empire, before her "incomparable beauty" subdued the heart of the Shahzâda, the son of Allah-ood-deen. She became his bride, and thus attained the rank for which many a Moslem fair one doubtless sighed in vain; yet, while the imperial court rang with the praises of her victorious charms, and the lyre of Umeer Khoosroo immortalised the illustrious loves of Khizr Khân and Dewul Rânee, who shall assert that no shade of sadness rested on her spirit at the thought of the disappointed affection of Shunkul Dev, or the deeper grief of her bereaved and dishonored father.

History records no more of the last and most unfortunate of the sovereigns of Unhilwârâ. He died, probably, a nameless fugitive; driven from his throne and his country; despoiled of the honor dearer to a Rajpoot than either power or home; deserted, in his affliction, by his wife, and even by the child whose fate it was to add the last and bitterest pang to his misfortunes. Yet were the sorrows of Raja Kurun far from unavenged. The plunder, which the victors had borne from the despoiled seaport of Unhilwârâ, concealed a viper which was destined to sting them to the heart. Years rolled on, and victory seemed chained to the blood-besmeared banners of Allah-ood-deen ; yet Nemesis hovered in the air with her slow-descending but inexorable sword. "The king, elated by the success "of his arms, abandoned himself to inordinate pride. He listened "no longer to advice, as he sometimes condescended to do in the "beginning of his reign, but everything was executed by his irrevo-"cable word. Yet, it is related that the empire never flourished so "much as in his reign. Order and justice prevailed in the most "distant provinces, and magnificence raised her head in the land. "Palaces, mosques, universities, baths, mausolea, forts, and all kinds "of public and private buildings seemed to rise as if by magic. "Neither did there, in any age, appear such a concourse of learned "men from all parts.

"But the king seemed to have now reached the zenith of his "splendour and power ; and as everything is liable to perish, and "stability belongs to God alone, so the fullness of the king's prosperity "began to decline, and the lustre of his reign to fade away." He resigned the reins of government entirely into the hands of Mullik Kâfoor, the thousand-deenar slave of Cambay, whom he blindly supported in every impolitic and tyrannical measure, thus giving disgust to the nobles, and creating universal discontent among the people. Mullik Kâfoor, who had long aspired to the throne, now began seriously to form schemes for the extirpation of the royal line. Khizr Khân, the bridegroom of Dewul Rânee, and Aluf Khân, the destroyer of her father's throne, were among his first victims, having been accused by him of conspiring against the life of the sultan, and involved in subtle and malignant meshes such as the hand of an Iago alone can weave. "At this time, also, the flames "of universal insurrection, which had long been smothered, began "to burst forth, and were first apparent in Goozerat, which rose in "insurrection," as if the very soil, which had so long obeyed the successors of Wun Râj, performed her last act of fealty in lighting the funeral pyre of their destroyer. To repress this rebellion the sultan dispatched a distinguished officer, named Kumâl Khân, but the followers of Aluf Khân, the murdered viceroy, defeated him with great slaughter. At the same moment, the Rajpoots of Cheetore, once again mindful of their ancient fame, hurled the Mohummedan officers from their walls and asserted their independence ; while Hurpâl, the husband of the sister of Shunkul Dev, raised the Dekkan in arms, and expelled the Moslem garrisons.

On receiving these accounts Allah-ood-deen, "the murderer," bit his own flesh in his impotent fury. His grief and rage tended only to increase his disorder, which seemed to defy the power of medicine; and, on the evening of the nineteenth of December, in the year of Christ thirteen hundred and sixteen, he gave up the ghost, not without suspicion of having been poisoned by the villain whom he had raised from the dust to filch from him the lives of his flesh and blood, and his own dearly bought imperial power.

BOOK II.

CHAPTER I.

FIRST MOHUMMEDAN PERIOD.

THE Mohummedan conquerors possessed themselves immediately of the capital city of Unhilpoor, of the ports of Cambay, Broach, and Surat, and of much of what remained of the crown lands of the dynasty of Sidh Râj. Large tracts of the country, however, continued to be for a length of time wholly independent, and though they were gradually rendered tributary to the Sultans of Ahmedabad, their complete subjection was never effected by those princes, nor have they, up to the present time, reverted to that natural relation to the paramount power which they bore during the sway of the dynasty of Unhilwârâ. A branch of the royal Wâghela race itself continued to hold much of the country to the west of the Sâbhermutee river, while other scions of the same house, separated by the Purmârs of Tursunghmo and the Râthors of Eedur, maintained themselves in different positions along the mountain line from Veerpoor, on the banks of the Myhee to Poseenâ, at the most northern verge of Goozerat, beyond the crag-embosomed shrine of Umbâ Bhuwânee. The Jhâlâs were firmly fixed in the plains which lie between the lesser Runn of Kutch and the gulf of Cambay; the Koolee branches of these clans, with frequent other tribes of pure or adulterated aboriginal descent, spread over the Choonwâl, and appeared in many remote and inaccessible lands of hill or forest; the banner of Kâlee floated under the protection of a line of Rajpoot princes, from the hill of Powungurh on the east; while on the west the descendants of Khengâr grasped with tenacity their famous fortress of Joonagurh, controlling, from within its walls, much of the peninsula over which they had long maintained the undisputed sway; and chiefs, deriving pretensions originally from them, showed themselves scattered over the remainder, distinguished among whom were the Gohils, lords of Gogo and Peerum, and of the sea-washed province which derived from them its name of Gohilwâr.

The story of these Hindoo chieftainships is our principal concern. The Mohummedan historians, for the most part, refer to them only under the titles of infidels, insurgents, or rebels. From the accounts, however, which these Moslems themselves have left us, and which we now give in nearly their own words, it is clear that Goozerat was very far from having been conquered even by the lieutenants of Allah-ood-deen. The task had to be attempted again and again by his successors, and was, in fact, as we shall afterwards see, never fully accomplished.

Moobârik Khiljy, the son of Allah-ood-deen, after the short-lived usurpation of Mullik Kâfoor, ascended the throne of Dehli in A.D. 1317, and in the first year of his reign sent Mullik Kâmil-ood-deen to allay the disturbances which had already commenced in Goozerat, in which country, as Ferishta relates, rebels had risen up in every direction. This officer having obtained the honor of martyrdom in war with the infidels soon after his appearance in Goozerat, a second army was sent thither under the command of the celebrated Ein-ool-moolk Mooltâny, an officer of great abilities, who defeated the insurgents, cut off their chiefs, and settled the country in peace. After this, the king conferred the government of Goozerat upon Zuffur Khân, whose daughter he had taken in marriage. Zuffur Khân soon after marched his army to Unhilwârâ, which had already been the scene of renewed disturbances; he reduced the rebels, confiscated their estates, and sent their moveable wealth to the king. This governor, though "without a fault, and the chief support of the state," fell a victim soon after to the caprice of his sovereign, being recalled, and put to death. He was succeeded by Hissâm-ood-deen, an officer of Hindoo descent and of the Purmâr blood, who had not long been established, when, in conjunction with a few nobles, he rebelled. The other commanders in Goozerat, however, rising in arms, defeated him, and sent him prisoner to Delhi. Mullik Wujeh-ood-deen Koreishy, a brave and active officer, was sent into Goozerat in the place of Hissâm-ood-deen, and succeeded in effecting the pacification of the country. On his recall, Mullik Khoosroo, a relation of Hissâm-ood-deen, and for some time the favorite of the king, was appointed to Goozerat, but his ambition leading him to aspire to the throne of his master, he does not appear to have exercised vice-regal power in person. Moobârik Khiljy, who was the last of his race, was murdered by Mullik Khoosroo in A.D. 1321.

In the reign of Gheiâs-ood-deen Toghluk, Tâj-ool-moolk was appointed to the government of Goozerat, "in order that he might "bring the same into subjection," and in that of Mohummed Toghluk, Ahmud Ayâz received the government of the province, and Mullik Mokbil was created its vizier. Some other officers at this time obtained estates in Goozerat, and one of these, who bore the title of Mullik-oot-Toojâr, or chief of the merchants, held the lands of Nowsâree, on the sea-coast below Surat. In A.D. 1327, Toormooshreen Khân, a Mogul general, having invaded Hindoostan, was bribed to retire, by Mohummed Toghluk, at almost the price of the kingdom, and in his retreat passed through Goozerat and Sindh, both of which countries he plundered, carrying off many of the inhabitants.

Twenty years afterwards Mullik Mokbil, who by this time appears to have been appointed to the government of Goozerat, taking alarm at the disaffection evinced by the Umeer Joodeeda, or officers of Mogul blood, made an attempt to secure the royal treasures, with which, and a number of horses collected from the royal stables, he was on his way to Delhi, marching by way of Baroda and Dubhoee, when he was intercepted and plundered by the Umeers, and compelled to fly to Unhilwârâ. The king, upon receiving intelligence of this outbreak, prepared to march in person to Goozerat; but first permitted Ayeez, the governor of Malwa, at that officer's request, to attempt the reduction of the rebels. Ayeez entered Goozerat accordingly; but was defeated, and slain by the Umeers, and the king, informed of his disaster, no longer delayed his own advance.

Mohummed Toghluk Shah, having reached the hills of Aboogurh, sent one of his generals against the Umeers. A battle was fought in the vicinity of the village of Devee (Deesa?), and the rebels were totally defeated. The king now proceeded by slow marches to Broach; another action was fought on the banks of the Nerbudda, which likewise terminated favorably for the royal troops—by whom the towns of Cambay and Surat were subsequently sacked. Mohummed Toghluk proceeded to invest Devgurh, which, under the Mohummedan name of Dowlutabad, he had twice insanely attempted to substitute for Delhi, as the capital of his empire. While employed in the siege, he received intelligence that the Umeer Joodeeda of Goozerat, joined by many of the zumeendars, or Hindoo landholders, had not only taken possession of Unhilwârâ, but had put to death the imperial deputy; had imprisoned the governor; and, after having plundered Cambay, were now engaged in besieging Broach. The emperor, quitting his lines before Dowlutabad, marched to Broach, the rebels retreating before him to Cambay, at which place they made a stand, and defeated the officers sent in pursuit of them by the shah. Mohummed Toghluk, breathing nothing but revenge, hastened to Cambay; the rebels again retired before him; but, in consequence of the state of the roads, and the unfavorable weather, the king was compelled to halt his army at Ashâwul, a town situated near the present city of Ahmedabad. The rebels, meanwhile, having recruited their army at Unhilwârâ, advanced to meet the king; a further action was fought at Kuree, in which the imperial arms were victorious; the rebels fled to Sindh, and Mohummed Toghluk entered the city of Wun Râj, where he remained some time employed in the restoration of order.

The king spent the greatest part of that year in Goozerat recruiting his army, and the year following he was employed in besieging Joonagurh and reducing Kutch. He was, however, attacked with a dangerous disorder at Goondul, in the neighbourhood of Joonagurh, which, though it proved eventually fatal, did not at the time prevent his marching with his army to the banks of the Indus, where he chastised the Soomuree Prince of Sindh, who had sheltered the fugitive Umeers.

In the reign of Feroze Toghluk, that sovereign, after his conquest of Nuggur Kot, had undertaken operations in Sindh which the rains compelled him to suspend. He moved his army, therefore, into Goozerat, where he remained until the season allowed of his returning to Sindh. Some years afterwards (A.D. 1376), the revenue of Goozerat being greatly deficient, the king was induced to listen to the proposals of an officer named Shums-ood-deen Dumghâny, who offered to give a large sum above the usual payment in case of his being appointed to the government. The king, after having enquired of the existing viceroy whether he would offer the same terms, and received a refusal, consented to the appointment of Shums-ood-deen, who accordingly repaired to the seat of his government; but soon after, being unable to fulfil his engagements, went into rebellion. The people, whom he had greatly oppressed, seizing this opportunity of revenge, joined the foreign Umeers of the province, and Shums-ood-deen was, by their united forces, defeated and slain. Furhut-ool-Moolk held the government from this time till A.D. 1387; and when, in that year, another officer was nominated to replace him, rose in rebellion, and, being joined by the foreign officers, defeated and slew his proposed successor. He was confirmed in the office of Governor of Goozerat by Gheiâs-ood-deen Toghluk, and retained it until A.D. 1390, when he again rebelled, with the view of establishing his independence. In furtherance of his object, Furhut-ool-Moolk strove to conciliate the Hindoos by encouraging their religion. His conduct, however, alarmed the orthodox Mohummedans, who addressed petitions to the throne, pointing out both the political views of their governor, and the danger to which he was exposing the faith of Islam. A nobleman of the court, himself of the Hindoo blood of the Tâk, or Takshac, race, was then appointed viceroy of Goozerat, under the title of Moozuffer Khân; and, to add to his dignity, was presented with the white canopy and scarlet pavilion, exclusively used by kings. Moozuffer Khân, having entered Goozerat, and advanced into the vicinity of the capital, was met at Sidhpoor by his rival with an army composed chiefly of Hindoos. An engagement ensued, in which Furhut-ool-Moolk was defeated and slain. Moozuffer Khân now, in the name of his imperial master, assumed the reins of government at Unhilwârâ (A.D. 1391).

CHAPTER II.

THE WÂGHELAS—LOONÂWÂRÂ—THE SHODÂ PURMÂRS—THE KÂTEES—THE JHÂLÂS—EEDUR—THE GOHILS OF PEERUM.

THOUGH the stem of the Solunkhees was uprooted, it was not before many of its branches, "like those of their own indigenous burr-tree," had fixed themselves in the soil. Beyond the limits of Goozerat, one branch of the Wâghela tribe is said to have given its name to the province of Wâghelkhund, or Bâghelkhund, in Gondwânâ; and the Thâkor of Roopnuggur, a chieftain of Mewar, whose stronghold commands one of the passes into that country, and whose family has been famed in the annals of border feuds, still lays claim to Solunkhee blood, and boasts his possession of the war-shell of the great Sidh Râj as an ancestral heir-loom.

As regards Goozerat, the Wâghelas, it appears, at first maintained themselves in the districts to the west of the Sâbhermutee, including "the Bhâl," and held also the country since called Jhâlâwâr, where we find one of their chiefs seated at Wudwân, with a powerful vassal at Syelâ. From this latter part of their possessions, however, they not long subsequently retired before the Jhâlâs and others; and in the reign of Ahmed Shah we shall find them seated at Kulol and Sânund, in the districts most exposed to the Mohummedan arms.

Another branch of the Solunkhees, under Veer Bhudrâjee, established themselves at Veerpoor, on the Myhee, where they settled at the hill of Owtul Mâtâ, and acquired the distinguishing name of Veerpoora Solunkhees. We have no further information in regard to this branch than the bardic statement that in A.D. 1434 they settled at Loonâwârâ, which town they founded by the blessing of Shree Looneshwur Muhâ Dev. Other supposed offshoots of the Solunkhee tribe are to be found among the Koolee chieftains of the Choonwâl, of whom hereafter.

The Shodâ tribe, a powerful branch of the Purmâr race, ruled part of Sindh from remote antiquity, and to a very late period were lords of Oomur Kot and Oomurâ-Soomurâ, in which division was Arore, the ancient capital of Sindh. The isolated and now dependent chieftainship of Dhât in the Indian desert, of which Oomur Kot is the capital, separates the Bhâtees from the Jhârejas, and is still held by a prince of Purmâr race and Shodâ tribe.[1] Another branch of the Shodâ Purmârs entered Goozerat at the time of which we are now treating. A branch of the Wâghelas, it is said, then held Wudwân, in after times the property of the Jhâlâs. Wudlâ, the Wâghela Raja of Wudwân, assigned Syelâ and other villages as a putto, or feudal grant, to the Chubâd Rajpoots, of whom the following story is related by the bards :—

A famine having occurred at Parkur, two thousand Shodâ Purmârs with their wives and children, under the leading of two chiefs named Moojo and Lugdheer, came to the Punchâl country, where they formed a collection of huts at a place called Ghâgureeo, a few miles to the east of Moolee. The Chubâd chief of Syelâ, fancying that the Shodâs were wealthy and unprotected, sought occasion for plundering them. He arranged a sporting excursion, and pretending that a partridge which he had wounded had taken shelter among their huts, demanded that it should be given up. Such a demand it was altogether inconsistent with Rajpoot honor to accede to; a contest, therefore, was the result, and many, both of the Chubâds and Shodâs, were slain. "A wild partridge came to the chief's door. " To oppose the Chubâd they mounted and stood in arms at the " gate. 'O! Moojo, this is my partridge,' the enemy demanded; " but, fired with pride, the Purmâr lord refused to surrender it. In " the morning, with the Chubâd the Shodâs fought; five hundred " Chubâds, seven score Shodâs fell. Moojo, risking his life for the " sake of a bird, won fame. The north star may move, Meroo fall, " Girnâr revolve, but the Purmâr cannot turn his back to the foe. " His dwelling Kundol, Choteelâ his fortress, his lands at Moolee— " give the Purmâr so much, he seeks no more." The chief of Syelâ, who had himself fallen, left a sister married to the Wâghela of Wud-

[1] Tod's Rajasthan, vol. i., pp. 43, 45, 92, 93.

wân. She pressed her husband to take revenge from those who had killed her brother; but Wudlâ had given his word of honor (kol) to the chief of the Shodâs, and was prevented, therefore, from openly proceeding against him. At this time two Bheel chieftains, named Aho and Phuto, were very powerful in Goozerat, and from their impregnable strongholds, in the ravines of the Sâbhermutee river, used to ravage the country of the Wâghelas. The Wudwân Raja, thinking to rid himself of the Shodâs, demanded that they should attack these Bheel fortresses. The Shodâs entered Aho Bheel's fort by stratagem, and put him to death, with many of his followers. They next proceeded against Phuto, and slew him also. In recompense for these exploits, the Wâghela of Wudwân conferred upon the Shodâs four "Choveeses" or districts of four-and-twenty villages each, those, namely, of Moolee, Thân, Choteelâ, and Choburee.

The Kâtees were vassals of the Soomuree King of Sindh, and lived in Pâwur-land. Once on a time a female dancer ridiculed the king as she performed before him, upon which she was condemned to banishment from his territories. The Kâtee chiefs, however, called the actress to their quarters, and amused themselves by causing her to sing the song which had offended the king. The Sindh chief being informed of this behaviour, issued sentence of expulsion against the Kâtees also. At this time a raja of the Wâlo race ruled at Dhânk, near Dhorâjee, in Soreth. The Kâtee chiefs flying from Sindh, took refuge in his dominions, and became his followers. One of the Kâtees, named Umuro Putgur, had a very beautiful daughter named Umurâ Bâee, whom the Wâlo fell in love with and demanded of her father in marriage. Umuro agreed to the celebration of the marriage, on condition that the Wâlo should eat at the same table with him. Hereupon the brothers of the Chief of Dhânk conspired against him as one who had lost caste, and drove him from his throne. He took refuge with the Kâtees, who accepted him as their leader, and laid plans, under his direction, for seizing territory from the Bhoomeeas—the men of the land. The Wâlo retained from his forefathers the worship of the sun, which religion was adopted from him by the Kâtees. Once when the Wâlo lay asleep, dreaming of his lost grâs or landed inheritance, Sooruj appeared to him and said, "Go forth to fight, trusting in me. I will aid you, and give you "victory, and you shall erect a temple for my worship." With the aid of Shree Sooruj, the Wâlo and his Kâtee followers conquered many villages, and amongst others, seized Thân and Choteelâ from the Shodâs. At Thân, which they made their capital, they erected a temple to the sun, whose deity is worshipped there to this day.

They attempted also to conquer the Moolee Chovees under the leading of Râgo Châwuro, one of the Kâtee chieftains, but the Shodâ Purmâr, Râjo Sutmâl, engaged them and slew Râgo.

"Collecting his army, he caused the Choodâsumâ and the Gohil "to tremble—a warrior that could not be tamed, he gallopped his "horse afar. Like a mighty Dev, valiant was the son of Sutmâl. "Had you not heard of this Râjojee, O! Râgo?

"Sometimes only, a man meets with a man. In the field, O! "Châwuro, you are a fighter, it is true; but the Purmâr, too, is a "warrior of might. Unless pierced by the point of the spear, how "should he resign his lands! What did he not endure for a partridge "only of old! Honor be to the race of Shodâ, the ever proud!"

The Wâlo chief had, by his Kâtee bride, three sons, Khoomân, Khâchur, and Horsur-Wâlâ, who shared his acquired territories between them. They took up their residences, respectively, at Choteelâ, Meetheeâloo, and Jetpoor; and were the founders of the three Kâtee tribes called after their names. The Kâtees were originally divided into eight branches; but these now assumed the common name of Ewurteeâs, or foreigners, distinguishing them from the Ghurderâs (seniors), or Wâlâ-Kâtees, the descendants of the sons of the outcaste Chief of Dhank and his wife Umurâ Bâee.

Next to the Wâghelas in nearness of relationship to the dynasty of Unhilwârâ, and like them in having acquired large territorial possessions at its fall, are the Jhâlâs. We first hear of them under the name of Mukwânas, at Keruntee Gurh, or Kero Kot;[1] at which place Veheeâs ruled in succession to numerous ancestors, when the Wâghelas were the sovereigns of Goozerat.

"When Veheeâs," says the bard, "took to his bed, at Keruntee-"gurh, his life would not pass from his body. Kesur, his son, said "to him, 'Father! how is it that your soul does not obtain "liberation?' Veheeâs answered—'There is a city named Sâmeiyoo, "in which Humeer Soomero, my enemy, rules. If you will promise "to carry off a hundred and twenty-five horses, bred in his stable, "and present them to the bards on the thirteenth day after my death, "I shall be released.' The brothers and brothers' sons of Veheeâs "stood around him, but no one of them made any answer. Then

[1] Kero Kot is, we are informed, a small village, still so called, near Butchow, in Kutch, where there are traces of an old city, extending as widely as those at Wulleh. The name does not appear in the maps unless the place indicated be "Kunt Kot," mentioned as the refuge of Mool Râj, of Unhilwârâ, during the invasion of the King of Sâmbhur. *Vide* p. 38.

"Kesur, although he was a minor, stepped forward, and, pouring "water into his father's hand, promised that he would perform his "command. Thereupon Veheeâs passed to Dev-Lok."

When the thirteenth day came round, Kesur put off his mourning, and invited his kinsmen to accompany him to Sâmeiyoo. Some one muttered—"No one will go to throw away his life with you." Kesur heeded them not; he trusted in his own strength. His arms reached below his knees; he wielded a spear that was fifty pounds in weight; he was armed with bow and arrow; he rode on a horse that resembled the eagle upon which Vishnoo is borne. He went to Sâmeiyoo and fulfilled his promise by bringing off the horses thence, and presenting them to the bards.

Kesur sent for his astrologer, and enquired how many days were allotted to him to live. The wise man, having consulted his horoscope, predicted his early death. Kesur said, "No one will know "of it if I die seated in the corner of the house; my name will be "famous if I die in fight." Thus considering, he went again to Sâmeiyoo, and finding seven hundred camels of Humeer's grazing beside the river Menee, he carried them off, and presented them to bards at Kerunteegurh. Still no army of Humeer's set out from Sâmeiyoo. Kesur went, therefore, upon a third foray. It was the Dussera festival; the wife and daughter of Humeer, seated in a chariot, repaired to a garden to take their pleasure. From thence Kesur carried them off; a hundred and twenty-five Soomuree ladies he carried off with them. Humeer now sent his minister to Keruntee-gurh, who, when he arrived, stated that the ladies were the wives and sisters of Humeer, and that it became Kesur to send them back with presents, in the fashion of married ladies returning from their parents' house. Kesur laughed, and said the property should not be given up; and that the ladies were his own wives. The minister returned with this answer to Sâmeiyoo.

Kesur sent for his kinsmen, as many of them as were at Keruntee, and distributed to them a Soomuree lady a-piece. He retained four for himself—in addition to his other numerous wives. Ten or twelve years passed away, and the feud still continued. Eighteen sons were born in this time to Kesur and his brothers, whose mothers were the Soomuree ladies. At length Humeer sent to say, "I would come to "fight with you, but Keruntee is a salt country; what subsistence "could my army find there?" Kesur sent answer, "I will sow a "thousand acres with green wheat for your army." Then Humeer "came to Keruntee-gurh, and in the battles that ensued, many Rajpoots lost their lives. Among the rest Kesur fell with his sons, of whom only Hurpâl survived. His brothers and nephews also fell, and Keruntee being destroyed, the Soomuree ladies burned themselves with their husbands.

Hurpâl, the son of Kesur, took refuge at Unhilwârâ Puttun, where Ghelaro Kurun, the Wâghela, ruled. The spear of Hurpâl was as heavy as his father's, and he and Kurun were sister's sons, therefore he was well received at Puttun. Kurun was at this time suffering much annoyance from a Bhoot, named Bâburo, who had taken to himself the favorite Rânee, Phoolâ Devee, of Jânjmer Tulâjâ. Hurpâl attacked the Bhoot, and seizing him by his lock of hair, which rendered him powerless, forced him to swear that he would never again cause annoyance at Puttun. He demanded a further promise from Bâburo, which was, that he should attend him whenever he was in difficulty and required his aid. The Bhoot assented. Hurpâl had afterwards a similar contest with a Shuktee Devee, whom he subdued, and compelled to become his wife.

One morning, Kurun being seated in his court, sent for Hurpâl, the Mukwâno, who came and stood before him; Kurun invited him to ask a boon in reward for his services; he asked for as many villages as he could bind garlands upon in one night. Kurun made him a written grant to that effect. When Hurpâl returned home, the Shuktee asked what present Kurun had made him, and, when she was informed, took upon herself the task of binding the garlands. Hurpâl also called in the assistance of Bâburo, the Bhoot, who attended him with his followers, a lakh and a quarter in number. They set out at nine in the evening, and fixed the first garland at Pâtree, then at its six hundred dependent villages. At four in the morning they had returned to Puttun, having bound garlands upon the gates of two thousand villages. Next morning the king having mounted a minister upon a dromedary, sent him out to make enquiry as to the number of villages which had become the property of the Mukwâno. The list contained two thousand names, and Kurun having read it, confirmed his previous grant.[1]

[1] The founder of a new village, after ascertaining from the astrologers the fortunate hour, erects two posts, between which he suspends a garland of leaves. This represents a Keerttee Stumbh. At the same time he sets up a water-vessel, which he worships as an emblem of his family goddess. He then worships Hunoomân, and concludes by giving a feast.

With the story in the text compare the following:—

"THE TICHBORNE DOLE.—The family of Tichborne date their possession of the present patrimony, the manor of Tichborne, so far back as 200 years before the Conquest. When the Lady Mabella, worn out with age and infirmity, was lying on her deathbed, she besought her loving husband, as her last request, that he

When Kurun went into his female apartments, at noon, the Rânee saw that something had occurred to cause him grief. She pressed him to tell her why he was sad, and was informed that Hurpâl had taken two thousand villages. The Rânee had adopted Hurpâl as her bracelet-bound brother, so she caused her chariot to be yoked, and set off to demand of him a bodice. Hurpâl met her at the gate of his mansion, and said, "Sister! for what purpose are you come?" She said she had come for a bodice, and he gave up to her the five hundred villages constituting the district called the Bhâl.

Bâburo Bhoot, in assenting to Hurpâl's demand that he should serve him when required, had added the following condition—"As soon as "the tasks you set me are performed, I shall devour you." Hurpâl was, therefore, now compelled to devise means for ridding himself of Bâburo—the Bhoot declaring his intention of exacting the penalty that had been provided. At length Hurpâl ordered Bâburo to bring a tall pole. The Bhoot brought one immediately. Hurpâl said, "Fix

would grant her the means of leaving behind her a charitable bequest, in a dole of bread to be distributed to all who should apply for it annually on the Feast of the Annunciation of the Blessed Virgin Mary. Sir Roger, her husband, readily acceded to her request, by promising the produce of as much land as she could go over, in the vicinity of the park, while a certain brand or billet was burning, supposing that, from her long infirmity (for she had been bedridden for some years), she would be able to go round a small portion only of his property. The venerable dame, however, ordered her attendants to convey her to the corner of the park, where, being deposited on the ground, she seemed to receive a renovation of strength, and, to the surprise of her anxious and admiring lord, who began to wonder where her pilgrimage might end, she crawled round several rich and goodly acres. The field which was the scene of the Lady Mabella's extraordinary feat retains the name of "Crawls" to this day. It is situated near the entrance of the park, and contains an area of 23 acres. Her task being completed, she was reconveyed to her chamber, and summoning her family to her bedside predicted its prosperity while the annual dole existed, and left her malediction on any of her descendants who should be so mean or covetous as to discontinue or divert it, prophesying that when such should happen the old house would fall, and the family name would become extinct from the failure of heirs male, and that this would be foretold by a generation of seven sons being followed immediately after by a generation of seven daughters and no son. The custom thus founded in the reign of Henry II. continued to be observed for centuries; and the 25th of March became the annual festive day of the family. It was not until the middle of the last century that the custom was abused; when, under the pretence of attending the Tichborne Dole, vagabonds, gypsies, and idlers of every description assembled from all quarters, pilfering throughout the neighbourhood; and, at last, the gentry and magistrates complaining, it was discontinued in 1796. Singularly enough, the baronet of the day had seven sons; and when he was succeeded by the eldest, there appeared a generation of seven daughters, and the apparent fulfilment of the prophecy was completed by the change of the name of the late baronet to Doughty, under the will of his kinswoman."—*Winchester Observer.*

"it in the ground and go on climbing up and down it; when that "task is completed you may devour me." Thus was Hurpâl relieved of his cause for anxiety.[1]

The race of Hurpâl and the Shuktee spread like the branches of a creeper of paradise; Shedo, Mângoo, and Shekuro were their sons; and they had a daughter, Bâee Oomâ Devee. One day the Shuktee's sons were playing in the courtyard of the palace, when an elephant belonging to the king got loose; she stretched forth her hand and laid hold of them (jhâlâ), whence they derived the name of Jhâlâ.

"I have heard of you as a warrior who conquered all the demons; I have "heard of you as a warrior who had a Shuktee for a Rânee; I have "heard of you as a warrior who took possession of two thousand vil-"lages. Hurpâl! great, with a hand like Yuma's, I behold your "power daily increasing. There is no warrior upon earth, O! son of "Kesur, equal to you.

"In Pâtree the Mukwâno built many a palace. The Rânee sat at "the window; no one knew that she was a Shuktee. The king's "elephant broke loose; she saw, from a distance, the princes playing. "Shedo, Mângoo, and Shekuro, extending her hand, she laid hold "upon; she gave them the title of Jhâlâ."

The fortress of Eedur is situated on the south-western face of the range of hills which connects the chains of Vindhya and Ârâwullee. It consists of a piece of table-land, elevated to a considerable height above the plains, and surrounded with eminences, the gaps intervening between which are artificially filled in, and strengthened by ramparts. The town of Eedur, which is surrounded by a handsome stone wall, with circular bastions, nestles at the foot of the hill; it is hardly perceptible from even a very short distance, being screened by small rocky hillocks, from which frown outworks, mounted with cannon, and manned respectively by the Jetâwuts, the Koompâwuts, the Chohâns, or other warlike vassals of the sovereign. From the residence of the Râthor princes, situated at the back of the town, beside a reser-

[1] Compare the following:—Michael Scott was, once upon a time, much embarrassed by a spirit, for whom he was under the necessity of finding constant employment. He commanded him to build a *cauld*, or dam-head, across the Tweed at Kelso; it was accomplished in one night, and still does honor to the infernal architect. Michael next ordered that Eildon-hill, which was then an uniform cone, should be divided into three. Another night was sufficient to part its summit into the three picturesque peaks which it now bears. At length the enchanter conquered this indefatigable demon by employing him in the hopeless and endless task of making ropes out of sea-sand.—*Appendix to the Lay of the Last Minstrel.*

voir of water, a steep and easily defensible pathway conducts through more than one gateway and fortified work to the plateau of the fortress. The two most conspicuous peaks of the hill above are crowned by edifices; that on the left, a Hindoo temple, which tradition knows as the guard-room of Runmul, one of the old Rows of Eedur; that on the right, a small dome-covered structure, called "the Palace of the mourning Queen." The level plain in front of the town of Eedur was, until lately, covered by a thick and impenetrable forest of stunted trees, which completed the defences of the fortress, and assisted in giving to it that impregnable character which it bore of old, and which is attested by the proverbial saying used throughout Goozerat, to signify the successful conclusion of a hopeless undertaking,—

"I have captured Eedur-gurh."

Eedur is first known in tradition as Il-doorg, the residence, in the Dwâpur Yoog, or third age, of Ailwun, the Râkshus and his brother, Wâtâpee. These demons harassed the surrounding country, which the indulgence of their cannibal propensities rendered desolate; they were at last destroyed by Ugust Reeshee. In the Kul Yoog, or iron age, when Yoodishteer was fresh in men's recollection, and Vikrum had not yet arisen to free the world from the load of debt, Venee Wuch Râj ruled in Eedur. He was the possessor of a magical figure of gold, which furnished him with resources for constructing the fortress on the hill and its various reservoirs. The Queen of Venee Wuch Râj was a Nâgpootree, the daughter of one of the snake kings of Pâtâl, or the infernal regions. They reigned there happily for many years, and then, as the story goes, suddenly disappeared. "Once "on a time the Raja and the Rânee were seated together in an oriel "window of their palace in Eedur-gurh, when the corpse of a man "who had died in the city was carried past, followed by a mourning "train. The Rânee enquired the meaning of this melancholy pageant, "and was informed by her husband that the mourners lamented one "who was dead. 'Let us not remain in a place like this, where men "die,' said the Rânee. Wuch Râj and his queen then went to the "hill of Târun Mother, and entering a fissure in the rock, close by "the spot where the goddess is now worshipped, they descended to "Pâtâl. Thereafter the land lay desolate for many years."

When Wullubheenugger fell, Pooshpâwutee, one of the queens of Sheelâditya, was at the shrine of Umbâ Bhuwânee at Ârâsoor, which she had visited for the purpose of laying upon the altar of the goddess a votive offering in acknowledgment of her expectation of offspring. She was on her return, when the intelligence arrived which blasted all her future hopes, by depriving her of her lord, and robbing him, whom the goddess had promised to her prayers, of his ancestral crown. She took refuge in a cave in the mountains, where she was delivered of a son, thence called "Goha," or cave-born. The queen confided the infant to a Brahminee, and enjoined her to educate him as one of her own caste, but to marry him to the daughter of a Rajpoot. She then mounted the funeral pile to follow her lord. At this period Eedur was in the hands of the Bheels. The young Goha, soon abandoning his Brahmin mother, frequented the forest in their company, and by his daring character rendered himself their favorite. The Bheels, in sport, having determined to elect a king, the choice fell upon Goha, and one of the "children of the forest" cutting his finger, applied the blood as the teeluk of sovereignty to his forehead. Thus Goha, the son of Sheelâditya, became lord of the forests and mountains of Eedur. His descendants are said to have dwelt in these regions for several generations. The Bheels, at length, tired of a foreign rule, assailed Nâgâditya, the eighth prince of the line of Gohâ, and deprived him of his life, but his infant son, Bâppâ, then only three years old, was saved to become the founder of the dynasty of Mewar.[1]

After these events, some Pureehâr Rajpoots came from Mundowur in Marwar, and binding the garland upon its gates, refounded Eedur, where they ruled for several generations. In the time of Pureehâr Umur Singh, the Raja of Kanouj, Jeychund Dulé Pângulo, was performing sacrifice on account of the marriage of his daughter, Sunyogeetâ. He sent letters of invitation to all rajas. Eedur was then subject to Cheetor, and Sumurshee Râwul having been invited by his brother-in-law, Prutheerâj, to accompany him to the marriage, summoned his vassal, Umur Singh, to attend him. The Pureehâr chieftain, with his son and a body of five thousand horse, went to Cheetor, and soon after they were cut to pieces in the great battle in which Prutheerâj was defeated by the Mohummedans. When the tale was told at Eedur, many of the Rânees became Sutees, casting themselves from a precipitous cliff to the north of Eedur, which still bears the name of "the Rânees' leap," or "the hill of murders."

Umur Singh had left Eedur in the hands of a servant of his, named Hâthee Sord, a Koolee, in whom he had great confidence. Hâthee retained possession of the country until his death, and was succeeded by his son, Sâmulyo Sord, in whose time the Râthors first appeared in Eedur.

After the death of Jeychund Dulé Pângulo, Seeyojee Râthor, who

[1] *Vide* Tod's Rajasthan, i., p. 220.

is reputed to have been his son, left Kanouj and established himself in the sandy deserts of Marwar. He had three sons, of whom the elder, Âstânjee, succeeded him; Sonungjee and Ujjee, the two younger sons, "considered that they had better go to some foreign country "for their subsistence." They repaired to the court of Unhilwârâ, whose sovereign, probably Bheem Dev II., was their mother's brother. The Solunkhee prince assigned to them the fief of Sâmeturâ, in the district of Kuree. Ujjee Râthor soon after espoused the daughter of a Chowra chieftain, whose estate lay near Dwârkâ. This connection gave him an acquaintance with that part of the country, which led him to seek an establishment therein; soon afterwards, therefore, he slew Bhoj Râj Chowra, and possessed himself of Dwârkâ and of the province of Okâmundul. Ujjee left two sons, Wâgâjee and Wâdheljee, whose descendants are still numerous in that country under the names of Wâjâs and Wâdhels.

Sâmulyo Sord was, meanwhile, exciting the discontent of his subjects at Eedur by his tyrannical conduct. The Nâgur Brahmins were at that time very numerous in the Sord's dominions, and the leading man of the caste was also the principal adviser of the sovereign. The Brahmin had a very beautiful daughter, whom the raja, happening one day to see, became enamoured of, and demanded in marriage. The minister knew that if he ventured upon a direct refusal, Sâmulyo would take his daughter away by force; he therefore counterfeited acquiescence, and merely begged for half-a-year's delay, in order that he might make suitable preparations for the nuptials. In the interval he hoped to discover some powerful chieftain whom he might call in to his aid. The Brahmin, with this view, paid a visit at Sâmeturâ, at the court of Prince Sonungjee, to whom he introduced himself, asking him if he had the courage to take Eedur, with its nine lakhs of revenue. Sonungjee assented. The minister, returning home, gave out that he was making preparations for the marriage, and was, with the view to its celebration, assembling his relations. By twos and threes, a hundred carriages, supposed to contain Brahmin ladies, conveyed to the minister's mansion the Marwaree warriors and their leader. A number of Koonbees were employed to collect goats and supplies of liquor. The minister at length announced that his preparations were complete, and sent to bid Sâmulyo Sord and his relations to the feast. The bridegroom's party arrived, was duly welcomed, and freely supplied with intoxicating liquors and drugs. The minister then ordered his servants to serve the second course. This was the signal which had been agreed upon. The Rajpoots, therefore, rushed forward, and surrounded the room in which the revelling was held. The doors were then locked, that no one might be allowed to escape, but a party of Koolees from without forced them open, and brought out Sâmulyo Sord. The chieftain strove to cut his way through his enemies, and regain the fortress, but a number of his followers were slain on the steep ascent, and Sâmulyo himself fell within a short distance of the gate of Eedurgurh. When Row Sonungjee came up to the spot where the Sord chieftain lay dying, Sâmulyo raising himself for the last time, made the royal teeluk on the victorious Râthor's forehead with his own blood, and begged him, with his dying breath, to appoint, for the preservation of his name, that each Râthor Row, on mounting the royal cushion of Eedur, should be marked with the teeluk by a Sord, who should draw blood for the purpose from his own right hand, and say, " May the kingdom of Sâmulyo Sord flourish ! " Row Sonungjee assenting, Sâmulyo soon breathed his last.

The wife of Sâmulyo, who was pregnant, fled, and took refuge in a cave at the foot of the hill sacred to Muhâ Dev Khokurnâth. She was there sheltered by the recluse who served the temple, and gave birth to a son, from whom descend the Koolees, of Surwân, on the Mewar frontier, and of Khokur, in Puttunwârâ.

The spots on the ascent to Eedurgurh, which are supposed to have been stained with the blood of Sâmulyo and his slaughtered followers, are still marked by the Hindoos with vermillion on " the " dark fourteenth," and other days on which Hunoomân is worshipped ; and when the descendant of Row Sonungjee assumes the cushion of his ancestors in their last retreat at Pol, a Koolee of Surwân is, to the present day, employed to mark, with blood upon his forehead, the royal teeluk which asserts his yet unsurrendered title to the domains of Sâmulyo.

" The Gohils," says Colonel Tod, " claim, with some pretension, " to be of the race of the sun." The accounts to which we have had access, however, make them of the race of Chundra, or the moon, descending through Shâleewâhun, the conqueror of Vikrâmâditya. Their first residence was Joona Khergurh, on the banks of the Loony river, in Marwar, ten miles west of Bhalotra. They took it from one of the aboriginal Bheel chiefs, named Kherwo, and had been in possession of it for twenty generations, when they were expelled by the Râthors. Their long possession of this seat in the " land of " death," is asserted by the title of " Muroo," which their chieftain still assumes.

It was under the guidance of Sejuk, the son of Jânjurshee, that the Gohils retired from Marwar. The cause of their departure was a feud excited between them and their neighbours, the Dâbhees, by the Râthor clan, under Âstânjee, the son of Seeyojee II., then making their first settlement in the land of Muroo. "The Dâbhees," says the bard, "behaved treacherously to the Gohils—treacherously "did they seek to destroy Sejuk. To a feast they invited the "Muroo, intending to put him to death. Clever was the Dâbhee's "daughter; she was the Queen of Sejuk. The virtuous wife became "aware of the intentions of her kindred; yoking her chariot she "went forth; she came to Sejuk's house, and related to him the "whole matter. When Muroo set forth, he called his good warriors, "and acquainted them with the design; they armed themselves, and "attended him. To murder Sejuk the chieftains assembled; he "knew their treachery, and came to meet them. The warriors struck "at each other. Sejuk had been invited to a feast. Strange it was "that they should slay each other. In the hall the dishes remained "filled; in the hall the sword moved; the chieftains caused wounds "in each other's bodies, gaping like the opened windows of great "mansions. Jânjurshee's son, brandishing his dagger, struck it into "the breast of Mân. Fighting with the Dâbhees, as if hunting "game, the Gohil finished his sport, and went home joyfully to Kher. "Mân he sent to the house of Yuma." The Râthors, who had set the parties at enmity, finding them both weakened by the losses which their feud had occasioned, now stept in, and seized the booty for themselves, expelling the belligerent clans from the land of Muroo. Hence the proverb,—

"Dâbhees left, and Gohils right."

Sejukjee assembled his clan; and, taking with him his minister, Shâ Rajpâl Umeepâl, and his family priest, Gungârâm Wullubhrâm, of which latter the descendants still exist at Seehore, set forth to seek his fortune "in foreign lands." The image of his god, Morleedhur, and the trident of his family, Khetrapâl (or Lar), were placed upon a chariot which preceded the line of march; for Morleedhur had appeared to Sejukjee in a dream, and had informed him that he should halt, and found a city upon the spot where the chariot should break down. When the train arrived in the Punchâl country, the wheel came off the god's car. Sejukjee halted upon the spot, which is that where the village of Sâpur stands, and proceeded with Shâ Râjpâl to pay obeisance to the Râ of Joonagurh. The Râ Kuwât and Koonwur Khengâr received them, and enquired what had driven them forth from their own country. Sejukjee answered that the Râthors had given the Dâbhees bad counsel, and had excited them against him, and that eventually Âstânjee had expelled the Dâbhees also, and had taken Khergurh for himself. Râ Kuwât took Sejukjee into his service, and gave him a grant of Sâpur and eleven other villages, with a commission to protect that part of the country "against "the Kânt Bheels." At that time the Kâtees had not yet come out of Pâwur land, and Dhândulpoor, near Choteelâ, was the frontier town between the Wâghelas and the Râs of Joonagurh.

Sejukjee remained several days at Joonagurh, and, while he was there the Koonwur Khengâr, who was thirteen years old, went out on a hunting expedition. He came at length to the neighbourhood of Sâpur, and, while following his sport, started a hare, which, when pursued, fled, and took refuge in the Gohil's encampment. Khengâr demanded that it should be given up to him; but Sejuk's brother and nephews declined, saying, that no Rajpoot could give up what had taken refuge under his protection. A contest ensued; several of the Koonwur's followers were slain, and he was himself made prisoner. One of the Koonwur's party escaping hastened to Joonagurh, and informed Râ Kuwât of what had happened, adding, that he did not know whether Khengâr was alive, or whether he had been slain. Sejukjee was sitting in the court at this moment; he became very sorrowful, and considered that he would not now be able to retain the grant of the villages. He rose, and making obeisance, placed the putta in the Râ's lap. Kuwât asked why he did so. Sejuk answered, "My followers have slain your only Koonwur; how can "I remain in your territory?" The Râ returned the grant to Sejukjee, bidding him be of good courage. Sejuk hastened to Sâpur, and finding that the Koonwur was alive and well, he made submission to him, and, bringing his daughter, presented her to him to be his wife. The princess, whose name was Wâlum Koonwurbâ, was sent with presents for her bridegroom, and a suitable wardrobe for herself, to Joonagurh; and Sejukjee, with the Râ's permission, founded a new town near Sâpur, and called it Sejukpoor.

At this time Sejukjee's brothers also were settled at different villages that were assigned to them. Hunoojee obtained Bugud; Mân Singh, Tâtum, near Botâd; Doodojee, Toorkâ; and Depâljee, Pâlyâd.

Sejukjee was succeeded by his eldest son Rânjee. His younger sons, Sâhâjee and Sârungjee, obtained the villages of Mândwee and Urteelâ, and were the ancestors of the families of Gâreeâdhâr and Lâtee.

At this time, a chieftain named Ebhul, or Ubhye, of the Wâlo clan, held possession of Wâlâk-land and of its capital, the town of

Wulleh, situated among the remains of the ancient city of Wullubhee-poor; he possessed, also, the neighbouring town of Tulâjâ. The position of the latter place has been already indicated. It stands at no great distance from the sea, on the banks of the river Shutroonj, which flows down from the sacred mountain of the Jains, and at the foot of a beautiful and pyramid-like hill, which the followers of the Teerthunkers regard as part of the back-bone of Soreth—a cone of the range of which Girnâr and Shutroonjye are the most celebrated pinnacles. The hill abounds in caverns and excavations, chiefly situated on its northern and western sides, and about midway between its base and its summit. The most remarkable of these is a rectangular excavation of considerable size, the exterior face of which has been formerly supported by four square pillars—all of them now removed. The architrave above them is enriched with square facets, and with a battlement of five four-centred arches, for which, as ornaments, though apparently ignorant of their constructive value, the early Buddhist architects exhibited a singular predilection.[1] Tradition has, however, forgotten the connection between this cave and the sectaries, who, when Sheelâditya ruled in Wullubhee, filled so important a place in story, and now assigns as its founder, Ebhul the Wâlo. Another large cave, close at hand, is dedicated to the Devee Khodeeâr, (of whom hereafter); while of numerous similar smaller excavations, some are used as dwellings by wandering ascetics; and others, and by far the greater portion, as reservoirs containing the purest rain water, for whose conduct into them small channels are cut all over the hill. On the summit stands a Jain temple, erected in A.D. 1381, and on the flat shoulder, to the west, a similar building of very modern date; the ascent to both of which is rendered easy by steps formed of masonry, or hewn out of the living rock. On the northern and eastern sides the peak of Tulâjâ is clothed with foliage, whose rich and varied coloring adds to the effect of the temples, which, from their rocky pedestal, stand out white and brilliant against the blue sky. The town, lying at its feet, is surrounded by a handsome battlemented wall, and a clear rivulet creeps beneath the northern bastions, which bears the same name as the hill, and which unites a little below the town with the river that descends from Pâleetânâ. In a small shrine, on the eastern face of the hill, a lamp is lighted every night in honor of Tâluv Dyte, from whom the hill derives its classic name of Tâl Dwuj Geeree. Tâluv was, as tradition asserts, the foe of Ebhul Raja, by whose arms he was

[1] *Vide* illustrations of the rock-cut temples of India, by Mr. Fergusson, p. 13.

subdued; but though his reputed conqueror is now impotent and well nigh forgotten, the Dyte still rules, seated on his rocky throne; the lamp which burns before his shrine must never be extinguished, even in the stormiest night of the monsoon, though the torrents of rain rudely wound the mountain's side; and when the loose fragments of rock roll down upon their dwellings, or pestilence rages among them, the inhabitants of Tulâjâ repent of having neglected the honor of Tâluv Dyte, and drawn down upon themselves this, his capricious vengeance.

In the days of Ebhul Wâlo, a merchant of the Jain faith had, it is said, filled so many store-houses with grain that he found it impossible to realize the value. He applied, in this strait, to his gooroo, one of the magic-skilled Jutees, who, writing a charm on an amulet, fastened it to the horn of a black antelope, which he set free to roam in the forest. After this the rain ceased to fall; famine raged for seven years; the cattle perished; the people fled to Malwa; and the land was desolate. The merchant's grain, however, was sold. Ebhul Wâlo, of all his numerous stud, had only five horses left. He was much distressed. A wood-cutter one day came into the court, and said that he had observed a black antelope in the jungle, which, wherever it moved, carried verdure with it. All then pronounced that some one must have bound the rain with this antelope. The raja and his followers went into the jungle, they caught the buck, and, unfastening the amulet tied to its horn, took out the paper, and read it. There was written thereon—"When this note shall be dipped "in water then shall the rain fall." They took water from a bouget, and moistened the note. Torrents of rain began immediately to fall. Some of the followers of Ebhul Wâlo perished in the storm. The raja himself rode a horse of celestial breed; he put it to a gallop, and made for a light which he observed twinkling in the distance, and which led him to the house of a bard who lived in a "Nes," or collection of huts. The men had, all of them, gone off to Malwa; but the women were left behind, and one of them, named Syhee, the Nesuree, took Ebhul off his horse. The king was senseless from the fatigue he had undergone; but Syhee restored him to consciousness by embracing him, and rubbing him with warm fomentations. Ebhul, recovering, asked Syhee who she was; she replied that she was a bard's wife. He informed her that she had saved the life of Ebhul Wâlo, and pressed her to ask of him a boon.[1] She said, "When a proper "opportunity arrives I will ask it." Ebhul then returned home to Tulâjâ.

[1] Literally "a bodice."

The famine disappearing, the bard returned home. He was informed that, during his absence, his wife had entertained a stranger in her house for three days. The bard was inflamed with jealousy; he began to accuse his wife, and threatened her. Syhee, placing the palms of her hands together, looked up towards the sun, and prayed, saying—"Sooruj, Sire! If I am guilty, may I be struck with leprosy, "or else may this bard!" Her husband became a leper. Syhee, satisfied with having, by this ordeal, established her innocence, carefully tended him, and carried him to Tulâjâ, to the gate of Ebhul Raja. She begged the doorkeeper to inform Ebhul that his sister, Syhee, the Nesuree, had come to ask for her bodice. When he received the message Ebhul was seated with his son, Âno, at dinner; he rose immediately, and coming to the door, greeted the Nesuree, and asked her what she desired. She said, "My husband has become "leprous; but if he be bathed in the blood of a man who possesses "the thirty-two marks of virtue, he will recover." Ebhul enquiring where such a man was to be found, was told that his son, Âno, was such. The Wâlo returned sorrowfully into his private apartments. The Rânee asked who had arrived, and what was the intelligence which caused him so much distress. Ebhul said, "A bard's wife, to "whom I made a promise, has come to demand its fulfilment, and "asks for Âno's life." Hearing this, Âno quickly answered, "She "says well, our names will live and be renowned." The Rânee also assented, and was pleased—thinking that men would say of her, "Such a jewel could have ripened only in the womb of such a "mother." At length Ebhul, determining to perform his promise, slew Âno, and washed the bard in his blood, upon which the leprosy immediately disappeared. By the favour of Yog Mâyâ, the bard's wife was enabled to restore Âno to life; but the devotion of himself and of his father still survives in verse—

"The giver of his head,
"Or the headsman should we praise?
"Men of Soreth! consider,
"Of the two Wâlos which was greater?"

In the time of Ebhul there lived at Wulleh a Chârun, or bard, named Mâmureeo, of the Mâd sect, who had seven daughters suspected of being Shuktees, and of sucking the blood of live buffaloes and calves. Ebhul Wâlo on this account sent for their father, and ordered their expulsion from the city. Mâmureeo called his daughters, and said to them, "You are Shuktees, no one will marry you, and the "Raja orders that you should depart hence." The seven sisters prepared to obey, and at starting agreed among themselves that whenever the temple of any of them should be found in a village, the other sisters should leave the place, and proceed onwards. The eldest of the sisters was lame, and hence named Khodeeâr. The others preceded her, and she limped after them, but to whatever village they came they found shrines already dedicated to the worship of Khodeeâr Devee, so powerful was her name.

Temples of Khodeeâr Mâtâ are still numerous in every part of Goozerat; vows are made, and offerings of buffaloes and calves presented to her. She has many "Bhoowos,"[1] and numbers the chief of the Gohils among her most devoted worshippers. Her sister, Âwud, has a temple at Mâmchee, in Kâteewar, and the other sisters are similarly worshipped.

There were formerly a thousand houses of Wâlum Brâhmins in Wulleh. They were the family priests of the Kyeusth caste, and had the care of the shrine of Wyejnâth Muhâ Dev. On the marriage of a Kyeusth maiden the Wâlum Brahmins exacted a fee of one hundred rupees, so that many maidens, though they had attained the age of thirty years even, remained unmarried in consequence of their parents' inability to satisfy the Brahmins' demands. At length the whole Kyeusth caste ceased to celebrate any marriage, hoping thus to compel the Brahmins to abate their claims. The priests, however, met this step by threatening that they would perform trâgâ, and inflict injuries upon themselves, of which the guilt should fall upon the Kyeusths. These, as a last resource, threw themselves at the feet of the raja. Ebhul Wâlo had been taught that the giver of a bride-gift acquired as much virtue-wealth as the performer of a horse-sacrifice. He caused the astrologers to search for a fortunate day, and declared that all the maidens should then be married, and that he would himself bear the expense that might be incurred. The Brahmins, however, refused to officiate unless their demands were satisfied beforehand; upon which, Ebhul, finding the power of these priests to be too great at Wulleh, caused all the maidens to be removed to Tulâjâ, where their marriages were celebrated by Brahmins of other places. The Kyeusths having thus effected their purpose returned to Wulleh, but the Wâlum Brahmins immediately repeated their demands as if the marriages had been performed by themselves, and resorted to trâgâ and other means of compulsion. The raja then called all the priests together, and held a council, with a view of settling the dispute to the satisfaction of all, but the Brahmins were

[1] For a description of the Bhoowos, see Conclusion.

much enraged, and allowed themselves to speak, even of the king, improper words. Ebhul Wâlo was very angry; he stood aloof while a number of Bheels, employed by the Kyeusths, attacked the priests, and committed many Brahmin murders. The priests who survived, carrying their families with them, retired from Wulleh, binding themselves by an oath that none of their race should ever after dwell in that town, or accept the office of family priest to any of the Kyeusth caste. Travelling towards Goozerat, the Brahmins arrived in the vicinity of Dhundhooka, where Dhun Mair, the Koolee, ruled. He, having no son, presented his property, as Krishn-gift, to the Brahmins. Four hundred of them settled at Dhundhooka; others, who refused the raja's gift, passed on into Goozerat, and took up their residence at Wâso, Sojeeturâ, and other towns. To those who remained, the raja granted the office of family priests to the Kshutrees and Vaishyas of Dhundhooka, and, though Modh Brahmins from other places came thither to act as family priests to the Modh Wâneeâs, this was not permitted, and up to the present time the Wâlum Brahmins are the priests of all castes in Dhundhooka.

Rânjee Gohil had meanwhile founded a town at the confluence of the Gomâ and Bhâdur rivers, no great distance from Dhundhooka, and had given to it the name of Rânpoor. He formed an alliance with the powerful Mairs, and to conciliate them, married a daughter of Dhun Mair, their chieftain, by whom he had a son, who acquired the village of Khus, and whose descendants still exist under the name of Khusheeo Koolees.[1]

Under pretence of avenging his oppression of the Brahmins, Rânjee Gohil and Dhun Mair combined to attack Ebhul, the Wâlo. The Gohil led two thousand Rajpoots, and five thousand Mairs followed their chieftain. It was, as some say, while Ebhul, according to his daily practice, worshipped the morning sun, that his enemies attacked him, and that, as he refused to leave his devotions, he was slain; but others assert that he fell, in the dusk of the evening, on the field of battle, and that he was deserted by Nârâyun, whom, when he went forth, he had entreated to remain unmoved until he should return victorious. Hence, his monumental stone, which still stands among the ruins of Wullubhee, is believed to avert its face from the deity which had betrayed him, turning to the west at the dawn of day, and moving gradually to the east until the time of the setting sun.

[1] Another account makes the Khusheeo Koolees to descend from the marriage of Veeshojee, one of the brothers of Sejukjee Gohil, with the daughter of a Mair Koolee of the Dhundhooka family.

The acts of Ebhul Wâlo are thus done into verse by Mâmureeo, the father of Khodeeâr:—

> " First, I brought back the departed rain,
> " The fear of a terrible famine allaying;
> " Next, I cured the leper's pains,
> " Releasing Nesuree Syhee from the curse.
> " Âno's head I gave—I who am called Ebhul!
> " A band of maidens in one day I gave in marriage—
> " I, the Wâlo, victorious among those who keep their word!
> " Tulâjâ, the ornament of my royal diadem;
> " Wulleh, my royal seat, a diadem among thrones.
> " A son of the sun, my father Soorojee;
> " An ocean of gifts; of Hindoos the boundary;
> " Waster of founded cities, builder of cities in the waste;
> " A Malwa to the poor, a raja like Dhurum."

Dhun Mair resigned to his son-in-law their joint conquest of Wâlâk-land; and Rânjee Gohil removed his royal seat to Wulleh, and reigned there until his death.

Rânjee Gohil was succeeded by his son, Mokherâjee, the most celebrated of his line, and the first who bore the far-famed title of "King of Perumbh." The earliest achievement of Mokherâjee Gohil was his taking up a strong position in the Khokurâ hills, which extend in a parallel line to the gulf of Cambay, between its waters and the mount of Pâleetânâ. From thence he made attacks upon different points on all sides, rendering himself the terror of the surrounding country. "When, in the caves of Khokurâ, the lion roared, "the dwellers in Vindyâchul abandoned their food, O! Mokehrâ." He possessed himself of Oomrâlâ and Bheemurâd, Modulgurh and Meetheeâloo; but his most important conquests were those of Gogo and Peerum.

Ghoghâ, or, as it is usually called Gogo, is at present a neat and thriving seaport town, containing upwards of eight thousand inhabitants, and possessing the best roadstead in the gulf of Cambay. Its seamen, called Ghoghârees, partly of the Mohummedan faith, and partly Koolee, or Hindoo, the descendants of the navigators fostered by the kings of Unhilwârâ, and to whom an entire square in that city was assigned, still maintain their ancient reputation, and form the best and most trusted portion of every Indian crew that sails the sea under the flag of England. Modern alterations have left in Gogo few remains of the times of Mokherâ, the Gohil. On the south-west corner of the town, and outside the circuit of the present walls, may, however, be observed the site of the ancient citadel. The towers may still be traced by large heaps of earth denuded of their mason-work, except where it is in some places grasped by the peepul-tree's tenacious roots. The situation was admirably selected for defensive purposes, being the highest in the neighbourhood, and commanding an extensive view of the gulf and the island of Perumbh, or Peerum, on the one side, and on the other of the whole country as far as the foot of the Khokurâ hills. It is also well supplied with the purest water.

The islet of Peerum is separated from the coast of Gohilwârâ by a channel about three miles wide, and, in the centre, about sixty fathoms deep—the outlet by which the river of Wullubhee makes its escape seawards. The belief that the island was once connected with the mainland is very prevalent, and may have originated in the existence of numerous and intricate reefs which the ebb of the tide discloses, especially in the direction of the port of Gogo. Neither history nor natural science has yet found means for adequately explaining the many and extraordinary changes which have been enacted on the shores of the gulf of Cambay; and the formation of Peerum, and the destruction of Wullubhee, connected as they probably are, in the most intimate manner, remain confessedly mysteries. The island is almost covered by a continuous range of sand-hills, resting on a scanty bed of black soil. These hillocks form a barrier against the sea, along the whole of the western face of the island, and are continually augmented by the drift occasioned, in the fair season, by the prevalent winds; but the eastern side is comparatively free from sand, and its soil affords a scanty subsistence to its few and temporary occupants. The asclepias, which covers the summits of the sand-hills, a few limb trees, whose flattened tops serve the inhabitants as storehouses for their straw, some stunted bushes, and a grove of mangroves on the eastern shore, are all that Peerum has to boast of foliage. The swell during the south-west monsoon is particularly heavy on this coast, and the dangerous effects of its strong tides are nowhere, perhaps, so powerfully felt as in the channel of Peerum. The first rush of the spring tide is irresistible in its force, and affords a scene which only the eye-witness can fully realize. A perpendicular wall of water, three or four feet in height, and extending across the gulf as far as eye can reach, approaches at the rate of twelve miles an hour in speed, and with an alarming noise, carrying certain destruction to the mariner whose ignorance or fool-hardiness leads him to neglect its warning voice.[1] Boats passing from the port of Gogo to Peerum, stand out

[1] *Vide* Forbes's Oriental Memoirs, vol. ii., p. 221; see also the papers "On "the Island of Perim," in the first volume of the Journal of the Bombay Branch of the Royal Asiatic Society.

as if with the intention of crossing to Dehej-bârâ, at the mouth of the Nerbudda, lest the strength of the current should carry them into the strait. They are exposed to an uneasy chopping sea, which frequently breaks over them, and are obliged carefully to avoid the sunken reefs over which the water boils up into little conical waves. The landing is usually effected upon a sandy beach on the northern side of the island, below a bank upon which a white flag points out a spot, marked by a pâleeyo, dedicated to Mokherâjee Gohil. The remains of the fortress of Peerum may still be traced, occupying nearly the centre of the island, and stretching across its entire breadth. A few bastions, and the site of a gateway on the western side, may be clearly distinguished; and one of the entrances was formerly ornamented by two monolithe elephants, with their pedestals cut out of a stratum of the conglomerate rock, which has been so great a subject of interest from the fossil remains it has preserved. Within the enclosure of the old castle, the remains of a tank and well are visible; broken pieces of Hindoo sculpture strew the ground; and a hamlet, consisting of about a dozen huts, occupies nearly the centre. At the south-western corner of the fortress is an elevated piece of ground, formerly, probably, the site of the citadel, but now occupied by a lighthouse. From this point the value of Peerum, as the stronghold of a maritime or piratical power of former days, may be vividly perceived. On the one side is seen the coast of Gohilwârâ, the port of Gogo, and many villages nestling among groves of trees, with the whole of the country sloping upwards towards the Khokurâ hills; on the other side may be clearly distinguished the mouths of the Nerbudda and of the Tunkâreea river; while, north and south, the eye sweeps the waters of the gulf of Cambay so completely, that of all that pass from ocean to the ports of wealthy Goozerat, no white sail by day, nor glimmering lantern by night, can escape the glance of the watchman of Peerum.

In these positions Mokherâjee Gohil at length established himself. "Rân's son, the powerful, the raja of rajas, built a new city for his "residence. On a hill he constructed a strong fortress; the waves "of the sea washed it on all sides. He made it famous under the "name of Perumbh, did the lord of earth, seizing the kingdom of "the Koolees. The Bâreâ was then the lord of it—of both Ghoghâ "and Perumbh. Both Perumbh and Ghoghâ took Mokherâ; seven "hundred mariners he put to the sword; he slew all the Koolees. "Subduing the two cities, he made splendid the throne of Perumbh, "did this great practiser of austerities in former birth, this chief of "great fortune. At Perumbh he kept many a ship, for the roads to

" many countries lay there; many a vessel did he plunder; in every " port he was an object of terror. From all that sailed he exacted " tribute, did the raja seated on the throne of Perumbh. The image " of Hunoomân he wore upon his armlet, the figure of Kâleekâ was " impressed upon the hand of Mokherâ."

The exactions and piracies of the King of Peerum at length drew upon him the weight of the imperial arms. His enemy is described in Hindoo tradition simply as Toghluk Shah; but though the Mohummedan historians mention nothing of the fall of Peerum, there can be no danger in identifying this Moslem leader with the prince, the outline of whose story, as far as it affects Goozerat, we have just related,—Mohummed, the son of Gheiâs-ood-deen.

It was, no doubt, while employed in restoring order to this part of his dominions that Mohummed Toghluk Shah turned his arms against Mokherâjee Gohil. The immediate cause assigned by Hindoo legend is the ill-treatment of a merchant of Delhi, who brought fourteen vessels laden with gold-dust to Peerum, which Mokherâjee plundered, though he had promised to protect them, and given the God of the Sea as his security.

" Much troops of Ghuznee came against Perumbh and Ghoghâ; " the kettle-drums and horns sounded; it seemed as if ocean had " deserted his bounds. Many Mohummedans of different races were " there—foot soldiers, horse, and elephants. With the ocean-lord to " fight, they pitched their tents at the edge of the ocean. The Gohil " alone in his den at Perumbh roared like a lion. His austerities had " been great, so he feared not a whit. The armies prepared, the " arrows flew into the sky, but no blow struck the city of Mokherâ. " Many days fought the Toghluk Shah with treacherous artifices, but " a lakh of attempts failed; the shah was tired with his labors; in the " water of the ocean his sight failed to reach; but Mokherâ grasping " his sword in his hand, maintained the honor of rajas."

The enemy could not reach Mokherâ at Peerum, being unable to pass the strait, though the aggrieved merchant fasted, and adjured the God of Ocean, who had become security to him, to withdraw his waters, and leave a passage for the Moslem army. Mohummed Shah then drew off his troops, hoping to entice the Gohil from his impregnable position, a stratagem which the Moslem often practised, and to which the Rajpoot chiefs as often succumbed.

" Between Ghoghâ and Goondee the Mohummedans frightened " remained. Then considered the raja, 'death must come some day " without doubt.' Ascending a ship, he came in the night from " Perumbh to Ghoghâ; he prepared to fight; taking in his hand his "sword, he bound upon his brow the crown of dying. Causing the "gate to be thrown open, the high-minded one led his army out, "giving his soldiers encouragement. Mokherâ, the Muroo, attacked "the padishah's army; he trampled the Mohummedans in the mud. "The pipe and the horn sounded; standards fluttered in the air; "streams of blood flowed. The warriors of both armies mingling "together, the sister's son of the padishah who led the Yuwuns was "perceived by Mokherâ; he struck him from his elephant down to "the ground. When Mokherâ Gohil began to strike, the Mohum-"medans thought of Allah. On the Usoor's army his blows rained; "half of Toghluk's soldiers did the son of Rân slay with the sword. "The enemy's array, torn by the sword of the king, seemed like a "mountain which the lightning had riven. Then Mokherâ fell, he "fell at the gate of Ghoghâ. The trunk of his body rushed on, "brandishing a sword; from the head which fell to the ground issued "the cry, 'Kill! kill!' The army of the enemy fled in a body, "many of the Yuwuns fell. The padishah himself escaped with "difficulty. A charmed string, blue in color, they laid on the ground; "then fell the trunk, then ceased the sword to move. The other "warriors then turned back. Perumbh's lord fell on the earth, "having performed to the full all his vows. Sejuk's grandson was "proved to be of the race of Devs; his life was swallowed up in "life, while the army of the padishah cried as it fled, 'Well done, "Hindoo! well done, Hindoo!'"

The fortress of Peerum was destroyed by the Mohummedans upon the death of its founder, and was never afterwards restored. Its association with his name is, however, still freshly preserved. The Hindoos delight to place a few grains of opium, under the name of a cup of Kusoomba, on the monumental stone erected to his honor, and the mariners who sail past the island of Peerum seldom neglect to cast an offering of food into the sea to propitiate the shade of Mokherâjee Gohil.

CHAPTER III.

MOOZUFFER SHAH I.—SHAH AHMED I.

MOOZUFFER KHÂN, immediately on his accession, undertook the task of reducing the Hindoo chiefs to the position of tributaries, and his first expedition of this nature was directed against Eedur.

Row Sonungjee had been succeeded, in their turns, by Emuljee,

Dhuwulmuljee, Loonkârojee, and Burhutjee, of whom nothing is recorded, except the remark, that "until the time of Row Burhutjee, "the kingdom was neither increased nor diminished." Runmul, the son of Burhutjee, is better known. He it is whose guard-room is pointed out, overtopping the fortress of Eedurgurh; and by him, and the eleven Runmuls who attended him, the bard is supplied with many a theme for romantic story. "Row Runmul took from a Yâduv "family the country called the Bhâgur, between Eedur and Mewar, "the capital of which, Jhârud-gurh, he made for some time his resi-"dence. From thence he removed to Pânowrâ. Runmul gave the "Bhâgur to a *puttâwut*, or feudal vassal, of the Solunkhee blood; he "received also a chief of the Sonuggera Chohâns who came to Eedur "from Jhâlor, having been despoiled by the Mohummedans; to him "the Row assigned the puttâ, or fief, of Jorâ Meerpoor. This Cho-"hân family for some time intermarried with that of the Row; but "after a time they connected themselves with Bheel women, and "became outcastes."

"In the year A.D. 1393," says Ferishta, "the Ray of Eedur having "refused to pay the customary tribute, Moozuffer Khân marched to "enforce it. Several skirmishes ensued, in which the new governor "was generally victorious, until he arrived before the town of Eedur, "which he closely invested. The siege being protracted, the garrison "became so distressed for provisions, that it is said they consumed "cats and dogs—not before these animals had begun to feed upon "each other. The Ray, at length, sent out his son to prostrate him-"self before Moozuffer Khân, and to beg the lives of the inhabitants; "a boon which was granted on condition of the payment of a quantity "of jewels, and a large sum in specie."

Moozuffer Khân was next engaged in vindicating the right of the sovereigns of Goozerat—a right dating, probably, at least as early as the reign of Sidh Râj—to the districts of Sultânpoor and Nundoorbâr, in Candeish, now attempted to be occupied by Adil Khân. On his return to his capital, he learnt that the Ray of Jehrend, in the western Puttun district, "an idolater," had refused allegiance to the Mohummedan authority. Moozuffur Khân accordingly marched against this chief, from whom he exacted tribute. He then proceeded to Somnâth, and once more overthrowing the Hindoo temples, converted them into mosques. The Governor of Goozerat next marched to Mundulgurh, which was surrendered to him; he then visited Ujmeer to pay his devotions at the shrine of a Mohummedan saint; and he returned home by Julwârâ, where he destroyed the temples, and exacted contributions.

In A.D. 1398, we find him engaged in another attack on Row

Runmul, of Eedur, who was obliged, as on the former occasion, to purchase forbearance by the payment of tribute. The terrific inroad of Teimoor having just occurred, the court of Dehli was now in a state of the utmost confusion, and many rivals were contending for the crown. Moozuffer Khân and his son appear to have advanced pretensions to the imperial throne; but these were not pushed to extremity, and the Governor of Goozerat contented himself with assuming royal state in the kingdom of which he was already the real sovereign. It was about this time that he caused himself to be proclaimed king, under the title of Moozuffer Shah; struck coin in his new name of royalty; and caused it also to be inserted in the Khootba, or public prayers.

In A.D. 1401, Moozuffer Shah again marched to levy the tribute of Eedur; but Row Runmul fled to Veesulnugger, leaving the king to occupy his capital. Next year the shah gained a bloody victory, at Somnâth, over a Hindoo prince, then apparently residing at Diu. The place was surrendered after the battle, and its prince and the greater part of the garrison were murdered in cold blood.

The last achievement of Moozuffer Shah was an invasion of Malwa, where he engaged Hooshung, its ruler, near Dhâr, defeated him, and took him prisoner. He died on the 27th July, A.D. 1411.

Moozuffer Shah was succeeded by his grandson, Ahmed Khân; but Feroze Khân, the cousin of that prince, disputed his title, and caused himself to be proclaimed king, at Broach, by an army of seven or eight thousand men, encamped on the Nerbudda. The rebellion was, for the present, easily extinguished; and Ahmed Shah, "who "had always professed himself extremely partial to the air and "situation of the town of Yessâwul (Âshâwul), situated on the banks "of the Sâbhermutee," inaugurated his reign by laying the foundations of a new city, of which Yessâwul formed a suburb, and which afterwards became the capital of the Kings of Goozerat; receiving, from its founder, the name of Ahmedabad (A.D. 1412).

In the latter end of the same year, however, Feroze Khân again set up his pretensions to the crown, and assembled a considerable force, among whom he raised his standard at Morâsâ. He was soon joined by Row Runmul, of Eedur, with five or six thousand horse, and their complement of foot soldiers. On the approach of Ahmed Shah, a garrison was left in Morâsâ, and Feroze Khân and the Row retired to Rungpoor, a town ten miles further off. Here they were besieged by the shah, and, the town being at length carried by storm, were compelled to fly for refuge to the hills. It is said that soon after Row Runmul and Feroze Khân had some disagreement, upon which the Râthor chief seized the horses, elephants, and other effects of his late ally, and sought, by delivering them up, to conciliate the favor of the shah.

Ahmed Shah was now engaged in a war with Sultan Hooshung, of Malwa, who supported the faction opposed to his succession to the throne. The shah was successful, and his enemies were dispersed. One of them took refuge with the Râ of Soreth, at Girnâr, and the attention of Ahmed Shah was thus directed to that Hindoo principality.

The country of Soreth has always been one full of attraction for the Hindoo; it is to him an earthly paradise, a land of clear rivers, of well-bred horses, of lovely women,—it is more, it is a holy land, to the Jain the land of Âdeenâth and Urisht Nemee, to the orthodox Hindoo the country of Muhâ Dev and Shree Krishn. The follower of the Teerthunkers turns his pilgrim-thoughts towards the holy mountains of Girnâr and Shutroonjye; the servant of Vishnoo thinks of Soreth as each morning he places on his forehead the teeluk of Gopee Chundun; the worshipper of Shiva sounds with a conch-shell of Soreth the praises of the victorious Shunkur;[1] while the Rajpoot and the bard extol the gallantry of Râ Khengâr, or lament the fate of Rânik Devee, or, perchance, at evening, meeting beneath the village tree, when the hooka bubbles, and the wandering stranger tells his tales of other lands, repeat the verse,—

"In Soreth are jewels five,
"Horses, rivers, women;
"Somnâth the fourth;
"Fifth, Huree's presence."

Nor is the Mohummedan less eager in his praise. "Fortune," says the Meerât Sekunderee, "seems to have selected this territory "from the most fertile spots of Malwa, Candeish, and Goozerat, to "present to the view at once all that was valuable in those countries; "but to all the advantages which it derives from its soil, in common "with those provinces, it possesses in its ports another, which they

[1] The port of Verâwul, on the coast of Soreth, is called by Hindoos "the field "of lamentation," because on the death of Sree Krishn and the Yâduvs, his companions, Rookmunee, the bride of Krishn, and the Yâduv ladies, sacrificed their lives there on the funeral pile. Near Verâwul is a tank, called, in memory of Krishn's favorites, the Shepherdesses of Vruj, the Gopees' or Shepherdesses' tank. The slime of this reservoir, which is white, and bears the name of Gopee Chundun, or Gopee sandal-wood ointment, is used by Vaishnavites, and especially by the Râmâ Nundee ascetics, to make the mark of the god upon their foreheads.

The shunkhs or conch-shells, which are used as horns in the temples of Shiva, are picked up on the coast of Soreth about Dwârkâ.

" cannot boast of, from which its merchants obtain wealth, and the " inland countries many of those luxuries so much in demand."

We have unfortunately little material for the history of " the race " of Huree,"—the Yâduv princes of Girnâr.[1] We have described their capital; we have related the story of Khengâr; we have seen the Gohils and others entering Soreth as vassals of the Râs, and the family of those princes itself subdividing into petty chieftainships; we shall now have little to record but long-continued and, at last, successful attempts at conquest by the Mohummedans, until we come to the closing scene, when, for a mere pittance, the Choodâsumâ waives his sovereign rights, and under title, derived from all that remains of the ancient line of Khengâr, the banner of the union crosses is unfurled in Soreth.

" Ahmed Shah," says the Mohummedan historian, " having a great " curiosity to see the hill-fort of Girnâr, pursued the rebel in that " direction; and as none of the rajas had yet bent their necks to the " Mohummedan yoke, he took advantage of the circumstance of the " raja having afforded an asylum to Sher Mullik, to make it a plea " for invading his country. On his arrival at the hills in its vicinity, " the king was opposed by the Hindoo prince, who, unaccustomed to " the brunt of Mohummedan warfare, was defeated, and pursued to " the fortress of Girnâr, now called Joonagurh. After a short time, " the raja, having consented to pay an annual tribute, made a large " offering on the spot. Ahmed Shah left officers to collect the stipu- " lated amount, and returned to Ahmedabad; on the road to which " place he destroyed the temple of Somâpoor, wherein were found " many valuable jewels and other property."

In addition to his attempts against the more powerful Hindoo princes, the efforts of Ahmed Shah were directed also against many of the numerous chieftains who held lands of greater or less extent in different parts of Goozerat. Some of these, sheltered in inaccessible natural fortresses of forest or mountain, were with difficulty compelled to pay a tribute, which was, from the first, always withheld, except when enforced by the presence of superior military power; others

[1] In the first volume of the Transactions of the Royal Asiatic Society (Bombay Branch) is a fragment of an inscription on a tablet at the entrance of Râ Khengâr's palace at Girnâr, which mentions the name of Nowghun, Khengâr, and Munduleek, and alludes to Sidh Râj Jye Singh Dev, " whose eyes were moistened and intoxi- " cated with the stream of the enjoyment of the bright pleasures afforded by earth; " the magnitude of whose glory dazzled the enemies; and whose feet were washed " by the fluid radiating from the gems on the brilliant crowns of kings who " humbled themselves before him." There is unfortunately no date.

who were less favorably situated for defence were driven wholly from their lands, and lived the life of outlaws, until their continual harassing incursions drove the proud conqueror to a composition, and they regained, on terms which included submission and tribute, a part of their hereditary domains. Some there were, who, urged by persuasion or compelled by force, exchanged the creed of their fathers for Islâm, and, treated on this account with more consideration, assumed the position of Mohummedan zumeendars. The work, however, was never fully accomplished; it was a labor of Sisyphus; allegiance sat as lightly on zumeendar as upon Thâkor or Row, and notwithstanding many a boast of the arrogant Moslem, the restoration of peace and unity to Goozerat was reserved for other hands, a wiser and more merciful policy, and a long future time.

"It must be known," says the author of Meerât Ahmudee, that at "the time of Allah-ood-deen, the Mohummedan faith was introduced "into the country extending from Nehrwala Puttun on the west, to "Broach on the east; but infidelity was still established in many "places. These, however, became purified and enlightened by "degrees, through the efforts of the Goozerat kings; and many of "them acquired the light of the faith through the labours of Shah "Ahmed." In the year A.D. 1414, one of the king's officers, ennobled by the title of Tâj-ool-moolk, received a special commission to destroy all idolatrous temples, and establish the Mohummedan authority through Goozerat; a duty which he executed with such diligence, that as Ferishta is anxious to believe "the names of Mewâs and Grâs "were hereafter unheard of in the whole kingdom."

It was not to be supposed that the bardic chroniclers should have passed over, without notice, such a revolution as was now attempted, nor have they done so, and though, in their usual temper, they have made the domestic features more prominent than the political or the religious, they have given us a picture of the times which we could not afford to lose, and much of the spirit, if not of the accurate details, of history, in the following picturesque tale of

THE COURTSHIPS OF AHMED SHAH.

When the padishah, says our present bardic authority, had taken the kingdom of the Wâghelas, there arose of that race two brothers named Wurhojee and Jetojee, who went out in rebellion.[1] In the

[1] The original term is "Bâhirwutoo;" the rebel himself is termed "Bâhir-"wuteeâ." "This term," says Colonel Walker, "is derived from *Bâhir*, outside,

country called Thul, near Unhilwârâ Puttun, there are two villages, named Bheeluree-gurh and Surdhâr, at which they placed their families for shelter, on which account the descendants of the former are called Bheelâreea, and of the latter Surdhâra Wâghelas. The chiefs left their families, and used to make forays as far as Ahmedabad, with about one hundred and fifty horsemen. Sometimes in the daytime and sometimes at night they plundered the villages of Ahmedabad; sometimes they carried off men. The padishah, Sultan Ahmed, took great trouble to apprehend them, but without success. At last, their means of subsistence being much reduced, they suffered greatly, and gradually lost most of their horsemen. There is a village called Nâshmud, on the road between Ahmedabad and Kuree, near Sântuj. At the tank of that village the brothers arrived one night. In the early morning, a Râjpoot of the village, named Bhundâree Ukho, was driving out a cartload of manure to his field. One of the Wâghelas' followers seeing him approach, concealed himself. The peasant who drove Ukho's cart perceiving this, said, "Sir! I think "the outlaws are come to the tank; we had better move on quickly." Ukho said, "Fear them not, there is no Rajpoot among them like "me, or they would have recovered their lands (grâs) within three "days." The Wâghelas' follower hearing this speech, went and told his chiefs; they sent him to invite the Râjpoot to come to them. Ukho Bhundâree having come to them, the brothers asked him what it was that he had said. He thought within himself that he had

"and *wât*, a road." "The offence consists in the Rajpoots, or Grassias, making "their ryots and dependents quit their native village, which is suffered to remain "waste, and the Grassia with his brethren then retires to some asylum, whence he "may carry on his depredations with impunity. Being well acquainted with the "country, and the redress of injuries being common cause with the members of "every family, the Bâhirwuteea has little to fear from those who are not in the "immediate interest of his enemy, and he is in consequence enabied to commit "very extensive mischief, until he may be extirpated, or his principal forced to "compromise the dispute. The number of small fortresses in the country, the "want of artillery, and little skill in its management, render it easy for a person "to obtain an asylum where he may defy the attacks of his enemies, while the "safety which these holds afford causes the commission of numerous acts of depre-"dation which otherwise would not be committed." In the hill country of Eedur, in the north-east of Goozerat, it is said of such an outlaw that he is "Wukhé," or "in trouble." We shall have many examples to produce in the following pages. A very similar course of proceeding to that of the Bâhirwuteea is described in the 14th chap. II. Samuel:—"Therefore Absalom sent for Joab, to have sent him to "the king; but he would not come to him: and when he sent again the second "time he would not come. Therefore he said unto his servants, see, Joab's field "is near mine, and he hath barley there; go and set it on fire. And Absalom's "servants set the field on fire."

meant it merely as a jest, but he would not deny his words. "Yes! "my lord," he said, "if you had a Râjpoot like me with you, you "would recover your lands in three days." The brothers said they would mount him on one of their horses, which was worth a hundred pounds, and give him anything else he asked for. They took him with them towards Ahmedabad.

The Hoormâ, or queen of the padishah, and the Begums of the Mohummedan chieftains, went every Friday to the holy place at Mukurbo, near Sirkhej, with five hundred chariots and a numerous escort. The attendants, however, remained at a short distance off, and the ladies alone went to the tomb of the saint. Ukho Bhundâree said to the brothers, "Unless you seize these ladies, you will not "recover your lands." When the ladies' carriages had entered the precincts of the tomb, the Rajpoot horsemen surrounded them. The Hoormâ asked who they were; they said they were Wurho and Jeto, who, having lost their hereditary estates, were determined to die, and announced their intention of driving off the carriages. The Hoormâ said, "If you take away my honor I must die. I will go "into the city and procure the recovery of your lands for you imme-"diately." She swore to this solemnly, and the horsemen then retired. In the meanwhile, the escort discovering the Wâghelas, prepared for an attack, but the Hoormâ forbad them to molest the Rajpoots. They obeyed her commands. The Hoormâ went into the city, and at night sat moodily in the palace, forbidding the lamps to be lighted. The padishah, being apprised of this, came to her, and asked what had happened. She told him the whole, and said, "I "have given my oath, therefore you must send for the two brothers, "and reinstate them in their lands. If they had driven off my "carriage, where would have been the padishah's honor?"

The padishah invited the brothers with great respect into Ahmedabad, and promised them dresses of honor. The Hoormâ had told them to remain at the white well near Pâlaree, and that she would send a hostage (bândhur) for them in the morning. They did accordingly, and in the morning the padishah sent his ministers, Mânikchund and Moteechund, who went to the spot, and, with the assistance of a gardener, called Wurhojee and Jetojee to them. The Wâghelas asked what security they had that they should not be seized and cast into prison. The ministers said they were securities for them themselves, and taking oaths to this effect, brought them towards the city. It was nearly sunset when they arrived at the gate, and observed a woman seated by the roadside in an indecent posture. The Wâghelas enquired of what caste the woman might be; the ministers said they supposed she was a Brahmin or a Wâneeo. The Rajpoots enquired further, of what caste the ministers themselves were; they answered that they were Wâneeâs. Wurho then said to Jeto, "Brother! these ministers are the sons of women who behave "thus in open day—what shame will they feel if the padishah throw "us into prison, or what hold can they have upon him? We had "better turn back from this place." They said to the ministers, "We cannot rely upon your security;" and then turning, went back to the white well. The ministers related what had happened to the padishah, who sent to ask the brothers the reason of their distrust. The Wâghelas said that they would not come without better security. The padishah then sent some of his Umeers as security, and the Rajpoot horsemen again advanced towards the city. It was evening, and the way was somewhat narrow. As they turned a corner they came suddenly upon a Puthân woman who was passing along, with her face veiled; and who, seeing the horsemen, endeavoured to conceal herself, but found no place. She considered with herself that it was not right that any man should see a Mogul's daughter, and having no other resource, jumped into a well. A number of people hearing the noise, ran together. The Rajpoots also stopped. When the woman was taken out, it was discovered who she was, and what was the reason of her falling into the well. Wurho and Jeto then felt confidence that the honor of the sons of such women would be a safeguard to them. Thus they came to the padishah's court. He ordered their old clothes to be taken from them, and presented them with new ones. From the old garments four pounds' weight of lice were taken out—such calamity had the Rajpoots endured in the jungle.

The brothers considered in what way they could please the padishah; they gave him their sister, Lâlâ, in marriage. Ahmed Shah gave them the five hundred villages of Kulol, and asked them how they would divide the estate. Wurho and Jeto said the elder brother would take the larger share, according to custom. The padishah asked what foundation the custom had, to which the younger brother replied, that its foundation was "force." Ahmed Shah said that as they had suffered alike they should share equally. Wurho, upon this, took Kulol and two hundred and fifty villages. The chief of his descendants now holds Lembor, and junior branches hold Pethâpoor and Pendairoo, with twelve villages apiece. The rest have been expelled by the Koolees. The younger brother had the two hundred and fifty villages of Sânund. The brothers had arranged that the elder should have the best land, but by-and-bye the younger brother's land began to produce fine wheat, while the elder could hardly grow vetches.

After these things a Thâkor, or chieftain, who possessed three hundred and fifty villages, named Beeolâ Sâmunt Singh, was one day passing along the road beneath the padishah's palace. It was the hot weather, and, as the sun was very powerful, he had thrown a cloth over his head, for at that time chutrees were not in use, and only the great Mohummedan omrah were permitted to use âftâbgeerees.[1] Wurho and Jeto were at this time seated in one of the windows of the palace. They said, in ridicule, "Who is it that goes "along hiding his face?" Sâmunt Singh, hearing this, said, "Why "should I hide my face? They may well hide their faces whose "daughters and sisters have been given to the Mohummedans." Wurho and Jeto were very much enraged when they heard this; they swore that Sâmunt Singh should give his daughter to a Mohummedan, or they would no longer call themselves Wurho and Jeto, but would submit to be dishonored. Sâmunt Singh, meanwhile, went on to his lodging. The Wâghela brothers, on the first opportunity, told the padishah that the chieftain of Beeol had insulted them, and that the only remedy was, that Ahmed Shah should take to wife the Beeolâ's daughter, a young lady fourteen years of age, and celebrated for her beauty. The king assented to their proposal; and said to some of his Mogul officers, "When Sâmunt Singh comes to court, "demand his daughter for me in marriage." They answered, "Your "Majesty! this Sâmunt Singh is a dweller in the forest; he will not "easily be brought to listen to what we say; and, indeed, it is a "difficult matter for us to speak to him on the subject." The padishah said, "Well, when he comes, remind me of the matter, and I will speak to him." One day Sâmunt Singh came to the court. The Mogul officers reminded the sultan, and he asked "Sâmunt "Singh, what children have you?" The chief answered, "Your "Majesty! I have one son and one daughter." Ahmed Shah asked how old the daughter was. He said, "She is seven years of age." The padishah enquired why the Rajpoots delayed so long marrying their daughters. The chief said, that it would cost him two or three hundred pounds to marry his daughter, and that it was difficult for him to spare so much; and further, that if he married her at too early an age, and she were to die, the money would be thrown away.

[1] Chutree *here* means the common parasol or umbrella of modern days; âftâbgeeree, a magnificent state umbrella. Chutree, however, equally means the royal canopy; it is the Hindoo, as the other is the Mohummedan word.

The king said, "Well! Sâmunt Singh, marry your daughter to the "padishah's throne." The Thâkor replied, "You say well, sire, I "know that many Hindoo raja's daughters are in the king's harem— "the Kulol Raja's, the Eedur Raja's, and others; therefore, if my "daughter be there too, it will be well, but she is too young as yet, "and, in appearance, far from worthy of the king. There may be "among my kinsfolk some maiden worthy of the king—her I will "marry to your majesty." The padishah said, "Marry me your "daughter, however things may be." Sâmunt Singh made many excuses as to her youth; but the padishah continued to insist, until he promised his consent. The chief went to his lodging; and the king calling for Wurho and Jeto, told them that Sâmunt Singh had agreed to give his daughter, notwithstanding their predictions to the contrary. They said, "He has so far agreed certainly, but among "Rajpoots it is the custom for the bridegroom to present a dress and "jewels to the lady, which we call '*wusunt;*' if the Beeolâ receive "'wusunt,' we may then reckon the affair as settled."

Some days afterwards, Sâmunt Singh having come into the court, Ahmed Shah said to him, "Sâmunt Singh, receive 'wusunt' on behalf "of your daughter." He said he would after his return home. The king said, "No! take it away immediately to your lodging." The chief was then forced to receive it. The king told the brothers that their prophecy, in regard to the Beeolâ's refusing to receive "wusunt," had proved as untrue as their first prediction. They said, "He has received 'wusunt,' but he will certainly not fix the day." The king upon this said to Sâmunt Singh at the next interview, "You must fix the day for the marriage." He replied, "I have "been here ten months; I must return home, and look after my "revenues; and it will take me a year to make preparations for the "marriage; I have not the means, at present, to pay for a wedding "with the padishah. Wait awhile." The king said, "Take what "sum of money you require from the treasury, but fix the day." He answered, "Your majesty! if I take money of yours for the "purpose, that will not be creditable to me." The padishah, nevertheless, ordered a camel's load of treasure to be conveyed to Beeol. With that money Sâmunt Singh built a fort at Beeol with bastions, and collected powder and ball, and soldiers. Then he sent word to the padishah to say, "Now be pleased to come, and be married."

About fourteen miles from Beeol is a hill, which is a very terrible place; there is a fortress there, called "Dhoree-Pâwutee." At that place, Sâmunt Singh had built a great mansion, and he had made a large cave under ground, in order that he might retreat thither if forced from Beeol. The remains of these still exist, and people say that there is much treasure buried there, but from fear of the bees no one can enter.[1] About two miles from the same place is Kedâreshwur Muhâ Dev, which is believed to be of the time of the Pânduvs, and twelve miles further on is Oontâreeya Muhâ Dev, which is far older than the time of the Pânduvs.

The king, taking a force with him, went towards Beeol, and pitched his camp four miles from the place. Sâmunt Singh sent his brother and nephew to the king, to enquire whether he intended to be married in the Mohummedan fashion or as a Hindoo. The king said he had never seen a Hindoo marriage, and would prefer that fashion. They said, "The king has come to our home to be married; we must, "therefore, perform the ceremony in a handsome manner. We will "fire off guns, and cast red powder into the air; and it is our Hindoo "practice to ridicule the bridegroom's party, and to sprinkle them "with salt and sand. If, perchance, your followers do not take it in "good part, and strike any one, there may arise a great fight out of "the marriage. You must, therefore, make them understand that "they are not to quarrel with any Beeol man who may ridicule them." The king gave orders accordingly to his followers. Sâmunt Singh's brother next said, "Sire! there is not room enough near Beeol for "your army to encamp. Let the great chiefs and nobles, therefore, "be sent on in advance; do you come yourself after them, and let "the troops come last." Having delivered the whole of their message, they returned into the town. The king sent on his chief officers, following them himself, his troops being in the rear. When they arrived near Beeol, they found five thousand Rajpoots waiting for them,

[1] In an eastern country, and in such a locality, *the bees* are an enemy by no means to be despised. Moses reminds the Israelites, in Deuteronomy, how the Amorites, which dwelt in the mountain, came out against them, and chased them "*as bees do.*" And Joshua relates how the wasps or hornets, "the forerunners of God's host," drove out the same enemy from before them. In his Western India, Colonel Tod tells a story of Mahmood Begurra, Sultan of Ahmedabad, and his iconoclastic attempts upon a brass bull of colossal size at the shrine of Uchuleshwur, upon Mount Aboo. "In descending from Aboo, after the reduction of Uchulgurh, his "banners 'fanned by conquest's crimson wing,' confusion waited on them from an "unlooked-for source. *A legion of bees*, issuing from their pinnacled retreats, at-"tacked and pursued the invaders even to Jhâlor. To commemorate this victory "over the spoiler, the name of *Bhumur Thul*, or 'Bees' Valley,' was given to the "spot. A temple was erected, and from the captured arms thrown away in their "flight, a vast trident was formed, and placed in front of the divinity who thus "avenged the insult to Nundee." *Vide* p. 87, *Tod's Western India*.

Not many years ago at Kaira, in Goozerat, the funeral procession of a British officer was as effectually put to the rout by an army of bees.

with guns loaded with ball. They closed the gate, and fired a volley from the ramparts, slaying many of the king's troops; but Ahmed Shah for a long time continued to think they were in sport. When he saw many men fall, however, he perceived that it was treachery. The fight went on for seven days, at the end of which time Sâmunt Singh having sustained a severe loss, carried off his family to Dhoree Pâwutee. The king's army entered Beeol, and plundered it; Ahmed Shah remained there three months looking after the wounded, preparing military stores, and collecting troops. At length he set off for Dhoree Pâwutee. He cut down many trees there, and continued to attack the place for two months. People say, that at last Sâmunt Singh fired balls of gold and silver at the Mohummedans. In the end, Sâmunt Singh, flying from Dhoree Pâwutee, took refuge at the mountain called Ghoonwo, and married his daughter to the Row of Eedur. The king seized his three hundred and fifty villages.

Sâmunt Singh remained in outlawry for twelve years, during which time he caused the Mohummedans much annoyance. At last the king sent security to him, offering an accommodation. Sâmunt Singh said he would live in peace if his lands were restored. The king then gave *wântâ* lands in eighty-four villages in the Dehgâm Pergunnah to Sâmunt Singh, and settled the dispute. Sâmunt Singh returned to Beeol, and took up his residence there; and, at the present day, descendants of his are existing under the name of Beeola Rajpoots, who hold *wântâ* lands in Dehgâm.

Lâlâ, the sister of Wurho and Jeto, died—some people say from drinking hot milk, which scalded her internally. The shah, who was very fond of her, and enchanted with her beauty and accomplishments, became distracted. He sent his ministers into different countries to procure him such another Hindoo wife, but they could find no beauty like Lâlâ among Hindoos or Mohummedans. The king, coming to Ahmedabad, made proclamation to this effect, and was more distracted than ever. He deserted the management of his affairs, and sat in a stupor of sorrow. The ministers thought there was no remedy but to procure for him another wife such as Lâlâ, the Wâghelânee. They sent a Brahmin, employed for such purposes, to seek another fair one. The Brahmin, after travelling through many countries, came at last to Mâtur, where there was a Seesodeea Raja, of the house of Cheetor, who bore the name of Sutrâsuljee, and the title of Râwul. He possessed sixty-six villages, and had a daughter, named Râneebâ, and two sons, Bhânjee and Bhojjee. Râneebâ was very beautiful. The Brahmin when he saw her was much delighted, thinking that, when he carried to court the good news that he had discovered her, he should receive a dress of honor. He went to the king's ministers, and told them that he had found a successor for Lâlâ Wâghelânee. They gave him a dress of honor, and made him detail the particulars. He said he had found at Mâtur, in the Churotur, a beautiful maiden, the daughter of Râwul Sutrâsuljee. The ministers sent for Sutrâsuljee to Ahmedabad, and with much respect, solicited him to marry his daughter to the throne. Sutrâsuljee answered that the daughter of a Hindoo could not be thus married. The ministers urged that the harem of the shah contained many Hindoo rajas' daughters. Sutrâsuljee merely answered, "They and I are different." The Deewâns said that if he did not give his consent willingly they should be compelled to extort it. The Râwul still refused, and, at last, was thrown into prison. His wife, when she heard the news, considered within herself, "I must look upon this daughter as one who is dead; but, by "some means or other, I must save the Chief's life and our *grâs*." She sent her daughter, accordingly, to Ahmedabad. When the lady, wearing her ornaments, was introduced to the king, he was astonished at her beauty, and exclaimed, "Is this Lâlâ returned?" She answered, "That Lâlâ has gone." The king recollected himself. The next day he held a court. He caused the fetters to be struck off Sutrâsuljee, and, calling him into court, presented him with a dress of honor. Sutrâsuljee thought lightly of his imprisonment, congratulating himself that he had escaped giving his daughter to the Mohummedan. He returned cheerfully home. When the time came for sitting down to dinner he called for Râneebâ. The Rânee pretended to go out for her, and, returning, said that Râneebâ was amusing herself, and would not come. Sutrâsuljee declared he would take no food until she arrived. Then the Rânee said to him, "My lord! when Râneebâ "was sent to the king at Ahmedabad your prison doors were opened." Hearing this, Sutrâsuljee was overpowered with grief. He said, "What mattered it had I died there? I am of the race of Cheetor; "I have myself been called Nukulunkee;[1] such a stain was never "before cast upon the Seesodeeas' honor. Fie upon you that you "have spotted it thus!" The Rânee said, "Your life would have "been lost; let us then look upon our daughter as one who is dead." The Rajpoot rose, quick as thought, and seized his sword; his wife cast her arms round him, but he dashed her from him down to the ground, and, drawing the weapon, plunged it into his belly, and fell a corpse.

Sutrâsuljee's sons, Bhânjee and Bhojjee, carefully performed his

[1] The "Stainless."

obsequies; they began to rule at Mâtur. When the matter became known at Ahmedabad, Râneebâ performed ablutions, and was very sorrowful. Beholding her grief, the king said kindly to her, "When "any one of the Hindoo rajas dies, and his sons succeed to the "throne, is there anything which a relation can do to help them?" Râneebâ said, "A rich relation may send a dress of honor, and replace "with it their white habiliments of mourning." The king said, "Let "me send for your brothers here to make them presents, and remove "their mourning." So was it done; the Thâkors came to Ahmedabad, and alighted at their own lodging. The king sent them hay, grain, and other necessaries; he said to the lady, "I will this day present "your brothers with dresses of honor." She said, "What brothers, "and what sister? I am no longer related to them." The king asked, "How? Are they not your brothers?" Râneebâ answered, "I am "now a Mohummedan, they are Hindoos, we cannot eat together or "drink of the same cup of water. How then any longer are we "brothers and sister!" The king replied, "Do you prepare dinner "for them to-day." Hearing this, the lady reflected, "I meant well, "but it has turned out otherwise." When the king sent for the "brothers, they came in expectation of receiving dresses of honor, and sat down at their sister's mansion. The lady, when they were alone, said to them, "Shame on you, brothers, that though our father "died on account of his grief at my being given up to the Mohum-"medan, you are come here to be made outcastes!" She then ex-"plained the intentions of the king. The younger brother, Bhojjee, at once dropped from the window, and made his escape; the elder brother, Bhânjee, remained. The king came out, and said, "Eat of "the food which your sister has prepared." Bhânjee said, "Sire! I "cannot." The king said, "Why stand you thus aloof?" Bhânjee said, "Sire! if I eat here, no Rajpoot will give me his daughter to "wife." The king said, "Think not of that, I will bring as many "Rajpoots as you please, and make them eat with you." He compelled Bhânjee to partake of the repast. The Thâkor was much grieved at this, and to assuage his grief, the king caused Rajpoots from fifty-two villages to be brought to Ahmedabad. At this time many Rajpoots hearing that the king meditated their forcible conversion, abandoned their villages and "grâs," and went away into other countries. Such as fell into the king's hands were compelled to forfeit their caste. Things went on in this way for many days; many a battle was fought, and many a Rajpoot lost his life.

Near Châmpâner is Râjpeepla, which is the capital of three hundred and fifty villages. The raja of it was Thâkor Hureesunghjee

Gohil. On one occasion a set of pearls of great value having been presented to him, he had made a necklace of them for his Thâkorine. He said to her, "There is water, truly, in these." When the struggle with the king occurred, the Raja of Râjpeepla, with the other chiefs, was compelled to fly into the jungle. At a time when they were suffering dreadfully from thirst, the Rânee, looking sorrowfully at her necklace, said, "Thâkor! you once told me there was water in these." On this incident the Châruns made the following verses :—

"O! shah, sultan, friend, when you became angry, the Shesh could "not support its burthen; the earth began to tremble. You slew the "warrior Rajpoots, full of pride—them of the Rewâ. On all sides "the dust was wetted with blood. O! sultan, from fear of you, "blistered were the feet of the Bhoomeeâs' Rânees; they wandered, "eating esculent roots; Upsurâs in form, they tore the pearls from "their necks, and, squeezing them into their husbands' mouths, cried, "'You said there was water in these.'" After twelve years spent in "outlawry, Hureesunghjee Gohil recovered his "grâs" from the shah, and his descendants still rule at Râjpeepla.

The Rajpoots who were thus put out of caste, concludes the bard, formed a separate caste, called "Molesulâm," because they had bowed (or made sulâm) to the Mohol, or palace of the sultan. These still dress as Hindoos; some of them practice the Hindoo religion, and some the Mohummedan; but among them the corpses of the dead are always buried, and not burned. Their women also dress as Hindoos. Other Hindoos look down upon them as Mohummedans; but they retain the names of the clans they formerly belonged to; and have Bhâts for their Wyewunchâs, who read their pedigrees. At marriages they do not use the fire-sacrifice; but are united with prayers; they retain, however, the "Gunesh-poojâ," and some other Hindoo rites. Some Rajpoots, who escaped notice from their unimportance, retained their caste, and are known as Kârudeeas; others, who were too powerful to be subjected, but agreed to become tributary to the sultan, remained rajas, and were still addressed by the title of Jee. A number of poor Rajpoots, remaining aloof "nurwa," and seeking nothing further than permission to cultivate the land, became Nârodas. The Wâneeas and Brahmins, who were made outcaste at the same time, joined the sect of the Borahs.[1]

[1] "But there is another tribe of Mohummedans, which cuts a considerable "figure in this collectorate (Broach) as agriculturists : these are the Borahs; but "they are quite a distinct sect from the trading Borahs. Agriculture is their sole "pursuit and occupation, although they sometimes hire out their carts, and accom- "pany them as their drivers. They are the most active, industrious, and skilful

The elder branch of the Wâghelas soon after these times melted away. Ânund Dev, the grandson of the first chief, held the undivided estate of Kulol, but his younger son, Rânik Dev, received as his patrimonial inheritance Roopâl, with forty-two villages. In A.D. 1499, when Mahmood Begurra, the grandson of Shah Ahmed, was upon the throne, Roodâ Rânee, the consort of Veer Singh Wâghela, the then Lord of Kulol, constructed, at an expense of "five lakhs of tunkhas," the magnificent well which still exists at the village of Udâlej. Veer Singh and his brother Ujetra Singh were at war with the Mohummedans, who slew the elder brother, and placed a garrison in his

"cultivators in the Zilla, as the appearance and resources of their villages fully indicate; their dress, manners, and language are the same as those of the Koonbee "and other Hindoo cultivators; they were, indeed, themselves originally Hindoos. "Their ancestors are supposed to have been for the most part Koolees and Rajpoots, with perhaps a few Koonbees; and their conversion, they think, took "place in the time of the Mohummedan monarch of Goozerat, known by the name "of Sultan Mahmood Begurra. The Goozeratee is the language spoken among "these Borahs, and not the Hindostanee, as in the case of those among the "Mohummedan cultivators, called Mulleks, Khans, &c. All the cultivating Borahs "are Soonees."—*Colonel Williams's Memoir on the Zilla of Baroche*, p. 91.

The following account of the origin of the Borahs is from an article on Oujein by Connoly, in the Journal of the Asiatic Society (Bengal), vol. vi. p. 842:—

"A man, named Yakub, obliged to quit his country from some domestic or "party feud, was the first of his sect who put his foot in India, having left Egypt "and landed at Cambay, A.H. 532 (A.D. 1137). At this time the chief Mulla of "the sect (which had been for some years settled in Yemen) was Zohribbin Musa. "Egypt obeyed the rule of the Caliph Mostemsir Billah, and *Sadras Singh* "governed the Hindoo kingdom of *Pirân-pattan*. Now Mostemsir, say most "authorities, died A.H. 487, and his grandson, Hafedh, the 11th caliph, reigned "from 524 to 544. The Guzerat chronicles, though very confused at this period, "agree better with the above date, for Siddha, or Jaya Singh, of which Sadras "may be a corruption, was King of Anhulwara patan in 1094."

See, however, the remainder of the article. It appears that Yakub landed at Cambay, and lived with a gardener, whom he converted. He subsequently converted the son of a Brahmin. "The King Sadras," and his two dewans, the brothers, "Târmall and Bârmall," used frequently to visit a temple at Cambay, where an iron elephant was suspended in the air by a magnet. Yakub removed the magnet, and was also victorious in a contest with the Brahmins. "Sadras and "his court, won by such a succession of miracles, embraced the religion of their "author." Their example was soon followed by many others. The sect kept up an intercourse with Arabia, and assumed the name of Vyuvuhârees, or Borahs.

There seems to be a strange jumble of real names and events in this story. "Sadras Singh" may well be *Sudderâ Jesingh*, the name by which Sidh Râj is popularly known in Goozerat, but the two dewans, Târmall and Bârmall, must be the brothers, Tej Pâl and Wustoo Pâl, the ministers of Veerdhuwul Wâghela. Again, the story of the king's conversion would apply better to Koomâr Pâl, or Ujye Pâl, of whom such tales are elsewhere related.

patrimonial town. Kulol was, however, held for several generations after by Veer Singh's descendants, until it was at length lost, in A.D. 1728, by Bhugut Singh. That chief retired to Lembodurâ, a village which he took from the Ânjunâ Koonbees, and which is still held by his descendant, who claims, and apparently with reason, the honor of being the chief of the Wâghelas.

Two or three generations after the death of Rânik Dev, the younger son of Ânund Dev, the estate of Roopâl was subdivided between the sons of Sâmunt Singh, the then chieftain; the eldest, Wuje Kurunjee, retained Roopâl, but a mansion was built at Kolwurâ for the younger son, Someshwur, who received fourteen of his father's villages. Wuje Kurunjee appears to have lost Roopâl, for his eldest son, Bheemjee, retired into the Eedur country, where he founded the families of Poseenâ and Hurâd, vassals of the Rows of Eedur, while Wunojee, the younger son, settled at Âloowâ, on the banks of the Sâbhermutee, at which place his descendants still remain.

Someshwur's grandson, Chândojee, still held Kolwurâ. He had a son, Heemâlojee, whose mother's brother, Pethoo Gol, possessed the estate of Sokhuroo, near the Sâbhermutee river. Pethoo Gol was afflicted with an incurable disease, and as he had no offspring, he looked with an eye of apprehension on Heemâlojee; it being no uncommon thing in those times, says the bard, for nephews to put their uncles to death for their grâs. Pethoo's fears were not without foundation, but the precautions taken by him prevented any open attack by his nephew. At length, however, Heemâlojee, pretending a pilgrimage to Sokhureeâ Muhâ Dev, entered Sokhuroo with a band of Rajpoots concealed in the closed carriages used for the conveyance of women. These warriors made their way into the mansion of the chief, whom they put to death. "Sut" having then come upon the Rânee, she cursed Heemâlojee, and prophesied that the children of even his daughters should meet an untimely death. The Thâkor implored her forgiveness, and said, "Mother! you have no child; I "am your son; what has happened has happened; be kind to me, "and I will obey any order you may give." The Sutee commanded him to found a new village in the name of his uncle, and promised that his descendants, in the male line, should maintain themselves there, but declared, that as her word could not be altered, the daughters of his race should be childless. Such was the origin of Pethâpoor, a handsome town on the Sâbhermutee river, a few miles to the north of Ahmedabad, distinguished to the present time by its manufacture of matchlocks, and by the valor and fidelity of its mercenary bands. The curse of the Sutee has, however, been accomplished, and the daughters of the Lords of Pethâpoor, it is said, have never reared a child.

The Sânund branch of the family has been more fortunate than that of Kulol, and still retains its possessions, subdivided into the two principal estates of Sânund (called also of Kot) and Gângur.[1]

CHAPTER IV.

AHMED SHAH I.—MOHUMMED SHAH I.—KOOTB SHAH.

In the year A.D. 1418, Ahmed Shah was drawn to the defence of the districts of Sultânpoor and Nundoorbâr, then threatened by the ruler of Asseer, in conjunction with Sultan Hooshung, of Malwa. When the rains had already set in, the shah received intelligence that during his absence the Row of Eedur, the Râwul of Châmpâner, the chiefs of Mundulgurh and Nadot, had combined to invite Sultan Hooshung to an invasion of Goozerat, and that the Râ of Soreth, having heard of the projected invasion, had refused to pay his tribute.

[1] There is much confusion, which it is now impossible to remedy, in the bardic account of the Wâghelas. One authority makes the first holders of Kulol and Sânund to be sons of Kurun Wâghela, and even mentions the names of their mothers. The account is as follows:—"Kurun's sons, Sârung and Wurshung, "were born at the same time, and were, therefore, both 'Pâtuwees.' Sârung's "mother was Tâj Koonwureejee, daughter of Gujsunghjee Bhâtee of Jesulmer; "Wurshung's mother was Umur Koonwerbâ, daughter of Desuljee Jhâreja of "Kerookot. Wurshung had Surdhâr assigned to him in the life-time of his father, "with six hundred and fifty villages. Sârung received, in like manner, Bheeluree, "with six hundred and fifty villages. Meeting at Bheeluree, the brothers took "Kuree from the Mohummedans, but continued the Begum on the throne, and "and went to meet the padishah at Puttun without taking any security. The "padishah was pleased, and gave them five hundred villages. Sârung Dev took "Kulol, with two hundred and fifty villages, and Wurshung took Sânund, with "the like number." The inscription on the well at Udâlej gives the following pedigree:—1. Mokul Singh; 2. Kurun; 3. Mool Raja; 4. Mahip, whose sons were Veer Singh and Ujetra Singh, the former Roodâ Rânee's husband. These two brothers are doubtless the Wurho and Jeto of the bards, to whom a family tradition has been assigned. Another inscription is to be found in a well at Mânsâ. It gives the following pedigree:—1. Mool Râj; 2. Vijye Ânund; 3. Velo; 4. Dhuwul; 5. Wânkâ; 6. Chumpuk, who married Chumpâ Devee, daughter of Loonkâ, the son of Sârung Devjee, and had by her a son Dhârâ, the person who constructed the well, A.D. 1526. This branch of the Wâghela family was seated at Ogânej, near Kulol.

Ahmed Shah immediately crossed the Nerbudda, notwithstanding the unfavorable season, and encamped his army on the banks of the Myhee, from whence he himself, with a light force, rapidly advanced to Ahmedabad, and thence to Morâsâ. Troops were detached against the Râ of Soreth, the Raja of Mundulgurh, and others of the confederates; and the shah himself, when the season opened, advanced from Morâsâ into Malwa, where he defeated Hooshung, and pursued him to within a few miles of Mândoo. In the following year a peace was concluded between the Kings of Goozerat and Malwa, and the former seized the opportunity of revenging himself upon his nearer neighbours. He occupied Eedur, and he invested Châmpâner, and compelled the Râwul to consent to an annual tribute. He next "re-"turned to settle the boundaries of his own country, dispersed the "refractory, and, destroying the Hindoo temples, built mosques in their "place. Having also founded forts in such places, he left garrisons "in them, among which may be mentioned the fort at the town of "Jinoor, in the Pergunnah of Bareah, and that of Shivpoor. After "this he established the market town of Dahmod, among the moun-"tains, where he erected a fortification. After this the fort of Karieh "(Kaira or Kuree?) built in A.D. 1304, by order of Alp Khân, who "governed the country for Allah-ood-deen Khiljy, was repaired, and "named Sultanabad."

Ahmed Shah was subsequently engaged in a war of some duration with Malwa, in which he was, on the whole, successful, though his troops suffered so much during the campaign as to oblige him to abstain from any foreign attacks for some years. In A.D. 1426, he marched "to retake Eedur," but being apparently convinced of his inability to hold that capital, the citadel of which, it is probable, had never been surrendered to him, he, on this occasion, with the view of more fully overawing the country of the Rows, commenced the construction of a large and handsome fortress on the banks of the Hâtmutee river, and within sight of the mountain-peaks that rise above Eedur-gurh, to which he gave the name of Ahmednugger. Tradition states that he also founded the fort of Sâdrâ, situated about half-way between Ahmednugger and his capital, in a strong position, on the banks of the Sâbhermutee, defended by deep ravines. Row Poonjâ, the then chief of Eedur, however, obstructed the shah's operations by night attacks on Ahmednugger, and by marauding expeditions into the country held by the Mohummedans. A reward was therefore set upon his head. On one occasion, when he had attacked Ahmednugger, the Row was repulsed, and pursued by the Moslem cavalry. He gallopped towards Eedur, but, as he passed at a rapid pace along a path at the edge of a ravine, his horse shied with him, and fell into the chasm below. The Row falling below the animal was killed. Next day, a woodcutter, who discovered the corpse lying in the ravine, having heard the proclamation of a reward, cut off Row Poonjâ's head, and brought it to the audience tent of the sultan. Ahmed Shah now sent a detachment to lay waste the country of Beesulnugger, in the hills about which Row Poonjâ had been wont to take refuge.

Row Poonjâ was succeeded by his son, Nârondâs, who, as Ferishta states, agreed to pay an annual tribute of three lakhs of tunkhas of silver into the treasury of Goozerat. From Eedur the king marched into the district of Gudwârâ, and next year, A.D. 1428, his pacification with Row Nârondâs having already been broken, "he marched again "to Eedur, and on the 14th of November carried by storm one of "the principal forts in that province, wherein he built a magnificent "mosque."

A contest now ensued with the Bahmuny sovereign of the Dekkan, in which his usual success attended the arms of Ahmed Shah. An interesting fact is here disclosed—the possession by the sovereigns of Goozerat of Salsette and of the islands of Mahim and Moombâ Devee, which, in their united form, constitute the present island of Bombay. Mahim was then held by a tributary Hindoo prince, with the title of Râee, who afterwards gave a daughter to the harem of the son of Shah Ahmed. There is no record of the separate conquest of this territory by the Mohummedans, nor does it appear that either the viceroys or the sultans of Goozerat were ever sufficiently unemployed up to this time, or possessed of sufficient resources to have enabled them to undertake an extension of their dominions into this detached and distant quarter. We have seen, however, that the sovereigns of Unhilwârâ pushed their armies deep into the Dekkan; that they not only held possession of the northern part of Candeish, in which Kurun Wâghela long maintained himself after Goozerat had been overrun; but that they also occupied the Konkun, and threatened the kingdom of Kollâpoor. We may therefore conclude that Bombay and the northern Konkun fell into the possession of the Mohummedans on the extinction of the Wâghela dynasty, as part of the recognised territories of the lords of Unhilwârâ,—a fact which, taken in connection with the glimpses we possess of their naval supremacy, is calculated to add no little interest to the illustrious line of Sidh Râj.

Kootb Khân, the governor of Mahim on the part of Ahmed Shah, dying, the Bahmuny sultan, seizing the favorable opportunity, occupied that island without loss, and also took possession of Tannah, in Salsette. Ahmed Shah immediately assembled a fleet of seventeen sail at Diu, Gogo, and Cambay, which, in co-operation with an army advancing along the northern Konkun, attacked and recovered Tannah. The Bahmuny general retreated to Mahim, and on the face of that island, which was exposed, constructed a very strong wattled breast-work. This stockade was carried, not without considerable loss, by the troops of Ahmed Shah, who now found themselves opposed to the whole of the Dekkan line. A bloody and indecisive action ensued, which was terminated at nightfall; but while darkness lasted, the Dekkan general abandoned his position, and retreated to the contiguous island of Moombâ Devee. The Goozerat fleet blockaded the island, and effected a landing upon it for the troops, and the general of the Bahmuny shah was compelled to fly to the continent. After another action, fought under the walls of Tannah, the Dekkany troops were ultimately defeated and dispersed, and the fleet of Goozerat returned home, carrying with it "some beautiful gold and silver embroidered "muslins," taken on the island of Mahim.

The Bahmuny sovereign, in A.D. 1431, sought to revenge his defeat by an irruption into the Goozerat provinces of Candeish; but he was encountered by Ahmed Shah in person, and met with his former ill-success.

Next year Ahmed Shah marched into Rajpootana, exacted tribute from the Râwul of Doongurpoor, proceeded through the Bheel country into the territories of Rânâ Mokuljee of Mewar, and levied contributions from the Rows of Kotah, Boondee, and Nudoolaye. The close of his reign was occupied by an unsuccessful attempt to preserve the throne of Malwa to the descendants of his ancient enemy, Sultan Hooshung. He died at Ahmedabad on the 4th of July, A.D. 1443, and was buried there in a sumptuous tomb in front of the Friday mosque.

Mohummed Shah, the son and successor of Ahmed, in the year of his succession led an army against the Row of Eedur, who for a time took to the hills; but "having soon after sent ambassadors to ask "pardon for his faults," was accordingly forgiven, and gave his daughter in marriage to the sultan. Mohummed Shah continued his advance into Bhâgur, and after exacting tribute returned to Ahmedabad. In A.D. 1449, he marched against Râwul Gungâdâs of Châmpâner, and, defeating him, drove him to take refuge within his fortress. The Râwul, however, prevailed upon the Khiljy sovereign of Malwa to march to his assistance, and Mohummed Shah made a disgraceful retreat before this new enemy.

Sultan Mahmood of Malwa now threatened the subjugation of Goozerat; Mohummed Shah died or was poisoned, and his son, Kootb

Shah, succeeding, found the invader between the villages of Sirkhej and Butwa, within a few miles of his capital. An action was fought, and the Sultan of Malwa, though nearly successful, was compelled at last to retire. A peace was concluded between the two sovereigns, who bound themselves by a special article to wage henceforth perpetual war against Hindoos, an engagement afterwards partially redeemed by an offensive alliance against Rânâ Koombho of Mewar.

Koombho Rânâ was one of the best of the many energetic princes who successively ruled Mewar, and to him is attributed that augmentation of her resources which enabled her to make so gallant a stand against the Mohummedan power under Sung, his heroic grandson. To Koombho Rânâ are attributed thirty-two of the eighty-four fortresses erected for the defence of Mewar. The greatest of these was Koombhomer, or Komulmer, whose natural position, aided by the works which he constructed, rendered it impregnable to a native army. He also erected a citadel within the ancient fortress of the Purmârs at Aboogurh, in which he often resided. Its magazine and alarm tower still bear Koombho's name ; and, in a rude temple, his effigy, in brass stills receives divine honours. Koombho Rânâ also fortified the passes between the western frontier and Aboo ; he erected the fort of Wusuntee, near Seerohee ; a second at Koombhâreea, beside the shrine of Umbâjee ; and others which protected his territories against the Mairs of the Ârâwullee, or the Bheels of Jhârol and Pânowrâ. The temple of Koombho Shâm, on Mount Aboo, is another monument of the Seesodeea prince, who contributed largely also towards the erection of the celebrated shrine of Rishub Dev, which occupies the Sâdree pass, "a deserted glen running into the western slope of "the Ârâwullee, below his favorite fort of Komulmer."[1] He was himself a poet, and the husband of a poetess, the celebrated Râthor princess, Meerâ Bâee.

Kootb Shah was called upon for assistance against the Rânâ of Mewar by his relation, Shums Khân, the descendant of a brother of Moozuffer Shah, then possessing Nâgor. The first expedition in which

[1] There is an inscription on this temple which furnishes a pedigree of Koombho Rânâ, or, as he is there called, Rânâ Shree Koombh Kurn, from Shree Bupya or Bâppâ, for an account of whose origin see p. 235. In this inscription (which is dated A.D. 1440), among other epithets applied to Koombho Rânâ, are the following: he was "The eagle which destroyed the crowd of snake-like barbarian princes, the "forest conflagration which burned the jungle of injustice, the Sultan of the Hin-"doos." The temple stands at a village called Rânpoor, about five miles from the town of Sâdree, or Sâduree, in Marwar. For a description of it, with illustrations, see Fergusson's Illustrated Hand Book of Architecture, vol. i., p. 79, and the same author's Illustrations of Indian Architecture.

the shah was not himself personally engaged was eminently unsuccessful, the troops of Goozerat being completely defeated by the Rânâ. Kootb Shah, hearing of this disaster, advanced in person: he defeated the Rajpoots of Seerohee, at this time vassals of Mewar, entered the hills, and made his way to Komulmer. In this position he was attacked by the Rânâ, who, being unsuccessful in several engagements, at length sued for peace.

Sultan Mahmood, of Malwa, now proposed to Kootb Shah the partition between the two Mohummedan powers of the whole territories of Rânâ Koombho, and a treaty to this effect was solemnly signed by their respective envoys, at the town of Châmpâner. Next year Kootb Shah marched towards Cheetor, carried the fortress of Aboogurh, in which he left a garrison, again reached Seerohee, and entered the hills, where, after two successful general actions, he a second time compelled the Rânâ to submission. In the following year, A.D. 1458, Rânâ Koombho was, however, again in arms with the view of reducing Nâgor. Kootb Shah, after a long delay, marched against him, and continued his victorious progress, until it was once more arrested by the impregnable fortress of Komulmer. He returned to Ahmedabad, where he shortly afterwards died, and was buried by the side of Mohummed Shah, his father, in the mausoleum of Sultan Ahmed.

CHAPTER V.

MAHMOOD BEGURRA.

Kootb Shah was succeeded by his uncle, Dâwood, who proved wholly incapable, and reigned only a few days, and then by his younger brother, Mahmood, surnamed Begurra, the greatest of the Mohummedan sovereigns of Goozerat. Though fourteen years of age at his accession, he speedily evinced the courage and ability which distinguished his future career. Having displayed a determination to protect against his enemies a faithful minister, whose destruction would have been but the prelude to his own, the young sultan was assailed in his palace by a body of thirty thousand rebels. His friends thought only of shutting themselves up in the citadel, or of escaping with the royal treasures, but Mahmood was of a different temper. The gates of the citadel were thrown open, and the boy king gallantly sallied forth, with quiver at his back and bow in his hand, and proceeding through the main street, in slow procession, in the midst of his enemies, the royal music sounding before him, gave his faithful nobles an opportunity of rallying round his standard. The commanding points were, under his personal direction, quietly and skilfully seized, and the rebellion was at once rendered hopeless.

Three years after this brilliant commencement of his reign, Mahmood assumed in person the command of an army, with which, marching into the north of Candeish, he saved the Bahmuny Shah of the Dekkan from the Sultan of Malwa.

In A.D. 1468, the holy prophet, Mahomet, having appeared to him in a dream, and invited him to the conquest of infidels, by spreading before him, in a vision, a magnificent banquet of the most delicious viands, Mahmood Shah prepared to achieve the conquest of Soreth, which Mohummed Toghluk, and his own great ancestor Ahmed, had attempted in vain. The most magnificent preparations were made for this expedition: the treasure chest contained fifty millions of gold, the commissariat was supplied with eighteen hundred gilded-handled swords, the manufacture of Egypt, Arabia, and Khorasân, with three thousand eight hundred of the celebrated blades of Ahmedabad, and the daggers in similar profusion, mounted with gold and silver; the master of the horse led with him two thousand steeds of Arabia and Toorkistan, and lest these rewards should be insufficient to recompense the warriors who attended him, Mahmood promised also the plunder of Soreth as the prize of their victorious valor.

On arriving within eighty miles of Girnâr, Mahmood detached a force of seventeen hundred men, under his uncle, Toghluk Khân, to occupy two outworks called Mohabilla, before his arrival. The Rajpoots, who were entrusted with the post, were surprised and cut off; but the Râ of Soreth, hearing of the event, descended from his hill-fortress, and attacking Toghluk Khân, was upon the point of repulsing him, when the arrival of Mahmood Shah in person changed the fortune of the day, and the Râ retreated, himself severely wounded. Mahmood cleared the country in the neighbourhood; sent out forage parties, who procured abundant provisions for his camp, and prepared for a siege; but the difficulties were probably greater than he had anticipated, and the Râ was allowed to purchase a cessation of hostilities by present submission, and by the payment of a large amount in jewels and in specie.

Mahmood, however, only required a pretext for attacking Girnâr a second time, and next year discovered one in the fact that "the "Row Munduleek visited the temples of idolatry, and went there "with all the ensigns of royalty." An army of forty thousand horse marched to Girnâr to punish this presumption; and the Râ, who was neither able nor willing to oppose the Mohummedan arms, paid the tribute which was demanded of him, and surrendered his royal umbrella and other kingly ensigns to the sultan. These concessions, however, were unavailing. The Râ of Soreth might have exclaimed, with his predecessor in misfortune, the gallant Prutheerâj Chohân, "Like a fly scared away, again and again the enemy returns." In the latter end of the same year Mahmood again marched in person to Soreth. The Râ declared his willingness to pay any sum of money he could produce, to protect his subjects from the horrors of war; but Mahmood replied, that "there was no greater fault than infidelity, "and that if he was to expect tranquillity, he must acknowledge the "unity of God." The Râ made no answer; but shut himself up in the fort of Joonagurh, to which Mahmood laid siege. Finding his position untenable, the Râ, leaving Joonagurh, retired to the upper fortress, on Girnâr; but his garrison was starved into submission, and seeing no end to his misfortunes, he quitted the fort, delivered the keys to the sultan, and repeated the confession of faith in imitation of the conqueror. His conversion is, however, by the author of the Meerât Sekunderee, made subsequent to his fall, and owing to the example of the saint rather than of the sovereign. "The Munduleek Raja," says that author, "being taken prisoner, was sent to Ahmedabad. "One day perceiving a grand procession going towards the residence "of the holy Shah Alum, at Russoolabad, the Râee enquired who "Shah Alum was, and in whose service. He was told that this holy "person acknowledged no master but the supreme Being. Struck "with admiration at the reply, he resolved to visit him, and was "afterwards persuaded by him to become a proselyte to the faith." The last of the Râs of Soreth was *dignified* by the title of "Khân "Jehân," or "lord of the universe," by the Mohummedans, and, under the guise of a saint of Islâm, is to the present day, at his tomb in the city of Ahmedabad, worshipped (like many other saints) by the descendants of those who had unremittingly persecuted him throughout his life.

Mahmood Shâh, having effected this much desired conquest, called together the Syuds and learned men of every quarter in order to settle them in Soreth. He caused also a city to be built, which in a little time also equalled the capital, and was called Moostufabad. While superintending the building of this new city, the sultan heard that the inhabitants of Kutch had made inroads upon Goozerat. In the year A.D. 1472 he therefore proceeded against them, and compelled their submission, and soon afterwards marched against the Jutts and Beloochees of Sindh, on which occasion he penetrated as far as the Indus.

The following bardic relations belong to the times at which we have now arrived:—

Gohil Bheemjee, the descendant of Sârungjee, possessed Lâtee and Urteelâ. He had three sons, and a daughter who was married to the Râ of Soreth, and, on account of this connection, the family usually lived at Joonagurh. When the army of the Mohummedans, breaking down the Hindoo temples as they advanced, came near Lâtee, Humeerjee, the youngest son of Bheemjee Gohil, was the only male of the family who was at home. The bad news having arrived, Humeer said to his brother's wife, "The Mohummedan army "is coming on with the intention of destroying Somnâth; but if "there were any seed of the Kshutrees left, the Mlech would not be "able to destroy the Hindoo temples." His sister-in-law replied, "If "there be no other seed of the Kshutrees, there is one seed at least— "yourself." When he heard these words, Humeer's blood boiled within him. He said not a word; but off he went, taking two hundred followers with him, to a hill called Surod, a few miles west of Seehore, where his friend Veguro, the Bheel, lived. Humeer told his story to Veguro; but the Bheel said, "None of the great râjas are "setting forth to the battle; why should you go? This Mohummedan army is very powerful; you cannot hope alone to drive it back." Humeer said, "I am going against them, that I may die in the fight; "but I am troubled much about this one thing—that I am still unmarried."[1] Upon this, Veguro Bheel, with the consent of his wife, married one of his daughters, who had attained the age of puberty, to Humeer Gohil. Humeer staid there one night, and left his wife pregnant. Descendants of theirs are still to be met with at Nâgher, in the Diu district, bearing the name of Gohil Koolees.

Veguro Bheel collected three hundred bowmen, and, joining Humeer and his two hundred Rajpoots, hastened to the defence of Somnâth. When the battle was at its hottest, Humeer cried to Veguro, who fought outside, to come in by a postern door; but the Bheel replied, "I am the Veguro (the long-horned bull), why should I enter

[1] The Shâstras have laid it down that

"The son-less obtains not liberation;
"Paradise is not for him—not for him."

"the postern?" Veguro fell— So they fought on, each in his own fashion, until

"Vegud the great fighter,
"Within the fort's postern entered not,
"But, tossing aloft his horns,
"Against the sky he struck them."

Humeer, too, was slain very soon after in the same battle :—

"Come quickly, brother!
"To the aid of Somaiyo:
"Drive them as the wind drives the waves,
"At the point of the spear.
"O! son of Bheem.

"To Shiv-Puttun advanced the flood
"Of rattling weapons.
"Among them sported the Soor,
"Like an untamed bison,
"Did the son of Bheem!

"Like a wave, O! Veer,
"Advancing, you turned not back,
"Against the cliffs you dashed,
"Of the army,
"O! son of Bheem.

"Sieve-like though became
"The form of your body,
"Your steps still, as befitted your race,
"Kept advancing,
"Son of Bheem!

"A forest of thorns, O! Veer,
"They who survived beheld,
"For the eye-protecting lid—Humeer
"Was first destroyed,
"Was the son of Bheem."[1]

Châmpâ, the son of Ebhul Wâlo, Lord of Jetpoor, near Joonagurh,

[1] "Many powerful Mahometan chiefs followed the example of Mahmood (of "Ghuznee). Sultan Mahmood Begurra, of Ahmedabad, is stated as the last who "sent an army against this place. On this occasion, the Gohil chief of Latee, "opposed the sultan, but without effect. He was killed, and Mahmood suc-"ceeded in reducing it, when he built a mosque on the spot where the temple "had formerly stood. Another temple was lately built by Ahilya Baee, a wife of "one of the Holkars, in which another symbol of Muhâ Dev has been placed."—*Colonel Walker's Reports.*

died in the same battle, leaving a name at which the Mohummedans long afterwards trembled :—

> "O ! padishah, rest not secure,
> "That that flower has departed ;
> "The Chumpâ[1] from the basket,
> "May start once more,
> "May the son of Ebhul."

In the time of Mahmood Begurra, says another bard, Rânpoor was held by a Gohil chieftain named Rânjee, who resided in a fort situated at the confluence of the Gomâ and Bhâdur rivers, upon the spot where stands the present edifice, subsequently erected by Azim Khân Oodâee.[2] Rânjee Gohil and the padishah had, it is said, married sisters, daughters of a raja of Marwar. The queen of the padishah, being once at her father's house on a visit, met there Rânjee's Thâkorine,[3] whom she invited to dine with her. The Gohil's wife excused herself, saying, "You have married the padishah, and my husband is "called his servant, therefore I am not worthy to sit at dinner with "you." This, and many other excuses, she offered ; but the elder sister, pressing with great urgency, she entreated her forbearance, and then confessed her real reason—that the queen, having married a Mohummedan, she should lose caste by eating with her. The queen, however, was very angry, and determined that she would, by whatever means, have her sister brought to Ahmedabad, and there cause her to dine with her.

After her return to the capital, Rânjee Gohil, being then present upon duty, the queen related the story to her husband, and begged him that he would send for her sister in any way that would secure her attendance, At this time Rânjee's groom of the chamber, having fallen into disgrace with his master, had been dismissed. The queen took him into her service, and instructed him to go for the Thâkorine.

The Thâkor's servant said that without a letter from Rânjee the lady would refuse to come. Upon this, the padishah one day asked Rânjee for his sword to look at, another day for his dagger, and again

[1] A play upon the words Chumpâ and Châmpâ, the former being the name of a flower tree (Michelia Champaca).

[2] Azim Khân Ghâzee was an officer of the later Mohummedan governments. In addition to the handsome fort of Rânpoor, he erected (in A.D. 1630) a building intended for a college, at Ahmedabad (which has since been degraded to the condition of a jail) ; and other edifices so numerous as to have given rise to his popular surname of "Oodâee," or "the white-ant," in allusion to the constructive habits of that insect, which is said never to move without building a house over its head.

[3] The usual title of a chieftain's wife in Goozerat is "Thukurâloo," or "Thukurânee," but as that employed in the text is also used, we have preferred it, as being more agreeable to European ears.

for his armlet. These he gave to the servant and sent him off. The servant went to Rânpoor, and said to the Thâkorine, "I am your "groom of the chamber, as you are aware; Rânjee has sent me to "summon you, and has given me these three articles as tokens. If "you disobey Rânjee, he will abandon you. You should, therefore, "join him speedily." The Thâkorine, hearing these words, ordered her chariot to be prepared, and set off with the servant. When they reached the neighbourhood of Ahmedabad, some of Rânjee's people met them, and recognizing the carriage, went up to it. The discharged servant then took to flight. Rânjee's followers conveyed the lady to his lodging, and when he enquired the cause of her coming, she said that it was at his order, and produced the tokens she had received. Then Rânjee knew that there had been treachery.

Soon after the padishah sent to say, "Let your Thâkorine come "hither to pay a visit; if you refuse, I will bring her by force." The Gohil refused, and a fight thereupon ensued; but Rânjee soon found that resistance was hopeless, and therefore had recourse to stratagem, and, with the aid of a Chârun's daughter, who remained to personate the Thâkorine, he brought her off in safety.

This Chârun's daughter was no common woman, but was, in truth, a Shuktee. She was the daughter of Doodo, of Oometâ, and Rânjee had become acquainted with her powers when on an expedition to collect tribute in that part of the country. A storm of wind and rain coming on, he was separated from his horsemen, and wandered alone to Oometâ, and being very much afflicted with thirst when he arrived there, he called to a girl who stood near for some water. She extended her arm from where she stood until she reached him as he sat on his horse, and thus handed him the cup. Rânjee, beholding this prodigy, dismounted from his horse, and, performing circumambulation, prostrated himself before her. Râj Bâee, for such was her name, upon this, said to him, "Ask a boon!" He answered, "That I may call "upon you for aid whenever a time of calamity occurs." She consented, and when Rânjee found himself in such straits at Ahmedabad he bethought himself of her, as has been related. On his return to Rânpoor, Rânjee prepared a place for Râj Bâee in his fort, and installed an image of her there as his Kool Devee, or family goddess.

After these things an old Mohummedan woman, with her son, lodged one night at Rânpoor, on their way to Mecca on pilgrimage. The boy rose early in the morning and began, as was his custom, to cry the "bâng," or call to prayers. Some Brahmins, hearing it, went to the Gohil and said, "This barbarian's crying the 'bâng' at such a "time, portends that the sovereignty of this town will pass to the bar-"barians." The Gohil was enraged at the idea, and seizing the old woman and her son, asked them how they presumed to cry the "bâng" at his gate. The woman entreated pardon, and protested that no harm was meant; but Rânjee was not satisfied, and he slew the boy with his sword. In revenge the old pilgrim retraced her steps to Ahmedabad, and laid her complaint before the padishah. Mahmood Begurra mentioned what had happened to all his Umeers, but they received the news very coolly, and no one thought proper to set out to fight with the Gohil. At length the padishah's own sister's son, Bhunderee Khân, notwithstanding that his nuptials had only that day been celebrated, determined to go forth against Rânpoor. The padishah and his officers spoke to him to dissuade him, but he said that he would certainly strike a blow for Allah. He advanced with an army as far as Dhundhooka, where he was met by Rânjee Gohil, and a desperate conflict ensued. The fight lasted for a long time, and Rânjee was driven continually backwards, until he reached the gate of Rânpoor. He sent to his Thâkorines, to order that when they beheld his royal umbrella go down they should destroy themselves, to avoid being captured by the Mohummedans. As the fight went on, the bearer of the umbrella set it down for a moment to drink water. The ladies thought their husband had fallen, and at once precipitated themselves into the well of the fort, and perished. Rânjee continued the battle after this catastrophe, but fell at last at the gate of Rânpoor; and the Mohummedans entered the fort, not, however, without the loss of their brave young leader, Bhunderee Khân. Mahmood Begurra afterwards presented Rânpoor to Hâloojee Purmâr, of Moolee, who was the son of the sister of Rânjee.

The story of Hâloojee is as follows:—A chief of the Jutts, who at that time lived in Sindh, had a very beautiful daughter, named Soomuree Bâee, whom the Sindh padishah attempted to take by force into his harem. The Jutts, therefore, fled from Sindh, about seventeen hundred in number, and came to Moolee, then held by two brothers of the Shodâ Purmâr blood, named Lugdheerjee and Hâloojee. The Jutts said that the padishah would certainly pursue them from Sindh, and that if the Purmârs could protect them they would remain, otherwise they would go on further. The Purmârs swore they would not allow them to be injured as long as their own heads stood on their shoulders. So the Jutts remained at Moolee.

The Sindh padishah's army soon arrived, and as it was very powerful, the Purmârs considered that having no fortress they would find difficulty in holding their ground. They retreated, therefore, to a hill named Mânduv, thirty miles to the west of Moolee, and strengthened themselves in the jungle there. The padishah's army followed them, and the fight went on for a length of time, until at last a link-bearer of the Purmârs treacherously went over to the enemy, and pointed out to them the single well which supplied the Purmârs with water. The Mohummedans cut off a cow's head and cast it into the well. The Purmârs were now forced to come to terms, and Lugdheerjee, the elder brother, gave Hâloojee as a hostage instead of the Jutt's daughter, whom he told to make her escape. She fled, and buried herself alive at Wunod, where her tomb may still be seen.

Lugdheerjee, going to Ahmedabad, procured the aid of the King of Goozerat, whereupon an army advanced from Ahmedabad. A battle was fought in the Bhooj country, when the Sindhis were defeated, and Hâloojee released, and carried to the capital.

Hâloojee Purmâr became a convert to Islâm, upon which Mahmood Begurra offered him lands in several districts. He refused them, however, saying that his family would wonder what had become of him, and begged for the wasted town of Rânpoor, which had belonged to his uncle, Rânjee Gohil, and had been ploughed and sown with salt by the padishah. This being given to him, Hâloojee begged for a grant on copper plate, but the padishah said that the fact of his conversion was not likely to be forgotten, and that no grant was required.

Lugdheerjee Purmâr retained his religion and the Moolee estate acquired by his ancestors. The following story explains how he met his death :—

The Chief of Sânund had given the village of Râneesur, as rent-free land (pusâeetâ) to a Chârun, from whom descended Ruleeo Guduvee, who was celebrated for his wit and sarcasm. At this time there was much plundering in the country, but no one molested the Chârun's village, on which account people of the surrounding villages placed their property there for protection. Being aware of this, a Mohummedan leader, named Boree Mogul, came to plunder Râneesur. After sacking the village, the assailants bound Ruleeo Guduvee with his children and family, and other people of the village, and carried them off. The first night they halted, Ruleeo, at midnight, began to howl and weep. The Mohummedans asked why he wept : he said it was for a great cause of mourning, with which he would acquaint none but their commander. Boree Mogul's servants told him of this, and he came up in person. Then the Goduvee told him he would give any sum that might be demanded for the ransom of himself and family. The Mogul asked where he could have any money left to him now. He said he had discovered a note in a locket, in which was described a place where his father had buried a hoard. The Mogul sent five hundred men with him, ordering that he should be released on giving up a lakh of money. After two or three marches they arrived at the edge of the Runn at Teekur, near Hulwud. The Guduvee then said that his property was buried in an island to which he pointed, and proposed that the party should gallop over the intervening level ground, and reach their destination at once. He set his pony in motion, and the heavy horsemen followed him at a gallop, but he led them into a quagmire, and when they were fairly entangled he got clear away, and ran off to Wudwân. He represented to the raja that he was the Rajpoot's Chârun, and persuaded him to recover his family from the Mogul. The Wudwân Raja bade him seek further assistance from the Shodâs of Moolee, and said that he would in the meantime march against the Mohummedans, which he did. Ruleeo went to Moolee, and told his story, and Lugdheerjee immediately set off in pursuit, with five hundred Purmârs. There is a tank called Punungsur in the Null Kântâ, near which Lugdheerjee met Boree Mogul—the Wudwân Raja not having yet come up—and fought with him a great battle. At last the Mogul was left with but few men, and he therefore fled, taking with him, on his horse, the daughter of a Brahmin of Râneesur. Lugdheerjee pursued, and came up with him at about a mile's distance. The Mogul turned and looked round, and perceiving that Lugdheerjee was alone, he wheeled round his horse and aimed a blow at him, but missed him. Lugdheerjee struck also, and missed his opponent; both of their horses rearing, they fell to the ground, and, getting up, wrestled. First Lugdheerjee was down, but the lady assisting him, he got the Mogul below him; the Brahminee then told him to use his dagger. He drew it, and stabbed the Mogul, but not before he had himself received a thrust from his antagonist's weapon in the belly. Both perished. Lugdheerjee's men plundered the Mogul's camp, and then searching for the corpse of their chief, committed it to the pile, and set up a monumental stone (pâleeyo). The Brahminee they restored to her father, at Râneesur.

The Moolee Purmârs are to this day celebrated for their courage, and treated with peculiar respect by the Jutt chiefs, in remembrance of the protection afforded them. A younger brother of Lugdheerjee and Hâloojee, following the example of the latter, became a Mohummedan, and received a grant of the twenty-four villages of Botâd, which his descendants held for several generations. They were in subsequent times well known in Goozerat, under the title of Tâlookdârs of Dholka.

CHAPTER VI.

MAHMOOD BEGURRA.

MAHMOOD'S next effort, after his expedition to Sindh, was an attack directed against the pirate chiefs of Jugut and Beyt, to which he was induced by the injuries they had inflicted on a holy man—"one of "the most learned philosophers of his age," who, being on board a vessel bound to his native country of Ormuz, had been driven into the port of Jugut, and there plundered "by the infidels, misled by "the infernal-minded Brahmins." The Mohummedans, with considerable difficulty, made themselves masters of both Jugut and Beyt; and Raja Bheem, the chief of the Rajpoots, being taken prisoner, was, at the instigation of the philosopher, dragged around the city of Ahmedabad and put to death, "in order to deter others from similar "conduct."

Shortly afterwards a conspiracy was set on foot among the Mohummedan nobles, having for its object the destruction of Mahmood, and the elevation of his son, the Prince Moozuffer, to the throne. It was at this time that the king was recommended to give employment to his officers, by proceeding against the fortress of Châmpâner. The conspiracy, however, proved abortive, and Mahmood's proposed expedition was postponed for some years. In A.D. 1482, he prepared for its accomplishment; but at this time his attention was diverted to the pirates of Bulsâr, on the coast below Surat, who had gained an ascendancy at sea which had not only interrupted trade, but even excited apprehensions of invasion. Mahmood now appeared in the character of a sea-captain; he collected a fleet at Cambay, on board of which he embarked a force consisting of archers, musketeers, and gunners; and giving chase to the enemy, sustained a running fight for some hours, during which several of the piratical vessels were captured. It was not until the close of the year that he was prepared to march against Châmpâner. Before we accompany him to the siege of this fortress, however, it is necessary to revert for a time to the affairs of Eedur.

Row Bhân, the brother of Nârondâs, appears to have been the prince who was compelled to give his daughter in marriage to Mohummed Shah, the father of Mahmood. The Mohummedan historians speak of him under the name of Beer, or Veer Raja. He is mentioned in an inscription on a well at Jebhârâ, in Eedur-wârâ, which not only furnishes us with a date, but also with a solution of the discrepancy regarding his name. The Row, it appears, had accidentally killed a cow, for which crime he endeavoured to atone by building the well in which the inscription is preserved. "In Sumwut, "1532 (A.D. 1476), on the fourth of the moonlight half of the month "of Phâlgoon, on Monday, Kâmdooghâ Mâtâ,—O Râm, Shree "Râm !—having come to drink water, Raja Shree Shree Bhân Veerjee "forced her to take shelter with Râm. Therefore, to remove his sin, "a gold cow, as a gift, he presented; a place of water he caused to "be constructed" * * * "Row Bhân," say the bards, "soon after he "had assumed the royal cushion, began to fix his boundaries. He "first struck the Seerohee village of Lâs, and fixed a stone (pâleeyo), "with a horse sculptured upon it, which still remains at a spot between "Roherâ and Poseenâ. Next he fixed his boundary at Row Jethee's "funeral temple, on the Nyhee river; and beyond that he took the "Chupun-pâl-land, which now belongs to Oodepoor. Thence he "advanced to Thâno, formerly called 'the Row's Thâno,' on the "Somâ river, about four miles from Doongurpoor. Thence he con-"tinued his march along the banks of the Somâ, to Mâlpoor and "Mugoree, which he included in the Eedur territory, as well as Kup-"perwunj and the Bâwun districts, as far as the river Sâbhermutee. "That river he made his boundary line as far as Târingâ, which he "included; and thence he went again to the stone at Seerohee." The boundaries thus laid down include, we may observe, a very ample territory.

Târingâ, here alluded to, is one of the celebrated sacred mountains of the Jains. Though it possesses neither the magnificence of Shutroonjye, nor the beauty of Tulâjâ, it is yet picturesque and interesting. The temple of Ujeetnâthjee, built by Koomâr Pâl, stands on a considerable piece of flat elevated land, in the bosom of a chain of mountains. It retains more of the venerable appearance of age than either of the shrines of Pâleetânâ, though, like them, it has suffered much from the modern innovator; it is surrounded by several small temples of recent date, and in its vicinity are, as usual, reservoirs of the purest water. On the hill there remains a shrine sacred to the Devee Târun Mâtâ, from whom is derived the name of Târingâ; it is associated with the times of Venee Wuch Râj, and his Nâg Pootree consort, and the site was probably occupied by a building long before the royal convert of Unhilwârâ installed Shree Ujeetnâth. A jungle, of the thickest character, surrounds the hill on all sides, and renders access difficult to all, and nearly impracticable to a party unprovided with a guide, much more to an invading enemy. Two easily defensible paths alone give access to the plateau on which the temples stand, and which, like that at Eedur, is fortified by the filling in of the few gaps nature had left exposed. On three of the surrounding peaks are built little whitened chutrees or pavilions, which, from their exceeding brightness, when a glimpse of them is now and then obtained through black ravines and tangled forest, serve as lanterns of the day, pointing out to the way-worn pilgrim the site of the holy dwelling of the "Invincible Lord."

In A.D. 1471, Mahmood Shah having withdrawn his court to his new city of Moostufabad, near Girnâr, a powerful officer, ennobled by the title of Mohafez Khân, occupied a viceregal position at Ahmedabad, and his son, Mullik Khizr, in the king's absence, marched without orders, and exacted tribute from Row Bhân of Eedur, as well as from the chiefs of Wâgur and Seerohee.

Row Bhân was about this time engaged in a contest with the Râwul of Châmpâner, whom he took prisoner, and carried with him to Eedur, but released after a six months' captivity. The cause assigned for the feud is characteristic; it is said that Row Bhân was attenuated in person and swarthy in complexion, and that the Râwul enraged him by causing a buffoon to personate him in some dramatic entertainment, in which the company were amused at an exposure of the Row's defects. The following verses, supposed to be spoken by the consort of the Râwul, express the terror with which the prowess of Row Bhân had inspired his enemy:—

"When, wearing ankle-bells, I walk,
"He thinks 'tis armour clanking,
"When ornaments I wear,
"They seem to him to be mail,
"When my bracelets clatter,
"He thinks 'tis the clash of swords,
"My ear-rings, when they glitter,
"Remind him of the blaze of fire.
"From fear of Row Bhân my husband starts,
"Even when safe in his home remaining,
"How can I sport with my husband
"Who has no moments' respite from fear."

To Row Bhân and his Rânee, is attributed the construction of the Bhânsur and Râneesur tanks at Eedur, with that of several other reservoirs at Wurâlee, Dudhâleea, and other places. The bards further assert that Row Bhân was mainly instrumental in the conquest of Châmpâner, effected by Mahmood Begurra, and though no mention of the circumstance is made by the Mohummedan historians, it is very probable, especially considering the former feud, that the forces of Eedur formed part of the army of the shah.

The fortress of Châmpâner, so called from Jâmb or Châmpâ, the companion of Wun Râj, and its reputed founder, is also known as Powan-gurh, "the castle of the winds," a name not undeservedly attributed to it from the stormy blasts that continually howl around it. It has the reputation of being a favourite residence of the goddess Kâlee, whose temple occupies its summit, and more than one Rajpoot chieftain, regarding himself as her feudal vassal, bends with respect to the authority which holds possession of the venerable hill. The mountain-rock of Powan-gurh stands nearly isolated, frowning over the eastern districts of Goozerat, and on some sides presents to view little but perpendicular cliffs; its steep ascent is everywhere strongly protected, and that which to the observer from the plains appears an artificial fortification is found to be a natural defence, consisting of rock scarped to a depth most formidable. At its northern base lie the remains of the city of the Hindoo princes, and there a remnant of falling domes and broken minarets, protruding through the dry and dusty jungle, evinces that as a Moslem capital the city once bore the ame of Mahmood-abad.

Of the Hindoo princes of Châmpâner, as of the great Scottish house of Marr, it may be said "their origin is lost in its antiquity." At what period the castle of Châmpâ passed into the possession of the Chohâns it is needless to conjecture, but the "Pâwaitchas of "Powan-gurh" it may be asserted were not unworthy scions of a race to which has been assigned the palm of martial intrepidity among all the royal houses of India. Râwul Gungâdâs we have mentioned as the opponent of Mohammed Shah; the prince of whom we are now to speak was his son, Jye Singh, by Ferishta entitled "Beny Ray," and widely known in Hindoo tradition under the name of Phutâee Râwul.

The Râwul of Châmpâner, hearing of Mahmood's preparations to attack him, at first sallied fiercely forth, and carried fire and sword into the territories of the shah, and then, as if terrified at his own temerity, sent ambassadors to implore forgiveness. Mahmood, irritated by the devastation which had been committed, refused to listen to any terms of accommodation, and the advanced guard of the Moslem army arrived at the foot of the hill of Kâlee on the 17th March, A.D. 1483. The shah himself soon afterwards joined with the main body of his army. Râwul Jye Singh once more made offers of submission, but as these were not received, he commenced a desperate resistance. The lines of the besiegers were continually attacked by the Rajpoots, who at length appeared in such force that Mahmood was compelled for a time to abandon the siege in order to give them battle. The action was sanguinary and obstinately contested, and the Hindoos, though ultimately repulsed, effected their retreat in order. Mahmood now resumed the siege, and the Râwul, notwithstanding a partial success in cutting off a convoy of provisions and stores for the besiegers, found himself hard pressed, and, in despair, had recourse to his old ally, the Sultan of Malwa. Gheiâs-ood-deen assembled an army, and showed a disposition to aid the Râwul, but on Mahmood's advancing against him he abandoned his intention; and the shah returning to his lines before Châmpâner, caused a mosque to be built therein, in order to convince his troops of his determination to persist in the siege. The approaches were now carried so near the place as to admit of the besiegers discovering the sally-port through which the Rajpoots passed each morning to perform their ablutions. A breach in the western wall was about the same time effected. On the morning of the 17th November, A.D. 1484,[1] the sally-port was seized by the Mohummedans, while Mullik Eiaz Sooltany, afterwards famous for his naval contest with the Portuguese, escaladed the western wall. The Rajpoots made desperate attempts to expel Mullik Eiaz, but without success; Mahmood Shâh in person supported him with fresh troops, the standard of the crescent waved upon the ramparts of Châmpâner, and a Moslem shell—emblem of Kâlee's anger—fell upon the palace of its sovereign. A funeral pile now rose within the walls; the wives, the children, the wealth of the Rajpoots were placed upon it; the fire rose, raged, and died away, and then the defenders of Powan-gurh, with bodies bathed in water and wrapped in saffron robes, flung themselves desperately upon their enemies. Few of the Rajpoots survived, the victors also suffered severely both in killed and wounded, and the Râwul of Châmpâner and his minister, covered with their own blood, fell into the hands of the shah.

Mahmood caused public prayers to be read for his victory, and while the sick and wounded were recovering he was employed in building "a beautiful mosque," and in giving a Mohummedan character to the city now termed Mahmoodabad. He stained his victory, however, by the murder in cold blood of Râwul Jye Singh and his minister, who, after recovering from their wounds, were vainly solicited to purchase life by embracing the Mohummedan faith.

Such is the Mohummedan account of the fall of Châmpâner. The names of the chief Hindoos who perished in the final sacrifice—so

[1] *Vide* Briggs's Ferishta, vol. iv. p. 68.

congenial to the blood-loving Kâlee—have been preserved by the bards :—

> " In Sumwut, fifteen hundred and forty-one,[1]
> " In the month of Posh, on the third day, the day of the sun,
> " Six rajas perished. First, Vershee fell,
> " Then Sârung Jhâreja, Kurun, and Jetmâl.
> " Survaiyo Chundrabhân, for Phutâee gave his life,
> " When Mahmood Shah, the great king, took Pâwâgurh."

It would seem, however, that the city only, and not the fortress on the mountain, had been as yet captured by Mahmood, and though the Mohummedan historians say nothing further on the point, there is probably truth in the common Hindoo traditional account, which states that the castle of the winds yielded only to a lengthened blockade.

Phutâee Râwul, says another bardic tradition, was king of Châmpâner. Once at the festival of the Nowrâttra, he went to see the women, singing "gurbhos." Kâleekâ Devee, of Châmpâner, on this occasion having assumed a human form, was singing among them. The raja, beholding how beautiful she was, fell desperately in love with her; he laid hold on the Mâtâ's scarf, with lustful intention. Kâlee pronounced the curse upon him, that his royalty should pass away.

Once on a time the padishah, in the course of a journey, passed within sight of Châmpâner, and, when he beheld the fortress, he stroked his moustache with his hand. There was a Brahmin in the city who had a son called Lowo, which Lowo witnessed this action of the king, and knew thereby that the king had formed the intention of taking Châmpâner. He went to Phutâee Râwul, and told him that the padishah would take his throne that year. The raja constructed five lines of fortification around the city—of stone, of water, of wood, of mud, of jungle. He prepared ammunition also, and sent Lowo to Ahmedabad to keep a watch upon the padishah. Lowo hired a mansion, which belonged to a merchant, opposite the padishah's palace. Once on a time the king sat at a window, looking in all directions. When he looked towards Châmpâner he stroked his moustache with his hand, and spoke of preparing an army. Lowo became aware that the padishah was now about to attack Châmpâner;

[1] On this occasion the bards are accurate in their date; Châmpâner fell, according to Ferishta, in A.D. 1484. If Mr. Prinsep's opinion be adopted, and fifty-seven years allowed as the difference between the Sumwut and the year of our Lord, the bardic date will exactly agree with the Mohummedan. If fifty-six years be allowed, as is more usual, there will be a difference of one year between them.

he returned to Phutâee Râwul, and told him that the padishah's army was coming against him. The Râwul took all possible precautions with a view to defence. The army of the padishah, five hundred thousand in number, advanced to within a short distance of Châmpâner, but no one knew what the object was which the king had in view. At midnight the padishah assembled his Sirdârs, and commanded them to plant his flag upon the city. The army attacked the city, and cannonaded it, but the fire from the city was heavier than the fire of the assailants, and the city could not be taken; so the padishah blockaded it for twelve years, but still without success. He then made peace with Phutâee Râwul, and called him to his own quarters to an interview, in the course of which he enquired of the Râwul how he had discovered his intention of attacking him. The raja answered that his priest, Lowo, had discovered his intention, and informed him of it. The padishah agreed never to interfere with Châmpâner, and asked to be presented with Lowo. Phutâee Râwul agreed, and the king caused a pâleeyo to be sculptured with the figures of two donkeys, and underneath to be written, "If any Mo-" hummedan take this city, there is the donkey's oath (gudheree gâl) " to him." He carried Lowo away with him, and made him his minister; and though he did not take the city of Châmpâner, he seized the districts and surrounding villages, and established it as a rule, that no one should carry anything into or out of Châmpâner. The inhabitants were distressed on this account, and took shelter in Ahmedabad.

The padishah, continues the bard, went from Châmpâner to Oomrâlâ, and seizing the raja of that place, carried him to Ahmedabad, where he threw him into prison. The raja remained in confinement for two years, and at the end of that time, a potter, of the village of Bhundâreeo, in his territory, went to Ahmedabad, and made acquaintance with a potter of that city, who was employed about the prison, with whose assistance he succeeded in bringing the raja out in a donkey's panniers, and placed him among a band of Uteets, who carried him to his father's sister, at Châmpâner. She paid his ransom to the sovereign of Ahmedabad, and replaced him on his throne of Oomrâlâ. From that day the Oomrâlâ rajas took the name of Râwul, in imitation of Phutâee's title, and they still retain it, and at their enthronement a descendant of the potter of Koombhâreeo makes the royal mark upon their foreheads.

The latter part of this tradition carries us back to the Gohils of Peerum.

Mokherâjee Gohil had by his wife, Wâdun Koonwurbâ, a Râjpootnee, of the Survaiyo clan, and of the family of Hâthsunee, near Pâleetânâ, a son, named Doongurjee, who succeeded him. He had also two other sons, Semursunghjee and Gormâljee, both of them born at Peerum. Semursunghjee went to reside with his mother's family, at Râjpeepla, and eventually succeeded to its possessions. Gormâljee left no descendants.

Doongurjee, the elder brother, abandoned Peerum, and made Gogo his residence. He was succeeded by his son, Veeyojee, who left three sons, Kânjee, Râmjee, and Roodojee. Kânjee succeeded, and left two sons, Sârungjee and Gemuljee, who were minors when their father died.

Râmjee, on the arrival of a Mohummedan army under the leader whom the Hindoos call Boree Mogul, made submission to that officer, and, surrendering his nephew, Sârungjee, as a hostage, seated himself on the royal cushion at Gogo as if in his own right. Sârungjee was conveyed to Ahmedabad; but a potter, named Pâncho Goojur, of the village of Kooleyâk, having gone thither, succeeded in carrying him off in a pannier, on the back of one of his asses. The escape of Sârungjee becoming known, some horsemen followed the fugitives. At a time when he was nearly overtaken, the potter fortunately fell in with the jumât, or band, of a gosâee, named Pertâp-gur-Bhâwo, and, having explained to their leader that the boy was the Gogo raja's heir, who would be able at a future time to recompense a service now paid to him, he placed him under the Gosâee's protection. The potter, continuing his route with his asses, was overtaken and seized by the horsemen; but these, disappointed in their expectations of discovering Sârungjee, went on but a little further, and then, giving up the pursuit, returned. Pertâp-gur-Bhâwo conveyed the young prince to Phutâee Râwul, of Doongurpoor, who had married his father's sister, and Sârungjee remained in concealment there until he had attained the age of twenty years. He then begged of his aunt that she would give him a few attendants, and allow him to proceed homewards. Râwul Phutâee supplied him with a force for his protection, and his aunt dismissed him, saying, "Go and recover your rights, and "your descendants shall bear the title of Râwul as a memorial of the "protection you have received from Doongurpoor." Sârungjee, agreeing to this, set out, and made his way to Oomrâlâ. His uncle, Râmjee, at Gogo, hearing of his arrival, sent for the Lords of Gâreeâdhâr and Lâtee, the descendants of the younger sons of Sejukjee, and heads of the two earliest branches of the Gohil house, and offered to resign to them twelve villages each if they would assist him against Sârungjee. Trâpuj and eleven other villages he passed to the chief of

Gâreeâdhâr ; and to the Lâtee Thâkor he offered the twelve townships of Wâlookur. These leaders at first assented to Râmjee's designs ; but afterwards, while returning together from Gogo, they considered that they had not done well in making such an agreement, and preferring a cadet's right to the cushion to that of the lineal heir ; they determined, therefore, to go together to Oomrâlâ. Having arrived there, and being admitted to an audience of Sârungjee, they said to him, " Râmjee Ghoghâree has sent us to oppose you, promising us " twelve villages each, but as you are the owner of the royal cushion, " we present the grants to you." Sârungjee said, " Bring me the " grants, I will sign them." He did so, and secured their loyalty. Râmjee Ghoghâree, hearing of what had occurred, felt that his opportunity was lost ; he therefore set off for Oomrâlâ, and himself also made submission to Sârungjee. The chieftains drank the red cup together, and agreed to forget the past. Sârungjee advanced to Gogo, and took possession of the royal cushion. His uncle, Râmjee, making obeisance before him, received as a grant for his subsistence the villages of Ookhuloo, Ugeeâlee, and Bhurelee, the grâssiâs of which still bear the surname of Ghoghâree. Râmjee held also the village of Monpoor.

In A.D. 1494, a revolted officer of the Dekkan government, having seized some Goozerat trading-vessels, and also taken possession of the island of Mahim, Mahmood Shah sent a fleet and army against him. The fleet, having arrived off the island, was destroyed by a tempest ; the admiral, and as many of his sailors as escaped, were washed ashore, and either made prisoners or massacred by the enemy. The officer who commanded the army, having marched through the northern Konkun, as on a former occasion, heard of the naval disaster on his arrival near Mahim, and, halting his troops, despatched a messenger to Mahmood Shah for instructions. The rebels were afterwards subdued by the King of the Dekkan, and their fleet delivered over in compensation to the Goozerat admiral, who was released from prison.

Next year, Mahmood Shah " marched towards the countries of " Wâgur and Eedur, from the rajas of which places he exacted large " offerings, and returned laden with treasure to Mahmoodabad Châm- " pâner." Soorujmuljee, the son of Row Bhân, appears to have been at this time the Prince of Eedur ; he reigned eighteen months, and left a son, Râeemuljee, whose throne was, in his minority, usurped by his uncle Bheem.

In A.D. 1507, Mahmood Shah again appeared as an admiral. " The " infidel Europeans, who had of late years usurped the dominion of "the ocean, endeavoured at this time to occupy for themselves "some part of the coast of Goozerat, on which they wished to settle." Umeer Hoosein, the admiral of the Turkish emperor Bajazet II., arrived off the coast of Goozerat with a fleet of twelve sail, carrying fifteen hundred men; and Mahmood Shah, anxious to aid in the expulsion of the foreigners, sailed in person with his fleet to Damaun and Mahim. The Umeer-ool-Oomra Mullik Eiaz Sooltany sailed also, from the port of Diu, and, having united his squadron with that of the Turkish admiral, attacked the Portuguese fleet, then lying off the harbour of Choul, a few miles to the south of Bombay. Victory declared for the Mohummedans; and the Portuguese fled, with the loss of "three thousand or four thousand infidels," as their adversaries assert; or, as they themselves admit, of their flag-ship, their admiral Don Lorenzo Almeida, and one hundred and forty men. The combined fleet was, however, afterwards defeated, and the Mamlook part of it annihilated in a battle fought close to Diu, on the coast of Soreth.

Sultan Mahmood, if not the greatest, is certainly the most popular of the kings of Ahmedabad; he is to the Moslem as Sidh Râj is to the Hindoo—a nucleus around which gathers romance and tale. His personal bravery and strength, his justice, his beneficence, his strict observance of Mohummedan ritual, and the excellence of his judgment, are alike extolled. He was also, it is said, "a great eater." Many are the anecdotes which are related of him; nor is there a fragment of Moslem architecture in Goozerat which popular feeling does not connect with the name of the great king—Mahmood Begurra. In additon to the two Mohummedan cities of Moostufabad and Mahmoodabad Châmpâner, he founded a new city on the banks of the Wâtruk, which, also, he called by his own name; "and "having fortified a rising ground on the banks of the before-mentioned "river, he ordered noble palaces to be built, of which the marks and "remains," says the author of Meerât Ahmudee, "are yet to be seen "at the time of writing, being the year A.D. 1756." At one or other of these he frequently resided; but he was punctual in "going to "Ahmedabad during the hot season of ripe melons, and returning "again after enjoying himself there for six months." The same writer goes so far as to assert that "all the fruit trees in the open "country, as well as those in the city, towns, and villages, were "planted in the reign of this sultan." It is said that his surname was derived from the capture of those two, as yet impregnable, Hindoo fortresses[1]—Girnâr and Châmpâner, a derivation which

[1] *Be* meaning two, and *gurh* a fort.

appeared to Ferishta to be "sufficiently rational and probable," and which, as we have none equally good to offer, we may adopt upon his authority. It was, perhaps, his naval warfare which won for him an European reputation. "The travellers of his day," says Mr. "Elphinstone,[1] seem to have formed a tremendous idea of this "monarch. Bartema and Barbosa are both full of him. One of "them gives a formidable account of his personal appearance; and "both of them agree that a principal part of his food consisted of "mortal poisons; and so impregnated was his system with this diet, "that if a fly settled upon him, it instantly dropped down dead. "His usual way of putting men of consequence to death was to blow "upon them after he had been chewing betel. He is the original of "Butler's 'Prince of Cambay,' whose

> " ———daily food
> " Is asp, and basilisk, and toad."

The following account of his death is derived from the Meerât Ahmudee:—"In the close of the year A.D. 1510, the sultan set out for "Puttun, and, as this was the last time he appeared in public, having "collected together all the great men of the state, he told them that "his life was near a close. On returning from Puttun he came to "Ahmedabad in four days; when, having made a pilgrimage to the "burial-place of Sheik Ahmed Khuttoo, he wept tears of repentance "over his own tomb, which had been built at the foot of the Sheik's "mausoleum. Subsequently to this, having entered the city of "Ahmedabad, he fell sick; and continuing so for three months, sent "for the Prince Khuleel Khân, from Baroda. After informing him "of his approaching dissolution, he finally took his leave for another "world on Monday, the 3rd of Rumâzan, in the year of the Hijra "917 (A.D. 1511); and his remains were deposited in the mausoleum "which still exists at Sirkhej."

CHAPTER VII.

MOOZUFFER II.—SIKUNDER—MAHMOOD II.—BUHÂDUR SHAH—MAHMOOD LUTEEF KHAN—CLOSE OF THE DYNASTY OF AHMEDABAD—THE EMPEROR AKBAR.

MAHMOOD BEGURRA was succeeded by his son Moozuffer II., whose opening reign was rendered remarkable by an earnest appeal to him

[1] *Vide* History of India, vol. ii., p. 206. Edit. 1841.

for assistance, which proceeded from the Sultan of Malwa. Mednee Râee, the Hindoo minister of that prince, had, it was represented, acquired such authority, that nothing beyond the name of king was left to the sultan, and infidelity was therefore rapidly regaining its dominion. Moozuffer II., moved with zeal for the true faith, immediately commenced his march for the land of Bhoj; and Ein-ool-Moolk, the Governor of Unhilwârâ Puttun, was ordered in consequence to move his division to Ahmedabad. The opportunity was not neglected by the still unconquered chief of the Râthors. Row Bheem, of Eedur, the younger son of Row Bhân, whom we have beheld usurping the throne of his nephew, Râeemuljee, taking advantage of the governor's absence, plundered and laid waste the surrounding country as far as the river Sâbhermutee. Ein-ool-Moolk, on the receipt of this intelligence, marched to Morâsâ, where he was attacked by Row Bheem and defeated, with the loss of an officer of distinction and two hundred men. Moozuffer Shah hearing of this, instantly returned to his own dominions, and taking up a position at Morâsâ, laid waste from thence the whole of the Eedur territories. Row Bheem himself took refuge in the hills; but the garrison of Eedur, consisting, as the Mohummedans assert, of only ten Rajpoots, defended the place with obstinacy against their enemies. Eedur was, however, taken; its temples, palaces, and garden-houses were levelled with the dust, and its heroic defenders put to the sword. Meanwhile, the Row, having deputed a Brahmin, named Mudun Gopâl, as his envoy to the Shah, had, through him, expressed his regret at the warfare which had arisen, and which he attributed to unprovoked outrages committed by Ein-ool-Moolk. He sent also one hundred horses and two hundred thousand "tunkhas" as an offering, and Moozuffer Shah, in consideration of the deferred expedition to Malwa, thought proper to overlook his defection and accept the treasure, which was applied to the purposes of the projected campaign. Moozuffer Shah now proceeded into Malwa. Row Bheem, of Eedur, was at his death succeeded by his son, Bârmul;[1] that prince was, however, soon after deposed by Sung Rânâ, of Cheetor, whose daughter had been married to Râeemuljee, the son of Soorujmul, now grown up to manhood. Bârmul, in the year A.D. 1515, sent envoys to Moozuffer Shah to solicit his aid, and the Mohummedan

[1] There are two inscriptions of these princes on wells at Teentoee and Reetorâ. The first was constructed in Sumwut, 1566 (A.D. 1510), by order of "Shree Muhâ "Râee, Shree, Shree, Shree Bheem, and Koonwer Shree Bârmul;" the second in Sumwut, 1599 (A.D. 1543), "when Muhârâjâ Râee Shree Bârmul" was ruling victoriously.

sovereign, displeased at the intervention of Sung Rânâ, and glad of the opportunity of asserting "that Bheem Row ruled Eedur by his authority," determined to send a force to the country of the Râthors. Nizâm-ool-Moolk, his officer, accordingly advanced, and replaced Bârmul on the throne; but, having pursued Râeemuljee into the hills, he was brought to action, and defeated with severe loss. The shah reproved Nizâm-ool-Moolk severely for having exceeded his instructions, and recalled him to the capital, but on his arrival there, appointed him to the government of Ahmednugger. In A.D. 1517, Râeemuljee again appeared in the Eedur territory, and defeated, with the loss of two hundred and seven men, Zeher-ool-Moolk—the Jher Khân of Hindoo tradition—a Mohummedan officer who had been sent against him at the head of a body of cavalry. Mullik Noosrut-ool-Moolk was upon this directed to march to Veesulnugger, and to plunder and lay waste the whole of the surrounding country, which the shah, in his orders, styles "the receptacle of renegadoes, and the "asylum of rebels."

The two following years were honorably employed by Moozuffer Shah in restoring to his throne the Sultan of Malwa. The Rajpoots were more than once defeated. Mândoo-gurh was taken by assault, and Rânâ Sung, who had attempted its relief, was forced to retire. Moozuffer Shah, having received marked expressions of gratitude from Sultan Mahmood, returned to his capital, which he had scarcely reached when he received intelligence that Râeemuljee, of Eedur, had sallied from the Veesulnugger hills, laid waste the Puttun district, and sacked the town of Gilwârâ. The Râthor prince had at length, however, been compelled to retire by Mullik Noosrut-ool-Moolk, who commanded at Eedur. The shah determined to seize Râeemuljee; he advanced in person towards Veesulnugger, and laid waste the country. He did not, however, succeed in effecting his object. Râeemuljee soon after died of disease, and Bârmul, as his heir, acquired an undisputed title to the royal cushion.

At this time intelligence was received that Sultan Mahmood, of Malwa, having ventured, in company with his Goozerat auxiliaries, to attack the combined forces of Mednee Râee and Rânâ Sung, had been defeated, and taken prisoner. Soon afterwards, Noosrut-ool-Moolk having been removed from the government of Eedur, and Moobâriz-ool-Moolk nominated to that office, some person ventured to extol, in the presence of the new governor, the bravery of Rânâ Sung. Moobâriz was incensed at this praise, and to show his contempt for the gallant prince of Cheetor, he caused a dog to be tied up at the fort gate, which he directed to be called by his name.

Sung Rânâ, hearing of this insult, was so much enraged, that he immediately marched with the intention of attacking Eedur, and had soon pillaged the country as far as Seerohee. Having arrived at Wâgur, he was joined by the raja of that country, with whom he advanced to Doongurpoor. The Governor of Eedur now thought it necessary to send for reinforcements; but his enemies at court prevented their despatch, representing to the shah that Moorbâriz, after having wantonly insulted the Rânâ, was now pusillanimously seeking for assistance, even before he had sustained an attack. Moorbâriz-ool-Moolk was therefore compelled to evacuate Eedur, and retire to the fortress of Ahmednugger. The next day Sung Rânâ took possession of the Râthor capital, where he was joined by several Rajpoot chiefs from the vicinity of Ahmedabad, who had fled from the oppression of its governor. With his new allies he advanced towards Ahmednugger, swearing that he would not draw rein until he should be able to water his horse at the Hâtmutee river. Moobâriz-ool-Moolk, though his force was far outnumbered by that of his opponent, quitted the fortress of which he held command, and formed in battle array outside its walls, on the opposite bank of the stream. The troops of Rânâ Sung received an attack from the Mohummedans with great steadiness, and then charged. The array of Islâm was broken by the fury of the Rajpoots, several officers of distinction were killed; Moobâriz-ool-Moolk himself was severely wounded; his elephants were taken, and the whole force was driven in confusion towards Ahmedabad. Sung Rânâ now plundered the surrounding country at his leisure: he spared the Brahmins of Wurnugger; but finding Veesulnugger defended against him, he took it by assault, slaying the Mohummedan governor. Having thus revenged himself for the insult which had been offered to him, he returned, unopposed, to Cheetor.

The viceroy of Moozuffer Shah, then absent on the Malwa frontier, having succeeded in reinforcing his army, and the dog, Rânâ Sung, having retired, Moobâriz-ool-Moolk attempted to re-assume his government. On the way to Ahmednugger he was opposed by a body of Rajpoots and Koolees from the Eedur territory, whom he defeated, but, having reached that city, he found the country around so enfeebled by the ravages to which it had been lately subjected, that he was compelled to fall back for supplies upon Poorântej.

Moozuffer Shah, determined not to allow of the abandonment of Ahmednugger, directed his officers to hold it at all hazards during the rains, and in December, A.D. 1520, he marched thither in person, with an army destined eventually for the reduction of Sung Rânâ.

The Eedur country was again subjected to the ravages of Mohummedans; but no decisive success was obtained by them over the Rânâ of Cheetor, with whom "a peace was patched up," as the author of Meerât Ahmudee relates, "in consequence of the hypo-"critical conduct of the officers commanding the troops."

The Rows of Eedur, during the occupation of their capital by the Mohummedans, lived, it is said, with their families at Surwân—the village held by the descendants of Sâmulyo Sord, situated in the hilly country on the frontiers of Mewar. Row Bârmul, as the Reetorâ inscription proves, outlived Moozuffer II., as well as his sons, Sikunder and Mahmood II., and was alive in A.D. 1528, when "Buhâdur Shah marched towards the countries of Eedur and Wâgur, "from whence he returned, by Châmpâner, to Broach;" and also in A.D. 1530, when the sultan again "marched towards Eedur; but "himself retired, after despatching two of his officers, with a large "force, to Wâgur." Row Bârmul died after A.D. 1543, and was succeeded by Row Poonjâjee, respecting whose career no incidents have been preserved.

It is unnecessary to our purpose to enter into a detailed account of the fortunes of the dynasty of Ahmedabad, whose history, as related by the Mohummedan writers, contains henceforth nothing which bears directly upon the story of the Hindoo princes of Goozerat. The reign of Sultan Buhâdur was one marked by the most violent contrasts. At one time we behold him emulating the glory of his great predecessor, Sidh Râj, his supremacy acknowledged by the kings of Candeish, Berar, and Ahmednugger; his rule extending over the kingdom of Malwa, once again subdued by the arms of Goozerat; and his victorious banner waving from the lofty battlements of Mândoo. At another time we find him driven from his kingdom by the Emperor Hoomâyoon, whom, in his prosperity, he had provoked. And, at last—a miserable affray with the Portuguese, sullied by more than the suspicion of treachery on either side, resulting in his death—we behold his murdered corpse cast upon the waters of the ocean; while the annalist who relates his story can close it only with admissions of weakness, and presages of decay. "After the death of Sultan Buhâdur, much disorder and sedition "found their way into the affairs of Goozerat; and, from that time, "the tribute from the kings of the Dekkan, and the ports possessed "by the Europeans, was no longer received."

Several years afterwards, in A.D. 1545, Mahmood Luteef Khan, the nephew of Buhâdur Shah, being then the occupant of the royal cushion, the extinction of the rights of the Hindoo landholders, formerly attempted in part, and with circumspection, in the vigorous days of Shah Ahmed and Mahmood Begurra, was now sought to be effected over the length and breadth of Goozerat, by hands as feeble as they were presumptuous; and a course of policy was entered upon, which, had other causes of dissolution been wanting, could hardly have failed in producing the total subversion of the throne of the sultans. "At this time the shah abandoned the "pleasures of the harem, and the government having thus received "an accession of power, both nobles and soldiers fell so completely "under its management that they had not the power of disobeying. "There was now some desire manifested of seizing upon Malwa; "but when the sultan consulted his minister, Âsuf Khan, in this "matter, he was told that he might obtain a country equal to Malwa "by merely attaching a fourth part of the Goozerat province, or "that part called the apportioned (Wântâ) lands, then possessed by "Rajpoots, Grâssiâs, and Koolees. 'If,' said the minister, 'that "fourth was only brought under government management, it is "sufficient, as a jagheer, to maintain twenty-five thousand horse;' "and the order was accordingly given for its resumption." The result was one which might have been expected—an universal, and, as subsequent history proves, a successful insurrection; for whatever deeds of oppression and of blood may have been enacted at the time, and however the Mohummedan rulers may have chosen to believe, or the Mohummedan historians to represent, the Hindoos to be a crushed and subdued people, the fact remains beyond dispute that their descendants, in spite of many a subsequent danger, still possess the soil of which it was sought to deprive them; while little but squalid poverty, and tottering ruins, represent the once proud sway of the dynasty of Shah Ahmed. "The Grâssiâs of "Eedur, Seerohee, Doongurpoor, Bânswârâ, Loonâwârâ, Râjpeepla, "the banks of the Myhee, and Hulwud (Jhâlâwâr), began on this "account to disturb the country. The parties of soldiers stationed "at Seerohee, Eedur, and other places, were therefore ordered to "extirpate the very name of Rajpoot and Koolee from such places; "excepting, however, those who were the armed police of the "country, or such as were engaged in trade, and who were to be "distinguished by a specific mark on the right arm. Should any of "this class be found without this mark, they were to be executed. "In consequence of such orders, the Mohummedan faith obtained "such a superiority in those parts, about the latter end of this reign, "that no Hindoo was allowed to ride on horseback through the "city; and those on foot were not allowed to wear clothing unless

" distinguished by a patch of red cloth sewed on the shoulder. " They were, moreover, prevented from exhibiting any public marks " of infidelity—such as the idolatries of the Hoolee and Dewâlee " festivals. It is, therefore, related that after the villain Boorhân " murdered the sultan, the Grâssiâs and Koolees set up an image " of the murderer, which they worshipped and addressed, saying, " 'This is our protector, who has saved us from perdition.' "

Whoever in the present day visits Goozerat, and in particular that capital city of Ahmedabad, which was the principal scene of these tyrannies, may behold the subterranean temple of the persecuted Hindoo, and the tall minaret of the Moslem in his day of power and intolerance, and may compare the state of affairs which these recall with things that are. The falling mosque strews the earth with its ruins, while, beside it, emerging from their dark hiding-places, the images of Shiva or of Pârusnâth are installed in newly erected temples; and the descendants of the swaggering Putâns and Moguls inlay the marble floors of the Hindoo shrines, or, for a pitiful hire, wave the torch and beat the drum in those idolatrous processions which gaily move along to re-establish in state the mute gods which their fathers fancied they had destroyed.

Sultan Mahmood was put to death in A.D. 1554; his dynasty lingered through the reigns of two feeble successors until the 18th November, A.D. 1572, when the great Akbar displayed his imperial banner within sight of the city of Ahmed, and a crowd of its inhabitants, of all ranks, went forth to welcome him as their sovereign.

" The learned and observing," says the author of Meerât Ahmudee, " well know that a cause for the decline of every empire " which has existed since the beginning of the world may be found " in the animosities of its nobles, assisted by rebellious subjects, " whose mutiny and endeavours, thank God! generally revert on " themselves, so that some more fortunate rival steps in and profits " thereby. Such was the end of the kings and nobles of Goozerat. " Fate having decreed the destruction of the government, its servants, " by disregarding all sacred ties in the midst of rebellions, went to " war among each other; so, under the semblance of friendship, they " openly committed acts of hostility, until at length, those parties " being set aside, the powers and seals of this kingdom were " transferred to the hands of the illustrious descendant of Teimoor— " Jelâl-ood-deen Mohummed Akbar."

The period which immediately preceded the establishment of

Akbar's authority was indeed one of the most melancholy in the history of Goozerat. At this time the Mohummedan nobles of the country, who had set up a supposititious son of Mahmood II. under the title of Mouzuffer III., divided, in reality, the country among themselves. Itimâd Khan, the most powerful of their number, held the capital city of Ahmedabad, with the port of Cambay, and the intervening territory; a second leader possessed the ruins of Unhilpoor, with much of the country between the Sâbhermutee and the Bunâs; to a third had been assigned the harbours of Surat and Broach, the fortress of Châmpâner, and the provinces south of the Myhee; Dhundhooka and Dholka had fallen to a fourth; and a fifth, seated in a fortress of Khengâr, affected to extend his rule over the peninsular of Soreth. Of Hindoo military vassals of the state there were at this time many. The northern districts, ranging from Kuree to Deesa, supplied a body of three thousand Rajpoot horse; Bohrjee, the zumeendâr of Bâglânâ, possessed the forts of Mooler and Sahler; and, served with the same number of cavalry, the revenues of two districts in the province of Godhrah were settled on the zumeendâr of Sonth and "Chuttârâl Koolee" for the services they performed; other "Wuttundârs," or hereditary landholders, in the district of Nâgor, served with a large force of mounted Rajpoots, and Poonjâ Râthor of Eedur, Râee Jye Singh of Râjpeepla, the Râwul of Doongurpoor, the chief of the Jhâlâs, the Jâm, with his four hundred grâssiâ dependants, and Khengâr Jhâreja of Bhooj supplied contingents, which, in cavalry alone, were estimated at sixteen thousand men. These powerful Rajpoot chiefs, who had maintained their lands and much of their independence against all the encroachments of the dynasty of Ahmedabad, had, of course, little to fear from the fragments of its shattered power, and the wild aboriginal tribes began again to break forth like a fire which had been restrained, indeed, by superincumbent weight, but had never yet been extinguished.

On the conquest of the country by Akbar, a viceroy or soubahdâr was appointed over the whole, under whom served the district revenue and military officers. The soubahdârs were usually men of the highest rank. The office was held by Khân Uzeez Kokâ, the foster-brother, and by Sultan Morâd Bukht, the son of Akbar; by Shah Jehân in the life of his father, Jehângeer, and by the Prince Morâd, his son, during his own reign. The annals of these times belong, however, to the general history of the empire of Delhi, and the pages of the Mohummedan writers contain little information in regard to the Rajpoot chieftainships, whose story is the object of this work. We find that Raja Todur Mul, when deputed by the emperor Akbar to effect a revenue settlement in Goozerat, seized every opportunity of conciliating and attaching to the throne the Rajpoot chiefs, in furtherance, doubtless, of the wise and generous desire of his master to rule no longer only as the chief of the Mohummedans, but as the head of a great and united Indian nation. On his arrival on the frontier of Goozerat in A.D. 1576, "the zumeendâr of Seerohee," we are informed, "presented a tribute of "five hundred rupees with one hundred gold mohurs.[1] Raja Todur "Mul gave him in return an honorary address, a jewelled head "ornament, and an elephant, after making an agreement with him, "on the part of the Delhi government, that he was to serve the "governor of Goozerat with two thousand cavalry. Raja Todur "Mul went from thence to Surat, and on the way thither, having had "a meeting at Broach with the zumeendâr of Râmnugger, who "presented a tribute of twelve thousand rupees and four horses, he "made him suitable presents in return. The zumeendâr was at "this time permitted to assume the rank of fifteen hundred horse, "and agreed to serve the Governor of Goozerat with one thousand "cavalry.

On Todur Mul's return from Goozerat towards Delhi, "he received "a visit from Rânâ Sâhsmul, zumeendâr of Doongurpoor, when this "chief was presented with an honorary dress, and the rank of two "thousand five hundred cavalry. He was also permitted to take "leave at Meertha after having agreed to serve in the province "of Goozerat."

From a statement made in the Ayeen-i-Akbery, that Row Nârondâs, of Eedur, commanded five hundred cavalry and two thousand infantry, it would appear that he also, like the chiefs of Seerohee and Doongurpoor, had been retained to aid the Viceroy of Goozerat with a subsidiary force. In the bardic Churittra of Veerum Dev also, the Row of Eedur is represented as a military vassal of the Delhi emperor. Ubool Fuzil alludes to others of the chiefs of Goozerat as similarly situated. "Chalawareh," he says, "formerly was an independent "territory, containing two thousand two hundred villages, which "extended seventy coss in length, and forty coss in breadth; and it "had ten thousand cavalry, with the same number of infantry. Now "it has two hundred cavalry and three thousand infantry; it is sub-

[1] This must have been "nuzur," the usual offering made at a visit, and not a payment of tribute. Here, and in the extracts which we shall afterwards have to produce, there is, however, much difficulty in regard to the numbers.

"ject to the Governor of Goozerat, and inhabited by the tribe of "Chaleh (Jhâlâ). Although now formed into four divisions, it is only "reckoned as a single pergunnah of Ahmedabad. It has a great num- "ber of towns." The four divisions here alluded to were those of Hulwud, Wudwân, Lugtur, and Limree, the formation of which will be described in a succeeding chapter. Soreth was, according to the same author, divided into nine divisions. The first of these, commonly called "new Soreth," had not been explored for a long time on account of the thickness of the forests and intricacy of the mountains. Joonagurh was situated in this division. New Soreth, as well as the second division of Puttun Somnâth, was inhabited by "Rajpoots of "the Gehlote tribe;" and the chiefs commanded, each of them, one thousand cavalry and two thousand infantry, "together with a num- "ber of Aheers (or cowherds), meaning, probably, Kâtees, of whom it is said in another place that they are of the Aheer caste, and that it is their business to look after horses. Of the third division, Ubool Fuzil informs us that, "At the foot of the mountains of Sironj (Shut- "roonjye), is a large city now out of repair, although the situation is "very desirable." The allusion is, probably, to the remains of Wul- lubheepoor. "Maabidcheen," he continues, "and the port of Gho- "geh are dependent upon it. The island of Birum is also in this "division; it is a square hill of nine coss in the midst of the river, "and formerly was the seat of government. The zumeendâr of this "division is of the Gohil tribe, and commands two thousand cavalry "and four thousand infantry." The fourth division was inhabited by Wâlâ Rajpoots; it included the ports of Mhowa and Tulâjâ, and supplied a contingent of three hundred cavalry and five hundred infantry. We need not follow our author through the remaining divisions, his description of which is not at all times intelligible. The Wâdhels, he mentions, possessed the port of Arâmrâ, which was a very strong place, and their contingent numbered one thousand horse and twice that number of foot. The kindred tribe of Wâjâs held a seaport called Jhânjeer, and supplied two hundred cavalry and the same number of infantry. By "the tribe of Cheetore," who mustered one thousand horse and two thousand foot, the author probably meant the Jetwâs of Bhoomblee. "The Bagheyleh tribe" inhabited one division, and commanded two hundred horse and the same number of foot; while the Kâtees, of the same part of Soreth, mustered six thousand horse and ten thousand foot; and another tribe of Aheers, who lived on the banks of the river Doondy, and were called Poorunjah, mustered half that number. The military force of the Jhârejas of Kutch Bhooj was ten thousand cavalry and fifty thousand infantry;

they were tall and handsome men, and wore long beards. The Jâm "Suttersal," a relation of the ruling family of Kutch Bhooj, was the grandson of a chief, who, having been driven out of that country by the Râwul, sixty years before, had settled in Soreth, "between the "territories of Chatwah, Badhil, and Nowneel," in a fertile country to which he had given the name of "Little Kutch," and in which he had founded his capital city of Nowânugger. The Jâm's contingent was seven thousand cavalry and eight thousand infantry.

In the Meerât Ahmudee we find it mentioned, that the Jâm of Nowânugger was at one time the supporter of Moozuffer III., the last of the sultans of Ahmedabad, but that he eventually betrayed him to his enemies. Moozuffer and the Jâm were defeated by the viceroy Khân Uzeez Kokâ, in A.D. 1590, and compelled to take refuge in the hills. The viceroy, subsequently to this victory, plundered Nowânugger, and besieged Joonagurh, which was defended by adherents of Moozuffer III., but being unsuccessful for a time in taking the latter place, he returned to Ahmedabad, when, as the historian remarks, the nobles were, for once, permitted to remain quiet on their own estates. Next year, Joonagurh fell into the hands of the viceroy, and Moozuffer was driven to take refuge with Khengâr, the Row of Kutch, who also had supported him. Uzeez Kokâ sent a force in pursuit of him, under the command of his son, who, during his march received the submission of the Jâm, and concluded a treaty with him, and the forlorn sultan, being soon after seized by the aid of the Jâm, that chief received, as his reward, from the imperial officers, the Pergunnah of Moorbee, which had formerly constituted part of his territory.

The following notice of the Rajpoot chieftainships, which lay on the eastern frontier of Goozerat, is to be found in the work of Ubool Fuzil :—"Near to Merow and Mungreetch is a territory called Pall, "through which runs the river Mehindery. On the Goozerat side of "this territory is an independent zumeendâr, who resides at Doongur- "poor. On the Malwa side of this country is Banswaleh, whose "chief is independent. Those two last mentioned chiefs have each "five thousand cavalry and one thousand infantry; and they were "both of the Seesodyah tribe, and relations to the Ranna, but now "the possessors are of another tribe.

"In the vicinity of Sirkar Putten is a country of which Serowhy is "the capital. The chief commands one thousand cavalry and five "thousand infantry. He has a fort on the top of a mountain called "Iyugurh (*vid.* Aboogurh), encompassing twelve villages, with great "plenty of water and pasturage. There is also another territory "situated to the east of Nudeebar, to the north of Mendow, to the "south of Madowt, and to the west of Chumpaneer, measuring sixty "coss in length, and forty in breadth. The chief is of the Chowhan "tribe, and his capital is Alymohan. Here are many wild elephants. "The military force is six hundred cavalry and fifteen thousand "infantry.

"Between the Sircars of Surat and Nuderbar is a mountainous "country, well inhabited, called Buglana. The chief is of the Rathore "tribe, and commands three thousand cavalry and two thousand "infantry. Here are apricots, apples, grapes, pine-apples, pome-"granates, and citrons in great perfection. Buglana has seven forts, "of which number Mowleer and Saleer are exceedingly strong.

"Between Sirkar Nadowt and Nuderbar is a hilly country, mea-"suring fifty coss in length, and forty coss in breadth. It is inhabited "by the Gowhil tribe of Rajpoots. At present the management of pub-"lic affairs is in the hands of one Tewary, a Brahmin, and the raja, "who possesses nothing but the name, resides sometimes at Rajpeep-"lah and sometimes at Ghoolwa. He has three thousand cavalry "and seven thousand infantry. The water of the latter place is very "bad; but there is produced very good rice and honey."[1]

The chieftainship last alluded to is that which, as we have seen, was founded by Semursunghjee, the son of Mokherâjee Gohil, the king of Perumbh, who succeeded to it in right of his mother.

CHAPTER VIII.

AFFAIRS OF EEDUR—ROW NÂRONDÂS—ROW VEERUM DEV—ROW KULEEÂN-MUL.

Row Poonjâ, of Eedur, was succeeded by his son, Row Nârondâs, who is mentioned (A.D. 1573) as having aided in creating disturbances against the government of Khân Uzeez Kokâ, the Mohummedan nobleman appointed by Akbar to the viceroyalty of Goozerat.[2] The insurrection was suppressed by the emperor, in person, and a large army was sent to punish the Row of Eedur. Two years afterwards,

[1] *Vide* Meerât Ahmudee, by Bird, pp. 325, 339, 343, 349.

[2] *Vide* "Ayeen Akbery," translated by Gladwin, vol. ii., article, "The Soobah "of Gujerat," pp. 75 to 96.

Uzeez Kokâ having been succeeded in his government by Meerzâ Khân, "a suitable army was sent to subdue Eedur," and in A.D. 1576, Row Nârondâs, being overwhelmed by the multitude of the imperial army, took refuge in the mountains. At length, leaving his place of security, and advancing to give the Mohummedans battle, he was defeated, and his capital fell into the hands of the emperor.

The following notice of Row Nârondâs is to be found in the Ayeen-i-Akbery :—"The Zumeendâr of Eedur, who is named Nâron-"dâs, lives with such austerity that his only food is grain which has "passed through oxen, and been separated from their dung; and "this kind of aliment the Brahmins consider as pure in the highest "degree. This Nârondâs is one of the principal chiefs of the Râthor "tribe; and he commands five hundred cavalry and two thousand "infantry."

Row Nârondâs was succeeded by his eldest son, Veerum Dev, a favorite hero of bardic tradition. A somewhat lengthy ballad poem records the adventures of his youth, and narrates how, at the age of five and twenty years, he found his way to Poongul, in the north of Marwar; how he won the love of the beautiful Punnâ, the daughter of a wealthy merchant of that place; how he triumphantly carried off the lady by force of arms, and how he slew many a valiant chieftain, when the array of Poongul "came upon the wâr." Another bardic account continues the story of Veerum Dev to its close, and this latter we propose to present to the reader, in as literal a translation as possible. It is entitled,

THE CHURITTRA OF ROW SHREE VEERUM DEV.

A year and a half after Veerum Dev had returned from Poongul, the Emperor Akbar summoned all the rajas of India to Delhi. The Princes of Oodeipoor, Jodhpoor, and Boondee, with others, obeyed the command. They remained three or four months at Delhi. Row Nârondâs and Prince Veerum Dev also went there. One day a tiger, which the emperor had in a cage, made its escape. Akbar gave orders that it should be caught, but his warriors answered, "Sire! a tiger "cannot be laid hold on." Prince Verum Dev said, "A Rajpoot "might lay hold on him, but he could not be sure to do so. The "tiger might kill the Rajpoot, or the Rajpoot might kill the tiger.' The emperor said, "You have well spoken." Then Veerum Dev went to lay hold on the tiger; he held a little shield in his hand, and advancing it before him, soon came to fisticuffs with his enemy; he struck down the tiger, and wrapping a scarf round his left arm, he thrust it into the brute's mouth, and with his right hand stabbed it with the point of his sword, so that it died. Then the emperor was delighted beyond measure, and gave him a magnificent dress of honor. Akbar said, too (alluding to Nârondâs, who was spare in person), that he had thought less than he ought of the gaunt Row, not knowing him to be the father of such a son as Veerum Dev.

Now Veerum Dev asked only one boon of the emperor, "When I "shall have come here, and it shall happen to be my wish to return "to Eedur, let me have leave to go at once." Akbar promised that he should. The Row and his son then made their obeisance, and went home to Eedur, and soon after Nârondâs died, and Veerum Dev sat on the royal cushion. Nârondâs left four Rânees :—one was the sister of the Rânâ Pertâp Singh, of Oodeipoor, who bore to him his two elder sons; the second was the daughter of the Bhâtee Prince of Jesulmer, and the mother of Râee Singh and Kishor Singh; the third was a lady of the Shekhâwut clan, the mother of Gopâldâs. The Row left, besides, a fourth Rânee, the daughter of the Hârâ of Kotah, and three concubines. The whole seven became sutees with Nârondâs. After this, a chief of the Row's, Hemut Singh, the Beeolâ, had gone to Doongurpoor on a visit, because his sister was married there to the Râwul Râm Singh. Dinner time having come, Râm Singh sent for him, and, with much urgency, pressed him to dine off the same dish with him. The chief had weak eyes, and they watered as he sat at dinner. Râm Singh said, "There's nothing I have such an aversion "to as this; if I had known of it, I would not have invited you to sit "beside me." Hemut Singh, hearing such insulting words, got up and left the room; he returned to Eedur, and said to Row Veerum Dev, "I am not strong enough of myself to strike Doongurpoor, may it "please your highness to accompany me? If not, with the men and "money I have, I will go and fight with Doongurpoor, and die there." Veerum Dev said, "Do you stay here until after New Year's-day, and "then I will accompany you." After the festival they mounted accordingly, and set forth. Meanwhile, a famine having occurred in Marwar, two bard's sons, who were on their way from thence to Goozerat, met them. One of the boys was going along on the road carrying some food with him, when Veerum Dev's cavalcade came up; he then moved on one side, and stood close to the hedge till it should pass. The Row, seeing him, cried out, "Halloo there! who are you? "and what are you standing beside the hedge for?" The boy answered, "Muhârâj! I am a bard's son, and I have heard that Vee-"rum Dev rains gifts even upon the hedges, so I am looking to see "what he has rained on this hedge." Then Veerum Dev took from his wrists his golden bracelets, and, throwing them into the hedge, said, "Go on looking, you'll find something in the hedge." As they went on, the boy's brother was standing by a well. The Row asked him, "Is this well yours?" He answered, "Sire! how should it be my "well? the well is your highness's." The Row then gave order, "I "have presented this well to you." Veerum Dev caused both of these boys to be suitably married, and descendants of their's still enjoy the said well. After this, the Row halted eight or ten days at Wurâlee.

Now, while Veerum Dev's camp was pitched beside the Sumuleshur tank at Wurâlee, it so happened that his brother Râee Singh also came by chance, as he was engaged in hunting, to that place. This Râee Singh, it must be noted, was a most eager sportsman. When Veerum Dev saw him, it came into his mind that if Râee Singh remained alive he would take his throne. Afterwards, when he had returned from Wurâlee to Eedur, he involved that brother of his in some fault, and slew him with his sword. This Râee Singh had a sister who was married at Jeipoor, and who, retaining this cause of feud in mind, put Veerum Dev to death, as will afterwards be related.

As things went on in this manner, another new year came round, and the Row collected his army, which with the following of his chiefs, amounted to eighteen hundred horse. They set out, and advanced by stages to Vincheewârâ; their warlike stores, such as armour for men and horse, cannon and swivels, being carried on the backs of camels. Hemut Singh, too, was with them with his force, for whose sake, indeed, it was that it became necessary to advance upon Doongurpoor. The Chief of Vincheewârâ, who was a vassal of Doongurpoor, made enquiries as to whither the Row's cavalcade was advancing. Answer was made to him that the Row was on his way to his father-in-law's at Râmpoor, which is on the banks of the Chumbul, on the borders of Mewar and Malwa. However, the chief knew that Hemut Singh and his sovereign were at enmity, and he thought to himself, "Here is Hemut Singh with them, with all his "men, and guns and other warlike stores, what reason can there be "for taking all these to Râmpoor?" So he was lost in doubt. Then the Eedur chiefs said to Veerum Dev, "Some one will say that "the Row came like a thief and struck Doongurpoor, but if he had "come openly he would not have struck it, therefore the matter "should be made public." The Row said, "It is well!" Then they told the chief of Vincheewârâ that they were advancing against Doongurpoor, and that he should go and make known publicly that the Row was coming against them at Doongurpoor, and that they should get ready to fight with him. The chief went, accordingly, and made the matter known, and the Râwul called his vassals together, and got ready to fight, and sent a messenger to Veerum Dev to say, "Come at your leisure to fight, we are ready." The Row remained eight days at that halting place, and then advanced to the neighbourhood of Doongurpoor, and the battle commenced by a discharge of cannon on both sides. The assailants knocked down a good deal of the fort and palace of Doongurpoor, which remain in the same broken state to this day. After ten days spent in this way, they put armour on men and horses, and assaulted the place, upon which occasion each side lost a hundred men. The Râwul, with his family, fled, and the Row, having remained three days and a half at Doongurpoor, and plundered the town, and taken all the treasure he could find, returned to Eedur. When he was gone, the Râwul returned home.

After this the emperor's army came against Oodeipoor, and the Rânâ, Pertâp Singh, fled to Venchâwârâ (this is the Venchâwârâ, which is near Pânowrâ) for the Rânâs were, from father to son, in outlawry against the emperor, and that sovereign had carried away the doors of the gate of Cheetor, and had set them up in the gate of Delhi; fifty-two rajas had perished, and the Rânâs, in their troubles, lay at nights on counterpanes spread on the ground, and neither slept in their beds nor shaved their hair, and if, perchance, they broke their fast, had nothing better to satisfy their hunger than beans baked in an earthen pot; for which reason it is that solemn practices are to this day observed at Oodeipoor; a counterpane is spread below the Rânâ's bed, and his beard remains unshorn, and baked beans are daily laid upon his plate. To this day, too, no new doors have been made for the further gate of Cheetor; and when the English government proposed to the Rânâ that he should cause new doors to be made, or that, if he liked, his own doors should be sent for for the purpose, the answer received was, that the Rânâ would set up his own doors again when he should have brought them from Delhi, by force of arms.[1] However, to return :—When the Rânâ fled to Venchâwârâ, a Mewar Bheel, named Châmpo, who was in outlawry against the Rânâ, was making great disturbances in that part of the country.

[1] For the story of Rânâ Pertâp Singh of Mewar, see chap. xi., of the Annals of Mewar. Tod's Rajasthan, vol. i., pp. 331 to 350.

The Rânâ drove him out, and he lived in the wild part of the Eedur territory, where he maintained himself by highway robbery and breaking into houses at night. When he began to give great trouble in Eedurwâra, the Row, Veerum Dev, said to his chiefs, "I will give a reward "to any one who will seize this Châmpo Bheel." Then the chief of Dudhâleeâ said, "I'm the man, I'll seize him." So saying, he went off to his village. When Châmpo Bheel heard this, he left off all other excursions, and began to ravage Dudhâleeâ only. The chief thereupon sent privately to him to say, "You must not plunder "my village; I will not seize you." Some months after this the Row again spoke to his chiefs. This time the chief of Mohunpoor said he would seize the Bheel. After having so said, he was on his way home, and had arrived at the tank at Sâbulee, where he lay down under a sacred fig-tree, putting off his arms. He sent also three or four horsemen that were with him into the village to procure necessaries. As the shadow of the tree moved, so he moved also, pulling the coverlet spread under him, until, at last, he had left his weapons at a long distance. Meanwhile, Châmpo Bheel came there; he had heard what had passed, and therefore thought he would kill the chief. He said to him, "So you have come out to seize me, have you?" The chief was afraid, and said, "It is not to seize "you that I want, but I have been very anxious to have an inter-"view with you." So saying, giving him confidence, he invited him to sit beside him, and gave him opium to drink. Afterwards, when Châmpo got up, and was going away, the chief considered with himself, "If he gets out of my hand at this time, when will such another opportunity arrive?" So considering, immediately he sprang upon Champo, and seized the sword he had in his hand, and the dagger that was in his waist, and with one hand stabbing him with the dagger, and with the other striking him with the sword, he put him to death. After this his own horsemen came up, and with them he sent the Bheel's head to Eedur, himself returning home. The Row presented him with the place which had been the haunt of Châmpo Bheel, where he founded a village called Châmpânâlya, which still forms part of the Mohunpoor estate.

At this time, Veerum Dev determined upon attacking the fort of Ahmednugger, and with that view assembled his vassals. Of these the principal was Rutun Singh Wâghela, of Poseenâ. The force was got ready, guns and stores were prepared, and Ahmednugger attacked for ten or twelve days, and at last taken; the market-place was plundered, and hostages were seized. When Veerum Dev returned back, the merchants of the town began to repair their losses. The Row then said that he would not obstruct them, on condition of their preserving the name of Eedur, whereupon they called one of the gates of the town "the Eedur gate."

The Pethâpoor chief was with the Row on this expedition, and from enmity on that account, an army from Ahmedabad attacked Pethâpoor. The Row hastened to his assistance, and repulsed the Mohummedan army, upon which the Pethâpoor chief gave his daughter in marriage to Veerum Dev. The Row was very fond of this lady on account of her great beauty, so he presented her brother with the village of Gudhâ, which is still part of the estate of Pethâpoor, after which the chief continued for a length of time to act as the Row's minister.[1]

After this, an army from Delhi came to levy tribute upon Râmpoor, the seat of Veerum Dev's father-in-law. The latter thereupon wrote to Veerum Dev to say, "This army comes against me to-"day, but to-morrow it will come against you. Do you, therefore, "hasten to my assistance." Veerum Dev assembled a thousand horse, which he sent with his vassals of Mohunpoor and Dudhâleeâ. At this time, Rutun Singh, of Poseenâ, staid at home in anger, the reason of which was this:—Some one had said to the Row, "It was because your highness had such a follower as Rutun Singh, "that you took Ahmednugger;" to which Veerum Dev answered, "What can Rutun Singh do? Is it a kingdom founded by him that "I rule over?" The chief, hearing this, was enraged. Now the two above-mentioned leaders went to Râmpoor. The Row of that place had sworn an oath that he would employ no Rajpoot who was either unwounded, or wounded in the back. A battle was fought with the invading army, which was driven back; but many Rajpoots, both of Râmpoor and Eedur, came to use there, and it is doubtful whether a single one escaped unwounded. Veerum Dev presented villages to the heirs of the deceased "for their heads." Some say that it was on account of the assistance thus afforded, that Veerum Dev obtained the daughter of the Row of Râmpoor for his wife.

[1] The Pethâpoor bardic account is as follows:—"The chief Doodojee, with "seven hundred Rajpoots was slain when Shukurdeen came to attack Eedur, at "which time many Toorks also fell. Twelve Wâghela chiefs, a Gohil, and a "Purmâr fell with Doodojee. Eedur was victorious. The Eedur Row, on this, "gave to Wâghjee, the son of Doodojee, the twenty-five villages forming the estate "of Gudhâ, which is still enjoyed by Pethâpoor."

After this, the Mohummedan army came against Cheetor, and the Rânâ of Mewar made a desperate stand; fifty-two rajas came to use, and Rânâ Pertâp Singh received many wounds; at last the imperial army was compelled to fly. This Pertâp Singh was the mother's brother of Veerum Dev, on which account the Row went to pay him a visit. He staid many days at Oodeipoor, until the Rânâ recovered. At Oodeipoor there is a great tank called "the Peecholoo," in the middle of which are grand palatial buildings, called "Jug Mundeer."[1] The Rânâ and the Row used to go thither in a boat. One day a kingfisher, hovering in the air, dashed into the water after a fish. The Row was very much delighted, and said, "Wâh! wâh! what spirit the little bird has!" Then the Rânâ asked where the bird had dived into the water, upon which the Row, taking a jewelled armlet off his arm, pitched it into the water, and said, "There, that's the place." The Rânâ cried out, "The armlet's gone, the armlet's gone." Then the Row threw in the other, and said, "We must "give a present that will please it to such a gallant little bird, "must we not." This the bards have celebrated as a great act of generosity.

Afterwards Veerum Dev returned to Eedur. At that time a Marwar bard, whose name was Âlojec, came to ask alms of Veerum Dev. Now it was the Row's practice not to go in turn to any Rânee on the day of the full moon; but to stay at the palace of the Râmpoor lady, and to sit at the eastern window till the moon appeared, when he distributed gifts, called "lakh pusâv." On this occasion he was seated, as usual, and called out, "Bring the lakh pusâv, here is some bard." The minister said, "Yes, there is this one bard come; call "him." The bard came, accordingly, and said, "At night time a "prostitute or a female ascetic might receive alms. I won't receive "them at such a time." The Row said, "Take them now, for in "the morning I will not give them." The bard swore an oath to leave Eedur at day-break, and said, "If you would give me two "lakhs, I would treat it as a defiled thing." The Row then said, "If it be my fault that you turn away, then may you get a sub-"sistence; but if it be your own fault, and if you go away leaving "me in blame without right, then may you get no subsistence." Thus he cursed him. At the same time he gave the lakh pusâv, and the village of Reheroo, to another bard. Now the first-mentioned

[1] See, for a description and view of this reservoir, Tod's Rajasthan, vol. i., p. 373.

bard rose in the morning, and took the road; with him were forty horses, five camels, and tents and equipage of all sorts; but wherever he went in Râjwârâ he met with disrespect, and at last he found his way home to Marwar, having sold the whole of his equipage to fill his belly.

Now, as to Rutun Singh, of Poseenâ, who had been enraged:—The Row, day by day, began more and more to hate him; on which account, the chief mounted his horse, and caused his cavalcade to get ready, and went off suddenly to Seerohee. Then the Row reflected, "If I were to seize on any of the seventy-two villages of "Poseenâ, I should drive him out into rebellion; but, on the other "hand, I get no service from him." Thus considering, he sent a bard to Seerohee to invite Rutun Singh to come in. The chief, however, refused to come to Eedur; but agreed to come to Gudhâ. So the Row set off thither, and a meeting took place. Then Veerum Dev pretended great affection externally, and he and Rutun Singh sat down together in an old temple which is in that place; but two Rajpoots, of Seerohee, who were in the Row's service, had been prepared beforehand, and they, accordingly, all at once rushed in, and killed the chief with the sword. His estate was given to his son, who was eighteen years of age. A bard made a song on this, addressed to Veerum Dev, the meaning of which was—"Had you not entrapped "Rutun Singh, and slain him, after inviting him, he would have "swung you and the temple round with one hand, as Bheem swung "round the elephant." The Row returned to Eedur; but this song rang in his ear. He set to work, and found out who had made the song. The Row swore he would slay the bard if he could get him into his power, and proclaimed that he would give a reward to any one who should bring news of him. One day when the bard had gone to Wurâlee to buy opium, the Row, too, happened to come there. As soon as the bard knew of Veerum Dev's arrival, he started off at the top of his speed. Some one told the Row of this, and he mounted and pursued the bard; and, after going some distance, came up with him. The Row then said, "How far will you run away, mounted on that wretched pony of yours?" The bard dismounted, and drawing forth a dagger, and pointing it towards his belly, said, "Your highness will get no praise for killing a poor "man like me. Better than that, that, if necessary, I should die by "my own hand." The Row adjured him not to kill himself, and said, "How is it that you, knowing you were under my displeasure, "should go about on such a poor animal as that?" The Chârun said, "Sire! where should a poor man, such as I am, get a good "horse from?" The Row gave him his own horse, and a dress of honor, and the village of Veevâvya, which his descendants still enjoy. He then returned to Eedur.

The Row, after this, made an expedition to Pânowrâ, the cause of which was that the Bheels of that place having made a night attack upon Delol, and carried off the cattle, the chief of Delol, one of the Row's vassals, mounted, and went on the "wâr;" and, regaining the cattle, slew many of the Bheels and the leader of the foray, whose head he sent to Eedur. The Bheels who escaped, and the heirs of those who died, began to plunder many villages of the Eedur territory, to balance this feud, and caused great annoyance to Delol. The Wâghela of Delol, on this account, made petition to the Row that he would effect a settlement. The Row Veerum Dev thereupon wrote to the Rânâ of Pânowrâ to restrain his Bheels, who made answer that they were not under his control. The Row then prepared to advance against him, and went by way of Pol to Surwân, and thence to Pânowrâ. The guns played for one day, and next day they used the musket and sword; and the Rânâ of Pânowrâ "came to use," with many other warriors, on both sides. The Row staid a month at Pânowrâ, and slew many of the Bheels of those parts; while others he seized and fined, or released on their giving security. He then placed the Rânâ's son on the cushion, and returned to Eedur. The Koolee chief of Surwân was with the Row in this expedition.

After this the Row set off to perform pilgrimage at Dwârkâ, to expiate the sins of killing his brother, Râee Singh, and the chief of Poseenâ. His Rânees and vassals accompanied him. They went to Dwârkâ, and on their way home halted at Hulwud. The Row seeing there a vast number of Sutees' shrines, asked the Râj of Hulwud, "Have all these Rânees become Sutees?" The Râj answered, "These are the cobblers' wives of this place, who became "Sutees." The Row asked, "Where, then, are the shrines of the "Râjwârâ Sutees?" The Râj said, "I never heard that any one in "my family had become a Sutee. The Row said, "There must be "some fault in this ground. Make yourself a palace on the spot "where the cobblers' houses are." The Râj had tried that, he said, but still there had been no Sutee. Then Veerum Dev said, "What! "has no one of your family married a true Râjpootnee. See, then, "here is my sister, a virgin, you shall have her in marriage." The betrothal was soon arranged, and when the Row returned home, the Jhâlâ chief came to be married, and the sister of Eedur, at her husband's death, followed him through the flames.

While the Row was absent at Dwârkâ, the son of Lâl Meeâ, of

Mândoowâ, who was a wanton fellow, happened to go for a time to Kupperwunj. He saw there a trader's daughter, who was very pretty, and seduced her, and carried her off to Mândoowâ. His father was very angry with him, but the mischief was done, and the girl had lost caste. Kupperwunj was in the Row's possession, and therefore, as he was on his way home from Dwârkâ, the trader came and complained to him. Veerum Dev carried his cavalcade to Mândoowâ, which he struck, and seizing Lâl Meeâ's son, put him to death. Lâl Meeâ himself fled, and the Row, after staying three days at Mândoowâ, which before and after that time paid revenue to Eedur, returned to his capital.

Now the Row, having no son, made many vows to many Devs and Devees, and performed many pilgrimages, but no prince made his appearance. At last some one said to him that if he would go to the ford, called Omkâreshwur's, on the Rewâ river,[1] and there bathe with his chief Rânee, with the same scarf wrapped round them both, he would obtain a son. The Row accordingly made a progress thither, accompanied by his family. Meanwhile, the following of a shahzâda[2] of the emperor's, had encamped there, and some butchers had collected eight or ten cows for them, which they were driving along the road. Some of Veerum Dev's servants saw them, and asked them who they were, and where they were taking the cows to. They said they were butchers, and were taking away the cows for the shahzâda. When the Row got intelligence of the matter, and was informed by the butchers that they had brought the cows from a distance of a hundred miles, he offered them from ten to a hundred pounds for each cow, but they refused his offer. Then the Row thought within himself, "I am styled protector of cows and Brahmins, so "it is a good thing to die at a place of pilgrimage in defence of "cows." Thus considering, he took away the cows by force, and then sent off his family immediately towards Eedur, the Rânee saying that if he came to use in protecting the cows, she would not remain a moment in the world behind him. Now the butchers went to the shahzâda, and complained, and the prince sent a herald to demand the cows. The Row humbly replied, "I am a Hindoo and

[1] This is the place commonly called Unkulesur, on the Nerbudda River, opposite Broach.

[2] The "shahzâdas" mentioned here and in other bardic chronicles of the time are, no doubt, the Mirzas, for an account of whom see Elphinstone's India, vol. i. p. 266, &c.

"in a place of pilgrimage like this I cannot give up the cows as long "as there is life in me, but whatever price you may command me to "pay for them I am ready to give." Then the shahzâda ordered his guns to open on the Row's party, but Veerum Dev and his followers immediately rushed upon them, and drove nails into the vents, and then the sword played. Many men fell on both sides, and after a time the Row retired to a place two miles off, where he halted. He had, before the fight, let the cows loose in the jungle, solemnly entrusting them to the care of Sooruj Dev. In the night time he reflected that there were very many butchers with that cavalcade, and that if he were to kill them, that would save the life of many a cow, so he fell upon them while it was yet dark, and slew numbers of the butchers. In this action a Khuwâs, of whom Veerum Dev was excessively fond, was killed. The Row, taking up his corpse, retired a few miles and committed it to the flames on the banks of the Rewâ. He then remained secretly at the village of Wudwânee, belonging to a Seesodeea, which is in that neighbourhood, for some days, and every night he went and slew or plundered some of the shahzâda's people. At length the cavalcade, which was going to Ahmedabad, suffered so much knocking about that it turned back to go homewards. The Row performed *Supindee shrâd*, and other funeral rites, on behalf of the Khuwâs, and erected a pavilion, which is still to be seen, over the spot where his body had been consumed. He then returned to Eedur.

Now the shahzâda, having gone to the emperor and complained, there was a mighty army sent against Eedur, which came and encamped at the Rumulesur tank, and erected batteries against the town. The contest of artillery went on for ten days, but the Row, remaining in Eedur-gurh, the emperor's army found that no strength of their's prevailed against it. They therefore set sentries, and encamped there for six months. At the end of this time, the Row, taking with him his Rânees, and their establishment, and eighteen hundred horse, left Eedur-gurh by a secret way, and retiring to Pol, took up his residence there. He left, however, his younger brother, Kuleeânmul, with a few soldiers, in Eedur-gurh. The emperor's army took the town of Eedur, and plundered it, but could not take the fortress. They discovered, also, that the Row had retired to Pol. The shahzâda, therefore, leaving a small force at Eedur, advanced to Bheelorâ, and encamped there with another division of his army, having placed his posts at Wurâlee, Guloroo, Ahmednugger, Morâsâ, Meghruj, and other towns, and thus taken possession of the whole Eedur country.

The Row lived six months at Pol, provisions ran short, and for two whole days he had been fasting; on the third day he went to the temple of Muhâ Dev, and with the intention of performing the "lotus-" worship," he aimed his sword at his throat. At this moment the word "forbear" issued from the temple. The Row looked round, but could see no one; he thought therefore that from his weakness of body, consequent on want of food, his mind had been playing tricks with him. He again prepared to kill himself, but three several times the word "forbear" issued from the shrine. The Row then asked, "Who is it that forbids me?" The answer was, "I am Muhâ Dev! "why do you seek to slay yourself?" "Because I have nothing to "support life with," said Veerum Dev. "You shall have that which "you seek to-morrow," was the reply. The Row, upon this, returned to his quarters. At this time the formerly-mentioned Âlo Guduwee, the Chârun, who had gone away, angrily refusing to accept the *lakh pusâv*, came back to the Row, at Pol, in a state of destitution, and sang a good song in his praise, and begged for alms. Those who stood by said, "Are you not ashamed to ask alms at such a time as this?" To this the Chârun only answered by an extempore stanza. Meanwhile news had been carried to Oodeipoor that "Veerum Dev is in trouble (wukhé) at Pol, and has no food left." A supply of money and necessaries was then put upon camels, and sent off, and at this very moment the convoy arrived. Veerum Dev gave all the treasure out of it to the Chârun.

Afterwards the Row considered that it would be out of his power to defeat the emperor's army, and that even if he drove a post out of a position, it would be soon replaced; so he got up one morning, and put a knife and a dagger in his waist, and tied on his sword, and mounted his horse, and set out without telling any one. He took only a single horseman with him, and went to Bheelorâ. There was a high building there, upon which the shahzâda was seated. The Row pulled up his horse below, and gave the bridle to his follower, enjoining him not to stir from the spot. He went on and said to the sentinel, that he wished to have an interview with the prince. The sentinel made his request known, and he was directed to lay down his arms and proceed. He went up and engaged in conversation, when he perceived a cat that had seized a pigeon drop with it from the roof of the building to the ground. The cat was above and the pigeon below, so that the latter was killed while the former escaped. Veerum Dev thought within himself, "If I take him, and fall with him, I shall perhaps survive." He seized the prince by the throat, and threw him down out of the window, falling himself upon him. The shahzâda was killed, but the Row, mounting his horse, escaped to Pol. When the shahzâda's death was known, the whole army retired. Then the Row returned home to Eedur, and lived there many days.

Meanwhile, a merchant brought horses to sell them, among which were two horses, named Nuthwo and Jâlâhur, upon which the merchant set a price of forty-four thousand rupees. Veerum Dev purchased them. When the Dusserâ came, and they went to worship the Shumee-tree, and kill the "Chogâneeo buffalo," these two horses were much admired. They set free, according to the Eedur practice, a large and well-fed male buffalo; the Row struck it with the blunt edge of his spear so as to make it run, and then the nobles gallopped after it to spear it. The buffalo killed, and the shumee-tree worshipped, each exhibited the excellence of his horse and his own skill in riding. This amusement finished, the Row and his nobles rested themselves on swinging seats, fastened to the trees, until dark, when torches were lighted and the procession prepared, and the whole party marched in great splendour to the court. On the fourteenth, the Row presented the horse, "Jâlâhur," to Sâyâ Jhoolâ Guduwee as a present, and kept "Nuthwo" for his own riding. That day it was the turn of the Wâghelee lady, of Pethâpoor, to entertain her husband. The Row, having gone to her apartments, said to her two or three times, "To-day I gave away my horse, Jâlâhur, in a present." The Rânee said, "Why do you keep on telling me time after time that "you have made a present of a pony?" The Row then grew angry, and said, "When your father shall give the Chârun a horse like "Jâlâhur, I will come back again to your apartments, and not "before." So saying, he got up, and went out. The Rânee, directly she got up in the morning, ordered her chariot, and, going to Pethâpoor, told the story to her father. He then sent men to get a horse of similar value, to Kâteewâr, to Moolee, to Choteelâ, to Thân Râddhuroo, and every other place he could think of where fine horses are produced; but a horse of such value was nowhere to be found. Then the Thâkor went in person to the Chârun's house, and, buying the horse from him for a very large sum, brought it home. Six months afterwards he sent for the same Chârun, and (a thing which made every one stare and look angry) made him a present of the horse. When the Row was made aware of this, he went in person to the Pethâpoor, and, after saying "bravo!" to his father-in-law, brought the Rânee home with him.

Afterwards the Chârun wanted to give the horse to the Row to take care of during the rainy season, but the Row said, "My Sirdâr, Mâljee "Dâbhee, is on duty at the out-post, at Brumh Kheir, do you give the horse to him to take care of." So the Chârun gave it to the Thâkor Mâljee. Soon after this, Rânâ Wâgh, of Tursunghmo, made a foray as far as Kheir, and the Dâbhee, mounting the same horse, set off on the wâr. He was successful, and recovered the buffaloes, but the horse was wounded, for the forayers had taken to the hill Mundowuree, near Wâdhuwâ village, and the horse had galloped half-way up the hill, as may be known by marks that are still existing in that place—and a difficult place truly it is—not such as a horse might ascend. Afterwards the horse died of his wounds; on which subject the Chârun composed some verses. This Rânâ Wâgh, it must be told, was very valiant, and he used to say—

"I am Rânâ Wâgh,
"And up the Hurnâv is my share (bhâg)."

That is the river Hurnâv, which flows into the Sâbhermutee, at Bhânpoor of the Bhâtees, near Sutlâsunâ, and the Rânâ claimed it as his boundary.

After this, when another Dusserâ came round, the Row, with his own hand, killed the "Chogâneeo buffalo." That day it was the Rânee Chundrâwutjee's turn to receive her husband. The Row said to the Rânee, "To-day there was a very large buffalo, and I killed it "myself." Then the Rânee said, "A male buffalo is a different sort "of an animal—this was nothing of a buffalo." Then the Row became angry, and said, "When you can show a different sort of a "buffalo, then you may be pleased to return to Eedur; until then, be "so good as to go to your father's house, and stay there." So saying, he got up. Then the Rânee said, "Let your highness be pleased to "come to Râmpoor before the next Deewâlee. Make me a promise!" The Row made the promise and went away. The Rânee, too, in the morning set off to her father's house. When she arrived there she sent for a wild buffalo, as strong a one as she could get, and began to feed it up to the highest point. Afterwards, about the Deewâlee time, the Row set out from Eedur, to go by way of Doongurpoor to Râmpoor. Meanwhile, a cadet of Jodhpoor, named Umur Singh, when out hunting, wounded a boar, which, running away, got into the lands of Vikâner, the raja of which place killed it. Then Umur Singh got angry, and said that he would, without doubt, slay the man who had killed the boar wounded by him. He prepared to attack Vikâner, but, in the meantime, the Delhi Emperor, hearing of the matter, sent a shahzâda to put a stop to the feud. This shahzâda and

Veerum Dev met on the road. Then the prince thought of taking revenge for his brother; but, in the meantime, he received a letter from Umur Singh, who had heard of his coming, and thought he would take part with Vikâner, to say, "I am ready for you, too, if "you choose to come and fight me;" and so he was obliged to leave the Row unmolested, and go to the aid of Vikâner. While the fight was going on between these two parties, the Row went on to Râmpoor. When he arrived within thirty miles of the place, he sent forwards to say that he was coming. Now the family bard of Râmpoor had some time or other been to Eedur, where he had not received the respect he was entitled to. On account of that enmity, when he heard that the Row was coming, he caused the above-mentioned wild buffalo to be let loose on the road by which he was to come, pretending that it was doing too much mischief at Râmpoor. When the Row saw the animal coming, he thought that it was let loose to meet him on his arrival, so he killed the buffalo. He then became very angry, supposing that it had been the intention to ridicule him. He said to himself, "If I had not killed it, I should have "lost my character." In his anger, on this account, he turned back, and put up for the night at a village two miles distant. When the Râmpoor Raja heard of the matter he set out to meet Veerum Dev, and, making apologies to him, brought him back with him, and said, "It was not I who caused the buffalo to be let loose." When they came to examine into the matter, they found that it was the bard who had set the buffalo loose, upon which he was reprimanded. After this the Row staid there a month, and then began to talk of going away. The Rânee said, "Since my father died, the Row of Boon-"dee, knowing my brother to be a minor, has seized upon some of "his districts. As your highness has come, be pleased to cause them "to be given up." Then Veerum Dev wrote to the Row of Boondee to say, "Restore the districts, or else get ready to fight, and come to the boundary line." The two chiefs thereupon met at the boundary line, and a battle ensued, in which many on both sides were slain. The districts, however, were won back, and the Row, returning to Râmpoor, took the Rânee home with him to Eedur. Afterwards he gave to Sâyâjee Guduwee an elephant and "lakh pusâv."

A very short time after this, Veerum Dev set off on a pilgrimage to Gungâjee; he bathed at the Sorum Ghât, and turned homewards. Now, his half-sister (the sister of Râee Singh) was married at Jeipoor. She sent her own Koonwur, her minister, and others to meet Veerum Dev, and invited him with great urgency to Jeipoor. The Row was apprehensive that she would poison him, to take revenge for her brother, therefore he used every precaution in regard to what he eat or drank. At the time of taking leave, a very valuable dress of honor was presented to the Row, which, however, was poisoned. When Veerum Dev got back to Bheelorâ, within the Eedur country, he forgot his fears, and put on the dress. He was immediately seized with excruciating pains, and within an hour became a corpse. His funeral pile was erected at the gate of Bheelorâ, and the Rânees at Eedur, when they heard of the event, became Sutees.

Row Veerum Dev left no son. Of the younger sons of Row Nârondâs, however, several survived—Gopâldâs, Keshuvdâs, Sâmuldâs, Kuleeân Mul, and Pertâp Singh. Keshuvdâs and Sâmuldâs received the estates of Subulwâd and Hâtheeâ Wussye. Pertâp Singh, whose mother was of the Tursunghmo family, generally lived at Tursunghmo. On one occasion he was the cause of some injury to the Râna, who, thereupon, put him to death, and it was partly in revenge for this deed that Row Kuleeân Mul, when he took possession of the cushion, struck Tursunghmo.

Previously to the death of Veerum Dev, Gopâldâs and Kuleeân Mul had together made a pilgrimage to Dwârkâ, and, while they were worshipping there, the silver teeluk, on the forehead of the image of Shree Krishn, had fallen into the lap of Kuleeân Mul, who was therefore considered to have been specially appointed by the god to succeed to the royal cushion. When Veerum Dev died, however, Gopâldâs, as the rightful heir, prepared to seat himself on the throne, and the astrologers were employed to calculate the auspicious hour. Kuleeân Mul, then at the house of his mother's family at Oodeipoor, was summoned to be present at his brother's inauguration. When the proper time arrived, Gopâldâs seated himself to be invested with the royal jewels. He put on first one and then another, and took them off again, and was not able to make up his mind. Meanwhile, the auspicious hour had passed away. The ministers and chiefs were complaining to each other that such a person as this was not fit to manage the kingdom, when, at the very moment, Kuleeân Mul came up from Oodeipoor, attended by five horsemen. The whole court welcomed him, and placed him on the throne. When the royal drum began to sound, Gopâldâs enquired what was the matter, and was informed that Kuleeân Mul had assumed the cushion.

Gopâldâs went to Delhi, and took service with the emperor, in the hopes of procuring assistance to enable him to regain Eedur. At length he advanced, bringing an army with him, and struck Mândoowâ, of which he took possession, and from thence he meditated advancing upon Eedur. Lâl Meeâ, of Mândoowâ, however, concealed his men in a ravine, in ambuscade, and Gopâldâs fell into the net, and was slain with fifty-two Rajpoots. He had left his family when he went to Delhi at the hamlet of a cowherd named Wolo, and, after his death, they remained there, and founded a village called Wulâsunâ, after the cowherd. They gradually encroached upon the surrounding country, and at length Huree Singh and Ujub Singh, the two sons of Gopâldâs, divided their lands into the greater and lesser estates of Wulâsunâ.

During Veerum Dev's absence at Benâres, the districts of Pânowrâ, Puhâree, Juwâs, Jorâ, Pâtheeâ, Wullechâ, and others had been brought under Mewar. Kuleeân Mul, raising an army, conquered them back again. Rânâ Umur Singh, of Oodeipoor, opposed him with an army; a cannonade commenced the engagement, and then the sword played; there was great slaughter on either side, but victory remained with the Row. Kuleeân Mul also struck Tursunghmo, for the following reason.

Rânâ Wâgh, of Tursunghmo, had heard that the Rânee of Kuleeân Mul, who was the daughter of the Row of Bhooj, was very beautiful. He therefore conceived a great desire of seeing her. On the Dhunâl estate there is a village named Gudheroo, in the lands of which the Row's Jhârejee Rânee had constructed a temple to Shâmlâjee, at an expense of five thousand pounds. Hearing that the Rânee had come to that temple on a pilgrimage, Rânâ Wâgh, assuming the dress of a Brahmin, went thither among a number of Brahmins. The Rânee marked the Brahmins on the forehead, and made them presents; she offered a present to Rânâ Wâgh, among others, but he declined to receive it, and when a discussion arose, disappeared. Row Kuleeân Mul became aware of what had happened, and, in revenge, struck Tursunghmo.

Afterwards, the Guduwee Sâyâjee formed the design of erecting a fort, at the village of Koowâwoo. The Row was not pleased with this proceeding, and therefore he persuaded the Guduwee's astrologer to tell him that his allotted term of life was expired, for the Guduwee had enjoined the astrologer to inform him upon this point, that he might retire to Vruj. The Guduwee, thereupon, set off to Vruj, and presented to Shree Nâthjee a salver containing thirteen pounds' weight of gold. Thence he went on to Benares, and, as he had faith in the astrologer's words, he staid there awaiting his death. However, he had to wait ten years. When at length he fell very sick, he wrote to the Row of Eedur, to say that he greatly desired to see him. The Row set off to Benares, and was within one stage of that city when news was brought that Sâyâjee had cast off the body. The Row then considered that if he were to continue his journey to Benares people would say that he had come on a pilgrimage, and not on account of Sâyâjee. He therefore sent for water of the Ganges to the place where his encampment was, and having bathed therein, turned homewards by way of Oodeipoor. From that place he brought Guduwee Gopâldâs, to whom he presented the villages of Therâsunoo and Râmpoor, which are still held in twelve shares by his descendants. To another Chârun, who accompanied him, he gave the village of Thoorâ-wâs, which his descendants hold, divided into four shares.

After this, the Row had a quarrel with Seerohee, and went to war about a boundary. Twenty or thirty men on either side were slain, between Roherâ and Poseenâ; at length the Thâkor of Poseenâ stept between the combatants, and an arrangement was effected. Kuleeân Mul was succeeded, at his death, by his son, Row Jugunnâth.

CHAPTER IX.

THE SHRINE OF UMBÂ BHUWÂNEE.—DÂNTÂ.

Immense of bulk, her towering head she shews,
Her floating tresses seem to touch the skies,
Dark mists her unsubstantial shape compose,
And on the mountain's top her dwelling lies.
As when the clouds fantastic shapes disclose,
For ever varying to the gazer's eyes,
Till on the breeze the changeful hues escape,
Thus vague her form, and mutable her shape.
Illusive beings round their sovereign wait,
Deceitful dreams, and auguries, and lies,
Innumerous arts the gaping crowd that cheat
Predictions wild, and groundless prophecies;
With wondrous words, or written rolls of fate,
Foretelling—when 'tis past—what yet shall rise;
And alchymy, and astrologic skill,
And fond conjecture—always formed at will.

Lorenzo De' Medici, translated by WILLIAM ROSCOE.

THE temple of Umbâ Bhuwânee lies embosomed among the hills of Ârâsoor, at the south-western termination of the Ârâwullee range. From Unhilwârâ and the sacred Sidhpoor, the river Suruswutee may be followed up to its source, at Kotheshwur Muhâ Dev, near Umbâjee, through a wild, but picturesque, and fertile valley, upon which the forest-covered hills gradually close. Beside this lonely streamlet, when evening darkens around him, adding to the mysterious gloom of the untracked jungle, the lair of the hyæna and the tiger, with the dusky, unclothed forms of the children of the forest around him, and the harsh and wooden rattle of their drums, sounding from some distant village, the stranger need tax his imagination little to realize to himself his dreams of the Fetish-haunted banks of African Niger. Nor long, perchance, before a strange illumination lightens up the scene. The Bheel is offering his rude lustration to the mountain under whose form he worships the goddess of his faith; and flames, feeding on the dry brushwood, creep from hill to hill, slowly undulating like a huge fiery serpent, and recalling the imagery of the Psalmist,—"as the stubble before the wind, as the fire burneth the "wood, and as the flame setteth the mountains on fire."

Small bands of worshippers arrive daily at the temple of Umbâjee, from the whole surrounding country, and even from remote parts of India; but the great Sunghs, or caravans, approach it three times a year, and principally in the month of Bhâdrapud, during the rainy season, on the birthday of the Goddess. Not seldom from even Europeanized Bombay,—its air dusty with commerce, its waters white with many a western sail,—from beneath the shadow of the Cathedral which bears the name of the great Eastern Apostle, perhaps from the very precincts of the Court where ermined judges sit to administer the strange law of a foreign land—a land whose shadowy form, if ever it rise before his mental vision, looms far beyond the horizon which his hereditary faith has drawn around this mortal scene—the Hindoo pilgrim, quitting as it were a phantom-peopled world, for one, to him more real, measures with penitential feet the toilsome road to Ârâsoor.

The sacred caravan, which is usually very numerous, is entertained at whatever spot it makes its nightly halt, by members of it who have bound themselves by vows to consecrate sums of money to the service of "the mother." The last halt is at Dântâ, a small town nestling at the base of wild and rocky hills, at which reside the Purmâr chieftains who have been the most favoured followers of "the illustrious Umbâ." From thence the ascent to the shrine is lengthened, and for the most part very gradual, though occasionally sufficiently steep and rugged—for no human hand may smooth the difficulties which obstruct the pathway to Doorgâ's throne. Proceeding along this varied route, he holy band shining in the bright sun-light, with scarlet, and white, and yellow, with glittering steel, and softer gold, exhibits a gallant show; now traceable in lengthened, winding line upon the broken plain, now partly hidden by many coloured rocks, or concealed from view by the tangled forest's shade. At a place called "the well of Nânâbhâee," about half-way up the steepest portion of the ascent, the Sungh makes a temporary halt, and on quitting this spot, it soon emerges from amidst the gloomy rocks, and reaching more open ground, begins to scent the perfumed breezes of Ârâsoor. By-and-bye a shout from the head of the line of march proclaims that the temple is in sight. Then, dismounting from their horses, or descending from their litters, the whole pilgrim band prostrate themselves upon the ground, and as they rise again, the hills re-echo with their cries of, "Conquer! Umbâ, Mother!"—"Victory to the illustrious Umbâ!"

The temple itself is small and much surpassed by many a less venerated fane; it is surrounded by a fortified wall, inclosing buildings occupied by the priests and servants of the Goddess, or tenanted by her pilgrim worshippers; it contains also a garrison, but that she may not be thought to owe the inviolability of her dwelling to any aid from an arm of flesh, Umbâ Mother has refused to permit the erection of an external door. It is Doorgâ, the daughter of Hemâchul and Meenâ, the consort of the mighty Shiva, who is worshipped in this shrine; not, as in her storm-rocked temple on the hill of Châmpâner, under the shape of the blood-delighting Kâlee, but rather in the milder and more mysterious form of an Isis or a Cybele, as Bhuwânee, the active expression of the self-existent principle, and as Umbâjee, the mother of Creation.

The Shrine of Ârâsoor lays claim to the most remote antiquity. Here, it is said, was offered in vicarious sacrifice the hair of the infant Shree Krishn, and here, in after days, his bride, Rookmunee, worshipped Devee, when he bore her from the threatened embrace of Shishoopâl. The threshold has been worn away by the feet of the pilgrims of many a century. The worshippers, when they are admitted to a sight of the idol, lay before it offerings of garments, money, or jewels. They present also, among other articles, cocoa-nuts, as vicarious offerings, instead of the lives of themselves or of their friends.[1]

[1] The reason why the cocoa-nut is constantly employed by Hindoos to represent a human being, is to be found in the strange story of Vishwâmitra. That saint, it is said, in imitation of Brumhâ's creative power, produced, himself, several sorts of grain—he also formed a cocoa-nut tree, and at length began to create men growing out of this tree, commencing with their heads. Brumhâ, fearful that his occupation of creating would be taken from him, worshipped the saint, who thereupon consented to desist, but, in commemoration of his exploit, permanently affixed the human heads to the tree, under the form of its fruit.

The most solemn worship is performed on the eighth night of the Nowrâttra, when the Rânâ of Dântâ, in person, celebrates fire-sacrifice before the Ârâsooree Mother, and fills with sweetmeats a large cauldron, which the wild Bheels of the mountain empty on a signal the Goddess gives, by letting fall from off her neck her garland of flowers. The same chief receives the pilgrim-tax and the duties levied for the protection of caravans. If a Thâkor arrives as a worshipper, the best horse in his suite must be presented to the Rânâ. He removes also the whole of the offerings which are made by the pilgrims during their stay at the shrine, and which consist of vestments, banners, vessels of the precious metals, bells, and other necessaries for the service of the temple. Seven silver clogs stand continually before the idol.[1]

Notwithstanding the more beneficent form in which the goddess here appears, she receives the sacrifice of animals which are slain before her image, and also offerings of spirituous liquors. The use of oil is forbidden in the service of the temple, nor may it be employed by a worshipper as long as his pilgrimage lasts. The lamps which illuminate the shrine, and those which are waved before the idol, are supplied with clarified butter. The Rânâ of Dântâ, when present at the evening worship, himself fans the goddess with a "châmur" of horse-hair, but the ordinary officiating priests are three in number—Owdich Brahmins of Sidhpoor, who farm their office, paying a revenue to the Rânâ. It is their duty to mark pilgrims with the châdlo on the forehead, at the commencement of the pilgrimage, and with a red hand, on the shoulder, at its termination; they are fee'd by the worshippers according to their means, and sometimes, it is said, refuse the indispensable mark of dismissal until their claims are satisfied.

In a temple to "the Invincible Mother," on the edge of a reservoir near the principal shrine, called Mânsurowur, is an inscription of the Muhâ Rânâ Shree Mâl Dev, dated Sumwut, 1415 (A.D. 1359.) At the door of the adytum of the temple of Umbâjee is a tablet, which records offerings made in Sumwut, 1601 (A.D. 1545), by the Rânee of Row Bârmul, of Eedur, probably on the death of her husband. There are several other inscriptions on the pillars of the temple, principally of the sixteenth century, recording the gifts of private individuals, and one dated in Sumwut, 1779 (A.D. 1723),

[1] The numbers three, five, and seven, are considered auspicious by the Hindoos, and particularly the two latter. They represent heaven, earth, and hell; the five elements; and the seven Sages.

when "the lord of the land, Râj Adheerâj Rânâjee, Shree one "hundred and eight times repeated, Shree Pruteesunghjee," was ruling, states, that a wâneeâ family built a dhurum-sâlâ, or house of accommodation for pilgrims, "for the sake of a son," and adds "by the kindness of Umbâ, the hope was fulfilled."

The Rows of Seerohee, whose territory approaches the shrine of Umbâjee, once held a share in its revenues, but subsequently resigned it, on the ground, it is said, that Gosâees alone can with credit receive the offerings made at a temple. A daughter of Dântâ was once married to a bridegroom of the house of Seerohee. She proceeded to the house of her father-in-law, dressed in a scarf, which, as ill luck would have it, had been presented to the goddess by one of her bridegroom's family. Her husband therefore declared that as she wore the mother's dress, he could henceforth regard her only as a mother to him. The lady was compelled to return home,

"Widowed wife and wedded maid;"

and, from that time, a rule was made that the daughters of Dântâ should abstain from the use of garments which had been offered to Umbâjee.

About two miles to the west of the temple of Umbâ Bhuwânee, is a hill upon which a fortress was formerly situated called Gubbur-gurh. The rocks there form themselves, when seen from a distance, into the semblance of a huge arched portal, a fact which, perhaps, gave rise to the legend that Mother Umbâjee keeps her state in the hollow of the hill. "At one time," it is said, "a cow belonging to "the Mâtâjee used to graze with the shepherds' cattle all day, and "return into the hill at night time. A cowherd wondered whose "the cow could be, and gradually came to the determination that "he would, at all risks, discover the owner, and claim from him his "fee. One evening, when the cow set off as usual homewards, the "cowherd followed, and with it entered the hill. He found himself "in the interior of a splendid palace, full of magnificent apartments. "In the principal hall the Mâtâjee herself appeared, reclining on a "swinging couch, and surrounded by numerous female attendants. "The cowherd, mustering up courage, approached her, and enquired "whether the cow was hers. She answered in the affirmative, and "the cowherd was encouraged to continue. He said that the "animal had been tended by him for twelve years, and that he had "now come for his fee. Mâtâ Umbâjee directed one of her "maidens to give him some of a heap of barley that lay upon the

" ground. The servant took up a winnowing fan full of the grain, " and presented it to the cowherd. He took it, and went out " disappointed and angry, and as he passed the threshold he threw " the barley from him. On reaching home, however, he discovered " some grains of the finest gold adhering to his dress. The cowherd " attempted next day to regain the entrance of the hill, but was " unable to discover it, nor did the Mâtâjee's cow ever again make " its appearance."

A more modern legend is attached to another hill hard by. " A few " years ago, a cultivator belonging to the Seerohee country went from " home to find a purchaser for a pair of bullocks. As he wandered " about a gosâee met with him, who said, 'If you will follow me, I " 'will enable you to dispose of your bullocks.' The cultivator " accordingly followed the ascetic, who led him, taking his bullocks " with him, into a cave in the side of the hill. After proceeding " onwards for some distance within the cave, they came at last to a " magnificent hall, with a large stable beside it, in which many " horses were stalled. There were many men at work there, too, " making armor for men and armor for horses, and weapons, guns, " and other warlike stores; there were also piles of cannon balls, and " heaps of musket bullets. The gosâee now asked the cultivator what " price he expected for his bullocks, and, having ascertained it, " brought the sum demanded from the hall, and gave it to him. " Then the cultivator asked, 'Whose mansion is this, and whose " stores are these, and who lives here?' The gosâee said, 'You shall " know of this two years hence. These stores are for war with the " English government.' The cultivator returned home, and made " known in his village what he had seen. Other people of the " village then, taking the cultivator with them, went to see the cave, " but it was nowhere to be found."[1]

[1] Traditions, similar to these, are to be met with in all countries. The Eniheriar dwell in Valhalla, and at the destruction of the world are, under the guidance of Odin, to come forth again in arms. King Arthur rests in the Isle of Avalon, awaiting his destined time for the overthrow of his enemies. Frederick Barbarossa sleeps in the Kiffhaüser, in Thuringia, until the hour of his deliverance strikes, and a better time ensues, which will be, it is said, when the ravens no longer fly round the mountain, and an old withered worn-out pear-tree on the Rüthsfeld again sends out shoots, and bears foliage and blossoms. In the Wunderberg, near Salzburg, dwells the great emperor, Charles V., with golden crown and sceptre, attended by knights and lords. His grey beard has twice encompassed the table at which he sits, and when it has the third time grown round it, the end of the world and the appearance of Antichrist will take place. The Jaloff inhabitants of the mainland of Africa, opposite the isle of Goree,

Near Umbâjee, beside a rivulet, and among natural shrubberies of wild jasmine and other scented flowers, is a little village founded by Koombho Rânâ, of Cheetor, and called after his name, Koombhâreea. Beside it are some handsome white marble temples of the Jain faith, constructed by Veemul Shâ. "The Mâtâ," as the legend relates, "gave much wealth to Veemul Shâ, and he constructed here "three hundred and sixty temples to Pârusnâth. The Mâtâjee "asked him by whose aid he had built them; he said, by the aid of "his spiritual preceptor. She repeated the same question thrice, "and each time received the same answer. She then said to him, "'Escape as quickly as you can.' The Shâ fled into the crypt "below one of the temples which is connected with the crypts of "those at Dailwârâ, and travelling by the subterranean passage,

believe in a species of beings called Yumboes, who resemble the Gothic fairies. Their chief abode is a subterraneous dwelling in the Paps, the hills about three miles from the coast. Here they dwell in great magnificence, and many wonderful stories are told of those persons, particularly Europeans, who have been received and entertained in the subterranean residence of the Yumboes; of how they were placed at richly furnished tables; how nothing but hands and feet were to be seen, which laid and removed the various dishes; of the numerous stories the underground abode consisted of; the modes of passing from one to the other without stairs, &c. &c. As to gifts made on such occasions, and rejected, compare the following story:—

"A dwarf came down one night from the chesnut woods on the side of the "mountain over the village of Walchwyl (in Switzerland), and enquired for the "house of a midwife, whom he earnestly pressed to come out, and go with him. "She consented, and the dwarf, bearing a light, led the way in silence to the "woods. He stopped at last before a cleft in the rock, at which they entered, "and the woman suddenly found herself in a magnificent hall. She was thence "led through several rich apartments to the chamber of state, where the queen "of the dwarfs, for whom her services were required, was lying. She performed "her office, and brought a fair young prince to the light. She was thanked, and "dismissed, and her former conductor appeared to lead her home. As he was "taking leave of her, he filled her apron with something, bidding her on no "account to look at it till she was in her own house. But the woman could not "control her curiosity, and the moment the dwarf disappeared, she partly opened "the apron, and lo! there was nothing in it but some black coals. In a rage she "shoke them out on the ground, but she kept two of them in her hands, as a "proof of the shabby treatment she had met with from the dwarfs. On reaching "home, she threw them also down on the ground. Her husband cried out with "joy and surprise, for they shone like carbuncles. She asserted that the dwarf "had put nothing but coals into her apron; but she ran out to call a neighbour, "who knew more of such things than they did, and he, on examining them, "pronounced them to be precious stones of very great value. The woman "immediately ran back to where she had shaken out the supposed coals, but they "were all gone."—*Vide* "Keightley's Fairy Mythology," "Thorpe's Northern "Mythology," &c.

" emerged upon Mount Aboo. Then the Mâtâjee consumed all the " temples by fire, with the exception of five, which she left as " witnesses to the tale, and the calcined stones of those which were " destroyed may still be seen strewed over the ground." This legend probably contains a certain amount of truth, in as far as it relates the destruction of temples founded on the spot by Veemul Shâ, through a volcanic agency which has evidently at some time or other been very active throughout the hills of Ârâsoor. The Shâ himself seems to have fully believed that his loss was occasioned by the vengeance of Shree Umbâjee, for the inscription on the temple which he subsequently founded at Dailwârâ, of Aboo, contains the following stanzas in propitiation of that goddess :—

" IX. Thou whose leaf-like hands are red as the leaves of the " Ushok tree, thou who appearest in resplendent beauty, borne in a " carriage drawn by Keshree-Singhs, thou who bearest two children " in thy lap, such in person, Sutee Umbeekâ, destroy the calamities " of virtuous men!

" X. Once on a time to that viceroy at night-time, Umbeekâ the " wise, gave this order—' Upon this mountain do you erect a good " temple for Yoogâdee Nâth, a place pure from sin.'

" XI. When one thousand and eighty-eight autumns had passed " since the time of Shree Vikrumâdit (A.D. 1032) on Urbood's " summit, Shree Âdee Dev was by Shree Veemul seated. Him I " worship."

Among more modern inscriptions in the temple of Nemeenâth, at Koombhâreea, occurs one, dated Sumwut, 1305 (A.D. 1249), recording additions to the edifice made by Brumh Dev, the son of Châhud, the minister of Koomâr Pâl Solunkhee, who, as is here mentioned, " at " the village of Pâdpurâ, caused to be erected the temple called Oon- " deer Wusâheekâ." [1]

On a pâleeyo close by is another interesting record, dated Sumwut, 1256 (A.D. 1200), which states, that " Shree Dhârâwursh Dev, the lord " of Urbood, the thorn to all Munduleeks upon whom the sun shines," constructed a well " in this city of Ârâsanâpoor."

From these particulars, relating to the shrine of their patron goddess, we now turn to the story of the race of Rânâ Wâgh, the Purmârs, of Dântâ, and Tursunghmo.

[1] Or " the Rat's temple." It is mentioned in the Prubundh Chintâmunee, that Koomâr Pâl caused a temple of this name to be constructed in commemoration of the injury he had inflicted on a rat, by taking away its pieces of silver. *Vide* p. 139.

Ruvpâljee Purmâr was the fortieth in descent from Vikrum. He went on a pilgrimage to Dwârkâ, and thence was on his way to Kutch. He had a vow neither to eat nor drink without having first worshipped Mâtâ Umbeekâ, on which account she was pleased, and permitted him to behold her, and promised to grant whatever boon he might ask. He asked for the throne of Nugger Tatta and the rule over Sindh, which the goddess granted to him; and he erected three royal seats, at Nuggur Tatta, Bâmunoowâ, and Belâ. Twelfth in descent from Ruvpâljee was Dâmojee, who, having no Koonwur, made vows to Umbâjee for the purpose of obtaining one. The goddess drew blood from her own finger, and, with this and dust from her body, produced a prince, to whom she ordered the name of Jus Râj to be given. She also declared that she had created him that he might protect the place where she was worshipped. Nuggur Tatta was in in this reign invaded by the Mohummedans, who, after a struggle of nine years' duration, took the city, and slew Raja Dâmojee. Koonwur Jus Râj, however, continued the contest, and recovered the city.

Raja Jus Râj, also, was a devoted servant of Umbâjee, and received great strength from the goddess. In his reign, however, the Mohummedans again returned, and, making wells with the bones of animals, and perpetrating other Mlechisms, so polluted the land, that Umbâjee said to Raja Jus Râj, "I have no pleasure in remaining here any "longer; I will retire to my dwelling which is at Ârâsoor." The raja said, "I am your servant, wherever you go I will follow." She listened to his prayer, and said, "It is well! Come with me, and I "will give you the throne of that country." So saying, she vanished. Jus Râj after this again engaged the Mohummedans, but was defeated, and lost Nuggur Tatta. He then, taking his family with him, went to the Mâtâjee, at Ârâsoor. Umbâjee gave him the tiger upon which she rides, and said to him, "Seat yourself upon this tiger, and "make a circuit—whatever territory you encircle shall be yours." The raja did so, and made the circuit of seven hundred and sixty villages. On the south he included the Doturso Puttâ, as far as Kherâloo; on the north-east the territory up to Koturâ; on the east as far as Derol; on the north the country up to the Bhârjâ's well, which is in the lands of Seerohee; on the south-east he went as far as Gudwârâ; on the north-west as far as the village of Hâtheedurâ. He found buried treasure in the Bhundhâro hill, which people now called "Gubbur," with which he raised an army, and went to Nuggur Tatta to take revenge for his father. Jus Râj drove the Mohummedans out of the city, and slew many of them; he remained in that country until his death, but his Koonwur was all this time at Gubbur-gurh with the Mâtâjee.

Jus Râj's son, Kedâr Singh, or Keshree Singh, fought with Tursungeeâ Bheel, who reigned at Tursunghmo, and, having slain him, removed to that place his royal seat, which had been before at Gubbur-gurh. Kedâr Singh's son was named Juspâl, or Koolpâl. He attempted to perform a great sacrifice at Rorâ village, but the attempt failed, and the Brahmin who was employed was so mortified that he threw himself into the fire pit, and perished, having laid a curse upon the race of Juspâl, that they should have no power of providing for the future, but should always lose their opportunity, and then repent.[1] Several generations after this, in the time of Rânâ Jugut Pâl, the army of Allah-ood-deen Khoonee took Tursunghmo. The Rânâ went and entreated the Mâtâjee's assistance, who told him to fight again the next day; he did so, and won Tursunghmo back again. Sixth in descent from Jugut Pâl was Kânur Dev, whose brother, Âmbojee, seized upon the puttâ of Koturâ. Kânur Dev had two Rânees; to one of them, Râm Koonwuree, a Jhâleejee of Hulwud, the Doturso, or Kherâloo puttâ, was assigned for her subsistence. The Rânee lived there with her Koonwur Meghjee, and built the eastern door of Kherâloo, and a well and tank, which are to this day known as "the "Jhâlees." The second wife was Rutun Koonwuree, a Seesodunee, of Oodeipoor, who founded Rohilpoor Puttun, now called Rorâ. The raja went to Oodeipoor to be married a third time to the Rânee Lâl Koonwuree Seesodunee. As he returned with her, his brother, Âmbojee, of Koturâ, was anxious to entertain the bridal party, but Kânur Dev was not inclined to stay. Then Âmbojee spoke humbly to Rânee Lâl Koonwuree, and said, "There has been a quarrel between us "two brothers about the puttâ; if this be not reconciled now that you "are come, when shall it be reconciled?" The Rânee then persuaded her husband, and it was agreed that they should stay there. When the time for dinner came, the two brothers sat down to dine together. Suddenly Âmbojee got up, and, striking Kânur Dev a blow on the head with his sword, ran upstairs. Kânur Dev rushed after him, and, catching him by his dress, gave him twenty-one wounds with his dagger, so that he died. Thus both brothers were slain. The newly-married Rânee became a sutee in the same place, and a funeral pavilion was built over her remains. The Jhâlee Rânee also became a sutee at her father's house at Hulwud.

When Rânâ Kânur Dev set out for Oodeipoor, his two sons,

[1] The present Rânâ Jhâlum Singh makes the following comment upon this story:—"Yes! that curse remained in force up to the time of my uncle Jugut "Singh."

Meghjee and Wâghjee, were left with their mother's family at Hulwud, while Tursunghmo was entrusted to a Khuwâs of the Rânâ's, named Mâroo Râwut. The Row Bhân of Eedur had married the daughter of Âmbojee, and when he heard of the death of the two brothers, he collected a force, and went to Tursunghmo, which he took, and seizing Mâroo Râwut, carried him to Eedur. The Row left a garrison at Tursunghmo. Opposite to the palace at Eedur there is a prison, into which the Row thrust Mâroo Râwut, and every day he used to amuse himself, by sitting at the window, and ridiculing him in every possible way. At last the Khuwâs made answer, "Row, you have "seized upon the principality, because the Koonwurs are infants, but "do not suppose that there is no one to help. A tiger even, when "he's caged, can do nothing; but if you were to let me out, I would "cause this palace of yours to be dug up, and thrown into the Rorâ "Hurnâv river." The Row was enraged when he heard this, and cried to the guard, "Turn that dog out!" However, the Row's Rânee, Âmbojee's daughter, knew of the exploits that Mâroo Râwut had performed, so she would not permit that he should be let out of the prison. Another day, when she was not present, the Row released him. He remained two days at Kulnâth Muhâ Dev's, and then went to Hulwud. As he sat beside a tank, a Wudhârun, or female slave, of the Rânee Jhâlee's suite, came there for water, through whom he made his story known. The raja sent for him, and soon afterwards Mâroo Râwut, with the two Koonwurs and a large sum of money, were on their way to Ahmedabad. Mâroo first saw the padishah's minister, and arranged matters with him; then he took the two Koonwurs, one on each hip, and, with a brazier of lighted coals on his head, went to make his complaint to the padishah. When the padishah saw him, he said, "The children will be burned, put them down." Both the Koonwurs then cried out with a loud voice, "Sahib! when we have "got down where shall we stand? The Eedur Row has seized posses- "sion of our ground, and this is the padishah's ground; if we get down "upon it, we shall make an enemy of him." The padishah told them to take courage, and having caused them to be set down, and made himself acquainted with their story, was pleased to send an army against Eedur, on the agreement that the Koonwurs should pay him ten thousand pounds as an offering. The army advanced, and encamped near Eedur. Row Bhân then said to the leader of the army, "I am ready to pay the padishah whatever offering these Tur- "sunghmo people have agreed to pay; so do you take your army "back again." But the Mohummedan said, "I have the padishah's "orders, and must act up to them." Row Bhân upon this fled with his family, and the army struck Eedur, and cast the Row's palace down to the ground. Then Mâroo Râwut said, "I will give a gold "mohur to every one who will take a stone from hence, and throw it "into the Hurnâv." Many of the soldiers, therefore, took stones and piled them beside the Hurnâv, and with these was built the temple of Shâmlâjee, which is upon the banks of the river, near the village of Gudhâ. From thence the army went on to Tursunghmo; the Eedur garrison abandoned the place and fled, and it was restored to a prosperous state, and made over to the Koonwur. Then the leader of the army said to Mâroo Râwut, "Now produce the money which "you promised." Mâroo answered, "I have no money here, my "treasure is in the hills of Soodâsunâ: if you will come thither, I will "pay you the money." So saying, he put the Koonwurs under the care of Mâtâ Umbâjee, and set out himself with the army. He caused the army to encamp at the Wursungh tank, which is between Tembâ and Bhâtwâs, in Gudwârâ; he then said, "I will go and get "out the treasure, and bring it." So saying, he went into the Soodâsunâ hills, and there lay concealed. The Mohummedans for a day or two waited for him, but as he did not come they set out to look for him. However, they could not find him. At length he sent to the commander of the army, and said, "If you will give me a "hostage, I will come in and settle the matter with you." Having received a hostage, the Râwut came into the encampment, and said, "I have not got the money, but here is this Kherâloo district, I will "mortgage it to the padishah, and whenever I can pay the money the "district shall be released." Thus saying, he passed a deed of mortgage for the Kherâloo district, but retained "wântâ" lands in several villages.

In the time of Âskurunjee Rânâ, one of Akbar's shahzâdas fled from Delhi, having committed some offence. He went to Oodeipoor, Jeipoor, and other places in Râjwârâ; but found no one to shelter him. At last he came to Tursunghmo. Âskurunjee offered him shelter, and he remained there, and built a fortress upon the hill called Kâlwân, which is north of Tursunghmo about three miles. One day, when the shahzâda was very much pleased with the Rânâ, he began to give him his ring, which was of great value, and set with precious stones; but the Rânâ said, "I will not take it now, when "your highness's affairs are arranged, and you go hence in peace, I "will receive whatever you may choose to offer." His servants, however, told the Rânâ that he had made a mistake, for that princes' minds were not always the same, and that he should have taken the opportunity while he had it. Then the Rânâ recollected the Brahmin's curse upon his ancestor—that the lords of Tursunghmo should never have a provident mind. Next day he went to the shahzâda, and said, "Will your highness give me the ring which you were going to give "me?" but the prince replied, "When I am going I will give it." However, he went away to the west without giving it, and Bârmul Row, of Bhooj, seized him, and sent him to the padishah, at Delhi; for which service Row Bârmul got the Moorbee district.[1] Afterwards, when the padishah and the shahzâda were on good terms again, the padishah asked him who they were that had given him shelter, and who that had entertained him hospitably. He said, "Âskurunjee, of Tursunghmo, was the only one who sheltered me or "treated me with hospitality." The padishah, when he heard this, sent Âskurunjee a dress of honor, and the title of Muhâ Rânâ. The shahzâda also sent the before-mentioned ring, which was set with diamonds worth a large sum of money. Âskurunjee left three sons—Wâgh, Jeimul, and Pertâp Singh.

In the time of Rânâ Wâgh, the two Rânees of Row Kuleeân Mul, of Eedur, (that is to say), Bhânwuntee, of Oodeipoor, and Veenuyâmuntee Jhârejee, of Bhooj, used to come every Monday to worship at the temple of Muhâ Dev, at Brumh Kheir.[2] That place is called Bhrigoo-kshetra; the Hurnâv river is there, and Rânâ Wâgh claimed it as his boundary line—as the couplet says—

"I am Rânâ Wâgh,
"And up to the Hurnâv is my bhâg."

Some one told Rânâ Wâgh that the Eedur Row's Rânees were very beautiful, and so he determined he would see them. He dressed himself like a Brahmin, and went with the Brahmins, one Monday, to Bhrigoo-kshetra. The Rânees, after worshipping Muhâ Dev, made marks on the Brahmins' foreheads, and gave them alms. Among the rest, they marked Rânâ Wâgh, and offered him alms, which he refused to receive. They asked him what was the reason for his refusal. He said he had taken a vow at Benares that he would not receive alms from any one. The Rânees went away, and the Rânâ also returned; but the matter came to the knowledge of Row Kuleeân Mul. The Row then entered into an alliance with Jeimul, Rânâ Wâgh's brother, whom he kept with him at Eedur. He also enter-

[1] This is probably an incorrect allusion to the story related at page 302. The "shahzada" would then be Sultan Moozuffer III., of Ahmedabad.

[2] The account here given is the Dântâ version of the story, as that given at p. 320 is the Eedur version of it. Each has been translated literally.

tained Vegurno Jemâdâr, a Nâgur Brahmin, who had lost caste, and become a Mohummedan; but had quarrelled with the padishah, and leaving Ahmedabad, had come to Eedur. The Row promised to entrust to this officer the village of Wurâlee, if he would seize Rânâ Wâgh, and give him up to him. Vegurno agreeing, went to take charge of Wurâlee, and laid himself out to be the best of friends with Rânâ Wâgh. Once on a time the Jemâdâr invited Rânâ Wâgh to drink opium with him at the ford of Lânk, on the Sâbhermutee. The Rânâ went there, taking two horsemen with him. Munjee Wâchâwut, Thâkor of Deepuree, one of the Rânâ's sirdârs, thought with himself, that the Rânâ setting out alone that day, would surely be made prisoner, so he went to remonstrate with him. The sage's curse, however, lay on the family, so the Rânâ could not see beforehand, to provide against the danger. He not only persisted in going, but desired Munjee Wâchâwut not to accompany him. The Thâkor, however, was so impressed with the danger, that he followed him at a distance. Rânâ Wâgh reached the ford of Lânk, and feasted with Vegurno and drank liquor. After that, Vegurno's men seized him; one of his followers was slain, and the other escaped. Munjee Thâkor came to the rescue, and killed one or two men with his spear, but was then slain. The Jemâdâr carried the Rânâ to Wurâlee, and threw him into prison, and wrote off to the Row to say, "I have seized "Rânâ Wâgh, do you, therefore, confine his brother Jeimul." When the Row received the letter, he was playing at draughts with Jeimul in an upper room; and below, at the foot of the stairs, a Rajpoot named Sâloo Bhoot, Thâkor of Châmpoo and Khâpurethâ, was seated. The messenger, going to him, said, "Where is the Row? I have brought "this letter from Wurâlee." The Thâkor said, "What is the letter "about? you need not fear to tell me, for I am one of the Row's servants." The messenger said, "The letter is about the capture of "Rânâ Wâgh." Then Sâloo Bhoot said, "The Row is lying down, sit "you here till I go and take a look. If he be awake, I will call you; "but if he be asleep, and you wake him by talking too suddenly, he "will be angry." So saying, he made him sit down, and going up stairs, stood behind the Row and in front of Jeimul, and drawing a knife across his throat, made signs to the latter that the Row would take off his head. Jeimul, not understanding this signal, the Thâkor made signs to him to come down stairs. Then Jeimul understood, and, making a pretence for his absence, went below. Sâloo Bhoot told him what had happened; and he went home to his lodging, and, mounting his horse, gallopped off, northwards, towards Bâleshee (Mhow). He kept his horse at full speed for twenty miles, so that when he reached the gate of the village of Âkordeeâ, the horse dropped. Jeimul went into the village on foot, and took shelter with a Chârun, named Wurjâng Bâdooâ. Wurjâng's son, Sudhoojee, asked what had happened, and who he was. Jeimuljee said, "The "Row's men are pursuing me; therefore, if you can protect me, do "so; if not, forward me on to some distant place." The Chârun said, "I will protect you with my head; but though I die, the Row "will not quit you. Do you, therefore, take the better of these two "mares, and make your escape; and when you get back to your "country think of me." Then Jeimul took the mare, Keshur, and fled, and got safe to Kherâloo.

Now the Row, having received the letter from the messenger, and read it, sent in pursuit of Jeimul. When the pursuers got to Âkordeeâ, and saw the horse lying dead, they felt sure that the fugitive was in the village. They went to the Chârun's house, and made great uproar there, saying, "Give up our thief to us." The Chârun said, "He has deceived me and fled, taking my mare with "him. I don't know who he is." The pursuers went after him to the distance of twenty or five-and-twenty miles, and then returned to Eedur.

Jeimul assembled men in the Kherâloo district, and went to Tursunghmo, of which he took possession, and began to collect stores there. Meanwhile Row Kuleeân Mul came thither with an army. A battle took place, and the Row, being unsuccessful, returned to Eedur. The dispute with the Row lasted a long time. There were in the Rânâ's service two brothers, Mehepo and Râjdhur, Thâkors of Muhâwud, and the Koolee Thâkor of Wujâsunâ, named Depo, who had eighty men. This Depo asked permission to make an attack upon Eedur, which was granted him. He placed his followers in little hamlets in the Eedur country, and went himself, with two or three men, to Eedur. At this time some actors were playing before the Row, in his court. The Thâkor went, and sat down among the lookers on, and ascertained that the Row's brother, Keshuvdâs, was present. The daughter of this Keshuvdâs was throwing pebbles, from the window, at Rânâ Wâgh, and when they struck him on the head he uttered something like a cry, upon which all present, actors and spectators, laughed. The Rânâ Wâgh said, "I "shall never be at peace in another world unless my heir, whoever "he be, cause this woman to weep." Depo Thâkor was very much grieved when he saw the Rânâ suffering such affliction. Now when the play was finished, they brought the plate round; then Depo took the gold armlet off his arm, and threw it in. The actors said, "Who "is it that gives this, whose fame shall we celebrate?" but Depo made no answer. Then the by-standers said, "Some drunken fellow "has given it; but what business is that of yours, the Supreme Being "has given it to you." Afterwards they brought round the plate again; then the Thâkor gave the other armlet. It was now midnight. At this time the Row's brother, Keshuvdâs, went out. Depo followed him, and struck the torch out of the hand of the torch-bearer who was with him. He then stabbed Keshuvdâs, and, cutting off his head, made his escape with it. Then there arose a cry of "The Row's brother has been murdered! The Row's brother has been murdered!" The girl before-mentioned now began to weep, and beat her breast; and Rânâ Wâgh, when he heard this, immediately killed himself. As long as the Rânâ was alive, the Row used daily to say to him, "If you will pass a deed assigning some of your "villages to me, I will release you;" but the Rânâ would never agree to this, and only answered—

"I am Rânâ Wâgh,
"And up to the Hurnâv is my bhâg."

Now, Depo, as soon as he had got clear off, set fire to a hill, upon which his men, posted in different places, directly they saw the glare, set fire also to the villages they were in.

Afterwards, Depo came to Tursunghmo, and having made obeisance to Jeimul, said, "Umbâjee Mâtâ has preserved my honor." Jeimul gave him the village of Bheemâl. Depo's descendants are still to be found at Wujâsunâ, in the position of cultivators. Rânâ Jugut Singh took back the village of Bheemâl from the family, but left them a fourth share of it, which they still hold.

The Row sent for the Chârun, Bâdooâ Sudhoojee, and said, "You "caused my thief to escape, therefore you shall not remain in my "country." When Rânâ Jeimul heard of this, he sent for that Chârun to Tursunghmo, gave him the village of Pâneeâlee, and, making him his family-bard, kept him near himself.[1]

Now the two Gudheeâs, Mehepo and Râjdhur, who were in the service of Rânâ Jeimul, asked for a few days' leave, and set off homewards. Meanwhile they came to the river, at the gate of the village of Gothurâ, when a shepherd came out with some goats. They asked him whose the goats were; he answered that they belonged to the Rânâ. They said, "We belong to the Rânâ, too, so give us one of the goats." The shepherd refusing, they took one by force, and

[1] The Chârun from whom this account was derived is a descendant of Sudhoojee's, and holds a sixteenth share of the village of Pâneeâlee.

killed it. Then he went to Tursunghmo, and complained to the Rânâ, that the Gudheeâs, though warned not to do so, had taken one of the goats by force, and killed it. The Rânâ when he heard this said, "These people are getting very proud, they must be looked "after." Some friend of theirs wrote this information to the Gudheeâs, and told them that if they came back without making a thorough arrangement they would be put to death. Upon this the Gudheeâs remained six months at home idle; at the end of this time the Rânâ summoned them. They said they had not confidence in the Rânâ, but that they would come if they received Bâdooâ Sudhoojee's security. The servant came back with this message, upon which the Rânâ called his minister, and assembled his sirdârs, upon whose advice he sent off a letter giving Sudhoojee's security unknown to the Chârun. When they read this letter, the Gudheeâs, Mehepo and Râjdhur, came to Tursunghmo, and put up at a garden at the gate of the town, preparatory to presenting themselves to the Rânâ. Then Bâdooâ Sudhoojee went to pay them a visit, in the course of which he observed, "It is a very good thing that you, master and "servants, are at one again." They said, "Yes, but it was only on "receiving your letter of security that we came." Sudhoojee answered that he knew not a word of any security; upon which they showed him the letter. He repeated that he knew nothing of the matter, and said that they had better determine upon what they were to do at once. The two brothers then made up a plan between them, and the younger soon after set off, pretending that he had quarrelled with the elder. All the people then surrounded the elder brother, and said that he should go, and make up with his brother, and bring him back. Mehepo accordingly mounted his horse, and set off under pretence of bringing Râjdhur back again; and when they came together, they shook their horses' reins, and galloped off to Muhâwud. When the Rânâ heard that the Gudheeâs had gone back again, he asked what was the reason. Then the people told him that there had been a quarrel between them, and that one had gone away angered, upon which the other had followed him to bring him round. The Rânâ, however, thought within himself that some one must certainly have told them. He asked the Guduwee whether he had gone to visit them, and whether he was the person who had commenced the subject, or whether another had done so. Now there was a Koolee, named Wâleeo, a servant of the Gudheeâs, who was given to opium, and who used to live about the Rânâ's presence, and make leaf-plates. The Chârun said that it was probably Wâleeo who had told them, and that they had therefore made off in alarm. Then the Rânâ threatened this Koolee very much, and turned him out, and he too went to Muhâwud. Afterwards Bâdooâ Sudhoojee said to the Rânâ, " Well done, Thâkor ! you caused me to quarrel with the Eedur " Row, and brought me here, and then you laid a plot to take away " my character, by secretly sending security in my name, and bringing " the Gudheeâs here. Now, I am not going to remain any longer in " your country." He then went off in anger, and the Thâkors, Mehepo and Râjdhur, having secretly invited him, he, too, went to Muhâwud. Then the Thâkors were considering about giving the Guduwee a village, but meanwhile the Rânâ got information of the matter, and he sent to make friends with the Guduwee, and induced him to return, and replaced him at Pâneeâlee.

Now, the Eedur army came against Tursunghmo, and a battle was fought, and many on both sides were slain. At length the army turned homewards. At this time they seized a Nâgur of Tursunghmo, whom they took to Row Kuleeân Mul. The Row ordered that his nose should be cut off. Then the Nâgur said, " It is well ! it will be known " then that I was with Kuleeân Mul's army." The Row asked what was meant ; the Nâgur answered, " When you have cut off my nose, " having taken me alone, it will be as if your whole army had lost its " nose." The Row turned him out without maiming him.

As the army turned back a Koonbee woman was going along with her husband's dinner. The Row saw her, and, as he was hungry, he said, " What have you there ? " She answered that it was rice-pottage, He took it and began to eat, but, as the pottage was hot, his fingers were burnt. The woman said, " Why, you're as bad as Kuleeân Mul." The Row asked how that was. She said, " The Row, instead of " taking possession of the outlying villages, attempts to take Tur- " sunghmo itself, a thing which he cannot accomplish in ten years. " So you, instead of beginning upon the pottage round the edges, " which has become cooled, must needs thrust your fingers into the " middle and get them burnt." The Row thought, " What she says " is true ; I have found my tutor ! " He sent for the Gudheeâs to his camp, and asked them to take the direction of the army. They said, " We have eaten the Rânâ's salt, and drunk water from his wells " for many a day. You must permit us to make one attempt to bring " him to terms, and, if he will not listen, we will do as you desire." Mehepo then went to Tursunghmo, and said, " Cut away these sacred " fig-trees that overhang the fort of Tursunghmo, otherwise the enemy " will climb the trees, and fire from them into your palace." The Rânâ said, " Who is there strong enough to come as far as this ? " Besides, to cut down a peepul-tree, and to murder a Brahmin, these "two sins are equally abominable;[1] therefore, I will not cut one." When the Gudheeâ pressed very much, the Rânâ said, "Go! do you "too, climb up with them, I care not for you." Then the Gudheeâ returned to the Row's camp, and said, "The Rânâ refuses to listen." They divided the army into three divisions, of which the Gudheeâs each of them led one, the Row commanding the third. They advanced upon Tursunghmo by different roads and invested it, and, climbing the surrounding heights, descended into the town. Then the Rânâ, taking his family with him, fled to Dântâ. The following are the principal sirdârs on the Rânâ's part, who came to use in this war:—Khet, Mehedâs, Pârkhân, Pertâp, Gopâl Singh, and Veerbhân. Jugmâl, one of the Rânâ's chiefs, slew Shenkhân, a sirdâr of Eedur.

The Rânâ Jeimul and Koonwur Jetmâl, having retired to Dântâ, were followed thither by their enemies, upon which they took shelter at the Mâtâjee's, and went out against the Row. Kuleeân Mul left posts at every village, and returned to Eedur. At Tursunghmo, Mâlâ Dâbhee commanded the post; at Surrâ, the Rehwurs; at Thânâ, Meghâ Jâduv. Rânâ Jeimul lost all his men and horses by degrees, and at last died.

After his father's death, Koonwur Jetmâl sat at the Mâtâjee's gate, and fasted for many days without procuring any sign from the Mâtâjee. At last he made preparations for performing the "lotus worship." Then the Mâtâjee seized his hand, and said, "Mount your horse, and "set forth; I will be your helper. Whatever land you shall pass "round in this day's ride shall be yours, and where you draw rein "your territory shall cease." Then Jetmâl, with the few horsemen he had left, mounted, and set off. They came first to the post of the Rehwurs, who, perceiving the approach of an immense cloud of horsemen, took to flight, leaving their horses and baggage. The next post they came to was Meghâ Jâduv's. Here, by the Mâtâjee's aid, the enemy saw a horseman in every bush on the hill-side, so they fled in dismay; Meghâ, who was engaged in washing his horse, was taken by surprise and slain. They went on to Tursunghmo, and drove away the post from thence; next they cleared Ghorâd and Hurâd of the enemy. Then Rânâ Jetmâl was wearied, and prepared to dismount; the other Rajpoots entreated him to forbear, but he answered

[1] In the Bhugwut Geetâ, Krishn declares that he is represented by the following:—

"Among trees, the sacred fig;
"Among holy sages, Nârd;
"Among Gundhurvs, Chitrâruth;
"Among Siddhs, Kupeelâ Moonee."

that he could sit his horse no longer. He dismounted, and the Mâtâjee's gift was at an end. After this, Tursunghmo lay desolate, and the royal seat was removed to Dântâ; which town derived its name from Dântoreeo Veer, whose shrine is situated two miles to the west of it, on the road to Nowâwâs, where the people make offerings of horses formed of clay. Soon after, Rânâ Jetmâl died.

CHAPTER X.

EEDUR.

On the death of Row Kuleeân Mul, of Eedur, his son Row Jugunnâth assumed the cushion. During the reign of Kuleeân Mul two parties had been formed amongst the Eedur ministers; the one consisted of the Desâee zumeendârs, of Wusâee, Mondeytee and Kureeâduroo, who were supported by the Wâghela Thâkors of Poseenâ, and the Derol sirdârs; the other was composed of Ghureebdâs, the Rehwur Thâkor, of Runâsun, the chiefs of the Mohummedan Kusbâtees, of Eedur, and Moteechund Shâ Muzmoondâr, of Wurâlee. In these times the Mohummedans began to send armies to levy the tribute of Eedur with more regularity, and Vetâl Bhârot, of Baroda, who bore the title of Row, was security to the emperor for the Râthor princes. The imperial tribute was levied through the Governor of Ahmedabad. No annual payment was yet established, but every five or ten years, when the governor found himself in sufficient strength, he sent an army, and effected a levy. After the accession of Row Jugunnâth, however, the Mohummedan power increased every day, and the Eedur tribute became, by degrees, an annual levy—Vetâl Bhârot being still the go-between. The Bhârot at length became so large a creditor of Row Jugunnâth's, that that prince resolved to get rid of him. For this purpose he sent a female slave to his lodging, and, exciting against him a false accusation of fornication, expelled him from the town. The Bhârot retired to Baroda, and subsequently went to Delhi, as will be seen in the sequel.

Row Jugunnâth[1] had, after this, a quarrel about precedence with the Seesodeea Râwul, of Doongurpoor, whose name was Poonjâ. About the year A.D. 1650, they met at the temple of Shâmlâjee, which

[1] There is an inscription of Row Jugunnâth's on a well at Eedur, dated A.D. 1646.

is on the boundary of their dominions. On this occasion Râwul Poonjâ's handkerchief happening to fall to the ground, the Row, who was junior to the Râwul, took it up, and presented it to him. It was then pronounced that the Râwul had forced the Row to touch his feet. In this matter Mohundâs Rehwur, Thâkor of Mohunpoor, did good service, for he attacked Doongurpoor, made the Râwul prisoner, and kept him in confinement until he compelled him to make submission to the Row, upon which he dismissed him with presents. It was at the time of worship that the Râwul was seized, and the image he used was taken by the Thâkor, and is now at Mohunpoor. Upon this, the bards have the following verses :—

" Poonjâ he forced to submit,
" Did the Eedur Row ;
" Jugunnâth performed a deed of strength,
" He inflicted great disgrace.
" The Row imprisoned the Râwul,
" He exalted the honor of the line of Kumdhuj,
" With his sword subduing the Lord of Powan-gurh.
" The honor of Doongurpoor was lost,
" The Râwul trembled with fear,
" Taking the Seesodeea by the hand,
" Jugunnâth caused him to touch his feet."

One day, while Row Jugunnâth was at Morâsâ, a physician came thither from Delhi, who gave him medicine to restore virility, telling him not to use it until he rejoined the Rânee. When Jugunnâth arrived within a few miles of Eedur, he took the medicine, which had nearly been the cause of his death. He escaped, however, but from that time forth was never able to stand upright.

Now Vetâl Bhârot, having gone to Delhi, presented to the padishah, as an offering, a gold dish filled with water, and containing the leaf of a mango tree, a piece of sugar cane, a leaf of a khâkuro tree with a representation of a squirrel upon it, which held in its mouth a piece of sugar. The padishah, enquiring the meaning of this gift, the Bhârot made answer,—" There is a country which is like a gold " dish, where there is plenty of water, and where mango trees and " sugar cane flourish, but the animal that dwells among the khâkuro " trees[1] eats the sugar. If your majesty will give me five hundred " horse I will bring this country into subjection to you." The padishah, upon this, sent orders to the Shahzâda Morâd, who was then governor of Ahmedabad, and commanded him to assist Vetâl Bhârot

[1] An allusion to the Khâkuro jungle, which then surrounded, and formed one of the defences of Eedur.

with five thousand horse. There was at this time at Delhi, a vukeel, or agent, on the part of the Row Jugunnâth, who sent off an express to say that an army, under Vetâl Bhârot, was ordered to advance against Eedur. The Row had by this time forgotten his ill-treatment of the Bhârot, and he therefore wrote to him in a friendly manner, to say that he had perfect confidence in him, and to enquire whether the force were indeed directed against Eedur. Vetâl Bhârot returned answer, that the Row need feel no alarm; but the army under Prince Morâd nevertheless advanced, and Eedur was taken without a blow being struck.

> " In Sumwut seventeen hundred and twelve (A.D. 1656),
> " On the third of the month, on Sunday,
> " In the month of Âsho, in the light half of the month,
> " The Shahzâda Morâd came to take Eedur.
> " To fight against him, Jugunnâth prepared,
> " Treacherously the Bhât prevented him from fighting,
> " Treacherously did Vetâl expel the Row;
> " But when Poonj Râj was slain, then it was that the
> " Mohummedan took Eedur-gurh."

The last line is an allusion to Row Jugunnâth's son, Poonjâ, who " went out " against the Mohummedans. Indeed, as long as he lived they could not call Eedur their own.

> " Poonjâ slew many a Puthân,
> " His force to Eedur leading,
> " Night and day the Puthânees shed tears for their lords,
> " For Poonjâjee struck down the base ones in the field.
> " Those whom Poonjâ struck needed no physician.
> " When in the field the Kumdhuj warrior fights,
> " How can I retain any confidence in my bracelets?
> " Thus cried the Mogulânees, losing all hope,
> " Alas! alas! no one's lord will return."

Row Jugunnâth retired to Pol after his expulsion from Eedur, and died there soon afterwards.[1]

Morâd Shah having taken Eedur, continued the ministers in the management of affairs, and having placed a Mohummedan officer,

[1] There is a ballad account of this Row, which thus commences:—

> " Jugunnâth Row, you sunk your house,
> " Base son of Kuleeân!"

The bard, who began to recite it to us, however, had no sooner repeated the above two lines, than his arms, which had been raised for gesticulation, fell to his sides, his head sank upon his bosom, the tears started to his eyes; he murmured, " Why should I speak ill of the Rowjee!" and, neither at that nor at any future time, could be persuaded to resume his tale.

named Syud Hâtho, in command, returned home. Syud Hâtho commenced his government by resuming all the grants (shâsuns) which had been made by the Rows; and the Bhâts and Châruns thereupon deserted their villages, and took refuge with the Thâkor of Mâlpoor, by whom they were protected.

The following is a further account, given by the bards, of Poonjâ, the son of Jugunnâth:—

Poonjâ, being a minor, proceeded to Delhi to receive investiture. The Jeipoor Raja, remembering the old feud of the time of his great uncle, Veerum Dev, was unwilling that Poonjâ should be invested, and accordingly persuaded the padishah that the young Row of Eedur was very turbulently disposed, and that his present minority would be a good opportunity for seizing upon the principality. The padishah asked how he could be satisfied that the young Row was turbulently disposed. The raja advised that he should ask for a handsome horse, which the Row possessed, and remarked that if this were given up, Poonjâ would be proved to be loyal, but if not, that it would clearly appear he meditated treachery. The padishah accordingly sent to demand the horse, but the Jeipoor Raja had meanwhile persuaded Row Poonjâ that the padishah intended a disrespect, and had indeed determined to destroy him, and that it would be better for Poonjâ to return home at once. The Row, therefore, fled. He was pursued by the padishah's troops, and surrounded at a village twenty-five miles from Delhi. He managed, however, to conceal himself in the house of a carpenter, and to join a band of Uteets, in company with whom he wandered about for a long time. Meanwhile Eedur was taken by the padishah's troops, and Row Poonjâ's mother, supposing that her son was dead, had retired to the house of her own family at Oodeipoor. Some time after, Row Poonjâ found his way, in company with the Uteets, to Oodeipoor, where he made himself known to his mother, and to the Rânâ, who gave him a force to assist in recovering his hereditary dominions. Row Poonjâ accordingly advanced and conquered back Eedur, where he took up his residence, placing, however, his Rânees and treasure at Surwân. It was in Sumwut, 1714 (A.D. 1658), that Row Poonjâ regained Eedur; he reigned there about six months, and was then taken off by poison.

Urjoondâs, the brother of Row Poonjâ, lived at this time at Dhâmod-nee-Nâl, where he gradually assembled a thousand men, with whom he harassed the Ahmedabad Pergunnahs. Once on a time, the Râj Koonwurs, or princes, of Dewulya, Bânswârâ, Loonâwârâ, and Doongurpoor, were on their way from Ahmedabad to their own homes. They halted at Runâsun, where they were well received; and as they continued their journey from thence, Row Urjoondâs, hearing of their arrival, sent an express to invite them to pay him a visit. They went, therefore, to Dhâmod. While they were there, it occurred to them that Runâsun, being a difficult place, would be a good point for the Row to take post at, and make incursions upon the lands of Ahmedabad and Eedur. They agreed, further, to take part with the Row, and mustering their united forces, found that they amounted to five thousand men. They went, therefore, to Runâsun. Now the Rehwurs had been on the look out ever since the Koonwurs had seen Runâsun, lest they should join Row Urjoondâs, and cast a longing eye upon the place. Though the Row and his confederates arrived suddenly therefore, the Rehwurs were prepared, and under cover of the houses, fired upon them as they were entering Runâsun. Four rajas were at once slain—Urjoondâs Row, and the Koonwurs of Doongurpoor, Loonâwârâ, and Dewulya. The Koonwur of Bânswârâ fled, carrying the corpses of his companions with him, to Dhâmod, where he performed their funeral rites. Row Urjoondâs left a son, then five years old, whom the Koonwur took with him to Bânswârâ, where he gave him the puttâ of Tooteeâbul in Wâgur for his subsistence during his minority, and this puttâ is still enjoyed by his descendants.

Row Urjoondâs having fallen, Jugunnâth's brother, Gopeenâth, remained "out," and made excursions as far as Ahmedabad. The padishah's power was at this time on the decline, and Syud Hâtho thought fit to call upon the Desâees and Muzmoondârs to go to the Row, in order to arrange for the payment to him of a certain sum, on condition of his forbearing to harass the country. The ministers said that such a purpose could not be effected without the aid of Bhâts and Chârun. Syud Hâtho, therefore, recalled the Bhâts and Châruns, who had held grants from the Rows, and restored their villages. Jogeedâs Chârun, of Koowâwoo, was then despatched to the Row, and arranged for the payment of the "Wol," which the Rows still hold upon Eedur. Syud Hâtho was soon after replaced by Soubah Kumâl Khân, an indolent person, who paid no attention to his government. Gopeenâth Row was therefore enabled to drive him out, and thus, at length, recovered possession of Eedur, where he ruled for about five years. Ghureebdâs Rehwur, the Thâkor of Runâsun, was, however, afraid that if the Row held Eedur, he would, sooner or later, take vengeance for Row Urjoondâs. Ghureebdâs was, as has been mentioned, at the head of a powerful party in Eedur, which included the Kusbâtees. With their aid he brought an army from Ahmedabad to expel the Row. Row Gopeenâth had two Rânees, a daughter of Oodeipoor and a daughter of the Wâghela of

Pethâpoor; he had also two concubines. Taking these ladies with him, he retired into Eedur-gurh, but the Kusbâtees pursuing him, and forcing their way in, he was obliged to descend the hills, in the direction of Kulnâth Muhâ Dev. The ladies, at the same time, fled to the "hill of murders," where they determined to die, supposing that all was lost; and accordingly perished, by drowning in the reservoir called "the broken tank." Row Gopeenâth, meanwhile, was sheltered at Kulnâth Muhâ Dev's. A Brahmin, of Wurâlee, came there to worship Kulnâth, and Row Gopeenâth, who was accustomed to eat a pound and a quarter of opium every day, took two gold bracelets off his arms, and gave them to him, saying, that one was a gift, but that he should sell the other, and bring opium, to enable him to get on to Surwân. He also promised the Brahmin, that when he was restored to Eedur, he would give him a village. The Brahmin took the bracelets, and, going home, related to his wife what had happened. She advised that he should not return, for that the Row would some day lay claim to the bracelets, if he survived. Gopeenâth, being unable to procure opium, died, and from that time the Rows have never recovered Eedur.

The affairs of Eedur now fell into the hands of Moteechund, the Muzmoondâr of Wurâlee, and the Desâees of Wusâee, Ghureebdâs Rehwur, holding the office of Prudhân, or chief minister, Gopeenâth's son, Row Kurun Singh, lived at Surwân until his death. He left two sons, Chândo or Chundra Singh, and Mâdhuv Singh; the mother of the former was a Jhâlâ lady, of Hulwud, and that of the latter, a daughter of Dântâ. Row Chândo grew up at Surwân, and Mâdhuv Singh, at Udheyrun, which had been assigned to his mother. Mâdhuv Singh at length went out, and engaged the padishah's troops at the village of Châmpulpoor, in the Poseenâ district. From thence he went to Verâbur, which he took possession of, and his descendants remain there still.

In the same year, Sumwut, 1752 (A.D. 1696), Row Mân and Gowind Râthor, relations of Row Chândo, joined him from Mewar, and "went out" with him against Eedur, and in Sumwut 1774 (A.D. 1718), the Desâees brought Row Chândo back to Eedur, having driven out the Mohummedan garrison. Row Chândo, however, did not rule well, and the Wâghelas and Rehwurs encroached upon all the crown villages of Eedur; the former occupying the country as far as Wurâlee, and the latter advancing their territories to Sâbulee. At this time, the Thâkor of Pâlya having died, it became necessary to present a sword and dress of honor to his successor. Row Chândo attempted to leave Eedur, under pretence of making this investiture, but his mercenaries interrupted his departure, and demanded their arrears. The Row gave them as security Sirdâr Singh, the Thâkor of Wolâsunâ, who was then at Eedur, and entrusting him with the government, as his representative, quitted his capital, never to return. Sirdâr Singh ruled at Eedur for a time in the name of the Row, until, at length, the Desâees and zumeendârs placed him on the royal cushion. Sirdâr Singh's minister was Shâmlâjee Thâkor, of Lehee, a "brother "of Wolâsunâ," a man of great ability and courage, who recovered the villages which had been encroached upon by the Rehwurs and Wâghelas. His success raised him many enemies, and the leading men of the Kusbâtees at length persuaded Sirdâr Singh that Shâmlajee meditated his and their destruction. The Row believed them, and dismissed Shâmlajee, who went his way. Buchâ Pundit was invited from Baroda, to be his successor. Soon after, however, a quarrel arose between Row Sirdâr Singh and the Kusbâtees, and the former meditated attacking them, and openly declared that, unless he were able to put them to death, he would not remain at Eedur. Finding himself unable to effect his purpose, he retired in discontent to Wolâsunâ. Buchâ Pundit then ruled in Eedur, with the Kusbâtees, Moteechund Muzmoondâr, and Rehwur Udhey Singh, of Runâsun, the interest of the Desâees having declined. Buchâ Pundit paid tribute to the governor of Ahmedabad, and continued to rule in Eedur; but the Desâees were discontented with the state of affairs, and Lâl Singh Oodâwut having arrived at Wusâee, on his way from Soreth to Marwar, they went to him, and made him their confidant. He said, that if they chose, he would bring them a good raja. The Desâees agreed, and entered into a written engagement, upon which Lâl Singh went to Poseenâ, and brought Muhâraja Ânund Singh and his brothers to Eedur. It was in the year Sumwut, 1787 (A.D. 1731), that Ânund Singh took Eedur from Buchâ Pundit.

To return to Row Chândo:—This prince retired to Pol, which was in the possession of his wife's family, the Pureehâr Rajpoots, with the expressed intention of bidding them adieu, and proceeding to Kâshee, to die there. After remaining at Pol about two months, Row Chândo set out to retire to Benares. There is a village named Surchow, about ten miles from Pol. The Row halted there, and wrote to his friends at Pol, to come and eat a last feast with him, and return home. They came and feasted, and drank with Row Chândo. When the Pol Rajpoots were overcome with drink, the Row caused them all to be put to death, and returning to Pol, seated himself on the royal cushion, and his descendants remain at Pol to this day.

CHAP. XI.

THE GOHILS.

We have thus followed the fortunes of Northern Goozerat, to the time when the transient dominion of the Moslem ceased, when the Muezzin's call to prayers began to die away, subdued by the sound of the liberated bells, which once more tinkled in each Hindoo temple, and the flag of Shiva, under the form of the national banner of the Mahrattas again floated supreme throughout the land, from that deity's much oppressed shrine at Prubhâs, to the still inviolate mansion of his consort, the inaccessible Umbâ Bhuwânee. The sovereigns of the Dekkan we shall again behold, as in the days of the Solunkhee Kings of Kuleeân, extending their dominion over Goozerat and Soreth. Before, however, we pursue their story, we must return once more to the scene with which our drama opened—to the site of forgotten Wullubheepoor, to the minarets of Loleeyânah, already crumbling into dust, and to the neighbouring spot on which is now to rise the Shaivite spire, inscribed with the dreaded name of Dâmâjee Guikowâr.

Sârungjee Gohil,[1] was succeeded in turn by his son, Shivdâs, and his grandson, Jeytjee. Jeytjee had two sons, Râmdâs and Gungâdâs, which latter obtained, as his portion, the village of Chumârdee.

Gohil Râmdâsjee, say the bards, visited Benares as a pilgrim ; he feasted there fourteen thousand Brahmins, and presented each of them with a gold coin in alms. When he had completed his pilgrimage, he sent the Sungh home, and proceeded alone to Oodeipoor. Koombho Rânâ inquired what Rajpoot clan he belonged to, and what lands he was possessed of. Râmdâs replied, "I am the Gohil Rajpoot, lord "of the port of Ghoghâ and of Gohilwâr." Then Koombho Rânâ gave his daughter, Sukomul Bâ, to Râmdâs. At this time, Momud Shah's army attacked Oodeipoor, and a battle was fought, in which Râmdâs slew many men, horses, and elephants. Râmdâs had a Shâlagrâm stone in his head which was cut in two in the fight ; an elephant's bell falling upon it concealed it for the time, and after that a snake built his heap upon it. Koonwur Sutojee heard the news of

[1] See page 289.

this fight, at Ghoghâ; he performed the funeral obsequies of his father. At this time, the Shâlagrâm appeared to him in a dream, and said, "I, your Isht Dev, am buried in the ground at Oodeipoor; "bring me from thence." Sutojee sent Duvey Rughoonâth and others to the spot pointed out at Oodeipoor, and brought thence the Shâlagrâm; and the stone, the pieces of which have adhered together, is now worshipped in the house of the Duvey's descendants at Seehore, who enjoy annual grants on that account.

Râmdâs left two younger sons, Sudooljee and Bheemjee, to the former of whom was assigned, as his portion, the village of Udheywârâ; and to the latter, that of Thânâ, the present possessors of which, Bheemjee's descendants, bear the title of "Thâneeâ Râwuls."

In the annals of Mewar, mention is made of "the Gohil from "Peerum," as one of the defenders of Cheetor, on the occasion of its capture by Allah-ood-deen, in A.D. 1303,[1] and the historian of Rajpootana applies the incident to the time of Râmdâsjee Gohil. The bards of the Bhownugger family, however, connect, as we have seen, Râmdâsjee Gohil with the reign of Koombho, Rânâ of Mewar. That prince encountered Mahmood, Shah of Malwa, and defeated him, as Ferishta mentions in his Malwa history, in A.D. 1454. This latter date even, can hardly be brought to synchronise with Râmdâsjee, whose great grandson, Dhoonâjee, died in A.D. 1619. It is, perhaps, more probable that the Gohil prince was one of "the numerous "auxiliaries from all parts of Râjwârâ," who endeavoured to maintain Cheetor against Buhâdur Shah, of Goozerat, by whom it was taken in A.D. 1532-33.[2]

Sutojee, the son of Râmdâs, left four sons, Veesojee, who succeeded him, Devojee, Veerojee, and Mânkojee. The younger brothers obtained, as their portions, three villages each, forming the estates of Pucheygâm, Uwâneeya, and Nuwâneeya. The descendants of Devojee form the family called Devânee Gohils, from his own name; those of Veerojee, are known as the Vâchânees, from Veero's son, Vâcho. They now hold Ḳhokhurâ, Mâmchee, and Kunâr.

The town of Singhpoor, or Seehore, was, as we have seen, granted by the sovereigns of Unhilwârâ to Brahmins, who appear to have maintained possession of it, without admitting any external authority, until the times at which we are now arrived, when dissensions among themselves gave them a master in the person of Veesojee Gohil.

The situation of Seehore bears some resemblance to the crater of

[1] *Vide* Tod's Rajasthan, vol. i. p. 266. Tod's Western India, pp. 258-9, 266.
[2] *Ibid.*, vol. i. pp. 310 et seq.

a volcano; it is a flat plain, surrounded by a girdle of rugged hills. In the centre of the ancient town, of which no single dwelling now remains, is a small conical hill, called the hill of the seven streets, on the summit of which is a pavilion, in which, as tradition relates, the Brahmins of Seehore met of old in council, and for the administration of justice. Not very far from the base of this hill, is a handsome reservoir called "the Brumhkoond." It is of considerable size, square in form, and surrounded with niches containing Hindoo sculpture, and it descends from all sides, towards the pool in the centre, by flights of steps, relieved at regular intervals by landings. Around the terrace of the koond, a row of temples forms a kind of cloister, and outside these a wall surrounds the whole. To the south of the koond rises a singular hill, called, from the number of its peaks, "the three-horned mountain."

The circumvallation of old Seehore is still, in some places, discernible; the new town is placed on the north of these, and touches very closely the feet of the surrounding hills. A river, called the Gomutee, or Goutumee, washes the western side of Seehore, whose banks are dotted with numerous funeral memorials. A short distance from the town, near the river, is a second reservoir, called "the Goutumeshwur koond."

The old town of Seehore was, it is said, divided between two sects of Brahmins, the Runâs and the Jânees, who occupied respectively its southern and northern portions. A Jânee Brahmin's daughter, who had married into a Runâ family, was, it is said, one day churning milk in the yard of her husband's house, wearing her long hair loose over her shoulders, and her head uncovered. Her husband was seated at this time among other Brahmins in the pavilion on the hill of the seven streets which overlooked the whole of the city. One of the Brahmins, remarking that the woman did not cover her head though she was exposed to their gaze, said, without knowing that her husband sat beside him, "The man must be an effeminate fellow "whose wife is so careless of decency as this." Her husband, hearing the remark, was full of shame and anger; he went home, and cut off his wife's hair and her nose. The woman ran weeping to her father's house to complain of the cruel treatment she had suffered; her male relations took up arms, and hastened to exact revenge. A conflict ensued, in the course of which many Brahmins were slain, and the spot, thus stained with so much sacred blood of the priests, became henceforth accursed and desolate. It still retains the name of the "field of murders."

The Jânees and Runâs each of them now sought foreign assistance. The former set off to Gâreeâdhâr, to the descendant of Sâhâjee, the brother of Rânjee Gohil, and offered to make over to that chieftain the town of Seehore, with its twelve dependent villages. The chief of Gâreeâdhâr accordingly assembled a force, and advanced upon "the lion city," but, a bad omen occurring, he halted on the way, and lost his opportunity, being soon after attacked by the head of his house, Râwul Veesojee Gohil, whom the Runâs had brought with them from Oomrâlâ. Veesojee repulsing his kinsman of Gâreeâdhâr, entered Seehore, and took possession of the royal rights connected with it, leaving, however, the land to the Brahmins; and from this time Seehore became the capital of the Gohils, until Bhow Singh erected the new city, called after his name, on the ruins of the old town of Wuduwâ.

"No enemy," says the bard, "ever subdued the strength of Oomur "Kot (Oomrâlâ). Through Soreth walked the son of Sutmâljee, "grasping his sword. Veesul was like a tiger; an acre of his land "was to him as his liver—no enemy could take it, though striving "with great labour, from the son of Sutojee."

Veesojee was succeeded by Râwul Dhoonâjee; he left also two younger sons, Bheemjee and Kusheeojee, to whom were assigned the estates of Huleeyâd and Bhudulee.

While Dhoonâjee ruled in Seehore his kinsman, Noghunjee of Gâreeâdhâr, was attacked by Lomâ Khoomâ, the Kâtee chief, of Kherudee, and deprived of his estate, or, as the bard says, "his "grâs was taken from him." Noghunjee fled to Seehore for assistance, and Râwul Dhoonâjee prepared to support him with all his power; for, however willing the head of a Rajpoot house may be to infringe in his own interest upon the rights of the cadents of the family, his assistance is sure to be afforded them in case of an attack from without, which, if successful, must tend to his own eventual disadvantage—the teelâyut being in the last resort the heir of the phutâyo. The Kâtee chief, however, taking two hundred horse with him, made a night attack upon Wulleh, where Dhoonâjee's levies were assembling, and, in the course of the action, the Râwul was slain.

Noghunjee Gohil now fled to Rujo Bâreâ, the Koolee chief of Juwâsh, and, espousing his daughter, brought a force of Bâreâ Koolees to Seehore, and, procuring further aid from thence, advanced on Gâreeâdhâr. The Putel of the town came to his camp, and informed him that Lomâ's force was too strong to be attacked with success. A stratagem was determined on, and the Putel, returning into the town, raised an alarm that his cattle had been carried off by a party of horse who had retired in a westerly direction. The Kâtees hastened in pursuit, and Noghunjee, seizing the opportunity, entered the town with his family and followers. The inhabitants were favourable to the cause of the Gohil, and Gâreeâdhâr was therefore won; but Noghunjee, on the advice of his wife, fearing that Lomâ would retake the town, went to that chieftain, and gave up his sword. His wife became the adopted sister of Lomâ Khoomâ, but both she and her husband merely dissembled until an opportunity offered for revenge. At length a marriage occurred at the court of the Jâm of Nugger, who was Noghunjee Gohil's son-in-law. The chief of Gâreeâdhâr and his Thâkorine were invited, but the lady refused to go unless attended by her brother, Lomâ Khoomâ. A letter, sprinkled with red water, was therefore sent from Nugger to Lomâ, though he and the Jâm were at enmity at the time, in consequence of the Jâm's having been betrayed by Lomâ in an engagement with the Mohummedans. The Kâtee chief, however, went to Jâmnugger, and was present at the marriage; but, being afterwards invited to an entertainment in the Jâm's apartments, and prevailed upon to lay aside his arms, he was treacherously seized upon by Noghunjee and the Jâm, and put to death. Several of his relations also shared the same fate.

When the Kâtee chief was bound and disabled by wounds, the Jâm tauntingly asked him what he would do if he were then released. Lomâ answered, "I would overturn Nugger, as a woman turns cakes on the girdle."

The following is the bardic version of the story of Dhoonâjee Râwul:—"Lomâ Kâtee and Noghun, proud in fight, contended; "the drum beat in the limits of Wulleh. The Gohil mingled in the "fray; many arrows and musket-balls were discharged; the edge of "the sword played. Eesh came thither quickly to string heads in his "Roondmâlâ; flesh-devouring Shuktees and carrion birds came thither; "Upsurâs, too, and the thirty-three crore of Devs. Says Sooruj to "Uroon, 'Stop the chariot, O! Uroon; behold Dhoonâjee dies on "the field of battle.' A thousand horses were neighing there; "banners were waving; Dhoonâjee turned not his heel to the foe. "Angrily the Muroo Raja fought, and broke the Kâtee's army. "None but he would give his head; Noghun escaped, but Dhoonâjee "remained on the field. The king adorned the Kshutree race like "another Râm, the supporter of the 'birud.' Veesul's son, making "his sword to play, wed an Upsurâ, and passed to Swerga."

On the banks of the river at Seehore stands the funeral pâleeyo of

Râwul Dhoonâjee; he is represented as a mounted warrior brandishing his lance, and, beside his monument, are those of two of his wives who followed him through the flames. The name of one only of the sutees is legible, "Bâee Shree Kurmâ Devee." From this monument we derive the date of Dhoonâjee's death, "the light half of the month of Kârtik, in the year of Vikrum, 1675" (A.D. 1619). Close beside the pâleeyo of his father stands the monument of "Shree "Rutunjee, the son of Râwul Shree Dhoonâjee," which is dated only one year later (A.D. 1620.) There are two sutees' monuments beside that of Râwul Rutunjee; the names are obliterated, but on one of them may be traced the record that "Mother Shree —jee departed "with her beloved." Of the circumstances of Rutunjee's death nothing is known, except that it was the death of the warrior. The bardic account is as follows:—"When Rutun fixed his foot for the "fight, the Upsurâs crowded from heaven to the spot to claim the "hand of the son of Dhoono. On the spire, his family, Lâ Gohil,[1] "placed the finial 'generosity.' The son of Dhoono added to it the "banner of Kshutree-worthiness in war, and went his way."

Râwul Rutunjee had a brother, named Ukherâjjee; he had also three sons, Hurbhumjee, Gowindjee, and Sârungjee, and a daughter, Leelâjee Bâ, married to Râ Bhâro, of Bhooj. Râwul Hurbhumjee succeeded his father; he married the Rânee Unâjee Bâ Survaiyânee, and had by her a son, named Ukherâjjee. The Koonwur was two years old when his father "became a Dev." Gowindjee, his uncle, took possession of the royal cushion, and Rânee Unâjee Bâ, for fear of him, fled to Bhooj, taking with her the young prince.

The Vâchânees Keshuvjee, and Mukunjee, and the Devânee Mâljee at this time took counsel together, and, calling in a shepherd, named Bhânguro, to their aid, determined to oppose Gowindjee in the interest of their young lord, Ukherâjjee, then sheltered at Bhooj. They commenced a system of incursions upon Seehore. Gowindjee went to Ahmedabad to procure assistance from the Mohummedan government, and died there. When the news arrived at Seehore and Sutrâsuljee, the son of Gowindjee was engaged in celebrating his father's obsequies; Keshuvjee and his confederates, taking advantage of the crowd and confusion, made their way to the Râwul's residence, and, surprising Sutrâsuljee while asleep, seized him, and carried him out of the town to Old Seehore, where they had left their horses. They placed him before one of their party on horseback, and were

[1] Lâ Gohil is a fabulous ancestor of the family, celebrated by the bards as having presented gifts even from the tomb.

making off in the south-west direction, when they observed a party of Kâtee horsemen approaching Seehore, to join in the funeral ceremonies. Keshuvjee and his friends attempted to gain the three-horned hill, but were not able to avoid the Kâtees; they therefore determined on accosting them, and said, "Gowindjee has taken our master's "cushion, so we have seized his Koonwur, and brought him off. If "his friends will give up the town to the true raja, we will restore the "Koonwur." The Kâtees promised their assistance, and recommended that Ukherâjjee should be brought to Seehore, when they would place him on the cushion. Râwul Ukherâjjee was thus brought home and restored to his rights, and Sutrâsuljee was released, and presented with the estate of Bhundâreeo as his portion. His descendants are the Gowindânee Gohils.

While Ukherâjjee was yet a minor, and the power of the Gowindânee of Bundhâreeo was still felt in Seehore, the young Râwul's mother, Unâjee Bâ, became acquainted with Desâee Mehrâj, a servant of the Mohummedan government, at Loleeyânah. His son, Mehtâ Râmjee Mehrâj, was brought to Seehore, and installed as minister to the Râwul, his authority being supported by a party of troops from Loleeyânah, and the influence of the Gowindânees was thus counterbalanced. Ukherâjjee was succeeded by his eldest son, Râwul Rutunjee; his younger sons, Hurbhumjee, Vrujrâjjee, and Surtânjee, received as their portion the estates of Wurtej, Thorudee, and Muglânoo. Dhoonojee, another son, left no descendants.

Râwul Rutunjee employed, as his minister, Dâmjee, the son of Râmjee Mehrâj; he left one son, Râwul Bhow Singh, the founder of Bhownugger.

While Bhow Singh was yet a youth, some of his companions excited his anger against Wullubhjee, the son of Dâmjee, by jestingly remarking that the Mehtâ was the raja in fact. Bhow Singh upon this slew Wullubhjee Mehtâ with his spear. The minister's brothers and their partisans prepared to leave Seehore, but Bhow Singh's mother came to their house in her chariot, and entreated them to remain protesting that she was herself perfectly innocent of the deed, and that her son, as soon as he should be made aware of the truth, would repent what he had done. The Rânee also declared that if they left Seehore, she was determined to accompany them. Wullubhjee's brothers were thus prevailed upon to remain, and Mehtâ Runchor, the eldest of them, was appointed minister, and presented with the turban and silver inkstand, as usual.

In A.D. 1723, Râwul Bhow Singh founded a town near the ancient Wuduwâ, to which he gave the name of Bhownugger. It is a picturesque sea-port town, situated on the banks of the creek, or Kâree, already alluded to under the name of "the Bhownugger," or "the former" river, and which is navigable for small craft up to the point called Gheluree Bunder, about half-way distant between the port and the town of Wulleh. The residence of the Gohil Râwuls, with its clock-tower and campaniles, one or two large round towers on the walls, a reservoir constructed by Râwul Wujesunghjee in the suburbs, and several temples and funeral monuments of the ruling family, are the objects which first attract notice at Bhownugger. The houses are well built, usually of stone, but sometimes partly of brick, and enriched with woodwork, very elaborately ornamented.

From a slight elevation near the town, on the land side, a view is obtained of the port of Gogo,—between which and Bhownugger lies a dreary flat and sea-deserted tract,—of the Khokurâ hills, and those of Pâleetânâ, Seehore, and Chumârdee, with the Kâree winding towards the gulf. On the banks of the creek, a little below the town, placed upon a gentle eminence studded with shrubs, is the temple of Roowâpooree Mâtâ, which derives its origin, as tradition asserts, from the inhumation of the potter's wife, who turned back to look upon the falling city of Wullubheepoor. The shrine of Roowâpooree has no object worthy of notice, but in its immediate vicinity is an oblong stone, derived apparently from the funeral monument of an ascetic, which has long been celebrated as an ordeal stone, under the name of the "window of truth and falsehood."

Still nearer the waters of the creek is a bank bearing the name of "Doono," the scene of a legend, which tells that a merchant, refusing to fulfil a vow made by him to Roowâpooree Mâtâ, was sunk there, with his ships, laden with oil and madder. The bank emits discoloured water, which is pointed to in confirmation of this tale of Roowâpooree's vengeance.

In the creek, opposite the town, a few tall masts are visible, the remnant of the naval power of the Kings of Perumbh; and beneath their keels lies the submerged city of Dhootâr Puttun, the out-port perhaps, of Wullubhee Nugger, whose foundations of stone and brick may yet be exhumed when the low state of the tide offers opportunity.

The description of the capital of the Gohil Râwuls, given by their own bards, must not, however, in this place be omitted: "In this "Kulyoog," say they, "in the year of Vikrum, 1779, in Wyeshâk 'month, when the moon shone bright, on the 3rd day of the month, "the pundits were sent for, and the auspicious hour ascertained. "Beholding the conjunction, the learned men were much rejoiced; "'Bravo! bravo!' said they, 'this city will be like Indra's.' The

" word issued from their mouths, and the name of Bhownugger was " given to the city. The Brahmins prophesied that jewels and pearls " would adorn the city; that its enemies would be discomforted. " What Brahmins predict is sure to be fulfilled! Believing this, the " Râwul placed his throne; gardens he caused to be laid out; man- " sions he built that reached into the sky; a fort whose battlements " were overtopped by the palaces. Over the towers, kite-like, fluttered " the flags; in the narrowest streets polished lime was spread upon " the walls; the women, that out of each lane went forth to fill water, " seemed like herds of the elephants of Ceylon. With many different " plans, the artificers built houses of many stories; the cornices pro- " jected on either side; flower trees peeped through the lattices and " embrasures; elephants, with their collars of bells, created a jingling " noise, footmen followed them, and horsemen bearing lances; large- " bellied merchants wandered about with their dress loose; in lines " of thousands, on both sides, were the shops; from shop to shop " purchasers without number; the merchants trafficking, destroyed " the trade of other cities. In no other place were such lakh-lords " to be found; from place to place were the houses of those who " displayed the 'crore-banner.' The beauty of the Râwul's mansion " was such as none could estimate; it was covered with creepers " bearing gold-coloured flowers; the windows were studded with " costly stones; it was adorned with many kinds of sculpture; instru- " ments of music sounded there; every one exclaimed, 'Bravo! " bravo! to this princedom!' The lamps were lighted, the courtiers " assembled, the great drums rolled, the dancers danced, the pugilists " contended, every spectator was full of delight, foreign fruits were " brought in plenty, the Upsurâs danced with loosened vestments, " the teeluk of the Gohil race shone like the sun, poets chaunted songs " before him, the whole eight watches of the day passed in delight. " The sands of Jâhnuvee may be numbered, or the drops of rain; " but what pundit's son could describe how great was your lordliness, " O! Padishah of Perumbh!"

BOOK III.

CHAPTER I.

FROM THE FIRST APPEARANCE OF THE MAHRATTAS IN GOOZERAT TO THE CAPTURE OF AHMEDABAD.[1]

EARLY in the eighteenth century, Khundee Row Dhâbâree, the Senâputee of the Mahratta empire, began to pour his predatory horse into Goozerat, and exact tribute from that province. At first he hung about the neighbourhood of the city of Shah Ahmed; but afterwards, retiring for a time therefrom, he effected a more permanent establishment in the strong country about Nandode and Râjpeepla, from whence he commanded the principal routes for traffic between Goozerat and the Dekkan. At the battle of Balapoor, fought in A.D. 1730, the troops of Dhâbâree distinguished themselves by their bravery, and on that field a chieftain first obtained renown, whose name was destined to exercise no unimportant influence on the affairs of Goozerat. Dâmâjee Guikowâr was now appointed to command under the Senâputee, and was ennobled by the title of Shumsher Buhâdur.

Both Khundee Row and his newly-appointed lieutenant died soon after they had attained this success. Trimbuk Row Dhâbâree was then honoured with the dress of Senâputee, in succession to his father, and Peelâjee, the son of Junkojee Guikowâr, obtained the command which had been held by his uncle, Dâmâjee. A few years afterwards, Oodâjee Powâr, another active partisan leader, brought his Mahratta horse into Goozerat and Malwa, plundering the former province as far as Loonâwârâ, and laying the foundations, in the latter, of a power imitating the name and possessing the royal seat of the dynasty of Bhoj. Shoojât Khân was at this time appointed the deputy in Goozerat of Sur Boolund Khân, the imperial viceroy, and he was opposed by Hâmed Khân, on the part of his nephew, Nizâm-ool-Moolk, who had lately been deposed from the government of the province. Hâmed Khân, by a promise of "*the chouth,*" succeeded in procuring the assistance of the Mahratta leader, Kuntâjee Kuddum Bhanday, and these two officers, joining their forces, attacked, defeated, and slew Shoojât

[1] The information contained in this, and the next following chapter, is almost entirely taken from Grant Duff's History of the Mahrattas and Forbes's Oriental Memoirs.

Khân, within a few miles of the capital of Goozerat. When this event occurred, Roostum Ulee, the brother of Shoojât Khân, held the office of military governor of Surat, and had just gained advantages over Peelâjee Guikowâr, in the neighbourhood of that city.

Hearing of his brother's defeat and death, Roostum Ulee made a truce with his Mahratta opponent, and invited him to join in an attack upon Hâmed Khân. The wily Mahratta accepted his overtures, though already engaged by the emissaries of his adversary, and accompanied him towards Ahmedabad until he could ascertain precisely which side it would be most advantageous for him to join. The confederates crossed the Myhee at Fuzilpoor, and advanced to Ârâs. Hâmed Khân here attacked them, but was driven back by the fire of Roostum Ulee's artillery. By this time, however, Peelâjee Guikowâr had chosen his side; he therefore recommended Roostum Ulee to charge the fugitives, leaving the guns to his care. The gallant Mohummedan had no sooner followed this fatal advice than his guns were overturned, and his troops attacked in the rear by his treacherous ally. Roostum Ulee defended himself for some time with bravery, but his reduced numbers showed him the impossibility of escape, and dreading the ignominious treatment to which he knew he should be exposed as a prisoner, he stabbed himself to the heart.

Peelâjee's treachery was rewarded by an equal share of the chouth with Kuntâjee; and both, in conjunction, proceeded to levy their assignments; but the division of the money led to perpetual disputes. For some time these differences only produced heavier impositions on the towns and villages. When, however, the Mahratta leaders approached Cambay, and began, as usual, to burn the suburbs for the purpose of intimidation, the inhabitants, aware of their dissensions, and affecting to consider Kuntâjee the superior, sent a messenger to Peelâjee hinting this circumstance, and offering him a sum of money to retire. Peelâjee, exasperated by the insult, confined the messenger; Kuntâjee insisted on his being released, and both flew to arms to assert their prerogative. After a severe conflict, within sight of the walls, Peelâjee was discomfited, and retired to Mâtur, near Kaira. The contribution from Cambay was levied by the victor. The sum of five thousand rupees having been demanded from the English factory, the agents pleaded exemption, in consequence of privilege of trade from the "Shao Raja," but at this "the armed villains," as Mr. Innes, the chief of the factory, in bitterness of heart, terms them, "only laughed."

Hâmed Khân, foreseeing the desertion of one or other of his allies, made them sign an agreement, by which the chouth east of the

Myhee was assigned to Peelâjee, and that to the west to Kuntâjee. The Mahrattas still preserved their original custom of retiring to quarters during the rainy season, and soon after the battle at Cambay, Peelâjee retired to Songurh, near Surat, and Kuntâjee to a district which he held in Candeish.

Sur Boolund Khân, an excellent and popular officer, who had been unjustly removed from Cabul, was at this season of difficulty courted by the emperor, and earnestly solicited to repair to his government in Goozerat, for the purpose of suppressing the formidable insurrection of Hâmed Khân. A large army was soon assembled under his command, and he proceeded on his route to Ahmedabad in A.D. 1725. Hâmed Khân, despairing of being joined by the Mahrattas, left Ahmedabad defended by a weak garrison, and retired before the advanced division of the army of Sur Boolund. The Mahrattas had, however, crossed the Myhee, and as they joined him at Mahmoodabad, he retraced his steps to the capital. A party in the city, favorable to the new governor, having overpowered his garrison, and forced them out, Hâmed Khân encamped at the Shâhee Bâgh on the same day that the advanced guard of Sur Boolund Khân arrived at Udâlej. The rebel leader obtained a victory over this force, which had been pushed too far in advance, but his advantage was dearly purchased, and the Mahrattas could not be brought to risk another battle. Hâmed Khân became therefore a mere plunderer like themselves, and though military officers were appointed to the command of each district, and arrangements made with more than ordinary vigour by the new governor, Kuntâjee and Peelâjee continued to plunder during the remainder of the season, until at the approach of the rains they took their annual flight. "A deceitful calm," says the historian of Muhârâshtra, "succeeded;—the fall of the rain brought back the "cheering green; and the beautiful province of Goozerat, which, for "hundred of miles, may vie with the finest parks of the nobles of "England, was clothed, in all its natural beauties, by rapid verdure "and luxuriant vegetation. Tranquillity seemed to reign, where, a "short time before, nothing was to be seen but perpetual skirmishing, "murder and robbery in open day, caravans pillaged even when "strongly escorted, and villages burning or deserted."

Sur Boolund Khân exerted himself to check the incursions of the Mahrattas, and he repeatedly applied to Court for a supply of money, the exhausted state of the country under his care rendering it impossible to raise at first any revenue of consequence. His demands, however, being entirely neglected, he next endeavoured to conciliate Peelâjee and Kuntâjee by grants of chouth, but this attempt also failed, the Mahratta leaders collecting all the revenue, but affording no protection to the country. At length Chimnâjee Âppâ, the brother of the Peshwah Bâjee Row, arriving with a large army, plundered Dholka, and exacted a heavy contribution from Pitlâd. He promised, however, on the part of his brother, that if concessions were made to him, the country should be effectually secured from the depredations of all other freebooters. Sur Boolund Khân at length agreed to the Peshwah's proposals, after stipulating that two thousand five hundred Mahratta horse should constantly be kept up, and that every assistance should be afforded in maintaining the imperial authority. Bâjee Row further agreed, on the part of Raja Sâhoo, to prevent Mahratta subjects from taking part with or in any way supporting disaffected zumeendârs and other disturbers of the public peace, a clause apparently particularly aimed at Peelâjee Guikowâr, who had leagued himself with the Bheels and Koolees of the country, and was on that account considered particularly formidable by the Mohummedans.

No sooner had the Peshwah obtained these terms from Sur Boolund Khân than Trimbuk Row Dhâbâree commenced to negotiate with the other Mahratta leaders, and to assemble troops in Goozerat. At length, finding himself at the head of thirty-five thousand men, and having secured the support of Nizâm-ool-Moolk, he arranged his plans for an invasion of the Dekkan. He was supported by Peelâjee Guikowâr, by Kuntâjee and Rughoojee Kuddum Bhanday, by Oodâjee and Ânund Row Powâr, and by many other officers, and he proclaimed that he was proceeding to the Dekkan, to protect from the Peshwah's ambition the authority of Sâhoo Raja. Bâjee Row determined to anticipate his opponents. His army was far inferior in numerical strength, but was composed of the old Pâgah horse, and some of the best of the famed Mahratta Mânkurees. He advanced therefore rapidly towards Goozerat, and had soon crossed the Nerbudda. Here his vanguard came into collision with a party of the enemy under the command of Dâmâjee, the son of Peelâjee Guikowâr, and was completely defeated. This check, however, did not discourage Bâjee Row. He continued his advance, and at last met his enemy at a place between the cities of Dubhoee and Baroda, both then held by Peelâjee Guikowâr, where he gained the decisive victory which gave him all but nominal control of the Mahratta sovereignty.

This important battle was fought upon the first of April, A.D. 1731. Bâjee Row, when about to engage his countrymen, determined, contrary to his usual plan, to close with them immediately. The new levies of the Senâputee did not await the shock, but fled at the first charge. Kuntâjee Kuddum Bhanday joined them in their flight, and soon the veterans of Khundee Row Dhâbâree were alone left to protect his son. Bâjee Row fought on horseback, and exerted himself with all the energy so great an occasion required. His opponent was mounted on an elephant, and, beholding the flight of his troops, commanded the animal's legs to be chained. The field was disputed with obstinacy, and the issue was still doubtful, when Trimbuk Row, as he drew his bow-string to his ear, was slain by a random matchlock ball.

The victory gained, Bâjee Row, at the suggestion of Sur Boolund Khân, prepared to reduce Baroda,—the possessor of which, Peelâjee Guikowâr, had escaped wounded from the field. An accommodation was, however, come to in the month of August, and the Peshwah, at the close of the rainy season, returned to Satara.

The victory over Dhâbâree, like the issue of every civil war, left impressions on the minds of many which were not easily effaced. The Peshwah, however, adopted every means of conciliation in his power. Among other measures, Yeshwunt Row, the young son of the deceased, was raised to the rank of Senâputee, under the guardianship of his mother; and Peelâjee Guikowâr, their former lieutenant, was confirmed in that situation, assuming the title of Senâ-Khâs-Kheyl, in addition to his hereditary one of Shumsher Buhâdur. In order to prevent disputes, an agreement was drawn up under the authority of Sâhoo Raja, and subscribed by the Peshwah and the Senâputee, which stipulated that neither party should enter the possessions of the other in Goozerat and Malwa. Within the limits of the former province, the Senâputee was to have the entire management; but he bound himself to pay one-half of the revenue to the Satara government, through the Peshwah.

Although no attempt had been made to assist Sur Boolund Khân, or to avert the calamity and disgrace which that officer foretold must be the consequence of neglecting his applications for assistance, the concessions made in Goozerat were highly disapproved of by the imperial Court, and the Khân was superseded by Ubhye Singh Râthor, Raja of Marwar, who proceeded with an army to take possession of his new government. Sur Boolund Khân opposed him for some time, but at last retired to Delhi, where he was extremely ill-used, and unworthily disgraced.

The district of Broach was at this time held by an officer named Abdoolah Beg, as military governor under Sur Boolund Khân. It had formerly been assigned to Nizâm-ool-Moolk, as one of the districts of his personal estate, and Abdoolah Beg now placed himself under the authority of the Nizâm, from whom he received the title of

Nek Alum Khân, and neither acknowledged Ubhye Singh nor admitted the pretensions of the Mahrattas.

In A.D. 1732, Ubhye Singh's officer recovered the fort of Baroda. The cause of Peelâjee Guikowâr was, however, popular. He took the field, gained several victories, and occupied many of the principal fortified places. The Râthor chief at last determined upon despatching him, and, on pretence of arranging a final agreement, sent emissaries to him with that intention. These persons met Peelâjee at Dâkor, a village in the district of Tâṣrâ, celebrated for its shrine of Shree Runchor. They had frequent interviews with him, to disarm suspicion. At length, having sat one evening at dusk, they took leave, and quitted the Guikowâr's tent. One of the number, on pretence of having omitted some communication of importance, returned, and, affecting to whisper in Peelâjee's ear, stabbed him to the heart with a dagger.

The assassination of Peelâjee Guikowâr failed, however, to secure the advantages expected by Ubhye Singh. The Koolees and Bheels, instigated by the Desâee of Pâdurâ, near Baroda, who had lived in friendship with Peelâjee, rose all over the country; Mahâdajee Guikowâr, the brother of Peelâjee, advanced from Jumbooseer, and re-took Baroda, which has ever since remained in the hands of the Guikowâr family; and Dâmâjee, the eldest son of the murdered chief, advanced with a large force from Songurh, occupied many of the principal districts in the east of Goozerat, and pushing his incursions as far as Jodhpoor, compelled Ubhye Singh to resign Ahmedabad to a deputy, that he might return homewards for the protection of his hereditary dominions.

Dâmâjee Guikowâr now established himself in Goozerat, and two years afterwards compelled his father's rival, Kuntâjee Kuddum Bhanday, to quit the province. Kuntâjee, however, the next year, A.D. 1735, persuaded Holkar to join him in an inroad upon Goozerat; they appeared unexpectedly; plundered several towns to the north of Ahmedabad, levied contributions at Eedur and Pâhlunpoor, and as far as the Bunâs; and departed as suddenly as they had come. Ubye Singh was shortly afterwards formally removed from the government of Goozerat, but his deputy, Bhundâree Rutun-shee, refused to evacuate the city of Ahmedabad, and Nujeeb-ood-Dowlah Momin Khân, the newly-appointed governor, was compelled to solicit the aid of Damâjee Guikowâr in order to expel him. The Guikowâr and Momin Khân exchanged turbans, and the Mahratta chief sent a force under an agent, named Rungâjee, with his new ally to expel Rutun-shee; the confederates were repulsed in an assault upon the city, but Rutun-shee at last surrendered. Rungâjee and Momin Khân obtained possession of Ahmedabad about the 20th of May, 1737, and an equal share of authority and revenue was assigned to the Moguls and Mahrattas, an arrangement which, as might have been expected, occasioned constant disputes. In the same year, the emperor having at last prevailed on Nizâm-ool-Moolk to repair to court, the governments of Malwa and Goozerat were once more restored to that chieftain in the name of his eldest son, Ghâzee-ood-deen,—the conditions being that he should drive the Mahrattas from those provinces. These conditions, however, he was unable to fulfil, and after a contest with his able opponent the Peshwah Bâjee Row, Nizâm-ool-Moolk was compelled to sign a convention by which he promised to procure the emperor's confirmation to the grant to Bâjee Row of the whole province of Malwa, and the complete sovereignty of the territory between the Chumbul and the Nerbudda.

Dâmâjee Guikowâr henceforth possessed very considerable resources. He wielded, as agent of the widow of Trimbuk Row, the whole power of the party of Dhâbâree, for Yeshwunt Row even, when his age entitled him to claim that position, was altogether incompetent to act as its leader. Dâmâjee continued to levy all the usual Mahratta dues in Goozerat, and an annual tribute from Kâteewâr, until the death of Momin Khân, in February, 1743. Ubdool Uzeez Khân, the new governor, appointed by an imperial edict, was then at Aurungabad, in the Dekkan; he raised immediately a few thousand men, and, marching to assume the charge of his new government, passed Surat, and arrived at Unkulesur, near Broach. At this place, however, he was suddenly attacked by the partisans of Dâmâjee, and his party totally destroyed. Fukheer-ood-Dowlah was next sent from Delhi to take charge of Ahmedabad (A.D. 1744), but a detachment of Dâmâjee's troops, under Rungâjee, opposed him, and prevented his obtaining possession. Dâmâjee was at this time absent at Satara, and his brother, Khundee Row, taking advantage of the opportunity, made several important changes, removing Rungâjee, and appointing an agent of his own at Ahmedabad. He also gave some support to Fukheer-ood-Dowlah, but Dâmâjee, speedily returning, dissolved their connection before it had proved injurious to the Mahratta cause, by giving up to Khundee Row the fort of Borsud and the valuable district of Nerriâd, and appointing him his deputy at Baroda. By this judicious management Dâmâjee preserved an ascendancy over the numerous members of his own family, and thus surmounted the most important obstacle to the maintenance of his power. He refused to acknowledge Fukheer-ood-Dowlah, and supported in preference the brother and son of his old ally, Momin Khân.

In A.D. 1751, Dâmâjee Guikowâr, on the invitation of Târâ-Bâee, the widow of Raja Râm, the son of Seervâjee, marched to Satara to rescue the raja and the Mahratta state from the power of the Brahmins. As soon as accounts were received of the Guikowâr's approach, Târâ Bâee, who had before unsuccessfully urged the raja to assume the control usurped by his servant, Bâlâjee Bâjee Row, now invited him into the fort of Satara, where she made him a prisoner. Dâmâjee Guikowâr was at first successful in defeating the Peshwah's officers, and in joining Târâ Bâee, but he was immediately afterwards compelled to retire before them, and to open a negociation with Bâlâjee. The Peshwah finding Dâmâjee in his power, now demanded the payment of all the arrears due from Goozerat, and the cession of a large portion of territory. Dâmâjee represented that he was but the lieutenant of Dhâbâree, and that he had no authority for complying with these demands. On this reply the Peshwah seized some of the family of the Guikowâr and of Dhâbâree, and imprisoned them in a hill fort; he afterwards treacherously attacked and plundered the Guikowâr's camp, and seizing Dâmâjee himself, placed him in confinement in the city of Poonah. Before he would listen to any overtures for the release of his prisoner, the Peshwah bound him down by the strongest securities; he fixed a sum of fifteen lakhs of rupees as an acquittance for the amount then due; he also exacted a bond for an equal partition both of the districts then held by the Guikowâr family in Goozerat, and of all future conquests. Dâmâjee agreed to give up half the territory, and, after deducting his expenses, to render a fair account of half the surplus in situations where tribute, shares of revenue, contributions, or prize property were realized. He also engaged to maintain ten thousand horse, and to assist the Peshwah when necessary; to pay, as the lieutenant of Dhâbâree, an annual tribute of five lakhs and twenty thousand rupees for his share of the Goozerat province; to contribute annually a certain sum for the support of the raja's establishment; to aid the Peshwah in establishing garrisons in the districts ceded by this agreement; and finally, to join in enforcing their mutual claims to tribute over the whole peninsula of Soorâshtra. Rughoonâth Row, or Râghobâ, the younger brother of the Peshwah, now made an expedition into Goozerat with the view of completing the general arrangements comprehended in the settlements with Dâmâjee Guikowâr, and that chieftain, having been released, joined him with his army soon after he entered the province. They proceeded together levying tribute and reducing the country, and their progress was not interrupted until they arrived under the walls of Ahmedabad.

The capital of Goozerat was then in the hands of Juwân Murd Khân Bâbee, an officer originally appointed to the charge of the Mogul quarter by the brother of the deceased, Momin Khân, but who, during the confinement of Dâmâjee, had usurped the whole power of the city, permitting, however, the realization of the Guikowâr's dues. Juwân Murd Khân was absent at Pâhlunpoor when the confederated Mahratta chiefs appeared before Ahmedabad. He returned in time to save the city from being carried by escalade; and his presence communicating a new spirit to the garrison, the defence was maintained with great resolution. The conduct of Juwân Murd Khân Bâbee procured him an honorable capitulation, and the districts of Puttun, Wurnugger, Rhâdunpoor, Beejâpoor, and others, were conferred upon him on condition of his giving up the city. In April, 1755, Ahmedabad was finally taken possession of by the Mahrattas. The revenue was to be equally divided between the Peshwah and Guikowâr, but the whole garrison was furnished by the Peshwah, excepting that of the citadel, now called the Guikowâr's Huwelee, which was occupied by the troops of Dâmâjee.

CHAPTER II.

THE BRITISH FIRST APPEAR IN GOOZERAT.

From the time of Mr. Bourchier's succession to the government of Bombay, which took place on the 17th November, 1750, a more intimate intercourse commenced between the Mahrattas and the English. The latter were long urgent with the Peshwah to assist them in restoring order in Surat, the affairs of which had during the weakness of the imperial government fallen into a state of confusion, and in establishing their privileges and trade in that city on a secure footing. The Peshwah, however, failed to afford them the support they required; and when they attempted to effect their object independently of his assistance, he defeated their schemes by making a feint of attacking the island of Bombay. Surat Castle was notwithstanding taken possession of by the English, though with a considerable loss of both officers and men, on the 4th of March, A.D. 1759. It was not long before they were led to take a further step towards a territorial establishment in Goozerat. In A.D. 1771, they prepared to enforce against the Nowaub of Broach certain claims which they professed in right of sovereignty in Surat. A collision was, however, for a time avoided, and a treaty concluded with the Nowaub, which, as insufficiently favorable to the interests of the latter chief, was soon disregarded by him. The expedition which had been formerly projected was now carried into effect, and Broach, with the loss of the gallant and accomplished general, David Wedderburn, was taken by storm on the 18th November, 1772.

Meanwhile, the great Guikowâr chief, Dâmâjee Row, had died, leaving behind him four sons. Syâjee Row, the eldest of these, was the son of the second wife of Dâmâjee, and his title to the succession was therefore disputed by his brother, Gowind Row, who, though junior in age, derived his birth from the first-espoused wife of his father. The remaining sons, Mânukjee and Futteh Singh, brothers of whole blood, were the children of a younger mother. The pretensions of Gowind Row had been at first admitted by the Peshwah Mahdoo Row ; but, being afterwards disallowed in his court of law, were finally rejected by him in favor of those of Syâjee, who was invested accordingly with the titles of Senâ-Khâs-Kheyl, Shumsher Buhâdur. Syâjee Row was, however, an idiot, and his brother, Futteh Singh, was therefore appointed by the Peshwah to act as his deputy. After the death of Mahdoo Row, and the murder of Nârâyun Row, his brother, their uncle, Râghobâ, the younger son of Bâjee Row, succeeding for a time to the office of Peshwah, invested Gowind Row as successor to the Guikowâr possessions in supercession of the former installation of Syâjee. Gowind Row immediately set off for Goozerat, with the view of wresting the government from Futteh Singh, and a state of constant warfare commenced between the partisans of the rival brothers.

The continuance in power of Râghobâ was but brief. The ministers of the Poonah state, supported by the great military chiefs, Holkar and Sindia, opposed themselves to him, and in January, 1775, he arrived, almost a fugitive, at Baroda, in Goozerat, where his partizan, Gowind Row Guikowâr, was then engaged in besieging his brother. The deposed Peshwah had also a further object in retiring to Goozerat. He sought to renew a negociation which he had for some time had on foot, for obtaining the assistance of the Bombay government. A treaty was finally concluded between these parties on the 6th March, and the English became pledged to the support of

Râghobâ with a military force. A detachment sailed accordingly from Bombay, in expectation of forming a speedy junction with Râghobâ's army in Goozerat. On their arrival at Surat, however, the English found that their ally had already experienced a serious reverse. He had been compelled by a confederated ministerial army to raise the siege of Baroda, and to engage them on the plains of Ârâs, near the river Myhee, where he was totally defeated. The British detachment, which was under the command of Colonel Keating, proceeded nevertheless to Cambay, accompanied by the ex-Peshwah, and landed at that place on the 17th March. It was more than a month before they effected a junction, at the village of Durmuj, eleven miles north of Cambay, with the fugitive army of Râghobâ, and it was not until the 3rd May that the united force reached the town of Mâtur. The direction of their route was now changed. They left Mâtur on the 5th, with the intention of moving on towards Poonah, and on the 8th reached Nerriâd, where they remained a week, exacting a contribution from the town. The army, after quitting Nerriâd, continued its march towards the Myhee, and on the 18th, at Ârâs, near that river, the fatal scene of Roostum Ulee's defeat and death, and of Râghobâ's former discomfiture, an engagement was fought, in which the enemy was defeated, not, however, without severe loss to the British detachment. Colonel Keating arrived at Broach on the 29th, and having deposited his wounded in that town, made an attempt upon the enemy, who were encamped near the Nerbudda. They became aware of his approach through the irregular movements of his Mahratta auxiliaries, and throwing their guns into the river, retreated along the northern bank. It was now finally resolved to remain in Goozerat during the rainy months, and to proceed to Poonah at the commencement of the fair season. The fortress of Dubhoee was the place destined for the winter quarters of the British detachment, and on the 8th June Colonel Keating accordingly marched thitherwards from Broach, along the banks of the Nerbudda. After an attempt to surprise the enemy, at the ford of Bhâwâ Peer, the British troops at length quitting the river, turned towards Dubhoee. The monsoon, however, commenced with unusual violence, and though they had no other enemy to encounter, and no more than twenty miles to march to their destination, it was upwards of a fortnight before the officers and privates of the English detachment found themselves sheltered within the time-hallowed walls which had been erected by the Kings of Unhilpoor.

Such was the termination of the first British campaign in Goozerat. If not wholly unsuccessful in its progress, it was certainly barren of immediate results. The supreme government, seated with new authority in Bengal, disapproved in no measured terms of the alliance with the ex-Peshwah. A cessation of hostilities was the consequence, and as soon as the state of the roads allowed, the detachment under Colonel Keating, accompanied by Râghobâ, returned towards Surat.

A few years afterwards the English, on this occasion as principals, were again at war with the Poonah government, of which the master-spirit was the celebrated Nânâ Furnuvees. On the 1st of January, A.D. 1780, General Goddard, in command of an English army, crossed the river Taptee, from Surat, and moved slowly northwards. His battering-train and stores having at last reached him, he marched to attack Dubhoee, then held in the name of the Peshwah, while the civil officers of the British government, raising irregular troops, expelled the partisans of Nânâ Furnuvees from the districts of Surat and Broach. On the 18th of January the army of General Goddard arrived before Dubhoee, and two days afterwards, a battery being in readiness to open upon the place, it was evacuated during the night by its Mahratta garrison. Futteh Singh, the acknowledged head of the Guikowâr state, with whom negotiations had been already commenced, signed, a few days afterwards, a treaty of offensive and defensive alliance, in virtue of which he was henceforth to possess the Peshwah's territory north of the Myhee, ceding at the same time to the British government his own lands in the districts of Surat and Broach. General Goddard accordingly pursued his march to the north, and on the 10th of February displayed, for the first time, the British colours before the Moslem capital of Goozerat. The Mahratta governor declining to surrender, a battery was opened on the 12th, and a breach was on the following evening declared practicable. From motives of humanity, and the fear of excesses in the city, the assault was during next day delayed, in hopes that the garrison might be induced to surrender. The endeavour was, however, unavailing, and on the morning of the 15th a forlorn hope, followed by the grenadiers of the Bombay division, rushed up the breach, which the garrison, after a determined stand, and when three hundred of their number had fallen, at length relinquished. The capital of Goozerat was scarcely reduced, when Goddard heard of the approach of Sindia and Holkar, who crossed the Nerbudda on the 29th with large bodies of horse, and advanced into the neighbourhood of Baroda. On the British general's marching against them they retired, however, towards Powangurh.

Dubhoee, which had been entrusted to the care of Mr. James Forbes, of the Civil Service, since known as the author of the "Oriental Memoirs," was meanwhile surrounded by the Mahratta horse, who encamped within sight of the walls, though not within reach of the cannon of the town. The garrison consisted only of three companies of sepoys, commanded by three European officers, a few European artillerymen and lascars, with five beruks or battalions of Arab and Sindhian irregular infantry. Two English gentlemen, a civil and a military officer, then hostages in the Mahratta camp, contrived to send a secret message to their countrymen within the town, counselling surrender, and pointing out that all resistance would be vain. Within Dubhoee, however, a different spirit prevailed, and though various articles of capitulation, culled from the Annual Registers and Encyclopædia, which were the principal treasures of James Forbes's scanty library, were looked over, that, in case of necessity, honorable terms might at least have been made, the treatises on fortification, gunnery, and similar subjects were more carefully studied, and preparations were made for strengthening the ramparts, repairing the towns at the Diamond-gate, and rendering the old Mahratta guns of service. The approach of General Goddard with his army from Ahmedabad, however, deprived the defenders of Dubhoee of an opportunity of testing the value of their preparations, and the Mahratta army broke up its encampment and retired.

The war continued with various fortune through a series of events, only indirectly affecting the interests of Goozerat, until the 17th of May, 1782, on which day a treaty was concluded at Salbhye, under the mediation of Muhadajee Sindia, between the British and the chiefs of the Mahratta nation. By this treaty, which was not finally ratified until the 24th of February, 1783, the position of the parties in Goozerat was to revert to that which had existed previous to the war of 1775; the territories of the Baroda state were secured from dismemberment, and no claim of tribute was to be preferred by the Peshwah against Futteh Singh for the period during which hostilities had continued. The valuable district of Broach was at the same time bestowed on Muhadajee Sindia, "in testimony," as was stated at the time by the Governor-General in Council, "of the sense which "they entertained of the generous conduct manifested by the said "Muhadajee Sindia to the government of Bombay, at Wargaum, in "January, 1779, and of his humane treatment and release of the "English gentlemen who had been delivered as hostages on that "occasion." Among the pergunnahs of Goozerat thus restored to the Mahrattas were those of Dubhoee and Zinore, and the other districts under the jurisdiction of Mr. Forbes, who was now directed to surrender them to such officer as might be deputed by the Mahratta state to receive them. At the same time the chief and council of Broach were ordered to deliver up that important city and its valuable pergunnah to Bhâsker Row, the agent of Muhadajee Sindia. The description which the author of the "Oriental Memoirs" has left us of the surrender of Dubhoee and Broach, contains so many characteristic and interesting features that we shall doubtless be excused if we present it in his own words :—"When," says Mr. Forbes, "it was "publicly known that Dubhoee and its dependent pergunnahs were "to be given up to the Mahratta government, and the day approached "which was fixed for my departure, a deputation from the Brahmins "and principal inhabitants visited me at the durbar, and sincerely "condoled with me on the change of affairs. They offered presents, "and were so hurt at my refusing anything tendered for my accept-"ance, that I was at length induced to mention a gift which I could "receive without conscientious scruples, if they could bestow it, "which from delicacy alone I had not before asked. Expressing "some surprise, and at the same time manifesting the greatest desire "to oblige me, I told them, that as Dubhoee contained many re-"mains of Hindoo antiquity, in broken columns, mutilated images, "and remnants of basso-relievo scattered among dilapidated build-"ings in the city, I requested they would allow me to select a few of "the smallest specimens from the exterior fragments, which I would "bring with me to Europe, and erect a temple for their reception in "my own garden. Their astonishment increased at this communica-"tion, and was followed by a solemn silence. They expressed no "apprehension of my ridiculing their religion, but seemed anxious to "know why a Christian wished to possess Hindoo idols. I found a "little difficulty in convincing them of the general curiosity of Euro-"peans, the gratification it would be to show them those specimens "of oriental sculpture, and the delightful association of my own ideas, "when I should behold in my own country the precious relics "transported from a distant spot endeared by a thousand tender "recollections.

"Their tears flowed when they requested to retire for a few hours, "during which they would assemble the recluse religious Brahmins, "and in a conclave consider the first request of the kind which "they had ever heard of. They returned the next morning with "countenances indicating mingled sensations of regret at my ap-"proaching departure, and of delight at having it in their power to "grant my request, to which they acceded in the most liberal "manner, desiring I would send my own people to select such "specimens as I thought proper, and place them in a temple to "friendship in my own country. I did so; and deputed some "*Hindoo* workmen to collect such small images as I pointed out in "the dilapidated walls of forsaken dewuls, and from the exterior "ornaments at the Gate of Diamonds, which, in eight groups, now "adorn an octagon building at Stanmore-hill, erected for that "purpose, under a linden-grove, on the margin of a lake profusely "adorned by the nymphea lotus, which, when its snowy petals and "expanded foliage are gently agitated by the southern breeze, re-"minds me of the sacred tanks in Goozerat."

The author, at length, took his departure for Broach, where he was witness to a similar scene :—

"The inhabitants of Broach, accustomed to the lenity of British "jurisdiction, execrated the approaching change, and dreaded the "arrival of Bhâsker Row, which had been delayed in consequence "of a mistaken renewal of hostilities on the Malabar coast; the "people of Broach, in the meantime, indulged a vain hope that the "intended cession would not take place. No prayers, no cere-"monies, no sacrifices, were left unperformed by the different castes "and religious professions, to implore the continuance of the British "government. It is with extreme satisfaction I recollect the un-"feigned sorrow which pervaded all ranks of society when the fatal "day was fixed for our departure. Broach, before its conquest by "the English, had belonged to the Moguls, and was governed by a "Mohummedan nowaub : the inhabitants well knew the difference "that awaited them. Of all oriental despots, the arbitrary power "of the Mahratta falls, perhaps, with the most oppressive weight; "they extort money by every kind of vexatious cruelty, without sup-"porting commerce, agriculture, and the usual sources of wealth and "prosperity in well-governed states. The Mohummedans, although "equally fond of money, spend it with more liberality, encourage "useful and ornamental works, and patronize art and science.

"On the ninth of July, 1783, the day appointed for the cession of "Broach to Muhadajee Sindia, the chief and council received his "agent, Bhâsker Row, with proper ceremony, in the durbar, and "there delivered to him the keys of the city-gates. We immediately "repaired to the water-side, to cross the Nerbudda in our way to "Surat, and were silently followed by the principal inhabitants of the "city. While embarking on the Company's yacht, a dark cloud "passed over us, and a shower of rain fell; our afflicted friends, no "longer able to keep silence, and forgetting the impending terrors of "a Mahratta despot, pathetically exclaimed, 'These drops are the "tears of heaven for the fate of Broach!'"

"I oppose this fact to a thousand unfounded prejudices, and un-
" supported calumnies, against the English, which were once so easily
" credited in Europe. Among the many who occupy eminent stations
" in India, some, no doubt, deserve censure; the characters of all
" who fill similar situations at home are not immaculate; the tempta-
" tions of wealth and power sometimes subdue the strongest minds;
" but the hour approaches when they cease to charm, and when a
" conscience 'void of offence' will be the only comfort. Whether
" the European or Indian peculator is now amenable to human laws
" or not, a secret monitor corrodes every present joy, and an un-
" erring Judge hereafter will avenge the breach of His own laws, esta-
" blished in truth and equity! The general opprobrium was unjust
" on a set of men whose prevailing characteristics were philanthropy,
" generosity, and benevolence."

Broach remained in the possession of Sindia from this period until the time when that chieftain engaged in war with the British government. It was taken from him by storm, by a part of the Baroda subsidiary force under the command of Colonel Woodington, on the 29th August, 1803.

Futteh Singh Guikowâr died in consequence of a fall from the upper story of his house, on the 21st December, 1789. A contest for the regency now occurred between Mânâjee, the full brother of Futteh Singh, and Gowind Row, which was only set at rest about four years afterwards by the death of Mânâjee. Though his title was now undisputed, Gowind Row Guikowâr found it, nevertheless, difficult to obtain permission to quit the Peshwah's capital. Nânâ Furnuvees sought to impose upon him stipulations to the advantage of the Poonah government, in addition to those exorbitant ones which had been already forced upon his family. The British government, however, intervened to prevent a dismemberment of the Guikowâr territories, contrary to the stipulations of the treaty of Salbhye, and the Furnuvees admitting the validity of their objections, Gowind Row was at last permitted to depart, for the purpose of assuming the regency at Baroda, on the 19th December, 1793.

Gowind Row Guikowâr died in September, 1800. He had been at war for two years with Âbâ Shelookur, the deputy of Chimnâjee Âppâ, Bâjee Row Peshwah's brother, as Governor of Goozerat. Shelookur, during the term of his government, made himself most obnoxious to the people by his tyrannies and exactions. The house now employed as the Session Court at Ahmedabad was built by him on the foundations of royal buildings of the Mohummedan sultans, and at the expense of the population whose materials he seized, or whose labour he compelled. Among other cruel deeds, he is accused of having seduced into his power a soldier of fortune, named Monsieur Jean (or, as he is commonly called, Moussa Jân), and of having caused him to be blown from the mouth of a cannon, in order to possess himself of his wealth. In 1800, Mr. Duncan, the Governor of Bombay, having arrived at Surat for the purpose of assuming the government of that city, on the demise of the last nowaub, vukeels were despatched by Gowind Row Guikowâr with the ostensible view of congratulating him on his arrival, but with the real object of procuring British assistance for the reduction of Shelookur. Mr. Duncan was himself prepared with requests that the Guikowâr government should cede to the British the pergunnah of Chourâsee, which surrounds the city of Surat, and their share of the Mahratta chouth of the revenues of the port. The application on the part of Gowind Row for assistance against Shelookur was, however, evaded, and no satisfactory result was at the time obtained in regard to the pergunnah of Chourâsee, or the chouth. The Guikowâr government now resolved upon reducing Shelookur with their independent means, and an army advanced from Baroda against Ahmedabad. Shelookur called in his lieutenants from Dâkorjee and Kâteewâr, and engaged the Guikowâr army near the Rozah of Shah Alum, outside the city. He was unsuccessful, and was compelled to take refuge in the citadel, where, being eventually deserted by his mercenaries, he was made prisoner. The Peshwah, who had been hostile to Shelookur on account of his connection with Nânâ Furnuvees, now granted his share of the revenue of Goozerat in farm to the Baroda government, at an annual rate of five lakhs of rupees for five years, and Rughoonâth Myheeput Row (commonly called Kâkâjee), the cousin of Rowjee Âppâjee, the Guikowâr minister, was appointed Governor of Ahmedabad.

CHAPTER III.

ÂNUND ROW GUIKOWÂR.[1]

THE death of the Muhârâjâ Gowind Row Guikowâr having occurred

[1] We depend henceforth upon bardic authority, and upon the unpublished papers in the Record Room at the East-India House, in London.

after midnight, on the 19th of September, 1800, Bâbâjee Âppâjee and Meer Kumâl-ood-deen Khân, the principal military officers present, joined with the two great bankers, Mungul Pâreekh and Sâmul Bechur, who held the Arab mercenaries in dependence, to effect a settlement of affairs. Early in the morning the ladies of the family were all assembled, and Ghenâ Bâee, the widow of the Muhârâjâ, a Jhâlâ Rajpoot lady of the house of Lugtur, declared her intention of burning with the corpse of her husband. From this step she was, however, dissuaded by the officers, who assured her, taking oaths to that effect on the Korân or in Hindoo modes, that they were determined to maintain the honor and influence which she enjoyed during the lifetime of her husband. The corpse of Gowind Row was now carried to the funeral pyre, and Ânund Row, his eldest legitimate son, commenced his reign. Rowjee Âppâjee, the late Gowind Row's minister, soon after arrived from Ahmedabad, and resumed the administration of affairs. The minister's first endeavour was to prevail upon the bankers and officers to take means for restraining the ambition of Kânhojee Row, an illegitimate son of the late raja, whom he accused of having already raised disturbances in the life-time of his father. This proposition was not, however, assented to; and soon after, Kânhojee Row, with the aid of some of the officers who adhered to his party, made himself master of the government, and of the person of his brother, Ânund Row Guikowâr. The tyrannical disposition of Kânhojee now had full opportunity for exhibiting itself. He conducted himself with so much violence towards all the officers of the government, and with so much contempt, if not actual severity, towards the Raja Ânund Row, that a general combination, with the apparent consent of his brother, was soon formed against him. On the night of the 27th January, 1801, his house having been surrounded, he was, after some resistance, seized, and brought before Ânund Row, under colour of whose authority he was disarmed and put in irons, and subsequently conveyed as a prisoner to the fortress of Râmpoor Roteah, among the hills which divide Goozerat from Malwa. Rowjee Âppâjee, from this time, became the real head of the executive government.

As early as April following, however, Gujrâ Bâee, the daughter of Futteh Singh Guikowâr, for reasons unknown, quarrelled with Rowjee Âppâjee, and sought shelter in the city of Surat, and before the end of the year a still more formidable malcontent was arrayed against the government of the minister. Peelâjee Guikowâr had conferred the government of Kuree upon his younger son, Khundee Row, who was confirmed in that possession by the Senâputee Dhâbâree, whose officer Peelâjee then was, and invested also with the title of Heemut Buhâdur. His son and successor, Mulhâr Row, was, on the rise of his family to sovereign power, confirmed in both his possessions and his rank by Futteh Singh Guikowâr, while, at the same time, his future allegiance to the head of his house was provided for by his agreeing to serve the state with four hundred horse. This service was, however, commutable for a payment of 120,000 rupees, and the Jâgheerdâr of Kuree, though admitting a feudal dependence on the sovereign of Baroda, was within his possessions as wholly independent of him, as was the Guikowâr himself, within his own territories, of the head of the Mahratta State. Mulhâr Row Guikowâr urged, as the minister represented, by demands lately made on him for arrears of tribute due to the state, or, as he himself asserted, and as the party of Gujrâ Bâee affirmed, by sympathy for the unmerited situation of Kânhojee Row, now began to assemble troops, and publicly declared his intention of punishing Rowjee Âppâjee and his brother, Bâbâjee, for their several unwarrantable and despotic acts, and of reinstating Kânhojee Row and the other ill-used members of the Guikowâr family in their just rights, which were withheld from them by those tyrannical ministers. Mookund Row, another illegitimate son of the late raja, had shortly before, under pretence of visiting the shrine of Shree Runchorjee, at Dâkor, retired from Baroda, carrying with him a large amount of jewels and treasure. The ministerial party endeavoured to procure his return; but as he would not listen to their remonstrances, and began to excite disturbances, they sent an army against him, upon which he fled into the Kuree territory, and took shelter with Mulhâr Row. Mulhâr Row had already taken forcible possession of the fortresses of Veesulnugger and Beejâpoor, which he affected to hold for Muhârâjâ Ânund Row, and he vaunted that forty thousand troops were in readiness at different points to espouse his cause. Shivrâm, an old officer in the Guikowâr service, disgusted, as it was said, at the conduct of the ministers, had gone over to him, and it was given out that several others, who held considerable commands, were about to follow this example. The forces of the contending factions already faced each other. Bâbâjee Âppâjee was encamped at the Shâhee Bâgh, near Ahmedabad, with his advanced guard at Kâlee-kâ-kot. Mulhâr Row himself remained at Kuree with a part of his force, but his brother, Hunmunt Row, with another division, was encamped at Kulol, eight coss in advance of Kuree, and about seven from the outposts of Bâbâjee's army. Three skirmishes had already taken place, in all of which Mulhâr Row claimed the advantage. Under these circumstances, both parties applied for assistance to the British governor. Gujrâ Bâee and her minister offered, on behalf of Kânhojee, not only the cession of the Chourâsee pergunnah, and the Guikowâr share of the chouth of Surat (the previous cession of which, by Gowind Row, had up to the time of his death been rendered ineffectual by the Peshwah's disapprobation), but also the pergunnah of Cheeklee, which they represented as more valuable than that of Chourâsee. Rowjee Âppâjee, on the other hand, in January, 1802, in the name of Muhârâjâ Ânund Row, deputed Meer Kumâl-ood-deen Khân, and two vukeels, to Mr. Duncan, who formally delivered a deed of relinquishment of the Chourâsee pergunnah and the Surat chouth, in fulfilment of the late Gowind Row's incomplete engagement. The British governor weighed, for a considerable period, the pretensions of both parties, but eventually determined on lending his assistance to the ministers who wielded power in the name of Ânund Row. Several reasons concurred to induce Mr. Duncan to adopt that course. There appeared to him to be, on the whole, no more reasons for relying on the veracity of Mulhâr Row's representatives than on that of their opponents, who were, moreover, in possession of the whole country, with the exception of the districts which the Jâgheerdâr of Kuree had overrun, in the vicinity of his own territory. The ostensible, and perhaps real sanction of Ânund Row Muhârâjâ, the undoubted head of the Guikowâr state, was given to the proposals of the ministers; and these officials called upon the British government in the most formal manner to comply with the terms of the treaty of Salbhye, by interfering to prevent the dismemberment of the Guikowâr state. Mulhâr Row was, as the governor was informed, endeavouring to introduce a foreign force from Sindh, the presence of which might have completely neutralized the influence of the British in Goozerat; and Mr. Duncan was further apprehensive that the ministerial party, should their demand for British assistance meet with an unfavorable reply, might throw themselves into the hands of Sindia. A detachment was therefore formed for the purpose of giving weight to the British arbitration, and of maintaining the integrity of the Guikowâr dominions. It consisted eventually of about two thousand men, four hundred of whom were Europeans, and the command was conferred upon Major Alexander Walker,—a name afterwards deservedly famous in the annals of Goozerat. This officer it was, however, determined should, as soon as possible, quit the military character, to assume the position of British resident at Baroda, a provision which Mr. Duncan (whose hope it still was to bring matters to a settlement without employing force) considered would render him the more disinclined to urge matters to extremity.

Major Walker was instructed to proceed in the first place to Baroda with the Guikowâr vukeels, his ostensible mission being that of presenting compliments and condolence, on the part of the British government, to the Muhârâja Ânund Row, on the death of his father, this ceremony having been delayed pending the cession of the Chourâsee and chouth. His real object was to ascertain the true state of Ânund Row's mind, and whether Hunmunt Row, the son of that prince, had received his father's consent to his joining the army under Bâbâjee. The military detachment was in the meantime to proceed by sea to Cambay, and to be joined there by Major Walker on the termination of his mission to Baroda.

Major Walker left Surat on the 24th of January, 1802, and reached Baroda on the 29th. The mission passed through Broach, where it was received with distinction by Sindia's officers. A deputation from the minister met them at the distance of a few miles from Baroda; and at a coss from the town they found Rowjee Âppâjee, attended by all the civil and military officers, waiting to receive them, in a spot where carpets had been spread, in the open air, for the meeting. Major Walker was presented to every person of consequence, including the Arab Jemâdârs, the whole displaying the greatest cordiality. He proceeded thence to Baroda, where he was conducted to a suite of tents that had been prepared for him, a body of troops receiving him with rested arms, and a salute being fired from some field-pieces on the spot. Next day, the minister repeated his visit to the British envoy, and at once exhibited his great anxiety for the reduction of Kuree and the total expulsion of Mulhâr Row. The British envoy, unwilling to discuss the matter at that time, turned the conversation to the subject of the supplies required for the efficiency of the detachment at Cambay. It was agreed at this interview, that Major Walker should attend the Muhârâjâ that afternoon. This design was, however, prevented by Ânund Row's declaring that he felt it incumbent on him to pay the first visit. Major Walker, in return for this courtesy, met the Guikowâr prince on the road, and Ânund Row, descending from his elephant, embraced him, and proceeded with him to the tents. The raja was attended by all the officers of his court, and by an escort of horse and foot, and was received with a salute of artillery. He retired, at Major Walker's request, into a private apartment, with such of his sirdârs and chiefs as he selected to accompany him. The governor's compliments and message of condolence on the death of the late Gowind Row were now offered. The Muhârâjâ received them without the least attention, and it was soon apparent to the envoy that his mind was in a state which incapacited him for close application of any kind. The following graphic description of the scene which ensued is given in Major Walker's own words :—

"Ânund Row appears about thirty or forty years of age, of a robust "person, and a body that has no visible signs of feebleness, but an "unmeaning countenance and heavy eyes betray at once perhaps a "natural imbecility, and the ruinous effects of intoxicating drugs, to "which he is said to be addicted. Probably both these means "operate to depress the mind of this prince, but his incapacity for "business is here imputed more to the pernicious habit of smoking "bang, than to constitutional weakness. Notwithstanding these "marks of mental debility, Ânund Row appeared in possession of "his recollection, he named several of his officers, and was not "without a general knowledge of the affairs of his state. If at any "time he appeared embarrassed, Rówjee and Kumâl-ood-deen were "always ready to assist. The ornaments for his person were the only "part of the presents that engaged any part of his attention. He "repeatedly adjusted the surpech to his turban, and removed the "dustbund from his wrist to his ângrukhâ.[1] Âghâ Mohummed's "watch attracted his notice, and he examined it childishly. Towards "the conclusion of the interview, he appeared for a moment to re-"cover himself, and observed that he had many enemies, who spread "false reports of his situation and of the state of his mind, but that "he hoped by my means, the governor would be undeceived, and "that I would write him the truth. In this request, Rowjee and "Kumâl-ood-deen repeatedly joined, observing it was now easy to "see how much the raja had been injured by report. Ânund Row "next adverted to the hostility of Mulhâr Row, and expressed his ex-"pectation that the major would hasten to punish his enemies. He "mentioned several times their expulsion from Kuree, as an object "which he earnestly desired; this desire was re-echoed by the at-"tendants. The raja was assured that the Company's government had "the advantage of the Guikowâr states always in view, and that the "justice of his cause and the English forces would effectually pro-"tect him against his enemies. During this interview the Raja "Ânund Row conducted himself with humility, frequently declaring "his dependence on the English government, and his respect and "attachment to the Company, founded on the intimate connection "formed by his ancestors. After the customary offering of rose-water "and betel, the Guikowâr Ânund Row took his leave and returned."

[1] The *ângrukhâ* is a body-coat; the meaning is, that he pulled the sleeve of his coat under the bracelet on his wrist—not an uncommon mode of fidgetting.

On the 1st of February the envoy visited the Muhârâjâ in his palace. "The demeanour of the prince," says Major Walker, "was "much more collected than on the former day; he was cheerful, and "the stupidity of his first appearance seemed to give way to a consi- "derable share of benevolence, and even of intelligence. After the "public conversation, Ânund Row presented the mission with presents, "and requested our attendance in a private apartment. An indiscri- "minate number of the leading men, with their attendants, forced "themselves into the apartment. Ânund Row pronounced an eulo- "gium upon Rowjee, and evinced a strong desire to inflict a due "punishment upon Mulhâr Row. He said that the presence of his "son, Hunmunt Row, with the army was entirely his own act; men- "tioned that he was twelve years of age, and spoke of him with satis- "faction. He positively denied that Mulhâr Row had in any manner "obtained his sanction to prosecute war; but when he was asked "whether Kânhojee was imprisoned with his consent, he made no "reply—he hung down his head, rolled his eyes, and maintained an "expressive silence. The officers then attempted to answer for him, "but he still remained silent. He whispered to me that the Arab "Jemâdârs were all his mortal enemies, and that they would not per- "mit him to converse freely. The mission soon after retired." Major Walker was afterwards informed by the Muhârâjâ's confidant, Mungul Pâreekh, that it was a religious feeling which made him silent when questioned respecting the confinement of Kânhojee. He had continued to consider the imprisonment of his brother as a crime, and an act of impiety, notwithstanding the public necessity for it, and when the event first happened he had allowed his beard to grow, as a sign of mourning, and had for a long period afflicted himself with mortifications.

The Guikowâr government, as it appeared to Major Walker, was in so absolute a state of weakness and disorder, that it must have dissolved, unless strengthened by external support. The confusion of authorities, and the misery thereby entailed upon the people, were hardly to be conceived—nothing but the absence of order everywhere prevailed; the pay of all departments was in arrears; the country was mortgaged to money-lenders, who collected from it what they pleased; a single mercenary leader travelled about with more authority than the prince; and an armed aristocracy had possessed themselves of the government, holding the Muhârâjâ himself completely under their control; while, from their own administrative incapability, they were, in their turn, wholly in the hands of the bankers. The expenditure at this time of the Guikowâr government exceeded its means by four or five lakhs of rupees during the year. The minister, Rowjee Âppâjee, was a person fitted by his acuteness and prudence for the management of public business, but he had been familiar with revolutions, having witnessed or taken part in the changes that, during forty years, had shaken the numerous branches of the Mahratta empire. His character had thus become tinged with suspicion, his caution degenerated sometimes into timidity, he was not at liberty to pursue his own plans, and wanted firmness to wrest their usurped power from the Arab officers. He appeared sometimes to distrust the intentions of the British, while at others he exhibited a degree of candour and openness in his conversation which had all the appearance of security. The Deewân was said to be frequently too communicative, and to prejudice, by this disposition, both his own affairs and those of the state.

The Arabs were, in Major Walker's opinion, the only material obstacle to the complete establishment of the British influence in Goozerat, but he did not consider them to be in reality formidable. Though they were brave, their ferocity rendered them incapable of subordination; though they were attached to individual chiefs, that very attachment prevented their union under any common system. Their real number was less than seven thousand, of whom no more than one thousand were concentrated in any single position. About a fourth part only of these were natives of Arabia, the remainder were men of Arabian extraction, but born themselves in Goozerat. Their arms, which were chiefly match-locks, were bad, and their knowledge of war was contemptible; of the forts which were in their possession, Baroda, considered to be the best, was in no state to resist a regular attack. Two battalions of British troops stationed at Baroda were sufficient, Major Walker thought, effectually to counterpoise the power of these mercenaries, and he was sanguine that, when their influence was thus reduced, their situation would appear to themselves to be less desirable, and their numbers would decline. The Arabs were divided into two parties, at the head of which were the bankers, Mungul Pâreekh and Sâmul Bechur. The latter was reputed to possess a cunning, avaricious, and intriguing disposition. He was not well affected towards the British, and the party of Arabs which was under his control was the more numerous.

Rowjee was at first very much dissatisfied when he learnt that the British government had it in view to accommodate matters with Mulhâr Row, instead of punishing him by military force. He contended that nothing was to be done without taking Kuree. Major Walker urged, in reply, that this mode of proceeding might be the means of perpetuating the disorder of the country, for, although it would be an easy matter to take Kuree, Mulhâr Row would probably escape, and for a length of time harass the borders by a predatory warfare. Rowjee said that it was his intention to request that two of the British battalions should remain to prevent the enemy's return, and added, that he proposed to repay this assistance by the cession of a convenient tract of country on the sea-coast. Kuree should, he said, be taken, with all Mulhâr Row's country, elephants, and horses; and a jâgheer, worth a lakh of rupees annually, might then be assigned to that chief in a different part of the country. The British envoy was, however, instructed to demand that the fullest authority should be given to him to settle disputes in an equitable manner, and it was intimated that if Rowjee were determined, at all events, on the extirpation of Mulhâr Row, it would be better, perhaps, that British intervention should proceed no further, and that the troops should be recalled. Rowjee, at length, professed that he would be satisfied if the English force would only encamp for a day or two within the limits of the Kuree Jâgheerdâr, in return for that chieftain's invasion of the territories of the Baroda state; he further offered to resign a large portion of the tribute payable by Mulhâr Row, provided that concession would ensure a peaceable demeanour on his part.

The opinions of Major Walker, as reported to his government, were, that justice and policy alike warranted the punishment of Mulhâr Row should he decline to make submission to his sovereign. Holding his jâgheer as a vassal of the Muhârâjâ, that chief had withheld the payment of his tribute; and when called to account, had taken up arms, under pretence of defending himself against a foreign enemy, and notwithstanding a declaration to the contrary, had been guilty of aggressions against his sovereign, with the ultimate view of dethroning him. Little weight could be allowed to Mulhâr Row's pretext that he was in arms in behalf of Kânhojee, as that prince had no real claim to the throne, and as Mulhâr Row himself had acquiesced in his deposition, and even celebrated it by a discharge of artillery. His invasion of the Guikowâr territory was also long posterior to that event, and it was accompanied neither by any declaration of hostility, nor even by any previous complaint. If Mulhâr Row remained obstinate the task of reducing him would be a popular one, and its successful accomplishment must necessarily be followed by the acceptance of a subsidiary force. It was, perhaps, even necessary to this object that the British should perform a service which would be at once apparent; and after a successful expedition to Kuree, the detachment, or a similar body of troops, might, by an easy arrangement, be moved to Baroda, and firmly established there.

The envoy quitted Baroda on the afternoon of the 8th of February, having been completely successful in his mission. Bâbâjee, with the Guikowâr forces, were put under his command, and he was fully authorised, in case of Mulhâr Row's applying for peace, to act in such a manner as he might deem suitable to the interests and safety of the government of the Muhârâjâ.

CHAPTER IV.

MULHÂR ROW GUIKOWÂR.

If we have given a more detailed account of these negotiations than may seem to be consistent with the character of our work, our excuse will be found in the fact, that upon them really hinged the future fate of Goozerat. Had the aid of the British been rejected, and had the troops advanced no further than Cambay, the territories of the Baroda government must inevitably have fast relapsed into a state of miserable anarchy and confusion, similar to that in which the dominions of Holkar and Sindia were subsequently involved. As it was, affairs progressed rapidly towards that settlement which formed the groundwork of all future political relations in Goozerat.

The British detachment disembarked at Cambay, from Surat, on the morning of the 2nd of February, and encamped in an open spot, which, in 1775, had been occupied by the troops of Colonel Keating, contiguous to the reservoir called Nârâyun Sur, a garden-house being assigned for the accommodation of the head-quarters. The forces of Bâbâjee and Mulhâr Row were meanwhile engaged in desultory and indecisive skirmishes, while negotiations, as profitless as the hostilities, still continued. Mulhâr Row's troops numbered altogether, it was said, about fifteen thousand men.[1] Shivrâm, who was the only officer of consequence, commanded about seven hundred Hindoostânees, who affected the semblance of regular discipline; he led also three hundred or four hundred Mahratta horse. An Englishman, named Parker, commanded a corps called the "Gosâeen's wife's troops," and one Joaquim, a Portuguese, led about two hundred men, among whom he had attempted to introduce some order, so

[1] This was Parker's account, though he himself varied in his statement. Major Walker estimated them at from ten to twelve thousand horse and foot, with ten or fifteen pieces of artillery, mostly of small calibre.

that "a few were in red jackets, but the greater part went agreeable "to their own fancy," as Parker writes, "both in dress and fighting." Sindhis and Puthâns, Kâtees and Koolees, made up the rest of this heterogeneous army. The latter, who were "armed horse," wearing the antique tunic of chain armor, were under the command of "a "famous leader, called *Boobât Singh*, who had lately distinguished "himself in two or three skirmishes with Bâbâjee's troops," and whom we shall hereafter introduce to our readers as the notorious Thâkurâ of Bhunkora. Bhooput Singh, though now the most distinguished of his partisans, had formerly been the constant enemy of Mulhâr Row. During the administration of Kânhojee he had been sent for to Baroda to be employed, as it was said, against the Jâgheerdâr of Kuree, but happening to be taken into custody at the same time that Kânhojee was seized, he had been released by Rowjee, lest he should, from future resentment, proceed to attack the territories of Mulhâr Row.

The 22nd of February had arrived without any step in advance having been made by the British troops. Meanwhile, Mulhâr Row had been carrying on with the Arab officers intrigues which had for their object the release of Kânhojee, while the adherents of the opposite party were dispirited by the delay made by the English, and by the fact that the resident at Cambay had despatched an agent to Kuree. Mulhâr Row refused to disarm his troops, or to give up Veesulnugger and the other places seized by him, which concessions, on his part, were deemed to be indispensable preliminaries to an arrangement. Mr. Duncan, who was now at Cambay, determined at length to direct the detachment to march at once, with a view of forming a junction with the army of Bâbâjee. Mulhâr Row was informed that the troops advanced to release from his grasp those parts of the Muhârâjâ's country which he had unjustly taken possession of; he was to be allowed, however, in case of his surrendering them, to come in to Mr. Duncan with an escort of not more than one hundred men, and was informed that he must expect no other terms. Major Walker marched, accordingly, on the 23rd; reached Ahmedabad on the 4th of March; and next day he was at Udâlej, where he left his heavy baggage and sick under a guard. Mulhâr Row still continuing to negociate, without affording any satisfactory proof of his sincerity, the British detachment entered the Kuree territory on the 10th, leaving behind them the Guikowâr troops, whose irregularities might have afforded ground of complaint. They encamped at Seretah, at which place Mulhâr Row, of his own accord, proposed to have an interview with Major Walker. The meeting took place accordingly, but was attended by circumstances such as, to the mind of the British commander, precluded every hope of a peaceable adjustment. The insincerity and distrust of Mulhâr Row were established by the extraordinary number of armed attendants with which he appeared at the interview, amounting to more than two thousand horse and foot, with three pieces of artillery. He also evaded his proposed visit to the British camp, and would proceed no further than a place two miles from the camp, where an awning had been spread for the preliminary interchange of compliments. Next evening, however, Mulhâr Row, after many excuses, visited Major Walker, when he promised immediately to disband his new levies, and to comply in every point with the wishes of the British government. He urged, however, that to save his dignity, the terms should be arranged privately through confidential agents, a request with which Major Walker complied. The terms demanded were, that Mulhâr Row should make full satisfaction to the Muhârâjâ, by an entire restitution of all his conquests, by restoring to freedom all Guikowâr subjects who had been seized by him, and repaying all sums levied from them by arranging for the payment of his arrears of tribute, and of the expenses of the war, and by giving security for the future good conduct. His new levies were to be disbanded and his ordinary forces drawn within the walls of Kuree, in the vicinity of which town the British army was to encamp, until such time as Major Walker should be satisfied of his sincerity. The British troops, it was settled, were to move at once to Kulol, the Guikowâr forces following at an interval, and the commanding officer was at that place to have a final interview with Mulhâr Row. Major Walker having arrived on the 15th at Kulol, found the place deserted, and meeting with no intelligence of Mulhâr Row, advanced on the 16th to Boodâsun, a village about three miles distant from Kuree. On the approach of the British troops, a few of Mulhâr Row's horse were observed, who retired immediately, without committing any act of hostility. An adjoining height was soon taken possession of, and a picket, with a field piece, was placed in the most commanding position. From the heights thus occupied, Major Walker had a full view of Kuree, with the camp of Mulhâr Row and the whole of his army, which appeared in motion, spreading itself over the plains. The fort of Kuree was small and irregular; it possessed four gates, of which one only, the Futteh gate, was protected by defences newly raised, and mounted with cannon. The residence of Mulhâr Row, inclosed in a sort of citadel, was conspicuous from a distance, especially its large minaret-like tower, the open pavilion on the summit of which commanded a good view of the surrounding country. About noon, messengers arrived from Mulhâr Row, who presented letters expressing sentiments of so much moderation, if not submission, that Major Walker was far from suspecting that they were to be made the cloak of an act of treachery. An answer was despatched by the hands of a native agent, named Soondurjee, and of Captain Williams, an officer of the detachment. They had not been gone twenty minutes, and had hardly time to reach the outposts of Mulhâr Row's army, when they were made prisoners, and two guns belonging to that chieftain immediately opened fire upon the British camp. Major Walker held a short consultation with the chiefs of the allies, assigned them their places, and arranged with them that the whole force should advance and assault the enemy's camp. Kumâl-ood-deen Khân, reinforced to nearly a thousand horse, formed accordingly on the right flank of the British detachment; while Bâbâjee himself, with the infantry, the rest of the cavalry, and some artillery, was appointed to move on the left. The British detachment, on the allies giving notice of their readiness, began, between two and three o'clock, to advance in line with its field-pieces, two howitzers, and two eighteen-pounders. It moved forward slowly, but in excellent order, inclining to the right, in order to gain some heights, and to reach the front of the main body of the enemy. The fire of Mulhâr Row's artillery increased as the British advanced, and the ground was unfortunately favorable to its effect. About five o'clock, however, Major Walker found himself opposite to the enemy's encampment, in full view of it, and about half a mile distant. He was now anxious to have carried out the assault which he had meditated, but a report was at this time brought to him, that Bâbâjee's division had advanced little beyond their encampment, and that his Arabs refused to move in the direction of the British troops; while it became at the same time evident that Kumâl-ood-deen, who had for a time continued to maintain pretty well the station allotted to him, had now fallen behind, and was unable to keep that flank clear against the superior bodies of the enemy's cavalry. Major Walker was now compelled to relinquish his meditated enterprise, which, without the effectual support of the allies, was of too hazardous a nature, he therefore inclined still further to the right, a step which, while it removed the detachment gradually to a greater distance from the enemy's fire, enabled it also to occupy some rising ground which was possessed by bodies of their horse. In this position the detachment halted until dusk, when it returned, without any interruption from the enemy, to its former encampment. The loss of the enemy was reported to have been considerable, but the casualties on the British side were also heavy. Lieutenant Creagh, of His Majesty's 80th Regiment, and Captains MacDonald and Lovell, of the Honorable Company's service, were killed. The total loss in killed and wounded was one hundred and forty-six, twenty-five of whom were Europeans; and a six-pounder, the carriage of which had fallen to pieces, was left upon the field.

Major Walker was now satisfied that the war could not, with the forces at his disposal, be terminated by a *coup-de-main*. He resolved, therefore, to adopt the system of the Mahrattas themselves, and agreed, after consulting with Bâbâjee, to erect batteries, and to proceed against the enemy's camp as if it were a fortified town. Meanwhile Mr. Duncan, at Cambay, and his colleagues at the presidency, exerted themselves to push forwards the largest reinforcements which could be assembled. The whole of the disposable force at Bombay was immediately embarked, and a pressing requisition made to Colonel Sir William Clarke, the British commanding officer at Goa, to join the army before Kuree with the European brigade under his orders, and a battalion of native infantry. His Majesty's ships "Intrepid" and "Terpsichore," the Honorable Company's ship "Cornwallis," and the "Upton Castle," were employed to convey the additional troops to the northwards.

For some time a desultory warfare continued before Kuree, the enemy for the most part respecting Major Walker's force, and directing their hostility chiefly against the army of the Guikowâr commanders. Major Walker, on the other hand, finding that his own ammunition was insufficient, that the artillery of Bâbâjee's army was unserviceable, and that that leader's troops, if not actually wanting in courage, nor destitute of fidelity, were still lukewarm, and far less disposed to the cause they had espoused than the brave, though undisciplined Puthâns, Gosâeens, and Koolees, who composed the force of Mulhâr Row, deemed it his duty to confine himself to defensive measures, or at least to undertake no enterprise which his detachment could not execute without the support of the allies. Negotiations were at the same time going on between Major Walker and Mulhâr Row. The former, who was anxious to relieve Captain Williams from the ill-treatment to which as a captive he was exposed, even made concessions, but Mulhâr Row only rose in his terms, and the whole conference was productive of no effect.

Sir William Clarke arrived and took command at Cambay on the 12th April. It had at first been intended that the detachments as they landed should have been sent on at once, but it was ascertained that a thousand of the enemy's horse, under Bhooput Singh of Bhunkora, lay in wait to intercept them, and it was judged prudent to avoid the risk. Sir William Clarke, therefore, marched with the whole force, and joined Major Walker at Boodâsun, on the 24th of April, when he found himself at the head of a body of troops which, independently of the allies, amounted to between five and six thousand men, more than two thousand of whom were Europeans. The first task of the British commander was to despatch a message to Mulhâr Row, offering him, for the last time, an opportunity of peaceably submitting to the terms which had been demanded of him. During the consultation which was held at Mulhâr Row's, when the news of Sir William Clarke's arrival was announced, Mookund Row Guikowâr upbraided Shivrâm, Bhooput Singh, and the chief of the Puthâns, with having prevented the peaceable settlement of affairs, and stigmatized them as the authors of the approaching calamity. The other leaders of the party "looked at each other with much concern;" Mulhâr Row himself was fearful and agitated, but, for whatever reason, no answer was returned to the summons, and affairs were allowed to take their course. Preparatory to an attack on the town of Kuree, Sir William Clarke found it necessary to disperse the army of the enemy, which was strongly entrenched in its front. The strongest of these works was a battery with a cavalier, forming the right of the enemy's position, defended, as it was said, by twelve hundred or fourteen hundred Puthâns, commanded by an European officer. On the 30th April, a force consisting of His Majesty's 75th Regiment, with the flank companies of the 84th, and the Honorable Company's grenadier battalion, supported by the remainder of the 84th Regiment and four guns, the whole under the command of Lieutenant Colonel Woodington, prepared to attack this post: they arrived unperceived in the rear of the battery just as the day broke, and immediately carried it at the point of the bayonet. Some of the captured guns were instantly directed against the enemy. The British troops vigorously pursued their advantage, and the whole of the entrenchments in front of Kuree were, before eleven o'clock, in their possession, while the army which had attempted the defence was completely routed and dispersed. This success would have been effected, in so far as the resistance of the enemy had been concerned, with inconsiderable loss, but a tumbril, loaded with ammunition, which had been taken from Mulhâr

Row's troops, unfortunately exploded, and was the cause of nearly the whole of the casualties which occurred.[1] Mulhâr Row's camp and the neighbouring village of Cudale were plundered and set on fire, and his troops flying to the gates of the town, found them barricaded against their entrance, and received orders to disperse. They re-formed for a moment on the opposite side of Kuree, but were soon again in the greatest confusion. In the moment of alarm Mulhâr Row released Captain Williams, whom he had treacherously seized and detained, and that officer, accompanied by Soondurjee, arrived in the evening at the British camp.

Bâbâjee, who immediately despatched an account of this success to his brother, was in raptures with the valour of his allies, and the happy prospect thereby opened to himself and his friends. "I was "quite astonished, Bâbâ Sâhib!" he says, "to see the manner in "which the English fought. I do not suppose anybody in the "world can fight like them. They completed their intention in six "hours, and Kuree, by the good fortune of Shreemunt, must fall in "two days. From Cudale to Kuree is about half a coss. The "English line is close to the ditch. The effect of bringing the "English here will diffuse a proper and just sense of your wisdom, "and will make them respected and feared, not only by your enemies, "but by all the world, for their great bravery, by which means all our "care is over, for now we shall have it in our power to do all we "like."

The release of Captain Williams and Soondurjee, by Mulhâr Row, led to a further intimation to him from Sir William Clarke; and the day after the action that chief, having sent word that he would surrender, a small party was, by his own desire, sent to one of the gates of the town to escort him into the British camp. He had even taken his place in the palanquin at the gateway, when he was prevented from proceeding by the remonstrances and apparent resistance

[1] The following is the

Return of Killed and Wounded,—

	killed	wounded		
Europeans	22	82	=104	=162
Natives	6	52	= 58	

including

Officers Killed,—

Lieutenant Francis Ivie, Her Majesty's 84th Regiment
,, David Price, ,, 86th ,,

Officers Wounded,—

Lieutenant Henry Polcher, 1st (or Grenadier) Battalion
,, Henry Roome, 1st Battalion 6th Regiment.

of his own people. A breaching battery was therefore commenced, and made rapid progress, and on the 3rd of May, Mulhâr Row actually surrendered himself on no other terms than those of safety to himself and family. Two days afterwards the fort of Kuree was completely evacuated by the enemy, and taken possession of by the allied forces, the British and Guikowâr flags being displayed together thereon. It was found to contain thirty-seven pieces of ordnance of various calibre, besides elephants, camels, and a great quantity of ammunition and stores.

The fall of Kuree was immediately followed by the establishment of British influence at Baroda. As early as the month of March a convention had been concluded between Mr. Duncan and Rowjee Âppâjee, by which the Guikowâr state confirmed for ever its cession of the Chourâsee pergunnah and the chouth, and assigned, in security for the payment of the expenses of the British troops, its share of the Uttâveesee district, near Surat. By a secret article, which was not to be carried into effect until the end of the war, the Baroda government also agreed to permanently subsidize about two thousand native infantry, one company of European artillery, and its proportion of Lascars, the expenses of which force were also to be made good by an assignment of territory in such part of the Guikowâr dominions as might best suit the convenience of the contracting parties. The Arab force was also to be reduced. On the 4th of June, the government of Ânund Row Guikowâr, in testimony of their sense of the assistance offered to them by the British, made a free present to the Company of the district of Cheeklee, in the Surat Uttâveesee; and two days afterwards a further agreement was entered into, by which the convention of March, and the cession of Cheeklee, were formally confirmed, and it was provided that the British government should advance money for the payment of the Arabs who were to be reduced, —the loan being secured on the pergunnahs of Baroda, Korul, Zinore, Pitlâd, and Ahmedabad. On the same day, a deed was executed by Muhârâjâ Ânund Row, in which he agreed to assign the pergunnah of Dholka towards defraying the charges of the subsidiary force for future services, and to place it in possession of the British from the commencement of the Hindoo year 1860 (A.D. 1804). A further bond was at the same time passed for the expenses of the troops during the first year, being 780,000 rupees. It stipulated a "jaydad," or assignment of land, for 50,000 rupees, in the villages of Nerriâd, and pledged for the discharge of the balance the revenue of Kuree, with the Moolukgeeree collections from Kâteewâr, for the years 1857-8 (A.D. 1801-2). On the 7th of June, Major Walker was directed to enter upon his duties as resident at Baroda. He arrived accordingly at that place on the 11th July, and was received with great attention by the Guikowâr government. His tents were pitched, at Rowjee's suggestion, in a suburban garden, within sight of the minister's own residence, and in that situation he hoisted the British flag.

A few days before, news had arrived of the successful termination of a second revolt against the government of Ânund Row. Gunput Row, a relative of the Guikowâr family, had long ago endeavoured to possess himself of the supreme power, in preference to the late Muhârâjâ Gowind Row, notwithstanding which the good nature and easy temper of that prince had assigned to him the small district and stronghold of Sunkheira, at a moderate revenue, which he had of late withheld, intending, in co-operation with Mulhâr Row, to establish his independence. Since the fall of Kuree he had, however, been compelled to shut himself up in his castle, which, though mounting only a couple of guns, and otherwise contemptible in point of means of defence, had sustained an attack by the Guikowâr troops. Gunput Row had also been joined by Morâr Row, one of the illegitimate brothers of the Muhârâjâ. A detachment of British troops under Captain Bethune soon joined the Guikowâr force, and on the 7th July the fort of Sunkheira surrendered under a capitulation, which secured the lives and private property of the garrison. Gunput Row and Morâr Row had, however, escaped on foot, with a few attendants, the night preceding the capitulation, and now took refuge at Dhâr, with Bappoo Powâr, a son-in-law of the late Gowind Row, and a considerable Jâgheerdâr in Malwa.

The attention of both the Guikowâr ministry and the British resident was now for some months occupied in the difficult task of dispersing the Arab militia, who had for so many years controlled every movement of the state. Into the details of these transactions it is unnecessary for us to enter,—sufficient to observe that the aid of British troops was found indispensable, and that the Arab chiefs, besieged in the town of Baroda, were at length compelled to capitulate to a force under the command of Colonel Woodington, on the 26th December, 1802.

The steps by which British influence was introduced into Goozerat have thus been sketched. We may take the present opportunity of briefly noticing its future progress.

A definitive treaty of general defensive alliance was concluded with the Guikowâr on the 21st April, 1805, for the purpose of consolidating the stipulations contained in preceding agreements, and making some additions and alterations which were deemed expedient. The Guikowâr had previously received a subsidiary force of two thousand men, and he now engaged to maintain three thousand, who were to be stationed within his territory, but employed only on occasions of importance. Districts yielding 11,70,000 rupees were assigned for their support. The districts of Chourâsee, Cheeklee, and Kaira, together with the chouth of Surat, were ceded to the British, and the revenue of other districts was appropriated for liquidating the debt due to them by the Guikowâr's government.[1]

No settlement between the governments of Baroda and Poonah had taken place since the accession of Gowind Row. On the suppression of the rebellion of Âbâ Shelookur, the Guikowâr agreed to hold Ahmedabad in farm from the Peshwah, including the tribute of Kâteewâr, with the districts of Pitlâd, Nâpâr, Choorâ-Rânpoor, Dhundhooka, and Gogo, and some rights in Cambay. By the treaty of Bassein, however, the districts of Rânpoor, Gogo, and Dhundhooka, and the Peshwah's rights in Cambay, were ceded to the British government. A lease of the remainder was granted by the Poonah government to the Guikowâr for ten years, from June, 1804. But on the expiration of this term, the proposed renewal of the lease was positively rejected by the Peshwah, who had now become anxious to increase his political influence in Goozerat and Trimbukjee Dainglia, in 1815, having obtained the appointment of Sur-Soubahdâr,

[1] The following is a "Statement of the cessions from the government of Ânund Row Guikowâr, and Jaydad, to the Hon. East-India Company," being one of the papers by Gungâdhur Shâstree, appended to Colonel Walker's Report of 1st January, 1806.

Enams.			
Killahdary of Kaira ... rupees	42,000		
Pergunnah of Cheeklee	76,000		
Chouth of Surat Bunder	50,000		
Pergunnah of Chourâsee	90,000		
		2,58,000	
Jaydad.			
Pergunnah of Nerriâd	1,75,000		
Dholka	4,50,000		
Beejâpoor	1,30,000		
Mâtur	1,30,000		
Moondeh	1,10,000		
Tuppa of Kuree Pergunnah	25,000		
Customs of Kimcatodrah	50,000		
Annual Wurâts on Kâteewâr	1,00,000		
		11,70,000	
			14,28,000

took possession of the districts in that province in the Peshwah's name, and began to use the influence thus obtained in intriguing against the British power. By the treaty of Poonah, in 1817, the Peshwah, however, bound himself to disavow this turbulent chieftain; he relinquished at the same time all future demands on the Guikowâr, and compromised all past claims, and he ceded his revenue in Goozerat, with the exception of Oolpâr, to the British Government.

On the 6th November, in the same year, a further treaty was concluded at Baroda, by which the Guikowâr, who had secured important advantages by the treaty of Poonah, acceded to a plan for the consolidation of the territories of the respective governments in Goozerat, engaged to increase his subsidiary force by an addition of one thousand regular infantry and two regiments of cavalry, and assigned to the British government, for defraying the increased expense, districts lying conveniently for the meditated consolidation.

CHAPTER V.

MOOLUKGEEREE IN KÂTEEWÂR.

We have already seen that the Kings of Unhilpoor and the Sultans of Ahmedabad pursued in the main a very similar policy in regard to their neighbours. When they found themselves strong enough to do so, they effected a complete conquest, but, in the more numerous cases, where subjugation was impracticable, they contented themselves with the exaction of a tribute, rather than prosecute a doubtful contest to extremity. During the government of Goozerat by the Sultans, and afterwards by the Imperial Soubahdârs stationed at Ahmedabad, the Mohummedan authority was supported by garrisons, placed in fortified positions throughout the country, which ensured to some extent the regular collection of the tributary revenue, and rendered expeditions for its enforcement, except in special cases, unnecessary. These posts were, however, gradually withdrawn or driven out, and amid the frequent scenes of anarchy which were witnessed during the last days of the Mogul government, not a few were the result of endeavours to collect the revenue due from the tributaries by annual military expeditions. This course, which with the Mohummedans was compulsory and exceptional, was with their successors congenial and regular. It was a prominent feature in the policy of the Mahrattas that their sole object, in almost every country to which their arms extended, was the enforcement of a payment. It was not until some time after experience had taught them the advantages, towards the creation of a revenue, which a permanent settlement would yield, that their thoughts were even directed to a regular administration of the countries which they had subdued. "When the Mahrattas," says their historian, "proceeded beyond their boundary, to collect revenue "and to make war were synonymous; whenever a village resisted, its "officers were seized, and compelled by threats, and sometimes by "torture more or less severe, to come to a settlement; ready money "was seldom obtained, but securities from bankers, with whom all "the villages had dealing, were preferable, as they were exchanged for "bills payable in any part of India. When the garrisons of fortified "places made an unsuccessful resistance they were put to the sword." These expeditions, so peculiarly suited to the mercenary temper of the Mahrattas, were called "Moolukgeeree," or circuits of the country. On their first appearance in Goozerat, the example of their Mohummedan predecessors and the circumstances of the country, as well as their own predilections, led them to the adoption of these tributary expeditions. Bodies of three thousand or four thousand predatory horse, without guns or camp equipage, pursued their plundering march through those parts of the country which were still possessed by Rajpoot chiefs, and adjusted the amount of their demands to the ability of the Bhoomeeâ to comply, or their own power to enforce. As the government of the country became more settled, the Molukgeeree expeditions were undertaken with a certain number of irregular infantry, and began to assume more permanent features. It was a principle of the Mahratta commanders to increase the amount of their exactions, if possible, or at least not to recede from the demands of their predecessors, and so tenacious were they of this latter rule, that, in cases of arrears of tribute, a payment for two years at the former rate was preferred by them to a complete settlement on more moderate terms. With the Rajpoot chieftains, on the other hand, it was equally a point of honor to resist as long as possible the levy of any tribute whatever, and, in the last resort, to secure the most favorable terms in their power. A Moolukgeeree army seldom possessed power sufficient to subjugate a country, or to reduce its fortresses, which were sure to be defended with obstinacy; it carried on its operations therefore against the open towns and villages, selecting the season of harvest for its period of action, with the view not only of compelling the more speedy acquiescence of the chieftain, but also of securing the more ready means of subsistence for the troops. As the Mahratta army approached the territory of the chief from whom the tribute was demanded, it was his duty, if he meditated no opposition, to despatch an accredited agent to the boundary line, furnished with the means of affording security for his compliance with all reasonable demands. His estate was thereupon secured from predatory acts on the part of the invading army, by the presence, in each village, of one or more horsemen of the advanced guard, called "Bândhurs." When, however, the chieftain evinced a determination to resist, or even exhibited no indication of an early settlement, the Pindârees were thrown out on all sides, and the march of the army was thenceforth marked by every species of plunder and desolation; the ripe crops were swept from the fields, the villages were wantonly fired and destroyed, nothing was allowed to remain but the bare walls of the houses, and it frequently happened that every acre of his lands was left bare, and every hamlet in his territory reduced to a heap of smouldering ruins, before the Rajpoot chieftain condescended to the payment of the tribute demanded.

The Moolukgeeree tribute was in process of time (principally under the direction of Shivrâm Gârdee, the officer of regular troops already mentioned) raised very considerably above its original standard. In addition, also, to the tribute, properly so called, and which had been realized by the former paramount powers, the Mahrattas exacted payments under a variety of other heads, as for instance, that of grass and grain for the horses of their cavalry, and that more comprehensive item still of "extra expenses." The tributary country was subsequently divided into two districts—*Kâteewâr*, which included the Peninsula of Soreth, with the lands of the Jhâlâs and other contiguous territory, and the *Myhee Kântâ*, which extended from the banks of that river to Umbâ Bhuwânee and the Runn of Kutch.[1]

Several causes, arising from the usurpation of the Arab mercenaries, the death of the Muhârâjâ Gowind Row, and the insurrections of

[1] An estimate of the Moolukgeeree revenue from these two provinces, furnished to Colonel Walker by the Guikowâr authorities, in A.D. 1802, showed the following amounts :—

Province.	Guikowâr Share.	Peshwâh Share.	Total.
	Rupees.	Rupees.	Rupees.
Kâteewâr	4,09,521	5,38,019	9,47,540
Myhee Kântâ . .	3,00,622	15,000	3,15,622

Kânhojee and Mulhâr Row, had contributed to prevent the dispatch of the usual army into Kâteewâr, and the tributary revenue in that province had accordingly fallen into arrears since the year A.D. 1798-9. It fell to the lot of Bâbâjee Âppâjee to collect these arrears of tribute, and he accordingly proceeded on that service shortly after the fall of Kuree, in A.D. 1802. During the intervening period, the chieftains of Kâteewâr had fortified themselves and prepared for resistance, and the treasure which might have been appropriated in payment of the tribute was dissipated in various pursuits, particularly in the prosecution of their own dissensions. Their apprehensions were also further excited by the report that it was Bâbâjee's determination to enforce the whole of his demands at once. Having subjugated the Desâee of Pâtree, who was a partisan of Mulhâr Row, Bâbâjee entered Kâteewâr, and after a series of successful operations in which he was engaged with Mâleeâ, Moorbee, Joonagurh, Bhownugger, and Wudwân, and suppressing a dangerous insurrection of the Jâgheerdâr of Kuree, by taking that person and his son prisoners, he finally liquidated the whole arrears of tribute due from the country, and established in it a state of subordination and order superior to any that had been witnessed for centuries. In the course of this circuit of the Guikowâr general, however, successful as it was to an extent far beyond expectation or the real strength of his government, there were not wanting sufficient indications that the chieftains of the peninsula submitted the more readily to Bâbâjee's terms, from their knowledge of the dependence of himself and of his sovereign on the far greater resources of the British power. They feared, in fact, to use their own words, "that the army of the Feringees might be spread abroad." Under these circumstances, motives of sound policy, as well as those of humanity, and a due regard to British reputation, rendered it necessary that an influence already powerful, though unseen, should be openly acknowledged and fully defined.

At an early stage of the British connection with the Guikowâr government, it had been discovered that a considerable portion of the resources of the Baroda state depended on a punctual realization of its tributary revenue in Kâteewâr, while the large arrears due at that period rendered their recovery an object of no common importance. The Guikowâr ministry were extremely diffident of their ability to recover this revenue, unless with the aid of the British; and the increase of the subsidiary force to three battalions of native infantry, as well as the stipulation in the definitive treaty that one of the battalions should proceed to Kâteewâr whenever real necessity required it, principally arose from this impression of their weakness.

The British government thus found itself indirectly pledged to the realization of an object which, if pursued in the mode expected by its allies, would have to be effected at the price of a departure from its usual principles and policy. As early as 15th December, 1802, the supreme government, of which the Marquis of Wellesley was then the head, was therefore induced to express its opinion, that if an amicable arrangement could be made with the several chieftains of the peninsula for the regular payment of their tribute, without the necessity for the periodical advance of a military force, an acceptable service would thereby be rendered alike to the Guikowâr state and to the British interests in Goozerat. There were thus, in truth, concurring circumstances, which operated to render necessary such an interference on the part of the British in the affairs of Kâteewâr. To the voluntary payment of their tribute by the chieftains, the Guikowâr government looked forward for the means of effecting a large reduction in its overgrown military establishments; it anticipated also a valuable addition to its resources from funds which hitherto had been swallowed up in the enormous expenses of collection; but it looked to its allies for the means of effecting these desirable objects. The British authorities, on the other hand, while formally engaged and sincerely desirous to assist the Guikowâr state, felt repugnance to lending their aid for so questionable an object as the carrying out a Moolukgeeree expedition, though they could contemplate, with honest satisfaction, the advantages which the principalities of Kâteewâr would derive from an arrangement that ameliorated a custom so oppressive; though they had reason to believe that their mediation would be readily accepted by the chieftains, and though they were well aware that, as matters then stood, the Baroda state must, in default of their active interference, continue to carry out its objects in the peninsula of Goozerat by means which, however opposed to the principles of the British government, still derived the greater part of their efficacy from its presumed support.

Though these principles had been for some time admitted, it was not until the 3rd April, 1807, that the government of Bombay found themselves in a position to enter upon a task of carrying them into effect. Colonel Walker, having been selected as the officer uniting the essential qualifications of requisite information and local influence, was on that day instructed to assume the command of a detachment destined, in co-operation with a sufficient contingent of the Guikowâr troops, to proceed with those special objects into the peninsula of Soreth.

Means had previously been adopted, as has been noticed, for the purpose of sounding the chieftains of Kâteewâr in regard to their willingness to accept of British mediation for the permanent arrangement of their tribute, and the discontinuance of military expeditions for its realization. Though the result had been favourable, it was not long after the appearance of the detachment in Kâteewâr, before Colonel Walker discovered how little the chiefs contemplated a really disinterested course of action on the part of the British government. "The circular addresses to the chieftains," says that officer, "were "hardly believed to be sincere, and some extraordinary and curious "communications were the result of the advance of the troops, and "discovered the sentiments of the country. It was most natural to "suppose that our object was a Moolukgeeree circuit on our own "account, and I accordingly received some proposals extolling the "acquaintance of the parties with the arts of exaction and the bravery "of their troops, which would be exerted, without exposing those of "the Company, for a participation in the spoils. The Mâleeâ Raja "wished to turn the command of a passage over the Runn to account, "and proposed a joint plundering excursion into Chor Wâgur, "Kutch, and Sindh. Others, again, conceived our object was to "supplant the rights of the Guikowâr government, and these were "prepared to offer the most lavish assurances of dependence upon "the Company, and exhibited some attempts to neglect the Gui-"kowâr. Some insidious attempts were even made to raise our "suspicions of the fidelity of the Guikowâr government. It was "necessary to be prepared against these attempts, and discourage "them on their first appearance. Their intention was insidious, and "would have been productive of every serious consequence that "could flow from disunion of conduct and want of cordiality in the "pursuit of an object of joint interest. My endeavours were there-"fore directed to convince the Bhoomeeâs that the Company's troops "appeared in Kâteewâr as the allies of the Guikowâr, and that their "object was to promote an ultimate arrangement of the country, "under the Company's mediation, having in view the advantage of the "Guikowâr state, and the permanent interests of the Bhoomeeâs "themselves."

The efforts of Colonel Walker, which were ably seconded by Wittul Row Deewân, the commander of the Guikowâr troops, soon revived the confidence of the Bhoomeeâs; and an opportunity was found for establishing incontestably the disinterested intentions of the British, in the restoration to its owner of the fort of Kundornâ, which, having been seized by the chief of Nowânugger, was rescued by the detachment from his hands. The feeling of the Bhoomeeâs now sustained a complete revulsion; and some of the weaker chieftains began to entertain chimerical expectations, and to look forward to an indefinite redress of injuries from the justice of the British government. Though anxiously embracing every opportunity of affording protection to those to whom it could be extended to advantage, and though actually successful in restoring many outlaws to their homes, and in preventing many acts of oppression, the British envoy found it necessary to confine his attempts, as a general rule, to the one object of providing for the Bhoomeeâs security in time to come, without entering into the discussion of cases of doubtful or irremediable misfortune. His chief difficulty lay in assuming a just standard for a revenue, which had hitherto been so fluctuating and undetermined. It was evident, on the one hand, that the Baroda government had reason to expect, if not an increase to their revenue, at least its maintenance on an undiminished footing—the rather under the intimate knowledge which the British possessed of their necessities. The Bhoomeeâ chieftains, on the other hand, were induced to rely upon British influence for their protection from excessive exactions, and from the permanent establishment of a tribute beyond their means to defray.

The existing rate of tribute had been increased under the administration of Bâbâjee and others, principally under the item of "extra expenses," to an amount to which the Bhoomeeâs had submitted with reluctance, which had been calculated upon the utmost revenues of their territories, and which was unfit for the basis of a permanent settlement, both because it had not been in existence for a sufficient length of time to constitute a precedent, and still more, because, as was evident, it could not have been realized in successive years without recourse to coercion. A small reduction was therefore granted to almost every chieftain, principally under the item above mentioned. Engagements were then entered into, under the guarantee of the British government, which assured to the Baroda state the punctual payment of the tribute upon the rate determined, while they bound the chieftains of the country to refrain from those mutual aggressions and acts of depredation and violence which had formerly kept the country in a state of continual suffering; the petty states on the sea-coast covenanted to relinguish piracy, and resigned the right to property in wrecks that might happen within their territories; the Jhâreja and Jetwâ Râjpoots at the same time, by a solemn act, proclaimed the abrogation of their inhuman practice of female infanticide; while the mediating power pledged itself to protect the country from oppression, and to relieve it from the injuries which it had hitherto annually sustained from the circuit of a Moolukgeeree army. In order, however, to ensure permanency to these engagements, and to confirm to the Guikowâr government that ascendency on which so many advantages depended, it was determined to station within the peninsula a military force, composed of a contingent of Mahratta horse and one battalion of the British subsidiary troops.

As the result of the arrangements thus ably concluded, through the influence of the British envoy, the chieftains of Kâteewâr were gratified by seeing one of the most oppressive sources of exaction considerably ameliorated, and its future amount finally determined, while, on the other hand, the rights of the Guikowâr government (no longer, as formerly, based upon the mere superiority arising from more powerful resources) were now solemnly and formally recognised by the voluntary acts of the chieftains of the country themselves, and established, for the future, upon the same foundations as those engagements which connect more civilized states with each other,—"an advantage," says Colonel Walker, "in the most complete sense of the "term, which no government preceding that of the Guikowâr had yet "been able to obtain."

CHAPTER VI.

THE WÂGHELAS—THE KUSBÂTEES OF DHOLKA—THE JHÂLÂS.

We may now pass in review such of the Rajpoot houses as were found in existence by Colonel Walker, when the various districts of Goozerat which have been mentioned passed into British hands, and when the influence of the British government was, through the engagements lately concluded, extended over other parts of the country.

Of the younger branch of the royal Wâghelas, we have had nothing to record from the time of Ahmed Shah to the present period.[1] The chief of Sânund, or of Kot, was now discovered by Colonel Walker, holding the first position among the independent "grâssiâs" of the district of Dholka, and though possessor of but twenty-four villages,

[1] *Vide* p. 267.

still assuming the title of raja, and boasting of his high descent from the forgotten kings of Unhilpoor. His principal town of Kot, though undefended by fortifications, was encircled by an impenetrable belt of jungle, and he retained in his service a force of two thousand irregular infantry, and one hundred and fifty horse, who mounted guard at his residence, and were engaged to defend his person or to wage hostilities, "like the troops of a sovereign prince." His relation, the chief of Gângur, possessed villages, which though only eight in number, constituted a very valuable estate, and maintained an armed force of one thousand men.

Each of these chiefs paid to the paramount power a yearly tribute, the amount of which, however, varied according to circumstances. The general government, as was stated by Colonel Walker, possessed no right of interference with their internal administration beyond that of enforcing the payment of their tribute, and preventing any disturbance on their part of the peace of the country.

In the immediate vicinity of the Wâghelas were the Kusbâtees of Dholka, a numerous and warlike body of Mohummedans, inhabiting the chief town of the district, and who were regarded by the Mahratta governments as an useful counterpoise to the power of the Rajpoot grâssiâs. The Kusbâtees were of three classes—Menâs, Rehens, and Purmârs; the two former were reputed to have come from Delhi at the close of the sixteenth century; the last were, as their name implies, of Rajpoot blood, and were in fact the descendants of that branch of the Purmârs of Moolee, which, we have already beheld, settled at Botâd, as converts to the Mohummedan religion.[1]

In A.D. 1654, say the bards, a quarrel having arisen between the brothers who then held Botâd, one of them, named Mullik Mohummed, went off in anger to Dholka. His grandson, Kumâl Mohummed, left seven sons, who, with two hundred horse, which they commanded, served Ubhye Singh Râthor during the time of his government of Ahmedabad, and afterwards followed the Nowaub Kumâl-ood-deen (or Juwân-Murd Khân) Bâbee. When the latter was compelled to surrender Ahmedabad, the Purmârs retired to Joonagurh, where they served for many years. At length, as they were in arrears of pay, the Nowaub of Joonagurh assigned to them his rights of tribute upon Gâreeâdhâr, which he found himself unable to realise. The brothers had been previously on very intimate terms with the Gâreeâdhâr people, and therefore they set off thither joy-

[1] *Vide* p. 281.

fully, taking with them their families as well as their military retainers. The villagers were very much distressed, and determined to rid themselves of their burden; but in the meantime, in order to prevent any suspicion, they each of them received a horseman, and entertained him hospitably. At length, one night when the horsemen had retired to rest a signal was given by beat of drum, and each householder put to death his guest. Mullik Futteh Mohummed and Mullik Uchâ, two of the Purmâr brothers, were the only survivors; the remaining brothers, and the whole of their retainers, perished.

When the news reached Dholka the cry was that great oppression had been committed. The two Tâlookdârs also said, "If they "had been slain in fight we should not have grieved, but they have "been oppressed fraudulently. We will become Fukeers." Their friends persuaded them not to become Fukeers, but to take revenge. They agreed, and when they had purchased new horses, they returned to Joonagurh to serve the Nowaub with new men. For a few years they found no opportunity for revenge, but at length the Guikowâr army going its rounds in Kâteewâr, Neewâz Khân Rehen, the Dholka Kusbâtee, went with the Mahrattas, and as the Rehens and the Purmârs were on good terms, Mullik Futteh Mohummed and Mullik Uchâ accompanied him. Neewâz Khân paid the tribute due to the Guikowâr from Gâreeâdhâr, and then attacked and destroyed the village in revenge for the Tâlookdârs, ploughing it up with donkeys, and sowing it with salt. The Purmârs seized the village head-man, and his two daughters, whom they made their concubines.

Kumâl Mohummed had acquired wealth; but his eldest son, Mullik Nâmunt, had used his sword so well as to add to the family riches, and he had obtained several villages also. He was called the Tâlookdâr of Keshree, an estate of sixteen villages. After his death at Gâreeâdhâr, his brother, Futteh Mohummed, became his heir; but he, too, died in A.D. 1746, and was succeeded by his son, Sher Meeâ, who ruled his Tâlook well, made good use of his sword, and increased his possessions.

Sher Meeâ died in A.D. 1799, and was succeeded by his son, Bhâwâ Meeâ.

Mullik Uchâ, the brother of Futteh Mohummed, received no part of his father's property, but by his good fortune he acquired villages of his own, and having founded a new house, was styled Tâlookdâr of Dhunwârâ, which estate is also in the Dholka district. He died in A.D. 1765, and left three sons. The eldest son, Nânâ Meeâ, succeeded his father, and died in A.D. 1799, without a successor. His brothers received no share of their father's property, but acquired villages by their own strength. Their sister, Mool Beebee, had been married to Sher Meeâ, and though Bhâwâ Meeâ was the son of another wife, yet as he was thus in a manner the nephew of Nânâ Meeâ, he became his heir, and inherited five villages, an elephant, two hundred horses, and other property.

Soon after Bhâwâ Meeâ's succession, a body of plundering Jutt horsemen, four hundred in number, attacked one of his villages, supposing that as Sher Meeâ was dead they could do so with impunity. Though they had often been beaten off by Sher Meeâ, yet this time they carried off the cattle, and brought them to Keshree, where they drew rein. Here they oppressed the people much, and though the villagers said, "This is Sher Meeâ's village, if his horsemen arrive "you will suffer for it," the Jutts paid no attention, but only said, "Sher Meeâ is gone, and his son is in the cradle." Bhâwâ Meeâ heard, at Dholka, what had happened; he immediately mounted his horse and set out, followed by about sixty horsemen. At this time he was twenty-two years old. When he came up with the plundering horsemen he went in among them without any consideration, and used his sword in a manner beyond his years. The forayers soon took to flight, leaving five of their number dead and many wounded. When the people at Dholka knew that the Tâlookdâr had set off to attack the Jutts, a large body of horsemen mounted and hastened to his assistance; but they were not in time for the battle, and before they even reached the ground, they met Bhâwâ Meeâ and his party returning with the horses they had captured, and the heads of the five Jutts that had been slain.

At this time the Jutts and Katees roamed about the country in large bodies, as freely as if they had been government troops. The ancestors of Bhâwâ Meeâ had often defeated them, and there was a deadly feud between them on that account, but as he had shown so much valor at so early an age, and his reputation went on increasing day by day, the Jutts feared to encounter him.

Sher Meeâ had served the Peshwah, but Bhâwâ Meeâ had attached himself to the Guikowâr, and gained great distinction. When the Baroda army advanced against Ahmedabad, in A.D. 1800, to drive out Shelookur, Bhâwâ Meeâ was with them, followed by two hundred horse; and when, in A.D. 1802, the Guikowâr called in the British to aid him against Mulhâr Row, and the British force which had disembarked at Cambay, found difficulty in advancing from thence to Kuree, the Guikowâr wrote to Bhâwâ Meeâ, who attended the troops to Kuree with two hundred horse, and was on very good terms with the British.

Bhâwâ Meeâ, after having attained great reputation, died in A.D. 1812, leaving two sons, Bâpoo Meeâ and Mullik Meeâ, of whom the elder succeeded him. The Tâlooka consisted at this time of thirty villages.

Such was the leading family of the Kusbâtees of Dholka, alluded to by Colonel Walker. He mentions that they were a bold and turbulent people, some of whom commanded the services of a considerable number of horsemen, whom they hired out to such of the neighbouring powers as required them. They held almost all of the peaceable part of the Dholka district in mortgage for payments of revenue in advance, and had thereby much extended their influence.

We have little to record of the fortunes of the Jhâlâs for many years after their establishment at Pâtree.[1] In the time of Muhârânâ Chundrasunghjee, who is said to have been the fifteenth in descent from Hurpâl, through his eldest son, Shedo, or Shodojee, the chief seat of the Jhâlâs had already been removed from Pâtree to Hulwud, another town on the banks of the lesser Runn of Kutch; and during his reign, or immediately afterwards, this branch of the house of Hurpâl was again subdivided into chieftainships, which still retain their independence. Prutheerâj, the elder son of Chundrasunghjee, lost his inheritance, but became the founder of the houses of Wânkâner and Wudwân; Umur Singh, the second son, succeeded his father at Hulwud, and is represented by the present chief of Dhrângudrâ; the third son, Ubherâjjee, founded the house of Lugtur. The family of Syelâ is a branch from that of Umur Singh, of Hulwud; and that of Choorâ descends from a cadet of Wudwân. The Muhârânâ Chundrasunghjee, here alluded to, is mentioned, by name, in the Meerât Ahmudee, as having, in the year A.D. 1590, had a meeting, at Veerumgâm, with Khân Uzeez Kokâ, the imperial viceroy in Goozerat. Shekhurojee, the second son of Hurpâl, established himself at Shunchânâ (or Susânâ), in the Veerumgâm district, and held an estate composed of eighty-four villages, which were subsequently re-annexed to the crown-lands, but in which his descendants still hold "wântâs." Mângojee, the youngest son of Hurpâl, founded the family of Limree, which was seated first at Sheeânee and next at Jâmboo.

The following is the story of Prutheerâj, the son of Chundrasunghjee, as given by the bards:—

Râj Shree Chundrasunghjee, who reigned at Hulwud, had three

[1] *Vide* p. 231.

sons, of whom Prutheerâj was the eldest. Udâjee, the Rajpoot of Sheeânee, having quarrelled with the Governor of Ahmedabad, determined to quit his territories, and in that view removed towards Hulwud. Prutheerâj had been out riding, and happened to bring his horse to the tank to drink water at the same time that Udâjee came thither for a similar purpose. Some persons who were at the tank cautioned Udâjee not to approach Prutheerâj, because he was in the habit of striking horses with his whip if they came near him. Udâjee went, notwithstanding, close to the Koonwur, and when the latter raised the whip to strike his horse, Udâjee brought his spear to the rest, and said, that if Prutheerâj struck the horse he would spear him. Prutheerâj was unarmed, and so he went back to the town, and there began to prepare a party to plunder Udâjee's camp. Chundrasunghjee, hearing of this, sent immediately to the Koonwur, to forbid his plundering people who had taken refuge in the territory of Hulwud. Prutheerâj, however, paid no attention to these remonstrances, but when he had completed his preparations set forth to attack the camp. Chundrasunghjee upon this mounted his horse, and riding to the camp of Udâjee, dismounted there. On being informed of the step taken by his father, the Koonwur forbore from his intended attack, and angrily went away to Wudwân, from which place he plundered the surrounding country. After a time, he had collected about two thousand followers, and having been informed that camels laden with treasure were on their way from Joonagurh to Ahmedabad, he prepared an ambuscade, and carried off the treasure. The persons in charge having made a complaint, the Mohummedan government set a reward upon Prutheerâj's head, and sent after him a Jemâdâr with two thousand horse. This officer, when he found what the strength of Prutheerâj's force was, determined to employ stratagem against him. He sent a man to Wudwân to say that he had been detached for the purpose of levying tribute, and requested Prutheerâj to accompany him. The Jemâdâr took an oath upon the Koran that he would commit no act of treachery unless Prutheerâj should first deceive him; and Prutheerâj upon this joining him, they planned an attack upon Sheeânee, which they successfully carried out, slaying Udâjee. Then "sut" came upon the wife of Udâjee, and she despatched her servants to Prutheerâj to beg for the head of her husband. The Koonwur, however, had cut off Udâjee's head, and caused it to be hung from a tree, and he sent word to the lady, in reply, that he would not give it to her unless she came herself and took it down. The wife of Udâjee came, and, girding up her clothes, climbed the tree, Prutheerâj meanwhile abusing Udâjee, and saying, "Son! you raised your spear against me, true; but see "now, how nimble I've caused your wife to be at climbing trees." The sutee, when she heard these words, cursed Prutheerâj in her fury, and said, "Yes! I have been compelled by you to mount a "tree, but no wife of yours shall ever wash her body in mourning for "you."[1] Other people, as well as the sutee, blamed Prutheerâj for what he had done, and it was not long before he was himself repentant. However, he went on with the Jemâdâr, collecting tribute. On one occasion, some of his people, being in the van, arrived first at a halting ground, and, as water was scarce, they pitched a tent over the well, and declared there was none in the place, so that though they got water from the well, the Jemâdâr's men had to travel six miles to get any. The Jemâdâr was informed of this; he said, "Prutheerâj "has been deceitful first, now I am absolved of my oath." He seized Prutheerâj treacherously, and carried him off, and no one in this country knows what became of him.

Prutheerâj being thus absent at the time of his father's death, his younger brother, Umur Singh, seized upon Hulwud. Prutheerâj, however, left two sons, Sultânjee, from whom descends Wukhutsunghjee, the present Râj of Wânkâner, and Râjâjee, who was the first of the house of Wudwân. Râjâjee married Som Koonwur Bâee, daughter of Rathor Shree Eesubdâsjee, the son of Row Nârondâs, and brother of Veerum Dev—the same lady, probably, who is alluded to in the Churittra of the prince of Eedur. The Râthorânee departed with her beloved through the flames of the pyre in A.D. 1643, as we are informed by the inscription on her funeral monument, and her image, under the respectful title of "the Sutee Râthor Mother's," is placed in a shrine at no great distance from that of the unhappy Rânik Devee, and on days of holiday, dressed in queenly marriage attire and jewels, receives the salutation of her descendants.

Among the Sutees' temples at Wudwân is one called "the Hâree "Mother's." This lady, whose name was Bâee Shree Dev Koonwur, was the daughter of a Hârâ chief named Umur Singh, and the wife of Muhârânâ Shree Urjoon Singh, whom she followed through the flames in A.D. 1741. The temple was erected by Urjoon Singh's son and successor, Muhârânâ Shree Subul Singh, who was not, however, descended of the Hâree Rânee, his mother being a lady of the Purmâr clan, by name Shree Uchoobâ. In a line with the Hâree

[1] She meant that his wife should never receive information as to when or where he died, so as to mourn for him.

Mother's shrine is the funeral temple of Muhârânâ Shree Chundra Singh, erected in A.D. 1779, by his son and successor, the Muhârânâ Shree Prutheerâj, whose mother was Bâee Shree Kooshul Koonwur, the daughter of Shree Jorâjee, a Wâghela chief of Pethâpoor. These scanty memorials supply the only information which we possess of the fortunes of the Jhâlâ house for many years.

Regarding the last mentioned prince, Muhârânâ Chundra Singh, of Wudwân, the bardic chroniclers, however, furnish us with the following narrative :—

A Lohânâ of the village of Memkâ, near Wudwân, took a bullock load of pulse, which in Kâteewâr they call "Jhâlur," to Rozkoo, in the Bhâl country, near Dhundhooka, to sell it. The Choorâsumâ grassia of Rozkoo, whose name was Mepjee, had married one of his daughters to a Jhâlâ bridegroom, but was nevertheless at feud with that house. He said jeeringly to the Lohânâ, "What's the worth of "that Jhâlâ of your's?" The Lohânâ answered, "A hundred "Bhâleeâs[1] go to one Jhâlâ." When the Choorâsumâ heard that, he was very angry; he beat the Lohânâ, took his bullock from him, and turned him out of the village. The Lohânâ went to complain to his prince, Chundrasunghjee Raja, of Wudwân. The raja enquired what the value of the bullock and its load was, and paid the Lohânâ the sum he named, but determined in his own mind that he would some day or other be quits with the chief of Rozkoo.

Now the Choorâsuma had a village called Morseeoo. Thither went Chundrasunghjee soon after with two thousand horsemen. He plundered the village, piled the wood of the houses upon carts, and set off homewards. Mepjee's sons, Lâkhâbhâee and Râmâbhâee, went to their brother-in-law, Hurbhumjee Raja, of Limree, and told him of their feud with Wudwân, and of what they had suffered on account of it. Hurbhumjee set out to their aid with seven hundred horse and eight hundred foot, and took with him Bhugwânbhâee, the Guikowâr's lieutenant, who was at Limree at the time, at the head of a body of twelve thousand horse, which he had brought into the province. The allies halted for the evening on the banks of the river Bhâdur, and as they had a number of guns with them, they determined to defend the passage against Chundrasunghjee. The raja of Wudwân meanwhile came up, and pitched his camp near them. He thought that it would now be impossible for him to carry off his booty, and that his honor would be lost if even a single cart were left behind; so he set the whole on fire. At three o'clock in the morning,

[1] Bhâleeâs are large earthen jars, or inhabitants of the Bhâl.

Chundrasunghjee rose and took "the red cup." He felt sure that he should be slain in the fight that was about to ensue, so he drank Ganges water, put a leaf of the sacred basil-tree in his mouth, and assumed some coral ornaments.[1] When he was ready, an Arab Jemâdâr in his service, whose name was Gorimbho, came to him, and said, "Thâkor! if it seem good to you, I will attack their guns "with my five hundred Mukrânees, while you charge the main body. "Or, if you please, I will charge them in the centre while you take "their guns." Chundrasunghjee thought the first plan the best. He dismounted from his horse, and took a sword and shield. One of his chiefs came to him and dissuaded him from fighting on foot, but the Durbâr replied, "Is there any hope of surviving now?" The chief "answered, "Sire! that is in the hands of the Supreme Being. May "Bâburo Kool Dev and Shuktee Devee protect you! But while you "have yet a horse, what need is there for your fighting on foot?" In this way he persuaded him to remount, and the rest of the horsemen having also mounted, they moved off to attack the enemy. Meanwhile Gorimbho Jemâdâr was advancing against the guns with his five hundred infantry. The guns were charged with round shot, and placed at the edge of the opposite bank over the river. The artillery men fired as quick as they could, but the Jemâdâr's men had already got down the bank into the bed of the river, and the balls went over their heads. The Jemâdâr immediately attacked the gunners, who fled, leaving their pieces in his possession. Meanwhile Chundrasunghjee charged the main body of Hurbhumjee's troops, and they, discouraged by the flight of the gunners, turned and fled also. Hurbhumjee escaped to Limree, pursued all the way by Chundrasunghjee, who killed about fifty of his horsemen.

When the battle was over, the Guikowâr's lieutenant, Bhugwânbhâee, sent an officer with a silver rod, to claim the guns as his master's property. Chundrasunghjee said that he had not been aware that that was the case, and that the lieutenant might come for the guns, or that he would himself send them. The Mahratta horsemen came for the guns and took them away, and Bhugwânbhâee went back to Baroda, while Chundrasunghjee returned home to Wudwân.

After the deaths of Chundrasunghjee and Hurbhumjee, the Limree Râjâ Hureesunghjee, the son of Hurbhumjee, attacked Pâthâbhâee (Prutherâj), son of Chundrasunghjee, in revenge. He came against Wudwân, with five hundred horse and two hundred foot. The horse were divided into three bodies, one of which encamped on the banks

[1] These are ceremonies of interment.—See account of funerals in the Conclusion.

of the Kâree river, six miles from Wudwân, and the other two beside reservoirs at Kherâloo and Pâleeâwullee. It happened that five and twenty of the Limree horsemen had skirmished up to the gate of Wudwân, and had killed a cultivator, and done some further mischief, when they were suddenly attacked by fifteen of Pâthâbhâee's horse, who were going their rounds. The Limree men took to flight, and the others pursued them to the place on the banks of the river where the foremost division was. The Wudwân horse fired into the encampment and killed five men, and the rest taking to flight they pursued them as far as Kherâloo. Raja Pâthâbhâee, receiving information of what had happened, set out immediately with two hundred foot and three hundred horse, and attacked the enemy posted at Kherâloo, whom he defeated and put to flight. In this action, Râmâbhâee, of Parburee, and Lâkhâbbâee, Hureesunghjee's mother's brothers, were killed. Their funeral temples may still be seen in that place.

There was another fight, also, at the Kâree river, in which Hureesunghjee was present in person. On this occasion, Pâthâbhâee's mother's brother, Sherbhâee Wâghela, of Pethâpoor, was carried by his horse through the midst of Hureesunghjee's troops. Hureesunghjee pursued him, and slew him. The armies afterwards separated and returned to their homes.[1]

A few years afterwards, in Sumwut, 1863 (A.D. 1807), the Jhâlâs were again at war among themselves. On the borders of the Wudwân territory there is a village named Khorâ, containing a very old

[1] The two following documents will throw light upon the text. The first is "a Runwutee deed," or grant, in compensation, to the successor of a murdered person; the second is an engagement entered into by outlaws, on obtaining permission to return to their homes.

I.

To Muhârânâ Shree Hurbhumjee, salutation from Jhâlâ Gopâljee, and Jhâlâ Veesojee, and Jhâlâ Bhâwajee, and Jhâlâ Bhâeejee, and Jhâlâ Ujâbhâee, and Jhâlâ Moolojee, and Jhâlâ Râmsunghjee, and Jhâlâ Rutunjee, and Jhâlâ Sungrâmjee, and Jhâlâ Rutunjee Lâkhâjee, and all the brothers.

A quarrel occurred among the brothers at the village of Bârejurâ, and Jhâlâ Mâljee and Jhâlâ Humeerjee cut off Jhâlâ Râmsunghjee's head. Therefore, Jhâlâ Mâljee and Jhâlâ Humeerjee are expelled from the eighty-four townships (of Limree), and Jhâlâ Mâljee's and Jhâlâ Humeerjee's grâs (hereditary lands), consisting of a share in the villages of Bârejurâ and Jhâleeâ, are given ughât (without opportunity of revocation) to Jhâlâ Kusheeâjee, as the price of Jhâlâ Râmsunghjee's head, the grant to last as long as the sun and the moon last. Jhâlâ Kusheeâjee is to receive the revenues of these two villages, and enjoy the "grâs." Further, no descendant of Jhâlâ Mâljee or Jhâlâ Humeerjee is to be permitted to reside in the eighty-four villages. Whoever entertains such a person is an offender

castle, the erection of which is attributed to Sidh Râj. Six miles from thence is Goojurvedee, a village belonging to the Raja of Dhrângudrâ. At these two frontier points the chiefs of Wudwân and Hulwud had their outposts. On the day of the festival of the goat, the Mohummedan soldiers belonging to the post at Goojurvedee went round their own village to procure a goat, and being unsuccessful then repaired to Khorâ. At this latter place they agreed with a shepherd to purchase a goat from him for three shillings, but having got possession of the animal they carried it off without paying the price. The shepherd went immediately to the Limree post in the village and complained of what had happened, and the Limree men turned out and went to Goojurvedee to demand the goat. The Dhrângudrâ soldiers now agreed to pay for the animal, but the others

against the Durbâr (the court, literally, meaning the chief, the Muhârânâ, of Limree), and if the Durbâr punish him no one shall complain. We will, all of us, act up to this agreement, and for us so doing the undersigned are security—Râbâ Wâsung, of Bodânâ, and Râbâ Bhugâ, and Râbâ Nâron, and Râbâ Dhunnâ, and Guduwee Undâ. We will act according to what has been here written. Sumwut, 1833 (A.D. 1777), Mâgsheer shood 6, Monday.

Signatures.	*Witnesses.*
Gopâljee, &c.	Shree Jugdeesh (*i. e.* the sun).
	Jhâlâ Mâljee.
Written by Jhâlâ Sungrâmjee.	Jhâlâ Meghâbhâee.
	Jhâlâ Chândâbhâee.
	Râthor Kândâ.
	Goletur Râjâjee.
	Desâee Luloobhâee.

Written by Bhowâneedâs, in the presence of the parties.

II.

Shree Bheemnâthjee is security for the performance of the under-written agreement. We will perform it.

To Muhârânâ Shree Hureesunghjee, salutation from Jhâlâ Kusheeâjee Râmsingh, and Keshâbhâee, of the village of Bârejurâ. In payment of debts due by us we mortgaged the village of Bârejurâ, to Shâ Nânjee Doongurshee. Afterwards, we had a quarrel with Shâ Nânjee, and leaving the village, went to Ookhrâlâ, from whence we annoyed the Durbâr. In atonement for these acts we hereby pass the village of Bârejurâ to the Durbâr, for seventy years, up to the end of which time the Durbâr is to enjoy it; and after that, we will arrange in regard to the debt due to Shâ Nânjee, as any two men may decide. On the above terms, the Durbâr has called us in and given us jeewâee lands in the village (lands for their subsistence), which we will enjoy, and create no disturbance for the future. For our keeping the above agreement, we give the following as security:—The Chundhooka Kusbâtees, Syud Boolâkee Azumbhâee, and Shekh Sâhib, and the Choorâsumâ of Parburee, Râmsunghjee; they are to be responsible in their property. Sumwut, 1853 (A.D. 1797). Bhâdrapud shood 2, Saturday.

refused the money, and taking away the goat returned with it home. When the Dhrângudrâ men went to their master, the Râj, at Hulwud, and informed him of what had happened he was angry, and said, "Why did you allow them to take away what you had purchased on "your holiday?" He determined to attack Wudwân, and sent for assistance to the Râj of Wânkâner, the chiefs of Syelâ and Choorâ, and to Huree Singh of Limree. The former declined joining him, but the latter assembled their forces and attended him. Huree Singh is said to have endeavoured to induce the chief of Wudwân to make submission:—"Do you suppose," was the message, "that there "is any difference between Hulwud and Limree? If you fight with "Hunoomân you will certainly be defeated. Does a wise man invite "Yuma to his gate? What has happened has happened, but if you "now persist, your fort will be destroyed and the army of the "Feringees will be spread over the country." Prutheerâj of Wudwân, however, determined to resist, and he collected a force which he maintained by plundering alternately the villages of Dhrângudrâ and Limree. When the allies were assembled, the Râj of Dhrângudrâ at first paid the expenses of the whole, but this was subsequently discontinued, and each chief supported his own troops. After some en-

Further, Mehta Bhugwândâs is security, the above-mentioned securities having declined; also Guduwee Dulâ Jeewun, of the Tâpureeâ branch, and Guduwee Jeewun Sâhoo, of Khumbhulâv, and Guduwee Ujâ Udâ, of the Dethâ branch, of the village of Puchum, and Râwul Devkurshun Wâlâ, of the village of Pansheenâ. They are to be responsible in their property.

Guduwee Dulâ,
agrees to the above.

Guduwee Ujâ Dethâ,
agrees to the above.
Guduwee Jeewun Sâhoo,
agrees to the above.

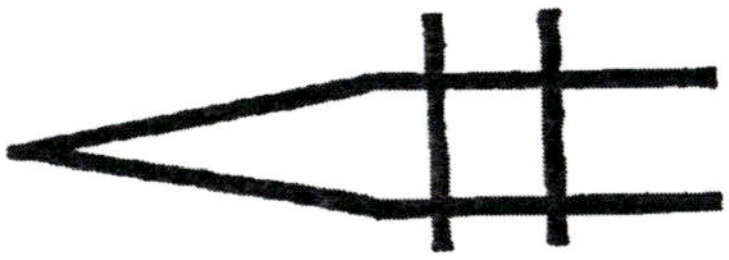

Râwul Devkurun Velâ,
agrees to the above.
Written by Myârâm, in the presence of the parties.

Witnesses.

Shree Jugdeesh (the sun).
Râthor Kândâ.
Jhâlâ Bâjeebhâee, of the village of Gedee.
Wâghela Hutheebhâee Bhowânjee, of the village of Loleeyânah.
Shâ Peetâmbur Bhowânee.
Sholunkee Kâkâ Jetarah.
Putel Mooloo Âshâ.
Gohil Hujoojee Jethâjee, of Dokurlâ.

gagements in the field Prutheerâj was compelled to retire within the walls of Wudwân, and the allies then besieged him and effected a breach with their artillery. At this period, however, the Bhâts and Châruns came between the combatants, and an arrangement of the dispute was by their means effected.

Thus far on bardic authority. Colonel Walker, who was in Jhâlâwâr shortly after these occurrences, gives the following account of them :—

"Another cause" (of the wretched state of the country) "is the war "which lately existed between the Rajas of Limree, Wudwân, and "Dhrângudrâ. This war arose from the ridiculous circumstance of a "party of Dhrângudrâ horse having taken a goat from a shepherd, "for which they offered to pay, but the shepherd went and com-"plained, and a party of Wudwân people took the flesh of the goat "from the horsemen while they were preparing to cook it. This pro-"duced retaliation from Dhrângudrâ; one outrage provoked another; "the Limree Rajâ was implicated in the quarrel; nor was it settled "until every village of the Wudwân Tâlook, consisting of upwards of "sixty, was laid waste save four, and the walls of Wudwân itself "breached. The other Tâlooks suffered in proportion."

According to the bards, the feud cost the Râj of Hulwud a lakh of rupees, or ten thousand pounds, the chief of Limree two thousand five hundred pounds, and the chiefs of Choorâ and Syelâ one thousand each.

The country of the Jhâlâs was at the time of Colonel Walker's settlement of the Mahratta Moolukgeeree district of Kâteewâr, in which it was included, involved in a state of great depression, produced by several causes. A fruitful source of dissension, not, however, confined to this part of Goozerat, was the system under which the property of a chieftain was divided and subdivided among his descendants. A constant state of enmity among the Rajpoot families themselves had resulted from the endeavours of the superior chieftains to preserve their territories from dismemberment, by force or fraud employed against the junior branches of their families. Nor were the external difficulties of the country less serious. Kâtees, Jutts, Meeyânâs,[1] and

[1] The Meeyânâs, who were men of Sindhi extraction, and much renowned as warriors, were numerous at Mâleeâ. Their character, as popularly estimated, may be gathered from the following story :—

One day, while an Arab soldier of the Guikowâr's was at his prayers, a Meeyânâ passed by, and enquired of him who he was afraid of that he bent his head that way. The Arab replied, with some indignation, that he feared no one but Ullah (God). "O ! then," said the Meeyânâ, "come along with me to Mâleeâ; we don't fear even Ullah there."

other predatory tribes, kept the inhabitants of its few and miserable villages in continual alarm. The deficiency of cultivation was rendered still more strikingly visible by the nearly total absence of wood, or even of foliage. In most parts of Jhâlâwâr the cultivator went armed to the scene of his labours, and in every village a tall tree, or other elevated station was employed as a watch-tower, from which a sentinel gave instant notice of the approach of the much dreaded predatory horse. The cattle, which, with their domestic utensils and ploughs, constituted the sole property of the villagers, were now hastily driven off from the fields to such shelter as could be afforded by the scanty defences of the village, or if overtaken by the freebooters in the open country were soon wending their way across the Runn to a ready market in Kutch or Chor Wâgur. The annual Moolukgeeree expeditions of the Peshwâh, the Guikowâr, and the Nowaub of Joonagurh had further contributed to render waste and depopulate a country which had received from nature almost every requisite of fertility. Its state of desolation may be vividly perceived in the fact, that when the Mahratta Soubahdârs were passing through it the want of firewood was sometimes so great as to render it necessary for the Bhoomeeâ chieftain of a place to cause one of his own villages to be deserted in order that its materials might supply the invading army with fuel. More special causes of suffering were found at this particular period in the late exaction of arrears by Bâbâjee, in the state of war which had been produced by Mulhâr Row's presence in the country after his escape from Nerriâd, and in the exhausting feud among the Jhâlâ chieftains themselves, which we have just described.

Jhâlâwar was divided into a number of independent chieftainships, the principal of which were those of Hulwud or Dhrângudrâ, Limree, Wudwân, Wânkâner, Choorâ, Lugtur, and Syelâ, whose formation we have already noticed. A family respect was still paid to the Râj of Dhrângudrâ, who on state occasions received the first act of civility, and was seated on an elevated cushion above the other chieftains of the race of Hurpâl. The affairs of this chieftain had been very ill managed, and his district plundered by an unworthy minister, who had lately absconded. Nor had the other estates of the Jhâlâs experienced a happier fate, and those of Choorâ and Lugtur in particular had temporarily fallen under the direct control of the Mahrattas. Heerjee Khuwâs, the minister of the chief of Lugtur, had advanced money to his master, and having obtained the entire control of the estate, proceeded to erect fortifications, and showed a disposition to establish his own authority. The Jhâlâ chief, in alarm, sought the aid of his daughter Ghenâ Bâee, the widow of the Muhârâjâ Gowind Row Guikowâr. The Baroda state was induced to interfere, and discharge the demands of Heerjee Khuwâs, but it became necessary for the Guikowâr officers to assume the management of the Lugtur estate, in order to defray the debt thus incurred, which step they had accordingly taken, reserving a portion of the produce for the subsistence of the chieftain.

CHAPTER VII.

THE CHOORÂSUMÂS OF DHOLLERA—THE GOHILS.

THE first settlement of the British in the peninsula of Soreth was made, as we have already hinted, under the auspices of presumed descendants of the ancient and princely line of Girnâr. A younger son of one of the Râs of Soreth, named Bânjee, is said to have received, as his patrimony, four "chorâshees," or districts, each containing eighty-four villages; one of which, the district of Dhundhooka, was inherited by his son, Râeesuljee. From Merjee, the fourth son of Râeesuljee, descended the Choorâsumâ grassia Syesuljee, who, at the time of Ânund Row Guikowâr, possessed, or laid claim to, the villages of Dhollera, Râh Tulow Bunder, Bhângur, Bheem Tulow, Goomah, and Saibellow, comprising in all an area of about a hundred thousand beeghas. Three of these villages were, however, uninhabited.

The district of Dhundhooka had fallen, after the division of the country between the Viceroy of Ahmedabad and the Mahrattas, to Kuntâjee Bhanday, who held it as a separate estate. It was taken from Kuntâjee by Dâmâjee Guikowâr, and, on that chief's compelled submission to the Peshwah, passed into the hands of the court of Poonah. Under the Mahratta government the unsettled state of the country, and the continually recurring pecuniary embarrassments of its rulers, compelled the komâvishdars, or farmers of districts, to contract upon terms which could be fulfilled only by the most oppressive exactions. The territory entrusted to them was also exposed to the depredations, not only of the surrounding states, but of every predatory leader who could attract to his standard fifty or a hundred men. The villages therefore fell to ruin, and a large part of them became wholly deserted. Many of the smaller landholders had at this time become anxious to place themselves and their possessions under the protection of any government sufficiently powerful to prevent the neighbouring chiefs from encroaching on their estates, and the powers to which they were tributary, from exacting a larger revenue than that which had been stipulated for by the Mogul rulers, at a time when the country was in a far more flourishing condition. The British government, which now appeared upon the stage, presented to the view of the grassias a power such as they desired, and to it therefore were addressed their applications for aid.

"In the view of improving our commercial, and, eventually, our "political, intercourse with the peninsula of Goozerat," says Mr. Duncan, in a letter addressed to the Governor-General, from Cambay, on the 11th June, 1802, "I have accepted the offer of the port of Râh "Tulow, or Dhollera, situated about twenty miles to the south of this "place, the grassia proprietors of which, viz., Mânâbhâee Gorbhaee "and Syesuljee Suttâjee, and their brethren, have been pressing me "for the last four years to accept of this spot, on condition of their "continuing to receive one-half of the net future income; their object "in which has been the procuring protection for themselves against "the depredations of their neighbours, and particularly from the "encroachments of the Raja of Bhownugger, who wishes to possess "himself of this excellent sea-port, to prevent its becoming a rival to "his own less convenient one of Bhownugger; and he has, for that "purpose, been tampering with some of the brethren of these grassias, "to make over their shares to him, which he has accordingly obtained "from one of the inferior among the brethren, named Hâllojee, in a "proportion too insignificant (not exceeding eleven parts in a hundred "in the village of Dhollera) to affect their general engagements with "us for their whole interest; besides that, one brother cannot make a "valid grant of the joint property, and that even this trifling attempt "to supersede our claims is of a date posterior to, and may no doubt "be justly considered as the immediate consequence of the previous "tender made to us by the united body of the grassias in question, whose territory, situated under the pergunnah of Dhundhooka, "is subject to a fixed khundunee (tribute) to the Peshwah, who does "not, however, appear to exert any interference in the internal "management, as seems, indeed, sufficiently implied in the recent "attempts of the Bhownugger chieftain to acquire this possession, and "the terms on which a small proportion thereof had been actually "made over to him."

The example set by Syesuljee and Mânâbhâee was not long after followed by numerous other holders or claimants of villages in the

Dholka and Dhundhooka Pergunnahs, whose applications were strenuously supported by Sir Miguel de Souza, through whom they were made. As, however, most of the villages, which were thus proposed to be ceded to the British government, had been held for periods of twenty years or more by the Râwul of Bhownugger, the Thâkor of Limree, or some other chieftain, and as the claims thus revived were, in his opinion, far better consigned to oblivion, the Resident opposed, with success, the acceptance of the proffered cessions. "Vague, uncertain, and disputed claims," said Colonel Walker, "to the sites of villages, of which the recollection scarcely exists, are generously ceded to the Honorable Company, upon condition of displacing the immediate possessors from the waste lands they have brought into cultivation, and relinquishing one-half of the advantages to be gained solely by the Company's means to the grassia claimant, and undertaking to rebuild and repeople villages for their benefit. * * * In the prosecution of our views in Kâteewâr, humanity is a principal consideration, and the Honorable Company's advantage, honor, and reputation will consist in reconciling the animosities of the rival chieftains, instead of availing ourselves of the precarious benefits to be derived from their dissensions."

We return now to the affairs of the Gohil clan, who were the nearest neighbours to the newly-acquired British possessions on the coast of the peninsula of Soorâshtrâ.

When the seal of the padishah, says the bard of the Gohils, was exchanged for that of the Sâhoo Raja, bands of Arabs consorted with that king; his rule extended as far as Mecca, and, on the east, to Bhudreekâ; his soubahdârs were so powerful that they exacted double rates of tribute. They returned to his presence from subduing the country. When the roll was called and the royal assembly held, the Gundhurvs sang songs and related tales; dances were exhibited; the king sat on his throne. Said the Sâhoo to Seevâjee, "We have broken Delhi, and taken possession of much territory. What countries have been conquered by us, and what remain?" Seevâjee said, "Eating your salt, I have taken several countries, and have subdued the Bhâtee Raja, but Sorethland is a country where there are many men and many forts armed with guns. This country has not been subdued." The Sâhoo beheld there, like peers, two soubahdârs seated, Kuntâjee and Peelâjee; he granted them a puttâ for a lakh of years. "If you can conquer Soreth I give it to you—wherever there are cities I will assign you jâgheers." He gave them crowns and dresses of honor; the army set off immediately; it went onwards, laying waste the habitable places; it came to Goozerat, and took possession. The officers of Delhi, taking with them a park of artillery, advanced; they drew the Mogulâee sword. In that battle Roostum Ulee was slain, he who was the leader of eighty thousand men. Then the zumeendârs, bending the head, began to say, "You are our lords, "to you every village will pay 'sulâmee;' we are humble, who will "contest with you? But, if you subdue Bhâwo, you will obtain a "reward at Sattara. Bhâwo caused us much annoyance; then we "bowed the head to him, and said, 'You are our lord.' In many "places he has seized forts." When Kuntâjee heard these words he was distressed; he came and pitched his tents within two coss of Seehore. Calling for a Brahmin, he sent him with a letter to Bhâwo: "Give up the fort of Seehore, or Shumbhoo's[1] oath to you. In the "morning coming I will plant my flags on all sides of your city. I "will give you four watches of the night." Bhow Singh beheld the note he had written. He was angry; he said to the Brahmin, "Show "me your back, that I may not incur the sin of slaying you." The Brahmin went away, and said to Kuntâjee, "Go forth in the morning, "and fight with him."

The great drums sounded, the army set forth, Kuntâjee approached to where that Indra among men was seated in Seehore. The fire-arrows[2] began to fly, the balls of the swivels to travel, the hills began to re-echo. The balls flew on both sides. They did not injure those who dwelt in the fort, though they scattered its assailants like pigeons. Many of those who were outside fell, and eat the dust. The dwellers in the fort remained immoveable. Rutun Singh's son, Bhow Singh, did not fear a whit; the Mahrattas were tired. The Deewân said, "Why are you vexing yourselves? little is left of our ammunition or "of our army. Listen to my advice. Muroo, who is as lofty as the "sky, has not come into our hands." Thus speaking, they struck their tents and retreated. Kuntâjee did not return home. On the journey he died. He did not go to his raja. He went to the house of Yuma.

Another year came round. The Sâhoo again summoned his Râwuts. "Have all come home, subduing territory? Have Peelâjee "and Kuntâjee been defeated anywhere, that they have not returned? "What has become of them?" The Râwuts answered, "He who "goes to Java perhaps may return, and bring back as much wealth

[1] A name of Shiva. [2] *Kokbân*, rockets.

"as may support his children's children; but he who goes to fight "with Bhâwo never returns."[1]

Bhow Singh Gohil, as we have seen, founded the new capital of Bhownugger, in A.D. 1723.[2] He was a chief of enterprise and sagacity, and before his death had the satisfaction of seeing his city established as a commercial emporium. At that period the disturbances consequent on the decline of the Mogul empire had rendered navigation dangerous, and subjected commerce to oppressive exactions. The trade of Gogo and Cambay had proportionably decayed as those ports were deprived of protection and unsupported any longer by the lucrative communication with Ahmedabad. A number of small communities had been established; the coast from the mouth of the Myhee to the Indus had fallen into the possession of robbers, who subjected the property of the merchant to their lawless rapine; and the sea had become infested by pirates. There were, therefore, great advantages to be derived from the establishment of a comparatively powerful ruler at Bhownugger, who was both able and desirous to extend protection to commerce. From this period we are to date the intercourse of the Gohil Râwuls with the government of Bombay, "and at a time," says Colonel Walker, "when the resources and "commerce of the presidency were more limited than at present "(A.D. 1807) the friendship of the chieftain of Bhownugger seems to "have been cultivated with assiduity and attention."

Bhow Singh was succeeded, in A.D. 1764-5, by his son Râwul Ukherâjjee, commonly styled Bhâwâjee, who was of an unambitious temper and averse to war. From the necessity of affording the trade of his port encouragement and protection, the Râwul, however, joined with a body of his troops an armament from Bombay, and assisted in the reduction of Tulâjâ and Mhowâ, then possessed by Koolees, who supported themselves by piratical attacks upon the merchants and vessels of every nation. The moderate policy of Râwul Ukherâjjee made him reject the possession of Tulâjâ, which, after its conquest, the British would have conferred upon him. In consequence of his refusal, Tulâjâ was delivered to the Nowaub of Cambay, A.D. 1771

[1] It is a saying in Goozerat,—

> "Who goes to Java
> "Never returns.
> "If, by chance, he return,
> "Then, for two generations to live upon,
> "Money enough he brings back."

[2] This is the statement of the accredited bards of the Gohil clan. Colonel Walker says the town was founded in A.D. 1742-3.

or 1772; and, about a year after this event, Râwul Ukherâjjee died, and was succeeded by his son, Wukhut Singh.

Râwul Wukhut Singh, better known by the familiar title of Âtâbhâee, was far more ambitious and enterprising than his father. He increased his territories by various acquisitions, while at the same time he encouraged and protected commerce. "In Sumwut, 1836" (A.D. 1780), say the bards, "Shree Wukhut Singh drove Noor Mo-"hummed out of Tulâjâ, and took possession of it; he also seized "Jânjmer. In the same year he drove Jusso Khusheeo Koolee out "of the port of Shree Mhowa, and took possession." Colonel Walker mentions that both force and artifice were employed by Wukhut Singh in dispossessing the Nowaub of Cambay of Tulâjâ; he states also that the Râwul soon afterwards established his authority over the district of Wâlâk (so called from its having been of old the property of the Wâlâ Rajpoots), with the exception of a few villages, the property of the Survaiya clan, and re-settled and fortified Mhowa, which had been destroyed by the expedition in which the British troops were engaged, and rendered it a flourishing port. "It is to "be observed," continues the resident, "that this acquisition of a "valuable country and of an extensive coast was made from tribes "who exercised piracy, and that whatever share of violence and "ambition may have been united in the measures of the Bhownugger "chiefs, their ultimate object was the protection of commerce. The "good effects of this policy were extensively felt, and the coasting "trade of the honorable Company's subjects derived every advantage "from this regular plan for the security of commerce. The Râwuls "of Bhownugger were the first chiefs who had the discernment to "discover the advantages of this policy, and they have the singular "merit of reforming the predatory habits of their subjects, of direct-"ing their attention to industrious pursuits, and of affording security "to the persons and property of merchants, which have reclaimed "an extensive line of coast from the practice of piracy, and been "productive of many permanent benefits. It must at the same time "be admitted, that in other instances the ambitious policy of Wuk-"hut Singh has been but little restrained by any of the considerations "of honor and justice. His measures have been executed with "vigour, and generally with judgment; but they have been influenced "alone by his interest, and pursued with perseverance and spirit, em-"ploying indifferently force, intrigues, and artifice to increase his "power and ensure success to his schemes."

Under these auspices Bhownugger became the channel of the import and export trade of Goozerat, Soreth, and Marwar, and the encouragement which merchants received induced many opulent people to settle there, while the neighbouring port of Gogo, with the advantage of a much more convenient harbour, soon fell into decay.[1] As an example of the superior judgment and policy of the Gohil chiefs, Colonel Walker mentions the remarkable fact, that while at the port of Gogo, at that time under the Peshwah's government, shipwrecks and stranded vessels were annually farmed as a source of revenue, everywhere on the coast subject to the Gohils they were protected, and restored to the merchants.

In A.D. 1792, according to the bards, "Wukhut Singh became at " feud with the Kâtees, and led an army to Cheetul, from which the " Kâtees retreated. He plundered the fort of many horses, camels, " carts, and other property. He raised his standard at Koondulâ. " The Kâtees went to Ahmed Khân, Nowaub of Joonagurh, and " complained that the Râwul Wukhutsunghjee had seized their grâs. " The Nowaub advanced therefore with an army, but the Râwul met " him with forty thousand men. Arriving at Pâtunâ he drove away " the Nowaub with his cannon, and took the village of Râjoola from " him. The Jetwâ Rajpoot, Jeeâjee, effected a reconciliation between " the Nowaub and the Râwul, and they drank the red cup together, " but the Râwul was at feud with the Kâtees for twelve years."

Joonagurh was at this time, we may mention, in the hands of the family of Kumâl-ood-deen, or Juwân-Murd Khân Bâbee, the latest Mohummedan ruler of the capital of Shah Ahmed.

These events are commemorated also by the following ballad:— "Quickly advanced the Nowaub, bringing with him an army of " Kâtees; not a man was left in fort, or castle, or village. As he " came on angrily, Wukhutesh, like another Indra, mounted to " oppose the Yuwun. The kettle-drums sounded, and the great " drums too, the peaks of the mountains re-echoed, the earth-sup- " porting snake began to writhe, the ocean to dash its spray up to the " sky. The spear in his hand was glancing like a ray of the sun; " against the Nowaub none but the son of Ukherâj could go. " Countless Rohillas, Sindhis, and Puthâns came on, many Arabs " sounding the drum: Âtâbhâee, with his brothers, advanced to " meet them—'You have come with a good object, Bâbee! mount " 'and come on to the fight.' He gave him a sulâmee of cannon; " erecting batteries, he threw him into sorrow. Hemud considered " that he should get more blows than money. Without sounding the " kingly drum, off he fled in the middle of the night. The Kâtees, too,

[1] This state of affairs has since been reversed: the trade of Gogo has revived, while that of Bhownugger has fallen away.

"began to fly, hither and thither, like crows. The son of Mohobut "Khân fled; he heeded not what road he took. After the Yuwun "went Âto, following him by his track. The lord of Seehore cried "as he advanced, 'Slay! slay! take care of the honor of Sulâbut "Khân.'[1] Expelling friendship from his heart, he angrily encamped "at Pâtuna, within a coss of the enemy's frontier. 'Huree! Huree!' "exclaiming, he pitched his camp.

"As Devs and Dytes prepared for encounter, so stood the black "elephants and long-maned horses. Five kinds of music sounded; "sword, lightning-like, flashed ready for the fight; it seemed as if "the last day had arrived; tubes began to be discharged; in double "lines the Arab beruks advanced, shouting 'Deen! deen!'[2] the "valiant followers of Wukhut Singh irregularly were fighting. With-"in an hour Meeâ cried out for quarter; he began to be himself "the suitor. 'I swear to you by the Koran I will not attack you "again. I give you Râjoola, Koondulâ, and Cheetul; the Almighty "has given you all the country.' He caused a grant to be written, "and above it he placed his seal. The chief of Porbunder, Jeewojee "the Jetwâ, tried to give him courage; all that were with him were "dismayed; the Soubahdâr of Soreth was left without honor. With "him were the Koompâwut of Jetpoor, Wujsoor the Kâtee, of "Jusdun, the Dâhâ also: what strength had they to contend against "the King of Perumbh, over whose palace floated the flag of victory. "The strength of the Bâbee was broken, what of the Kâtees' "strength! Bhow Singh's descendant and his Koonwur—performers "of deeds of wonder—re-burnished the water of the sword of "Rutunesh, Bhâwo, and Ukherâj. Songs were sung throughout the "land. The princes rained on all around a shower of gold. Wuk-"hutesh, having obtained the victory, came joyful home."

In the early part of the month of October, 1803, Mulhâr Row Guikowâr, then for a second time in insurrection, came into collision at Sâbur Koondlâ, near the frontier of Gohilwâr, with a body of horse belonging to the army of Bâbâjee Âppâjee, who was employed at the time in his Moolukgeeree expedition in Kâteewâr. Mulhâr Row's followers were defeated and his baggage was plundered; he fled himself to Bhownugger, and solicited protection from Wukhut Singh Gohil. The Râwul was by no means disposed to espouse his cause, and contented himself therefore with permitting his embarkation on board a boat in which he purposed to make his

[1] An ancestor of the Nowaub's.

[2] *Deen* means "religion," and is a usual Mohummedan party-word.

escape to Dwârkâ or Bhooj. Two English boats however hove in sight before Mulhâr Row had proceeded far on his voyage, and fired two shots at his vessel. Mulhâr Row therefore again sought the shore, and re landed at Bhownugger, but the Râwul continuing to refuse him an asylum, he and his son, apprehensive of the consequences, abandoned their banner and drums, their horses and elephants, and betook themselves to flight, nor halted until they had reached the sacred hill of Shutroonjye or Pâleetânâ. There they remained with a single attendant for several days, and were almost starved, when some of the inhabitants of the adjacent country discovering their retreat, disclosed it to Bâbâjee. The Guikowâr general sent a party of one hundred horsemen, with led chargers, to bring them in. The three fugitives, on the approach of the horsemen, made no resistance, having abandoned all hope, and endured the pains of hunger almost to the death. They were supported to within a short distance of the Guikowâr camp, where they met the litters which had been sent out by Bâbâjee to receive them. Such were the circumstances which attended the last appearance in Goozerat of the talented, ambitious, headstrong, and unfortunate Jâgheerdâr of Kuree. With his son, Khundee Row, he was transferred, in the month of May following, to the charge of the British government, and by their orders conveyed to the fort of Bombay, where he was detained as a prisoner at large until he ended his days.

Early in A.D. 1804, a British agent was deputed to the Râwul of Bhownugger to induce him to agree to an amicable settlement in regard to his Moolukgeeree tribute to the Court of Baroda,—a measure which the Guikowâr government had adopted at Colonel Walker's recommendation, and to which Wukhut Singh also had for some time listened favourably. Influenced, however, principally by his ministers, the Râwul for some time evaded, and at length wholly rejected, the proposal. This conduct compelled Bâbâjee, who had waited for some time on the frontier in hopes of an accommodation, to enter the Râwul's territories, in the month of August, and hostilities in consequence ensued. The Guikowâr general advanced to Seehore, and his Pindârees harassed the country around, and carried off the cattle of the villagers. As the lands of the Gogo pergunnah were principally divided between the British and the Râwul, and were so intermixed that one share could hardly be injured without the other being affected, Wukhut Singh seemed to Colonel Walker to have formed some expectation from these circumstances that Bâbâjee would not venture to molest him. "I "have found it necessary," says the resident, "to undeceive him on "that head, and to apprise him that he shall be answerable for the "damage which may befal the Company's division of the pergunnah "from his resistance to the customary demands of the Guikowâr "government. I have not received an answer to this communi-"cation, and it may perhaps produce some good effect, as I under-"stand that the raja is displeased with his present advisers, and has "threatened to dismiss them for the injudicious course they have led "him to pursue." It was not, however, until the month of October that the Gohil Râwul, succumbing rather to British threats than to Mahratta valour, intimated his consent to settling with Bâbâjee for three years' tribute at the customary rate. The successful defence of Seehore against the Guikowâr army is thus celebrated by the bards:—

"The whole earth began to resound, such was the noise of the "royal drums of the strong and renowned Ânâbâ of Baroda. Fight-"ing with his enemies he broke down their boundaries. An unshaken "pillar was Mulhâr Râee in Kuree. An enmity arose between the "lords of Kuree and Baroda. Bâbâ's army set forth against Kuree "with fluttering banners, dust rising in clouds into the air. The "Bâbâ brought against Kuree an English army. An innumerable "array of warriors shouted. For two or four months they fired at "Kuree with their guns; at length Mulhâr Row, abandoning Kuree, "fled. Bâbâ conquered the impregnable Kuree. No one could "fight against him; all came to make their sulâms, seeing that he had "quickly captured such a fort as Kuree.

"The army advanced to Pâtree, which was held by Desâees, who "bowed to none. Fighting, they took from them lakhs of treasure; "things left lying on the road could be lifted by none; such was the "fear of Bâbâ. As he served Kuree, so he served Pâtree; he de-"stroyed many forts of the Mewâsees; he laid Juttwâr under contri-"bution, also Lutâd. When the Soubah arrived at a place, it was as "if a gang of plunderers had fallen upon it. Preparing his army, he "came to Jhâlâwâr to fight. First, he levied a contribution upon "Dhrângudrâ, the lord of eighteen hundred villages. Wudwân he "fined most certainly; he fined, too, Wânkâner; Limree and Syelâ "he fined; he collected whatever he demanded with his mouth. "The Soubah fined all Jhâlâwâr, defeating them; he fined the lord "of Moorbee; he fined Mâleeâ. The unbending Jâm he fined; "four thousand chiefs were fined by the Soubah. Hâlâr he took "possession of; firing cannon balls, he fined the Joonagurh Nowaub. "Fining the Kâtees, he reduced their land to weakness. The lord "of Por he fined, the Mânâ, the Jetwâ; he fined the Choorâsumâ;

"none could contend against him. All Soreth fining, he advanced "against Seehore; the earth began to shake, so mighty an army "advanced. Five coss distant he encamped at Âmbulâ. 'Âto has "conquered much territory. I must have money in proportion.' "Then, on each side, the guns were fired—wall-pieces and swivels. "Bullets flew like rain; the Mahrattas grew weary; streams of blood "flowed from their bodies; they lost courage. Many were slain, "many had their heads cleft asunder, the eyes of many were "darkened. Wuktâ's warriors plundered the Bâbâ's army like lions "unchained; the ground was covered with corpses and heads; they "sought to escape in all directions.

"This misfortune befel Bâbâ in Sumwut, 1860 (A.D. 1804). For "five months he could find no means of escape; the Soubah was "very much distressed. Of collecting tribute he lost the recollection; "all he thought of was escaping. In his tent he sat, and hid his "head. When he passed an acquittance, then he obtained permission "to retire. To what Bhâwo's grandson proposed he was forced to "agree; he came to exact a fine, but discovered he had one to pay, "for the two-and-a-half lakhs which he carried away had cost him "full five."

At the time of Colonel Walker's appearance in Kâteewâr, the Râwul of Bhownugger, in addition to the ports of Mhowa and Tulâjâ, and the districts already mentioned, had established his authority in nearly the whole of Wâlâk and in the district of Sâbur Koondlâ, and other places of less note. The disturbed state of society rendered the realization of his revenue very precarious, and he was supposed to be deeply involved in debt, from the necessity which he had experienced of increasing his forces to support himself against the Kâtees. His military establishment consisted of five hundred Arab, and two thousand five hundred Sindhian infantry, with about five hundred regularly maintained horse. He could also collect from the villages of the Bhyud, or cadets of the Gohil clan, three thousand Rajpoot horse; and to assist in predatory expeditions, though incapable of military operations, he could muster, also, two thousand five hundred "weavers." He had also of late entertained a body of a hundred horse belonging to Bhâwâ Meeâ, the Purmâr Kusbâtee of Dholka, for whose payment he had assigned the ancient possession of that family—the village of Botâd, in the pergunnah of Rânpoor, which stood opposed to Jusdun, a principal seat of the Kâtees, across the border. The town of Gogo, as a port of the Moguls, had been subject to the governor of Cambay. It had assumed the name of bârah—a title nearly synonymous with "harbour," but usually implying the possession of some portion of landed territory. On the division of Goozerat between the Guikowâr and the Peshwah, Gogo bârah fell to the latter authority, while the Moolukgeeree revenue of the remainder of Gohilwâr was assigned to the former. The whole was, however, eventually transferred to the British.

The Gohil clan possessed in the whole about eight hundred villages, of which about six hundred and fifty belonged to the Râwul Wukhut Singh. The chieftains generally resided in places of difficult access, and some of them had built extensive stone fortifications, which were, however, but indifferently provided with cannon, as well as deficient in other means of defence. Of the junior branches of the clan, the principal were those of Wulleh, Lâtee, and Pâleetânâ. The first of the Wulleh family, who were seated amidst the ruins of the ancient city of Sheelâditya, was Veesobhâee, the second son of Bhow Singh Râwul, the founder of Bhownugger. His grandson, Megh Râj or Mugobhâee, now held thirty-two villages. The chief of Pâleetânâ was descended from Sâhâjee, one of the younger sons of Sejukjee Gohil, to whom had been assigned the estate of Gâreeâdhâr; he possessed forty-two villages, of which, however, nearly the half were uninhabited. Oomurjee, of Pâleetanâ, had been obliged a few years before to solicit the support of the Guikowâr government, and his territories were at the time in a state of complete subjection, many of his villages had been mortgaged, and the enemies he had provoked had deprived him of others. The tranquillity of his district was now maintained by the presence of a Mahratta garrison in his ancient capital of Gâreeâdhâr. Soor Singh, the chief of Lâtee, and representative of Sârungjee, another of the younger sons of the first Gohil chieftain, retained but five villages of his original estate. The total destruction of this branch of the family had, indeed, been prevented only by the marriage of Dâmâjee Guikowâr with the daughter of Lâkhâjee, the then chieftain. By this connexion the Gohils of Lâtee secured the support and protection of the Baroda government, and an exemption from the payment of their Moolukgeeree tribute, which was commuted for the yearly offering of a horse in acknowledgment of supremacy. The dowry of the Gohil lady was, however, the district of Chuburra, since called after the name of her Mahratta bridegroom, Dâmnugger.

Numerous other Rajpoot estates, principally belonging to scions of the Jhâreja house of Kutch, were included in Colonel Walker's settlement of Kâteewâr, in addition to the chieftainships to which we have alluded, but to these we do not propose to refer, as we possess no original information in regard to them, and as their affairs have been as yet unconnected with the events of our story.

CHAPTER VIII.

BOUCHERÂJEE—THE CHOONWÂL.

As the Purmârs of Dântâ, with the Ârâsooree Mother, so the tribes of the Choonwâl are indissolubly connected with a more modern, but scarcely less famous Devee, Shree Boucherâjee. Some Chârun women, says the tradition, were travelling from Sulkhunpoor to a neighbouring village, when the Koolees attacked and plundered them. One of the women, whose name was Boucherâ, snatched a sword from a boy who attended her, and with it cut off both her breasts. She immediately perished. Her sisters, Boot and Bulâl, also committed suicide, and they, as well as Boucherâ, became Devees. Shree Boucherâjee is worshipped in the Choonwâl; Boot Mother, at Urnej, near Kot; and Bulâl Devee, at Bâkulkoo, about fifteen miles south of Seehore.

Upon the spot where Boucherâ perished, one of those rugged, cairn-like memorials, called "Khâmbees," was erected. This was afterwards supplanted by a temple of the smallest size, which is still in existence. A second temple, of somewhat larger dimensions, was erected in front of the first building, and so near to it as almost to close the entrance. The first of these erections is attributed to an apparently fabulous personage, Sulukh Raja; the second, to a Mahratta Furnuvees. Beside them, but turned in a different direction, is a large temple, possessing a spire and two domes, which was erected in A.D. 1783, by Mânâjee Row Guikowâr, the brother of Futteh Singh, and younger son of the great Dâmâjee. In front of this building is the pit used for fire-sacrifice, and beyond the fire-pit stands a pyramidal altar, called "châchur," or "the cross-roads," upon which animals are offered. Several houses of accommodation for pilgrims surround the temple, with lines of pedlar-like stalls, where the necessaries for worship, and various little knick-knacks for private use, are exhibited for sale. In one corner is an octagonal tower, of two stages, surmounted by an open, domed pavillion, called "Deep-mâlâ," or "the Lamp-garland." The two solid stages are chequered with niches for lamps, which, on days of festival, make a brilliant display of light. A battlemented wall, loop-holed for musketry, and protected by circular towers at the four corners, surrounds the temples and their subordinate buildings. The gateways are three in number. The principal one is contained in a rectangular tower, of which the upper portion forms a room, containing the royal drums and other instruments of music. From the terraced roof of the tower, the view extends on all sides over a flat, open country, studded with villages, each nestling in its clump of trees. Among them may be discerned Chundoor, Punchâsur, and Wunod, recalling the story of the first of the Unhilwârâ princes, Wâghel, the cradle of the latest scions of the race, and Kunsâgur, with its princely remains of their mid-day splendour. Sulkhunpoor stands hard by, and, nearer still, a hamlet bearing the goddess's name of "Bechur." A grove of bâbul and other trees of scanty foliage hedges the fort itself. Outside the walls is a small square tank, called the "Man Surowur," celebrated for the miraculous cures which have been effected by its waters, and at no great distance from it are other larger, but less celebrated, reservoirs.

The fame of Boucherâjee is said to be principally, if not entirely, owing to Wullubh Bhut, a Mewârâ Brahmin, of Ahmedabad, who, about the year A.D. 1744, composed many ballad poems in her praise, which, in a collected form, constitute the Boucherâjee Poorân. He celebrates her under the style of Doorgâ, a goddess to whom, however, the name of Boucherâjee is not otherwise attributed. No image is used in any of the numerous temples which have been, at different places in Goozerat, erected to the honor of Shree Boucherâjee. The object of worship is a square panel covered with pieces of tinsel, and placed in a niche which fronts the rising sun. At the Nowrattra, and similar festivals, Koolees and others, when their children or friends are threatened with death, present to Boucherâjee, in addition to the usual fire-sacrifice, vicarious offerings of animals, usually the goat or the calf of the buffalo. The sacrifice is performed in the open air, at the altar called "Châchur," in front of the great temple. At other times sacrifice of liquor and flesh is offered to Boucherâjee publicly by Rajpoots, Koolees, and others, and secretly, at night-time, by Brahmins and Wâneeâs, who practise a species of Shuktee-worship, and call themselves of the sect of the Mâtâ. These offerings are consumed by the worshippers after presentation. Brahmins and Wâneeâs also offer live cocks to the Mâtâ, placing them in the niche where she is worshipped. These accumulate, and are usually very numerous about the temple. A story is told of one of these cocks, which, having been cooked and eaten by an audacious Mohummedan, burst through his belly, and came forth alive :—

> "He eat a cock,
> "In oil having cooked it;
> "From the Mlech's body,
> "You called it, Bechurâ!"

Whence the people of Goozerat say to a person who keeps back from another what is due to him, "Take care, lest it prove a "Boucherâjee's cock to you." Lame, blind, and other impotent persons, persons desiring a son, or other blessing, make vows to Boucherâjee; they approach her temple, and there remain seated beside the Man Surowur, abstaining from all food, until they fancy that they have heard the Mâtâ promising to them the accomplishment of their desires, when they arise and return home. Those who are indebted to Boucherâjee for the gift of a son, gratefully call him after her name, "Bechur." Vows to Boucherâjee are made even by persons professing the Jain religion.

The officiating priests of this goddess are Brahmins, but the musicians and some of the other servants are Mohummedans. The owners of the temple's revenues are persons called Kumâleeâs, said to be about one hundred in number, of both sexes, and of all ages, and who assert themselves to have been created by the goddess. Though they worship Boucherâjee, and bear about her trident, they nevertheless profess the Mohummedan religion, a fact which they account for by pretending to have been forcibly converted by Allah-ood-deen. Only the less valuable offerings, however, are the property of the Kumâleeâs; those which are more costly being reserved under the care of the Guikowâr's officers, for the expenses of the temple. The right of the Kumâleeâs to even the share which they enjoy is, moreover, disputed by the Rajpoot landholders of the neighbouring village of Kâlree. A few years ago, these, to the number of about forty, simultaneously entered the precincts of Boucherâjee by the three doors, and put to death as many of the Kumâleeâs as they could find. Their victims, about ten in number, were buried outside the gate of Boucherâjee, the murderers having for the time effected their escape. A class still more degraded than the Kumâleeâs is also to be found in the service of Shree Boucherâjee—the Pâweeâs, who are eunuchs, and who, if universal belief be true, prostitute themselves to unnatural practices. They wear the dress of females, with the male turban. They are about four hundred in number, of whom the half reside at Teekur, near Hulwud, while others rove about the country extorting alms, by the usual means of intimidation and annoyance employed by other classes of wandering ascetics, both Hindoo and Mohummedan. Some of the Pâweeâs, it is commonly asserted, have amassed considerable wealth.

A few miles from the temple of Boucherâjee is the town of Detroj—"the Heart of the Choonwâl." The Devee has another temple there, which some consider to be her original shrine. She is the family goddess of the Kolee chiefs, called Thâkurrâs, of that neighbourhood, and, until lately, a festival was held annually at Detroj, on the day before the Nowrâttra, when the assembled Thâkurrâs sacrificed thirteen buffalo calves upon her altar. The wild chieftains used, however, on these occasions to inflame themselves with drink, and quarrels, frequently terminating in bloodshed, invariably ensued. The fair of the Mâtâ, at Detroj, has therefore of late years been suppressed, but the Thâkurrâs still, on the appointed day, repair separately to the borders of Detroj, and sacrifice, each of them, a buffalo calf in Boucherâjee's honour.

The head of a branch of the royal Solunkhee house became connected, say the bards of the Choonwâl, with a Kooleen of Detroj, but at what time this took place is not known. His descendants intermingled with the Koolees, and one of them, Kânjee, surnamed the Rât,[1] or barber, held forty-four villages, from whence was derived the name of "Choonwâl."[2]

[1] A corruption, probably, of the word "Rawut," meaning a war-like chief.

[2] *Choonwâlees-gâm*, meaning forty-four villages. These Rajpoot chiefs, heading tribes of aboriginal descent, afford an exact parallel to the foreign leaders of Highland clans in Scotland. "It is a circumstance worthy of notice, that when "the great families at the head of the Highland tribes have been traced far back, "they have generally been found to be of Teutonic race. The chiefs of the "Macdonalds, Macleods, and Mackintoshes were of Norwegian blood. Those "of the Frasers, Gordons, Campbells, Cumins, and many others, were Norman. "It seems as if the Celtic people—energetic, brave, and enduring as they were, "as followers—required, like some oriental races, the leadership of captains "issuing from races better fitted for organizing and commanding. In some "instances, the foreign family adopted a purely Celtic patronymic, from the "name of the sept of which they were the leaders. In other cases, such as the "Gordons and Frasers, the sept, probably absorbing various small tribes, and "admitting to its bosom many stray members, owning strange varieties of uncouth "Celtic denominations, took the name of the leader; hence we find the purest "Erse spoken by people enjoying the Norman names of a Gordon or a Cumin. "But, whether the chief adopted the name of the tribe, or the tribe that of the "chief, the unyielding influence of old national customs and peculiarities prevailed "over the higher civilization of the leaders, and their families gradually adapted

Once on a time, it is said, a bard from Jâmnugger, named Jhâr Guduwee, came to Detroj, on his return from a pilgrimage to Benares, and put up at Kânjee Rât's house, where he was very well received, and presented with a horse. The Chârun going home praised Kânjee Rât very much in the Jâm's presence, mentioning that it was because he was the Jâm's family bard that he had been so well received. The Jâm upon this sent a dress of honor to Kânjee Rât. The Putel of Detroj, whose name was Gopee, was all-powerful in the town at this time. He was envious of the honor paid to Kânjee Rât, and sent him orders to quit the town. Kânjee retired accordingly from Detroj, and took up his residence at Jângurâ-pura, four miles off. When the day devoted to the obsequies of deceased progenitors came round, Kânjee Rât sent a torch-bearer into Detroj to ask for milk, as he was preparing for the performance of his father's anniversary ceremonies. The torch-bearer procured milk from house to house, and at last went to Gopee putel's, and told him that he too must give milk. The putel flew into a passion, and caused his servants to break the vessel in which the torch-bearer carried the milk he had collected. Kânjee Rât's servant, therefore, was obliged to return to his master, weeping for the failure of his mission. The Rât was very much hurt at the putel's conduct, but thought it better to dissemble for the present. At this time a Chârun came to Kânjee's lodging, and when he had sung a song, he begged the Rât for a silk scarf. This Kânjee had it not in his power to give: he sorrowfully repeated a verse—

> In recompense of what sin was I born,
> The son of a great father?
> A mendicant asks me for silk;
> At home I have not even cotton.

" themselves in speech and method of life to the people over whom they held " sway. The same phenomenon was exhibited in Ireland, where the 'degenerate " English,' who, living from generation to generation among the native Celtic " Irish, had adopted the customs and costume of those they were expected to " civilize, elicited the ceaseless denunciations of the English government, and the " penal wrath of Parliament."—*Vide* Burton's Life of Simon, Lord Lovat.

The following is a list of the Rajpoot-Koolee Thâkurrâs of Goozerat:—*The Solunkhees*, of Kookwâv, Bhunkorâ, Chuneeâr, and Dekhâwârâ, in the Choonwâl; *the Mukwânâs*, of Kutosun, Junjoowârâ, and Punâr; *the Râthors*, of Ghântee and Wâghpoor, on the banks of the Sâbhermutee; *the Dâbhees*, of Ghorâsur, in the Churotur; *the Chohâns*, of Umleeârâ, in the Myhee Kântâ; and *the Wâghelas*, of Kâkurej. In the case of each of these families, their first connection with the Koolees separated them at once from the Rajpoot clans to which they belonged, and reduced them of necessity ever after to the adoption of the manners and customs of the Koolees, though, in most cases, modified so as to approach more nearly to those of the pure Hindoo tribes.

Kânjee resolved within himself that he would go and sacrifice his life before the Mâtâ at Detroj. Meanwhile he lay down to rest. In the night the Mâtâ appeared to him in a dream, and said, "Be not "afraid. Come to Detroj the day before the Nowrâttra. A buffalo "calf will meet you outside the village: this you must sacrifice to "me, and then you may plunder the putel's house victoriously. As "a proof of the reality of this dream, I give you a silk scarf, which "you may present to the mendicant." Having thus spoken, the Mâtâ became invisible. Kânjee awoke, and found a silk scarf lying beside him. In the morning he gave it to the Chârun. When the day before the Nowrâttra arrived, he assembled his friends, two hundred in number, well mounted and armed, and with them advanced to Detroj. At the gate of the town he found a very fine buffalo calf belonging to the putel. He killed it before the Mâtâ, and sprinkled her with its blood. At this time the padishah had a garrison in a fort outside the gate of Detroj. Kânjee Rât posted a hundred horsemen to observe the garrison, and taking the remaining hundred with him, went to the putel's house, and ordered him to pay him obeisance. This Gopee putel refused to do, whereupon Kânjee slew him, with six of his sons. The seventh son he saved alive, and Kâleedâs, the present Putel of Detroj, is that son's descendant.

A complaint was made at Delhi that the putel had been put to death, and the padishah sent Azim Khân to reduce Kânjee to submission. There was at that time a very extensive forest about Detroj, called the "Jânguro Forest," of which the following story is related:—When Dhârâ Shah fled before his brother, he came to Detroj, and Kânjee Rât offered to protect him there. Dhârâ asked where the fort was in which he was to be sheltered. To which Kânjee replied that the forest was stronger than any fort. Dhârâ answered, "The padishah's camels would eat this forest, and the tim-"ber of it would make stakes for fastening his horses. However, it "is well in you that you have so much courage." Thus speaking, Dhârâ Shah pursued his journey to Sindh. Now Azim Khân, when he arrived, lost no time in clearing the forest, upon which Kânjee fled to Kutosun, where a connection of his, named Jeswunt Singh, was living. They jointly opposed Azim Khân, but were at last obliged to fly to Junjoowârâ, where they were received by Jehojee Mukwânâ. The whole of the allies were, however, at length compelled to fly to Thurrâ, in the Kâkurej country, where a Koolee Thâkor, named Koompojee, then ruled. Koompojee joined them, and they continued their retreat to the hill called "Kurjâ," where they held out for twelve years, living the life of outlaws, until at length a wâneeâ of

Chundoor, named Kurum Shee, who was employed by Azim Khân as his revenue minister, effected a reconciliation between them and the padishah, and procured the restoration of their pergunnahs. The Thâkurrâs bound themselves therefore to Kurum Shee, that none of their race should gallop a horse near Chundoor, nor injure any of its inhabitants.

The Shah's court listened to the complaint about Gopee.
They said, "Will no one seize Kân?
"Let us send a stout Umeer to Goozerat
"To crush this Jânguro Kânuro."

With honor Azim Khân was sent
To set crooked things straight.
Kân and Jeswunt, fighting, he drove out;
With them fled Raja Jesheeo.

Kumo[1] was made Deewân by Azim.
Several rajas submitted to him.
From fear of Azim, Thurrâ's lord fled;
The rajas, all of them, fled to Kurjureeâ.

At Kurjâ they held out—praised be their valour!
Why should I make the story long?
Jeswunt, Kân, Koomprâj, and Jesheeo,
The Râthwee[2] protected like a hedge.

From this time Kânjee Rât held Detroj without interruption, and attained to great power and fame. It is even said that the padishah conferred upon him royal insignia, a drum, bearers of silver rods, and a state umbrella.

Kânjee was succeeded by Râmsunghjee, Udebhânjee, and Nâronjee. The plinth of the funeral temple of this latter chief still exists at Bhunkorâ, in the Choonwâl, and an inscription thereon states, that "Rât Shree Nâronjee's chutree" was erected by his brother, Shree Hureesunghjee, and his Koonwur, Shree Kânâjee, in A.D. 1720.

Kânâjee, the younger, appears to have emulated the fame of his predecessor of the same name:—

O! Kânâjee, Kânâ's quiver,
Thou didst bind on thee in thine youth.
Another could not support its weight.
O! Dev-descended chief of Detroj!

[1] Kurumshee of Chundoor.

[2] A title of Kurumshee's.

Like Kânjee Rât, he was at war with the Mohummedans.

The world with outcries went before the Shah,
The padishah heard the true word they said,
"As before in Agra, Jânguro Kânuro was famed,
"A Kânuro Jânguro has arisen again."

He has wall-pieces and warriors, his kettle-drums resound;
Black elephants he keeps with him, does Nundo's son;
His subjects cry, "What great matter is it to slay footmen?
"He slew a nowaub with his banner and flag."

He is a striker of many blows, he is of great strength,
Three kinds of army he leads to crush his enemies,
He makes war-music sound, he destroys difficult forts,
He adorns his father's seat, does the grandson of Udebhân.

Against the padishah continually he carries on war;
The padishah's subjects suffer fear not to be allayed.
"Wah! wah!" cried out the courtiers of the Jâm;
"Kâno padishah destroys the troopers of the Shah."

Another verse thus celebrates his generosity—a virtue as necessary to the bardic hero as valour itself:—

Indra rains but four months,
You rain the whole twelve;
He sends prosperity sometimes,
You are ever relieving the poverty of poets;
He thunders in the sky,
You thunder upon earth;
He rains money and grain,
You rain horses;
Detroj Rân! giver of gifts,
I behold you increasing like the moon;
O Kânâ, son of Nundo,
I pronounce you to be equal to Indra!

Kânâjee appears to have held only a fourth share of the Choonwâl, which had been already divided—at what time is unknown—into the estates of Kookwâv, Bhunkorâ, Chuneeâr, and Dekhâwârâ. He divided his own share among his sons during his life-time. Nuthoobhâee, the eldest, received the villages of Râmpoorâ, Kânpoorâ, and Kânj; Dâdo, the second son, had Duslânoo and Nâronpoor; Bhooput Singh, the youngest, Koeenteeoo and Ghuteshânoo. Kânâjee retained the rest of the estate for himself, consisting of the villages of Bhunkorâ, Kântrodee, Chooneenoo-puroo, Dângurwoo, Bâlshâshun, Endurâ, and Kudwâhun.

On the death of Kânâjee, Bhooput Singh, who was then twelve years old was driven from the estate by his elder brothers, and retired to the house of the Thâkurrâ of Chuneeâr, who was his distant kinsman. He had a favorite goat, which on one occasion fought with a goat belonging to the Thâkurrâ of Chuneeâr, and, being beaten, ran away. Bhooput Singh was much enraged with his goat, and said to it, "Shame on you, that you have taken away my character." He cut off the goat's head. The Chuneeâr chief was afraid that Bhooput Singh might some day be angry in a similar way with his children, and might do them injury. He therefore determined upon sending him away. Bhooput Singh retired to Koeenteeoo, one of the villages which had been assigned to him by his father, and took up his residence there. Now Koompojee Mukwânâ of Punâr was advised by his minister, Puthoo, to give his daughter in marriage to Bhooput Singh. Koompojee, who was a chief very famous throughout the country, asked how such a thing could be thought of while Bhooput Singh had no lands. The minister replied, that if Koompojee were to assist him, Bhooput Singh would soon recover his estate. So the lady was married to the young Thâkurrâ, and his father-in-law, Koompojee, collecting two thousand Koolees, put to death his brother, Dâdo, and Dâdo's son, Bunesung, at Duslânoo, upon which Nuthoobhâee, the other brother, fled away for fear, and took shelter first at Kutosun and then at Ghântee. Bhooput Singh upon this seized his father's and brothers' estates, and seated himself at Bhunkorâ.

An Uteet of the Gosâee monastery at Bhunkorâ used to come and go to the apartments of the mother of Bhooput Singh. The Wâneeâ ministers took advantage of this to tell tales to Bhooput Singh, and say that, from the Wâneeâ's coming to the durbâr, the Thâkor's name was spoken ill of. Bhooput Singh was enraged at the thought, and slew his mother with his sword. The Uteet thereupon fled, and never returned, but his disciple took possession of the monastery.

At this time the "Meleekurs," or forayers, of Koompojee Mukwânâ of Punâr ranged the whole country from Wudwân and Limree on one side, to Ahmedabad on the other. The Raja of Sânund gave Koompojee a horse every year at the Deewâlee, and arranged that his territories should be exempted from forays. Koompojee levied black-mail on many other villages also. Now Jethâ Putel, of Mândul, was in great favor with the Mahrattas, and used to precede the Peshwah's army when it came into the country to levy tribute from the Bhoomeeâ chiefs. At one time two lakhs of rupees of tribute were due to the Peshwah by the Râj of Hulwud. Jethâ Putel went there to arrange for the payment of these arrears. At that time the Bâee was managing the estate in the minority of the Koonwur. She told

Jethâ Putel that she had not the means of paying the arrears at that time, her country having been but lately wasted by the chief of Wudwân, who allowed her not a moment's respite. Jethâ Putel threatened that if his demand were not complied with he would enforce it by firing the town. So saying he went away. Now Koompojee was the adopted brother of the Bâee, and she sent for him, and told him that she should never be at rest until Jethâ Putel was dead. Jethâ came about the same time to a Punâr village, called Chureeâloo, to fasten a garland on behalf of the Peshwah. Koompojee took the opportunity to quarrel with him, and slew him with his sword—a deed which gave great satisfaction to all the Bhoomeeâs.

After this Koompojee made a foray upon Od-Kumod, near Ahmedabad, with a hundred and fifty horsemen in chain armor. He drove off the cattle. There was, however, in the village a post of sixty Mahratta horse. These horsemen came upon the "wâr," but Koompojee engaged them, and repulsed them with the loss of twenty of their number, he himself losing only four of his followers. There was, however, another post at Sirkhej, and a Wâneeâ minister, with only six horsemen and a pair of kettle-drums, came suddenly upon the Koolees, during one of their halts. The Meleekurs, when they heard the drums, supposed themselves to be attacked by an officer at the head of a large force, and so took to flight. Koompojee Thâkurrâ, as he galloped off, was struck through from behind with a spear, and fell dead. The Mahrattas carried off the corpse, and refused to give it up until Shâmtâjee, Koompojee's son, promised that he would never make a foray upon their village again. Having obtained the body, Shâmtâjee committed it to the flames at Punâr, and erected a pâleeyo at Od-Kumod.

To return to Bhooput Singh. Mulhâr Row Guikowâr sent from Kuree to claim the villages of Kântrodee, Koeenteeoo, and Ghuteshânoo as Guikowâr property, but Bhooput Singh refused to surrender them, and the dispute lasted for a number of years. At one time several cart loads of silk goods, the property of a Puttun merchant, passing along under the protection of the Chuneeâr Thâkurrâ's people, were seized by Bhooput Singh between Duslânoo and Bhunkorâ. Bhooput Singh allowed the merchant to ransom his property for fourteen thousand rupees. This conduct produced a great feud between him and Chuneeâr, in the course of which many men on both sides were slain, and Bhooput Singh himself was, on one occasion, wounded with a matchlock ball. Hunmunt Row, the brother of Mulhâr Row, advanced towards Bhunkorâ at this time with a Mahratta force from

Kuree, and sent to Bhooput Singh to say, that as the Thâkurrâ was about to throw water on his head,[1] he had come to bind a turban for him. Bhooput Singh replied that he did not want the turban, and had no intention of allowing the Mahrattas to enter his town. Hunmunt Row, therefore, quartered his troops in the neighbouring villages, and sent to Kuree to say that Bhooput Singh was not to be caught by stratagem. Upon. this, Mulhâr Row forwarded Bhooput Singh a safe conduct, and invited him to Kuree. On his arrival he repeated his demand for the three villages, which was again rejected by Bhooput Singh. It was near harvest time, and the grain was ripening in the fields. Bhooput Singh laid them all waste, and, leaving his village, placed his wife and children at Veerumgâm, and "went out." He had three hundred horse of his own, and his allies swelled his force to the number of two thousand. He plundered the Guikowâr's villages.

Bhooput Singh used the royal drums and umbrella which had been granted by the padishah to his ancestor, Kânjee Rât. While he was "out," Mulhâr Row began to destroy his house with his cannon. A Chârun sneeringly said, "What wonder is there that Bhooput Singh "should fight; but now the very bricks of his house are turned war-"riors!" Mulhâr Row was ashamed of his proceeding when he heard this, and retired. Bhooput Singh continued for a long time to be a terror to the Mahrattas:—

"Kuree and Bhunkorâ fought,
"Sattara and the Jâm heard it,
"Bhooput went to the battle
"As Râm against Râwun.

"Descendant of Kânâ! the enemies'
"Flesh-devourer,
"Your sword
"Has become a terrible Dâkin.

"Women of the Mahrattas,
"How can ye wear ornaments?
"Over your heads hangs a great terror,
"For ready to engage stands Bhooputo.

"Mulhâr Row did not perceive the snake's house,
"Unwittingly he set his foot thereon:
"The mighty serpent awoke,
"Bhooputo, the invincible warrior.

[1] That is, to bathe for the first time after recovering from his wound.

" Kuree he will dig up by the roots,
" He will force them to sue for peace;
" Bhooputo will enjoy the land,
" He will strike Row Mulhâr.

" Senselessly many swaggered,
" Mahrattas and Toorkoras,[1]
" On all four sides your servants—
" You made them, O! Bhooputo."

When a son was born to Mulhâr Row, at Kuree, a servant of his went into the market to purchase ginger for the use of the Rânee, that root being much used by Hindoo women as a tonic after child-birth. The servant kept on saying, "We must have the very best "ginger in your shop." The grocer said, "Bhooput Singh's mother "has eaten all the best ginger, there's none left now but what's dry." The damsel went home, and mentioned what the grocer had said to Mulhâr Row. He was enraged, and plundered the grocer's house. When Bhooput Singh heard this, he made up to the grocer his loss. In this way, Mulhâr Row and Bhooput Singh were opposed for many years. At length, when Mulhâr Row went to war with the English and the Baroda state, he called in Bhooput Singh from Junjoowârâ to his aid; and when Mulhâr Row was made prisoner, it was to Bhooput Singh's care that he confided his family.

The following anecdotes are related of this chief:—

The Kâtee of Dhândulpoor, named Godud, was attacked by the Nowaub of Joonagurh. He sought aid from the Râj of Hulwud, but that chief was afraid of the nowaub, and refused to assist him. Godud Kâtee then sent for Bhooput Singh, who went to Dhândulpoor, and defended it successfully.

The chief of Hulwud had encroached upon the lands of the grassia of Methân, who is the head of a younger branch of his family. Upon this the Methân Jhâlâ gave his daughter to Bhooput Singh, as other chiefs had given daughters, on like occasions, to Mohummedans; and the Râj of Hulwud, from fear of Bhooput Singh, withdrew immediately from the lands which he had seized.

Bhooput Singh used to give feasts to Brahmins on the twelfth days of both divisions of the month. He maintained also a charitable establishment in his village for the poor, and forbore from plundering the poor, though he made war upon rajas. He died in A.D. 1814.

In the neighbourhood of the Solunkhee-Koolees of the Choonwâl

[1] A name of contempt for Toorks or Mohummedans.

are the Mukwânâ-Koolees, who possess the estates of Junjoowârâ, Kutosun, and Punâr. Kesur, the Mukwâno,[1] had, in addition to his son Hurpâl, the ancestor of the Jhâlâ clan, two other sons, Wujepâl and Shâmtâjee. Wujepâl was wounded and taken prisoner in a battle against the Mohummedans, and became a Molesulâm. His descendants are the Mohummedan chiefs of Mândoowâ in the Myhee Kântâ, who bore the family title of Lâl Meeâ, and have been alluded to in the story of Row Veerum Dev of Eedur.[2] Shâmtâjee took forcible possession of the town of Sânthul, at which his descendant, Kânojee, resided in the days of Mahmood Begurra. Kânojee married the daughter of a Bheel chieftain, and thus lost caste; he served, however, with distinction under the sultan, and Mahmood therefore made him a grant of the estate of Kutosun, which consisted of eighty-four townships. Thirteenth in descent from Kânojee was Nâronjee, Thâkor of Kutosun, from whose time the fortunes of the family may be very minutely traced, exhibiting, perhaps, the best example which Goozerat can furnish of the effects of the Hindoo custom of subdividing landed property. It is not, however, our intention to enter upon this task, as the subject, though interesting to the student of land-tenures, is unattractive to the general reader. The exploits of the Kutosun Mukwânâs do not furnish so good a field for bardic tale as those of their neighbours of Bhunkorâ, but the names of Ujbojee and Ugrojee, grandsons of Nâronjee, are not without fame in their way, and are celebrated in a ballad, from which we select, in conclusion, a few passages. The following is a picture of Ujbojee's court at Kutosun:—

"Drums sounded in the durbâr; water was sprinkled on the "ground; many chiefs came thither to seek sanctuary, standing with "their palms joined, they made their petitions. Before the descendant "of Kânojee, as before Indra, sounded the thirty-six kinds of music; "before him learned men read the Veds; sugar was supplied to the "guests, goats flesh, and flesh of hog; opium and saffron were daily "distributed; dancers performed before Ujbo; always in 'color and "'music'[3] he sported; a pair of bugles sounded before him; the "singers, swinging, elephant-like, from side to side, sang songs; in "spending money, the chief was as free as Bulee Raja; at his cook-"room, daily, rice and milk, and all kinds of ambrosia-like food "were prepared; over his house always floated the flag of Dhurum;[4] "such was the lord of the Choonwâl, who issued his commands even

[1] *Vide* p. 229. [2] p. 320, &c.

[3] "Rung-râg," festivity.

[4] That is, to invite comers to receive charity or religious gifts.

"to the padishah. Well didst thou rise Sun-like Mukwâno! son of "Jusâ! the father of Hindoos, and the boundary! Nor less famous "was his brother, Uguresh; the brothers recalled to men's minds the "sons of Dusruth."

Ujbojee was, according to the bard, an universal conqueror, he defeated alike "the Show Raja's army, the army of the Dekkanees," and "the army of Delhi;" but he did not neglect still more congenïal achievements; "from village to village he *fixed his grâs*," or imposed his black-mail; "every day he gained great fame in plun-"dering. His Umeers were the Vishrodeeâ, the Punâra, the Murto-"leeâ," and a vast number of other half-clad lords of hamlets; he was not, however, deficient in wardrobe himself, for the bard particularly specifies that "he dressed in silk and jewels."

Ujbojee established his claim to a more honorable reputation, by throwing open his granaries to the poor, on the occasion of that terrible famine of A.D. 1813, the recollection of which, like the echo of some mournful strain that will not pass away, is sure to darken the most joyous verse of the bard:—

"The earth was distressed, rajas were without food, Rows and "Rânâs had not a grain to bestow, husband and wife deserted each "other, parents abandoned their children, the practice of religious-"giving was forgotten; charitable establishments were broken up; the "places of water were dry, not a drop fell from the heavens. At the "time when daily from each village came such news as this, when all "the country was a beggar, at that time did the descendant of Kâno "unfurl his flag; open he threw his stores; though other rajas "would not admit strangers to their villages, Ujubesh received them "all. If Indra remained angry in Swerga, this Indra upon earth, at "least, was propitious; he strove to drive the famine from the land."

The following is an account of a war with the Mohummedans:—

"At this time two Toorks ruled at Kuree, Âmbo Khân and "Lembo: they oppressed the country. When they heard of the "fame of Ujbo and Uguro, they wrote to Kutosun to demand "tribute and submission. Ujbo was furious when he heard the "message. Uguro restrained him from slaying the messenger. "They sent for the minister, Deepchund, the son of Mudunshâ; an "irritating answer they made him write to the Toorkurâs, reminding "them of the exploits of Kesur, and of the lords of Keruntee-gurh. "The big-bearded Moslem assembled full of pride, they pitched "their camp at Dângurwoo. When the news reached Kutosun, "Ujbo called in his brothers, Tejul, whose sword had never broken, "Meghrâj, Jugto, and Sooruj Singh. Uguro, stroking his moustache, "addressed them; the brothers swore they would do the duties of "brotherhood. Vikumshee, the poet, cried, 'Wâh! wâh!' He was "pleased when he saw their courage; he incited them by singing the "songs of their fathers; he sang of Shâmtâjee of Sânthul, of "Hurkhâ Showâee, of Kâno. Many Koolees came together; the "twanging of bows sounded, each bore his quiver at his back; "some were horsemen, some footmen, some soldiers of the night. "Jhorâ and Jussâ came with the men of Jukânâ; Hemo came, of "Ugurjâ; Mâno, of Murtolee," and many others. We need not, however, enter upon the description of the battle, which is put together after the established bardic receipt; the Shesh Nâg trembled; Hindoo met Mohummedan as mountain meets mountain; the stream of blood flowed like a river; Shiva appeared, as usual on such occasions, with his staff of Veers, goblins, flesh-eaters, &c. Sooruj held in his horses, the chariot of the sun was stayed. "Upsurâs and Howris came to carry to their celestial homes "Hindoos and Moslem. Âmbo and Lembo, who turned not to "flight, strove with the sword-armed Kshutree."

All this is usual, the following, however, is peculiar :—

"When Uguresh excited him, Ujbo determined upon falling on "the enemy by night, tiger-like, as well as fighting them by day. "From tent to tent he dug mines; money and jewels, arms and "clothes he carried away. In both ways the enemy received blows; "having nothing to eat, away they scampered; of men and horses "were left but a few." Reduced to such straits as these, the Mohummedans were glad to avail themselves of the offers of the Thâkor of Wursorâ, who now came forward, and, effecting a settlement of the matter in dispute, "caused the strife to cease."

CHAPTER IX.

THE MYHEE KÂNTÂ.

THE fiscal and military division of Goozerat, known to the Mahrattas by the name of the Myhee Kântâ, was not, as the name implied, confined to the banks of the Myhee, but extended northwards from that river to Poseenâ, Umbâjee, and the Bunâs, and included, in fact, all that portion of Goozerat proper which required the presence of a military force for the realization of the Guikowâr's tribute. The natural features, which we have described in the opening of this work, were, in a great degree, the causes of the very different state of subjection into which the various parts of the province had fallen. The level country was almost entirely reduced under the direct government of the Mahrattas, though the jungles of the Choonwâl, and the banks of the Myhee, as far south as Baroda, still furnished shelter to independent tribes, and many villages in Mondeh, Nâpâr, Dholka, and others of the richest districts, including those which belonged to the Rajpoot landholders, and in particular to the Wâghelas, required an annual armament to enforce payment of their tribute. As the smaller streams branched off, many independent communities appeared among the ravines and jungle on their banks; as these rivulets increased in number, and the forest grew thicker and more continuous, the independent territories also became more frequent, and were found in more solid masses, until at length the still-untamed principalities of Eedur and Loonâwârâ were reached amidst the mountains of the north-east.

Many Koonbees, waneeâs, and others of the peaceable classes, were included among the population of the Myhee Kântâ, but the castes which bore arms, and in whom the whole authority of the country was vested, were Rajpoots, Koolees, or Mohummedans. Of these, the Koolees were by far the most numerous, though they were, for the most part, found under Rajpoot rule. The Rajpoots themselves were of two descriptions—the Marwarees, who had accompanied the reigning family of Eedur in its emigration from Jodhpoor; and the adherents of the ancient Rows, whom we have already beheld driven to a last retreat at Pol. The former resembled the clans of Marwar in their costume and manners, but, in their present sequestered situation, had contracted an additional ruggedness. They were said to be very brave, but stupid, slothful, unprincipled, and devoted to the use of opium and intoxicating liquors. The Rehwurs, and other clans who still professed allegiance to the descendants of Row Sonungjee, were considered to be more civilized than the Marwarees, more honest, more submissive, but less active and warlike. All the Rajpoots used swords and shields, matchlocks and spears. They often wore defensive armor, either of leather or of chain, and placed it upon their horses; they sometimes, but rarely, carried also bows. Their plan of war was to defend their villages; they seldom, except after an ineffectual defence, took to the woods like the Koolees, and were quite incapable of the desultory warfare so congenial to the temper of the latter tribe. The Koolees, or Bheels (for, though the former would resent the classification, the distinctions between them need not here be noticed), were, as has been observed, by far the most numerous of the inhabitants of the Myhee Kântâ. They were more diminutive in stature than the other inhabitants, and their eyes wore an expression of liveliness and cunning. Their turbans, if they used any, were small; their common head-dress was a cloth carelessly wrapped round the temples; their clothes were usually few and coarse; they were seldom seen without a quiver of arrows, and a long bamboo bow, which was instantly bent on any alarm, or even on the sudden approach of a stranger. The natives described them as wonderfully swift, active and hardy; incredibly patient of hunger, thirst, fatigue, and want of sleep; vigilant, enterprising, secret, fertile in expedients, and admirably calculated for night attacks, surprises and ambuscades. Their arms and habits rendered them unfit to stand in the open field,[1] and they were timid when attacked, but had, on several occasions, shown extraordinary boldness in assaults, even upon stations occupied by regular British troops. They were independent in spirit, and although all professed robbers, were said to be remarkably faithful when trusted, and were certainly never sanguinary. They were averse to regular industry, exceedingly addicted to drunkenness, and very quarrelsome when intoxicated. Their delight was plunder, and nothing was so welcome to them as a general disturbance in the country. The numbers of the Koolees would have rendered them formidable had they been capable of union, but though they had a strong fellow-feeling for each other, they never regarded themselves as a nation, nor ever made common cause against an external enemy.

The revenue of the state of Eedur amounted to four lakhs of

[1] The Scottish Lowlanders entertained a similar opinion of the Highland clans. A ballad, entitled "Bonny John Seton," has the following verses :—

"The Highland men they're clever men,
"At handling sword and shield;
"But yet they are too naked men
"To stay in battle-field.

"The Highland men are clever men,
"At handling sword or gun;
"But yet they are too naked men
"To bear the cannon's rung.

"For a cannon's roar in a summer night,
"Is like thunder in the air—
"There's not a man in Highland dress
"Can face the cannon's rair."

rupees, without including its dependencies of Ahmednugger and Morâsâ. In the time of the Rows, the Eedur territory had been much more extensive, but the pergunnahs of Kherâloo and Poorântej had been conquered by the Sultans of Ahmedabad, while other districts had been absorbed by the Rânâs of Mewar, or the Râwuls of Doongurpoor. The Muhârâjâ of Eedur possessed himself no more than a revenue of one lakh, or one lakh and a half, the remainder was assigned to eight Rajpoot chiefs, who held of him, under the designation of "puttâwuts," on condition of military service, and a small pecuniary payment. There were, besides, between twenty and thirty Rajpoot and Koolee chiefs, many of whom had held lands of the old Rows for military service, but who now paid, instead, an annual tribute to the Muhârâjâ. The whole Eedur country was tributary to the Guikowâr, the levy being made in the first place upon the Muhârâjâ and his puttâwuts, but falling ultimately on the people of the country, upon whom an extra cess was imposed to meet it. The Muhârâjâ's personal force consisted of only fifty horse and one hundred and fifty foot; but as occasion required, it was increased to a much larger number, by the employment of mercenaries, of whom bands were never wanting. The puttâwuts' contingent was about one thousand strong, horse and foot, and there existed a further force of six hundred military vassals.

The chiefs of Ahmednugger, Morâsâ, and Bâyur were relations of the Muhârâjâ of Eedur, and held territory which was included in that principality, though they were in reality almost entirely independent. The chief of Ahmednugger, in particular, was the mortal foe of his kinsman of Eedur, and their enmity had of late been raised to the highest pitch by a dispute regarding Morâsâ, which the Muhârâjâ claimed as a fief that had reverted to him on the death of the last chief, while the Ahmednugger prince continued to hold it for his son, who was, as he contended, the rightful heir by adoption.

The eight "puttâwuts" of Eedur were (with the exception of one, who was a Chohân) of Râthor blood, distinguished by the family names of Jodhâ, Châmpâwut, Koompâwut, and others, which marked their respective descent from Jodhâ, the founder of Jodhpoor, his brother, Châmpâ, his nephew, Koompo, or other members of the reigning family of Marwar. Their respective rank was strictly settled, and the honors assigned to each were carefully defined. The Koompâwut of Oondunee, the highest in rank, was preceded by a silver rod, and was allowed to sound the kettle-drums at the head of his train; he was entitled to recline in a litter, and to use the royal "châmur," or fan of horse-hair. His lands were free of all revenue payable to the head of the state; when he appeared in the presence, or retired from it, the Muhârâjâ rose from his cushion and embraced him, and his place in the court was the first on the right hand of the sovereign. Perhaps the most highly valued of his privileges, however, were two, which will doubtless appear strange ones to the European reader—he was entitled to wear a heavy anklet of gold, and to smoke a golden hookah in the royal presence. The noble of lowest rank, who possessed, however, the most ample estates, was the Chohân of Mondeytee. He enjoyed the fewest privileges granted to any of his order—the kettle-drums, and the state-embrace of the Muhârâjâ.

Next in rank to the nobles of the first class was the Bârutjee, or royal bard, whose seat was in front of the Muhârâjâ's cushion, and who received the prince's salutation, both on entering and on retiring from the court.

There were other military vassals, who, holding lands in the districts (or zillahs) of the great nobles, were called "Zillâyuts." Some of these were received by the Muhârâjâ on entering the presence, but no notice was taken by him of their departure. They maintained each of them a small number of horsemen, which never exceeded ten, and followed the noble of the zillah.

The revenue affairs of the state were conducted by a minister called Kârbhâree or Deewân, usually a member of the commercial classes. Other relations, however, were entrusted to one of the Sirdârs, who bore the title of Prudhân, and whose constant presence with the Muhârâjâ was indispensable. No step could be taken by the prince, which affected one of the nobles, without the concurrence of the Prudhân, and a summons for attendance signed by the Muhârâjâ, but wanting the counter signature of this minister, would have been disregarded by the puttâwut, or even considered as evidence of a treacherous intention.

The Eedur territory, though open towards the west, was generally very capable of defence. It abounded in rivers, hills, and forests. The soil was fertile, and innumerable mango trees evinced that it had once been cultivated; the greater portion was now, however, overgrown with jungle.

The Myhee Kântâ district contained also the Rajpoot principality of Loonâwârâ, of whose fortunes we possess unfortunately no record. It included, in addition, the territory of Dântâ and the possessions of numerous small chiefs, (each of them leading from fifteen hundred to three thousand fighting men, and seated in the neighbourhood of fastnesses of very great strength), of whom the most considerable may be divided into four or five clusters. The Koolee chiefs of

Umleeârâ, Lohâr, and Neermâlee, with the Mukwâñâ landholders of Mândoowâ, Poonâdurâ, and Kurâl, occupied an area of about fifteen miles in the neighbourhood of the river Wâtruk : a second cluster, of nine Koolee villages, lay on the Sâbhermutee, in the pergunnah of Beejâpoor; immediately to the south of these were the Rajpoot estates of Wursorâ, Mânsâ, and Pethâpoor. The Koolees of the Kâkurej, near the Bunâs, and those of the Choonwâl, were estimated at the respective strength of eight thousand, and five thousand bowmen; but their country was not strong, and they had ceased to be troublesome to their neighbours.

The ruins of numerous and extensive castles, built by the Mohummedan monarchs with the view of checking the "Mewâsees," or refractory tribes, are still to be seen in unfrequented parts of the country. Such measures were probably not very effectual, even when the Moslem power was in full vigour, and in the decline of the Mogul empire the garrisons were withdrawn, and the country was abandoned to its turbulent inhabitants. The state of affairs was altered on the appearance of the Mahrattas, who, without building forts or attempting to assume the direct government, carried on their usual harassing inroads until they extorted a tribute, which they continued to increase as opportunity offered.

The Mahratta Moolukgeeree force, in the Myhee Kântâ, used to canton during the rains wherever its presence seemed most required, and for the whole of the remaining eight months of the year it was constantly in motion. When the tribute was not paid on demand a horseman, entitled to levy a fixed sum every day, called a Mohul, was despatched to the chief. In case this measure proved ineffectual the force moved to the chief's lands, when, if the presence of such undisciplined visitors, by its own inconvenience, failed to bring him to terms, they proceeded to cut down his crop, spoil his trees, and waste his lands. These measures were generally rendered necessary by the imposition of some addition to the tribute; but many villages also made it a point of honor not to pay unless a force came against them. In cases of extreme obstinacy in refusing tribute, or in committing or encouraging depredations, the Guikowâr officer entered on open hostilities. He generally endeavoured, by a forced march, to surprise the Mewâsees in their villages, and seize their chief or their women. If he succeeded, the Mewâsees submitted; but if he failed, he "struck" (that is to say, burned) the village, and the people, especially if they were Koolees, retired to the jungle, and set his attacks at defiance. The strongest Koolee villages were open on the side furthest from the river, and the only object of such defences as they erected on other points appeared to be to secure a retreat to the ravines. The facilities afforded by these recesses, whether for flight or concealment, inspired the Koolees with the greatest confidence, while the roads leading along the supposed ridges were by no means equally encouraging to the assailants. In such cases the Koolees, with their bows and matchlocks, would often keep the Guikowâr troops for a long time at bay. But if they were dislodged they scattered, and, by long and rapid marches, united again at a concerted point beyond the reach of their enemies. In the meantime they sometimes attempted night attacks on the camp, in which the suddenness of their onset often struck a panic into the undisciplined troops opposed to them; but they more frequently avoided the enemy, and annoyed him indirectly by the depredations they committed on the villages in which he was interested. In the meantime the Guikowâr chiefs endeavoured to obtain intelligence, and to cut up the Koolees or seize their families. They also tried by all means to prevent their receiving provisions, and otherwise punished all who supported them. If this plan were successful, the Koolees would subsist for a long time on the flowers of the Mowra tree, and on other esculent plants; but in time the bulk of their followers would fall off and return to their villages, while the chief, with the most determined of his adherents, remained in the jungle, and either was neglected or easily eluded the pursuit of the Mahrattas, until he could, by some compromise, or even by submission, effect his restoration to his village. There were many instances in which quarrels with the Koolees had terminated still less favorably to the Guikowâr. The village of Umleeârâ, though defended on one side only by a narrow strip of jungle and a hedge of dry thorns, stood a siege of six months against a body of seven thousand men. The village was carried by assault; but a part of the Koolees rallied, and the besiegers fled with the greatest precipitation, leaving their guns and four of their principal leaders on the field. On another occasion the inhabitants of Lohâr, about one thousand strong, enticed a Guikowâr force of ten thousand men through a long defile into the bed of the Wâtruk, and while a small party made a show of resistance on the opposite bank an ambuscade started up and opened fire on the rear in the defile. The whole army immediately took to flight, and Bâbâjee Âppâjee, who commanded it, with difficulty escaped by the swiftness of his horse.

When the affair was with Rajpoots these almost always defended their village; and that of Kurrorâ, situated among strong ravines, on the banks of the Sâbhermutee, once beat off several assaults of the Guikowâr troops, and compelled them to raise the siege. The Rajpoots sometimes, though rarely, hired foreign mercenaries, and often called in Koolees, but the Koolees never had recourse to the assistance of any other tribe.

The Mahratta power was at its highest in the Myhee Kântâ about the end of the eighteenth century, at the time when Shivrâm Gârdee, the commandant of regular infantry, whose name has been already mentioned, was employed in the settlement of the province. The disorders of the Guikowâr government, subsequent to the death of Futteh Singh, did away with the effects of Shivrâm's successes; but about the year A.D. 1804, order was very effectually restored by Rughoonâth Myheeput Row (or Kâkâjee), the cousin of Rowjee Âppâjee, and although the Guikowâr troops had since then met with some reverses, they had never encountered any general spirit of resistance. The first interference of the British government in the affairs of the Myhee Kântâ took place in A.D. 1813, when Major Ballantine, following up the system which had been so ably introduced by Colonel Walker, entered into engagements, on the part of the Guikowâr, with all the tributary chiefs of the province. By some unaccountable mistake, however, those terms were never either conformed to or formally annulled. The Myhee Kântâ was, during the period that ensued, entrusted to Buchâ Jemâdâr, an officer of the Guikowâr government, who kept up a considerable force, and maintained the authority of the Mahrattas with some energy. He greatly increased the pecuniary payments of the chiefs, and he chastised such of them as went into open rebellion, but he was unsuccessful in preventing depredation, and loud and frequent complaints of the outrages of the Koolees were heard in the British districts. In A.D. 1818, the larger part of the Jemâdâr's force was called off on foreign service, and afterwards, the whole of the Mahratta troops having been withdrawn, the province relapsed into nearly its former state of disorder. Three years afterwards the Myhee Kântâ was visited by Mr. Elphinstone, who then held the reins of government at Bombay, and under his direction a British agency was established in the province, with the general views of securing its tranquillity and of providing for the peaceful realization of the tribute possessed by the government of Baroda.

CHAPTER X.

THE MUHÂRÂJÂS OF EEDUR—ÂNUND SINGH—SHIV SINGH—BHUWÂNEE SINGH—GUMBHEER SINGH.

UJEET Singh, say the Eedur bards, speaking of the Jodhpoor Raja of that name, was very famous. He placed seven shahzâdas on the throne, and unseated them again. In the end he placed Momud Shah on the throne. For seven days Ujeet Singh's order was obeyed at Delhi, and five great rajas came to him for protection—those of Jeipoor, Jesulmer, Buhâwulpoor, Seerohee, and Sheekur. After placing the padishah on the throne, Ujeet Singh remained three years at Delhi, and then returned to Jodhpoor, leaving Koonwur Ubhye Singh, with five thousand horse, to serve the padishah. One day the padishah took Ubhye Singh with him for a sail upon the Jumna. When they reached the middle of the stream, the padishah ordered the Koonwur to be thrown into the water. Ubhye Singh asked what was the reason. The padishah told him he must write to his brother, Wukhut Singh, to put his father to death. Ubhye Singh upon this caused Bhundâree Rughoonâth to write to Wukhut Singh, and tell him that he would give him Nâgor on condition of his at once putting Ujeet Singh to death. When the letter reached Wukhut Singh, he went in the middle of the night, and put his father to death.[1] The Rânees prepared to become sutees; they took with them Ubhye Singh's younger brothers—Ânund Singh, Râee Singh, and Kishor Singh,—in order that their eyes might not be put out, according to the Jodhpoor custom. The Jodhpoor Raja's place of cremation was at Mundowur. When the Rânees arrived at that place they made the Koonwurs over to the Sirdârs. Now Râee Singh and Ânund Singh were the sons of a Chohân Rânee, and Kishor Singh of a Bhâteeânee. They were entrusted to the care of the Chohân Sirdârs, Mân Singh and Deveedâs, and of Mân Singh's Koonwur, Jorâwur Singh. These Chohâns held the Roeechâ puttâ, the produce of which was one lakh; they abandoned it and went away with the Koonwurs, and halted at Chândelâ, fifteen coss east of Jodhpoor. Thâkor Mokum Singh, the puttâwut of Baroda in Marwar,—a puttâ of ten thousand rupees,—was ordered by Wukhut

[1] See this story in detail in Tod's Rajasthan, vol. i. pp. 744, 745.

Singh to pursue them and slay them, or bring them back. He mounted, therefore, and proceeded with eight hundred horse to Chândelâ. The three chiefs, beholding his approach, girded up their loins, and seated themselves in council, their twelve hundred horse being encamped around them. Mokum Singh dismounted at their tent, and asked for the Koonwurs. Mân Singh said that they had been entrusted to him by the sutees, and that he now made them over in the same way to Mokum Singh. As he spoke these words he presented also a dagger, and said, "If you intend to slay "them, do so now." Mokum Singh said, "Thâkor! you have done "much, that you have drawn me in along with you. Now, what "befalls you must befall me." The four chiefs retired together to a hill called Âdowâlo, in Marwar, and became outlaws. Their families were left at Kurneejee Mâtâ's, at a Chârun village called Desânot in Bikaner,—this Mâtâ being very powerful to protect those who fly to her for refuge.

Now before this time the Châmpâwut puttâwuts of Sunulâ, viz., Showâee Singh, Mân Singh, Pertâp Singh, and Jeewundâs, who held a puttâ of seventy thousand rupees, had had a quarrel with Raja Ujeet Singh, and their puttâ had been placed under attachment. They also had become outlaws, and were at this time at Âdowâlo, their families having been left at Kurneejee Mâtâ's. They had lately plundered a caravan of treasure passing from Ujmeer to the padishah at Delhi. When the Râj Koonwurs arrived at Âdowâlo, the Châmpâwuts made an offering of this treasure, and volunteered their services. Koonwur Ânund Singh accepted the offer, and at this time he made a promise to Mokum Singh Jodhâ, Mân Singh Chohân, and Pertâp Singh Châmpâwut, to the effect that if he obtained a kingdom he would confer a puttâ upon each of them, as they were faithful to their lord. From Âdowâlo the Koonwurs and their partisans began to make forays upon Marwar, and it is still said of Mân Singh Chohân, in songs, that he churned Muroo-land as the Devs churned the ocean.

When Ubhye Singh, from fear of the padishah, wrote to Wukhut Singh to put his father to death, the padishah gave him the Eedur pergunnah as a present, and a deed with nine seals. A Brahmin named Jugoojee, the Pooroheet or family priest of Ubhye Singh, while on his way from Delhi to Jodhpoor, was seized by the outlaws, and carried to Adowâlo. He informed them of the grant of Eedur to Ubhye Singh, and swore to them that if they would permit him to go to Delhi he would bring the grant back with him. They agreed to the Brahmin's proposal, and he went to Ubhye Singh, and informed him that his brothers were plundering and distressing Marwar, suggesting that the grant of Eedur should be given to them, instead of one of the twenty-two pergunnahs of Jodhpoor. Ubhye Singh gave him the grant, and he carried it to Âdowâlo.

At this time, Sumwut, 1785 (A.D. 1729),[1] Oodâwut Lâl Singh, who served the Nowaub of Borsud with three hundred horse, was on his way to Marwar on leave, and, arriving at Eedur, pitched his tents by the Rumulesur tank. It was then that the Desâees came to visit him, and offered to make him master of Eedur. Lâl Singh said that the padishah had granted Eedur to Muhârâjâ Ubhye Singh, and that he could not himself take it, but that he would bring Ânund Singh and the other brothers of the Muhârâjâ who were in outlawry. This being agreed to by the Desâees, Lâl Singh went to Âdowâlo and related what had passed. The Râj Koonwurs had in the meantime been joined by Jethâwut Uderâmjee and Koompâwut Umur Singh: they now set out at the head of about five thousand horse, and proceeded to the pass of Roherâ, leading from the Seerohee country into the province of Eedur. The Wâghela Thâkor of Poseenâ, a puttâwut of the Row's, however, blocked up the pass, and would not permit the Râj Koonwurs to advance, for the Rowjee had by no means abandoned his claim to the possession of Eedur. At length it was arranged that Ânund Singh should marry the Thâkor's daughter,

[1] The following is an extract from a report by Major Miles, then in political charge of the Myhee Kântâ, dated 21st September, 1821:—

"In Sumwut, 1785, Ânund Singh and Râee Singh, two brothers of the Rajah "of Jodhpoor, accompanied by a few horse from Vanoo and Pahlunpoor, and the "Koolees of Gudwara, took possession of Eedur without much difficulty. They "are said to have had an order from Delhi, but the truth seems to be that they "were invited by the state of the country, and most likely assisted by the Marwar "princes, who at that period held the Soubahdaree of Ahmedabad. Some years "after, at the instigation of the Dessye above-mentioned (who had been placed in "charge of Eedur after its capture by Morad Buksh), who appears to have been "displaced by the Marwarees, an officer in the service of Damajee Guikowâr, "named Buchajee Dewajee, was dispatched, on the part of the Peshwah, to take "possession of Eedur, which, assisted by the Rehwur Rajpoots, the servants of "the late Row of Eedur, he did. Ânund Singh was killed in an engagement, "fought for the recovery of Eedur, about Sumwut, 1809 (A.D. 1753), and Buchajee, after leaving a detachment there, returned to Ahmedabad. Râee Singh, "however, collected a force, and again obtained possession of Eedur. He died "in Sumwut, 1822 (A.D. 1766). Shiv Singh succeeded his father Ânund Singh, "and is said to have governed about forty years. Shiv Singh had five sons— "Bhowanee Singh (or Laljee), who succeeded him; Sungram Singh, who received "the puttah of Ahmednugger; Jalum Singh, of Morassa; Indur Singh (no "puttah); and Umur Singh, of Gorewara. Bhowanee Singh governed only one "month after the death of his father, and was succeeded by his son, Gumbheer "Singh, the present raja, in Sumwut, 1849 (A.D. 1793); Gumbheer Singh has one "son, named Oomed Singh, or Laljee, who is about twenty years of age."

and that that chief should have twelve villages in addition to those which he held of the Row of Pol. The villages of the Dhunâl estate were accordingly made over to the Thâkor, and his daughter was married to Ânund Singh, and the army thereupon advanced to Poseenâ. To this place the Râj Koonwurs invited the Desâees, and on their arrival an arrangement was concluded, and the force advanced to Eedur, which place they entered on the seventh of the light half of Phâlgoon, Sumwut, 1787 (A.D. 1731), the same year in which Muhârâjâ Ubhye Singh came to Ahmedabad. Ubhye Singh was afterwards on good terms with the Eedur Muhârâjâs, and not only procured for them the grant from Delhi, but also put them in possession of the pergunnahs of Beejâpoor and Poorântej. As long as Ubhye Singh remained, Eedur had no jummâ (tribute) to pay to Ahmedabad.[1]

Two years after Muhârâjâ Ânund Singh's arrival at Eedur the

[1] We do not know how this statement is to be reconciled with the following letter, quoted by Colonel Tod (Rajasthan, vol. ii., p. 769):—

"*Letter from Raja Jey Sing, of Amber, to Rana Singram Sing, of Mewar,* "*regarding Edur.*

"SRI RAMJI.

"SRI SEETA RAMJI.

"When I was in the presence, at Oodipoor, you commanded that Mewar was "my home, and that Edur was the portico of Mewar, and to watch the occasion "for obtaining it. From that time I have been on the look out. Your agent, "Myaram, has again written regarding it, and Dilput Raee read the letter to me "verbatim, on which I talked over the matter with Muharaja Abhe Sing, who, "acquiescing in all your views, has made a *nuzzur* of the pergunnah to you—and "his writing to this effect accompanies this letter.

"The Muharaja Abhe Sing petitions that you will so manage, *that the occupant,* "*Anund Sing, does not escape alive, as, without his death, your possession will be* "*unstable*—this is in your hands. It is my wish, also, that you would go in "person, or, if you deem this inexpedient, command the Dhabhaee Nuggo, placing "a respectable force under his orders, and, having blocked up all the passes, you "may then slay him. Above all things, let him not escape,—let this be guarded "against.

"Asar badi, 7th S., 1784 (A.D. 1728).

"*Envelope.*

"The Pergunnah of Edur is in Muharaja Abhe Sing's jagheer, who makes a "nuzzur of it to the Huzoor; should it be granted to any other, take care the "Munsubdar never gains possession. 8th S., 1784.

"On the margin is written, according to custom, in the raja's own hand— "Let my respects be known. When, in the Dewan's presence, he ordered that "Edur was the portico, and Chuppun the vestibule to Mewar, and that it was "necessary to obtain it. I have kept this in mind, and, by the Sri Dewanjee's "fortune, it is accomplished."

Nowaub of Borsud fled to him for shelter, in consequence of a rebellion of his brothers. The Muhârâjâ, having asked advice of his Sirdârs, sent his two brothers, accompanied by Châmpâwuts Showâee Singh, and Pertâp Singh, Jodhâ Mokum Singh, Jethâwut Uderâmjee, Châmpâwut Jeewundâs, and Koonwur Jorâwur Singh, with a force about two thousand strong, against Borsud. There was a great fight there, and cannon were fired from the fort, so that for ten days it could not be taken. At length the Borsud Kârbâree came over, and opened the gates of the fort. Koonwur Jorâwur Singh received two or three sword wounds during the siege, and fifty of the Marwarees fell, with about as many on the other side. The Nowaub, when he was replaced on the royal cushion, said to Muhârâjâ Râee Singh, "Stay with me until I am firmly settled." Râee Singh therefore remained for eight months.

At this time the Rowjee assembled his Sirdârs, the Rehwurs, the Thâkor Udesingh, of Runâsun, the Thâkors of Monpoor, Surdohee, Roopâl, and Ghorewârâ, and all the Bhoomeeâs around, with the exception of the Wâghela of Poseenâ. The Sirdârs said they would go and fight for the Row, and take Eedur if they could. They advanced to Deshotur, where there were five hundred houses of Dâbhee Râjpoots, and from thence to Eedur. At this time the Mohummedan Kusbâtees were very strong in Eedur; they were divided into two branches, called Naiqs and Bhâtees (in all about fifteen hundred houses), and to them the gates and batteries of Eedur were entrusted. The Rowjee's puttâwuts gained over the Kusbâtees, and took the town of Eedur. Muhârâjâ Ânund Singh had been left with only two Sirdârs, Koompâwut Umur Singh and Chohân Devee Singh; he retired with these Sirdârs and his zenana into the fortress on the hill, but being in danger even here he sent out the ladies under the Sirdârs' protection by a postern gate, and himself left the fort by the main gate which overlooks the town, and went on in the hope of joining the zenana. The Muhârâjâ had but few horsemen with him, and even these were scattered. At this time he perceived a body of Rehwur horse approaching, and immediately gave orders that his royal drum should be sounded to call together his followers. The nobut-beater[1] remonstrated, saying that the Rehwurs would come up if the drum were sounded, but that the Muhârâjâ's horsemen were too far off. Ânund Singh repeated his order, in an angry tone, and the drum was immediately sounded. The Rehwur horse galloped up, and overtook his scanty following,

[1] The "nobut" is the royal drum.

and a fight ensued. On the Muhârâjâ's side, Chohân Devee Singh first went down; then Koompâwut Umur Singh was wounded. Râmdân, the nobut-beater, was slain. The Muhârâjâ's horse was killed under him, and at length he himself was slain. A few only of his followers escaped, and the Rehwurs took the fort of Eedur.

Many arrows flew, many swords moved,
Great companies of elephants met each other
When Ânund Muhârâj, at Eedur-gurh, wedded the Upsurâ.
Of the bridegroom's party, the leader was Deveedân Mâmo.
The claims of all, he paid with blows redoubled.
Indrâ-like was Ujmâl, the bridegroom.
His best-man was the son of Phut Mâl.
Instead of a marriage song, they had the roar of battle.
Valiantly advancing, they pushed back their enemies,
Like elephants in rut, swaying from side to side,
Did the Kumud and the Muchureek strike down their foes.
The fort lords, Mâmo and Bhâneej, passed to Paradise,
For them had ceased the toil of being born in the womb.
Him who, in front advancing, fell, I praise—the Chohân! [1]

The Sonuggeree and the Wâghelee, Rânees of Muhârâjâ Ânund Singh, retired to the Seerohee village of Roherâ, and there became sutees. A slave-girl also burned herself with them. Their chutrees may still be seen at Roherâ.

When the matter was made known to Muhârâjâ Râee Singh, at Borsud, he prepared to advance upon Eedur. He took up his ground first at Mooneyoo, where he remained four months, plundering the Eedur country, without finding any opportunity of attacking Eedur-gurh. At length he sent Keshree Singh, of Beejâpoor, and Unop Singh, of Dâwud, two Bhârots, and planned with them to seduce the Sâbher Kântâ chiefs who were on the Row's side. The Bhârots accordingly made an arrangement with these chiefs that when the fight began they should fire in the air. Râee Singh now advanced from Mooneyoo to Bârolee, where he found himself at the head of ten thousand men. The Naiq and Bhâtee Kusbâtees were also seduced by promises of puttâs and jâgheers to desert the Row, though they still protested to him that they would defend the town. Râee Singh now advanced against Eedur, and surrounded the town with his troops. He himself, with Mân Sing Chohân, Koonwur Jorâwur

[1] *Mâmo* and *Bhâneej*, mean *mother's brother* and *sister's son*. *Ujmâl*, is Ânund Singh. *The son of Phut Mâl*, is Devee Singh. *Kumdhuj* or *Kumud* is a title of the Râthor clan, as is *Muchureek* of the Chohân.

Singh, Jodhâ Mokum Singh, and the Châmpawuts Pertâp Singh, Showâee Singh, Mân Singh, and Jeewundâs, ascended the hill called "Mudâr Shâ's toonk," which overlooks Eedur, and from thence descended into the town, which the Kusbâtees rendered without resistance. The Sirdârs asked the Muhârâjâ what was to be done next; he said, "Ask Mâmâ Mân Singh, who is the leader of the army." Mân Singh advised that they should kill the Kusbâtees, and enjoy a thornless râj. The Marwarees therefore attacked them, and killed about a thousand; they next attacked the fort, which they took, killing some of the Rehwurs. The Rowjee now escaped to Pol, and the Rehwurs went home to their own estates, having held possession of Eedur for about eight months in all.

Ânund Singh Muhârâjâ had left a son, Shiv Singh, who was six years of age. Râee Singh placed him on the throne, and began to act as his minister.

After this, Muhârâjâ Râee Singh attacked Ude Singh Rehwur, the Thâkor of Runâsun. As he advanced, a Bheel, who met his cavalcade, mentioned that the Thâkor had died, and that his son had taken his seat on the cushion. The Muhârâjâ, when he heard this, was so much enraged at his enemy's having died a natural death, instead of having been slain by him, that he shot the bearer of the tidings dead with an arrow. He proceeded, however, to Runâsun, and surrounded the town. The young Thâkor fled to Loonâwârâ, the Solunkhee of which place had married his sister. The Muhârâjâ remained a month and a half at Runâsun, and then retired, having made the twenty-four villages of the estate "khâlsâ," or crown-land, and placed a garrison there, under Koombho Bhâtee. Runâsun remained subject to Eedur for five years, and then, in consequence of the continual incursions of the Rehwurs, it was given back to them, twelve villages, of which Deshotur was the principal, being, however, retained as khâlsâ lands.

The following song relates to the contest which took place at this time between the Rehwurs and Râthors:—

"Night or day, the sound of the war-drum ceases not,
"But the Jodhâs are not lessened in number;
"Daily, with its elephants, an army advances,
"The feud with the Marwarees has no termination;
"All day long they seek the field,
"They fight, they charge, they mount, they fall;
"Without a warrior's death no evening comes;
"When many fall, then fall the shades of evening.
"On both sides, like roaring floods, rush on the armies;
"Great is the noise of broken trees, of armor broken.

"Ah! when will Kâlo[1] cause this calamity to cease,
"This dust-storm in the land of Eedur?
"Shall I praise the arms, or praise the wearers?
"Shall I praise the Sirdârs, or praise the followers?
"Is Rehwur good, or is Râthor good?
"Awe strikes the beholder as each chief charges on,
"And though the Sirdâr fall, the followers continue the battle,
"Yet falls not Eedur-land into the power of either."

Râee Singh now placed Shiv Singh at Eedur, and took up his own residence at Morâsâ, where he built a mansion and accommodation for his zenana. Five years afterwards a Mahratta army, led by the wife of Junkojee, came from Poonah to Morâsâ, and demanded tribute. The Mahrattas were about fifteen thousand in number, yet tribute was refused by Râee Singh. The lady who led the army sent, it is said, to Muhârâjâ Râee Singh, and requested that he would visit her, as she had heard that he was very handsome, and was disposed to remit the tribute. Râee Singh said, that if he was not handsome, he was a good archer, and asked the messenger, in sport, whether he thought an arrow would go through the buffalo and water-bags of a Mahratta water-carrier who was passing at the time under the walls of the fort. He drew his bow, and the arrow passed through both the animal and the bags. The water-carrier went off immediately to his friends, and complained bitterly, and the Mahrattas immediately attacked with their whole force. The garrison, which consisted of only one hundred and fifty Marwarees, fought till they were all slain, but Râee Singh, placing his wife on his horse behind him, and winding a scarf round her so as to fasten her to himself, galloped off to Râeegurh, a fort which he had constructed upon a hill near khâlsâ village of Unghâr, and which contained a garrison of two hundred horse and foot. He remained there two or three days, and then went on to Eedur.

When the Mahrattas took Morâsâ, the Châmpâwut Jeewundâs fell, and his brother, Pertâp Singh, was left on the field wounded. The Mahrattas, supposing that the latter was the Muhârâjâ Râee Singh himself, put him into a litter, and carried him off to Ahmedabad, where they placed him in confinement. Shortly afterwards they proposed to ransom him for eighty thousand rupees, and this sum was taken out of the Eedur treasury, and dispatched upon camels towards Ahmedabad, but when the escort reached Pethâpoor on its way, the Thâkor himself, who had managed to effect his escape, met them, and the money was brought back to Eedur. Râee Singh then said that the

[1] Krishn.

treasure had been taken out for the use of Pertâp Singh, and that the Thâkor should keep it. Pertâp Singh declined, urging that he had no need of money when the Muhârâjâ provided so well for him. The Sirdârs, at length, arranged that half that sum should be given to Pertâp Singh, and half replaced in the treasury.

In the year 1797 (A.D. 1741), says the bard, the Muhârâjâ granted "puttâs" to his followers. Mondeytee was given to Mân Singh Chohân, Chândunee to Châmpâwut Showâee Singh, Mhow to Châmpâwut Pertâp Singh, Gântheeol to Jethâwut Uderâmjee, Teentoee to Koompâwut Umur Singh, Wudeeâvee to Koompâwut Bâdur Singh, Merâsun to Jodhâ Indra Singh, and Bhânpoor to Oodâwut Lâl Singh. At this time Râee Singh and Shiv Singh were seated together upon the cushion of Eedur. The Sirdârs, however, considered that two swords could not be contained in one scabbard, and that some day treachery would be perpetrated. They assembled at the Chohân's mansion to deliberate as to how the Muhârâjâs could be separated, Shiv Singh having now attained the age of about eleven years. Koompâwut Umur Singh was at length deputed by them to Muhârâjâ Râee Singh. He said, "Muhârâj! if you will pardon me, I will speak." Râee Singh replied, "Say on." "All say," continued the Thâkor, "that one scabbard cannot contain two swords, nor one "throne afford room for two rajas.[1] Your highness should therefore "proceed to some other place." Râee Singh said, "No one but "yourself has mentioned anything of this kind to me, therefore both "of us must leave the Eedur territory." Râee Singh accordingly

[1] "You must not," say the Dutch, "have two mainmasts in one vessel:"— "Une nation se peint dans son langage, principalement dans ses expressions "proverbiales; celles de la langue française, en partie prises de la chevalerie, "indiquent l'époque qui contribua en France à former cette politesse exquise, "cette urbanité délicate, cette émulation de grandeur et de générosité, dont il "est resté quelque chose dans nos romans; celles de la langue hollandaise "montrent visiblement que le commerce et la navigation ont toujours été les "occupations principales des Bataves, et que l'économie, chez ce peuple industrieux, "a été de tout temps la première des vertus.

"Le Hollandais veut-il faire entendre qu'il ne faut qu'un seul maître dans une "maison, il a recours à cette figure: 'Il ne faut pas qu'il y ait deux grands mâts "dans un vaisseau."

"S'il veut faire connaître que ceux qui n'ont pas la charge ou la conduite, de "quelque affaire, pretendent souvent en raisonner mieux que les personnes à "qui on l'a confiée, il fait encore usage d'une figure prise dans ses habitudes, "en disant: 'Les meilleurs pilotes sont ordinairement à terre.'"—*Description of the United States of the Netherlands.*

retired to Râee-gurh, and Umur Singh went off to Marwar, his puttâ of Teentoee being assigned to Châmpâwut Mân Singh.

Râee Singh Muhârâjâ left no son, but he had a daughter, Bâee Eejun Koonwuree, who was married to Mâdhuv Singh, Raja of Jeipoor.

Umur Singh was not successful in his attempt at obtaining a puttâ in Marwar, and he therefore returned, six years afterwards, to Eedur, and was presented with the estate of Muneeol. He had two sons, Sher Singh, and Dheerut Singh, who served the Muhârâjâ Shiv Singh so well that he assigned to them the puttâs of Kookreeoo and Oondunee. Muhârâja Shiv Singh made also other grants. To Futteh Singh and Khoman Singh, the grandsons of Châmpâwut Pertâp Singh, he gave the estates of Mhow and Wânkâner, and he gave land to several other Rajpoots, who became zillâyuts of one or other of the Sirdârs.

When the Guikowâr army, under Âppâ Sâhib, with the Rowjee, the Rehwurs, and others, in St. 1844-5 (A.D. 1788-9), or thereabouts, came into the Eedur country, and began to kill and plunder, the Sirdârs retreated with their families to the hills. They all assembled at length at the "Ghoonwâ" hill, which lies between Dântâ and Poseenâ, and is accessible only by a narrow pass, from whence they made night attacks upon the Guikowâr army, slaying and plundering. The army then came against the "Ghoonwâ," upon which the Sirdârs fled to Pânowrâ, in Mewar, to the north of Eedur. The Mahrattas advanced upon Mondeytee, and plundered and burnt all the villages of that district, as well as many villages of Poseenâ, Mhow, Chândunee, and other districts. At length they advanced upon Eedur, against Muhârâjâ Shiv Singh, and encamped at the Rumulesur tank. They sent to the Muhârâjâ to say that if he did not come in to a conference, without loss of time, they would destroy Eedur. Upon this, Shiv Singh, with his five Koonwurs, went into their camp. The commander of the Mahrattas now demanded that the Muhârâjâ should sign a deed, passing half his country to them, on pain of the territory being laid waste. The pretence which they made for this claim was, that Shiv Singh represented Ânund Singh Muhârâjâ only, and that the share of Muhârâjâ Râee Singh, who had died without offspring, was theirs, the territory of Eedur having been taken possession of by these two princes jointly. The Muhârâjâ when he heard these demands made humble submission, but without effect. The Mahratta leader threatened to seize him and place a garrison of his own in Eedur. Then the Muhârâjâ, in his trepidation, said, "To "pass a deed for the territory is not in my hands, it is in "the hands of the Sirdârs. It is a kingdom acquired by "their means that I rule over." The Pundit demanded that the Muhârâjâ should summon his Sirdârs. Shiv Singh answered, "They will not come at my summons; besides, you have laid waste "their villages, and they, too, have done some harm to you—how, "then, can they come in?" The Mahratta officer then gave security, and the Muhârâjâ also wrote private letters to the Sirdârs, saying, "If you do not come in I shall be made prisoner." Upon this all the Sirdârs came in, with the exception of Soorujmul, the Thâkor of Chândunee, who went off to his own village, with his followers, numbering a hundred horse and two hundred foot. When they arrived the Pundit threatened them very much, and compelled them to pass a deed for Râee's Singh's share. The Muhârâjâ signed first, and then seven Sirdârs subscribed the deed.

This affair completed, the seven Sirdârs said, "When Soorujmul "signs then our signatures are to hold good, but not till then." The Pundit said, "Send for him." A horseman of the Muhârâjâ's and one of the Mahratta leaders were then sent to offer the security of Jân Mohummed, an Arab Jemâdâr, and Soorujmul soon after came in with a hundred and twenty horse. The Pundit received him courteously in his own tent, seated him beside himself, and then gave him the document that he might affix his signature, as the other Sirdârs had done. Soorujmul had no sooner read it, however, than he tore it up, saying, "The Muhârâjâ is lord of the pât (throne), but I am lord of the thâth" (district, lit. building). He said to the Jemâdâr, "You must conduct me back to Chândunee," and, immediately rising, went off home. The Mahratta leader was very much enraged, and threatened the Muhârâjâ and the Sirdârs, but they protested that there was no fault of their's, they had signed the deed. The Pundit then demanded that they should accompany him to attack Chândunee, to which all assented. Batteries were thrown up before Chândunee, and the attack was continued for the whole of one day, the Muhârâjâ and Sirdârs apparently taking part with the Mahrattas, though in heart they were with Soorujmul. In the night Soorujmul fled to the hills, and the Mahrattas plundered and burnt the town. They remained in that place for four days, during which time Soorujmul fell upon them when occasion offered, slew ten or twelve men, and carried off fourteen horses. The army struck its camp before Chândunee, and moved to Sâmbulee. There, too, Soorujmul fell upon them in the night time, and slew, among others, the Arab officer who commanded the artillery while he was making his bread and singing, "tân-a, tân-a, tân-a." The Muhârâjâ then said to the leader of the Mahrattas that this Rajpoot was a dangerous fellow, and there was no saying whom he might slay, and that if the army retired he would send the sum of money which had been agreed upon. A bond for twenty thousand rupees was then drawn up and signed, the Mahrattas retired, and the Muhârâjâ returned to Eedur. He sent immediately for Soorujmul and begged him to restore his village, and presented him with four thousand rupees to rebuild his mansion. Soorujmul did so, but after this he became full of pride on account of his valor, and used to say, "There is no strength in either Muhârâjâ or Sirdârs. "It was I alone that preserved the throne of Eedur."

When the Mahrattas retired, they left garrisons at Ahmednugger, Morâsâ, and other places. The Sirdârs drove out most of these posts, but in some places they held their ground, and in these the Peshwah acquired a half-share.

Now when Châmpâwut Soorujmul came to Eedur, the people had to make the roads clear for him, otherwise he threatened them. A nobut-beater of the durbâr's on one of these occasions having offended him by committing a nuisance on the public road, Soorujmul seized him, and, tying a rope round his ancle, ducked him in a pond, lowering him and pulling him out until he died. At this time Muhârâjâ Shiv Singh was old and infirm, and a great friendship existed between the prince Bhuwânee Singh and Soorujmul. On one occasion Soorujmul made a feast at Chândunee, and invited the prince; they were seated together in the durbâr, when one of the prince's attendants, a Bhojuk Brahmin, happened to spit on the floor. Soorujmul was in a fury, and ordered the Bhojuk to lick up the spittle with his tongue. The Bhojuk said, "I have done wrong, but now I will wipe "it up with my clothes." Soorujmul, notwithstanding, insisted upon being obeyed. Then the Muhârâj-Koomâr said, "He has done "wrong, therefore, if you please, I will wipe it up with my own shawl." Still Soorujmul insisted, "He shall lick it up with that very tongue." Then the prince was angry, and getting up he went away. Returning to Eedur, he related the whole story to the Muhârâjâ, and said, "There is such pride in this Sirdâr that he defies all authority." The Muhârâjâ heard, but made no answer. The prince, however, kept his anger in his heart.

The affair appeared to have been forgotten, and the Muhârâj-Koomâr sent to invite Soorujmul to a feast. He took him up to Eedur-gurh to inspect the fort, and brought him at length to the "palace of the mourning queen," where he slew him with the sword. The Thâkor, however, was a great loss to the Eedur state, as the verse says:—

> "The Châmpâwut, with treachery,
> "Had not the Nurend slain,
> "Goojur-land, his property,
> "Soojo Kumdhuj had made."

After his death, Soorujmul became a Bhoot, and occasioned great trouble for a long time.

Soorujmul's Koonwur, Subul Singh, hearing the news, fled away in alarm, and "went out." However, he was brought round, and induced to return, but the twelve villages of Hursol were taken from him. Mân Singh, of Mondeytee, was succeeded by his son, Koonwur Jorâwur Singh. He left also a younger son, Rughoonâth, to whom was given the estate of Gotâ, which he left to his son, Soorut Singh.

The Muhârâj-Koomâr, Bhuwânee Singh, made an attempt to take the Gotâ estate from Soorut Singh, because, as he declared, too many villages had been given to puttâwuts, and few remained khâlsâ. He sent to Soorut Singh, demanding that he should give up one or two of his villages. This demand, however, did not please Muhârâjâ Shiv Singh, but he was afraid of the prince, and did not say much to him. Soorut Singh replied to the demand by "going out." He carried his family to Jowâs and Puhâdun, villages of Mewar to the north-east of Pâl, and made incursions upon the Eedur country, seizing cultivators and village traders, from whom he exacted ransom, and carrying off cattle. On one occasion he attacked Brumh Kheir, which contained a garrison of Eedur troops, one hundred in number, horse and foot. There was a great fight there. Afterwards a body of the merchants of Eedur, proceeding on pilgrimage to the temple of Rishub Dev, in the Sâdree Pass, with an escort of twenty-five Koolees, halted at the village of Thânâ. Soorut Singh visited them, and asked what need they had of so large an escort. They answered that his being "out" was the reason. Soorut Singh said they need not be apprehensive of him, for Eedur was his mother, and he would not snatch at her scarf. He then accompanied them to the place of pilgrimage, and guarded them on the way home again. The merchants, when they reached Eedur, told the Muhârâjâ and the prince that Soorut Singh protected the people of the town of Eedur, and should therefore be called in. However, the prince did not receive this advice. The Muhârâjâ then, without the prince's knowledge, wrote to Soorut Singh, and said that Chooreewâr was his cook-room village, and that if the Thâkor struck it he would fast, and thus compel the prince to call Soorut Singh in. The Thâkor upon this assembled his men, and plundered Chooreewâr, which he burned, carrying off the prisoners and cattle. When the report of this event reached Eedur, the Muhârâjâ began to abstain from food. The prince immediately called in Soorut Singh, giving him an Uteet of Eedur for his security. When the Thâkor arrived the prince was very much enraged with him, and demanded his reason for doing so much mischief. Soorut Singh showed him the Muhârâjâ's letter. When the prince spoke to the Muhârâjâ about the matter, Shiv Singh was ashamed, and the enmity which already existed between father and son was augmented. The durbâr said to Soorut Singh, "Why should you have exhibited a "letter that I wrote to you for your own good? I think your death "must be near at hand, as your intellect is thus turned." Soorut Singh now got back his estate, but he died six months afterwards, in 1841 (A.D. 1785). He was succeeded by his son, Ude Singh.

On the death of Dolut Singh, the grandson of Jorâwur Singh, of Mondeytee, without offspring, Ude Singh succeeded also to the larger puttâ of Mondeytee.

In the year 1848 (A.D. 1792), Muhârâjâ Shiv Singh became a Dev.[1] Twelve days afterwards his son, Bhuwânee Singh, also died, in the thirty-sixth year of his age. Bhuwânee Singh Muhârâjâ was succeeded by his son, Gumbheer Singh, who was born in 1835 (A.D. 1779). The younger brothers of Bhuwânee Singh were Jhâlum Singh, Sugrâm Singh, Umur Singh, and Indra Singh. Jhâlum Singh had the management of affairs during the minority of Gumbheer Singh. After a time, however, the Sirdârs assembled at the mansion of the Châmpâwuts, with Bhârot Mohobut, of Veejâpoor, who was then the Deewân, and came to the resolution that, as two swords could not be contained in one scabbard, it was right that Jhâlum Singh should not sit upon the cushion, but beside it. Jhâlum Singh asked what course was left open for him to take. The Sirdârs said that he was a prince, and knew the customs. Upon this, Jhâlum Singh and his brothers, Sugrâm Singh and Umur Singh, retired with their followers, and took possession of Morâsâ, Ahmednugger, and Bâyur, without receiving any grants from the Muhârâjâ. Indra Singh, who was blind, remained at home, and to him was assigned the estate of Soor.

Sugrâm Singh was succeeded by Kurun Singh, and he by Tukhut Singh, the present Muhârâjâ of Jodhpoor.

[1] The following inscriptions supply authentic dates of the Muhârâjâs of Eedur:—

1. On a Jain funeral monument near Eedur, "Sumwut, 1840 (A.D. 1784), Shree Muhârâj Âdheerâj, Muhârâj Shree Shiv Singhjee, &c."

2. On the well of Wujur Mâtâ, in Eedur-gurh, "Praise to Shree Gunesh! "Shree Râmjee! In Sumwut, 1847 (A.D. 1791), Phalgoon shood 5, Wednes-"day, Shree Shree Shree 108. Shree Muhârâj Âdheerâj Shree Shree Shree Shiv "Singhjee, Shree Muhârâj Koonwur, Shree Bhuwânee Singhjee caused this well "to be constructed, &c."

3. On another Jain monument, near Eedur, "Sumwut, 1859 (A.D. 1803), Shree "Muhârâj Âdheerâj, Muhârâj Shree Gumbheer Singhjee, &c."

Indra Singh left four sons, who are still living. Jhâlum Singh and Umar Singh died without offspring.

When Gumbheer Singh Muhârâjâ was eighteen years old, he said that the three brothers should take two pergunnahs between them, and to enforce this determination he prepared an army, and advanced to Hinglâz, on the road to Ahmednugger. Jhâlum Singh and Sugrâm Singh joined in opposing the Muhârâjâ, and a battle was fought, in which, as both sides were provided with cannon, many fell on either part. They were separated by the evening. The next day, the Châmpâwut, Jodhâ, and Chohân Sirdârs came up and joined the Muhârâjâ, and a demand was sent to the enemy for the surrender of Ahmednugger. At this time, Bhowân Singh, of Teentoee, in discharging a pistol, which had been kept loaded for a long time, and would not go off without more powder, blew off his hand. The Muhârâjâ received this as a bad omen, and, giving up his expedition, returned to Eedur. Bhowân Singh was carried away in the direction of Teentoee, but died on the road, at Bhuvnâth Muhâ Dev, near Mhow.

After this, Jhâlum Singh, of Morâsâ, began to encroach upon the villages around him, belonging to the Thâkor of Umleeârâ, the Râthor of Mâlpoor, and the Rehwurs of Monpoor and Surdohee. His army consisted of Marwarees and others. In an attack upon Mâlpoor, about A.D. 1799, Jhâlum Singh Muhârâjâ had five thousand men to oppose to eight hundred of the Râthor's. The struggle continued for three days, and at last Mâlpoor was taken, and the Râwul slain. The Muhârâjâ garrisoned Mâlpoor, but the young Râwul Tukhut Singh, having gone out, and created much distress by burning the villages of the Morâsâ estate, it was at length agreed that Mâlpoor should pay the Muhârâjâ a sulâmee of six hundred rupees yearly, and Mugoree one of five hundred rupees, and the Râwul Tukhut Singh recovered his villages.

About the year 1864 (A.D. 1808), Shumsher Khân, of Pâhlunpoor, having had a quarrel with his brother, the Deewân, left home in anger, and came to Eedur. The Muhârâjâ pointed out to him, for his residence, his village of Châmpulpoor, in the Poseenâ district, and Shumsher Khân went thither to reside. Peer Khânjee, of Pâhlunpoor, upon this, wrote to the Muhârâjâ, and said, "You must not entertain "my brother." No attention having been paid to this demand, the Pâhlunpoor army advanced into Gudwârâ, and took possession of that district, placing in it a force of occupation. The Muhârâja thereupon assembled his troops, and driving out the Pâhlunpoor force, sat down in the Deewân's village of Sheeshrânoo, and sent thence to Peer Khânjee to say, "If it be your intention to fight, I will wait here for "you." As Peer Khânjee showed no signs of advancing, the Muhârâjâ began to talk about striking one or two of the Pâhlunpoor villages, in return for the occupation of Gudwârâ; but Koompâwut Nâr Singh, who was the Prudhân at that time, said, "Muhârâjâ! we "have come beyond the frontier of Pâhlunpoor, and the victory "therefore is our's. Striking these villages, as you propose, would "only extend the feud." The Muhârâjâ assented to this advice, and, turning back, advanced upon Dântâ, from which Rânâ Jugut Singh fled to the hills. The Eedur force plundered the villages of Nowâ Wâs and Bhemâl (from which the inhabitants fled), and, finding crops of sugar-cane on the ground, they cut the cane, and made huts for themselves of it, and remained there a month, living upon the neighbouring villages. At length it was agreed that the Rânâ of Dântâ should pay to the Muhârâjâ a tribute of five hundred rupees a-year, and the latter returned to Eedur.

CHAPTER XI.

DÂNTÂ.

RÂNÂ JETMÂL,[1] of Dântâ, left two sons. The elder was Jesingh; the younger, Poonjâ, whose mother was the daughter of the Wâghela of Dhunâlee, one of the Sirdârs of Dântâ. Poonjâ lived for a time with his mother's family, because the brothers did not agree. But when his father died, this being no longer a secure refuge, he was conveyed by his mother's brother to Chitrâsunee, in the lands of Seerohee. After Jetmâl's death, all the Sirdârs and relations slept in the durbâr for the twelve nights of the mourning, on coverlets laid on the ground, and Koonwur Jesingh Dev himself slept in a cot. When the servant came to prepare the cot for him, he threw out of its place the coverlet of Sudhoojee Bâdoowâ's son, Umurâjee, and began to make ready the cot there. Then all asked, "Whose cot are you "making ready here?" The servant said it was the durbâr's. The Sirdârs said, "Why, the durbâr died two days ago, and how is it that "there is another in so short a time?" The servant said, "The "Supreme Being has so arranged it, and it is not now to be set aside

[1] *Vide* p. 340.

"by you." When the Sirdârs heard this, it seemed very ill to them, and they considered that "he will not suit our purpose." Afterwards all the Sirdârs assembled, and, holding a consultation, said to Bâdoowâ Umurâjee, "Employ some means that appear to you good." He said, "I will go and take the weight of another master, but you must "all of you stand to my aid courageously." Then Umurâjee took two horsemen with him, and set off. When the three were setting out, Koonwur Jesingh Dev said, "Whither are you going?" They said, "We are upon the durbâr's business." Then he thought, "It may be "so; the Kârbhâree may have sent them on some business." The three went to Dhunâlee, and asked the Thâkor, Wâghela Mokum Singh, where Poonjâ was. He said he was at Chitrâsunee, They went thither, and staid the night. The next morning they called the Sindhee, to whom the village belonged, and said to him, "Poonjâ "has been living with you; will you, therefore, do him service?" He said, "I have three hundred or four hundred men; whatever service "you may point out I am ready for." He then got his men ready. Guduwee Umurâjee now said to Poonjâ, "Be pleased to accompany "us to Dântâ." He said, "I will not come, because he will put me "to death." The Guduwee said, "I am security that no one shall "put you to death." They turned back, therefore, taking Poonjâ with them, and came to Surrâ. The next day was the auspicious day for Jesingh Dev's taking possession of the cushion, and much splendid preparation was made. Jesingh Dev was putting on his clothes in the durbâr. Meanwhile Poonjâ made his appearance, and the Kârbhâree and Sirdârs placed him on the cushion. All said to the chief of the merchants of Dântâ, named Nânâbhaee, "Do you "make the teeluk;" upon which the merchant made the teeluk, and presented fifty-five rupees as an offering; after which all the others presented suitable offerings. At this time the soldiers from Chitrâsunee came, and said, "What service have you for us to per-"form?" They told them to put sentries on all four sides of the durbâr, that no one might come or go. This was effected in a perfect manner. Afterwards the royal drum was sounded, and cannon fired. Jesingh, hearing this, said, "Who caused that drum to sound?" Some one told him, "Poonjâ has assumed the cushion." Meanwhile the order arrived, "Whatever jewels belonging to the durbâr you may "have in your possession must be sent, and you must leave the place." Jesingh Dev asked, "Where am I to go to?" The answer was, "You "should go to the village of Gungwâ, which was assigned to your "mother for a subsistence." Jesingh Dev said, "Gungwâ is a single "village; that will not supply my necessaries." The village of Mân-kuree was then assigned to him in addition. He took his family with him, and retired to Gungwâ.

The same day that Poonjâ assumed the cushion he was attacked with vomiting. The Sirdârs considered what this omen might mean. Some omen-reader suggested, "The Raja suffers from "repletion—the meaning is that he will make many districts his own." Afterwards, when he reached mature age, he won back several rights of "wol," in Dhândhâr, which had been encroached upon. He won back also his wântâ lands in the Kherâloo puttâ, which had been seized. He also revolved in his mind the restoration of Tursunghmo, but found no leisure to restore it. At this time he gave the village of Rorâ, which has since become desolate, to Umurâjee Bâdoowâ; he gave him also the "Kereeo wântâ," in the village of Koondul, with five-and-twenty mango trees. At an after-time the Rânâ gave also certain fields in the village of Thânâ, which the Guduwee resigned to his half-brothers, Sâmojee and Sukhojee. Rânâ Poonjâ afterwards married, at the house of the chief of Lembuj, a brother of Seerohee. This Lembuj chief, whose name was Châindojee, was "out" against Ukherâj, the lord of Seerohee, on which account he came to Dântâ, and received from Poonjâ Rânâ the village of Wusâee to reside in, which is on the road to Umbâjee. Chândojee lived there, and prosecuted his feud with Seerohee, which was not arranged until after a five years' struggle. Chândojee then gave his sister in marriage to Rânâ Poonjâ, and assigned the lands in the village of Wusâee, which had been reclaimed by him as her dower. Thus did Poonjâ reign in a good manner. He left three sons—Mân Singh, Umur Singh, and Dhengojee, which last got the village of Guncheroo.

Mân Singh succeeded on the death of Rânâ Poonjâ. Umur Singh obtained the village of Soodâsunâ; but it happened that he once on a time went to pay a friendly visit to the Thâkor of Chitrâsunee, and was on his return thence, when the army of the Bâbee, of Rhâdunpoor, which was on an expedition, made its appearance. Umur Singh was slain by them at the forest near the village of Pulkhuree, in Dhândhâr. He left two sons, Hutheeojee and Jugtojee, who were slain by Mân Singh's Koonwur, Guj Singh, after he assumed the cushion. The story is as follows:—

Once on a time Guj Singh was seated in the palace at Dântâ, and said to those around him, "Is there any one who would leap down "from that limb tree into the court?" Hutheeojee climbed the tree immediately, and jumped down. Rânâ Guj Singh thought within himself, "This man will some day play me false." Some time after wards he said to a Chowra Rajpoot, who was in his service, "If you "will kill these two brothers I will give you a field in free grant." Then that Rajpoot killed the elder brother with a blow of a sword in the very hall of Dântâ, and the other he slew on the hill, opposite the window of the durbâr. There is a shrine of this younger brother, Jugtohee, at the same place, where prayers are made to him. He sometimes appears to people, and sometimes possesses them, in which case offerings must be placed there for him. Hutheeojee left a son, Khomân Singh, who received the village of Udeyrun, in place of Soodâsunâ, which was taken from him; for his mother, after her husband's murder, brought Khomân Singh, then a child, to Rânâ Guj Singh, and placed him in his lap, saying, "Do to this boy also as it "may please you." The Rânâ said to himself, "I have killed his "father, but if I give him something I shall be freed from the sin of "murdering a relation; so he gave him Udeyrun." Jugtojee left no son.

To return, however, to Mân Singh:—he reigned four or five years, and died, leaving two Koonwurs, Guj Singh and Juswojee. The village of Rânpoor was first assigned to Juswojee, but after the death of Hutheeojee and Jugtojee, he received also the estate of Soodâsunâ, retaining Rânpoor as well. Juswojee afterwards obtained Wusâee, in the Dântâ puttâ, and Juspur-Chelânoo.[1]

Guj Singh ruled in a good manner, and left two sons,[2] Pruthee Singh and Veerum Dev, who obtained the village of Nâgel. In Pruthee Singh's time, the army of Dâmâjee (Guikowâr) came to Dântâ. Pruthee Singh opposed him in arms for some time, and at last took to the hills. Afterwards he repaired to the Mahratta camp on receiving safe conduct, and agreed to pay something in the way of tribute, which, when the Mahrattas had received, they withdrew. Afterwards Hyder Koolee, the Nowaub, on the part of Delhi, came with an army. The Rânâ fought with him, too, and slew thirty of his followers. In the end the army retreated, and victory remained with the Rânâ. After this the Pâhlunpoor chief ceased to pay a claim, which the

[1] For Juswojee's descendants, see note "on Soodâsunâ," at the end of this chapter.

[2] The following is the inscription on the monument of Rânâ Guj Singh, at Dântâ:—

"In the year 1743 (A.D. 1687), on Mâgsheer shood 9, Sunday, when Rânâ "Shree Gujsunghjee went to Vyekoonth, three sutees burned; their names— "Vowjee Shree * *, Unund Koonwur; Vowjee Shree Wâghelee Roopâlee, "Unund Koonwur; Vowjee Shree Bhuteeânee Jesulmeree, Unop Koonwur— "these three became sutees. In commemoration of them this chutree of Rânâ "Shree Gujsunghjee was caused to be made. In the year 1748 (A.D. 1692), on "Muhâ wud 7, on Friday the chutree was caused to be made.'

Rânâ held upon the Pâhlunpoor village of Ghoreeâlya. The Rânâjee now considered how to strike the village. When the Pâhlunpoor chief knew of this, he sent for the Bhâts of Mehmudpoor (one of his villages), and said, "Do you keep guard in the village of Ghoreeâlya." They did so, and the news was carried to Dântâ. At this time a Wâneeâ, named Ruheeo, was the minister of Dântâ. This Ruheeo sent for the Bhâts to Dântâ, and asked them to take charge of the villages of Dhunâlee and Sheeshrânoo, on which the Pâhlunpoor chief asserted a claim, saying, "You are guarding one of the Pâhlunpoor "villages, so guard one of our's too, and we will give you as much "as they give." The Bhâts answered, "We cannot ride upon two "horses." Ruheeo said, "Well, then, go and keep the best watch "you may, we will mount and come." The Bhât thought he would go to Mehmudpoor for his own men, and then to Pâhlunpoor for men from thence, and thus garrison Ghoreeâlya. Meanwhile the Rânâjee mounted at once, and struck Ghoreeâlya, which he plundered, carrying off hostages and cattle, with which he returned to Dântâ. When the Pâhlunpoor chief heard the news he sent for the Bhâts, and reprimanded them, and said, "Now do whatever remains "in your power, and bring back my hostages which the Rânâjee has "seized." Then the Bhâts collected to the number of a hundred, and began to perform "dhurna." They set out from their own village, and at every coss, as they advanced, they burned a man, so that by the time they had arrived at Poonjpoor seven or eight men had perished. Then the Dântâ men, going out of Poonjpoor to meet them, brought the Bhâts round, and prevailed on them to turn back. But when the Rânâjee sent to offer gifts to the Bhâts, they said, "If we "receive anything, the Rânâjee will be washed from this sin, there-"fore we will receive nothing;" so saying, they went home. On account of this sin, though Pruthee Singh Rânâ had seven sons born to him, he died childless. At his death three of his wives became sutees, of whom one was the daughter of Sukhut Singh, the Deora of Lembuj; another was the daughter of the Wâghela of Pethâpoor.[1]

Pruthee Singh's line having failed, the minister and Sirdârs united

[1] There is an open funeral pavilion at Dântâ, which contains three pâleeyos. The centre one bears the figure of a horseman, beneath the usual sun and moon; the two side stones have figures of sutees sculptured upon them. Rânâ Shree "Kurunjee," as an inscription records, "caused to be made the chutree of Rânâ "Shree Prutheesunghjee." Another inscription runs as follows:—"Praise to "Shree Gunesh! When Rânâ Shree Prutheesunghjee departed to Shree Vyekoonth "two sutees burned, their names—Vowjee Shree Deoree, Phool Koonwur, and "Vowjee Shree Wâghelee Pethâpooree, Sirdâr Koonwur, in Sumwut, 1799) A.D. "1743, on Shrawun, Shood 2, on Wednesday."

to place upon the cushion Kurunjee, the son of Veerum Dev. This Kurunjee quarrelled with his own Sirdâr, Megh Râj, who held a puttâ, including the villages of Deewuree and Bhudder-mâlâ. At this time there was at Dântâ a Rajpoot named Kotheeo Wukto, who every day at opium time used to be the butt of the Rânâ's abuse. One day this Rajpoot, becoming enraged, wounded the Rânâ with his sword, and escaping, took shelter with Megh Râj. Then the Rânâ sent to Megh Râj to say, "Give up this offender to me." Megh Râj answered, "When one has taken shelter, it is not the Rajpoot practice to give "him up; therefore I keep him with my head." Afterwards, when the Rânâ importuned him very much, Megh Râj sent the Rajpoot away into the hills, and himself, going out in anger, went to Guncheroo, where he remained six months. However, the Rânâ took no steps to content him and bring him in. Megh Râj then thought with himself, "What shall I do remaining here?" so he went to Soodâsunâ. The Thâkor of that place, whose name was Umur Singh, received him, and he staid there a year, but the Rânâ still gave him no satisfaction. At length Megh Râj said to Umur Singh, "Come! I will "cause the cushion of Dântâ to be given to you." They collected a force of one thousand men and munitions of war, and advanced upon Dântâ, which they entered, and drove out Kurunjee, who, mounting his horse, fled, and went to Pempulodurâ, five coss from Dântâ, the village which is usually assigned to the heir-apparent for his subsistence. Umur Singh now assumed the cushion at Dântâ, and brought the whole country into subjection to himself. Things remained in this state for two or three years. At length Bâdoowâ Gorukdâs, of Pâneeâlee, and his brothers took counsel together, and agreed that it was not for their honor that their master, while they stood by, should be kept out of his throne. Afterwards they went together to Rânâ Kurunjee, and said, "Why have you become cold, and why sit you "here?—if you exert yourself you will win back the throne of Dântâ." The Rânâ said, "No way occurs to me, if any occur to you pursue it." The Guduwees said, "Summon your Sirdârs." He summoned them. Sâheb Singh Bhâtee came, the Thâkor of Ghorâd; Unop Singh Râthor, also, the Thâkor of Hurâd; and the Thâkor of Godhunee, Deveedâs Wâghela. These three Sirdârs met, and came to the conclusion that, "Without we procure the aid of Buhâdur Khân, "the Deewân of Pâhlunpoor, our object cannot be effected." However, they considered that the Deewânjee's assistance was not to be obtained without a great deal of money, which, under present circumstances, they could not procure. Afterwards Kurun Singh sent for his younger brother Oomed Singh, who was at Nâgel, and said to him, "You have a daughter who is a virgin; if you will marry her "to Buhâdur Khân we shall get back our place." Oomed Singh said, "If the place be got back, you will be the master of the cushion; "what gain will accrue to me that I should give my daughter to the "Toorkâ?" Then Kurunjee gave him a written deed for five villages, to be placed in his possession on the recovery of Dântâ. The gift consisted of half the village of Nâgel, the villages of Thânâ, Koondol, Pânoondurâ, and Wuroosun, and the present village of Gudh, which was afterwards founded in the lands of Koondol. Oomed Singh then agreed to do as they wished. Afterwards the three Guduwees went to Pâhlunpoor, and had an interview with Buhâdur Khân, and settled that he should help them to recover the place, and that, for his so doing, Oomed Singh's daughter should be betrothed to him. The Deewânjee was very much pleased, and said, "I "will recover your place for you, and the marriage shall be performed "afterwards." The cocoa-nut and a rupee were then presented, and the betrothal concluded. They took the Deewânjee's force with them, and went against Dântâ, and encamped among the mowra trees of Poonjpoor, from whence they sent a message to Umur Singh, demanding that he should quit Dântâ. Then Umur Singh considered, "The "Pâhlunpoor force has come, so that now I shall not be able to keep "Dântâ." So he sent to say, "I will give up your Dântâ to you, "but what do you assign to me for my subsistence?" It was then arranged that he should have five villages in addition to the fifteen he held already, namely, Jetpoor, Nânâ Surrâ, Torâ, Khâree, and Bâmuneeoo, and, besides these, a fourth share of the Mâtâjee's transit dues. At that time the Mâtâ received a rupee from each passenger. For some years four annas were paid to the chief of Soodâsuna, but afterwards confusion began to occur in the accounts, whereupon the Rânâ commenced to levy only twelve annas from each person, leaving the Soodâsunâ share out of the question, and said, "Do you take "your four annas from whoever passes the gate of your village." From this time they began to levy the four annas at Soodâsunâ.

Rânâ Kurunjee now came to Dântâ, and took his seat upon the cushion. When the force was ready to return home the lady was sent for from Nâgel to a spot in the lands of Thânâ, where four mango trees grow beside a hillock, and there she was married to the Deewânjee. The whole were escorted to Pâhlunpoor.

This Kurun Singh had two sons, Rutun Singh and Ubhe Singh. Rutun Singh ascended the throne. He had previously put to death the two Wâghela Thâkors of Dhunâlee, whose names were Lârkhân and Pârkhân, two brothers. The story is as follows:—This Lârkhânjee once on a time had come to Dântâ to pay his respects to Rânâ Kurunjee, because he too was one of the Dântâ Sirdârs. At that time Koonwur Rutun Singh was playing like a boy, though he was thirty years old. Lârkhânjee said, "How long are you to continue "a child?" and ridiculed him. The Koonwur went and repeated what the Thâkor had said to the Rânâ. Kurunjee said, "It is well! "then kill me, and be called Rânâ." The Koonwur said, "Sire! "may you be preserved, but him I will certainly kill." Then the Rânâ said, "You must get the strength first." As soon as the matter came to Lârkhânjee's ears he started off home. Two years after this, Rânâ Kurunjee went by chance to Nâgel. Thither the afore-mentioned two Wâghela brothers came to meet him. Then the Koonwur thought, "To-day I will put them to death." He arranged with some followers of his that they should take Lârkhânjee with them to the Suruswutee river to bathe, keeping Pârkhânjee with the Rânâ, and that the former should be killed there, and a gun then fired as a signal for the other brother also to be put to death. Accordingly the Koonwur set off to bathe, taking a javelin with him. He thrust Lârkhân through with his javelin, and his followers finished him; a gun was then fired, and the men who were about the Rânâ, as soon as they heard the report, put Pârkhân to death. When Buhâdur Khân, the Deewân of Pâhlunpoor, became aware of this matter, he said, "These two Thâkors had my safe conduct, I "must therefore take precautions lest the Rânâ should ill-treat their "families." He therefore placed two hundred horse in Dhunâlee and Sheshrânoo, and the possession thus acquired has been retained, so that the villages have fallen under Pâhlunpoor. The deceased left each a son, one of which sons went to live at a village of his own, named Godhunee, where his descendants still remain; the other went to the house of his father's sister at Soodâsunâ, and obtained "wantâ" from the chief of that estate.

Rutun Singh reigned about five years after the death of his father, and died, leaving no son. He was succeeded by his younger brother, Ubhe Singh. This Rânâ brought to Dântâ a Mahratta named Urjoon Row Chopuro, to whom he promised the "chouth" of the Dântâ possessions. The reason was that his Sirdârs and puttâwuts, and his brothers, too, were giving trouble, as were also the neighbouring Rajas. Urjoon Row brought a hundred Guikowâr horse with him: he lived at Dântâ, and at first was satisfied with a trifling exercise of authority, but when two or three years had passed over he began to rule as if in his own right, and to build a small fort at Dântâ for his residence, and to annoy the inhabitants. Then the

Rânâ began to be afraid lest his very throne should be encroached upon. Meanwhile this Soubah, while he was building his house, took by force for that purpose bamboo rafters that were lying at the doors of some Rajpoots' houses in the village. Then the eyes of the Rajpoots were split, and when the Mahratta soldiers began to jabber their "ikarum tikarum,"[1] ordering people here and there, a fight would have been the result had not the Rajpoots reflected that it would be hard upon the Rânâ if a struggle were to take place. They went to the durbâr, and complained that the strangers had begun to give them much annoyance. Then said the Rânâ, "What "is an annoyance to you, is first an annoyance to me." He summoned all his Sirdârs. The Koonwur Shree Mân Singh was at this time about five and thirty years of age; he said to the Rânâjee, "If it be your order, I will drive these people out." The Rânâ said, "Do so, as you are a good son." Then the Koonwur sent to the Chopuro to say, "Do you now quit this place." The Mahrattas paying no attention to the summons, the Koonwur blockaded them, and cut off their supply of water, grain, and grass, and threatened also to slay them unless they retired. At length they retired, but the Dântâ people moved with them, encircling them at a short distance off, until they reached Gudwârâ, where they left them, and returned home. The Thâkor Soojâjee of Bhâloosunâ then entertained them, and began to quarrel with the Soodâsunâ people, saying that they must give him possession of his wântâ lands in their limits. Then Futteh Singh, Thâkor of Soodâsunâ, came to Dântâ to seek aid from Koonwur Mân Singh, who, taking a force with him, went to the assistance of Soodâsunâ, and drove out the invaders. Then the Bhâloosunâ chief became alarmed lest, if a feud arose between him and Dântâ, he should be destroyed; he therefore dismissed the Guikowâr force, which moved off towards Ahmedabad. The Koonwur, having effected a settlement, returned to Dântâ, soon after which, in the year 1815 (A.D. 1795), the Rânâ Ubhe Singh died.

Ubhe Singh had three sons—Mân Singh, who succeeded him, and whose mother was a Chowree lady of Wusâee, and Jugut Singh, and Nâr Singh, whose mother was a Bhuteeânee, the daughter of Sâheb Singh, Thâkor of Ghorâd, near Tursunghmo.

Mân Singh's first exploit was to make a raid upon Dhunâl, a village of Poseenâ, from whence he carried off the cattle, but the "wâr," pursuing him, recovered the spoil. Six months after that he struck

[1] The words "ikaré," "tikaré," mean in the Mahratta language "here" and "there."

the Poseenâ village of Châangod, which he plundered. The village became uninhabited, and has up to this moment so remained. When the Muhârâjâ Gumbheer Singh, of Eedur, went with an army on an expedition against the Mewâsees, he sent for Rânâ Mân Singh, who joined him with forty horse. After this Moolukgeeree was completed, and the Rânâ was returning home, the Muhârâjâ presented him with a horse worth a thousand rupees. After a reign of five years, Mân Singh died, in Sumwut, 1856 (A.D. 1800), and, as there were disagreements among the brothers at that time, people said he had been poisoned.

His brother, Jugut Singh, on mounting the throne, made his inaugural foray (teelâ-dhâr) on the village of Nendurdee, in Gudwârâ, which he plundered and burnt, carrying off hostages, because the Bheels of that village had harried the buffaloes of Nowâ-wâs, and the putel had come to Dântâ, saying, "Give me a spade, that if anywhere "there is a bone left of my lord Mân Singh, I may dig it up. Had "that lord been alive, the Nendurdee Bheels had not carried off my "buffaloes." On another occasion he collected a force, and went against Poseenâ, when Keshree Singh, Thâkor of Poseenâ, came to meet him between Hurâd and his own village, and, presenting a horse to the Rânâ as an offering, gave security. The force, turning back, went to Gudwârâ, and advanced upon Muhâwud; upon which Thâkor Wukhtojee came, and presented a horse, and, making an agreement, gave security. After this the Rânâjee exacted a horse from Hâtheejee Gudheâ, of Nânâ Kothârun, against whom a claim existed on account of a robbery. The force returned home from thence.

Again, in the year 1170 (A.D. 1814), the Rânâjee collected a force, and carried off all the buffaloes of Dhunâl. He next struck the village of Bâwul Kotheeoo, belonging to the Raja of Derol, and plundered it. Next year he struck and plundered Kheroj, which belonged to a brother of the Thâkor of Poseenâ, on which occasion two of his men were killed. His brother, Nâr Singh, who was married to a lady of that place, came to him, and said, "I shall be "blamed at this time; people will say, 'Nâr Singh came with them, "and caused his father-in-law's village to be plundered.'" On that account they turned back, and went to strike the village of Dhuroee. At this place the enemy gained over a Bârud, named Keertâjee, who was with the force; upon which this Keertâjee, going to the gate of the village, said to the Rânâ that the omens were not good. On this account they turned back, and came to Thânâ, where they encamped. At this halting-place the Rânâ called together the Sirdârs and the minister, and asked from what source he was to pay the arrears due to the mercenaries. They answered, that Thâkor Rutun Singh of Pâwudee, and Thâkor Undojee of Undhâreeâ, incited the Mewâsees to enter the Dântâ country, and caused them to plunder, and that therefore their two villages should be plundered, and the means of paying the mercenaries procured. The Rânâ then prepared to advance upon Undhâreeâ, upon which the Thâkor of that village fled to Pâwudee, and he and the others who were threatened got ready for the fight. Now, in the end of the night the Rânâ's army broke up from Thânâ, and advanced to Undhâreeâ, when they found the village deserted. They went to Momun-wâs, where they received a fire of musketry from the defences. Upon this the mercenaries forming the advance of the Rânâ's force fired, and one of their balls killed Thâkor Undojee of Undhâreeâ; the rest of the people who were assembled at Momun-wâs then fled, and took to the hills, and the village was struck and plundered. The Rânâ immediately advanced, and halted at Pâwudee, which village also he plundered, and, carrying off the property, turned back, and encamped at Motâ Surrâ. At this place the Thâkor of Pâwudee came to the Rânâjee, bringing security, and it was arranged that a third share of Undhâreeâ should be the Rânâjee's property, to which effect bonds were interchanged. After this, security was taken from the surrounding Mewâsees, and in 1872 (A.D. 1816) the Rânâ broke up the army, and returned home to Dântâ.

Thâkor Wukhtojee Jeetojee said once to Rânâ Jugut Singh, "My "expenses are not supplied by the villages of Khâbhee-wâs and "Kunbee-was, therefore give me something in addition." The Rânâ said, "You will not get anything more than that which was assigned "to your father." Wukhtojee upon this went off in anger to Deesa, to Deewân Shumsher Khân, and said to him, "If you will give me a "force, I will go and do some injury to the Dântâ country, that I "may procure satisfaction of my demands." At that time, however, there was friendship between the Deewân and the Rânâ; therefore the former wrote to the latter to say, "Come to terms with Wukhtojee, "or he will do some mischief." The Rânâ then sent for Wukhtojee, and offered to give him a grant of the villages of Oonturee and Bhootâsur, if he would release them from an Uteet to whom they had been mortgaged. Wukhtojee assented to this proposal, and released the two villages, which were uninhabited, and founded there a single village, called Ubhâpuroo, where he placed his family, living himself at Dântâ, and performed service there as Prudhân. Two years afterwards he died, and Ubhâpuroo then fell to his sons and to his brother Bhuvjee.

At this time Sirdâr Singh, Thâkor of Koondol, died, leaving no son, upon which Rânâ Jugut Singh and his brother, Nâr Singh, attached the five villages of the Koondol estate, and brought all the moveable property of the late Thâkor to Dântâ. The funeral ceremonies of Sirdâr Singh were performed at Koondol, and his Thakorine received three wells for her maintenance. However, Bhuvjee Jeetojee made a claim on the estate, and said, "Something, at any rate, must "be given me from Koondol." Rânâ Jugut Singh said, "Do you "enjoy what was given to your father, Jeetojee—Khâbhee-wâs and "Kunbee-wâs; you will not get any of this property." Then Bhuvjee went off in anger to Pâhlunpoor, accompanied by Meheroo Sindhee, an old Jemâdâr of the Rânâ's, who was also on ill terms with the Rânâ. Now Bhuvjee having gone to Pâhlunpoor, made a petition to Miles Sahib about the right of succession to Koondol, which he contended was vested equally in the Rânâjee and himself, while the Rânâjee had taken possession of the whole. "Therefore," said Bhuvjee, "I will pass a deed assigning the whole village to the "English government, and whatever it may come into the mind of "that government to give me I will receive." Some adherent of the Rânâjee's wrote this intelligence to his master, who thereupon sent his brother, Nâr Singh, and Jeewâ Kulâl, a minister of his, to Pâhlunpoor, offering to make over a seven-anna share of the whole territory of Dântâ to the English government, and to permit the attachment of the state by that government. Upon this Bhuvjee's hand became powerless. After this Bhuvjee took service with Futteh Khân, the Dewân of Pâhlunpor, who gave him his fourth share of the village of Nâgel. The Rana subsequently gave Bhuvjee the village of Kurunpoor, and they drank the red cup together. The English government placed a garrison in the Dântâ country in the year 1876 (A.D. 1820).

In the time of this Jugut Singh, two hundred horse and five hundred foot of the Mewâsee Koolees, of the Kâkurej, made an inroad upon the Dântâ villages of Ruttunpoor and Poonjpoor, and carried off the buffaloes. Jugut Singh mounted on the "wâr," with fifty horse and two hundred foot. They met in the lands of Motâ Surrâ, and a battle was fought, in which twenty-five of the freebooters were slain, and Bheekho Jemâdâr, a Bhâttee Rajpoot, on the Rânâ's side, was wounded, and had his horse killed. The cattle were recovered, and when the Rânâ returned to Dântâ, he presented

Bheekho Jemâdâr with a gold anklet, a horse, and other gifts.

Now as Jugut Singh had no son, he proposed to Nâr Singh to adopt one of his two sons, Jhâlum Singh and Huree Singh. Nâr Singh thought, "If the son obtain the cushion, the father will have "to sit at his feet, and make obeisance to him." Some people, however, persuaded Jugut Singh that Nâr Singh meditated to take him off by poison, or to slay him with the sword; and as he believed the story, he began to keep within his house, which he fortified, and never came near the council-room: the consequence of which was that the Bheels and Koolees of the surrounding villages commenced a system of plundering. At length the people came to him, and petitioned, "If your highness neglect in this manner to keep up any "order, and remain within your palace, how can the affairs of the "country be carried on?" Now Rânâ Jugut Singh had no confidence in any Kârbhâree, but only in Kulâl Jeewâ, by whose advice he acted; and the people blamed him because he employed a liquor-seller as his minister. At this time there was a Seesodeeâ Rajpoot, named Gumân, at Dântâ, a slave-girl of whose establishment this Jeewâ carried off by force. On the other hand, this Rajpoot, Gumân, carried on an intrigue with one of Jeewâ's two wives. For these reasons there was a bitter enmity between these two. But Gumân could say nothing to Jeewâ, for fear of the Rânâjee. However, there were many other ministers, as well as people, who were very inimical to Jeewâ.

Once on a time the Kulâl set out to make the assessment of the year's crops, and he assessed a piece of rent-free garden land that belonged to Gumân; and when the Rajpoot protested against this, he paid him no attention, but, on the contrary, abused him. Gumân then became very angry, and began to consider how he could put the Kulâl to death. His first step was to carry his mother and brother to the Poseenâ village of Hurâd. The next morning, at dawn, he got up, and took his station opposite the Kulâl's door. Jeewâ soon came out of his house, and seeing the Rajpoot sitting there, asked where he was going to. Gumân said that he was going to a certain village, but that he waited to see what the omens were. The Kulâl was, in truth, a little alarmed, but he went on, and finished his business with all haste, and began to return quickly home. The Rajpoot followed him, and struck him from behind. A struggle ensued; the Kulâl struck Gumân on the head with a brass vessel he carried in his hand, but received from him two stabs of a dagger. He escaped, however, from his grasp, and ran off for shelter to the house of a Dher, which he was entering, when the Rajpoot, who had picked up his sword and shield, ran quickly upon him and slew him. Gumân took the ornaments off the corpse and ran away, threatening some people who raised an alarm that he would kill them too, unless they remained quiet. He got clear off into the hills. A servant went to wake the Rânâjee, who was still lying down, and told him what had happened. The Rânâ was very much distressed, and ordered that the slayer of Jeewâ should be put to death. On all sides horsemen then galloped off, but as they were all glad that Jeewâ had been killed, they merely went up and down for a time, and then returned and said that the murderer had not come into their hands. Upon this Jugut Singh felt satisfied that it was Nâr Singh who had caused his Kârbhâree to be put to death, intending to slay him also, and he began to say so before people. Nâr Singh then sent to the Rânâjee, to say, "Why do you give me a bad name in "this way? I will leave your town." He prepared to go off to Ahmednugger. The people, however, went to the Rânâ, and said, "Nâr Singh is going off in anger. You must bring him round and "get him to stay; for it will not be to your credit if he goes." Then the Rânâ sent men, and persuaded Nâr Singh to return, and the people made the two brothers drink opium together. A month afterwards, however, some one again excited the Rânâ's suspicion that Nâr Singh sought to kill him; so he went to Soodâsunâ, and stayed there two months with Thâkor Mohobut Singh. Nâr Singh and the ministers, all of them, went to give him satisfaction, and succeeded in bringing him back to Dântâ. He stayed, however, only ten or twelve days, and again flying, took refuge in the monastery of an Uteet, at Pethâpoor, whom he informed that Nâr Singh purposed to kill him. He stayed there a month, and was again persuaded to return home; and soon after he was attacked with fever and other disease, which, after a month's illness, carried him off, on the 7th Phalgoon wud, in the year 1879 (A.D. 1823).

Nâr Singh assumed the cushion after the death of Jugut Singh Rânâ.

In the year 1892 (A.D. 1836), Rânâ Juwân Singh, of Oodeipoor, came on pilgrimage to Shree Umbâjee, on which occasion he invited Rânâ Nâr Singh to visit him. Nâr Singh accordingly went to the Mâtâjee's, and took up his lodging there. The Rânâ of Oodeipoor now sent to inquire, "In what manner will your visit be made? "Have you any record on the subject in your durbâr?" Nâr Singh then inquired of all the Sirdârs and Kârbhârees, but no record was found. Then all the old men were enquired of, and among them, I, too (the narrator of this account), was questioned. I said that Rânâ Kânur Dev had married at Oodeipoor, and that the Seesodunee lady had become a sutee at the gate of Koturâ, where her monument might be seen to this day.[1] Upon this, Rânâ Juwân Singh sent for Nâr Singh to visit him, and rose to receive him. Nàr Singh presented a horse and a gun, worth a hundred rupees; and Juwân Singh gave him in return, a horse and a pearl necklace. He presented the family priest, also, with a pair of gold armlets. Juwân Singh, after remaining two days, set off homewards, on which occasion Koonwur Jhâlum Singh, with his horsemen, escorted him as far as Seerohee.

Nâr Singh and Jhâlum Singh went, in the year 189—, on the occasion of an eclipse of the moon, to Aboo, on a pilgrimage. On that occasion there were great sunghs assembled at Aboo, from Goozerat, Marwar, and Mewar. At the time of the eclipse people began to bathe in the Nukhee tulâv, when an ascetic came, and said, "Let not any one bathe in the tank at this time; whoever does so "will die." Some of the pilgrims believed this, and did not bathe; but the greater part disbelieved, and bathed. At the time, sixty-four Yogeenees' chariots descended from the sky, and the Yogeenees commenced bathing. In the morning the cholera broke out, and as many as had bathed died, with few exceptions. The Rânâ and the Koonwur had bathed after the eclipse was over, therefore they did not suffer, nor did any of the sungh that was with them die. They remained four days, and then went to Umbâjee.

After this the Governor Sahib came from Bombay to Sâdrâ, and invited all the Bhoomeâs of the Myhee Kântâ to visit him. Rânâ Nâr Singh and Koonwur Jhâlum Singh went with the rest to Sâdrâ, and presented to the Sahib a horse and a piece of gold tissue; in return for which the Sahib gave both father and son a pair of shawls and a turban. All the other Bhoomeâs gave and received dresses of honor. At length the Sahib returned to Bombay, and all the Bhoomeeâs went home. The principal Hindoo Rajas were Muhârâjâ Gumbheer Singh, of Eedur, Muhârâjâ Kurun Singh, of Ahmednugger, and Râna Nâr Singh; the principal Mohummedan Sirdârs were Futteh Khan, the Deewân of Pâhlunpoor, the Nowaub of Rhâdunpoor, and Shumsher Khân, the Deewân of Wurgaum.

After this, Rânâ Nâr Singh went to Major Miles, at Pahlunpoor, about an arrangement for his country, and represented that he had given a share in it to the English government to keep order; but

[1] *Vide* p. 330.

that instead of agents of the English government, there were sent employés of the Deewân of Pâhlunpoor, with whom he had made no agreement whatever. However, the Major gave Nâr Singh no satisfaction; and as the Nowrâttrâ was near, he was obliged to take leave to attend at the Mâtâjee's. At length, when Lang Sahib[1] came to Sâdrâ, the Deewân's attachment was removed, after it had been maintained for about twenty-seven years.

Nâr Singh died in Sumwut, 190—, and his corpse was committed to the flames by Jhâlum Singh, at Gungwâ. The young Rânâ also built a chutree at that place.

NOTE ON THE SOODÂSUNÂ BRANCH OF THE FAMILY OF DÂNTÂ.

When Guj Singh, the son of Rânâ Mân Singh, was the occupant of the cushion of Dântâ, and his brother, Juswojee, held the estate of Rânpoor, Umur Singh, the son of Poonjâ Rânâ, Mân Singh's brother, was at Soodâsunâ. At this time, the Soodâsunâ estate consisted of the single village of that name. Umur Singh, who was a valiant warrior, sought to bring into subjection to himself Juswojee's estate of Rânpoor, on which account he made frequent forays upon Rânpoor, and carried off the cattle. Once on a time, when he had made an inroad, and was driving off the buffaloes, Juswojee sent to him to say, "Uncle! it was not suitable that you should have driven "away the buffalo cow which supplies me with milk." Umur Singh answered, "There's many a male buffalo in the lands of Rânpoor, "if you want milk, drink from one of them." Then Juswojee came to Dântâ, and told this story to Mân Singh in great sorrow. Mân Singh said, "We cannot come round Umur Singh at the present "time, some day I will look after him." After this, Mân Singh, retaining enmity in his heart, incited the Mewâsees and freebooters to put Umur Singh to death, promising a reward, upon which their people began to annoy Soodâsunâ. On one occasion the Gudheeâs drove off the Soodâsunâ cattle, and Umur Singh going on the "wâr," overtook them at Bhâloosunâ, and recovered the spoil. One of his cultivators, however, came to him, and said, "You have recovered all "the cattle, but there was a bullock belonging to me, worth a hun-"dred rupees, which is not among them, so you have made no "'wâr' for me." On this Umur Singh turned back after the forayers

[1] Colonel Lang, an officer who for several years held the appointment of political agent in the Myhee Kântâ, and whose name is there widely and deservedly respected.

and recovering the bullock, began to drive it home, but the animal was restive, and would not be driven, but ran off continually. At last Umur Singh thought that if the bullock were carried off by the forayers he would lose his honor; so he killed it with his spear, and returned. On account of this murder, he met his death within four months of that time. It happened thus:—He had gone to Chitrâsunee to pay a visit of friendship to the Thâkor. As he returned, a meer (minstrel) joined his company. Umur Singh said to him, "There are many outlaws about at this time, and you cannot "keep up with us, so you must not come." The meer said, "Sire! "I must needs come with you." So saying, he went on as before. Meanwhile, at the village of Pulkhuree, Umur Singh fell in with a party of the Bâbee of Rhâdunpoor's horse, who were out on a plundering expedition. As the Rajpoot party retreated before them, the mare which the meer rode broke down. Then Umur Singh called to him to get off and kill the mare, and mount behind on his own horse, but before the meer could get down the pursuers overtook him. He cried out, "Sire! do not go away and leave me." Umur Singh turned back to help him, and at that moment received a ball in his chest and fell dead.

After the death of Hutheeojee,[1] the son of Umur Singh, his Koonwur, Khomân Singh, being only eighteen months old, Juswojee took possession of Soodâsunâ. Hutheeojee's Thâkorine came thereupon to the Rânâ, and said, "How shall I subsist now?" upon which the Rânâ gave her the village of Udeyrun, where her descendants still remain.

Juswojee continued to hold Soodâsunâ, and had five Koonwurs. Sirdâr Singh, the eldest, succeeded him; Ujbojee and Dhunrâjjee received from the Rânâ the village of Solânoo; Nâthjee and Jorjee received Juspoor, which was founded by Juswojee. In Juswojee's time, a Guikowâr army came, under the leading of a Soubah, named Vitoobâ, and caused annoyance to Soodâsunâ, at which time Bhoj Râj Râwul, Togo Wunol, and Ghelojee Bâdoowâ, the Guduwee of Pâneeâlee, came to use. The army struck the village and retired, and the people then returned from among the hills and rebuilt it. At this time the Guikowâr army used to come every three or four years, and when the people of the village heard of their approaching, which they did generally when they were about ten coss off, they caused the Trughâyâs to beat their drums, and raise a cry of "Fly, fly, the army is coming!" upon which the people fled, and, taking shelter

[1] See p. 465.

among the hills, concealed themselves there. When the force came up the village was plundered and set on fire; and then, if the Mahrattas maintained themselves there for any length of time, an arrangement was come to, and a certain sum of money, for which the villagers assessed themselves, was paid as tribute, or the jumâbundee, and the people returned and re-inhabited the village.[1]

When Juswojee died, Sirdâr Singh assumed the cushion. Now Rânâjee Guj Singh, having attained to old age, and having no son, took Sirdâh Singh into his lap, but after that a son, named Prutheerâj, was born to him. After Guj Singh's death, Sirdâr Singh founded upon this a claim to the cushion of Dântâ; and, in compensation for his abandonment of it, received Wusâee, Dâwol, Dâlesânoo, and several other villages. Sirdâr Singh's brothers "went out" for a subsistence, and obtained certain lands and fields.

Sirdâr Singh's eldest son was Oomed Singh. His four younger sons, Chundra Singh, Wukhut Singh, Surtân Singh, and Pertâp Singh, received the village of Wusâee, to be held jointly. Sirdâr Singh having made a foray upon Tembâ, and carried off cattle and hostages, the "wâr" came from Tembâ, and a conflict ensued, in which Koonwur Oomed Singh was slain. He left three sons, Umur Singh, the Pâthuwee Koonwur, Jugoojee, and Ugur Singh, who received five villages, to be held jointly.

On the death of Sirdâr Singh, he was succeeded by his grandson, Umur Singh. The Kheelor district, which lies between Soodâsunâ and Taringâ, was held by Hureeol Râjpoots, who were puttâwuts of Dântâ, but these, being much annoyed by the Mewâsees, left the district, and retired to the village of Kurbuthee, in the Wurnugger Talooka, upon which the chief of Soodâsunâ took possession of the district, with the consent of the Rânâjee. In Umur Singh's time, a Guikowâr army was repulsed with loss to them, but without a single man being killed on the part of Soodâsunâ. It was this Umur Singh who took possession of Dântâ.[2]

Umur Singh left a son, Futteh Singh, whose sons were Mohobut Singh and Punjee. In the time of Mohobut Singh, in Sumwut, 1860 (A.D. 1804), Kâkâjee brought a Guikowâr army, and a conflict ensued. The Mahrattas lost sixty men; but the Thâkor was assisted by the spirit of Mâniknâth Bhâwo, and did not lose a man, but gained the victory. This Mâniknâth is the same Bhâwo who permitted the erection of Ahmedabad, and who has two shrines on the hills at Tur-

[1] "Many times," says the narrator of this story, "do I recollect having to take "flight on such occasions as these."

[2] See p. 468.

sunghmo and Soodâsunâ, where he used to dwell. Mohobut Singh made a foray upon Runsheepoor, and carried off cattle and hostages, because the Bheels of that place had harried the buffaloes of his village of Dâwol.

Mohobut Singh left four sons, Huree Singh, Rutun Singh, Purbut Singh, and Mokum Singh. Huree Singh enjoyed the cushion four years, and was succeeded by Rutun Singh, who held it for two years and died. His son, Bhooput Singh, succeeded him, and lived a year afterwards. Then Purbut Singh, the present Thâkor, succeeded. Mokum Singh died in infancy.

CHAPTER XII.

MUHÂRÂJÂ GUMBHEER SINGH OF EEDUR.

Now Khomân Singh, a Châmpâwut, had done good service to the raja, who therefore said to him, "I have a great desire to promote "you, but I am doubtful whether, if you are promoted, you will not "turn against me." Then the chief took an oath that he would never draw sword against his prince; upon which the raja granted to him the estate of Wânkâner,[1] with the right of receiving the royal embrace on entering the Court.

The village of Pânol belonged to a bard, who died without a male heir. The mother and wife of the deceased maintained in his house relations of their own, a father and two sons, and procured wives for the youths. They also assigned a sixth share of the village to them, and gave them a separate establishment. However, the two brothers, in the hope of gaining possession of the whole village, formed the design of putting the ladies to death. They slew the elder lady with a dagger, but the bard's widow escaped, and making her way with great difficulty to Eedur, laid her complaint before the raja. Gumbheer Singh, upon this, sent for the principal bards of the neighbourhood, and commanded them to go to Pânol, and tell the two murderers that it was his order they should quit the place. This order was, however, disobeyed. The raja then sent for his chiefs one by one, and said, "Do you go and slay these two bards, and make Pânol

[1] This is Wânkâner in the Eedur country—not to be confounded with Wânkâner of Soreth.

"crown-land." Each chief separately replied, "If you please to take "one of my villages do so, but it is not fit to put a bard to death; "you should therefore pardon this offence." Upon this the raja sent money to Hyderâbad, in Sindh, and hired there fifty Abyssinians. When these made their appearance, all the chiefs, and others who knew what was intended, strove to change the raja's resolution. He did not, however, attend to their remonstrances. Then all repaired to Khomân Singh, and said, "The raja bestows his complete favor "upon you, so if you will exert yourself to persuade him, the bards "will certainly be saved." Khomân Singh went to the raja, and said, "Have the kindness to pardon the offence of these bards." The raja refused the request, upon which the chief of Wânkâner replied, "Henceforth I will never make a petition to you any more." The raja said, "Do as you please." Khomân Singh was pained at this reply, and immediately rising, departed to his home.

Now the raja sent the Abyssinians to put the bards to death; and these last getting intelligence of the matter, one of the young men cut off the heads of his two children. He slew also two of the Abyssinians, and maimed himself so frightfully that he died. His father also killed himself; but his brother, who was absent from home, escaped. The Abyssinians returned to Eedur. After these events the bard who survived, having collected from distant places five hud-dred of his caste-fellows, came to Eedur to compel Gumbheer Singh to make reparation; but the raja, with the aid of other bards, got rid of them. Khomân Singh took the death of the bards so much to heart, that he determined on retiring to the Himalaya mountains to die. The raja, with the chiefs of the state, proceeded to Wânkâner for the purpose of inducing him to change his resolution, and Gum-bheer Singh said, "If it is because of this bard that you are departing, "you shall have a larger village instead of Pânol." The chief, how-ever, made answer, "If you had listened to me when I came to entreat "you, I would have remained, but I will not now remain though you "adopt a million expedients." Khomân Singh left home, accompanied by eleven attendants—his relations, friends, or followers. In his train was a dweller among the hills, who had suffered so much annoyance from the Bheels of his village, that he went to lay down his life among the snows of the Himalayas, in order that he might become the chief of the district in another birth and take revenge upon the Bheels. The desire of all the rest, however, was to pass to the heaven of Vishnoo. They had adopted the saffron robe; they had laid aside their arms for staves twisted round with silver wire; the horses they rode were stripped of all warlike ornaments. The chieftain's wives and the inhabitants of his village were very much distressed at such a sight. Raja Gumbheer Singh, throwing himself in the way as the sad procession swept along the road, entreated Khomân Singh for the last time, and said, "I will lay my turban in the dust at your feet." The Châmpâwut answered, "Should you do so, I would slay myself on "the spot." The raja was unable to urge anything more.

Khomân Singh's son and heir, Dheerjee, who was at this time twenty years old, obtained the estate of Wânkâner, and served the heir-apparent, Prince Oomed Singh, from whose kindness he received an addition to his lands and the privilege of sounding kettle-drums at the head of his cavalcade.

Now, Raja Gumbheer Singh was very partial to Dheerjee of Wânkâner, for reasons which will appear from the following narrative. During the time that the Rows of Pol had made forays upon Eedur, in assertion of their claim to the cushion, they had plundered and burnt many villages. The raja therefore conceived the desire of retaliating by striking Pol. In A.D 1808, he entered six thousand matchlock men, and summoned all his vassals at Eedur, with whom he advanced as far as Wurâlee, without letting any of them know that the expedition was destined against Pol. Their next encampment, however, was at a pass four miles from that place.

When the raja's army left Eedur, the Row of Pol and the Rehwur and Wâghela chiefs, who had of old been vassals of his house, were all on the alert, and sent out scouts to bring intelligence. The only approach to Pol is by a pass almost in the bed of a river, which flows between lofty cliffs from east to west. The pass is defended, also, by two gates. The Row caused both of these gates to be built up, and at each of them he placed some of his "brothers" and mercenaries, armed with matchlocks, who picked off the raja's men whenever they showed themselves. Gumbheer Singh lost forty men in this defile, and after encamping near it four months, was still unsuccessful in discovering any means of overcoming the difficulties opposed to him. He was therefore in the greatest despondency. At this time he caused four hundred gold armlets to be made, which he distributed among the Bheels of the neighbourhood, and said to them, "Show me a way by "which I can get into Pol." The Bheels said, "There is no other "road than this one, but a party with scaling ladders might ascend one "by one a mountain path on the south side, though it would be a "very difficult task for them to carry even their arms." The raja sent at once for ladders, and, superintending the operation in person, caused his followers one by one to ascend. At this time the Eedur chiefs agreed that as the Koompâwuts were the raja's great favourites, they should lead the way on the occasion. Dheerjee, of Wânkâner, and other Châmpâwuts, however, privately agreed that their time was come for taking revenge against one of the chiefs, now with the Row, who had killed their relation. When the Koompâwuts mounted, therefore, Dheerjee and his friends mounted with them, and pushed on to Pol itself. They then called to the Arabs to wind their horns, and fired a volley of musketry. Upon this the Row and his family fled over the hills, and Gumbheer Singh, entering Pol with the horse-hair fans waving before him, caused a cushion to be placed in the mansion of the Row, and took his sent thereon. The raja, after remaining there a month, was disposed to send for his family, and make Pol his residence; but the Row began to make daily inroads upon the Eedur villages, and the chiefs said, "Your Highness has "taken Pol and increased your fame, let all the dwellings, with the "exception of this mansion, be given to the flames, and let us return "to Eedur lest the Row enter therein." Then the raja, following their advice, struck his camp, and came to Bheelorâ. At this time the mercenaries became urgent for their pay, which was two or three months in arrears; they surrounded the raja, and for two days prevented his smoking his hookah or taking any food. At last he sent for the head-men of all the crown-villages, and said to them, "You "swallow up the whole produce of my villages, and give me hardly "anything. Now, therefore, what remedy have you to propose, as "the troops have set a watch over me?" Then the head-men willingly paid fines, according to their ability. The raja returned to Eedur, and because the Châmpâwuts had done good service in the matter, he extended much favor to them.

At this time, a force of Sindhis, five thousand strong, had attacked Doongurpoor and taken it, and having seized the Râwul, and placed him in a litter, they carried him about with their army. They now advanced into Wânswârâ, and a severe engagement was fought there, in which many on both sides were slain. A number of the villages of Wânswârâ were subdued. Then Urjoon Singh, one of the feudal chiefs of Wânswârâ, assembled a force, with which he defeated the Sindhis and drove them out. These disturbances continued for five years, and the pay of Urjoon Singh's mercenaries having fallen into arrears, and no means existing for satisfying their demands, that chief moved his troops into Loonâwârâ and Bâlâsinor, where he exacted tribute, and at length, advancing into the Eedur country, came to Pâlya. Now Dheerjee, of Wânkâner, was at feud with the chief of Pâlya, but upon good terms with Urjoon Singh. He went, therefore, and had an interview with the latter. When the chief of Pâlya heard of this, he also went to meet Urjoon Singh, and said, "I am at feud "with Puhârjee, of Thodurâ; I will give you a sum of money if you "will put him to death." Urjoon Singh accepted this office. Now Dheerjee, who was a friend of the chief of Thodurâ, endeavoured, without success, to dissuade Urjoon Singh, and at last went away in a rage, saying, "I go to Thodurâ, to wait there for you. Come and "fight with me as soon as you can." He went to Thodurâ, and the chief of that place also began to collect mercenaries, but could secure the services of a few only. He therefore went to Eedur, and said to the Prince Oomed Singh, "If you do not support me at this time I "shall die fighting against the enemy, and then Thodurâ will pass "into their hands." Upon this the prince, too, advanced to Thodurâ with his forces. The assailants, now finding that they were overmatched, gave up their attempt, and all parties returned to their homes. On this occasion, also, the raja was much pleased with the conduct of Dheerjee.

When Subul Singh, the son of Soorujmul of Chândunee, became a Dev, his two sons, Sâm Singh and Mâlum Singh, struggled for the possession of the estate. The elder son, Sâm Singh, who had little ability, went off in anger to Wânkâner. Mâlum Singh, on the other hand, went to Teentoee, and said to Kunukâjee, the chief of that place, "If you will place me on the cushion at Chândunee, I will "take your Koonwur in my lap."[1] Kunukâjee thereupon went to Chândunee, and began to say, "Mâlum Singh shall sit upon the "cushion." However, Dheerjee, of Wânkâner, came and said, "Sâm "Singh is the rightful heir, he shall sit upon the cushion." The chiefs quarrelled for some time, and then went home. Soon after, Kunukâjee raised four hundred mercenaries, with whom he attacked Wânkâner. Dheerjee engaged him, and killed ten or twelve of his men; meanwhile the neighbouring chiefs came, and said, "Why do "you fight to the death about other people's quarrels?" They thus induced Kunukâjee to retire, but a feud, not easily to be extinguished, had arisen between the two opponents. Now, the Chândunee minister came to Raja Gumbheer Singh, and said, "Muhârâj! may it "please you to come in person to place the young heir of Chândunee "on the cushion." The raja said, "Did not Dheerjee and Kunu-"kâjee go to place him on the cushion?" The minister replied, "Muhârâj! he whom they seat on the cushion cannot sit there, but "the young chief whom you may be pleased to seat there." Then

[1] Meaning that he would adopt the Koonwur as his own son.

the raja said, "If the village of Kothurâ be given to me I will come, "and, in exchange, I will give you that of Seeyolee." The minister obtained Sâm Singh's consent, and passed a deed assigning Kothurâ to the raja, who thereupon went and seated the rightful heir on the cushion, and girt him with the sword; but as to the village about which he had spoken to the minister, that he never gave. To the younger brother of Chândunee, he caused a single village to be assigned for his subsistence.[1]

A month after the first affair at Thodurâ, Dheerjee collected a force and commenced an advance against Teentoee, on account of the feud about Chândunee; but the other chiefs interfered, and went to induce him to return. Kunukâjee upon this made an attack upon Dheerjee's ally of Thodurâ, and Dheerjee, hearing the news, hastened

[1] Major Miles, in his report on the Myhee Kântâ, of the 21st of September, 1821, has the following :—

"Soorujmul, father of Subul Singh, of Chandunee, died about forty years ago. "Subul Singh is said to possess a very moderate share of understanding, and, from "his bad management, Futteh Singh, Thakor of Mhow, subsequently assumed the "chief control among the Champawuts, Futteh Singh died in A.D. 1805, and "Anur Singh succeeded him, and also died in A.D. 1819. Gopal Singh, his son, "is an infant, and the affairs of this quarter have since fallen into great confusion. "Gopal Singh is about fifteen years of age. The putta of the Champawuts has "lately been partitioned, from some quarrel between the two eldest sons of Subul "Singh, Maljee and Samjee. The partisan of the first is Kunukâjee, Thakor of "Teentoee. The Raja of Eedur and Dheerjee have taken part with Samjee. "The result, after much disturbance and bloodshed, has been the assumption of the "town of Kher, and half the pergunnah of Hursole by the Raja of Eedur, with the "consent of Kunukâjee, who has taken charge of the remainder of the putta. The "proprietors, nearly destitute of support, complain of the conduct of all parties."

The following occurs in a report by Lieutenant-Colonel Ballantine, dated Sadra, 15th October, 1822 :—

"*Chandunee.*—The relinquishment of this puttah was first sought by the owners, "who had quarrelled, and its partition was the basis of the whole of the disturbances "excited by Kunukâjee and Dheerjee, which, with Gumbheer Singh's after-"measures to check their usurpation, led to the Champawut rebellion. Maljee "and Samjee are the sons of Subul Singh, and it appears that they are in every "respect incompetent to the charge of their puttah. The measure has since been "referred to a commission of the Sirdars, and the following is the substance of the "decision given by them :—

"'The case of Maljee and Samjee being referred to our decision, we find it "impossible to become their security, or to associate them in our arrangements and "obligations. Both brothers labour under the effects of excessive inebriety, even "to insanity; and both, under these failings, have committed the most atrocious "acts; nor are they, in our judgment, capable of improvement. Hence we give it "as our opinion, that under these disqualifications, the following provision seems "the most rational and equitable in their behalf, viz., &c., &c., &c.'"

to his assistance. A battle was fought, in which the chief of Teentoee was repulsed, with the loss of ten of his followers.

Kunukâjee, however, returning home, began again to collect a number of mercenaries, that he might attack Thodurâ a second time. Dheerjee, when he heard of this, called in Prince Oomed Singh to defend Thodurâ, who went thither, though the raja and others dissuaded him from doing so. Kunukâjee advanced with his force into the lands of Thodurâ, and then heard this intelligence. He reflected, "The heir-apparent is within, and if anything were to happen to him it would not be right." He therefore passed by the lands of Thodurâ and went to Pâlya, and took hostages therefrom. There was no reason for his going to Pâlya, except that he wanted to raise money. He went afterwards to other villages and took hostages, and from thence he wrote to the prince, saying, "Your highness is my lord, therefore it is not fit that you should remain in Thodurâ. When you oppose me in fight, I have neither eye, nor spear, nor bullet, therefore you make me appear low in the world's sight." The prince was enraged at this letter also, so he gave Dheerjee some of his troops, and sent him against Kunukâjee. Now, an Arab officer of the chief of Teentoee's force was exercising his horse, when Dheerjee's men fired upon him, and killed the horse. The Arab went to Kunukâjee, and said, "They have killed my horse, so I will now attack them." That chief said, "Do not you go there to fight with them; but set matchlock men secretly beside the road in this ravine, and let us draw up in front, so that they may be shot down as they come against us." They did so, and the result was, that Dheerjee lost seventeen horsemen, and was obliged to turn back to Thodurâ.

Dheerjee on this occasion had dressed one of the troopers in his own clothes, which trooper happened to be slain. Now, when Kunukâjee's men stripped the dead of their clothes, they found Dheerjee's clothes among the rest, and therefore thought that he was killed. Upon this the Teentoee chief mourned greatly, and taking the red turban off his head, put on a white one. His son, Lâljee, then said to him, "How is it that you did not think of the matter before, since you mourn in this way now?" He answered, "You, all of you, turned my head, therefore it has happened thus." Afterwards, when they made inquiry, they found that Dheerjee was safe, upon which Kunukâjee was very glad, and went home.

Now the prince, when he saw how sorrowful Dheerjee was, said to him, "Do not you entertain the least sorrow, those that have died will not return again, but I will not allow you to be a loser in any respect. I will give you back your horses and servants." Dheerjee said, "He has taken away my honor, I must strike Teentoee." The prince then took an oath, "I will not return to Eedur until Teentoee "shall have been struck." Then Dheerjee, taking the prince with him, went to Teentoee." Oomed Singh wrote to his father to say, "If you please to bring a force to my assistance do so, otherwise I "will die fighting against Teentoee." The raja was not pleased at the matter, but in order to protect his son he joined him with his forces. At this time a respectable bard of the Seerohee country, named Khoree Dânjee, was with the Thâkor of Teentoee, having been banished from Seerohee, because he had importuned the Row to fulfil an engagement which had been contracted on his security. When the raja's army came up, Kunukâjee took post in a fort he had caused to be made on a hill, and prepared to defend himself. However, Khoree Dânjee went to the raja, and said, "Sire! it is not "becoming that you should bring cannon hither to carry on war "against one of your own chieftains." He managed to satisfy the raja and Kunukâjee with his arguments, but the prince and Dheerjee continued inflexible. At last the Teentoee chief paid a sum of money, and, peace being concluded, the raja took his son with him and returned to Eedur.

Notwithstanding this apparent settlement, Dheerjee's mind was not satisfied, but his anger was transferred to the prince. He returned home, and soon after carried off the cattle from the village of Bheelorâ, which had been given to Oomed Singh for his private purse. The prince upon this wrote a letter to Dheerjee, upbraiding him, to which that chief answered, "Why did you cause my servants and horses to "be killed?" Afterwards Dheerjee carried off cattle and hostages from the crown village of Bhootâwud. He struck also Wusâee, another of the prince's personal villages, and wounded three or four of its defenders. He plundered Sheelâsun, Rentorâ, and other villages. At length the prince raised two thousand men, and taking the chiefs with him, and two guns, went to Wânkâner. Dheerjee, too, prepared for engaging. He entertained two hundred mercenaries. The prince came up, and halted fifteen days at Wusâee. Dheerjee made a night attack upon the camp at that place, and, after killing the Arab who had charge of the artillery, got off in safety. The next day Oomed Singh moved from thence, and encamped at Bheelorâ, from whence he went on to Wânkâner. At that place there was fighting for three days, in the course of which ten men were killed of the prince's party and three of Dheerjee's. Then the prince wrote to his father, saying, that after three days' time all attempts to take Wânkâner had been unsuccessful, and demanding that more men should be sent to him.

The raja upon this sent a reinforcement of two hundred foot and fifty horse. At this time many persons said to Dheerjee, "The raja's "heir has come here as a point of honour. Without striking Wânkâner he will not go away. In the end you, a chief of three villages, "will not be strong enough to continue the contest; and you have "deserved great applause that you have for three days resisted all "attacks. Now, therefore, you should retire." Upon this Dheerjee made preparations for a feast in his mansion. He set swinging beds in order, placed bottles of liquor and sweatmeats for the guests, with a sum of money as an offering, and all these arrangements completed, he retired. Then the prince plundered and burned the village, cut down the mowra and mango trees, and filled up the wells. He remained there three days, and returned to Eedur. Meanwhile Dheerjee, with his family, went to Doongurpoor. The Râwul of that place gave him a village, which he made his residence, and began to plunder and harass the Eedur country, doing a great deal of mischief. Atlength the raja, giving hostages for his safety, sent for him to Eedur, and came to terms with him. He restored his village to him, and the prince took him again into his personal service.[1]

[1] Dheerjee makes the following statement in a letter to Major Miles, dated 29th May, 1821:—

"I received your letter, and understood its contents. You write that you have "heard of some irregular conduct on my part. This report is very true, but no "depredations have been committed by me in the territory of the English govern-"ment, and no one has been molested without cause. I have a note written by the "Raja of Eedur, which, after having given me, he has altered his mind. He has "seized one of my villages, and has been the cause of the death of my brethren, "without making me any recompense. He has also caused me the loss of ten "horses, for which he has not paid me. Whatever the Muharaj promised has "proved wholly false. He has resumed my village, notwithstanding I have bor-"rowed and expended fourteen thousand rupees for his service, of which sum he "has not repaid me a farthing; and he has instigated my enemies to murder me. "If you wish to see the note written by the raja, I will send it, and you can read "and return it; and if any blame be imputable to me, I will conform to your "directions. I molest none but my enemies and those upon whom I have claims. "The British government is great, but my claims on the Muharaj should be "allowed, and all the villages of the Champawut puttahs seized by him should be "restored; after which I have no demands, and shall then be ready to perform "the service of the British government. I have many enemies in the Eedur "district. Send a man to me, and I will give him the paper before mentioned. "I shall wait four days for him. Do not give credit to my enemies: my quarrel "is with the Eedur durbar," &c. &c.

Bharot Damodhur Mohobut Singh having been despatched by Colonel Ballantine to Dheerjee, returned to camp on the 30th September, 1821, and furnished the following information:—

"Soon after my quitting this camp, I was visited by Thakor Dheerjee, who,

A year afterwards the prince gave Dheerjee a sum of money, and sent him into Kâteewâr, telling him to purchase as many good horses

"though he at first appeared satisfied in his own mind of the justice of his cause, "eventually admitted his error, which was a first aggression against Eedur; but "now expressed a sense of contrition, and solicited my agency in effecting a com- "promise with Laljee Muharaja (Prince Oomed Singh), who had by this time "advanced into the neighbourhood of Wankaner with a large force. On a "repetition of the Thakor's solicitation, I was induced to comply with his request, "and he authorised me to make the following terms:—

"1st. To restore all plundered property up to the present time.

"2nd. To pay a portion of the expense incurred in entertaining troops against "Wankaner.

"3rd. That he would compromise, by a gift of money or land, the death of a "Brahmin that had taken place in one of his enterprises. And,

"Lastly. That he would attend the Muharaja's service.

"On this I lost no time in repairing to Laljee Muharaj, and fully represented "these circumstances, soliciting at the same time his admission of the prayer, at "all events until the matter could be brought to the knowledge of the British "government. Laljee Muharaj at once declared that he would not, as Dheerjee "had attacked his private village; and only allowed me time to return, and inform "Dheerjee of his intention. The village (Wankaner) was in due course attacked, "and as Dheerjee on this occasion made no determined resistance, it was "completely ransacked, and burnt to the ground."

"*Laljee Muhârâjâ to Colonel Ballantine*, *9th September*, 1821.

"Dheerjee for the last twelve months has committed the most serious excesses "in our pergunnahs, from Wankaner, whence he has continued to send forth "banditti, having entertained a numerous body of mercenaries. Besides, he "carried off a Banian hostage from the walls of Eedur. Dheerjee, however, "disregarded our remonstrances for four months, when it became necessary for us "to entertain troops, with whom we attacked Wankaner, and Champawut Dheerjee "has been dispossessed, flying for refuge to the Doongurpoor territories."

"*Dheerjee to Colonel Ballantine*, *8th September*, 1821.

"I duly received your letter, which contains the misrepresentations of my "enemies; but, if it is your pleasure, I will send to you the writing of the Muha- "raja to peruse, to show that my acts were at his instigation. In one instance I "served him, and had eight or ten men and eight or ten horses killed and wounded. "These circumstances I previously represented to Major Miles. The Muharaja, "having deviated from the purport of the writing, led me to commit excesses in "his pergunnahs. The Muharaja has since attacked and destroyed my village, to "which I made no opposition, and he has plundered it of property to the amount "of fifty thousand rupees. For the truth of these assertions, you may apply to "the Muharaja of Ahmednugger, and Major Miles can also acquaint you with "many particulars. If you find me in fault you can hold me responsible in any "way you please. In the first instance the Muharaja instigated me, and then "left me to abide the consequences. I am now in the jungles. I have eight "hundred men and one hundred horse, who are starving, and if nothing is done "for me in the case of my village, I must commit depredations on Eedur. "Further, I am desirous of serving you with my men and horses, as I will not "again serve the Muharaja."

as he could for the money. Dheerjee went to Wursorâ, near Mânsâ, where he spent the money in marrying a wife. He had one wife before this. After purchasing jewels and clothes for his bride, he had a small sum left, with which he purchased two horses, and, coming to Eedur, presented them to the prince. Oomed Singh asked where the rest of the money was gone to. Dheerjee answered, "It was my "master's money, and I spent it in my affairs; I did not go to steal "from any other person's house." The prince said nothing to this, but the raja pressed him, saying, "Give up my money." Dheerjee said, "As to money, I have none in my house: you may do what you "please." The raja then quartered horsemen upon him, upon which Dheerjee passed a deed assigning the village of Ghântee instead of the money. However, he was very sore at heart upon the subject, and at length went out again in rebellion, taking his family with him. In the forest districts of the Mewar zillah there is a Bheel village, called Pâtheâ Wulechâ. Dheerjee lived a year in that village, making forays into the Eedur country. Once on a time he carried away the cattle from the village of Bâmunwâ, which belonged to Teentoee. He had only twenty horsemen with him, but in a single day he would plunder as many villages as he had followers. However, when he came upon Bheels who plundered in the Eedur country, he would cut off their heads, and send them in baskets as an offering to the raja. Among the villages which he plundered, burnt, or took hostages from, were Wusâee, Bulolee, Bheelorâ, and many others; in fact, with the exception of those which had been given to bards, there was scarcely a crown village which escaped his ravages.[1]

At this time the raja said one day in his court, "It was I who gave "this man power and promoted him, in return for which he despoils "my villages. Why does he not go to some other state of Râjwârâ "and procure a holding for himself there?" This observation was conveyed to Dheerjee, who thereupon went to Rânâ Shree Bheem Singh of Oodeipoor. Now Dheerjee had gained fame for himself in foreign parts on account of the valor he had displayed in his outlawry, and the Rânâ was also acquainted with him from the time that that prince had visited Eedur to be married to the sister of Gumbheer Singh. The Rânâ therefore drew out a deed for a valuable feudal holding, and gave it to Dheerjee. That chief accepted the grant, but would

[1] *Colonel Ballantine to Government, 22nd March, 1822.*

"Dheerjee has gone out again in rebellion, without assigning any cause. He is "implicated in the commission of many atrocities of the most serious nature. He "is reputed to have put to death or maimed fifteen or sixteen Brahmins of Bhee- "lora, and to have committed other very serious aggressions."

not receive the deed. He said, "If I remain here it will be said of "me that I could not recover my father's rights, and I shall lose my "honor." He remained at Oodeipoor four months, and then returned to the Eedur country, having placed his family at Koorâgâm, in Marwar.

At this time Colonel Ballantine sent for all the Eedur chiefs to Sâdrâ, in order to arrange for the settlement of the country. There was a very general discontent among the chiefs, and several of them refused to pay the raja's dues. Some of them offered their horses to be priced, and said that they had no money, but that they were the servants of the state, and their heads were the raja's. The Koompâwuts alone made a proper answer. After a month's consultation, the British agent put the chiefs of Mondeytee, Teentoee, Thodurâ, and Wânkâner in irons, and forced others to give up part of their estates to the raja. Dheerjee, of Wânkâner, had been called in on the security of a bard. He came, attended by thirty-five armed followers, who were, however, dismissed by the raja; his nephew, Udjee, who was quite a youth, being alone left to attend upon him. When the government soldiers came to seize Dheerjee, Udjee slew some of them, and wounded others, and was then slain.

When the load fell on his brother,
Fell upon Dheero,
Against their enemies wielding his sword,
Udo gained an Upsura bride.
The Arabs he cut to pieces;
The enemies beneath his feet he cast;
At one blow he cleft them in twain,
At one blow, did Udo!

After he had been confined six months, Dheerjee broke his fetters, scaled the wall of the fort, and escaped. The chief of Mondeytee was detained four months, and then released, having given security, and made concessions to the raja. The chiefs of Teentoee and Thodurâ were similarly released, about the same time.[1]

[1] *Colonel Ballantine's Memorandum of Dheerjee's Proceedings, 30th October,* 1823.

"Dheerjee's murder of Brahmins, and other crimes, having been formerly fully "communicated to government, he was ordered to be fined, and kept in constraint, "and his land to be made over to his nearest relative. Troops were sent to punish "him, but at this juncture he sent in Bharot Damodhur Mohobut Singh to make "submission, upon which Colonel Ballantine, when he assembled the other Sirdars "at Dubhora to make an adjustment of securities for Guikowar tribute, &c., sent "also for Dheerjee, and informed him that he might make known his complaints "against Gumbheer Singh. Dheerjee asked for safe conduct, which was, as an "indulgence, procured for him from Gumbheer Singh. He came in, and re-

While Dheerjee remained in confinement at Baroda, he had made a vow to Shâmlâjee that he would offer valuable offerings at that god's shrine if he should effect his escape. At length he escaped by climbing over the wall, and fled to the shrine, where he performed his vows. Thence he went secretly into Kâteewâr, where he purchased horses, and having mounted troopers upon them, again entered the Eedur country, and resumed his system of annoyance. Colonel Ballantine at this time set posts from village to village, but Dheerjee fell upon them at night time, and slew many of the soldiers. On one occasion, when he had seized hostages at a village, he was pursued by the government troops and the Eedur horse. A deep and broad ravine came in his way, over which Dheerjee, without hesitation, leapt his mare. Then, turning round to his pursuers, he cried, "Follow "now, whoever of you dares leap the ravine." No one followed.

"ceived encouragement, and money was advanced to him to live on, and the "settlement of the whole Champawut district obtained with great difficulty from "Gumbheer Singh. Security was then demanded from him, but Dheerjee, under "pretext of going to Dehgaum, made off, and on the road seized hostages at "Wussye, murdered a Borah of Ahmednugger, harried the cattle of Bheelora, and "committed other outrages. He now seduced Thakor Gopal Singh, then a boy "residing in the Danta country, to join him, and Puharjee (of Thodura), and, "soon after, the three combined wrote a letter, saying they would plunder the "country. Dheerjee took to the mountains, whereupon a strict search was made "after him; and Bhatee Puharjee, Kunukajee, and other villains were taken, "whereupon Dheerjee became apprehensive, and fled to Oodeipoor. There the "Rana and his Sirdars, being ignorant of the villanies Dheerjee had committed, "used their mediation with the resident there (Sir David Ochterlony), and he, to "gratify the Rana, addressed a letter to Colonel Ballantine in Dheerjee's behalf, "requesting him, for the sake of the Rana of Oodeipoor, to overlook Dheerjee's "offences, and to make such a settlement for the future in his favor with Gum- "bheer Singh as should be just and proper. Colonel Ballantine thereupon wrote "to the resident, calling Dheerjee to Sadra. Dheerjee, in that gentleman's "presence (the resident's), made arrangements to come in company with Gopal "Singh, and took leave of the resident, bearing his letter, and accompanied by "his attendants and a respectable servant of the Rana's, Pooroheet Laljee. Dheer- "jee had overawed Gopal Singh, and forced from him the resignation of a "share of his land. He left Gopal Singh at Oodeipoor, and on the road robbed "his servant of his jewels; and wherever Gopal Singh had left money or clothes "in deposit, Dheerjee seized them by force. When he arrived at Sadra, he said "he was empowered by Gopal Singh to act for him. He made submission to the "political agent in the presence of Pooroheet Laljee, promising to recall Gopal "Singh, and give security, and passing a bond to that effect, Kunukajee and Pu- "harjee being securities. Dheerjee now received money for his subsistence, and "was dismissed to return home. On arriving there, he petitioned for the removal "of the government post there, which was granted. However, he did not send "for Gopal Singh, and that chief, accidentally hearing that a settlement was in "progress, hastened to Sadra, and made submission. Dheerjee was then sum-

After this Lâljee, the son of the chief of Teentoee, joined Dheerjee, and the outlaws retired together to the forests of Doongurpoor, where they received shelter, and from that retreat continued to ravage the territories of Eedur.

Now at this period the Râwul of Doongurpoor was thirty-two years old, but he had taken it into his head that he would have no son, and that it was necessary for him to adopt one. He therefore sent for Dulput Singh, the heir of Dewulya, who was of the same descent with himself, and passed a deed appointing him his own heir. This young chief was not favorable to the outlaws, and they, perceiving the fact, lost confidence in their present situation, and removed their families to the neighbourhood of Shâmlâjee. However, they continued themselves to reside in the Doongurpoor country, and to

" moned, and sent by his servant an answer, written from Ahmednugger, but dated " Wankaner; and the servant, when asked where his master was, said, 'At Beejapoor.' Colonel Ballantine then applied to his securities, and placed Mohsuls " on them and him. Dheerjee, having arrived at Sadra, was daily called upon by " Colonel Ballantine for a settlement, but day after day passed without anything " having been adjusted; and his securities having arrived, and declined further " responsibility for him, Mohsuls were placed upon him. Dheerjee declared that " unless these were removed he would commit suicide, and that no one could tell " what might happen, for his men were not under his control."

"*15th November*, 1823.

" Since the Mohsuls were placed upon Dheerjee, now ten days ago, his conduct " has been insolent and threatening, declaring, that though he wished himself to " give the securities required, he could not answer for the conduct of his armed " mercenaries, with whom he has continued to parade camp in direct violation of " his word. * * * * As might have been expected, Dheerjee contumaciously " and determinedly opposed my measures for the reduction of his armed followers, " and in the affray that in consequence took place he received a wound in the back " from one of his own people attempting to cut down an Arab. In the affray, " also, one Arab was wounded, and two of his people—one severely, who has since " died.

Despatch from the Bombay Government to the Court of Directors, 1st September, 1826.

" The three Thakors (Dheerjee, Kunukâjee, and Puhârjee) were subsequently " removed to Baroda, as it was not considered safe that they should remain in the " Myhee Kanta, it being explained to the raja (of Eedur) that their removal to " Baroda did not in any way affect the allegiance they owed him. An arrange- " ment was also made for the management of their estates by their nearest rela- " tions, and a separate provision for themselves and their families, who were not " to accompany them to Baroda. On the 24th September, 1824, Dheerjee effected " his escape from Baroda, assisted by Laljee, the son of the Teentoee chief (who " remained in confinement), and began committing excesses in the Myhee Kanta, " which led to the despatch of a light force from Deesa in pursuit of him."

plunder Eedurwârâ. Upon this the young chief secretly offered to reward any one who would give him a sight of the outlaws. Once on a time Dheerjee and Lâljee came to a village in the Râwul's country, Dheerjee being in distress, and suffering from inflammation of the eyes. They procured a person to get ready dinner for them there. The heir of Doongurpoor, becoming aware of their arrival, set off with a hundred horse, who, when they reached the village, began to beat the royal drum. Dheerjee and Lâljee, hearing the sound, mounted their horses and fled; the Doongurpoor horse pursued them, and came in sight of them. They cried to the outlaws, "What "is this, are you Rajpoots, and do you run away?" Dheerjee said, "you are many, and we are but two; at this time it is necessary to "fly;" his companion, however, began to slacken the speed of his horse, and meanwhile the Doongurpoor men came up with him. Lâljee's horse now pulled up, and would not move a step. An Arab struck the horse a blow on the back with his sword, receiving at the same moment a blow from Lâljee's sword. Another horseman thrust at Lâljee with his lance, but he avoided the blow, and ran the assailant through, so that he died. As his horse would not move, he now dismounted, and, after killing two more of his assailants, was himself slain. Dheerjee, meanwhile, had galloped off, supposing that Lâljee was following him.[1]

Afterwards, whenever it was known that Dheerjee had procured refreshment at any one's house, fifty of the government horse would immediately put up there, and annoy the inhabitants very much. Once Dheerjee came to a village of his own, which was near to a bard's village, upon which the raja, suspecting the bard, quartered two horsemen upon him. Dheerjee, when he heard this, went suddenly to the village, and attacked the horsemen, of whom one was slain by him, but the other escaped. The bard immediately began to employ means of intimidation against the outlaw chief; he wounded his own arm and his thigh, and thrust a dagger through the throat of an old woman of his family. When the raja heard of the attack upon the horsemen he declared that it must have been instigated by the bard, and therefore ordered a force against his village, but on further enquiry the true state of the case was discovered.

Dheerjee now carefully avoided entering even the lands of one of his friend's villages—indeed, of avowed friends he possessed not one.

[1] A force under Major Thomas advanced to Doongurpoor in pursuit of the outlaws, and carried the fort on the 11th of March, 1825. Lâljee was killed by the young chief of Doongurpoor in the month of June following, a deed at which his adopted father was much incensed.—*English Records.*

He fixed his residence in the Mewar hills, but continued his harassing incursions, which he carried as far as Puttun, attacking the government troops, and carrying off cattle and hostages from the villages. Afterwards he directed his attacks against the country about Râeegurh. He continued in outlawry about fourteen years. At length, in the year A.D. 1827, while he was hiding among the Eedur hills, he had received a supply of gunpowder from his friends, and spread it out upon a cloth to dry, when a spark falling from the matchlock of one of his mercenaries, the powder exploded, and he thus received injuries of which he died. At the time of his death he was about forty-five years of age. Dheerjee was short in stature and spare in person. His deeds of outlawry have won him greater fame than has been gained by any chief of Eedur, and his exploits are celebrated throughout the Myhee Kântâ in the songs of the women as well as in the stanzas of the bard.

At the time of Dheerjee's death, his family were in the Marwar country. One of his two wives (who was of the Chowra clan), on receiving from his servant the turban which he had worn, burned herself on the funeral pile with that relic of her husband. She left no child. The other widow, with an infant son and daughter, returned to Wânkâner.[1]

CHAPTER XIII.

MUHÂRÂJÂ GUMBHEER SINGH OF EEDUR.

PRINCE OOMED SINGH died of small-pox in A.D. 1824, at the age of twenty-seven. Two of his wives followed him to the pile; they were

[1] All attempts on the part of the British authorities to apprehend the outlawed chief had proved fruitless, a fact which the government of Bombay mainly attributed to the almost general connivance of the chiefs in the Myhee Kântâ in his depredations. The resident at Baroda was therefore directed to offer terms to Dheerjee, and to promise that his grievances should be investigated, and those which proved reasonable redressed. Mr. Willoughby, who was then in charge of the residency, opened a communication accordingly with the outlaw, but while it was in progress news arrived of the death of Dheerjee, which was reported by that gentleman on the 6th August, 1827. The chief of Wânkâner survived the accident which led to his death six days, and on finding his end approaching, directed one of his Rajpoot followers to communicate the facts to Mr. Willoughby, and request that care might be taken of his family.

daughters of the Chohân chief of Dhurol and the Chowra of Mânsâ. A concubine also became a sutee. The prince had two other Rânees upon whom the desire of accompanying their lord to Paradise did not come. They were daughters of the Rajas of Wânswârâ and Dewulyâ, and retired as widows to their fathers' houses.

> "The giver of gifts to bards, of lands, of elephants, of horses,
> "Was Gumbheer's son, whose mind was filled with wisdom.
> "Desiring him, the Chohânee and the Chowree
> "Went to obtain the royal seat of the lord of the Devs.
> "A thorn to his enemies, the conqueror of the Mahrattas,
> "Who extinguished his flame-like foes by the strength of his arm,
> "Whose face was resplendent as the day-bringing sun,
> "Such was Lâl, with whom to Paradise went the sutees.
> "Huree [1] worked an evil work in the world,
> "The hope of the bards had not been fully satisfied.
> "The crown among Rânees, the Râthor took with him.
> "They became Upsuras! Oomed became Indra!
>
> "The horse-hair fans were waving of the Chohânee's lord,
> "He who was the wealth of bards. To attain to fame,
> "The heir of Jodhâ's race passed with his Rânees
> "To Indra's mansion—did the Sun of the Hindoos!
> "As long as sun and moon remain, the descendant of Guj Singh
> "Shall enjoy the great throne. So is it fit!
> "Indra's seat enjoyed to the full, in bright form,
> "To Vishnoo's eternal heaven he shall pass."

A Brahmin of Eedur was so deeply distressed when he heard of the prince's death, from thinking of what would become of the state, that he dashed his head against a grain jar, and dislodged a heavy weight lying on it, which fell upon him and killed him. The raja granted to his son the village of Mâtâsool, which he had taken from the Koompâwuts, and which still remains in the Brahmin's possession.[2]

After this, in A.D. 1829, Gopâl Singh, the chief of Mhow, went out in rebellion, because the raja had struck the villages of his estate. He retired with about twenty horsemen he had with him to his village of Cheetror. A trader of that place had died, and one of the merchants of Eedur, with his wife and family, had come thither to his funeral feast. They remained four nights, and then taking leave of the chief, set out home, forming altogether a party of

[1] Vishnoo.

[2] Colonel Ballantine reports, on the 17th May, 1824, "the death of the only son "of the Raja of Eedur;" and, on the 27th, writes, in continuation, that "three "females, the wives of Laljee Saheb, accompanied the body as sutees to the pile "and were burned. Gumbheer Singh is suffering from the deepest affliction."

a hundred persons. The Cheetror traders escorted them for a certain distance, and then turned back; but Gopâl Singh followed the strangers with his men, and, seizing the whole of them, carried them off to the hills. When the news was brought to Eedur, the merchants of the town set off in a body, with loud cries, to the palace. The raja, peeping out of an upper window, said, "What is it?" The merchants answered, "Our people went to a feast, and have all been seized "and carried off from the place by Gopâl Singh. What is it that you, "our master, have done? If there were any master over our heads "could such a thing happen?" Then the raja said, "Your master "sleeps beside the Rumulesur tank.[1] What master have you? I am "an old man." However, he collected his forces, and made an expedition as far as Mhow and Cheetror, from whence he returned without success. The traders now began again to raise a howling, and to complain of the calamities they suffered, for it was suspected that Gopâl Singh had violated the honor of the women who were his prisoners. The raja then took the turban from his head, and tied a cloth round it and said, "When I recover your hostages, I will reassume my "turban." However, mentally he vowed that it should not be until Gopâl Singh was slain. Now, that chief released the traders on receiving ransom for them, and himself living in the Mhow hills with his family made inroads upon the Eedur country. At length the raja, having assembled an army, encamped at Bhuvnâth, near Mhow, and sent for Dâmodhur Mohobut Singh, the bard, whom he offered as security to Gopâl Singh. The chief of Mhow came in, and was most warmly received by the raja, who, after they had drunk opium together, said, "You are my son; who is there of mine equal to you? when I see "you I rejoice as if it were Oomed Singh that I beheld." Having talked to him in this way, he replaced him in Mhow. However, after this the raja continually said, "I have no relish for my food, unless I "behold Gopâl Singh." Thus saying, he sent for him to Eedur.

In A.D. 1830, the raja set out with his retinue to travel through his country, at which time it was that he seized upon Bud Singh, the chief of Kherod, in the Poseenâ district, and threw him into irons. It happened thus:—

The chief of Hurâd-Poseenâ died in A.D. 1828, leaving a son, named Purwut Singh, who had attained the age of eighteen, but was an effeminate youth. His two nearest relations were Jâmut Singh and Bud Singh. The former wished to place the rightful heir upon the cushion, but the object of the latter was to seat himself there. However, as he

[1] Alluding to Prince Oomed Singh, whose funeral pyre was erected by the side of that reservoir.

found no means of effecting this object, Bud Singh came to Eedur, and said to the raja, "If you will place me on the cushion of Poseenâ, I "will pass a deed resigning a fourth of the estate to you." The raja agreed to this offer. The matter, however, came to the knowledge of the young chief and Jâmut Singh, and they also went to the raja and said, "It is not customary to place a distant relation on the cushion "when there is a son existing." The raja said, "He promises to pass "a fourth share to me, therefore it is him that I will seat." They saw there was no other remedy, so they also said they would pass a fourth share. Gumbheer Singh, however, said, "A fourth share is "what he offers me. What more than this do you offer, that I should "seat you on the cushion?" At length, after much discussion, the young chief passed a deed resigning a third share of the estate, and Jâmut Singh set off to Poseenâ, at the raja's order, to place him on the cushion. Bud Singh, however, when he was gone, offered to resign a six-anna share,[1] upon which the order was sent, "Return hither without "placing the chief's son on the cushion." Jâmut Singh returned. Then the raja said, "Bud Singh offers six annas, therefore Budjee "has the cushion." The contest went on in this way for two months, and at last the young chief resigned half the estate. Then the raja sent the Prince of Soor with fifty matchlocks and fifty horse, an elephant, royal drums, and silver rod, to seat the chief's son on the cushion, and at the same time to receive charge of the half-share that had been passed to him. The prince went accordingly, and placed Purwut Singh on the cushion. Bud Singh upon this went to his own house at Kherod to live there, and began to injure the villages of the Poseenâ estate, upon which the new chief complained at Eedur. The raja sent for Bud Singh to Eedur, but he did not obey the summons, being afraid that he would be put to death. Hostages were then given him and he came, but was still distrustful of the raja. At this time a minister of the Seerohee state happened to be at Eedur on some busi-

[1] With Hindoos everything is divided into annas, or sixteenths of a rupee. In Wales a similar custom still prevails. The registrar of the Bristol District Court of Bankruptcy was sitting in November, 1855, at New Quay, Cardiganshire, taking the examination of several witnesses in the matter of the bankruptcy of Thomas Davies, shipbuilder of that port. Most of the witnesses were Welsh people, and the subject of the inquiry being the extent of the bankrupt's interest in a certain vessel, some surprise was created by the witnesses speaking of their shares in the vessel as a matter of weight. The mystery was solved by the interpreter in this way:—A vessel about to be built is divided into sixty-four shares, the total being taken by the owners to represent a pound avoirdupois. Thus, the owner of four sixty-fourths is said to have an ounce; of two sixty-fourths, half-an-ounce; of one sixty-fourth a quarter of an ounce; and so on in proportion.

ness. Bud Singh went and lodged with him. The raja sent for him to the court and reprimanded him on this account, but Bud Singh paid no heed. The raja then determined upon seizing him, but deferred doing so lest the Seerohee minister might oppose him. Bud Singh was therefore lectured and dismissed, and, going home, set to work exactly as before to do all the harm he could to the Poseenâ estate. The raja again sent for him, giving him security, but the chief declined visiting Eedur again. However, Gumbheer Singh corrupted the chief's two ministers (a Brahmin and a bard), by promising to give them each a village, if they would persuade their master to revisit the court. Bud Singh was thus enticed to Eedur, where the raja received him with the greatest respect, and caused him to be brought into the presence, overcoming his first suspicions by continued attentions. Meanwhile, a Sindhi officer, named Meroo, was directed to seize him, which task he accordingly effected while Bud Singh was on the way from his lodgings to the court. Meroo carried the chief to his quarters, and there put him in irons.

Now when the raja set off on his tour, in A.D. 1830, Bud Singh was carried with him as a prisoner; but two months afterwards, on some change of policy, he was allowed to furnish security, and was then released, his lands of Kherod being restored to him, to be held free of all claims on the part of the crown, and satisfaction being otherwise afforded him. However, Bud Singh, when he reached home, sent for the two ministers, and having put them off their guard by kind usage, he first cut off the Brahmin's head, which he threw to the dogs, that they might crunch it, and then attempted to destroy the bard also. This latter, however, made his escape.

The raja left Eedur with his cavalcade, attended by Kurun Singh, the prince of Ahmednugger, Gopâl Singh, chief of Mhow, and the whole of the nobles. At this time the two chiefs above mentioned, with Jhâlum Singh, of Mondeytee, came to a private decision that the force should move upon Pâlya, with the chief of which place they were at feud; the raja and his ministers, Durjun Singh, had, on the other hand, planned an expedition against the Rehwurs. On Gumbheer Singh's announcing his intentions, the three chiefs pretended acquiescence, and remained in person with the raja, but sent their cavalry contingents on in advance, and struck Pâlya before the raja's arrival, burning all the dwellings in the town. Mohobut Singh, the chief of that place, took to the hills; and this chief indeed was not the man to take to flight, but it was because he supposed himself to be attacked by his master's troops that he fled. When the raja came up, and found the town a heap of smouldering ruins, he rebuked the three chiefs very earnestly. The camp was then pitched in the lands of Pâlya. Mohobut Singh, its chief, however, lost no time, but raising a large force of Bheels, blocked up the road by which the army was to retire. Meanwhile the army remained in its position, subsisting upon the spoils of the town of Pâlya. Durjun Singh's troops committed no act of hostility; but the three confederated chiefs plundered and burnt even the outlying villages, much to the annoyance of Gumbheer Singh. At this time news arrived that a string of camels laden with property, belonging to a banker who was with the army, had been plundered by the Bheels on its way from Eedur, and that the wild robbers had wounded both the camel men and their animals. At the same time came a message from Mohobut Singh, of Pâlya, who protested that the raja had struck his village without any just pretence, for that his revenue had been regularly paid, and threatened that he would make it a difficult matter for the army to get home again. Upon this the raja sent to say that he had no intention of striking Pâlya, and that the result had been brought about by the three chiefs. Mohobut Singh rejoined, "I could have given them an answer; but why was it that your "highness took the pains to accompany them?" The raja then sent for him to an interview, but the chief refused to attend, and Gumbheer Singh was at length compelled to agree that when Pâlya should be rebuilt no revenue should be demanded from the chief for two years. Upon this the raja struck his camp, and the event having displeased him, he proceeded no further with his tour, but returned to Eedur, and disbanded his army.

The raja, however, retained Gopâl Singh near him. Now there was a deadly feud between Gopâl Singh and Durjun Singh, the Prudhân. The raja said, therefore, to the former, "It is my intention "to make you minister of Eedur; and, what is more, if you can keep "a secret, I have one for your ear." Gopâl Singh promised secrecy, and the raja whispered, "I want Durjun Singh put out of the way." Gopâl Singh said, "Is it truth that you are speaking, or do you "merely ridicule me?" "It is nothing but truth," said the raja. "Then give me your oath." The oath was given. Gopâl Singh now asked permission to go home to Mhow, and not only received it, but was also loaded with presents. He went accordingly; and on his return to Eedur, the raja received him affectionately, and made him a present of the sword and shield which had been worn by the late Prince Oomed Singh. Many people, however, who observed all that was going on, warned Gopâl Singh that the raja would some day play him false. "Recollect," said they, "how Bhowânee Singh deceived

"Soorujmul, of Chândunee, to his death, and how he treacherously "slew the young chief of Merâsun. It is the very rule of their house "to do such things as these." Gopâl Singh, however, paid no attention to these warnings. Even when his own father-in-law, Puhârjee, of Todhurâ, entreated him to beware, he refused to believe, and said, "It was with such bugbears as these that Kunukâjee "and Dheejee were kept at a distance from the court. You want me to believe them, that you may keep me away too."

After this, Gopâl Singh's mother having died, he procured, with much entreaty from the raja, leave to visit Mhow, in order to perform her obsequies. At home, too, many people said to him, "Do not go "back to Eedur;" but he paid no attention to the advice of any one. His stepmother and his wife then arranged, so that when he prepared to go to Eedur he was met outside the village by a string of women carrying black and broken water-vessels, and by other ill omens. Nevertheless, the chief went his way to Eedur.

Many days after this, in the year A.D. 1831, the raja, having first administered a solemn oath of secrecy to the Kusbâtees who were in his service, said to them, "You must put Gopâl Singh to death this "day." Not one of them would, however, agree to undertake the task. The raja then sent for Meroo, the Sindhi, and having sworn him to secrecy in the same way, procured his consent to the deed. The day before, the raja had said to Gopâl Singh, "To-morrow is "the feast of Shivrâtree; so you must come early in the morning, "and then we will manage what we have settled about killing Durjun, "Singh." In the morning, therefore, Gopâl Singh got up, bathed, took his breakfast, and having made himself ready, went to the foot of the palace stairs, and sent word to the raja that he was arrived. The door-keeper then, according to the usual custom, received from him his arms. Now Meroo and his soldiers, with their matchlocks loaded, were ready to kill Gopâl Singh; and whatever men of good character, or whatever friends of the chief's party were about the court, had been sent away, on one pretence or another, into distant parts of the country. Gopâl Singh having arrived at the palace, the raja sent for him into the apartments of the elder Rânee,[1] where he was seated in state, having caused carpets and cushions to be spread. When dinner-time came, and a dish was brought in for the raja, he said to the chief, "Do you, too, sit down, and dine with me." Gopâl Singh excused himself; but with much urgency was prevailed

[1] Her name was Dolut Koonwerbâ, and she was the daughter of the Bhâtee chief of Oshwâ, in Marwar, a cadet of Jesulmer. She perished as a sutee upon the death of her husband.

upon to sit down. After dinner the raja presented betel-nut to him. At this time his father-in-law drew him on one side, and said to him, "I fear much that it is designed to put you to death this very day. "Remember, I have married to you my daughter, who is now only "fourteen years old, and for her sake I implore you to take means "for saving your life." Gopâl Singh only made answer, "You are "entertaining a groundless suspicion." Then the father-in-law, pretending that he went to smoke a hookah, got away with great difficulty to his lodging, and mounting his horse, gallopped off for his life. The Sindhi officer thereupon increased his precautions, and rendered it impossible for any one else to make his escape.

At this time the raja gave orders to a servant to bring him a bottle of perfume. When it was brought he said it was not the one he wanted. This was repeated several times, and at last the raja rose, under the pretence of procuring for himself the scent he required, and went out. The door was immediately locked behind him, and he whispered to the Sindhi, "Now if he escape, your head must "answer for his." The reply was a volley fired into the room where the chief was from the windows on each of the four sides. Gopâl Singh had twelve attendants with him, who threw themselves before their chief; but as the bullets poured in they fell dead one after the other, and he himself received many wounds. The raja then showed himself, and said, "Ah! Gopâl, tell me was it right of you to carry "off the Eedur traders? now show us what strength you can put "forth; see, here are two swords for you to wear, take them!" So saying, he threw two swords into the room. Now, Gopâl Singh cried out with a loud voice to the Rânee, and said, "I am in your palace, under your protection." The Rânee upon this went to the raja and said, "If you slay Gopâl Singh after what has happened, I will die "along with him." The raja said, "If I leave him alive now he will "slay me." "Let precautions be taken," replied she, "of whatever "strictness you please, but his life must be spared." All the night and next day Gopâl Singh was allowed to remain where he was. When night came round again he determined he would make an attempt to clamber over the palace wall and escape. With this intention he went out, and was immediately cut down by the sentinel on guard, and died. After this, outcastes were sent for, and the corpses were by their means dragged into the yard of the palace. The raja ordered the outcastes to cut the bodies into pieces, that the kites might eat them. When the principal merchants of the place heard of this intention, they came to the palace and said, "Muhârâj! "you have punished those who had offended, you have no longer "any quarrel with these lumps of earth; allow them to be burned." The corpses were upon this placed together in a cart, and removed to the funeral ground, where they were consumed by fire; and after this the inhabitants of the palace broke their fast, for since Gopâl Singh had entered it no one had tasted a mouthful of food. The chief of Mhow left two sons, Bhârut Singh and Purwut Singh, of whom the elder was, at the time of his father's death, only seven years old. The followers of the slain chief, with his children and the other members of his family, fled to the mountains on hearing of the catastrophe at Eedur. Then the raja marched towards Mhow, and, having encamped near it, sent to call in the children of Gopâl Singh, and replaced them in their inheritance.

NOTE.—We have not met with, in the English records, any mention of the fate of Gopâl Singh, of Mhow. There had been no resident political agent in the Myhee Kântâ since the withdrawal of Lieutenant Colonel Ballantine, and, under these circumstances, a deed of this nature was only too likely to have been concealed from, or misrepresented to, the British authorities. All that is upon the records in relation to Raja Gumbheer Singh tends to strengthen the belief that such a crime, upon his part, was by no means unlikely. The treachery of his disposition is still notorious in the Eedur country, and is indicated by many other actions recorded by the bards. In A.D. 1821, Major Miles thus wrote of Raja Gumbheer Singh:—"The character of the present Raja of Eedur is represented "by the natives to be a mixture of craft, inconstancy and deceit. "He is reputed to be quite indifferent to persons' merits and means, "provided he can obtain his object. His want of faith is proverbial, "and there is scarce a man in the Eedur territory, I am told, who "would take his oath as the most trifling security for the performance "of his promise or engagement. In the management of his revenue "he is said to be profuse and improvident; he, however, uses every "means in his power to cheat his creditors and soldiery. He is "completely in the hands of the Brahmins and Gosaees, who "advance money at enormous rates of interest, and absorb his "revenues by anticipation. This bad character is, doubtless, "justified in some particulars, but seems exaggerated in others. The "raja appears a man of abilities, with a peculiar turn for intrigue "and artifice. His knowledge of mankind has made him superior "to most of his ministers and connections, and, as they frequently "find themselves no match for him in the management of politics, "they are more willing to cast the blame on his dissimulation than to "allow any want of parts or foresight in themselves. Again, his "character must be considered with reference to his situation and "the persons by whom he is surrounded, and with whom he has to "contend." Making every allowance, however, it must, we fear, be admitted that Raja Gumbheer Singh was a rare and consummate hypocrite, who exhibited in perfection the mixture of craft and cruelty which, among Rajpoots, is attributed as a distinguishing characteristic to the Râthor race. With the Glo'ster of Shakespeare, he, too, might have thus soliloquised—

> "Why, I can smile, and murther whiles I smile:
> "And cry content to that which grieves my heart;
> "And wet my cheeks with artificial tears,
> "And frame my face to all occasions."

CHAPTER XIV.

MUHÂRÂJÂ GUMBHEER SINGH OF EEDUR.

JHÂLUM SINGH succeeded his father, Ude Singh, in the estate of Mondeytee, about the year A.D. 1804. The chief of Gotâ, the brother of the late chief of Mondeytee, dying, and leaving no son, Jhâlum Singh purposed to assign the estate which thus fell to him to his son, Oomed Singh, whose mother was a daughter of the Chowra chief of Wursorâ. As, however, the estate was held under a separate grant from the crown, it was necessary that the raja should receive the young chief's obeisance on his installation. Jhâlum Singh sent his minister accordingly to Eedur, and the raja, giving his assent to the scheme, intimated his readiness to proceed to Mondeytee whenever a day should be appointed for the purpose of binding the turban of investiture upon Oomed Singh's head, and granting to him the right of receiving the royal embrace. On the appointed day Prince Oomed Singh repaired, as his father's representative, to Mondeytee. However, the prince had been betrothed to the lady Golâb Koonwerbâ, the daughter of Jhâlum Singh by his Râthor wife, and sister of the whole blood to Soorujmul and Sher Singh. The mother of his affianced bride, therefore, prevailed upon him to invest his brother-in-law, Sher Singh, instead of the son of the Chowra lady, an act which was the seed of much future calamity, and produced a bitter enmity between Jhâlum Singh and his Râthor wife and her sons, as well as between that chief and his sovereign.

Sher Singh took up his residence at Gotâ. His village of Rutunpoor marched with the Wulâsun chief's village of Khâskee, and both parties had posts of armed men in these places. In the rains a dispute arose between the cultivators of the two villages in regard to the boundary. They were separated for the time, but both parties went to their masters to complain. Each chief made the same reply—"If you had been men you would have fought it out." Next day, therefore, when the cultivators drove their ploughs to the disputed boundary, they took arms in their hands, and a fight ensued. One man was killed on Sher Singh's side, and others were wounded; on the other side there were many men wounded. When the chief of Gotâ heard of the result, he went to his father at Mondeytee, and begged for assistance, adding that if he should not receive it he would go to Wulâsun, and maintain the fight to the death, though there was a numerous garrison in that place. Jhâlum Singh upon this assembled his men, and in person led them to Wulâsun, and a contest ensued. The chief of Mondeytee sent to the Raja of Eedur, who offered to supply him with money and mercenaries, and dismissed his messenger with the remark that if the Wulâsun chief were victorious, the Marwaree honor would be gone, and he would some day make himself master of Mondeytee as well. The chief of Wulâsun sent also to beg for succour because half his estate belonged to the raja, but Gumbheer Singh made him a reply similar to that which he had made to Jhâlum Singh; in fact, he would be equally glad whichever way victory should be decided, provided only that one party or the other were a loser. Now there lived at Wulâsun a female ascetic who wore male attire, and assumed the male name of Mândâs. She was famous as a negociator, and in that capacity she came to Eedur and stated in a boasting style, in the raja's presence, that the men of Wâlusan had driven away the Marwarees in a manner much to the disgrace of the latter. Durjun Singh, the Prudhân, who was seated in court at the time, was much stung at this remark, because his own son and his brother were with the chief of Mondeytee. He wrote to Jhâlum Singh to say that he had better never show his face at Eedur again than come back without striking Wulâsun. He proffered at the same time a supply of money. The day before his letter reached Wulâsun a skirmish had taken place, but a neighbouring chief had come between the combatants. When the Prudhân's letter arrived, Jhâlum Singh attacked the place in earnest, and plundered and burnt it, carrying off prisoners and cattle, and leaving the chief of Khâskee dead on the field. There was an end of the matter for the time, and the Marwarees returned home. The power of the British has prevented the Wulâsun people from balancing the feud since, but they say that whenever that power shall be withdrawn they will have their revenge upon Mondeytee.

In A.D. 1820 the last of a collateral line of the Chohân clan died, and his villages were claimed by Raja Gumbheer Singh, on the ground that as they had been granted separately from the estate of Mondeytee they should now revert to the crown. Jhâlum Singh, however, refused his consent to this arrangement, and threatened to go out in rebellion. It was about this time that Colonel Ballantine was engaged in settling the Eedur country. Jhâlum Singh was confined by him, and regained his liberty four months after on condition of resigning the disputed estate, making other concessions to the raja, and giving security for his good behaviour during the next ten years.[1]

In A.D. 1826, the chief of Gorul died, leaving only a daughter, named Chând, who was married to the Raja Gumbheer Singh. The raja proclaimed that his father-in-law had given him the village as the dowry of his bride, and that he intended to place a garrison there, and

[1] The following occurs in a general report by Colonel Ballantine, dated Sadra, 15th October, 1822 :"—

"The conduct of this chief (Jhâlum Singh, of Mondeytee) was brought to the "notice of government in my report of 7th April last, and his defection proved. "The chief has since compromised his differences with Eedur by fine, and has "been restored, and has received his puttah afresh. * * * Each puttawut has his "zillayuts, whose footing is the same as his own with the raja. They enjoy lands "for service, and have, of course, been included in these arrangements. In this "puttah are four zillayuts, but the lands of the zillayuts are also the gift of Eedur, "and therefore obtain a similar claim and footing (*sic. orig.*). It is thus accounted "for :—On the establishment of the present dynasty the ancestors of the present "zillayuts were the followers, relations, or partizans, of the raja's puttawuts, and "received from Eedur provision lands under virtually similar tenure. The puttawut "cannot dispossess, but commands the service of his zillayuts, and the only "distinction is, they render separate securities to their immediate superiors, who "are thereby distinctly responsible for them. * * * This chief is allied to "Gumbheer Singh. His daughter is married to Oomed Singh, the heir apparent, "but the connection seems rather to have produced discord than union. "Jhâlum Singh is himself married to the daughter of the Row of Pol, and has by "her a son, his heir, Soorujmul. The son and mother have been long at variance "with him. For some time they took refuge at Eedur, and Gumbheer Singh "appears to have interested himself to obtain Soorujmul and his mother a subsist-"ence with no avail. Jhâlum Singh resented this, and was actually going into "rebellion at the time I summoned him. The son has since gone into service at "Seerohee, and the mother has returned to Pol."

either annex the estate to the crown, or give it to the rânee for her pin-money. The chief's widow was disposed to acquiesce in this arrangement, as the raja promised her an income from the estate. However, Jhâlum Singh, of Mondeytee, asserted that he was the adopted son of the deceased, and, so saying, he shaved his moustache, and proceeded to perform the obsequies which the raja had been desirous of performing. Gumbheer Singh was afraid of driving him out into rebellion, and determined therefore to humour him for the present, and wait for an opportunity. Thus the Gorul estate fell to Mondeytee. A year afterwards, Jhâlum Singh said to his eldest son, Soorujmul, "It was my original intention to have given the estate of "Gotâ to Oomed Singh, but your mother caused that to be given "to your brother, Sher Singh. I will, therefore, give this estate of "Gorul to Oomed Singh." Soorujmul did not agree to this, and Jhâmul Singh, on his refusal, flew into a passion, and went off immediately to the court of Mân Singh, Raja of Jodhpoor, where he remained six months.[1] However, he was not successful in obtaining service there, and he found his own expenses, and those of Oomed Singh, who was with him, growing heavy, so he went from Judhpoor to Kotah. At this latter place he obtained service, and there he remained for a year. Jhâlum Singh had hoped that when he went away Soorujmul would have followed him, and acquiesced in his wishes, but such was not the case. His son remained at Mondeytee, and administered the affairs of the larger portion of the estate, three villages only being in the hands of Jhâlum Singh's servants. At the end of the year, therefore, the chief returned to the Eedur country, and sent to tell Soorujmul that unless Gorul were given to Oomed Singh, he was determined to resign the whole estate into the hands of the raja. Soorujmul paid no attention to this threat, and his

[1] On the 24th of December, 1826, Colonel Ballantine thus writes to the resident at Baroda :—

"I have, also, on this occasion, been requested by Gumbheer Singh and Koon-"wer Soorujmul, of Mondeytee, to bring to the notice of government, that Thakor "Jhâlum Singh has for some time past quitted Mondeytee, and is reported to have "taken refuge with Raja Man Singh, of Jodhpoor. The Thakor was also last "year, for the most part, at Kotah, and has there taken service for his second son. "The reason assigned for this is family disputes, and a wish on the part of the "chief to disinherit Soorujmul, his eldest son and heir." Colonel Ballantine accordingly recommended that Soorujmul should be installed "in the vacant "estate." The resident, however, thought that it would be sufficient if the *management* were entrusted to Soorujmul on his father's behalf. This latter proposition was approved by the government of Bombay, and the arrangement was carried into effect in April, 1827, but annulled in the following June.

father at last began to entertain mercenaries. When Soorujmul received intelligence of this step, he wrote to his father, to ask why he was assembling men, and to say that the estate of Mondeytee might be given to any one he pleased, for that he himself had determined on retiring to Bhownugger, or elsewhere, to procure service. The chief wrote in reply, offering to give his son two villages for the present, and assuring him of the succession to the whole estate on his own death, but demanding that he should in the meantime retire from Mondeytee. Soorujmul refused his consent, and went off in anger to Ahmednugger, where he assembled three hundred matchlock men, and such of his father's vassals as were on his side. In March, 1829, he came at midnight with his troops to the neighbourhood of Nâdree, where his father was, and having given strict orders that not a gun should be fired, prepared to surprise the village. However, the troops as soon as they approached the place fired a volley, and the arrival of Soorujmul thus becoming known, he was opposed by his father's followers, while Jhâlum Singh himself, conceiving the attacking party to be stronger than his own could engage with safety, retreated with his Chowra lady, and having placed her in security at a village in the Dântâ territory, fled himself to the hills. Soorujmul now took possession of Nâdree, and placed a garrison there. He then returned to Mondeytee, and made it again his residence.

It being now five years since the death of Prince Oomed Singh, the raja himself demanded in marriage the lady Goolâb, Soorujmul's sister, who had been betrothed to his son. The chief of Mondeytee and his Râthor wife were neither of them pleased at this proposal, as the raja was now an old man, but Soorujmul agreed to give his sister to Gumbheer Singh, on condition of receiving his support against his father. When Jhâlum Singh was driven to the hills, it occurred to him that Soorujmul would seize the opportunity for marrying his sister to the raja. He wrote privately, therefore, to the lady's mother, to send her to him, that he might arrange her marriage with a suitable husband. The young lady was sent accordingly, and her father caused her to be married to the chief of Sulâna, a cadet of Rutlâm.

Jhâlum Singh had by this time collected six hundred Arab and Mukrânee matchlock men, with whom he soon after made a night attack upon Nâdree. Kânjee, the captain of Soorujmul's garrison, however, fought with great bravery, and repulsed the assailants.

> "Like an angry tiger came on the son of Udmâl;
> "But Kâneeo, like a black snake, kept hold of Nâdree."

Jhâlum Singh retired to a position among the hills, where a thick forest sheltered his men, having in his retreat set fire to one of Soorujmul's villages. A few days afterwards he prepared to attack Mondeytee, where his son himself lay with a small garrison. The young chief's spies, however, informed him of his father's advance, and he wrote immediately to his agent at Eedur to call upon the raja for his promised assistance. Gumbheer Singh agreed to comply with the call, and assembled troops. All that day, however, wore away, and next day the raja moved with his troops in a northerly direction, intimating to the agent that it was his intention to interpose between Jhâlum Singh and Mondeytee. That chief had, however, attacked the place on the preceding night. Soorujmul's men were protected by the buildings, and under their fire thirty-five of the assailants fell, but six of his small garrison, who defended a round tower, which contained the ammunition, were destroyed by its explosion. The young chief himself was wounded in the hand with a matchlock ball, but he retained possession of the town. Next day one of the neighbouring chiefs came up, and some of the inhabitants of Mondeytee went out to Jhâlum Singh, and persuaded him to come to an agreement with his son, for that his face would be blackened in case Soorujmul were killed, and it was thus at length arranged that Soorujmul should surrender Mondeytee, on condition that two villages were assigned to him during his father's lifetime, and that the succession was secured to him. The young chief, upon this, taking his mother with him, quitted Mondeytee for the villages which were assigned to him, and Jhâlum Singh re-entered his town.

Soorujmul, however, for fear of his father, began at once to look out for a more secure place of retirement, but none of the chiefs would receive him. He retired to Koowâwoo, where there is a mansion, enclosed within a fortified wall. The village belonged to bards, who were not pleased at the presence of such a visitor. Soorujmul pacified them by saying that it was not his intention to remain a longer time than should suffice for his recovery from his wound. However, at this time, the raja happened to come into the neighbourhood, and the bards went to him, and obtained his written permission to their allowing Soorujmul to remain. The chief staid, therefore, at the bards' village for a considerable period, and at length, leaving his family there, went to Ahmednugger, and took service with Raja Kurun Singh, who gave him a village and a pair of kettle-drums.

In the year A.D. 1833, Raja Gumbheer Singh became a Dev. Fourteen Rânees became sutees with his corpse, but the mother of the present raja, Jowân Singh, remained alive to rear her infant son.

"Many stars fell to the earth,
"The earth quaked,
"Cows lowed in the night time,
"Terribly sounded their cry.
"Indra poured down little rain,
"Hail fell from the sky,
"Clouds obscured the face of the sun,
"Gusts of wind blew:
"From these omens they prophesied
"That a great man would fall:
"Then died the raja of the race of the sun![1]

[1] The earthquakes and the fall of meteors here mentioned were actual occurrences. A.D. 1833, was a year of uncommon scarcity, if not of famine. The Bombay government write thus to the Court of Directors, on the 10th of December, in that year:—

"The political superintendent of Pahlunpoor reports the entire destruction of "the monsoon crops, which had caused the price of grain to rise to a height "unknown since the famine of 1812-13. With a view to afford every facility to "the importation of grain, and to alleviate, as far as possible, the distress caused "to the poorer classes, the Dewan of Pahlunpoor had, at the suggestion of Lieu-"tenant Prescott, altogether removed the transit duties upon imported grain, and "the greater part of this district being, fortunately, favourable to irrigation, every "encouragement has been given to cultivators to sink wells for that purpose, by "which means the present scarcity will be partially removed. There is still, how-"ever, much reason to apprehend that the Koolees and other turbulent characters "throughout Goozerat, deprived of employment by the failure of their crops, and "rendered desperate by the present high price of food, will assemble in bands, and "threaten the public tranquillity, for the preservation of which every practicable "measure of precaution has been taken.

"On the 16th of August, Mr. Willoughby states, that up to that period there "had been a general failure of rain almost throughout Kateewar, and no prospect "of a timely supply to save the crops. A great scarcity of grain and forage was "the consequence, and large remissions of tribute, due to the British and Guikowar "governments, would become necessary. The price of grain had trebled in "amount, and was still rising; the want of forage was principally felt, great "numbers of cattle were dying daily. Mr. Willoughby further states, that in his "opinion, one half of the ordinary amount paid by the tributaries would have to "be remitted.

"The very bad accounts received from the districts to the N.W. and S.W. of "Bhooj, induced the resident to make a tour through them, to satisfy himself by "personal observation. These reports appear not to have been exaggerated. In "many places there had been no rain this year, and a very scanty supply last "season, owing to which the forage had totally failed, and cattle perished from "starvation in large numbers. On most other occasions of drought in this pro-"vince, the people had Guzerat, Kateewar and Sinde to retire to with their "families and herds, but this resource has failed them this year. The durbar has "resolved to alleviate the sufferings of the working class by giving them a seer of "grain daily for deepening the tanks near the city, to which the minister has "added a quarter of a seer at his own expense.

"Subsequent to the date of this report, some rain had fallen, but the hopes thus "excited were dissipated, and the prospects of the season rendered more gloomy

"Gumbheer raja fell,
"Whose splendour among Hindoos was unbroken.
"When the dwellers in the queens' apartments heard the news,
"The sutees, with delight, cried Hur! Hur![1]
"'For the salvation of my race,
"'To increase the splendour of the three lines of ancestors,[2]
"'I will accompany my lord,
"'That my fame may be blazoned in the nine divisions of the world.'
"Such a determination in their hearts fixing,
"They called the 'Great Splendour' to witness,
"'If I remain behind my husband,
"'Where is my queenly virtue?'

"From love of their husband, the women,
"Though many, were delighted in mind.
"From love of their husband, the women
"In their hearts allowed hope to expand.
"From love of their husband, the women
"Prepared a last procession.
"From love of their husband, the women
"Caused drums to be sounded and songs to be sung.
"True wives of the son of Bhuwân, then raised they the cry
"'The bright road let us travel,
"'With her husband who refuses to burn,
"'Where is her love to her lord?'

"At this time, so many
"With earnestness spoke the speech,
"Making the true wife's vow
"To bathe in the bath of fire:—
"First, Dolut, the princess,
"The Bhâtee's daughter, splendid as Doorgâ;
"Princess Jushoo, the Chohân,
"She whom the people called Mother;
"Of great truth, the Seesodeâ's daughter,
"Princess Ujub, an increasing moon;
"When the sutees joined the mighty raja
"Their fame cast light around them.

"Princess Lâl, the Uhuree,
"A sutee like Junuk's daughter;[3]

"by the appearance of large flghts of locusts, which have entirely overspread the "country, and utterly destroyed the crops of every kind. This scourge has reduced "the people to despair, they cannot be induced to sow the seed for the after-crops, "and the durbar, it is believed, will not recover more than one-fourth of its "accustomed revenue."

[1] A name of Shiva.

[2] The sutee's virtues benefit the families of her father, her mother, and her husband's father.

[3] Junuk's daughter is Seetâ, the wife of Râm.

"Wukhut princess, the Chowra,
"Like incarnate Gungâ;
"Chund, the Chohân lady,
"Who resembled Bhuwânee;
"Like a vision of Pârwutee,
"Princess Wudun, the vow-performer;
"Concubines both, Nâthee and Wunâ,
"With joy and hope prepared for the pile;
"With the fort-lord, Gumbheer,
"The women set forth to burn.

"Oomeydâ went with joy,
"For sut-performing she presented herself;
"Jusoobâee, the nurse's daughter,
"To burn her body prepared;
"An auspicious day perceiving it,
"To prove their virtue they went forth;
"A double line they formed,
"Each line touching their lord.
"With words of courage they spoke,—
"'This age of iron, frail as a creeping shrub, what is its value?
"'To the city of sutees going, we will there remain,
"'Our husband's service we will perform there.'
"With words of courage they spoke,
"At the time whose good deeds cannot be destroyed.[1]
"Each of them went to her chamber,
"To bathe in the Ganges water.
"Each of them dressed in handsome clothes,
"Each of them assumed her jewels,
"Necklaces of pearls
"Each with joy put on.
"In great splendour at that time,
"Knowing it to be a deed of religion;
"With the royal son of Bhuwân,
"The sutees set forth to burn.

"In the year called ninety,
"In the nineteenth century from Vikrum's time,
"In the time of rain, rain not having fallen,
"When the sun had finished half his course,
"In the month of Shrâwun, when the moon was dark,
"On the moon's day, on the eleventh of the month,
"Five hours after sun-rise,
"Departed the soul of Gumbheer.
"That whole day and night the corpse lay in the queen's apartments
"That the sutees might be ready to accompany it.
"When the night departed,
"In the morning, they set forth to the pile.

[1] At the time of death, that is, when good deeds cannot be cancelled by any future ill-deed.

" Sounded many noises :
" The copper drums sounded ;
" The smaller drums also ;
" Though the task was mournful, it was joyfully accomplished ;
" It seemed as if a raja with his rânees set forth on a pilgrimage.
" Gumbheer Singh and the queens,
" With smiles on their faces,
" Seemed the moon sinking to its setting
" Midst a company of stars.
" At each step they gained fame ;
" At each step they performed a 'horse sacrifice.'
" Virtuous gifts they gave as they went ;
" Abandoning the love of home,
" Thinking only of their lord,
" Regarding their bodies as blades of grass.
" What bardic honor shall I give these sutees ?
" Call other women '*tender*,' if you will ;
" These are *hardy*,[1] strong as warriors.

" At the last place
" The sutees arrived,
" They worshipped the sun,
" They uttered these words,—
" 'O, Day-causer ! O, Dev !
" 'That aidest always the sutee,
" 'In this good Eedur,
" 'May I be married in another birth,
" 'May my husband always be the son of Bhuwân.'
" Thus saying, they made obeisance to the sun,
" Remembering their husbands in their hearts.
" Turning back, they moved haughtily
" Towards the funeral pile.

" Praise to the Bhâtee race,
" Whose fame is in the earth !
" Praise to the Seesodeeâ clan !
" Praise to the clan Chohân !
" Praise to the clan Chowra !
" Whose daughters with their husband departing,
" In fire consume their bodies.
" Praise to the prince who married you !
" Wives such as you are ships that bear your husband across the ocean
" of existence.

" The fame of your race you have increased ;
" Great joy you have caused to spring up ;
" As you repeated the name of Vishnoo,
" Good men who heard your words
" Took vows to abandon the world ;

[1] The opposition in the original is between *Ubulâ* and *Subulâ*, two words compounded of the word *bul*, strength, with the affixes, *U* and *Su*, of negation and affirmation. *Ubula* is, however, commonly used to mean "a woman."

"Cowards began to tremble with shame;
"Kshutrees felt their courage inflamed;
"The fame of the Râthor was established.
"A great deed of virtue you exhibited to the world,
"With your lord abandoning the body."[1]

[1] The following account of the circumstances which attended and followed the death of Raja Gumbheer Singh is derived from a despatch of the Bombay government to the Court of Directors, dated 8th October, 1833:—

"We have the honor to communicate to your honorable Court the death of "Gumbheer Singh, the Raja of Eedur, which took place on the 12th August last, "on which occasion the political commissioner for Goozerat deputed his first "assistant, Mr. Erskine, to Eedur, with a view to prevent any disturbances arising "in consequence of this event, and at the same time to signify to the several chiefs "the desire of the British government to continue the succession in the person of "the only son of the late raja; and it is now our painful duty to report to your "honorable Court the deplorable tragedy which occurred in the performance of "the funeral rites of the deceased.

"The death of the raja, who had been for several days in a state of stupor, was "for some time concealed, and remained unknown to the mother of the young "raja until after the funeral ceremony; but the other seven rânees or wives took "the resolution of burning with their husband, and, accordingly, early on the "morning of the 13th August, these infatuated women, two concubines of different "caste from the raja, one principal personal servant, and four domestic slave "women, were taken down with the corpse, and burnt with it before the whole "assembled population of Eedur, the ministers and every person of authority "aiding in the horrid ceremony. Nor was any effort made by a single person con-"nected with the raja's family, or having any influence at Eedur, to dissuade any "of the parties from taking this fatal step. It is stated by Mr. Erskine that one "of the rânees was several months advanced in pregnancy, and another, who "throughout showed a disinclination to the sacrifice, had never cohabited with the "raja. The eldest in years, who was the second in rank, was aged sixty, and the "youngest, to whom the raja had only been married nineteen months, was only "twenty years of age. Notwithstanding the religious prejudices of the people, "an universal feeling of horror and disgust is said to prevail against the principal "actors in this atrocity, and it is the general belief that if proper means had been "taken, there would not have been more than three lives sacrificed. It is related "by an eye-witness, that just before the lighting of the pile, the eldest rânee "addressed the ministers, saying, that she herself had all along resolved upon im-"molating herself, and that no expostulations would have any effect upon her, but "that it was strange that she had not heard a word of dissuasion or compassion "expressed by any one, and she concluded by desiring them to go and live on the "plunder they were securing to themselves by the destruction of their chief's "whole family. The ministers were influenced by personal interest in sparing the "life of the surviving rânee, she being the mother of the raja's only son, and her "loss might have been prejudicial to their views."

CHAPTER XV.

SETTLEMENT OF THE MYHEE KÂNTÂ.

In the year A.D. 1828, the Raja Gumbheer Singh had struck the village of Keeree, which belonged to Futteh Singh, the chief of Roopâl. Futteh Singh laid a complaint before Major Miles, the British agent at Pâhlunpoor,[1] who then temporarily superintended the Myhee Kântâ, and that officer, after a time, decreed that the raja should pay a sum of money for having plundered the village. The sum was much too large, and hence it became a proverb in Eedur that "the ant (Keeree) has become an elephant." However, the raja never to the day of his death paid the money, and the chief of Roopâl began to think of going out in rebellion, or seizing some substantial hostage from Eedur, in order to procure a ransom for him. Now, Khemchund, one of the Eedur ministers, had a brother named Ukhechund, who was a merchant, and about this time Ukhechund put up for a night at Roopâl, on his way home to Eedur from Pertâpgurh, with a valuable investment of piece goods, opium, and other merchandise, under the protection of ten matchlock men. The chief of Roopâl entertained the merchant very attentively, and the next morning sent off the goods with the escort, and pressed Ukhechund to remain to dinner, promising to see him safe home to Eedur. After dinner he set off with the merchant, attended by ten horsemen, under pretence of an escort, but when he reached a place convenient for his purpose, he made his guest a prisoner, and carried him off into the forest. The merchant offered to pay any sum that might be demanded as the price of his liberty, but Futteh Singh said it was not money he wanted, but a letter to the minister, Khemchund, to ensure the payment of the sum decreed in compensation for Keeree, or at least an arrangement that nothing should be demanded in the way of tribute from Roopâl until that sum were absorbed. The merchant wrote, as he was required to do, to Khemchund, but that minister replied that he had no power in the matter, the Eedur state having been attached by the British government.[2] Upon this, the

[1] Lieutenant Prescott, and not Major Miles, appears to have been the Superintendent of Pahlunpoor at the time of this award.

[2] "After the death of Gumbheer Singh," say the Bombay government, in their despatch to the Court of Directors of the 16th September, 1834, "the powers of the

chief of Roopâl proceeded to give Ukhechund much annoyance; he kept him without food for days, beat him, put powder into his ear and set it alight. The merchant now offered to pay double the sum in dispute out of his own means, but Futteh Singh said that would be no use, as he should not be allowed to keep the money. At length Khemchund sent for Soorujmul, of Mondeytee, and told him that he would give him a large sum of money, for which he passed a bond, on condition of obtaining his brother's release. Soorujmul, therefore, set out from Koowâwoo, where he then resided, to look after the chief of Roopâl. Now, the Bheels of the village of Wâvree were at feud with Roopâl, because many of them had been killed by the Rehwur clan, to which Futteh Singh belonged. Soorujmul engaged these Bheels to bring him intelligence of the chief. They disguised themselves in the costume of various wandering tribes, and searched until they discovered where Futteh Singh was. Soorujmul having obtained this information, began privately to raise mercenaries, of whom he assembled two hundred at Ahmednugger and Morâsâ, and two hundred more at Teentoee. He remained himself at Koowâwoo until he was joined by his vassals' horse, and then taking the mercenary matchlock men with him, he advanced, guided by the

" state had been usurped by a person of disreputable character, named Chajooram, " who was formerly employed under the late raja's eldest son, Oomed Singh, and " succeeded in pillaging that young prince of a considerable property. He was " afterwards employed by Gumbheer Singh, on the death of Laljee Sahib, as his " Deewan, and was for some time nominally his prime minister. Gumbheer Singh, " however, who latterly managed his own affairs, had for some time before his " death entirely withdrawn all confidence in him, and though he nominally bore " the name of Deewan till the raja's death, he was never employed or consulted " by the raja on the affairs of state. Through the means of Peetojee, the ranee's " brother, he found means to ingratiate himself with her, and being assisted by " Jhâlum Singh, the chief of Mondeytee, who has long been associated with him " in his evil practices, he carried on the whole of the business, and continued the " system of plunder which he commenced on the occasion of the sutees, reported " in our letter, dated 8th October, 1833. He was the principal agent in that cruel " sacrifice of human life, and in consequence of his unfeeling conduct on that oc- " casion, and his oppression of the ryots in numerous instances, he had rendered " himself almost universally detested throughout the Eedur districts. * * * As " it was evident that under this management both the property of the young prince, " of which the British government is the guardian, would suffer most considerably, " and the public revenue be so plundered that the government would find it difficult, " if not impossible, to perform its engagement with H. H. the Guikowar, the " Political Commissioner recommended, and we accordingly sanctioned, the ap- " pointment of a regency during the young raja's minority, consisting of the follow- " ing persons, viz.: The Ranee, Durjun Singh of Kookreea (the Prudhan), Humeer " Singh (of Soor), cousin of the late raja, and Meerjee Shettya, Karbharee of " Jhâlum Singh, of Mondeytee."

Bheels, towards the Roopâl chief's retreat. As the Mondeytee force came up, a Brahmin, who cooked for Ukhechund, and a Bheel were standing together upon an eminence. Soorujmul's men fired at them, wounded the Brahmin in the foot, and shot the Bheel dead. When the Roopâl chief heard the report of the matchlocks he thrust the merchant into a pit, and stood beside him with a drawn dagger, ready to slay him if he uttered a sound. His son, Gokuljee, stood in like manner beside the Brahmin. Thus they were prevented from raising the alarm, and Soorujmul's men, having hunted everywhere without discovering them, at length gave up the search, and passed on to Roopâl and Chândunee, at which latter place they halted fifteen days. Soorujmul wrote from thence to Khemchund, telling him to forward money for the payment of the mercenaries, but the minister refused to make any advance, and said that Soorujmul had done him mischief instead of good. The troops now began to clamour for pay, and Soorujmul having no means of satisfying them, led them back to Roopâl, from which place he drove off the cattle, and took hostages. The animals were priced, and distributed among the mercenaries, and the money which was obtained as ransom for the captives was also shared among them, but their demands were still incompletely satisfied. Soorujmul therefore led his men to Bokhâr, a Roopâl village, and commenced plundering it. Now, the chief of Roopâl had shortly before seized a quantity of opium belonging to a merchant, and placed it in the house of a Brahmin of Bokhâr. Soorujmul being informed of the fact, demanded the opium from the Brahmin. The priest and his wife, however, immediately resorted to means of intimidation; they wounded themselves, and sprinkled with their blood those who attempted to enter the house. The Rajpoots, therefore, desisted from their attempt, but carried off the cattle and other property of the village, which was distributed among the troops, as before. The Mondeytee chief, after this, plundered two or three of the Eedur villages, because the minister refused to satisfy his demand. He now retired to a forest, called "Phârkee," in the neighbourhood of Mondeytee, and from thence levied contributions on the Eedur villages for grass, opium, tobacco, sugar-cane, and other necessaries. Whenever the villages refused submission to his demands, he plundered them: but the mercenaries' pay was not made up notwithstanding. The mercenaries at Phârkee now fasted for two or three days, compelling Soorujmul to fast also, and they threatened him. He made them promises, and induced them to accompany him to Wurâlee, where he encamped beside a reservoir, and laid the surrounding villages under contribution.

In the year A.D. 1835, Raja Kurun Singh, of Ahmednugger, died. Mr. Erskine, the British agent, was then at Wuktâpoor, a few miles from that capital. When he heard the news he went to Ahmednugger, to prevent the Rânees becoming sutees. The corpse lay for three days, the belly having been opened and filled with spices. On the third day, some Rajpoot chiefs were sent to Mr. Erskine to urge that the women would not be burned by force, but at their own desire, and that it was their custom from the time of their ancestors. Mr. Erskine detained the ambassadors, but sent no reply. The Rajpoots in the town, therefore, called in Bheels from the surrounding country, and sent word to Soorujmul to advance with his troops, determining that they would burn the women secretly if they could, or otherwise resist the British agent if he came to prevent them by force. Soorujmul, however, did not come up until it was too late. The Bheels secretly erected a funeral pile on the side of the town furthest removed from the British encampment; they placed within it much cotton, clarified butter, cocoa-nut shells, and other inflammable substances. Mr. Erskine had set guards at all the gates of the town, and the Rajpoots therefore opened a new one, and, in the middle of the night, armed themselves, and carried the sutees out by it. There were three Rânees upon whom the desire of accompanying their lord came; they were daughters of a Deora chief of the house of Seerohee, of the Chowra of Wursorâ, and of the Rehwur of Runâsun. The Rajpoots had taken the precaution of placing Bheels to watch Mr. Erskine's camp, and when the sutees were burned the flame of the pile, rising high into the air, attracted the attention of the British agent, who sent to ascertain the cause. The Bheels opposed this advanced party, and let fly arrows at them. The agent then mounted, and moved on with his force, but the affair was over, and the Rajpoots retired; however, one British officer was shot by the Bheels.[1]

[1] *Mr. Erskine to the Resident at Baroda, 9th February,* 1835.

"The camp was removed about eight o'clock, and all was quiet till an alarm "was given, about half-past two o'clock in the morning, that the pile was on fire. "The Guikowâr horse were encamped between the ground we formerly occupied "and the river, on the banks of which the pile had been erected, and I have been "informed this morning that the cries and supplications of the women were so "vociferous, that every man who was asleep started from his bed. Enough "people to perpetrate the violence were taken, but no more, and the women were "dragged over a broken part of the wall, on the river side, by these ruffians, "attended by Kurun Singh's two sons, and, with the utmost haste, hurried into "the pile, which, saturated with oil and clarified butter, was set fire to, and the

Soorujmul arrived in the neighbourhood of Ahmednugger the day after the death of the sutees, and sent forward a party of horse to reconnoitre. They came to Ahmednugger, and seeing what had happened, returned and reported to the chief, who thereupon moved back again to the reservoir at Wurâlee.

Mr. Erskine wrote to Soorujmul to say, that as he had fled like a hare he would follow him like a hound. The chief thereupon sent his family to Pânowrâ, and retired himself to the celebrated hill, named the Ghoonwo, which is surrounded by a thick forest. The British agent, when he had received reinforcements, moved upon Gotâ, accompanied by eleven officers. There was a sheep fastened at the door of Soorujmul's house. A trooper of the British detachment came to carry it off, and was shot dead. Many other men were killed, and among them, one of the British officers, but the village was not taken. During the night Soorujmul's aunt, the widow of the Row of Pol, made her escape, under the escort of some Bheels, to Pânowrâ. In the morning the attack was resumed, but noon came, and the village was not yet captured. The Koolee chief of Dhuroee, who was with the British, now asked for permission to break into the village, as he was at feud with Soorujmul. He broke into the place where the horses were picketted, and the troops entered the village and burnt it. Several Rajpoots were killed or wounded; among them, Rutno Râthor fell, after killing many of the assailants: the mark of his sword upon a tree is still pointed out by the villagers.

"People say that of old
" The headless corpse fought on,
" O! man-jewel Rutno! the tradition
" You preserved, brave son of Sher Singh!

When Soorujmul, who was at the Ghoonwo hill, a few miles off, heard the report of musketry, and saw the flames of the burning village, he sent out scouts, who learnt what had happened from people whom they met flying from the village, and, returning, gave information to their chief. Upon this, Soorujmul proceeded immediately to Gotâ, with his Rajpoot horse, and four hundred matchlock men. The British detachment was then at the village reservoir; many who had been wounded were already placed in litters and some were refreshing themselves beside the tank. Soorujmul sent

" abomination completed. Any attempt to prevent the sutee must have been too " late, as, when I was informed of the fire, I beheld the extensive blaze, and knew " that all was over."

For further details, supplied by the English Records, see the note at the end of this chapter.

forward his matchlock men to a ravine, through which the road from Gotâ to Wurâlee passes, and, when the British force moved, he followed them with his horsemen until they fell into the ambuscade, where many of them were killed and wounded. People say that another British officer was killed there.

The detachment reached Wurâlee, and from thence retreated by Eedur to Sâdrâ.[1] Soorujmul returned to the Ghoonwo, and, seizing

[1] The following account of the affair at Gotâ is derived from a letter addressed to Mr. Erskine by Captain Delamain, dated Eedur, 22nd February, 1835:—

"I have the honor to report that I reached the position stated to be occupied "by Soorujmul at daybreak yesterday morning, and found it deserted. Upon "enquiry, I was given to understand that he had moved off two days previously "to, or in the direction of, a village named Gotâ, about two coss distant, which is "held by his brother, and it was thought probable that he was staying with him "in the vicinity. I instantly directed the march upon that village, and on the "advance-guard riding up the principal avenue of the village, a shot was at once "directed upon them from a high ghurree, and in a few minutes firing commenced "in several quarters on both sides. The result has been twenty-five prisoners, "the whole of the men in the village at the time, exclusive of four or five that were "killed.

"I regret to have to state that the loss we have sustained in this affair is most "severe, and much more than the object would warrant, could it have been "anticipated. It was wholly caused by about seven men who had taken position "in a very strong and lofty ghurree, situated in the midst of a courtyard, without "the means of ascent, except by a small door which was commanded from the "apertures of the outhouses forming the court, in the intricacies of which some of "the enemy were posted. Their shots were unerring, and the whole of their "defence most creditable to them as men. I before lamented the number of "casualties. I must now acquaint you, with the greatest concern, that Lieutenant "Pottinger is among the number killed. He fell most gallantly heading an advance, "and although brought on to this place, expired about ten o'clock last night. "His body I have this moment dispatched to your camp to prevent delay, and its "arrival this letter will, I hope, precede.

"The village of Gotâ was for the most part consumed. I must beg here to "acquaint you that the intelligence received by you, and communicated to me, as "to the nature of the country, is most incorrect. It consists of rocky eminences "covered with dense jungle, and is altogether quite impracticable to cavalry, as "far as their use is concerned, placing, indeed, infantry at a serious disadvantage. "This was exemplified on our evacuating the village yesterday. Soorujmul "(who was at hand) came down with his followers, and opened a fire upon "the rear of the cavalry through the jungle, killing a trooper. To have attacked "him was impossible, and would only have added to the loss already sustained "from him. The infantry I had at this time detached a short way in advance in "charge of the prisoners, and they were not available.

"I had intended halting for the night at Wurâlee, but a mistake having caused "us to advance a coss on this side of it in search of a tank and open ground which "I had observed in the morning, but which would not answer our purpose, as I "afterwards found, we continued our march to this place and arrived at eight "o'clock, the men and horses extremely fatigued.

a trader of Gulorâ as a hostage for his subsistence, carried him off to Pânowrâ. The British agent came afterwards with two guns to Ahmednugger and Eedur. At the latter place he sent for Jhâlum Singh, of Mondeytee, and told him that he must call in his son. Soorujmul was at this time at Phârkee. Jhâlum Singh mentioned to the agent where he was, but at the same time sent to Soorujmul telling him to make his escape. When the force reached Phârkee, therefore, Soorujmul had escaped, but he fled so hastily that he left his carpet spread on the ground, and dropped the saddle off his camel; he left behind him, too, the trader whom he had seized. There is a lake called Ghorâduroo, between Phârkee and Pol, beside which Soorujmul halted. The British agent continued to threaten Jhâlum Singh, and he, thinking that the troops would not venture to follow him there, mentioned that his son was at Ghorâduroo. However, the British troops advanced thither, the chief of Mondeytee having hardly time to send word to his son. Soorujmul fired on the troops and then took to flight. In this retreat his brother, Sher Singh, who was with him, became giddy and had nearly been made prisoner; however, his followers carried him up the mountain side. Soorujmul again retired to Pânowrâ.

Meanwhile Jhâlum Singh, who was at feud with the villagers of Koowâwoo because they had sheltered his son when he was at enmity with him, persuaded the British agent that the chief of Roopâl and the Ahmednugger rajas, Pruthee Singh and Tukhut Singh, who were in outlawry about the matter of the sutees, and Soorujmul himself, were all of them at Koowâwoo. The agent moved to that place, therefore, with a body of cavalry. The bards to whom the village belonged (among whom was the narrator of this story) were summoned to the agent's presence, and questioned as to where Soorujmul was. They said they did not know, upon which the troops began to batter the town; the fort wall was destroyed by the cannon, and the village was plundered and burnt. Many of the villagers escaped, but many were taken and carried off with the cattle, which were also seized, to the head quarters of the British force at Wurâlee. The troops after this

"I herewith send a return of the killed and wounded; the men returned missing "have probably been taken or killed by the enemy. They were, I imagine, led by "the hope of plunder to continue in the village after the assembly had been sounded, "not being aware of the proximity of Soorujmul and his followers."

"To effect his capture or destruction will not, I imagine, be easy, as of course "he will retire from strong to stronger country. With two hundred infantry I do "not think I should be warranted in attacking his force in country of this de- "scription. I have no doubt I could make him retire, but the loss on our side "would be tenfold, and without, I think, corresponding benefit."

advanced to Pânowrâ to seize Soorujmul; a fight took place there, and an officer and fifty men of the attacking force were killed. Pânowrâ was taken and burnt, and the inhabitants fled from it. The troops next burned Mânpoor, in Mewar. Soorujmul and his family meanwhile fled to the hills, and his wife, whose name was Jodheejee, travelled in a miserable condition through these wild places, her feet pierced with thorns, and her strength exhausted with the weight of her little daughter (afterwards married to Raja Jowân Singh, of Eedur), whom she was forced to carry with her on her hip.

When the British force retired to Sâdrâ, the town of Pânowrâ was restored, and Soorujmul leaving his family there, returned to the neighbourhood of Koowâwoo, rushing occasionally from the hills to plunder the territory of Eedur. At this time the principal of an Uteet monastery at Sidhpoor having died, the succession to his authority was disputed by two of his disciples. One of them, whose name was Râj Bhârtee, changing his attire to that of a Rajpoot, went out in rebellion and joined Soorujmul. He promised to find pay for that chief's mercenaries, if he would espouse his cause. Soorujmul agreed, and commenced incursions upon the country around Sidhpoor. One day Soorujmul and Râj Bhârtee came with eighteen horsemen, and halted on the banks of the Suruswutee, near Sidhpoor, where they cooked their dinner, giving out to the passers-by that they were people of Eedur, on their way to a celebration of obsequies at Pâhlunpoor. In the evening, however, the Rajpoots entered the market-place with the intention of seizing the head merchant of the town. They could not discover this person, and, therefore, went to the house of another mercantile man, named Lukhoo Shet, and asked the clerk where his master was, stating that they wished to cash a bill. The clerk said that he would cash the bill for them without disturbing his master, who was at dinner upstairs. The Rajpoots dismounted, and going upstairs, seized the Shet, whom they hustled out of his house into the street, where one of the party put him on his horse, like a bundle of hay, and the whole gallopped off down the street. The alarm was raised in the market-place, and when the horsemen reached the town gate they found the door swinging on its hinges. One of the Rajpoots abused the doorkeeper, and drew his sword upon him, and he opened the door. Soorujmul and his party now took the road to Oduv. The Guikowâr commander in Sidhpoor sent his cavalry in pursuit, but as these had no hope of reward, they followed the Rajpoots leisurely for a time, and then returned home. Soorujmul went on from Oduv to the Ghoonwo and Pânowrâ. Lukhoo Shet petitioned that he might be well treated, and released on paying a ransom, but Soorujmul, though he assented to the first part of the proposal, declined the second, saying that the Uteet's affairs must first be settled. The merchant gave Soorujmul bills, which his followers cashed, aud supplied themselves and their prisoner. The mercantile body at Sidhpoor now complained to the government of Baroda, declaring that they would leave the town deserted unless Lukhoo Shet were restored to liberty. The Guikowâr ministry, thereupon wrote to Captain Outram, who was then the British agent in the Myhee Kântâ, to procure the release of the merchant. That officer advanced to Eedur, and called in all the outlaws on security for their good treatment. First of all came in Soorujmul, and threw down his sword, receiving a pardon from the agent. The chief then said that his mercenaries would harass him for their arrears of pay, and that he had not the means of supporting even himself. Two of the Mondeytee villages were therefore assigned to him, and he disbanded his troops, with the exception of twenty horsemen. He was appointed by the Eedur government captain of the garrison of Bheelorâ, and his troops were taken into pay. His vassals, also, who had been out in rebellion, were restored to their estates. His companion, Râj Bhârtee, surrendered to the Guikowâr government, who, after detaining him in confinement for some months, accepted a sum of money as an offering, and placed him on the cushion of the monastery at Sidhpoor, where he still resides, with the reputation of being a very wealthy man. In a similar manner the outlaws of Ahmednugger, Roopâl, and other places were restored to their homes, and peace was established throughout the territory of Eedur.

In the year A.D. 1838, Jhâlum Singh, the chief of Mondeytee, died, and Soorujmul succeeded him in the possession of his hereditary estate, while his brother, Sher Singh, retained the lands of Rutunpoor and Gotâ.

Appended Note on the Final Proceedings in the Myhee Kanta, as described in the English Records.

Bombay Government Despatch of the 17th of September, 1835.

"When Mr. Erskine arrived at Ahmednugger, on the 16th of February last, whither he had proceeded with a force of three hundred men at his disposal, to put down some disturbances quite distinct from this event, he was informed that Kurun Singh, the raja of that district, was not expected to live out the day. Mr. Erskine upon this endeavoured to ascertain whether a compulsory sutee with the raja's wives, who were seven in number, was contemplated, as in the case of the Eedur raja's death, in August, 1833. He could not procure any satisfactory information. The raja died late in the evening of the 6th of February, which fact was concealed until the following evening, when it became openly a matter of conversation that five out of seven widows would be sacrificed at the funeral pile. Early on the morning of the 7th, Mr. Erskine summoned to his presence Pruthee Singh, the raja's eldest son, a youth of about seventeen years of age, and Humeer Singh, of Soor, the deceased's first cousin, stated to them the detestation entertained by the British government of that inhuman practice, and declared his intention to oppose by every means in his power the observance of a revolting rite, which, if formerly tolerated, was now very justly enacted to be a crime, within its territories, by the British government. The whole of the succeeding day was spent on the part of Pruthee Singh and Humeer Singh in representations of the necessity of the ceremony taking place, and on Mr. Erskine's, in earnestly entreating their co-operation in his views. Mr. Erskine was perfectly unconscious that the sole object of this discussion was to gain time, and that emissaries had been sent to every village in the Ahmednugger zillah, to collect armed Bheels, and matchlock men, with a design of carrying the sutee into effect by main force. Towards the evening large bodies of armed men were observed pouring into the town from every direction, within sight of our camp, on which Mr. Erskine requested the officer commanding the detachment to disarm all such people, as it was plain they were congregating for some evil purpose, since there could be no occasion for that sort of force for the purpose of burning the raja's body. One or two parties were disarmed and allowed to go, with a promise that they should get their arms next day. In the meanwhile it was reported that a very large body of armed men was assembled in the fort, and a party of about fifty or sixty Koolees, matchlock men and others, headed by a man said to be kotwal to Kurun Singh, with lighted matches and slung bows, passed close to Lieutenant Lewis, who was on parade underneath the walls of the town. That officer addressed the kotwal, who was on horseback, told him the orders, and requested him to cause the men who followed him to surrender their arms, when the kotwal immediately ordered the men behind him to fire on Lieutenant Lewis. The men unhesitatingly obeyed, and Lieutenant Lewis was shot through the side. The party then ran into the town, the gates of which were immediately closed, and a brisk fire was opened from the ramparts upon our troops, who were within two hundred paces of the wall; and as there were pieces of ordnance in the town, which if mounted during the night, in the bastions, might have destroyed a great number of our men, it was judged advisable to fall back a few hundred paces, Mr. Erskine having in the meantime sent off an express to the military authorities at Ahmedabad and Hursole for artillery to storm the gate, and take possession of the town. Everything remained quiet until about half-past two o'clock the following morning (the 9th), when an alarm was raised that the pile was on fire. It was now too late prevent or impede the atrocity, which was in the act of being perpetrated. The measures taken by the cruel authors of the barbarous proceeding had been but too successful, and the unfortunate women fell a sacrifice to the savage prejudices of their destroyers. We abstain from laying before your Honorable Court the particulars of the horrid transaction, which will be found detailed in Mr. Erskine's letter, noted in the margin. (This letter will be found in the note at the foot of page 519.)

"The sanguinary deed completed, the late raja's two sons, attended by a band of Rajpoots and others, sallied out of the town. In the morning no symptoms of hostility were displayed towards the detachment, except a few shots fired from the fort at the water-carriers going and coming to and from the river, and most of the

Bheels and Koolees had withdrawn from the town during the night. Mr. Erskine's information, at this time, led him to believe that the sutee, which was undoubtedly a measure of compulsion as regards the victims, was perpetrated against the will of Pruthee Singh, who was disposed to follow Mr. Erskine's advice.

"An addition to the force, of fifty men from Hursole, arrived in the afternoon of the 9th, and Captain Lardner, the officer in command, had intended to have taken possession of the town that evening, which might have been done without much difficulty, had it not been for the following circumstances:—Some months previous to the occurrence of the sutee, Soorujmul, the eldest son of Jhalum Singh Chohan, chief of Mondeytee, had collected a large body of insurgents, and placed himself at the head of it. The ostensible object of the assembly of that force was to procure the liberation of the Doongurpoor Sowcar, brother to Khemchund, of Khooshalchund Nalchund's firm of Ahmedabad, and to oppose Heemut Singh and Futteh Singh, of Roopal, with whom he and his connections had long been at enmity. Some unsuccessful conflicts with his enemies, and the importunity of his troops for pay, involved him in trouble; and observing that excesses on the part of the Thakor of Roopâl, in the Doongurpoor territory, had not met with immediate punishment, he thought that he could best employ his followers in general depredation, and accordingly attacked Durrowee, one of the ghansdana villages, and distributed the pillage among his needy soldiery. Affairs at Eedur were in so disordered a state when this was made known to Mr. Erskine, that he thought it advisable to wait till their settlement before he had recourse to coercion towards Soorujmul, and merely wrote him a letter of advice; but he subsequently learnt that Soorujmul had attacked Hursole, in Nanee Marwar, another of the ghansdana villages. Mr. Erskine hereupon sent five mohsuls on him, requiring him immediately to disband his sebundy. He dismissed the five mohsuls, and refused to disband the force. On this twenty mohsuls were sent, but without any beneficial effect.

"On the 9th February, at four o'clock P.M., intelligence arrived by one of the five mohsuls whom Soorujmul had expelled from his camp that he had encamped at Wuktapoor, four miles from Ahmednugger, with about one thousand Mukranees and sixty or seventy-five horse, with the view of opposing the British troops. On the receipt of this news, Mr. Erskine advised the officer commanding the detachment to defer any operations against the town of Ahmednugger for a time, and requested the officer commanding the northern division of the army immediately to send such assistance as he might think fit for subduing Soorujmul's force and quelling these extensive disturbances which had arisen. * * * * *

"On the 3rd March the town of Ahmednugger was taken possession of by the British troops, and on the 6th March Mr. Erskine stated his expectation of being shortly able to settle the affairs of the Myhee Kântâ."

Bombay Government Despatch of 15th October, 1835.

"There were thus three parties of insurgents in arms in the Myhee Kântâ: 1st. Pruthee Singh and his adherents; 2nd. The Thakor of Roopâl, and his associate, the Thakor of Ghorewara, and their followers; and, 3rd. Soorujmul and his coadjutors. * * *

"Captain Delamain, with a combined force of two hundred infantry, a wing of cavalry, and a hundred and fifty Guikowar horse, marched to attack Soorujmul and on the 17th February reached Wurâlee in the Eedur country, where Soorujmul was said to be encamped. He was found to have retreated; and, as it was believed that he was at Gotâ, two miles off, the residence of his brother, Sher Singh,

Captain Delamain resolved on advancing to that town. The place was taken, and four or five of the enemy killed, and all the survivors in the village, twenty-five or thirty in number, were taken prisoners. But our loss was severe, and an officer, Lieutenant Pottinger, of the 17th Regiment, N.I., was killed. This lamented result was occasioned by there being a strong and high ghuree, or fortlet, at the place, which was desperately defended by the men who occupied it, and by our detachment not being provided with a gun, which, for the service in contemplation when the detachment marched, was not necessary. * * *

"The field force having been augmented, operations were then commenced against the Thakor of Roopâl. At the conclusion of February, 1835, detachments of our troops took, without loss on our side, and destroyed the villages of Kanora and Dodhur, and also a Gosaeen's mut in the neighbourhood of the latter village, and on the 5th March, 1835, the village of Peermalee, all strongholds of the Roopal Bheels, and occupied entirely by irreclaimable outlaws. The town of Roopal was also occupied by our troops. * * After the dispersion of the Roopal rebels, operations were resumed against Soorujmul by the field force under the command of Major Morris, of the 24th Regt., N.I., which, on the 11th March arrived before Gorul, one of his principal strongholds in the hills in the neighbourhood of Mondeytee and took it, and dispersed the garrison, with the loss to the enemy of eight killed and seventeen or eighteen wounded. Soorujmul had quitted the place, which was defended by his brother, Sher Singh, and about two hundred or two hundred and fifty Mukranees. * * Towards the middle of March, 1835, the force, penetrating further into the hills in pursuit of Soorujmul and his adherents, took and destroyed the strongholds of Pharkee, Panowra, Manpoor, and Badurwara. The town of Panowra was the residence of a Bheel chief, who had long been the terror of the neighbourhood, and who was Soorujmul's most persevering and devoted ally. In these operations we had an officer. Lieut. Cruikshank, 17th Regt. N.I., and seventeen sepoys wounded, and the enemy had about 370 men killed and wounded. * * *

"The transactions reported in this despatch have, we acknowledge, left a painful impression on our minds, that after the severest sufferings and privation on the part of the troops in toiling through a most rugged and difficult country, with which we are most imperfectly acquainted, the dispersion of the parties who appeared in arms against us has been effected, it is true, but the chiefs have not been captured, and the causes still exist which have always made it so easy in these quarters for an enterprising leader to assemble at any time a body of armed men ready to join him in projects of plunder and depredation. The mass of the population, in fact, in these tracts is warlike, and if not constantly predatory, at least always willing to be so; and while we have no more acquaintance with the country, which is one of such uncommon strength that a few courageous and well-armed men might successfully oppose at almost every step many times their number, and no more connexion with nor influence over the chiefs than those which we now possess, we can scarcely hope to keep in order so many ungovernable spirits without the employment of overwhelming force, and, in short, studding the country with military parties, the expense of which would be enormous.

"These considerations have led us to entertain thoughts of causing a correct survey of the whole of the tract in question to be made, and our president (Sir Robert Grant) has further brought forward a proposition, in which the other members of the Board have concurred, for making an attempt at creating an influence over the warlike population of the Myhee Kântâ, and providing for the tranquillity of the country, and fostering its eventual civilization by measures similar to those which have been followed with such success in Candeish."

Bombay Government Despatch of 31st December, 1835.

"The nature of Captain Outram's (now Major-General Sir James Outram, K.C.B., Chief Commissioner for the affairs of Oude) duties in Candeish, and the ability and address displayed by that officer in restoring tranquillity in the Dang a few years since, point him out as eminently fit for this important trust. Under these circumstances our president proposed that Captain Outram be directed to proceed immediately to Goozerat, furnished with instructions grounded on the above suggestions."

Bombay Government Despatch of 15th May, 1836.

"Captain Outram himself, in his able and interesting report of the 14th November, 1835, plainly expresses his judgment to be, that however desirable it might be to conciliate the malcontent or insurgent chiefs in the Myhee Kântâ, there are some of them whom it is impossible to treat leniently, men who having openly defied the authority of the British government, must be made a severe example of; who, in short, must be proclaimed outlaws, and given up, when identified, to be executed by the sentence of a drum-head court-martial. In this sentiment Captain Outram was substantially supported by the Political Commissioner, and by several other officers whose opinions are entitled to considerable weight, to the effect generally that further measures of coercion are imperatively called for to ensure the permanent tranquillization of the Myhee Kântâ.

"After having given the subject the consideration it so well deserves, we resolved to adopt the opposite policy, and to begin by proclaiming an amnesty for the past, and by admitting, without exception, all who are now out in Bahirwuteea to terms, provided they will submit themselves to our authority, and furnish security for their peaceable conduct in future. We are not only sanguine that this policy will be successful, but are fully impressed with the conviction that the pacification of the Myhee Kântâ will never be effected by any other means. * * *

"In the first place it does not appear to us that the principal malcontents (or, as they are called, insurgents), have embraced the lawless courses they pursue from pure love of them, but that they have engaged in them in consequence either of family dissensions, grievances unredressed, or misfortunes which British policy has occasioned. On this point the information before us is defective, but strong grounds exist for believing that the disturbances in the Myhee Kântâ owe their origin and long continuance to the above causes, singly or combined.

"In the second place we consider that the severe example which Captain Outram and other officers recommend as an essential preliminary to a valid pacification has already been made. Although in the course of the military operations of last year none of the disaffected chiefs fell into our hands, yet their strength was broken, their followers dispersed, several of their strongholds, towns, and villages burnt, or otherwise destroyed, and a considerable number of their adherents killed, wounded, or taken prisoners."

Bombay Government Despatch of 26th April, 1837.
(Abstract.)

Captain Outram assumed charge of his appointment as political agent in the Myhee Kântâ on the 20th January, 1836. On the 7th February, in compliance with the conciliatory instructions of the government, he dispatched letters to the outlawed chiefs, requesting their presence in his camp for the conclusion of a settlement on the principle of an amnesty for the past, under specific conditions. The period mentioned in the letters was extended in favour of Soorujmul for ten days, and on the 8th March that chief appeared in the agent's camp, expressed contrition, and promised, on the grant of pardon, to find security. He then withdrew for the purpose of providing sureties and dismissing his followers.

On Captain Outram's arrival at Eedur about ten days after, however, an agent from the town of Sidhpoor came to request his interference in obtaining the release of the merchant who had been carried off from that place three months before. The British agent immediately addressed a letter to Soorujmul, demanding that the merchant should be given up within three days, and threatening revocation of pardon on failure of compliance. The government altogether disapproved of this proceeding, which called forth from Sir Robert Grant the remark, "I have, from the "beginning, feared that Captain Outram took too warlike a view of the mission in "which he was engaged." Meanwhile, however, Soorujmul had made answer that the Uteet, who had employed him to assist in capturing the merchant, had carried that person away, and that he therefore could not produce him. The agent continued to demand the merchant's surrender notwithstanding this statement, and Soorujmul was compelled to seek refuge at Pânowrâ. Captain Outram at once proclaimed the chief an outlaw, set a reward upon his head, and started with a detachment of troops in pursuit of him. The Rânâ of Pânowrâ, on the advance of the troops, under the apprehension that his town would be again destroyed, as it had been in March, 1835, refused to afford either aid or protection to Soorujmul, and the chief therefore at once surrendered. "Although," said the government, "we "could not help rejoicing at Captain Outram's success, and at the fortunate result of "his spirited, though somewhat rash, proceedings, yet we deemed the outlawry of "Soorujmul to have been harsh, and the consequent march of our troops unneces-"sary, but the plan was executed with a skill worthy of Captain Outram, and we "have no doubt contributed to the event. We therefore caused him to be in-"formed that we were perfectly willing to admit that success was to be attributed, "not to his instructions, but to his departure from them, enjoining him, however, "to a strict attention to the spirit of our instructions for the future."

On the 7th May, Soorujmul (who had been treated in the interval as a prisoner upon parole) presented himself before the political agent, accompanied by the Sidhpoor merchant, and, as their statements of what had occurred agreed, Captain Outram thought it advisable to release Soorujmul from arrest without the infliction of any fine, for which unexpected act of clemency the chief appeared to be deeply grateful.

"We rejoice," say the government, "in being able to report the continued good "conduct of Soorujmul since his admission to pardon, and we feel pleasure in having "it also in our power to state to your Honorable Court, that his exertions have "been joined with those of Captain Outram in re-establishing peace and good order "in the Myhee Kântâ. To this chief's assistance must be, in a great measure, at-"tributed the destruction of the Bahirwuteea Khoomla, and the dispersion of his "formidable gang."

Before the 1st September, 1836, the remaining outlaws had surrendered, and an important object had been gained by the opening of a line of road from Oodeipoor to Eedur, by way of Pânowrâ, the chiefs interested having signified their consent to the exemption of travellers by this road from transit duties for a specific period.

During the stay of the political agent at Pânowrâ, the exertions of that distinguished officer "were most successfully directed to quelling border feuds, one of "which, a blood feud, had been handed down from father to son for forty years. "He likewise took advantage of his presence in the wilder part of the hills to "obtain the confidence of the border chiefs, who up to that time had experienced "but few opportunities of seeing Europeans, except as enemies at the head of their "troops; he succeeded in settling numerous disputes and feuds, some of many

"years' duration, which had been a source of endless correspondence with the poli-
"tical authorities in Goozerat. So great, indeed, was the confidence which Cap-
"tain Outram inspired, that several Bahirwuteeas spontaneously sought his media-
"tion."

We take pleasure in closing the present note with a passage from a letter of Captain Outram himself, dated 30th April, 1836, describing the friendly feelings with which, under his conciliatory management, the British troops were received in the districts they passed through:—

"Our troops have traversed the country as friends, instead of enemies. The "Bheels, who at first invariably fled at their approach, were encouraged to come "back, and astonished at the kind treatment they received. Or, when fears deterred "them from appearing during the stay of the troops near their villages, they were "agreeably surprised, on their return, to find nothing destroyed during their absence. "A personal intercourse was kindly encouraged between the men and the villagers, "the consequences of which were soon seen in the happy and confident manner in "which the detachment was met on its return. In fact, the march of the troops in "the Myhee Kântâ this year has been a progress of peace, and they have been re-"ceived as a blessing, instead of avoided as a scourge to the country."

BOOK IV.

OR

CONCLUSION.

CHAPTER I.

HINDOO CASTES.

HAVING brought our narrative down to the time when British influence became paramount throughout Goozerat, it is our object in these concluding chapters to present the reader with a general picture of the state of society among the Hindoos of that country as it now exists. The task is one of great difficulty, nor can we, even with the assistance which we possess, hope to perform it in otherwise than a very incomplete manner. Though India and Britain be not now, as once they were, opposed to each other as Antipodes,[1] still an observation made in reference to other Orientals six centuries ago may be repeated with, in many respects, equal applicability to the Hindoos at the present hour :—"Is it to be wondered at," said William Longuespee, on the eve of that bloody field of Massoura in which St. Louis fell a prisoner into the hands of the Saracen,—"is it to be wondered at if "we new comers, young men and strangers, are ignorant of the East? "*As far distant as the East is from the West, so far different are the* "*people of the West from these Orientals.*"[2] The numerous restrictions with which Hindoos in their private life are fenced round, render it almost impossible that much private intercourse should take place between them and strangers, and the difficulties of the stranger who wishes to become acquainted with them are materially enhanced if his situation be that of a government official. But the only alternative offered to him is one of still greater difficulty—it is simply this, that he should, without an effort to the contrary, remain ignorant of a people among whom the best years of his life must be spent, and so be perpetually misunderstanding and misrepresenting the feelings by which they are actuated, and the facts by which they are surrounded.

Englishmen seem hardly able to realize the truth that in this nineteenth century a people such as the Hindoos survives, the habits and manners of which bear so much greater an affinity to those which they read of in the pages of Adams and Potter, or ponder over in the dusty saloons of a museum, than to those with which, in daily

[1] "Nex ipsos Indos lateris a parte orientis, nec ipsos Britannos, a parte Occi- "dentis."—Arnobius, quoted by Bishop Beveridge.

[2] *Vide* Matthew Paris's English History.

life, they are conversant. We have some apprehension, therefore, that the following descriptions may seem to our readers to be derived rather from antiquarian research than from every-day observation of common life. This, we would respectfully urge, is not the case; much which we represent will doubtless wear an antique appearance, for Hindoo life is, in its outline, at the present time, much what it was in the days of Kurun and Jye Singh, but the things of which we treat are, nevertheless, things which exist.

The first institution of Hindoo society which forces itself upon the attention of the stranger is that of caste. When Mr. Borradaile counted the castes in Surat in A.D. 1827, at the time that he was employed in collecting and arranging information regarding the customs of the Hindoos (a work which has unfortunately been altogether discontinued), he found in that city no less than two hundred and seven. Each of these was more or less restricted from private intercourse with all the rest (a subject which we shall have to pursue in some detail); they could not intermarry, nor even eat the same food, nor drink the same water.

Originally there were, as is well known, no more than four castes in India,—the Brahmin, or priestly; the Kshutreeya, or warlike; the Vaishya, or agricultural and mercantile; and the Shoodra, or menial. It would appear that for some time at least these names designated classes rather than hereditary castes in the modern sense of the term. Shrungee, the Reeshee or Sage, was born, we are told, of a deer, Kousheek sprang from sacrificial grass, Goutum from a hare, Vâlmeek from a snake's heap, Dron Âchâryâ from a leaf plate; other sages were the offspring of sailors' daughters, of prostitutes, of outcaste mothers, of menial servants, but they were, nevertheless, all of them Brahmins. In the Muhâ Bhârut frequent mention is made of the sages sharing the same table with the warriors; and of Kâleedâs, the poet, who was a Brahmin, it is said in other books that he married the raja's daughter, who was of course a Kshutreeya.

The celebrated "seven Reeshees" were householding Brahmins, and possessed but one wife between them. These, transferred to the heavens as the stars, which we call the Pleiades, shine around Droov, the north star, the portal of Vishnoo's Paradise, and beside them, in a lesser light, shines their consort Uroondhutee. From the seven sages most of the Brahmins trace their descent. Perhaps the first tangible schism among the Brahmins (for the Hindoo scriptures contain none of the modern caste names) may be traced to the time of the great Brahminical reformer, Shunkur Âchâryâ, who appeared about a century and a half before Christ to oppose the Buddhist doctrines. He found dissensions existing among the Brahmins themselves, who held each to their favorite "Ved," and proscribed those who preferred another of the four. The great reformer recommended that flesh should not be eaten, thus, in concession to the popular appreciation of Buddhism, keeping out of sight the Veds which prescribe animal sacrifice; he also advised that Brahmins should follow the Ved which each held hereditarily, without enmity to the followers of the other three. However, though striving to compose schism, Shunker Âchâryâ was unintentionally the cause of it. After his death his name became a watchword of faction, and Brahmins who were hitherto separated only by the Vindhya range of mountains, became henceforth divided into two sects, one of whom adopted, and the other opposed the tenets of the reformer. The Goud Brahmins, who retained the use of animal food, and the Drâvid Brahmins, who relinquished it, would now no longer consent to drink from each other's cups.

The Brahmins of Goozerat are believed to be subdivided into more castes than those of any other part of India. The origin of the Owdich caste, which is the most numerous, has been described in the history of Mool Râj, King of Unhilwârâ.[1] They were called Owdich because they came from the north, and Suhusrâ, because those who came on the first occasion were about one thousand in number. From the places of their residence they assumed the names of Sidhpooreeâ and Seehoreeâ Owdich, and the branches thus formed gradually fell into distinct customs. The party who continued to refuse the gifts of Mool Râj formed a separate caste, called Tolukeeâ Owdich. Since that time some of the members of the caste, falling into poverty, and being compelled to accept of the office of family priest to cobblers, tailors, minstrels, and others, and even to Koolees, have been excommunicated, and have formed so many further subdivisions. Others, settling in the city of Surat, or passing into the countries of Kutch, Wâgur, and Marwar, and there gradually adopting distinct customs from those authorized at home, have separated from the main body of the caste, and assumed such local names as that of Marwar Owdich Brahmins.

The Shreemâlee Brahmins possess a scripture which they assert to be a portion of one of the Poorâns. It informs them that their

[1] See pp. 47-49.

ancestors were sent for from all quarters at the time when the city of Shreemâl (now called Beenmâl), in Jhâlor, was founded, and that they then first became a local caste. Mâgh, one of the most celebrated of the Sanscrit poets, was a Shreemâlee Brahmin. When the town of Shreemâl fell into decay, many of the Brahmins, bringing their family goddess with them, came to Unhilwârâ, then in the ascendant, and settled either there or in other parts of Goozerat, or in Kutch or Soreth. Others settled in Marwar or Mewar. A large number adopted the Jain faith for a subsistence, and were thence called "Bhojuks" or "eaters." The Shreemâlee Brahmins are divided into the followers of the Yujoor, and those of the Sâm Ved, and there are seven "gotras," or tribes, of each, which, however, except in Goozerat, associate and intermarry. As well as the Owdich, the Shreemâlee caste traces its descent to Goutum, the Sage. There is at the present moment a struggle for supremacy between the two castes in the western districts of Goozerat.

Brahmins will usually eat together, though they decline intermarriages. There is, however, one caste of Brahmins in Goozerat, the Nâgur, which will not even eat with another caste. The original seat of the Nâgur Brahmins in Goozerat was Wurnugger, one of the oldest cities in the province, the foundation of which has been assigned by tradition to the race of Kunuk Sen. When Veesul Dev Chohân built Veesulnugger[1] he caused to be performed a sacrifice, which was attended by many Wurnugger Brahmins. These refused to receive alms from the king, but Veesul Dev, resorting to a stratagem, forced upon some of them the acceptance of grants of land. They were excommunicated by the body of the caste, and founded the Veesulnugger Nâgur sect. Similar occurrences at Sâtod and other places produced the Sâtodra, the Cheetrodâ, the Prushunorâ, and the Krushunorâ Nâgur Brahmins. Of this caste there is a division called "Bârud," composed of persons who, finding themselves unable to procure a wife in their own caste, have taken one from another. They are much despised after such a marriage, and compelled to quit their native village; but the sect continues, notwithstanding, to increase. Their women, contrary to ordinary practice, are permitted to remarry.

These are the principal divisions of the Brahmin sect in Goozerat, though by no means the whole of them. It is usually said that there are eighty-four castes of Brahmins.

It is stated in the Bhâgwut Poorân that Mureechee Reeshee, the

[1] See p. 75.

son of Brumhâ, had a son, Kusyup, whose son, Soorya (the sun) or Veevuswân, became a Kshutreeya. Mureechee's brother, Utree, had also a son, named Som or Chundra (names of the moon), and he, too, was a warrior. The great majority of the Rajpoot clans deduce their descent from either Soorya or Chundra. In the commentary on a Sanscrit work called "Rutun Kosh," it is said that the first of the Kshutreeya race was Munoo, and that from him sprung thirty-six tribes, of whom some acquired surnames by valiant exploits, some attained the rank of kings, others fell to that of cultivators, or even became lost in the Shoodra caste. Chund Bhârot states that when the Sages dwelt on Mount Aboo, and were annoyed by the Usoors, or demons, Wushisht, one of their number, created from a sacrificial pit of fire four Kshutreeyas—Pureehâr, Solunkhee, Purmâr, and Chohân. From these sprung the thirty-six Rajpoot clans, which he thus enumerates:—

> The Sun, the Moon, the Jâduv[1] races,
> Kukoosth, Purmâr, and Tonwur,
> Châhoowân,[2] Châlook,[3]
> Chind,[4] Silâr, Âbheewur,
> Doyamutt,[5] Mukwân,[6]
> Gurooâ Gohil, Gahiloot,
> Châpotkut,[7] Pureehâr,
> Râv Râthor the angry,
> Deorâ, Thânk, Sindhuv, Unig,
> Yotik, Pruteehâr, Dudheekhuth,
> Kârutpâl, Kotpâl, Hoon,
> Hureetuth, Gor, Kumâd, Jutt,
> Dhyânpâluk, Nikoombh great,
> Râjpâl lords of earth,
> Kâluchur last of all.
> I have named the thirty-six races.

The common version now given by bards is that five Rajpoots—Purmâr, Râthor, Jâduv, Châhoowân, and Solunkhee—sprang from the fire-pit, and that from these descend ninety-nine clans. The Rajpoot tribes still maintain that they are true Kshutreeyas, though the Brahmins deny that the warrior caste has any longer an existence. The reason is to be found in the affected purity, as regards food and other matters, which has crept upon the Brahmins, and in the compulsory marriage of Rajpoot ladies with the Mohummedan princes. The Kshutreeya caste is now no longer considered by other Hindoos

[1] The Jâduv or Yâduv to which the Râs of Soreth belonged. [2] Chohân. [3] Solunkhee. [4] Chundel. [5] Dâheemâ. [6] Mukwânâ or Jhâlâ. [7] Chowra.

to be next in rank to the Brahmin; its place has been usurped by the Wâneeâs, a branch of the Vaishya caste, who will not even drink water with Rajpoots, and "Brahmin-wâneeâ" is now a synonymous expression for "oojulee-wustee," or high-caste population. The Rajpoots use animal food and spirituous liquor, both unclean in the last degree to their puritanic neighbours, and are scrupulous in the observance of only two rules,—those which prohibit the slaughter of cows, and the re-marriage of widows. The clans are not forbidden to eat together, or to intermarry, and cannot be said in these respects to form different castes.

At the residence of every Rajpoot chief are to be found a number of female servants, either themselves purchased as slaves when young, or the descendants of women who have been thus purchased. They are of all castes, and are frequently even Abyssinians; in Kâteewâr the usual name for them is *Chokree*, in the Myhee Kântâ it is *Wudhârun*. These women are reputed to be of easy virtue, and are hardly ever married at all, but if they are it is with a member of their own caste. An intrigue with them is considered disgraceful to a member of another class. When a Wudhârun is found to be with child, the Rânee, her mistress, will send for her, and compel her to disclose the name of the father, who, if a wealthy person, is compelled to pay a fine. No fault, however, is imputed to the woman. The children bear the name of Golâ, or, if they have been employed in high situations by the chief, that of Khuwâs. They remain, however, the slaves of the chief, notwithstanding their promotion. On the marriage of a chief's daughter, a certain number of male and female slaves form part of the young lady's dowry. They perform the menial duties of the household, and used sometimes to accompany the corpse of their chief to the funeral pile, and burn themselves thereupon.

Vaishyas are still employed principally in agriculture and commerce. The most usual cultivators in Goozerat are the Koonbees, who are divided into the three great branches of Lewâ, Kuruwâ, and Ânjunâ. They assert themselves to be of Kshutreeya descent, and many of them even use the surnames of Rajpoot clans. Of the trading classes, the principal are the Wâneeâs, already mentioned, who form eighty-four distinct castes, deriving names principally from districts or towns. These castes are again subdivided, as into right and left hand, or into Dushâ and Veeshâ, names implying degrees of rank, and derived from words signifying ten and twenty. The Wâneeâs are still further divided by religious differences, as into Meshrees or Vaishnavite Hindoos, and Shrâwuks or Jains. The genealogists of the Wâneeâs, Jain monks, or bards, as the case may be, derive their descent commonly from some Rajpoot clan. Intermarriage is not allowed where the parties are reputed to be of the same descent.

Persons who perform duties which are considered to be menial are classed as Shoodras,—such as barbers, link-bearers, washermen, and others. The aboriginal tribes, Bheels, Koolees, Meenâs, Mairs, and others, are also Shoodras, as are the classes sometimes considered to be outcaste. With these, difference of occupation constitutes difference of caste. In the territories of Hindoo chiefs, Shoodras are not permitted to abandon their hereditary occupations, nor are they allowed to dress themselves in handsome clothes, or to build houses of the better class. In former days, the lowest castes were wholly excluded from the towns, and compelled to exhibit a distinguishing dress.[1] The Shoodras have, notwithstanding, their bards and genealogists, who feed their vanity with the assertion that they were originally Kshutreeyas. Even the outcastes bear the surnames of Chohân, Wâghela, and others, and are attended by the Toorees, as their minstrels, and the Gurodhâs, as their family priests, which latter wear an imitation of the badge of the regenerate, and assert themselves to be of the blood of the Brahmins. The outcastes are, as to religion, frequently followers of Kubeer, who proclaimed the, to them acceptable, doctrine that one caste was in no way different from another. Even these, however, are subdivided into Dhers and Olgânâs, of whom the former would be defiled and excommunicated were they to eat with the latter. Lastly, it is necessary to observe, that even the Olgânâ is still a Hindoo, and superior, as such, to a Mlech, or one who is not a Hindoo. A Mohummedan sovereign, as the story goes, asked his Hindoo minister which was the lowest caste of all. The minister begged for leisure to consider his reply, and having obtained it, went to where the Dhers lived, and said to them, "You have "given offence to the padishah. It is his intention to deprive you "of caste, and make you Mohummedans." The Dhers, in the greatest terror, posted off in a body to the sovereign's palace, and standing at a respectful distance, shouted at the top of their lungs, "If we've "offended your majesty, punish us in some other way than that. "Beat us, fine us, hang us if you like, but don't make us Mohum-"medans." The padishah smiled, and turning to his minister, who sat by affecting to hear nothing of the matter, said, "So the lowest "caste is that to which I belong!"

Among the Jains, religion consists principally in the practice of

[1] *Vide* the story of Jusmâ, the Odun, p. 86.

austerities, and in the avoiding to destroy life; caste restrictions are not prescribed to them. The Shrâwuks, however, practice many usages common to other Hindoos. If one have come into contact with an outcaste, he touches fire or water to purify himself. Like other Hindoos, if he have occasion to receive anything from a Dher, he causes him to set it down on the ground, and then purifies it with fire or water, before he takes it up. Even shepherds and Koolees incur pollution by touching Dhers, which they remove in a similar manner.

"The shepherds, Bhugwân and Rodo," said a Koolee, in the course of his evidence before a criminal court, in Goozerat, in August, 1853, "came to me, and said they had both touched "Dhers, and become impure, and asked me to give them fire. I "took a lighted coal out of my hookah, and each of them touched "his forehead with it. I threw it down, and they then took my "hookah and smoked." In other words, they were then purified, otherwise he could not have given them his hookah.

An additional cause of subdivisions among castes, is the great expense incurred in their public entertainments. A rich person, who desires to render himself popular, will supply at one of these more costly entertainment than is usually provided, or continue the feast for a day longer. Others, unwilling to be outdone, exert themselves to follow the precedent, which at length becomes so completely established that even the poorer members of the caste are compelled to comply with it, even if they borrow the means of doing so. These latter are glad enough, in this state of things, to avail themselves of the first caste dispute which occurs, as an opportunity for seceding. If a considerable portion of the caste be of one mind, they have no difficulty in effecting a separation; but when the non-contents are few in number, they are subjected to great annoyance. The body of the caste refuse to associate or have any dealings with them, to contract marriages with their children, to furnish them with fire, or to permit them to draw water from the public well. The wives or married daughters of the excommunicated persons are kept from them, and their dead lie unburied, until by submission, or other means, they can prevail upon their caste fellows, who alone are competent to do so, to carry out the corpse to the funeral pile.

In some castes a man is allowed to marry as many wives as he pleases,—a Rajpoot sometimes marries twenty, an Owdich Brahmin frequently five or six; in other castes, a man may not marry a second time in the lifetime of his first wife. Rajpoots never permit the re-marriage of a widow, but in some of the other castes a woman may re-marry more than once. Sometimes it is allowed to a husband and wife, who disagree, to separate by mutual consent, which is signified on the part of the woman by her tearing the hem of her garment, and on that of the man by his giving his wife a deed of release. In some castes it is considered indispensably necessary that girls should be married before they are twelve years old; in others, a husband of high family is much sought for, and women remain unmarried at the age of thirty. Some castes consider the non-performance of certain funeral ceremonies a sufficient ground for excommunication; in other castes these ceremonies are wholly neglected.

There are various restrictions in regard to food, any departure from which subjects a person to excommunication. The general rule is that food which has been prepared for persons of another, and particularly of an inferior caste, must not be eaten. If food preparing for a Brahmin be touched by a Shoodra, it is henceforth fit only for Shoodras to eat. In some castes food may not be removed beyond the place in which it has been prepared. There are similar restrictions in regard to vessels. A Brahmin, having used a vessel, must wash it with water before he can use it again, but a Vaishya satisfies the rules of his caste if he clean it with ashes. Vessels of zinc, stone, tin, wood, or earthenware, belonging to people of other castes, cannot be used by Brahmins, and if any such vessel belonging to themselves happened to be touched by a Vaishya or Shoodra, it is rendered useless to them. Scruples in regard to water are sometimes compelled to give way by the necessity of the case. The general rule, however, is that Hindoos cannot drink water which has been placed in vessels belonging to persons of other castes, and that their own vessels are rendered impure by the touch of these. In Western Goozerat, however, where there is great difficulty about water in the hot weather, it is customary for Brahmins to use brass or copper vessels belonging to persons of other castes, after they have scrubbed them well with dust and water, and washed them. A leathern bucket need only be washed, because, having come originally from the house of the tanner, who is a person of very low caste, it is supposed that no further defilement can happen to it. Some puritanical Brahmins will neither drink water which has been drawn in a leathern bucket, nor even use it for ablutions. In parts of Western Goozerat there is frequently but one well in a village, in which case the outcastes draw water on one side of it and retire, and the Brahmins and other castes, when they are gone, come and draw water from the other side. It is usually the case that there are many wells in a village, and that one is specially set apart for outcastes. The well is defiled if a dog or other animal have fallen into it, and for its purification water must be drawn from it five times, and Ganges water or cow's urine poured into it. If a Brahmin or Wâneeâ woman, returning home with water from the well, meet a funeral, she will sometimes throw away the water at once as defiled, sometimes veil herself, and move aside, averting her face, and, if the corpse be not carried within a few paces of where she stands, the water is preserved from defilement. The dead body of an animal defiles also, and, if one happen to lay on the way to the well, no water is procurable until it has been removed and the ground has been purified. Some women will throw away the water if a crow alight on a vessel and put his beak into it, but, as the case is rather a common one, other women take no notice of it. The custom is, perhaps, connected with a superstition which prevails in Goozerat, as it prevailed in England and other European countries, that the crow is a bird of ill omen.

CHAPTER II.

THE CULTIVATORS.

THE cultivators of Goozerat do not live, as those of European countries do, each upon his own farm, but are invariably concentrated into villages. By the term village is strictly meant, not merely the collection of dwellings which the cultivators inhabit, but the whole area which is in their occupation. A large part of the province is, as we have said, covered with groves of stately trees. Where foliage is less common, as in the districts lying contiguous to the Runn of Kutch, a grove of trees is the usual accompaniment of a village. Like the towns, each village has its neighbouring stream or tank, and most frequently its mosque and temple. The fields are, in the richer parts of the province, enclosed with strong and high permanent hedges, which, with the noble trees that everywhere abound, render the country so close, that the boundaries of a field circumscribe the view, and unless the hum of voices, the whirr of the spinning-wheel, or the barking of dogs, gives him notice of its vicinity, the traveller may enter a village almost unawares. Hedges and trees here swarm with birds, of many varieties, from the peacock to the sparrow; game of all kinds is in the greatest abundance, and monkeys rove about in troops, or rather in armies. In other parts of the country, as, for instance, in the territories of the Jhâlâ chieftains, the eye ranges undisturbed as if over a sheet of water, many villages may be distinguished at a single glance, and the presence of a herd of antelopes or the approach of a score of horsemen may be easily perceived at a distance of miles.

The cultivators are an industrious and orderly class of people, simple in their mode of life. They rise before daybreak, and, throwing grass before their bullocks, busy themselves for a few minutes in certain domestic affairs. By the time the cattle have finished their food, they are themselves ready for the field, to which they now set out, driving the beasts before them. They remain the whole of the day employed in the agricultural operations of the season. About nine o'clock their wives, having prepared their breakfast at home, bring it out to them in the field, and they return home for their evening meal, which is served soon after sunset. Some of the Koonbees, however, eat four times a day.

The Koonbee, though frequently all submission and prostration when he makes his appearance in a revenue office, is sturdy and bold enough among his own people. He is fond of asserting his independence, and the helplessness of others without his aid, on which subjects he has several proverbs, as, "Wherever it thunders, "there the Koonbee is a landholder," or, "Tens of millions follow "the Koonbee, but the Koonbee follows no man."[1] The Koonbee and his bullocks are inseparables, and, in speaking of the one, it is difficult to dissociate the other. His pride in these animals is excusable, for they are most admirably suited to the circumstances in which nature has placed them, and possess a very widely-extended fame. When Prince Kurun, of Mewar, was received, after his defeat by the Emperor Jehangeer, and that prince was anxious to treat him with unusual respect, he seated him, it is said, on his right hand, and presented him, among other rarities and choice things of every kind, with a pair of the bullocks of Goozerat. The Koonbee, however, frequently exhibits his fondness for his animals in the somewhat peculiar form of most unmeasured abuse. "May the "Kâtees seize you!" is his objurgation, if in the peninsula of Soreth; if in the Eedur district, or among the mountains, it is then, "May the tiger kill you!"—all over Goozerat, "May your master "die!"[2] however he means by this, the animal's former owner—

[1] "Unde vivent oratores si defecerint aratores," says Ordericus Vitalis.

[2] *Vide* Dean Swift's Mrs. Harriss's petition—

"The *devil* take me (said she, blessing herself) if ever I saw't."

not himself; and when more than usually cautious, he will word his chiding thus, "May the fellow that sold you to me perish!"

When the festival called Ukhâturee comes round, which it does early in Wyeshâk (May), the chief of a village collects the cultivators, and tells them that it is time for them to commence work. They say, "No! the assessment was too heavy last year, you lay too many "taxes upon us; besides, we have in truth no master over our heads; "people burn our houses, and lay waste our lands, and you afford us "no protection, and do not go on the wâr." The chief makes sundry excuses, the most usual and convenient of which is, that everything is the fault of that rascal of a mehtâ (his man of business), whom he protests his intention of dismissing at once. As to the cultivators, no one can have greater affection for them than he has; they are, in fact, his sons and daughters. Nor does the chief altogether overstate his feelings on this point; for he is well aware that his lands are of no value to him without the aid of the cultivators, and that in Goozerat, as in other countries of the east, "In the multitude of "people is the king's honour, but in the want of people is the "destruction of the prince." [1] After much haggling, and when the chief has presented the head-men of the village with turbans, and made liberal promises of remission of rent, the auspicious day is at length fixed upon and cultivation is commenced. The first step is to remove the stalks of the last year's wheat or cotton, and to lay down manure, which the cultivators have collected in their dung heaps, or perhaps the slime of a dried-up tank, upon lands intended for irrigation. Plowing, sowing, and the other operations of agriculture follow in order, a general notion of which may be gathered from the following ballad, entitled "The Koonbee's Griefs," which is a favorite song of the wives of cultivators in Goozerat.

Hear Shree Krishn! our prayers;
The Koonbee's griefs we relate.
Our sorrows remove, thou who art the earth-sustainer;
Râm! as you place us we remain.
Hear, Shree Krishn! our prayers.

July comes, the clouds rise;
They begin to pour forth rain;
The cart-rope and the goad are in the Koonbee's hand;
Wet is the Koonbee's body.
Hear, Shree Krishn! our prayers.

[1] *Vide* Proverbs, xiv. 28.

In August it rains uncertainly;
Drenched through are both men and women;
Says the son's wife to her father-in-law,
"Bâbâjee! please to plant a little rice."
Hear, Shree Krishn! our prayers.

September comes in well;
Drenched are the Koonbee women;
The children on their hips are crying;
Rain-drops fall from the bundles of grass upon their heads.
Hear, Shree Krishn! our prayers.

In October, we hoped would come
The rain that we were looking for;
Jowâree and bâjuree[1] are filling in the head;
The rice is drying up from the drought.
Hear, Shree Krishn! our prayers.

In November comes the assessment-maker;
At the village boundary he makes up his book:
The raja's order is now proclaimed,—
"A plant of pulse or a stalk of jowâree you must not remove."
Hear, Shree Krishn! our prayers.

December has come in well:
The first instalment has begun to be levied:
Head-man and accountant mount to the town-house:
The Koonbee gets many a blow.
Hear, Shree Krishn! our prayers.

In January is sown the second crop:
The cotton pods begin to burst;
Old restrictions are removed,
But they only make way for new.
Hear, Shree Krishn! our prayers.

February month has well come in;
Green are the village fields:
The raja's dues are paid off,
But frost now threatens to fall.
Hear, Shree Krishn! our prayers.

March month has well come in,
But the blight has struck our wheat.
"Come, let us leave this place, and fly."
It is too late, for the head-man has set his guards.
Hear, Shree Krishn! our prayers.

In April they meet at the town-house;
"Come, let us have your rent."
They plunder the earnings of the widow's spinning-wheel;
They carry off all by force.
Hear, Shree Krishn! our prayers.

[1] Two kinds of grain, "large maize" and "Holcus spicatus."

In May come the landholders,
They plunder us of the produce of our cows :
For want of butter-milk the children are crying ;
But the cursed ones go on with their snatching.
Hear, Shree Krishn ! our prayers.

June month has come in well ;
The angry Koonbee is appeased :
Oaths and promises they pledge to him—
He spreads his fields with manure.
Hear, Shree Krishn ! our prayers.

The twelve months' round is finished,
In Roopâ the Koonbee's song,
Whoever learns it, or hears it sung,
Will be advanced towards Vishnoo's heaven.
Hear, Shree Krishn ! our prayers.

When the crop is ripe, the raja or chief goes in person, or sends his man of business, to assess the fields. This is done in different ways, of which the most common are the following :—The landholder, or his agent, taking with him the head-man of the village, goes to each field. The head-man points out what he considers to be the amount of the crop—for example, that in his opinion there will be so many measures of grain on each acre. The landholder, too, makes his own calculation. The cultivator, when he hears the amount of the latter, breaks in with the exclamation, "Lord of the "earth ! so much as that will never be produced ; and I, who am a "poor man, will be utterly destroyed !" Much haggling takes place ; and at length a conclusion is come to which the Koonbee is sure to protest against, though the result be far more favorable than he anticipated. The cultivator now furnishes security that he will pay the landlord's share, and receives permission to cut his crop.

The landholder's share of the produce is different in different places—sometimes, as in Jhâlâwâr, about one-third ; sometimes a half, or two-thirds. Rice-crops, and others which are watered from tanks or wells, pay frequently one-third ; autumnal crops of wheat and barley, on irrigated land, frequently a fourth. In some cases, the landlord's share of the produce is nominally very small ; but his revenue is made up by a poll-tax on the bullocks and labourers employed. In regard to autumnal crops of wheat, raised without irrigation (called châsheeâ), which are very common in the Bhâl and other districts, a wholly different system was invented by a Rajpoot landholder of the Choorâsumâ clan. According to this system the number of the triple furrows made by the plough in sowing are counted. One part of the field will probably bear a better crop than another part; and three divisions of the field are therefore generally made. The first, middle, and last furrows of each division are then cut, and the grain threshed out and weighed. The amount is multiplied by the number of furrows, and the average produce thus ascertained. A maund per acre is deducted for seed, and ten per cent. for the cultivators' labour. The remainder is divided into two equal shares, of which the landlord takes one, and the cultivator the other.

The most ancient system of assessment, however, is as follows:— The cultivators are allowed to cut their grain, under the restriction that they pile it in separate heaps in the village grain-yard. The grain is threshed out by bullocks. There is now a grand meeting of landlords, village head-men, men of business, wâneeâs to weigh the grain, cultivators, and watchmen, at the granary; and the grain is weighed and distributed. First, about a fortieth part is set aside as a fee to the chieftain; next, something less, for the man of business, the village-sergeant, pocket-money for the chief's heir-apparent, the village watchman, the wâneeo who weighs the grain, the head-men of the village, the temple of the Devee, or of Vishnoo, the tank, the dogs, and other petty claims, too numerous to detail. When the weighing out is nearly finished, the cultivator will lay hands forcibly on the weights, and cry, "That is enough now:" and the remnant is left to him, under the name of "spoiled." When all claims have been satisfied, the remainder of the grain is equally divided between the cultivator and the landlord. The ancient practice appears to have been merely to measure roughly with a basket, without weighing.[1]

When a chief has to portion a daughter, or to incur other similar necessary expense, he has the right of imposing a levy upon the cultivators to meet it. He sometimes also gives to the genealogical bard of the family, or to some other person of the mendicant class, the right of receiving a small duty upon each plough, or of taking a measure of grain from every heap in the grain-yard. These grants may be made for a single year or permanently. Sometimes the tax is laid in the shape of a certain sum to be realized out of the revenue of each of the chief's villages.

It is unfortunately matter of notoriety that, speaking generally, all the cultivators and holders of land in Goozerat are in debt to such

[1] An improved revenue system is gradually maturing in the districts subject to the British government, to which we can only here allude.

an extent that they have no means of their own of extricating themselves from their difficulties. The creditors are for the most part Goozerat wâneeâs of the Meshree (Vaishnavite) or Shrâwuk (Jain) classes. A wâneeo commencing life spends his time partly in a large town and partly in some remote country village. He borrows a few rupees at interest in the town, with which he purchases small supplies of clarified butter, oil, molasses, and other such articles, and thus stocks his village shop. The cultivators having no money at hand, barter small quantities of their grain or cotton for as much oil as will keep their evening lamp burning for an hour, or for little supplies of groceries. They are perfectly unaware of the market value of their raw produce, and are quite satisfied that they have made a bargain if the wâneeo, with a politic show of liberality, throws in a little more ot the article he is selling under the name of a bonus. Having collected a sufficient quantity of raw produce, the trader carries it to the town, and sells it there at a favorable rate, and his capital thus augmented, he returns to the village to commence operations on a larger scale. A cultivator, perhaps, has lost his bullock; the wâneeo steps forward immediately to lend him money, at interest, to supply his loss. Or, perhaps, the Koonbee is engaged in marrying his child, or in performing the funeral rites of his parent; the trader will advance him money to supply him with the clarified butter, molasses, clothes, or other articles which are indispensable on these occasions, charging for them twice their value. Sometimes the cultivator prefers to make his own purchases in the town, but he must then take the wâneeo with him to act as broker between him and the town dealer, for he feels that the latter will otherwise charge him anything he pleases, and besides he has no money, and cannot borrow it except from the village lender, for the curious feeling in regard to rights, which is so prevalent among the Hindoos, applies here, and the village wâneeo will consider his property invaded if any other trader propose to deal with his constituents. On these transactions the wâneeo of course gains largely. Sometimes, however, he will say to the cultivator, "I "have no ready money, but if you will tell me what you want we will "go together and purchase it, and it shall be put down to my account." He takes care, moreover, to hint to his victim what praises he has heard of the liberality of the family, and how necessary it is that their honor should be maintained by a large expenditure on the present occasion. He adds, that such celebrations do not happen every day, but only once or twice in a lifetime, that the money will not be thrown away, and that nothing is easier than to make it up again. He will also say, "I have every confidence in you, and am "ready to advance you any sum you wish." In this way, flattering his pride, he easily plunges him deeply into debt.

There is nothing more adverse to the prosperity of the Hindoos than this unfortunate feeling of theirs in regard to money and expenditure. With them a mercantile man has "âbroo" (honor), he is a respectable man, nay, a great man—"a muhâjun"—by which they merely mean that he is wealthy, though he may be, indeed he too frequently is, selfish meanness itself. Similarly, a landowner or cultivator is "dheerujwâlo"—a courageous, high-spirited man—that is to say, he plunges himself into irretrievable difficulties, merely because he has not strength of mind sufficient to enable him to despise the tittle-tattle of his neighbourhood.

But, to return to our wâneeo:—When the occasion for all this extravagant expenditure has passed away, the wâneeo demands his bond. He tells the cultivator, "You have so much to pay to the ghee-dealer, "so much to the cloth-seller," and so on, to all of which the cultivator assents. The wâneeo says, "Now give me my *kothulee chorâmun*," meaning a fee for loosening the purse-strings, which must be paid in ready money, for luck, or as a good omen. The cultivator procures one per cent., in ready money, from wherever he can, and pays it. He has further, also, to make a present, not only to the person who writes, but also to those who attest the bond. Interest is stipulated for at two per cent. per mensem, or, if the terms are unusually moderate, at one. The bond prepared, the cultivator scrawls beneath it his mark—a rude representation of a plough. When the next crop is ready, and the government share has been paid, the creditor exerts himself to carry off all that remains; the cultivator, with much entreaty, obtains enough to subsist upon for a short time, and he is credited on account of the remainder with whatever the wâneeo may be pleased to allow him. Sometimes the trader carries off nearly the whole, and, when the cultivator talks about a subsistence, says, "What "need you care? When yours is done you can have as much as you "like from my shop." Thus the cultivator is driven to the wâneeo's shop for grain to eat, and grain to sow his field with. The terms of lending are, that the borrower shall repay twice the quantity of grain he takes away, when his crop ripens. The next harvest comes round, but now all the grain which is left, after the payment of the government demands, goes to pay for that which was borrowed last year, and there is nothing left to pay the interest of the bond. This, then, must be added to the principal, and so the bond goes on swelling year by year—the trader (who is well aware of the practice of the courts of justice) taking care to have it periodically renewed, and carefully closing every loop-hole through which his victim might escape.[1]

The creditor will now probably reside principally in the town, and on his occasional visits to the village he puts up at the house of his debtor, who is obliged to maintain him as long as he remains there. If the wâneeo have a son to marry, or a pilgrimage to perform, the debtor is obliged to lend him his cart and bullocks, and on such occasions he must also come forward with the usual present. The money-lender has by this time begun to assume a very high tone, and to demand payment, threatening to sell the cultivator's house or his bullocks; in fact, as a villager would say, "He becomes more "oppressive than a raja."

In a few years the wâneeo, having thus made himself the master of numerous cultivators, amasses a large sum of money. He now turns his attention to a higher prey, and seeks to become the creditor of local chiefs and landowners. His first step is to get himself introduced to the chief's man of business, whom he gains over by gifts and promises. This agent accordingly takes the first opportunity of praising the trader in the chief's presence, and intimating his readiness to advance as much money as may be wished for. When occasion arrives, money is accordingly borrowed from the Sowkâr or Shet (at which dignity the wâneeo has now arrived), and the man of business prepares a bond, and brings it to the landowner for his signature. The chief haggles like a child for a sum of ready money to be presented to him as the price of his affixing his seal, but cares little or nothing about what there is in the bond, never reflecting for a moment that he is likely to be called upon to fulfil his agreement. A few transactions of this kind lead to the inevitable termination. The Sowkâr sues in the Court of Justice; the man of business (who has carefully abstained from keeping any account, lest his own peculations should be exposed) deserts his master in the hour of need; the chief attempts to defend the suit, and while he admits that he has signed the bond, urges that he is not really indebted to one-tenth of the extent asserted; he is informed that he must produce his accounts in order to prove his defence, and when he states that his agent never kept any, is told further that this is merely a false statement, made because the production of the books called for would prove the

[1] The very poverty of these usurers makes them unmerciful creditors. "A rich "oppressor," it has been said, "leaves a man poor, but a poor oppressor leaves "to him nothing."

"A poor man that oppresseth the poor, is a sweeping rain which leaveth no "food."—Proverbs, xxviii. 3.

validity of the plaintiff's claim. The chief has, of course, no further defence; a decree is therefore passed, and his estate is attached.

We shall return to this subject in a following chapter; meanwhile, we beg of our readers to believe that although we have selected a prominent case as best suited to the purpose of illustration, we have, nevertheless, truly described a system which, with local modifications, still exists throughout the province of Goozerat.[1]

[1] Mr. Elphinstone, in A.D. 1821, alludes to this subject, in speaking of "the "hardship felt by the ryots from the exaction of the debts contracted by them "during the Mahratta government, under the decrees of the Adawlut."

"The root of the grievance," he says, "seems to be in the readiness with which "a bond is admitted as sufficient evidence of the justice of a claim. In this case "it is by no means so, for a ryot is easily drawn by occasional advances and par-"tial payments into a complicated account, which it is impossible for him to un-"ravel. This account presents a great balance in the lender's favour, and as the "practice is for the ryot to give up his produce each year in part payment, and to "take an advance to enable him to go on with the next, he is so completely in the "lender's power that he would sign anything rather than disoblige him. The "remedy, therefore, is to settle that in new provinces a bond shall not be conclu-"sive when originating in an old debt of a ryot, but that his whole account shall "be examined as if no bond had been executed, and only the amount which shall "then appear fair decreed to the plaintiff. If the debts could be paid by instal-"ments, regulated by the amount of the ryot's payment to government, it would "complete the removal of the evil; but, at all events, steps should be taken to "prohibit the sale of a ryot's cattle and implements of husbandry in satisfaction "of debts."

The Mongol Tartars appear to suffer at the hands of Chinese usurers in the same way that the Koonbees of Goozerat do at the hands of the Wâneeâs:—

"'They came to us,' says a Mongol, 'imploring arms; we allowed them, out of "compassion, to cultivate a little ground, and the Mongols followed their example. "They drank the Chinese wine, and smoked their tobacco; on credit they bought "their cloth, and then, when the time came for settling accounts, all was charged "forty or fifty per cent. more than its value. Then the Mongols were forced to "leave all—houses, lands, and flocks.'

"'Could you not ask justice from the tribunals?

"'Oh, that is impossible! The Kitat knows how to speak and to lie—*a Mongol "can never gain a lawsuit from a Chinese.* My lord Lamas,—all is lost for the "kingdom of Gechekten.'"

See M. Huc's "Travels in Tartary, translated by Mrs. Percy Sinnett. In another part of the work we have a description of the same state of things by an "enormously fat Kitat," who describes himself as "*an eater of Tartars*," and thus accounts for the name:—

"'What! don't you know the Tartars? Don't you know that they are as "simple as children when they come into our towns? They want to have every-"thing they see; they seldom have any money, *but we come to their help.* We "give them goods on credit, and then, of course, they must pay rather high. "When people take away goods without leaving the money, of course there must "be a little interest of thirty or forty per cent. Then by degrees the interest "mounts up, and you come to compound interest; but that's only with the Tartars.

CHAPTER III.

TOWN-LIFE—BRAHMINS—WÂNEEÂS—RAJPOOTS—BARDS.

In Goozerat the same rooms occur in all town houses, and in the same order, but the necessities of the site frequently alter the general outline of the building. In country villages, the houses contain, commonly, only the two rooms called "ordo" and "pursâl," with a broad veranda, supported on wooden pillars, in front of the latter. Houses are built for the most part of burnt brick, and are covered with tiles.

The towns are usually surrounded by a wall, and divided, internally, into mehelâs, or wards, each of which contains many houses, but has only one public gateway, and constitutes a species of inner castle. The only public buildings, with the exception of government offices, are those which are devoted to religious purposes—mosques, temples, serais, Jain convents. A river, or large artificial reservoir, is

"In China the laws forbid it; but we who are obliged to run about the land of "grass—we may well ask for a little extra profit. Isn't that fair? A Tartar debt "is never paid: it goes on from generation to generation; every year one goes to "get the interest, and it is paid in sheep, oxen, camels, horses—all that is a great "deal better than money. We get the beasts at a low price, and we sell them at "a very good price in the market. Oh! it's a capital thing, a Tartar debt! It's "a mine of gold.'

"The *Yao Chang Ti* (collector of debts)," adds M. Huc, "accompanied this "explanation of his mode of doing business with peals of laughter."

It is not only among Tartars and Hindoos, however, that such practices prevail. What will our readers say of the following account of a very similar state of things? The extract is from "England as it is in the Middle of the Nineteenth Century," by William Johnston, Esq. Murray. 1851. Vol. ii., p. 200.

"'The cause of the high price of village shops,' continues this gentleman (Mr. Johnston is quoting from a clergyman of Kent), 'arises, I apprehend, from want "of competition. A labourer (it is considered) is allowed credit for a small "amount, and then obliged to deal, under fear of having his debt called for, and "of thus being left destitute for the time. It may be true that the shopkeeper, by "deaths and other causes, loses money, but with such large profits the effect is "slight; and as he knows everybody, he has good tact, and generally avoids a bad "creditor. Millers commonly pursue the same system. Blankets are double the "price of a wholesale shop in London; shoes, too, are excessively high. The "labourer, in consequence, finds himself ill off, and complains that he cannot live "upon his wages, when, in fact, he cannot lay them out to advantage. Averages "and quotations serve little purpose; 'Deal here, or pay your debt' is the practical "argument. I believe one great cause of the bad condition of the poor is to be "found in this."

the usual accompaniment of every town of any consideration, and places of worship are more or less numerous in its vicinity.

The daily routine of small householders of the Brahmin-Wâneeâ class in towns is somewhat as follows. They rise from their beds about four o'clock in the morning, repeating the name of their tutelary divinity, as, O! Muhâ Dev, O! Thâkorjee (Vishnoo), O! Umbâ Mother. The pundit, or Sanscrit scholar, mutters a verse—"I call "to mind in the morning, the lord of the deities, the destroyer of the "fear of death." The Bhugut, or religious layman, chants the praises of his deity in the vernacular stanzas of some poet; or, perhaps, in "mental worship," passes over such things as the following in his mind:—

"My Dev is asleep, in a fine mansion, upon a fine bed. I approach "him and rub his feet, upon which he awakes, and, throwing a shawl "over his shoulders, rises from his couch. I wash his feet with warm "water, and anoint him with scented oils and perfumes. I cause "him to bathe in warm water, and put upon him a garment of yellow "silk, and a pair of shawls, and fetch him a stool to sit upon. I "then make the teeluk upon his forehead, adorn him with gold "ornaments, and hang garlands of flowers about his neck, burn "incense, and light lamps before him, and set before him rice-milk "and sugar to eat. I then wave the *ârtee* before him, and put upon "him a crown, a body-coat, a waistband, and other clothes. I then "prostrate myself before him, and pray to him, and the Dev is "pleased with me."

The ceremony called *ârtee*, or ârâtreek, will be explained in a subsequent chapter.

Brahmins and Bhuguts are frequently under the vow to bathe before sunrise, in which case, as soon as they are risen, and have said their prayers, they either bathe in warm water at home, or set off for that purpose to the tank or the river. After bathing they assume a silk garment that has been washed the day before, and worship. Each Brahmin has, in the Dev-mundeer, within his house, a small throne, upon which seven or eight idols are placed, as the Shâlagrâm stone (a representative of Vishnoo), Bâl Mookoond (the same deity in the form of the infant Krishn), Shiva, Gunputee, Doorgâ Devee, Sooruj (the sun), Hunoomân, or others. These images are washed, dressed in clothes and crowns, presented with flowers and other offerings, and worshipped with the "sixteen services" which will hereafter be described. The morning worship of a Brahmin is sometimes thus performed:—He praises the sun, and offers to him oblations; he then thrusts his right hand into a cloth bag, called a "cow's-mouth," which contains a rosary of one hundred and eight beads of the *Roodrâksh* [1] tree, which he tells over, repeating the mystic Gâyutree for each bead, or the name of his patron god. Sometimes the Brahmin tells his beads four or five times over. He is now ready to take his breakfast.

The eating-room is on one side of the open court, in the centre of the house. The usual meals are two in number; but rich people sometimes eat four times a day. Breakfast is taken about ten or eleven in the forenoon, after ablutions and worship. Brahmins wash the whole body again before eating; Kshutrees and Vaishyas only the hands and feet. They then assume the yellow silk vestment, which covers them from the waist downwards, and is the sole article of dress worn at meals. Each person has a small oblong wooden stool to sit upon, and the food is placed on a similar stool or short-legged table. The vessels used are brass or copper brass—a flat round dish, containing bread and preserves, or condiments, and two or three cups of pottage and vegetables. The water-vessel, of silver or brass, with a small drinking-cup set upon it, stands on one side. The second course is composed of rice and curds, or similar food. On great occasions, however, the fare is more varied and costly.

Ablutions after meals are confined to the hands and face. The men of the family eat at the same table; then the women clean the same vessels, and use them for their own breakfast. The servants take their food after the family breakfast is finished, and they use different vessels. The men chew betel-nut after meals, to prevent their incurring defilement from the touch of a person of lower caste. Such pollution, however, when it occurs, is remediable by the use of "punch-guvya," or the five articles derived from the cow, and by fasting for the remainder of the day.

The second meal, which is a lighter one, is eaten at about eight in the evening.

A Brahmin preparing for dinner makes a place called "choko," the floor of which he spreads with cow-dung and earth, moistened with water. When at home, his own "rusodo," or cooking-room, is the place employed; but, if necessary, the choko may be made under the shade of a hedge by the way-side, or in any other convenient place. Upon the choko he raises a little temporary stove, which he smears in like manner with cow-dung, and thereupon he cooks his food. The Poorbeeâ, or Eastern Brahmins, carry their exclusive notions upon this point to such a length that brothers even

[1] Elœcarpus ganitrus.

are forbidden to use the same choko, nor may one take fire from the stove of another. Hence the saying, "Twelve Poorbeeâs and thir- "teen chokos," because with that number of Brahmins an extra stove would be required for the fire alone.

The Brahmin, when his food is ready, before eating, performs "Turpun;" that is to say, he fills a copper cup with water, and puts therein a few grains of barley, some sesamum, leaves of the sacred basil-tree, sandal, &c., then holding some sacrificial grass, he fills his joined hands with water, which he pours back again into the cup, saying, "I offer (make turpun of) this water to all the Devs." He proceeds to make similar offerings of water to men, animals, trees, rivers, seas, Bhoots, Prets, Reshees, progenitors, and others. Then he mentions the names, as many as he can recollect, of his father's ancestors, his mother's ancestors, and his own deceased friends. He now performs *hom*, or fire-sacrifice, by throwing a portion of rice and clarified butter into a little copper or earthen vessel, containing fire, repeating, while so employed, the names of the Devs. The Brahmin sets aside five portions of food, for cows, beggars, dogs, ants, and crows. He then takes a little of each dish, and offers it to the Dev, in a vessel containing five divisions. He now sits down to his break-fast; but, before commencing, repeats the Gâyutree over a handful of water, with which he sprinkles his own food, and three portions which he sets apart for Brumhâ, Vishnoo, and Shiva. The first five mouthfuls he swallows are for the "Punchprân," or five airs supposed to be in the body and necessary to existence. At the conclusion of his repast, he deposits upon the ground a little of what remains, as an offering on behalf of the spirits residing in hell. This will no doubt appear to the reader to be a very elaborate and painful cere-monial; but long practice enables the Brahmin to acquit himself of the performance in less time than is occupied in the description.

Brahmins frequently consider it necessary that they should observe practices of peculiar difficulty in order to maintain their superiority over the other castes. Of these the most strict is an observance of the Nâgur Brahmins, called "Nuven," or "purity in regard to food." The Brahmin, having bathed, dresses himself in silk or woollen clothes, or if he require to use cotton garments, these must be dipped in water, wrung out, and dried in some place where nothing impure can touch them. Thus habited, he sits down to dinner, but he must preserve himself from numerous accidents which would render him impure, and compel him to desist from his meal. If he touch an earthen vessel he is defiled, unless the vessel have never contained water. The touch of a piece of cotton cloth, or of a piece of leather or paper, which he may accidentally have sat down upon, renders him impure, but if Hindoo letters have been written on the paper they preserve him from defilement, because they represent "Surus- "wutee." If, however, letters be written on cloth or leather, these remain impure. Thus, if the Geetâ, or any other portion of scripture, be required for use at the time, it must be bound with silk and not with cotton; leather must be avoided, and instead of common paste of flour and water, the binder must employ paste of pounded tamarind seed. A printed book will not answer the Brahmin's purpose, because printing ink contains impure matter. Some think that the touch of deer-skin or tiger-skin does not defile. Raw cotton does not render the Brahmin impure, but if it have been twisted for the wick of a lamp by a person not in the state of "Nuven" it does; and again, if it have been dipped in oil or clarified butter it does not. Bones defile, but women's ivory armlets do not, except in those parts of the country where they are not usually worn, and then they do. The touch of a child of the same caste who has not learned how to eat grain does not defile, but if the child have eaten grain it does. The touch of a donkey, a dog, or a pig, defiles; some say that the touch of a cat also defiles, others are inclined to think that it does not, because in truth it is not easy to keep the cat out. If a Brahmin who is in "Nuven" be eating, or if he have risen from eating, the touch of his person defiles another Brahmin who is in "Nuven," but has not begun his dinner.

Wâneeâs, and trading people generally, set off early in the morning to have a sight of the Dev in his temple. Some persons entertain a superstitious notion that everything will prosper with them during the day if they behold a particular person's face the first thing in the morning, so they keep their eyes as completely closed as they can, and set off to see this person of good omen. It is very unlucky, they believe, to see a man who has no son, an outcaste, a donkey, or a quarrelsome person. Others worship the first thing in the morning the "sacred basil," or the holy fig-tree. After they have eaten breakfast and chewed betel, they set off to the public market, where they follow their occupation until evening time, when they return home to dinner, paying, perhaps, on their way, a second visit to the temple.

It is the men's business to make what purchases are necessary for the household in the market, and to keep the accounts. All other domestic duties devolve upon the women.

The wives of the poorer class of householders rise at three in the morning frequently to grind grain, and are occupied, perhaps for three hours, in preparing as much flour as will last until the third day. When they have no grain to grind they must still rise at the same early hour, to milk the cows, churn, and extract clarified butter. At six o'clock, after arranging their costume, they set off with their vessels to the river-side, where they bathe, and fill water, and then return home. Some women bathe at home, and fetch water afterwards, and rich men's wives have a servant specially for attendance on the bath. When the women return with their water-vessels filled they must set to work to prepare breakfast. The males of the family, when breakfast is ready, sit down in a line at short intervals, and eat; when they rise, the women sit down. Breakfast finished, and the men off to their various duties, the women are busily employed in cleaning the house, the fireplace, the plates and dishes, and other vessels, and in preparing grain for grinding. About three in the afternoon they have a little leisure, which they employ in attending to their children, or in combing out their own long hair, and oiling it. In the evening they are again busy getting ready lights, preparing dinner, and spreading the beds.

When a caste entertainment takes place, the guests either wash at home, and dress themselves in silk clothes, or if the distance be considerable, carry their dining dress with them to the house of their host, who provides them with water to bathe in. When they are dressed, the men sit down in two lines outside the entertainer's house and take their dinner; as soon as they have finished their repast, the women sit down in a similar manner. In some places the women dine at the same time as the men, but at a short distance from them. The persons who prepared the dinner set it before the guests, and dine themselves when the rest have finished. On the west of the Sâbhermutee river the women dress for dinner in cotton, which practice is the subject of much contemptuous remark among the people of the eastern districts, whose wives wear silk dresses. In some places no person, not even a man of the caste, unless he have bathed and dressed himself in silk, can pass between the two lines of guests at a public feast without defiling the company, and it becomes therefore necessary that the entertainer should procure permission to barricade the street in which he lives. In other parts of the country a person of the same, or of higher caste, may pass without removing his clothes, but he must leave his shoes behind him, and carry his turban in his hand, and above all he must be particular not to carry with him a book bound in leather, or any other leathern article. Five or six of the caste are usually stationed on either side of the lines to keep off the dogs, a task in which they are not always successful, and when a dog gets in, his appearance creates quite a scuffle: hands are raised on all sides to drive him away, and it generally ends in his putting his foot into some man's plate, and jumping over him, or else in his rushing between two men, rendering them both impure. The sufferers, however, put up with the affront quietly for the time being, and finish what is in their plates, that they may not be guilty of disrespect to Unn Dev,[1] or sometimes they call to the sentinels, who remove their plates, and bring them fresh ones.

In times of peace and ease the Rajpoot leads an indolent and monotonous life. It is some time usually after sunrise before he bestirs himself, and begins to call for his hookah; after smoking, he enjoys the luxury of tea or coffee, and commences his toilet and ablutions, which dispose of a considerable part of the morning. It is soon breakfast-time, and after breakfast the hookah is again in requisition, with but few intervals of conversation, until noon. The time has now arrived for a siesta, which lasts until about three in the afternoon. At this hour the chief gets up again, washes his hands and face, and prepares for the great business of the day, the distribution of the red-cup, kusoombâ or opium. He calls together his friends into the public hall, or perhaps retires with them to a garden-house. Opium is produced, which is pounded in a brass vessel and mixed with water; it is then strained into a dish with a spout, from which it is poured into the chief's hand. One after the other the guests now come up, each protesting that kusoombâ is wholly repugnant to his taste, and very injurious to his health, but after a little pressing, first one and then another touches the chief's hand in two or three places, muttering the names of Devs, friends or others, and drains the draught. Each, after drinking, washes the chief's hand in a dish of water which a servant offers, and wipes it dry with his own scarf; he then makes way for his neighbour. After this refreshment the chief and his guests sit down in the public hall, and amuse themselves with chess, draughts, or games of chance, or perhaps dancing girls are called in to exhibit their monotonous measures, or musicians and singers, or the never-failing favorites—the Bhâts and Châruns. At sunset the torch-bearers appear, and supply the chamber with light, upon which all those who are seated therein rise, and make obeisance towards the chieftain's cushion. They resume their seats, and playing, singing, dancing, story-telling go on as before. At about eight the chief rises to retire to his dinner and his hookah, and the party is broken up.

[1] Food personified as a deity.

As may have been already observed in the course of our narratives, the Rajpoot chief has always several ladies, each of whom is maintained in a separate suite of apartments. He dines and spends the evening alternately in the apartments of each of the ladies, who, with her attendants, prepares dinner for him, and waits upon him while he eats it, waving the punkah or fan behind him, and entertaining him with her remarks, which, if report speak true (for no stranger is admissible on such occasions), frequently constitute a pretty severe curtain lecture.

Closely connected with the Rajpoots are the Bards, the Bhâts, and Châruns. Of their origin nothing is known, but they assert themselves to have sprung from Muhâ Dev or Shiva. They are in some places cultivators, in others bankers, but their more legitimate occupations are those of acting as securities for the performance of engagements, and of recording the genealogies of their Rajpoot clients.

During the anarchy which has more or less prevailed in Goozerat from the time when the dynasty of Unhilpoor was overthrown by the Mohummedans, to the time when, under British influence, the settlement was effected which we have described, the security of a bard was one of the few available means of ensuring the performance of both political engagements and private agreements, and of providing for the safe transaction of commercial operations. Whether the paramount power sought a guarantee from the half-independent principalities for the payment of their tribute, or a private individual desired assurance of oblivion and personal safety from the chief whom he had offended,—whether the money-lender looked for a pledge of repayment, or the merchant for a safe transit of his goods through a country infested with robbers,—the bard was alike resorted to as the only person whose security could be accepted without danger. As the descendant and favourite of the gods, his person was sacred in the eyes of men, who reverenced but little else, and he had at his command means of extorting compliance with his demands which were seldom used in vain. These were the rites of "Trâgâ" and "Dhurnâ," which consisted,—the former, in the shedding by the bard of the blood of himself or of some member of his family, and the calling down upon the offender, whose obstinacy necessitated the sacrifice, the vengeance of heaven; and the latter, in placing around the dwelling of the recusant a cordon of bards, who fasted, and compelled the inhabitants of the house also to fast, until their demands were complied with. It was not until the establishment of British supremacy rendered the performance of these barbarous rites impossible, that the custom of employing bardic security fell into disuse.

In his heraldic and poetical capacity, however, it is that the bard has been longest and most favourably distinguished. When the rainy season closes, and travelling becomes practicable, the bard sets off on his yearly tour from his residence in the "Bhâtwârâ" of some city or town. One by one he visits each of the Rajpoot chiefs who are his patrons, and from whom he has received portions of land, or annual grants of money, timing his arrival if possible to suit occasions of marriage or other domestic festival. After he has received the usual courtesies he produces the "Wye,"[1]—a book written in his own crabbed hieroglyphics, or in those of his fathers, which contains the descent of the house, if the chief be the "Teelâyut," or head of the family, from the founder of the tribe; if he be a "Phutâyo," or cadet, from the immediate ancestor of the branch, interspersed with many a verse or ballad, the "dark sayings" contained in which are chanted forth in musical cadence to a delighted audience, and are then orally interpreted by the bard, with many an illustrative anecdote or tale. The Wye is not, however, merely a source for the gratification of family pride, or even of love of song; it is also a record of authority by which questions of consanguinity are determined when marriage is on the tapis, and disputes relating to the division of ancestral property are decided, intricate as these last necessarily are from the practice of polygamy, and the rule that all the sons of a family are entitled to a share. It is the duty of the bard at each periodical visit to register the births, marriages, and deaths which have taken place in the family since his last circuit, as well as to chronicle all the other events worthy of remark which have occurred to affect the fortunes of his patron; nor have we ever heard even a doubt suggested regarding the accurate, much less the honest, fulfilment of this duty by the bard.

The manners of the bardic tribe are very similar to those of their Rajpoot clients; their dress is nearly the same, but the bard seldom appears without the "Kutâr" or dagger, a representation of which is scrawled beside his signature, and often rudely engraved upon his monumental stone, in evidence

[1] Hence the bard is called "Wyewunchâ," reader of the "Wye."

of his death in the sacred duty of Trâgâ. The heraldic occupation is hereditary, and as the bard goes forth on his annual circuits, attended not only by his servants and retinue (the females only being left at home), but also by his sons, the latter have numerous opportunities of becoming acquainted with the history of their patrons, and of learning, beside the funeral monuments of the race, all that traditionary lore which forms their ancestral wealth.

Of the poetic value of the bardic chronicles we have in some degree enabled our reader to form his own estimate. Perhaps it may be thought of them (as Johnson thought of the so-called "Poems of "Ossian"), that "nothing is more easy than to write enough in that "style if once you begin." Where poets form an hereditary profession, the character of the poetry can hardly be secure from this criticism. Their exaggerations are awkwardly great, and all their little fishes are apt to speak like great whales,[1] their descriptions and their similes have so little variety that they might almost be stereotyped. Still it must, we think, be admitted that there is often in the bardic sketches much of spirit, and of effective, however rude, colour and drawing. Their historical value may be accurately measured by a rule with which the biographer of the "Queens of England" furnishes us: "No "one," says Miss Strickland, "who studies history ought to despise "tradition, for we shall find that tradition is, on the whole, accurate "as to fact, but wholly defective and regardless of chronology." The bardic accounts, where they are written, and *are intelligible without oral explanation*, may rank with the contemporaneous ballad poetry of other nations; where unwritten, they approximate to common oral tradition. The written genealogies, where they do not ascend to fabulous periods, are doubtless correct in the main. In matters of less strictness even the bards themselves, though they admit a certain laxity, assert their material accuracy. The following is their canon:

> Without fiction there will be a want of flavour,
> But too much fiction is the house of sorrow.
> Fiction should be used in that degree
> That salt is used to flavour flower.

And in another couplet they assert that—

> As a large belly shows comfort to exist,
> As rivers show that brooks exist,
> As rain shows that heat has existed,
> So songs show that events have happened.

There is one subject, at least, upon which bardic testimony cannot

[1] This was the criticism applied by Goldsmith to Johnson himself: "If he were "to write a fable of little fishes, he would make them speak like great whales."

be impugned—the subject, we mean, of manners and customs; and without contending for what is extravagant, we may remark that the bards, even if by an operation the very reverse of that which is performed by amber,[1] have enshrined in the rude casket of their tradition much of that for which history is more especially valuable. Fielding, in vindicating the use and dignity of the style of writing in which he excelled, against the loftier pretensions of professed historians, said that in their productions nothing was true but the names and dates, whereas in his everything was true but the names and dates. "If so," remarked Hazlitt, "he has the advantage on his side."

The bardic song, with all its virtues and its vices, its modicum of truth, and its far larger mass of worthlessness, is now nearly silent, and can never revive; the swords which it celebrated are broken or rusted, the race by whose deeds it was inspired is fast passing away. Perhaps it may be the fate of even these poor unworthy pages to call attention for nearly the last time to the verse which has been, for so many centuries, alike a solace in peace and a stimulant in danger to the sons of the Kshutrees.

CHAPTER IV.

RAJPOOT LAND-TENURES UNDER THE MOHUMMEDANS AND THE MAHRATTAS.

Though victorious in the field, the Mohummedan invaders had effected nothing towards the permanent conquest of Goozerat until the time of Allah-ood deen Khiljy. The inroads of Kootb-ood-deen Eibuk produced little more solid effect than the expeditions of Mahmood of Ghuznee, and, but for the demise of the first Solunkhee dynasty, the kingdom of Unhilpoor might still, perhaps, have resisted the arms of even the now established empire of Delhi. If the death of Bheem Dev II., however, did not leave a vacant throne, the royal authority was certainly henceforth either in abeyance or but feebly wielded.

[1] "Family tradition and genealogical history, upon which much of Sir Everard's "discourse turned, is the very reverse of amber, which, itself a valuable substance, "usually includes flies, straws, and other trifles; whereas these studies, being "themselves very insignificant and trifling, do nevertheless serve to perpetuate a "great deal of what is rare and valuable in ancient manners, and to record many "curious and minute facts, which could have been preserved and conveyed through "no other medium."—*Waverley*, chap. iv.

The kings, suffering, perhaps, under the defects of an incomplete title, held even the crown lands which they possessed with no firmness of grasp, and allowed the outlying territory to escape almost entirely from their control. Their Purmâr vassals of Chundrâwutee were overrun by the Chohâns; the conquered chiefs of Kutch resumed their independence; the Râs of Soreth reasserted their old supremacy in that peninsula, and entertained followers, who soon became as powerful as their lords. The aboriginal tribes, taking advantage of the feebleness of the throne, began again to raise their heads. The Mairs of Dhundhooka and the Sords of Eedur exhibited the state of princes; the Bâreeâs of Gogo and Peerum wielded all that remained of the naval power of the kings of Unhilpoor, and, while the Kânt Bheels pressed upon the Râs of Soreth, their kindred ravaged the lands of the Wâghelas themselves. At this time, also, circumstances forced into the country various foreign chiefs, who, gladly received at first as vassals of the crown, became in the end, from their unquiet ambition, the sources of additional weakness. A Râthor soon established a rival kingdom among the mountains of Eedur, and a Jhâlâ, acquiring possession of an important portion of the home territory, rendered himself independent in all but name, affecting even to have presented a province to his sovereign. The Gohils from the north, the Shodâ Purmârs and Kâtees from Sindh, and other tribes entering Goozerat, joined in marriage with Choorâsumâs, with Wâlâs, or even with aboriginal Mairs, and, aided by them, attempted to wrest land from the Bhoomeeâs, or, perchance, turned their swords against each other. Goozerat was, in truth, invaded not by Moslem alone; and the army, which should have defended her, had broken up into numerous divisions, eager, no doubt, to protect the ground which each independently occupied, but, as a whole, connected by no common interest, and acknowledging no common leader. Under these circumstances, the generals of Allah-ood-deen Khiljy met with a far more feeble opposition than had been encountered by their predecessors, while, at the same time, the booty which they at length succeeded in acquiring had lost a great part of its value.

The account which the Mohummedans themselves have left us of the first period of their possession of Goozerat exhibits a scene of anarchy, produced, no doubt, partly by their want of power to settle the country, but, in a great degree also by the selfish policy in which the emperors indulged in regard to, not only the Hindoos, but also their own officers. Their governors we find continually changed, obtaining, perhaps, "the honor of martyrdom at the hands of the "infidels," or, when more successful against their enemies, disgraced or murdered by the monarchs whom they served. Rebels meanwhile, we are told, rose up in every direction. These outbreaks were at first confined to the Hindoos alone, but after a time the foreign Mohummedan officers, and eventually the viceroys themselves, joined in rebelling against the authority of the emperors, and Mohummed Toghluk, though personally undertaking the task, was unable to effect more than a partial settlement of affairs. Afterwards the resuscitation of the revenue was sought to be effected by farming it out on exorbitant terms, and a serious attempt to detach the province from the imperial authority was met by the appointment of a viceroy, who, from the moment of his setting foot in Goozerat, virtually inaugurated that separate kingdom, the establishment of which it was his commission to prevent.

The only Rajpoot chiefs of note with whom the Mohummedans are known to have come into contact during this period are the Râ of Soreth and his vassal Mokherâjee Gohil. Joonagurh resisted the Moslem attack, and though Peerum was destroyed, and its founder slain, the power of the Gohil clan was unbroken; Gogo and the rest of their territories remained in their possession, and a younger branch had sufficient influence to render itself paramount in the hills of Râjpeepla.

We have observed the measure of success which attended the steps taken by the sultans to effect the completion of the conquest of Goozerat. The Râs of Soreth and the Râwuls of Châmpâner were dethroned by Mahmood Begurra; the Rows of Eedur, however, successfully defended their independence against reiterated attacks, and Chowras, Jhâlâs, Gohils, and others maintained possession of their lands. Nor were they only the great Hindoo landholders who thus preserved their existence, for in every part of the country the hereditary Rajpoot estates constituted no small portion of the lands of each district.

The following is the general account given by the Mohummedan author of Meerât Ahmudee: "The whole of the zumeendârs in the "time of Sultan Ahmed Goozeratee erected the head of rebellion and "disturbance. They were, however, punished, and driven from their "retreats, and the servants of the king were established in every place. "In consequence of being thus completely dispossessed of their habi-"tations, that band of unbelievers, being hopeless, began to infest the "roads and villages with their depredations. Anarchy increased, con-"fusion prevailed, the decay of cultivation became visible, and the "ryots were distressed. Those whose duty it was to advise, in their "foresight put an end to these calamities, and exacted from the "zumeendâr of every village security to discontinue his opposition. "Three parts of the land of each village, under the denomination of "'Tulput,' were acknowledged as the property of the king, and one "portion was given to the zumeendârs, under the denomination of "'Wântâ,' and they were engaged to furnish guards and protection to "their own villages, and were to hold themselves in readiness for the "service of the king whenever called upon. As these people, without "paying obedience to the prince, did not see it possible to establish "themselves, they attended to make their submission, and engaged to "pay the crown a *sulâmee* from their Wântâ; from this time sulâmee "and paishkush became established against them. Some of the "zumeendârs, such as those of Huldhurwâs, Ghorâsur, Âtursoombâ, "Mândoowâ, and others, were converted to Islâm, and entered into "agreements for the defence of their own tâlookâs, and their posses-"sions were conferred upon them by the imperial court, for the en-"couragement of the faith, but they consenting to pay the imperial "'paishkush.' From other principal zumeendârs over whom the hand of "conquest did not extend, the levy of a yearly paishkush was exacted."

We have seen, however, from the narratives of the Mohummedan historians, that this levy was not accomplished without difficulty, and the continual presence of an important military force. The armies of the sultans, year by year, advanced against these Hindoo chiefs (as the armies of the Kings of Unhilpoor had formerly advanced against Soreth, Kutch, or Malwa), with a view of completing their subjugation, if that were practicable, or otherwise of enforcing as large a money payment as they could.

A similar general account is given by the bardic annalists, in whose wild but homely tales we have perceived how some of the Kshutrees' sons apostatized to Islâm; how others, more resolute, treading the flinty pathway of the outlaw's life, regained a scanty portion of their lands; and how a happier few, though flying oft from smoking homes, the mountain cave their dwelling-place, and the shield their sleepless pillow, maintained the unequal contest until their oppressors were no more.

The emperor Akbar was inclined to adopt a more liberal policy than that of his predecessors. The great Hindoo chiefs, as we have seen, had already been engaged in the military service of the state,[1] and now they were freely admitted to the rank of imperial nobles, on the condition that they should place the government mark on their cavalry contingents, and attend the provincial governor on all im-

[1] See p. 299.

portant occasions. The power of the imperial viceroy, or soubahdâr, was supported by a large army, usually quartered at Ahmedabad, which city formed in fact one vast cantonment. The country immediately surrounding the capital, and in other places where the imperial power was undisputed, was "khâlsâ," or under the immediate management of the servants of the crown,—and the superior authority of the soubahdâr was acknowledged from Jhalor to Songurh, on the frontier of Candeish, and from Dwârkâ to the borders of Malwa.[1] In addition to the central army cantoned in Ahmedabad, there were also numerous fortified ports, called Tahnahs, occupied by the imperial troops, in different places. The whole extent of the country was, nevertheless, intersected by the possessions of the Hindoo chieftains, who all of them under the Mogul government, whether "Rajas, Rajpoots, Koolees, or Grassias," bore the general name of zumeendârs. The revenue which was derivable from the zumeendârs, or their villages, was a fixed and settled sum. It was not determined by a valuation of the produce, and the assignment of a portion as the share of government; but, on the contrary, each proprietor obtained the best terms that he could. In the times of the emperors, as in those of the Sultans of Ahmedabad, however, the collection of the revenue from the zumeendârs was always of necessity supported by the presence of a military force.

"If the governor of the Soubah," says the historian, "should "proceed with a large army towards the banks of the Wâtruk, which "is situated to the westward, and also towards the boundary in that "direction, as far as Wânswârâ and Doongurpoor, which may be "about one hundred coss from Ahmedabad, and should return from "Wânswârâ towards the south, the zumeendârs of Sonth and Jâlreeâ "and the Bâreeâ districts, and Râjpeepla, and Mânduvee, and "Râmnugger (which is upon the sea-coast) would settle for their "paishkush; should he proceed towards Doongurpoor, which is to the "north-east, he will effect the settlement of the Zillah of Eedur, "Seerohee, Dântâ, the hills of Geer, Ranna Bao Phaphur, Khundeya-"nugger, the tâlookâ of Kutch, and from thence the zumeendârs of "Jhâlâwâr, Moorbee, Hulwud, the Sirkâr of Islâmnugger (Bhooj), "Jugut Ranna Bhao, Sirkâr of Soreth, Porbunder, Chanyeh Kesoje, "Oonah, and others of Kâteewâr,—Gohilwâr, Loleeyânah, Dhun-"dhooka, and Dholka, and at length arrive at Khumbâyut, which is "situated on the sea-coast, through the above-named Zillahs."

[1] See verbal information relative to the state of Goozerat, communicated to Colonel Walker by Amrut Lall, agent for nearly thirty years on behalf of the Peshwah's governor of Ahmedabad.

Many of the great zumeendârs continued to perform service until the reign of Aurangzeeb, but regained after that time their complete independence. In the same period of disorder the small landholders also strove, and not without partial success, to recover the lands which they had been compelled to resign in favour of the crown.

"In the course of time," says the same Mohummedan author, the "Rajpoots and Koolees, who had become powerful, excited dis-"turbances, carried away the cattle from towns, and murdered the "inhabitants during the harvest season. The people having no "means of redress, purchased exemption from these evils by giving "the authors of them a yearly payment in money, or by yielding up "possession of one or more fields fit for cultivation, and such claim "for exemption is called *grâs* or *wol*. This custom, gradually "established, has been so matured through the weakness of the "provincial governors, that there are very few places in the pergun-"nahs where some of the Rajpoot, Koolee, or Mohummedan inha-"bitants do not possess the right to grâs.

"As these people are naturally disobedient, addicted to theft. "highway robbery, and sedition, they therefore excited insurrections "whenever the government of the provincial rulers indicated the "least weakness. On this account several of the governors, both in "past and present times, after strengthening the fortifications of the "province, stationed a sufficent party of soldiers therein, and these "posts are named Tahnahs. The payment of each Tahnah has "been fixed by government, and certain lands are set aside for this "purpose in order that the party of men may never leave the post, "lest disturbances might be set on foot. Now that the unsettled "state of the province goes on increasing, the seditious tribes already "mentioned have levelled the small forts, where there were formerly "Tahnahs, and by establishing themselves in others, have obtained "possession in many towns of the tulput government share instead "of *grâs*.

"At present (A.D. 1747-8 to 1756), the provincial governor raises "a force, and collects a tribute from the holders of *wântâ* in posses-"sion of the tulput, in proportion to the capability of each place, "while he takes security from his own amildars (or officers); but "when the great landholders refuse to pay the tribute, what power "has the provincial governor to enforce it? and so faithless have "they become, that he cannot pass the city gate without an escort "from them."

There were, however, causes wholly independent of the Mohummedan conquest, which tended to reduce the power of the Rajpoot chiefs. The younger brothers of a family were invariably considered entitled to a portion of the paternal estate. In the case of important chieftainships this right was restricted to a portion of land, assigned as a maintenance, the extent of which varied according to circumstances, and the cadet, or "phutâyo," was the vassal of the "teelâyut," or chieftain; but where the estate of a cadet was concerned, his sons either divided the lands equally among themselves, or the younger brothers, sharing alike, assigned a larger share to the elder. Had circumstances permitted the strict and regular action of this system, it is manifest that the land-holding families must have been in every case, as they really were in many, reduced in a very few descents to the position of mere cultivators. But where no central government existed, and where public and domestic war continually raged around them, the cadets, such especially of them as were themselves "good "Rajpoots," frequently found opportunity for increasing their inheritance at the point of the sword. Many, too, quitted their patrimony to take military service at a distance from home, and the greater mortality among the class, which was inevitably the accompaniment of a state of chronic warfare, aided in retarding the minute subdivision of lands. The chieftain was always of right the heir, in the last resort, of the cadet. Sometimes, where the share of the latter was insufficient to supply his wants, he disposed of it by mortgage or sale to the head of his family; sometimes, from choice or necessity, he assigned his land, or a certain portion of it, to a powerful neighbour, other than his chief, either to purchase protection or to buy off annoyance. A further drain upon the resources of the Rajpoot chiefs existed in the necessity under which they lay, from religious feelings, or the desire of reputation, of conferring gifts upon Brahmins, Gosâees, and other religious mendicants, or upon Bhâts and Châruns, the recorders of fame. These classes were called in some parts of the country by the general name of Yâchuks. We have observed the "lâkh pusâv," the extravagant donations made by Row Veerum Dev, of Eedur, and others. These were not confined to money, apparel, jewels, horses, or other valuable articles, but consisted also of lands, which, from the same word above employed, were called "pusâytâ," and were free from all demands of the original granter, except that which he preserved as heir in the last resort. Pusâytâ lands were also granted to soldiers for military following, and to potters, torch-bearers, and other domestic servants.

The term "grâs" appears, as has been already mentioned,[1] to

[1] *Vide* p. 186.

have originally applied to gifts made to religious persons, such as were afterwards more particularly denominated "pusâv." In the bardic chronicles, however, it is constantly applied to the lands given for their subsistence to junior members of the chieftains' families, and this sense of the word continued for a long time to be the prevalent, if not the exclusive one. At length the term "grâs" was also used to signify the black mail paid by a village to a turbulent neighbour as the price of his protection and forbearance, and in other similar meanings. Thus the title of "grâssiâ," originally an honorable one, and indicating its possessor to be a cadet of the ruling tribe, became at last as frequently a term of opprobrium, conveying the idea of a professional robber, "a soldier of the night," such as the Meleekur of Koompojee of Bhunkorâ.

It is very important that we should recollect these distinctions, as the disregard of them has been the cause of embarrassment, if not of injustice. The concessions which, under the names of grâs or wol, Row Chândo forced from the usurpers of his hereditary principality of Eedur, should not be confounded with the black mail, which, also under the names of grâs or wol, the banditti of the Râjpeepla hills extorted from the defenceless villager, or the receivers of the Choonwâl from the travelling merchant; much rather should confusion be avoided between either of these classes of claims, and the regular and legal title to a share of the family lands which was possessed by the grâssiâ cadet of a Rajpoot house. The following description, by Colonel Walker, of the titles borne by the different chieftains throughout Kâteewar may be applied more generally to the whole of Goozerat:—

"The title of Raja is applicable to the head of the family only. "He must be independent, that is, not pay jumma or tribute to another "of his family. The tribute payable to the Moguls or the Mahrattas "does not affect the independence of his character. The address of "a Raja runs, 'Muhârâjâ Raja Shree ———.' The origin of the "title of Rânâ, which is nowise inferior to that of Raja, cannot be "satisfactorily traced. (Similarly of the title of Row.) The title "which follows next in gradation is that of Râwul, which is the most "appropriate designation of the chieftain of Bhownugger—a distinction "which his ancestors assumed on receiving some assistance from the "Râwul of Doongurpoor. This address runs, 'Râwul Shree ———.' "The sons of Rajas, Rânâs (Rows), and Râwuls bear the appellation "of Koonwur (prince), and *their* sons the designation of Thâkor, pro- "vided they have succeeded to an estate. The sons of a Thâkor are "also called 'Koonwur' during their father's life. On his death the "eldest becomes a Thâkor, and the others 'Bhoomeeâs' and 'Grâssiâs.' "Thâkor, the next gradation after Râwul, is applied to all those who "are not powerful enough to assume and use the title of Raja, or "who are the heads of distinct, but inferior branches of a family. "To the head of a family, Thâkors owe a feudal submission, "exemplified in the payment of tribute, sending a horse, or the per-"formance of service. In their own possessions, Thâkors are, "however, as independent as Rajas. 'Bhoomeeâ' is applied to all "possessors of landed property who are not Rajas or Thâkors, of "which they are the inferior gradation. We have generally called "them 'Grâssiâs,' in consequence of their being the ancient heredi-"tary proprietors of the portion of territory they possess, in which "sense the word 'grâs' is used, and it is equivalent to 'Asil,' or "'Cudeem' (two Mohummedan words, which mean 'root, origin, "'foundation,' and 'ancient, old, former.')"

The establishment of the Mahratta power must be reckoned from the fall of Ahmedabad, in the year A.D. 1755. For some years previously their incursions had been annually repeated under Peelâjee and Dâmâjee Guikowâr, the Peshwah Bâjee Row, and others, and Baroda had been actually taken possession of. The Mahratta inroads up to this time were, however, merely predatory expeditions, in which plunder was the object; and though a chouth had been extorted from the authorities of the Mogul government, still its realization depended upon the extent of the Mahratta military power. Ahmedabad having fallen, the whole country was divided equally between the Peshwah and the Guikowâr, including the tribute payable by the zumeendârs, who, during the contest for supremacy between the Mogul and Mahratta powers, had observed a strict neutrality, paying with equal facility their revenue or jumma to whatever person possessed local authority in their own district. Neither Moguls nor Mahrattas interfered in their internal policy; and during the government of the latter power they continued to possess the same rights and privileges which they had possessed, and to occupy the same position which they had occupied in the time of Akbar, with the exception that a gradual increase to their revenue was imposed by the Mahratta arms.[1]

"In the plain to the south," says Mr. Elphinstone, "and in the "open spaces that run up between the rivers, the Mahratta govern-"ments had the right of administering justice in every village, by "means of its own officers, and it always took an account of the

[1] From the information furnished to Colonel Walker by Amrut Lall, the Peshwah's agent.

"produce of the village lands, of which it was entitled to a certain share. "All the other villages retained their independence on the payment "of a tribute. Most of those which lay on the rivers in the midst of "subjugated country paid it regularly every year to the nearest "revenue officer; but those whose situations were stronger, or more "remote, withheld their tribute until compelled to pay by the "presence of an invading army. The villages which submitted to "the administration of justice and the inspection of their produce "are called *Ryuttee*, those which only pay a tribute *Mewâsee;* but "this last term is not extended to princes, like those of Eedur and "Loonâwârâ. The tribute paid annually to the revenue officer is "called *jummâbundee;* that collected by an officer at the head of "an army is called *ghâns-dhânâ* (grass and grain). There are many "*Mewâsees*, who though they are willing to pay a small sum to the "revenue collector, will not submit to the exaction of a large one "unless supported by a force. These pay both *jummâbundee* and "*ghâns-dhânâ;* the former to the collector every year, the latter to "the commandant of the force that is occasionally sent to levy it. "Both descriptions are, however, equally *tribute*, and neither is a "fixed share of the produce."

In regard to the Rajpoot chiefs here spoken of under the general name of "the grâssiâs," Colonel Walker has the following:—"The "power of life and death, and the administration of justice within "their respective villages, are possessed by all, and it was never "thought necessary to make reference to the authority of the "superior government residing at the Kusbah of the pergunnah (or "principal town of the district) in order to obtain leave for the "punishment or to avert the effects of having punished a criminal or "disobedient ryot. And also, in the event of a crime against "government being committed, it was usual to demand of the grâssiâ "whose ryot might have committed the act, that he should take the "necessary measures for punishing the same. In respect to exterior "relations, they appear to have exercised the same freedom. The "external interests of such petty states could not have extended far, "and may be supposed confined in great measure to their own "neighbourhood. But they enjoyed the right of peace and war with "each other. They formed such connexions as might be necessary "for the extension and security of their commerce; they built "fortifications and maintained troops. Nor does it appear that any "of the states to whom they paid tribute ever interfered in their "transactions, whether foreign or domestic, so long as they were "not inimical to themselves. It is generally admitted that the "payment of a tribute does not deprive the tributary of his independence." * * *

"With their hereditary possessions also they receive a variety of seigneurial rights and privileges. The grâssiâ proprietors of villages assign lands to Rajpoots and others for military services in the defence of themselves and property; they call for the services of all the artificers of the village whenever they require them; they possess the right to all trees which may fall down, although the produce may belong to the tenant who occupies the ground. Fees are paid to them for permission to contract a marriage, and some collections are made on the birth of their children; they abate and increase the revenues they derive from their ryots at their own pleasure."

The principal source of revenue possessed by the chiefs was the share of the crops which they received in kind. In the case of garden crops, sugar-cane, cotton, tobacco, opium, and other crops, in regard to which it is difficult to make the kultur or assessment which has been described, they levied a money rent. They sometimes received a tax upon ploughs as part of their land revenue. Sometimes, where the share of the produce was small, they exacted a trifling money payment in compensation. When land was assigned to the cadets of a family, it was the practice in certain parts of the country that the chief retained the money payments, leaving only the share of produce to the cadet. Cultivators reclaiming land, instead of paying in kind, made for a few years only a small acknowledgement to the chief in money. The produce of all trees usually belonged to the chief; waifs and strays also belonged to him. He levied transit duties on traders' goods, taxes on liquor shops, and on tanners and curriers, which latter tax, however, was in compensation for the perquisite allowed to those trades of removing the hides of all animals which died in the village.

The tax on marriages was trifling, varying from one shilling to four shillings. The chief received all fines imposed for criminal offences, and sometimes a fourth of the sum awarded in civil suits.

The whole administration of such parts of each district as were *ryutee* was confided, by the Mahrattas, to a komâvishdâr, a collector, or rather a farmer, of revenue. The residence of this person in the district was only temporary—he was, at any time, liable to be displaced by any other who was prepared to offer higher terms for the possession of his authority; it was, therefore, his interest to accumulate as much money as possible, without reference either to the permanent revenue of the pergunnah, or to the happiness of its inhabitants. One means of enriching himself was that of exacting fines for criminal offences; and with no severer punishment, therefore, crimes of the most heinous and flagitious nature were passed over. Civil disputes, which consisted principally of claims for the possession of land, for the recovery of debts, or for the assertion of caste rules, were, under the government of these farmers, referred to arbitration, the komâvishdâr interfering only by lending the aid of his authority for the enforcement of the award, and by appropriating to his own use a fourth of the sum awarded.

On the estates of the Rajpoot chieftains, justice, both civil and criminal, where it was administered at all, was in the hands of the grâssiâ. The influence of the Bhâts and Châruns was very powerful, and usually compelled the proper execution of engagements, for the performance of which they were securities. Where they referred cases to arbitration, the conduct of the grâssiâs contrasted very favourably with that of the komâvishdârs. The chiefs levied only a very small sum from the disputants, which was proportioned to their means, and was always appropriated to charitable purposes.[1]

Justice was administered principally through a system of ordeals and oaths, which still remains in vogue, both in the crown-lands of the Guikowâr state and in the Moolukgeeree districts of Kâteewâr and the Myhee Kântâ. Whatever the evidence in his possession, the complainant, instead of using it, most frequently preferred compelling the defendant to undergo an ordeal or to take an oath; and the defendant, on the other hand, often sought to anticipate his assailant by referring the matter through him to the same *judicium Dei*. Thus the point in dispute was often determined by the success of one of the parties in putting the other upon his trial by oath or ordeal, for, especially in the case of persons of character, it was held more creditable to retire from the contest altogether than to maintain it upon the ordealistic ground. There is a description of the ordeal, which is remarkably consonant with existing practice, in Renaudot's Arabian travellers. "In the Indies," say they, "when one man accuses another of a "crime punishable with death, it is customary to ask the accused if "he is willing to go through the trial by fire; and, if he answers in "the affirmative, they heat a piece of iron till it is red hot; this done, "they tell him to stretch forth his hand, and upon it they put seven

[1] *Vide* Mr. Diggle's letter to Colonel Walker, forming an Appendix to that officer's report "On the Company's late acquisitions in Goozerat, from the Peshwah and Guikowâr," dated 18th June, 1804. In regard to the last statement, see however, above.

" leaves of a tree they have in the Indies,[1] and upon these leaves they " put the red hot iron; and, in this condition, he walks backwards " and forwards for some time, and then throws off the iron. Imme- " diately after this, they put his hand into a leathern bag, which they " seal with the prince's signet; and if, at the end of three days, he " appears and declares that he has suffered no hurt, they order him " to take out his hand, when, if no sign of fire is seen, they declare " him innocent, and delivered from the punishment which threatened " him; and his accuser is condemned to pay a *man* of gold as a fine to " the prince.

" Sometimes they boil water in a caldron till it is so hot that no " one may approach it; then they throw an iron ring into it, and " command the person accused to thrust his hand down, and bring " up the ring. The accuser is in this case also to pay a *man* of gold."

" In the vicinity of my village," says a Goozeratee author of the present day, " there is a tree called the 'thief's limbaro,' where the " *hot oath* is administered to thieves. When a thief has been appre- " hended, or in any case where a dispute has occurred, and it cannot " be ascertained who is the guilty party, then the hot oath is ad- " ministered to either one or both of the disputants. Fifteen years " ago the oath was administered to a goldsmith. I did not go myself " to see what happened, but I heard the following account of it:— " The Raja's Kârbhâree caused an iron ring to be heated at the " 'thief's tree,' and ordered the Koolee, who was the goldsmith's " opponent, to take it up. People say that the Koolee had bribed " the Kârbhâree, so that, at the time of lifting the ring, the Koolee, " worshipping the Sun, said, 'O! Sooruj, sire, if I am in the right " save me!' and so saying he touched the ring with his hand, where- " upon the Kârbhâree immediately exclaimed, 'The Koolee has " saved himself!' Then, turning to the goldsmith, he said, 'If you " are in the right, lift the ring.' The goldsmith took off his turban " and body-coat; and went to a well, called the Gungâ well, which is " in that place, to perform ablutions. He became very sad, and " considered within himself whether he should not jump into the well, " and give up his life. At that time a voice issued from the well, " which said, 'Take courage!' Hearing this, the goldsmith looked " up and around, but in that space he saw no one, so he considered " that it must have been some Dev that ordered him to take courage. " After ablutions, he went out of the well somewhat reassured, but

[1] The burr-tree is here alluded to. We have ourselves seen this ordeal employed. The leaves usually protect the person from injury.

" when he looked at the ring, and saw how very hot it was, his fears " returned in full force. At that time, however, he perceived a train " of ants passing over the ring, which sight gave him some con- " fidence. At last, worshipping the Sun, he said, 'O! father Sun, if " I be in the right, protect me!' So saying, he took the ring out of " the fire with his hand, and placed it on his neck. Then the Kâr- " bhâree said, 'You have saved yourself; now throw the ring down;' " but the goldsmith replied, 'No! let me go first to the Bâee Râj (or " Thâkorine), and after that I will take off the ring.' At that time, " one of two shepherds, who were standing by, took the ring off the " goldsmith's neck with his staff. In the place where it fell upon the " ground the dust began to be very much heated. Then they said " to the Koolee, 'Put the ring in the same way on your neck,' but he " was unable to lift it, and his hand was found to have been burned " and blistered from having touched it in the first instance; so the " Koolee was pronounced to be in the wrong, and the goldsmith in " the right, and a large number of villagers who had come to see the " oath administered separated, remarking sagely to each other, that " 'even in this Iron Age, the Supreme Being has not deserted the " earth.'

" Sometimes an iron chain or ball is used in the same way as the " ring, the accused being ordered to lift it; and, sometimes he is " directed to take a ring or three copper coins out of a vessel filled " with heated oil. I have heard that a person, having professed his " willingness to submit to the trial by ordeal, a vessel of oil was " heated, and a cocoa-nut thrown therein to test the heat, and that, " though this was immediately cracked, the suspected person was " enabled to prove his innocence by taking copper coins out of this " hot oil, which he said seemed to his touch to be cold water.[1]

" At the village of Bhureeâd, near Dholera, there is the shrine of " a very celebrated Mohummedan saint, who is called 'Peer Bhuree- " âdro,' to which many people are taken to be tried by ordeal. The " defendant is compelled to put on a pair of iron fetters, and is then " directed to walk past the Peer's tomb: if the fetters fall off, he is " held to be cleared. I have heard that some contrivance is resorted " to in the making of these fetters, so that they may fall off.

" Another kind of ordeal is used at Bhownugger. There is a " stone there with a hole in it, through which, if a suspected man can

[1] See the extract from Sonnerat's travels descriptive of a feast of fire in honor of Dhurum Râj, or Yoodishteer, and Droupudee.—D'Oyly and Mant's Bible, note on Leviticus, cap. xviii. v. 21.

" creep, his character is held to be cleared; if he cannot, he is pro-
" nounced to be a liar. The stone goes by the name of *the window*
" *of truth and falsehood.*[1]

" The mode of administering the cold oath is this: The person
" swearing, professes his readiness to take a flower off an image of
" Shiva, or to place his hand upon the foot of some Dev; if the
" opposite party agrees, then the defendant clears himself by taking
" an oath in this form. If it be wished to impose on a Hindoo a
" very binding cold oath, he is compelled to place his hand on the
" neck of a Brahmin; or if one still more stringent is called for, the
" swearer is required to touch with a knife the neck of a cow, the
" meaning being, that if he breaks the oath he incurs the sin of
" Brahmin, or cow-murder. All these oaths are considered to possess
" great force, and they are only employed when the matter in dispute
" is of considerable importance; for smaller matters, lesser oaths are
" used.

" A Brahmin swears by his junoee, or cord of regeneration; a
" Râjpoot by his sword; a Wâneeo by Sârdâ, or Suruswutee (by
" which he means *his account-book*); a cultivator swears by his bul-
" lock; a Mohummedan by some rozah, or the saint that dwells
" therein; a Shrâwuk swears by his religion, or else says 'puchkând.'
" Many people swear by their sons, by grain, by their hopes, by their
" youth, by their brothers, by their fathers or mothers, or by their eyes;
" they mean to imprecate upon themselves the loss of these in case
" of their breaking the oath. Women swear by their husbands and
" sons; a widow, when called upon to swear, says, 'If I speak false,
" may I have the same fate for seven lives.' A Vaishnavite swears
" by his necklace, an ascetic by his beads, an artificer by his craft, a
" sailor by the jewel-mine—the sea, a wealthy man swears by Luksh-
" mee, *a school-boy by learning (!)*. A goldsmith swears by Mâtâ,
" meaning any Devee, but particularly Doorgâ, in the form of 'the
" 'lady of the tiger,' but they get out of this oath (in the very spirit
" of the casuists) by saying they meant to swear by some stout man
" (mâto). If a person swear by his ancestors, or by any deceased
" person, his oath is not accepted. Boys fancy that if they swear a
" false oath with the tongue between the front teeth (like the English
" school-boy's '*over the left*') it is no matter. The person who swore
" a man for any particular purpose, may release him from his obliga-
" tion by saying, 'The oath is void.' In the small country villages a

[1] *Vide* p. 354.

"great deal of business is transacted on the faith of these oaths, and "many people never make them falsely."

There is another spot consecrated to Peer Bhureeâdro, near Ahmednugger, in the Myhee Kântâ, at which people are tried by ordeal. A second mode of taking an oath by the Peer, is to lift one of the earthern toy-like horses, which are set before him by his votaries. Melâdee Mâtâ has a shrine near Kuree. The mode of swearing by her which is usually employed is that of raising in the hands a lighted lamp from before her image, and saying, "If I speak "falsely, may Melâdee Mâtâ take an answer from me in so many "days!" At Dhuborâ, near Sâdrâ, there is a temple of Hunoomân, who is here surnamed "Dubhoreeo." If it be intended to swear a minor oath by this idol, the party merely touches its foot; if a more impressive oath is required, the swearer drinks a cup of Hunoomân's oil. At Shâmlâjee, the mode of swearing is to take up a flower which has been offered to the god.

In the districts about Pâhlunpoor and Dântâ, the following is a common mode of settling disputes. The defendant goes to the bank of a river, or other place where there is sufficient water, attended by a friend, and accompanied by the plaintiff, who is armed with a bow and arrow. In order to clear himself, the defendant must keep his head under water for a sufficient time to allow of his friend's returning with an arrow which the plaintiff has shot from his bow.

Colonel Tod describes a stone similar to that at Bhownugger, but possessing powers still more extraordinary, which is to be found on the adjacent mountain of Shutroonjye. "Near the Choree of Ne-"meenâth," he says, "there is a plain flat stone, having, about three "feet above its insertion in the ground, a square hole of fifteen inches "diameter, called the *mooktdwara*, or 'door of bliss,' and whoever "can so compress his body as to pass through this ordeal of purity, "is sure of beatitude (*mookt*). Few of the sons of Mammon, who "'lard the lean earth,' can bear this test, unless they greatly mortify "the flesh. Strange to say, there is a stone image of a camel, nearly "as large as life, in juxtaposition with the 'door of bliss,' and as all "these erect stones are termed *sula*, or 'needle,' our Scriptural text "could not but suggest itself to the mind."

There is another stone of the same kind at Dubhoee, which bears the name of "Mâmâ Dokuree," and is mentioned by the author of the "Oriental Memoirs."

In all these modes of trial, and many others which are of daily use in different parts of Goozerat, the principle is the same. The judges tacitly admitting their incompetency to sit in judgment upon the accused, require him to pronounce upon his own guilt or innocence, by refusing or accepting the trial which is proposed to him. They are all of them, therefore, equally appeals to the *judicium Dei*—are, in fact, ordeals.[1]

[1] William of Malmesbury mentions, as a proof of the sanctity of the "old church" of Glastonbury, "that within the memory of man, all persons who, before "undergoing the ordeal of fire or water, there put up their petitions, exulted in "their escape, one only excepted," of whose case, however, he declines to inform us. If the assertion be a true one, we fear that the sanctity of this "depositary "of so many saints" must occasionally have been prostituted to the support of falsehood.

Similar miracles were wrought at the shrine of St. Thomas-à-Becket, at Canterbury, as we are told by a monkish historian who lived at the time of the saint's martyrdom, and from whose work it may be gathered that the royal officers had then frequent recourse to the trial-by-water ordeal. "Two men," he says, "were "impeached upon the Forest Act for stealing deer; and being tried by the water-"ordeal, one was cast, and hanged; the other, by invoking St. Thomas's inter-"cession, escaped. Another, accused of having stolen a whetstone and pair of "gloves, was convicted by the water-ordeal, and had his eyes dug out, and some "of his members were cut off, but were perfectly restored to him by the interces-"sion of the martyr, which he implored."

It was not, therefore, only upon special occasions that the ordeal was used in England; it was, in fact, the soul of the original Anglo-Saxon system of law,—the only species of trial which existed. Nor was it until the reign of Henry III. that the trial by ordeal was abolished. Up to that time it had been sanctioned by the clerical as well as the temporal rulers, both in England and Sweden, being performed, as we are told by Blackstone, only in the churches or other consecrated ground. Notwithstanding this fact, it appears, however, that the Church was mainly instrumental in the abolition, for we find royal letters. of the third year of the reign of Henry, addressed to the itinerant judges of the counties of Lancaster, Cumberland, and Westmoreland (the northern circuit of that day), announcing to them that because it was not determined, previous to the opening of the circuit, what form of trial they should undergo who were charged with robbery, murder, arson, and the like, "since the ordeal of fire and water had been prohibited by "the Roman church" (cum prohibitum sit per ecclesiam Romanam judicium ignis et aquæ), it had been provided by the king in council that the judges should proceed in a particular manner then laid down, in regard to persons accused of those crimes. About the same time King Valdemar II. abolished the trial by ordeal in Denmark. Vestiges of the practice have, however, been traced by antiquaries in customs long afterwards used. Such was that of leaping over the fire on Midsummer Eve, a superstitious instance of agility, from which we are told grave clergymen had to be deterred by an interdiction of ecclesiastical authority. Such also were the long-continued customs of swimming people suspected of witchcraft, or weighing them against the Church Bible, of which former King James, in his "Dæmonologie," as quoted by Brand, observes, that "it appears that God hath "appointed for a supernatural signe of the monstrous impietie of witchcrafte, that "the water shall refuse to receive them in her bosom that have shaken off them "the sacred water of baptism, and wilfully refused the benefit thereof." Such a

Villages were, by the custom of the country, held responsible for the value of property stolen within their limits, unless the footsteps of the robbers could be traced on to another place. It was therefore the duty of the police to keep watch throughout the day in the village lands, in order to prevent suspicious persons harbouring there. At break of day they were further bound to examine and carefully preserve the marks of all unrecognised footsteps, which might have been imprinted during the preceding night, in order that, if called upon, they might be enabled satisfactorily to take up and carry on the traces.[1]

Besides the territory which was under the jurisdiction of the hereditary chiefs of the country, and that which was entirely controlled by the central government, there was a portion of the lands of Goozerat which occupied an intermediate position, under the sway of a class of men who, though not possessed of hereditary rights, had succeeded in assuming what was well nigh their equivalent. Of this

relic, also, is probably the proverbial expression of *going through fire and water to serve any one.* A further relic of the ordeal has been noticed in the replication which a prisoner under indictment was called upon to make, that he would be tried "*by God and the country,*" or more properly "*by God* or *the country,*" that is to say, either by jury or by *ordeal*—the *judicium Dei.*

In our County Courts in England, and Sheriff Courts in Scotland, where the case is often allowed to rest wholly or partly on the oath of the party, we have returned very much to the old ordeal trial.

"There are cases," says that philosophic jurist, Bentham, "in which no evi-" dence can be had—in which plaintiff and defendant stand on their mere affirma-" tion and denial: ought the plaintiff to be denied the only means left—an appeal" to the conscience of his adversary? I answer, that in all such cases (*and they*" *are not instances of true judicial procedure, but of a sort of ordeal, similar to that*" *of red-hot iron or boiling water*) it would be much better," &c.

[1] It is curious to notice the similarity between the state of things which we have thus described, and that which once existed in our own country. "The criminal " laws of the Anglo-Saxons," says Russell, in his History of Modern Europe, vol. i., p. 53, "as of most barbarous nations, were far from being severe; a com-" pensation in money being deemed sufficient for murder of any species, and for" the lives of persons of any rank, including the king and the primate, whose head," by the laws of Kent, was estimated at a higher rate than that of the king. The" prices of all kinds of wounds were also settled; and he who was detected in" adultery with his neighbour's wife was ordered, by the laws of Ethelbert, to pay" him a fine, and buy him another wife. The punishments for robbery were" various, but none of them capital. If any person could trace his stolen cattle" into another's ground, the owner of the ground was obliged to show their tracks" out of it, or pay the value of the cattle.

"But if the punishments for crimes among the Anglo-Saxons were remarkable," their pretended proofs were no less so." The author then goes on to describe the ordeal system.

class we may select as a prominent example the Kusbâtees of Dholka. "Previous to the fall of the Mogul government," says Colonel Walker, "the Kusbâtees, as soldiers of fortune who had acquired a compe-"tence, settled at Dholka. From their numbers and warlike character, "their influence was great, and they were feared by that predatory "race of men—the Kâtees. When the Mahrattas obtained the "supremacy in this part of the country they were useful to them. "At this time, owing to the frequent wars and revolutions in the "government, Goozerat was in a state of anarchy, and the district of "Dholka had nearly become an uncultivated waste. The Guikowâr "government was incapable of remedying these disorders, and of "restoring the revenue, without the assistance of men of influence "in the country, and who had a command of cash. The Kusbâtees "on this occasion offered to restore the population of the several "villages, on condition that each village which they brought into "cultivation should be leased to them for a certain number of years, "at a fixed rent. These offers were accepted, and since that time it "has been customary to grant leases to the Kusbâtees of those vil-"lages which have from time to time become waste."

CHAPTER V.

RAJPOOT LAND-TENURES UNDER THE BRITISH.

In a minute, dated 6th April, 1821,[1] Mr. Elphinstone describes the effects of the introduction of British power into Goozerat. Each of the collectorates of Ahmedabad and Kaira into which the British territory north of the Myhee is divided, contains, he says, "two sorts "of villages, *Khâlsâ and Grâssiâ*," the former being those which had been immediately managed by the Mogul and Mahratta governments, and the latter those which had been subject to the hereditary jurisdiction of the chiefs. "The former are directly under the government, "the latter are held by a grâssiâ chief, to whom the government looks

[1] For which, see "Selections of Papers from the Records at the East India "House, &c.," printed by order of the Court of Directors, in 1826, vol iii., pp. 677 to 697. The compiler states that "the original is, in many places, obscure "and defective." We have, therefore, had the less hesitation in restoring the correct names where these were apparent.

" for revenue, and formerly looked for maintaining order. The most " striking division of the grâssiâ villages is into those held by Raj- " poots or grâssiâs, properly so called, and those held by Koolees, " generally termed *Mewâs*. The former, though foreigners, were in " possession of Goozerat when the Mohummedans invaded it; they " retained some tâlooks (lordships) and villages at that time, and they " recovered others by encroachment on the final weakness of the " Moguls. They are at once a more civilized and a more warlike " race than the Koolees; and it is, perhaps, owing to those circum- " stances, as well as to their having more recently possessed the " government of the province, that their claims appear to be much " more respected than those of the Koolees. The latter, though " probably the aborigines, seem generally to be considered as rebel- " lious, or at least refractory villagers, who have, from the weakness " of former governments, eluded or resisted the just claims of the " sirkâr (government). Both pay a sum to government, which govern- " ment appears to have had the right to increase. It was not usual " to interfere with the internal management of their villages, or to " examine the state of their receipts. Our government has asserted " the right, without always assuming the exercise of internal inter- " ference; but it is only of late that it has begun to inquire into the " collections, by establishing tulâtees (subordinate revenue collectors) " in grâssiâ and Mewâs villages. The whole of the pergunnahs of " Dhundhooka, Rânpoor, and Gogo, except the kusbas (or chief " towns), are in the hands of grâssiâ Rajpoots, as is a considerable " part of Dholka; there were also a few in Veerumgâm, which have " been swallowed up during the exactions of the Mahrattas. The " Kusbâtees of Dholka, though Mussulmâns, and the chief of Pâtree, " though a Koonbee, and though both differ from the others in the " nature of their tenure, may yet be reckoned in this class; but by " far the greater number are Rajpoots. They resemble their neigh- " bours and brethren in Jhâlâwâr, but are more intelligent and re- " spectable. The chiefs of Limree and Bhownugger are among the " number of our subjects in those districts, though they have large " possessions elsewhere. They are all quiet and obedient. Tulâtees " have been introduced into the villages of those of Dholka, and all " their revenue, but twenty per cent. of their own share, after deduct- " ing that of the ryots, is now levied by government. The police, " also, has either been committed to mookhee putels (or village head- " men), in a manner independent of their authority, or left in their " own hands, subject to all restrictions of that humble officer of the " police. The others are still on their former footing as to revenue;

" but they are under the Adâwlut (or Court of Justice), and are " either themselves agents of the magistrates, or are superseded by " their putels. The principal Mewâsees are the Koolees of the " Choonwâl, and those of the Purântej, Hursole, and Morâsâ dis- " tricts. The former are quite reduced, have received tulâtees, and " pay all their revenue but twenty-five per cent.; but the latter main- " tain their independence, and in some instances their rebellious and " predatory spirit." * * * *

" The most striking circumstances in the progress of our govern- " ment are the extraordinary obstacles that existed to introducing " order, and the surprising success with which they have been over- " come. The continual intermixture of our territories with those of " the Guikowâr, the Peshwah, the Nowaub of Cambay, and the un- " settled tributaries of Kâteewâr and the Myhee Kântâ, the number " of half-subdued grâssiâs and Mewâsees within our own limits, the " numerous and ill-defined tenures in almost every village, and the " turbulent and predatory character of a large proportion of the " people, combined to make the country beyond the Myhee more " difficult to manage than any part of the Company's territories; yet, " by the caution of government and the judgment and temper of the " local officers, our authority and our system have been established " with the utmost tranquillity, without either irritating our subjects " or embarrassing ourselves by any sudden or violent changes. Of " late years our innovations have been proceeding with accelerated " progress; and although the danger of hasty improvement is now " diminished, it may still be necessary to retard their advance, or at " least fix the limit beyond which it is not designed they should " extend.

" When we first obtained the pergunnahs forming the old Kaira " collectorship, the whole were put in charge of Colonel Walker, and " managed by his assistants; everything was left entirely on its old " footing, and nothing was done but to gain some information regard- " ing the actual condition of things. When regular collectors were " appointed, the same system was for a long time pursued.

" The only change in the revenue department attempted among " the grâssiâs was the increase to their tribute, to which they were at " all times liable; but the principles of a tribute were observed as " long as they were under Kaira, and with the single and temporary " exception of Bâpoo Meeâ, Kusbâtee of Dholka, no scrutiny was " attempted into their resources or management.

" The introduction of the judicial regulations was certainly a great " innovation, and was very early adopted; but it seems doubtful "whether the effect was soon felt. It is not likely that many of the "inhabitants of the grâssiâ villages came to our courts to complain; "and where the plaintiff belonged to a khâlsâ village it would be "thought natural and proper for government to interfere in his behalf.

"The first changes that were much felt were produced by the "regulations for the appointment of mookhee putels and of tulâtees, "particularly the latter. The grâssiâs who held more villages than "one were compelled to appoint mookhee putels, who from the time "of their appointment became responsible to the magistrate alone. "Those who had one village were themselves appointed mookhee "putels; in other cases they were obliged to nominate another person "for each village, who was responsible to the magistrate, and not to "the grâssiâs. Tulâtees were introduced into all the villages of the "grâssiâs of Dholka, and it was proposed to introduce them into all "the grâssiâ villages in Dhundhooka, Rânpoor, and Gogo. A "further change has taken place in the alteration of the principle of "the Dholka payments from a tribute paid to government to a certain "proportion of the produce left to the grâssiâs, and that proportion "is only twenty per cent. of the *government share*, from which all "village expenses, including tulâtees' pay, are to be defrayed.

"The effect of this change on the income of the chiefs is shown "by the payments of the three principal grâssiâs, to which I have "added the two chief Kusbâtees, though their situation is somewhat "different.

	1802.	1817.	1820.
	Rupees.	Rupees.	Rupees.
The Chief of Kot	48,000	57,000	72,000
The Chief of Gângur	15,500	19,000	23,000
The Chief of Oonteleea	6,000	6,000	11,000
Bâpoo Meeâ Kusbâtee.........	50,000	73,000	89,000
Luteef Khân Kusbâtee	11,000	13,000	16,000

"Their payments, especially those of the grâssiâs, have greatly "increased, and more within the last three years than in the pre-"ceding fifteen.

"The appointment of a tulâtee is very disagreeable to the chiefs, "and those of Dholka assured me that they felt the presence of that "officer more than the increase of their tribute. They said he as-"sumed the character of a representative of government, received "complaints from their ryots, threw their whole village into confusion, "and utterly destroyed their consequence among their people.

"The Adâwlut, also, as we came into closer contact with the chiefs, "has been more felt; and we have reason to regret that some modi- "fications were not made in our code before it was applied to a "people in a state of society so different from that which our laws "contemplate, and employed to enforce agreements concluded at a "time when the strict execution of them was so little foreseen. The "Raja of Kot, who, at the time of Colonel Walker's report in 1804, "maintained a body of 150 horse, and 2000 seebundees, was sent to "prison for neglecting a summons from a magistrate; and the chief "of Pâtree, who once resisted for two months the attacks of the "Guikowâr army, was thrown into jail for his inability to pay debts "contracted in consequence of war and contributions during the "period of his independence. I cannot more strongly show the "change that has taken place than by pointing out that these are the "persons whom Colonel Walker, and I believe all the gentlemen "employed in the first introduction of our authority, declared to be "*sovereign princes*, with whom we had no right to interfere beyond "the collection of a tribute, and that they are now deprived of all "power and consequence, and nearly the whole of their revenue. "Almost all these changes have, in effect, taken place within these "three years. They cannot but feel a change so sudden, and it must "be owned that they have suffered hardships, though not perhaps in- "justice."

Whether the Rajpoot chiefs were or were not treated with justice is a point upon which Mr. Elphinstone appears to hesitate. Had the great literary task of that eminent man been completed, as all must so much desire that it had been, the historian of India might, perhaps, have pronounced upon a question which the Governor of Bombay was reluctant to decide. Under present circumstances we can but conjecture what the causes of his hesitation may have been.

In regard to the jurisdiction of the local chiefs, the British government had at least acted inconsistently. When, in 1802, they accepted the cession of the territory of Dhollera, forming part of the pergunnah or district of Dhundhooka, then subject to the Peshwah, and in the face of the Mahratta prince's rights, hoisted their flag therein, as sovereigns, they not only assented to, but positively asserted, that which they so often afterwards denied—the sovereign rights of the local chieftains. Thirteen years afterwards, however, when the jurisdiction of the Râwul of Bhownugger in the pergunnah of Gogo, now ceded to them by the Mahrattas, was in question, they endeavoured to prove, by laboured but untenable historical arguments, that that chief had been entitled to exercise no jurisdiction therein. The general question was confused by an unnecessary and impracticable attempt to maintain it as a fact that the state of subordination which we wished to establish had actually existed under the now fallen governments of the Mohummedans and the Mahrattas. Upon this point the preceding pages will enable the reader to form his own opinion. Perhaps he will agree with us that "the hand of conquest" had not reached so far as was now maintained, and that the Bhoomeeâ chiefs, though rendered tributary, had many of them preserved their local authority. We cannot, however, regard the Rajpoot chiefs in the light of "sovereign princes," at least in any sense of that term which would not be equally applicable to the Celtic chiefs of the Scottish Highlands, nor do we regard the annulment of their seigneurial rights as in itself an act of injustice, any more than we so regard the abolition of the heritable jurisdictions in Scotland. The Sultans of Ahmedabad, and still more the Emperors of Delhi, exercised a supremacy over the Hindoo princes perhaps at least as great as was ever maintained by the House of Stuart in Cromarty or in Argyle. And in the prosperous days of Unhilpoor there can be no doubt of the supreme power of the sovereign.

It is at least manifest that the feudal power of the local chiefs within the British territory could not have been long preserved; it was not in Goozerat alone, of the provinces of Hindoostan, that the banner of the golden leopards was displayed in assertion of sovereignty; and when the descendants of Seevâjee and of Teimoor had alike succumbed, it was not to be expected that a greater antiquity in their title, or a still more evident inferiority in their power, should long preserve others. Besides, the victory which democratic tendencies had gained within the conquering nation itself, could not have failed sooner or later to influence the conquered; the tempest which had broken upon the cliffs of England was sure before long to make itself felt in the higher rising of the surges which rolled upon the beach of Soreth; and the Wâghela of Sânund and the Gohil of Peerum could not hope to escape the arm which had reft their hereditary power from McKenzie and McShimei. Where royal power had ceased to exist, there royal rights also must be admitted to have perished, and a great supremacy must necessarily extinguish petty jurisdictions, as the sun does a little fire.

When, however, we regard particular cases, the grounds of Mr. Elphinstone's hesitation more plainly appear. We may take as an example the fortunes of the Raja of Kot, or Sânund, a chief who

was the heir of Jeto, or Ujetra Singh Wâghela, and the presumed descendant, if not the representative of Raja Kurun, the last of the sovereigns of Unhilpoor. It may be excusable to repeat here the exact words of Colonel Walker's testimony regarding his principality:—
"The Mewâs villages (of Dholka)," he says, "are in a state of in-"dependence, and pay with difficulty their contribution of *ghâns* "*dhânâ*. This is obtained or fixed by a large military force, or by a "negotiation with the chiefs who are concerned, which generally se-"cures them an abatement. Some of these chiefs are grâssiâs of "more or less influence, but the chief of Kot assumes the title of "Raja, and is said to claim a very high descent. Each of these "chieftains has a certain number of armed followers, who attend him "voluntarily, and subsist on his bounty, or on the fruits of their "mutual plunder. But the Kot Raja has in his service a force of "two thousand seebundees (or irregular infantry), and one hundred "and fifty horsemen, who mount guard at his village, and who are "engaged to defend his person, or to wage hostilities, like the troops "of a sovereign prince. The village of Kot is not fortified, but it is "in the middle of jungle, and surrounded by fastnesses. The Kot "Wâlâ (the Raja) has under his jurisdiction twenty-four villages, and "pays generally a jumma of Rs. 42,723 yearly, but this varies ac-"cording to circumstances. * * * * The Mewâsees, according "to the Mahratta term, are so powerful in Dholka, that they are "nearly on the footing of Moolukgeeree tributaries, and required an "annual armament to obtain payment of their jumma, or ghâns "dhânâ. If the troops were numerous, the harvest ensued imme-"diately, and the contribution was fixed on an increased ratio. If, "on the other hand, the force employed was not very strong, a "skirmish ensued, and whatever might be its issue, the resistance "was thought honorable to the Mewâs, and after the subjection of "their country to pillage, the affair ended in a composition for more "or less, according to circumstances."

There was in fact an almost imperceptible distinction between the Molukgeeree tributaries and such chiefs as those above mentioned, who paid not a revenue, but a tribute, and that only under the pressure of a military force. The fate of the two classes of chiefs was, however, widely different. Had the lordship of Sânund been situated a few miles farther to the west, and beyond the line which separated the pergunnah of Dholka from the neighbouring Moolukgeeree country of Kâteewâr, the hereditary jurisdiction and honors of the chief would have been preserved to him, and his tribute, perhaps slightly increased, would have been fixed at a permanent rate for all future time. It can hardly then be wondered at, that, with a tribute raised in the course of a few years from Rs. 43,000 to 72,000, with dependents of his own lording it over him almost in his own mansion, as the agents of an all-powerful foreign domination, deprived, as Mr. Elphinstone says, "of all power and consequence, and "nearly the whole of his revenue," and actually sent to jail for disobedience to a summons, the purport of which he probably very imperfectly understood, the descendant of the royal house of Unhilpoor should complain of injustice as well as of hardship, and envy the happier fate of the former vassals of his family, the neighbouring Jhâlâ chieftains of Limree and Wudwân, who had, by better fortune, fallen under the Mahratta, instead of the British rule.

It would require a far more extended discussion than we have space for, and would weary the patience of our readers, were we to pursue this subject in detail. We therefore allude to merely one or two points. There appears to have been no sufficient distinction drawn between such mere leaseholds as those of the Dholka Kusbâtees and the permanent titles of the Rajpoot chieftains to their lands, —titles of which Colonel Walker had with much truth said, that "they are derived to their possessors by hereditary descent from a "period of the most remote antiquity, of which there is no record; "but they are secured to them by universal assent, and are at this "day unimpaired in their privileges. These rights, which have been "maintained by arms and an unconquerable sentiment in favor of "them, have withstood the revolutions of ages, and outlived the Mo-"hummedan dominion, which did everything in its power to subvert "them."

The government of Bombay,[1] in speaking of the tenures of the Jhâreja grâssiâs, supply a very clear description of the position of a Rajpoot cadet. "The Jhârejas of Anjar," they say, "are the direct "descendants of the younger brothers of former Rows, who have had "grâs assigned to them, which has in the course of years been di-"vided and subdivided among their numerous descendants. They "are lords of their *kurum bhâg*,[2] or share, which they possess by "right of birth, and originally paid no pecuniary acknowledgment to "the Row; but their services in times of general danger have always "been considered as one of the terms on which they held their grâs, "and whenever the Bhyud have assembled, they received an allow-

[1] *Vide* Revenue Letter from Bombay, of 31st May, 1818, p. 750, vol. iii., of the "Selection of Papers."

[2] An expression which literally means, "Destiny-share,"—"the share which "fortune has assigned."

"ance of grain for their horses, and food and opium for themselves. " * * * The quantity of land assigned to them for their "exclusive benefit, and which they hold rent-free, provided they "cultivate it themselves, is designated *grâssiâ owga*, and is called in "Goozerat, *jeewâee* (that is, 'a subsistence'); but if cultivated by the "ryots, it is subject to a veera, or tax, to the government, the grâssiâ "receiving a rent as proprietor of the land."

Numerous instances of this state of things have been given in the course of the present work, and surely if there be such a thing as a right to landed property in the world (which some, we are aware, will hardly admit), it is difficult to make out a better title to land than that which was thus possessed by the grâssiâs of Goozerat. The Court of Directors, however, thought differently. They considered the lands of the Jhâreja grâssiâs to be held simply "on condition of "service." "The decision upon these rights," they say, "is involved "in the same difficulties as that upon the grants on account of "services in other parts of India, when the services are no longer "required. These grants, we think, ought not to amount to abso-"lute property; and when the services cease to be performed, or "cease to be required, the case is open to the decision of govern-"ment."

The Bombay despatch had only stated that service was "*one* of "the terms" upon which the grâssiâs held their lands; and the history of our own country would hardly lead to the conclusion that lands possessed hereditarily on tenure of military service could be considered to have escheated solely on the ground that the service was "no longer required" by the crown. It is more to the purpose, however, to observe that the practice of Goozerat was certainly very different, and that the rights of the grâssiâs were by no means dependent upon the pleasure of the sovereign in regard to their employment in his military array.

"The *right* of government," says the Court of Directors, in A.D. 1819, "to increase the sulâmee,[1] or tribute, payable by the grâssiâs, "is, in our apprehension, very clearly established. This right would, "indeed, naturally arise out of the decision previously passed on the "question of sovereignty, which has been determined to vest solely "in the Company, to the utter exclusion of the pretensions set forth "by the grâssiâs, Bheels, and Koolees. The effect of that decision "was to place these classes on the same footing as other subjects, and

[1] For the Mohummedan account of the origin of this tribute, *vide* p. 564, where the terms *sulâmee* and *wântâ* are explained.

"consequently to render their property liable to a proportionate "share of the public burden in all cases where a special exemption "from or limitation of demand on the part of the sovereign power, "either for a term of years or in perpetuity, cannot be pleaded against "such liability." The right of increasing the grâssiâ tribute (as a tribute) was hardly one which a British government could press. If it existed at all, it must have been derived from the Mohummedans; and if so derived, it was, by the Mohummedans' own account of it, based upon, and limited by, nothing but force. Upon the principles laid down in the latter part of the paragraph, however, the case of the Raja of Kot (to adhere to that example) would, as it appears to us, have stood more favorably for that chief than it did, and somewhat as follows:—His territory would have been subject to the British jurisdiction; his tribute would have been fixed upon a due consideration of what he had paid to former governments,—would, in fact, have been calculated in the manner in which the tribute had been calculated in the Myhee Kântâ or in Kâteewâr; and (if this were considered less than his fair contribution towards meeting the necessities of the state) he would, in addition, have been called upon to bear his "proportionate share of the public burden," by either providing for the police and judicial arrangements within his estate himself, or by paying his share of the expenses of the government courts and the government police; but he would have been left to settle with the cultivators of his lands without any interference on the part of the state, as had been the case under the sway of the Mahratta or the Mohummedan. It was the confusion we have alluded to which, perhaps, lay at the root of the harsher treatment which the grâssiâs received. "It is now clear, however," continues the Court, "that the privileges to which the grâssiâs lay claim may "be traced for the most part, if not altogether, to the venality, re-"missness, or imbecility of persons charged with the maintenance of the "rights of the sovereign; *that their wântâ lands are rarely held by any "better titles than are derivable from collusion, fraud or violence* (*!*); "that the contributions which they levy under the denomination of *tora "grâs* are generally of similar origin; and that in some instances, "having sprung from the most frivolous and whimsical occurrences, "they have been subsequently tolerated by weakness, and submitted "to through fear." In the remarks of the Court three years afterwards even there may still be observed that leaning against the grâssiâs as a body which we have supposed to have been originally occasioned by an incomplete appreciation of the distinction between tenures which, though both passing under the name of grâs, were entirely opposite in their nature and origin. " The alienations," it is said, " in behalf of the grâssiâs and those other tribes who have proceeded " by forcible methods, appear to have been either granted in former " times by the government as a retaining fee for military services no " longer required of them, or to be usurpations perpetrated upon the " people, who thus endeavoured to purchase exemption from the de- " predations which these fighting tribes were in the habit of practising " upon them. We cannot but look upon all their acquisitions with " an unfavourable eye; and though we can easily conceive that con- " siderations of expediency may forcibly recommend forbearance, we " shall always rejoice when the extent of their possessions is di- " minished."

Considerations of justice and fairness apart, much, no doubt, may be said against the local chieftains; their utility, it may be urged, had passed away; their "services" were "no longer required;" they were as little likely to be reclaimed from their slothfulness and indisposition to the arts of peace, as they were to accept of the discipline which would have rendered them once again valuable in the day of war. It must, however, be recollected that experienced officers have been found to maintain, even at the present day, that the internal tranquillity of Goozerat has suffered in consequence of the diminution of that influence, which the sons of the Kshutrees had so long maintained against such fearful odds; it is by no means certain that, under more generous treatment, the character of the grâssiâs might not have improved; and, even in these days, the opinion is not wholly without supporters, which considers that a body of landlords, commanding respect from their hereditary title, may be a valuable bulwark to their land. However these things may be, it must, at least, be permitted to a lover of his country, to regret that the introduction of British power into Goozerat should have been attended with such well-founded causes of complaint to any portion of the inhabitants, as those which it certainly afforded to the descendants of Ujetra Singh Wâghela or Mokherâjee Gohil.

The opinions above expressed, in favor of the local chieftains, are not at variance with those which Mr. Elphinstone appears to have held. He proposed to remove the tulâtees at Dholka, to fix the payments of the grâssiâs, so as to leave them thirty per cent. instead of twenty on the government share, subject to a quinquennial revision on the same principle; he recommended that certain personal immunities should be granted to the grâssiâs, in their relation to the courts of justice; and urged, "that all claims against them for old debts, " even if supported by bonds, should be examined, with reference "to all circumstances arising from the situation of the parties at "the time when they were contracted, by which the nature of the "debts might be affected; and that, instead of seizing and confining "the persons of the grâssiâs, the judges should issue a precept to the "collector to sequestrate as large a portion of the lands as might "suffice for the gradual payment of the debt, leaving a decent main-"tenance to the grâssiâ." Mr. Elphinstone further advised, "that "the grâssiâ should be employed as head of the police wherever he "conveniently could, and that he should have no formal appoint-"ment of mookhee putel, a title which a Rajpoot chief must look "on as a degradation."

In regard to the Mewâsees (which term he appears to confine to the Koolee chieftains), the recommendations of Mr. Elphinstone proceed still further, and to the full extent of the sketch which we have drawn in speaking of the affairs of the Wâghela chieftain. "It appears," says the governor, "that there is no trace in history of their "(the Mewâsees) ever having been on a footing of greater dependance "than they are at present; and it follows that we have derived no "claim to reduce them further from our predecessors, and must rest "our right to do so on the law of nature, which entitles us to control "our neighbours as far as is required by our own security; and this "ought, therefore, to be the limit of our interference. Considering "the want of military force in the territory, it is surprising how little "trouble the Mewâsees have given us since we first came into "Goozerat; and it would be equally inconsistent with justice and "policy to risk this tranquillity for a little addition to the revenue, or "a fancied improvement in the police. That the improvement would "be real, I think more than doubtful; for, unless where Koolees "have acquired habits of industry and order, they can only be "restrained by rendering the communities to which they belong "responsible for their conduct; and, if we could quietly succeed in "bringing each individual under the direct operation of our police, "the effect, I doubt not, would be a great increase of robberies. I "would therefore propose that in the Mewâsee villages we should "hold the Thâkor responsible for the tribute, and for the maintenance "of the public tranquillity. He might be required to give security, if "necessary, and should be required to restore stolen property, and to "give up offenders, but he should be under none of the regulations "applicable to mookhee putels, and it should rest with the magistrate "what offences to notice in his village. All serious crimes ought, of "course, to be noticed, and the criminal should be demanded of the "Thâkor. The demand should be enforced by a mohsul and a daily

" fine. Obstinate neglect might be punished by apprehending the " Thâkor, and resistance by attacking him as a public enemy. Com- " plaints of a serious nature against the Thâkor personally should be " investigated in a summary way by the collector, before he proceeded " to apprehend the accused: when it became necessary to apprehend " him, he should be made over to the criminal judge in the usual " manner. Thâkors habitually guilty of connivance at plunder might " be deposed and imprisoned, the office of chief being made over to " another member of the family; or their villages might be garrisoned " by troops, and deprived of all Mewâsee privileges.

" No tulâtees should be appointed, and the tribute should be kept " nearly stationary. A small increase might be put on suitable cases " to preserve the right of the government; but, in general, the " greatest profit should be left to the villages, to encourage their at- " tending to agriculture. Civil justice ought, in most cases, to be " allowed to take its course, but, in some villages, it would be expe- " dient for complaints to be made in the first instance to the " magistrate, who might decide whether to send them to the courts, " or to settle them by punchâyets, supported by mohsuls."

We must here take leave of the subject, to which we have already devoted more space than we can well afford, though far too little for its real importance. The practical value of Mr. Elphinstone's counsel has, we may remind our readers, by no means passed away at the present time, for the hour must come, be it sooner or later, when portions of the province of Goozerat, wherein grâssiâs and Mewâsees still exist, with influence not much impaired, and habits but little altered, shall necessarily pass under the direct dominion of the British Government.

It is satisfactory to observe that if one portion of the inhabitants of Goozerat was subjected to hardship as the result of the introduction of British rule, other and more numerous sections of the people were largely the gainers. " It is not to be supposed," says Mr. Elphinstone, " that my stay in these zillahs could enable me to form any opinion " of the real condition of the people. The facts that present them- " selves on a hasty view are that the grâssiâs are weakened and de- " pressed; that the Desâees and all the hereditary officers, including " the putels, are stripped of power and influence, and given security " of persons and property in exchange; that the bankers are deprived " of one large branch of their profits by the change in our system of " revenue, and of another by the decline of commerce, occasioned by " the downfall of so many native states, and the equal diffusion of " property; that the Bhâts, once so important in Goozerat, are now "almost too insignificant to mention, and that the ryots have gained "much wealth, comfort, and security among all the sufferers. Those "engaged in commerce, and perhaps the grâssiâs, are the only classes "that give rise to regret. There are no hereditary chiefs, no esta-"blished military leaders, and no body of men that claimed (*s. o.*) "respect from even an apparent devotion to learning or religion. "The property of those who have suffered was built upon a de-"pression of the people, and their fall has been compensated by the "rise of the ryots, the most numerous, most industrious, and most "respectable part of the community. To that order our government "has, beyond all doubt, been a blessing. It has repelled predatory "invasion, restrained intestine disorder, administered equal and im-"partial justice, and has almost extirpated every branch of exaction "and oppression. The appearance of the country on this side of the "Sâbhermutee, which has been long in our possession, is what might "be expected in such circumstances. The former affluence of the "upper classes is apparent in the excellence of their houses; and the "prosperity of the ryots appears in the comfort of their dwellings, "the neatness of their dress, and the high cultivation of their lands. "In the fertility and improvement of the fields, there are many parts "of the Bengal provinces which cannot be surpassed; but in the "abundance of trees and hedges, in handsome and substantial well-"built villages, and in the decent and thriving appearance of the "people, I have seen nothing in India that can bear a comparison "with the eastern zillah of Goozerat."

In order to understand the improvement which had taken place in the position of the ryot or cultivator, we must see what that was under the native rule. Colonel Walker presents us with a description, which we quote, simply premising that a similar state of things to that which he pourtrays exists at the present hour in parts of Goozerat which are not under the direct authority of the British government. "The "proprietors (of alienated lands)," says Colonel Walker, "possess the "right of assessing the ryots, and of leasing their lands to the best "advantage. They appear to exercise the same rights in this respect "as a proprietor in Europe, but their rate of assessment is commonly "under that of the government. It does not appear that the govern-"ment interferes in this matter, but it is well understood that in the "case of oppression on the one part, or of misdemeanor on the "other, either party has a right to complain, and the ryot, if he dis-"likes the terms of his landlord, may remove into another district. "This is the usual resource, and the whole of the inhabitants of a "village, or that part of them which may be aggrieved, whether on

" private lands or holding from the government, will remove into an-
" other district, and accept of new lands there, or remain until they
" receive redress and have obliged the landholders to accede to their
" terms. To prevent these emigrations the komâvishdârs sometimes
" agree among themselves not to afford those who quarrel with their
" landlords any employment within their districts; but it happens as
" frequently that they are ready to take advantage of their ill-treat-
" ment and to avail themselves of their services. It may be here
" remarked that even the ryot or cultivator of government land has
" rights by prescription, and to deprive him of the spot which he or
" his family had long cultivated would be considered as an arbitrary act,
" unauthorized by law, or custom, which is the same thing; such eject-
" ments therefore seldom happen."

The security which the ryot possessed lay, practically, in the fact that his caste-fellows were sure to espouse his cause, and that his landlord could not expel him, because he dare not venture upon an act which might cause them also to retire. The state of things was represented by the eastern proverb already quoted:—" In the multi-
" tude of people is the king's honor, but in the want of people is the
" destruction of the prince." Under the British rule, however, the ryot was not only protected from foreign invasion and intestine disorder, but was actually vested with (what he never possessed before) a proprietary right to the land which he occupied, which he might now sell without the consent of his so-called landlord, and from which the government itself had no power to eject him as long as he continued to pay his rent.

Another institution of their British rulers was not so favorable in its action upon the cultivating population, while it mitigated in no slight degree the disadvantages under which the commercial, which were also the usurious, classes had fallen. The premature introduction of a judicial system, founded upon European maxims, produced evil effects, which, as we have already seen, were deprecated by Mr. Elphinstone. Four years afterwards (in A.D. 1825) they were thus vividly depicted by one who (as far at least as his position was concerned), may be called a still more impartial observer—Bishop Heber. "The greatest evil
" of the land here (in Goozerat)," says Heber, " as elsewhere in India,
" is the system of the Adâwlut courts, their elaborate and intricate
" machinery, their intolerable and expensive delays, and the severity
" of their debtor and creditor laws. Even in the Adâwlut, however,
" a very essential improvement had been introduced by Mr. Elphin-
" stone in discarding the Persian language, and appointing all pro-
" ceedings to be in that of Goozerat. Still there remained many evils,

"and in a land so eaten up by poverty on the one hand, and usury "on the other, the most calamitous results continually followed, and "the most bitter indignation was often excited by the judgments, "ejectments, and other acts of the court, which though intended only "to do justice between man and man, yet frequently depopulated vil-"lages, undid ancient families, pulled down men's hereditary and "long-possessed houses over their heads, and made the judges hated "and feared by the great body of the people, as practising severities "in the recovery of private debts which none of the native governors, "however otherwise oppressive, either ventured to do or thought of "doing. One good effect has indeed followed, that by making a "debt more easy to recover, the rate of interest has been lessened. "But this is a poor compensation for the evils of a system which, to "pay a debt, no matter how contracted, strips the weaver of his loom, "the husbandman of his plough, and pulls the roof from the castle of "the feudal chieftain; and which, when a village is once abandoned "by its inhabitants in a time of famine, makes it next to impossible "for those inhabitants, who are all more or less in debt, to return in "better times to their houses and lands again."

No less disastrous results might, perhaps, have been expected from the attempt to mould all at once the habits of the torrid zone into those of "this nook-shotten isle of Albion," and to apply, without an intermediate step, institutions which suited the subjects of George IV. to a state of society bearing so much more near a resemblance to that of the reign of Alfred.

CHAPTER VI.

RELIGIOUS SERVICES—FESTIVALS.

In a Hindoo temple the adytum containing the object of worship is invariably covered with a "shikur," or bell-shaped spire; the mundup, or ante-chamber, is open, and contains in temples of Shiva a figure of the attendent bull, Nundee. Vaishnavite temples especially have frequently two ante-chambers, in which case the first is open and the second closed. These, as also the temples of the Jain religion, have occasionally three spires, the centre one rather higher than the other two. The temple is surrounded by a Dhurumsâlâ, or house of accommodation, for attendants and worshippers. The surrounding structure is, however, still sometimes, especially in Jain temples, formed of numerous small spire-covered shrines, and the lodging-houses are in that case detached, but the whole mass of buildings is frequently encircled by a fortified wall. A large temple presents, in fact, the appearance of a village; the auxiliary buildings look like substantial private houses, but are more liberally adorned with carved woodwork; and sometimes nearly the whole exterior of them is covered with rude paintings, representing marriages or other domestic festivals, or more frequently the achievements of the gods. Small reservoirs of water called koonds, circular wells, and more imposing wâvs or bowlees, and sometimes majestic tanks are the more or less indispensable accompaniments of places dedicated to the religion of the Hindoos. Like the Christian churches of the middle ages, the Hindoo temples of Goozerat are usually placed in situations highly favoured by nature. The awful gloom of the grove, the romantic beauty of the mountain glen, the brightness of the river's bank, the wildness of the cloud-enveloped peak, or the solemn calm of the ocean bay, are accessaries of which the religions of Shiva and of Âdeenâth know full well how to avail.

The officiating priests are in the temples of Shiva usually Gosâees; in those of Vishnoo, Brahmins or Wairâgees; in Devees' temples, low caste Brahmins or Gosâees—sometimes, as in the case of Boucherâjee, even Mohummedans. The priest in a Jain temple may be of any caste, with the curious provision that he be not a Shrâwuk, or layman of that religion. Low-caste Brahmins, especially the class called Bhojuk, who have already been mentioned, are frequently employed. The *Gosâees* are members of a monastic order which follows Shiva. They wear orange tawny clothes, and the *teeluk*,[1] or sectarian mark upon their foreheads, is horizontal. The *Wairâgee* is a Vaishnavite monk, and wears a white dress and a perpendicular teeluk. Those who are servants of the Devees add to the teeluk a *chândlo* or red spot, made with a preparation of turmeric. The Jain monk is commonly called a *Jutee*, but the general name applying to all these orders is that of *Sunyâsee*, or anchorite. The Sunyâsees are now for the most part persons who have lost their property, have been deprived of their children, or suffered some other calamity, against which they have not had resolution to bear up. The intended recluse having arranged with a *gooroo*, or monkish dignitary, for his reception into the

[1] "Ye shall not make any cuttings in your flesh for the dead, nor *print any marks upon you*. I am the Lord."—Leviticus, xix. 28. Bishop Patrick notes that this imprinting of marks or signatures was understood to be fixing a badge or characteristic of the person's being devoted to some false deity.

order, and having ascertained the favourable day by astrological calculation, breaks the sacred cord, if he be of the regenerate classes, removes the hair of his head, assumes the monastic dress, and with alms and prayers receives initiation. Sunyâsees are, however, sometimes consecrated at an early age; a person who despairs of having children not unfrequently vows to consecrate one son, if two be granted to his prayers; and among the Jains, when disciples are scarce, as they frequently are, the monks purchase children for the purpose of initiating them.[1]

Our readers will have gathered from the description already given of "mental worship," that the ordinary Hindoo religious service consists in performing for the idol such acts as a menial servant performs for his human master. The routine, which affords a tolerably distinct idea of Hindoo domestic life in former days, is most fully brought out in a carefully attended temple of Vishnoo, in which there are five daily services. At the time at which men rise from their beds in the morning, bells are rung in the temple; the royal drum and the conch-shell are sounded to awake the Dev from his slumbers. The officiating priest having performed ablutions enters the temple, and waves before the idol a lamp, having usually five or seven branches. At eight or nine in the morning the Dev is dressed in clothes suitable to the season of the year. In the cold weather he wears a quilted coat, and has

[1] The following is the account given of himself by Gosâee Shumbhoopooree, one of these ascetics, whom we met with a few years ago:—

"I was born in Bikâner, and am the son of Pruthee Singh Shiv Singh Thâkor "of Mooroo, in that country. The name which I bore as a Rajpoot was Khet "Singh, and my tribe was the Râthor. When I was four or five years old, Soorut "Singh, Raja of Bikâner, seized upon the estate of Mooroo, and my father 'went "'out' to recover it. I was with my father in outlawry until I attained the age of "thirteen. My father then placed me in the temple of Mâtâ Shree Kurneejee, "which is twelve coss from Bikâner. When the raja heard of this he sent for me "to court, and giving me a dress of honour, ordered me to remain with him; but, "as I suspected that his intentions were treacherous, I made my escape to Hotee, "near Pokurn, in Marwar, where there is a temple of Muhâ Dev, and a monas-"tery, of which Muhânunt Chundunpooree was then the superior. I remained ten "days at the monastery, and saw the mode of life there, and it came into my mind "that it would be better to live there than to continue in outlawry. My lock of "hair was therefore cut off, and I was admitted as a disciple, and instructed by the "gooroo. I remained at the monastery ten years, and afterwards went to Hinglâz on "pilgrimage, and since then I have wandered about from one Hindoo holy place "to another, and have visited Kâshee, Jwâlâ Mookhee, Hurdwâr, Dwârkâ, and "other places. I am now about forty years old. About ten years ago I went to "pay a visit to my own family. I found my elder brother, Beerjjee, alive, also my "uncle Mân Singh, and his son, Rughoonâth, but my father was dead. They "pressed me to remain with them, but I made my escape."

a brazier placed beside him to afford warmth; in the hot weather he is anointed with sandal-wood dust and water to produce coolness, and is dressed in clothes of fine linen, and adorned with flowers and jewels; he is placed beside a fountain, and is fanned by his attendants. In the rainy season the Dev is dressed in scarlet cloth and shawls. At this time his breakfast is brought to him, which consists of rice and milk, and such other articles of food as rich men use. This meal should, however, be accompanied by the whole of the "sixteen acts of wor-"ship," which will presently be described. The third service is at noon; the Dev is again rubbed with sandal, and adorned with fresh flowers. Lamps are lighted, and incense is burnt before him, and he is supplied with food according to the season of the year. He is now supposed to retire for a siesta, and silence must therefore be maintained in the temple. At three in the afternoon the royal drum announces that the Dev has finished his noon-day sleep, the attendants bring in fruit and confectionaries, a chess-board, dice, and other means of amusement. The most important of all the services is, however, the fourth, which takes place at sunset, and is accompanied by the whole of the sixteen acts of worship. The Dev is invited into the temple, a throne is set for him, water is offered him to wash his feet, an offering of water is sprinkled before him, and a cupfull is presented, that he may rinse his mouth. Preparations for the Dev's bath constitute the sixth act of worship; he is next provided with garments and with a sacrificial cord; sandal ointment is presented to him, scented flowers and incense are offered to him. The lighting of lamps is the twelfth act of worship; the various courses of a sumptuous dinner are then presented to him, concluding with the leaf of betel; the branched candlestick is waved before him as in the morning. The worshippers circumambulate the image several times, like warders going the rounds, which forms the fifteenth act of worship; and the whole service is concluded by a hymn of praise.

The "*Prudukshunâ*," or circumambulation, is performed by some persons once only, by others seven times, and by others as often as one hundred and eight times. At each circuit the worshipper repeats the following "muntra," or verse of power:—

"Sin am I! sin-doer I! sinful-souled, sin-born! Protect me, O! "thou of the lotus-eye, all-sin-destroying Huree! (Vishnoo). What-"ever sins of mine and others are in existence, though they attain the "height of Meroo-mountain, all these find destruction at each step of "the prudukshunâ."[1]

[1] Compare the following:—"No sacrifice, however, was to be made without "leaves or branches of the misletoe; and before they entered the circle to offer,

The last of the five daily services takes place at night-time. Sandal, flowers, and incense are offered to the Dev, lamps are lighted, and a supper of milk, biscuits, and other articles is set before him. He is then supposed to retire to rest, and, if moveable, his image is placed upon a bed; otherwise it is covered with shawls and garments.

In the temples of Vishnoo there are usually two images, representing Seetâ and Râm, or Râdhâ and Krishn; Lukshmun, the brother of Râm, has also frequently an image. On the birthdays of Râm and Krishn, and on other festivals, the idols are crowned, and arrayed in royal attire. At the Hoolee, the Dev is dressed in yellow clothes, supplied with red powder and a squirt, and supposed to take part in the festivities. On another occasion the image of Vishnoo is carried to a river or lake, where it is bathed, and if the sheet of water be sufficiently extensive, it is placed in a boat that it may enjoy a sail.

In the temples of Shiva, and in those of Devees, the first, second, and fourth services only are used. The Jains merely wash their images with water, brush them, smear them with sandal and adorn them with jewels. They wave the branched candlestick, however, in the evening. The Shrâwuks, and particularly the women of that faith, carry with them, when they go to worship, a handsome bag containing rice. Near the idol is set a box, with a hole in the lid, into which they drop the rice, and which every eight or ten days is opened that its contents may be thrown to the pigeons, or otherwise disposed of, before life is generated in them. Some persons drop money into the box, and it appears probable that this was the original practice—the box retaining the name of "Bhundâr," or treasury.

The Hindoos in Goozerat divide the year into three seasons, the *Sheeâloo* or cold season, the *Oonhâloo* or hot season, and the *Chomâsoo* or monsoon. The first of these includes the months of Kârteek, Mâgsheer, Posh, and Mâgh; the second those of Phâlgoon, Chyetra,

" they made a tour about it sunways; and the like they did when they had done " offering.

" The tour about the circle is called *Deas-soil*, from *Deas* the south, and *soil*, the " sun, q. d. South about with the sun. I have often seen at marriages, and " churchings of women, and burials, such a tour made about the church. This " ceremony was not confined to the Druids; we find it at the funeral pile of Pallas. " Virgil, Æ. lib. xi. 188-190.

" Ter circum accensos cincti fulgentibus armis
" Decurrere rogos; ter mæstum funeris ignem
" Lustravere in equis; ululatusque ore dedere."

Lachlan Shaw's History of Moray.

Wyeshâk, and Jeth; and the third those of Âshâd, Shrâwun, Bhâdrapud, and Âsho. Each month is again divided into *Shoọd* and *Wud*; in the former of which there are moonlight nights.[1]

The first festival which we shall have to notice occupies the three last days of the month of Âsho. The thirteenth of the dark half of this month is called "*Dhun Terush.*" In the morning, after ablutions, the Hindoos having carefully cleansed a few silver coins, and placed them on a table, worship them, anointing them with a preparation of turmeric, placing before them flowers and fragrant colored powders, with incense and lamps, and performing the other acts of worship. At the same time shepherds, cowherds, and others who are similarly employed, adorn the animals which they tend, and worship them. Fishermen in like manner color and worship their nets.[2] Their duties are performed fasting: on their conclusion each household holds a private festival. In the evening the people of the town or village assemble outside the gate to see the cowherds drive their flocks and cattle in from the fields at full gallop. On their return into the village they illuminate their houses. The next day, which is called *Kâlee Choudush*, is dedicated to the worship of Hunoomân, and the night is the favorite time for the practice of magical rites. The illumination is repeated this night also, but is far more brilliant and general on the succeeding evening, which is called, from the lines of lamps which are then exhibited, "the Deewâlee."[3]

[1] The corresponding English months may be thus (roughly) stated :—

Sheeâloo . .	Kârteek.	=	November.
	Mâgsheer.	=	December.
	Posh	=	January.
	Mâgh	=	February.
Oonhâloo . .	Phâlgoon.	=	March.
	Chyetra.	=	April.
	Wyeshâk.	=	May.
	Jeth	=	June.
Chomâsoo. .	Âshâd.	=	July.
	Shrâwun	=	August.
	Bhâdrapud.	=	September.
	Âsho	=	October.

[2] "Therefore they sacrifice unto their net, and burn incense unto their drag; "because by them their portion is fat, and their meat plenteous."—*Vide* Habakkuk, i. 16. To which the author of the "Christian Year" refers in the following lines :—

"To our own nets ne'er bow we down,
"Lest, on the eternal shore,
"The Angels, while our draught they own,
"Reject us evermore."

[3] Deep or Deev, a lamp, and Âlee, a line.

On the first day of the month of Kârteek, which is also the first of the year, the Hindoos build before the Devs an Unnkoot, or store-house of every kind of food. It was the practice of old to worship Indra upon this day, but Shree Krishn, during his incarnation, caused the mountain King Gowurdhun, to be substituted for the Sovereign of Paradise,[1] and the Hindoos of the present day therefore erect a model of Gowurdhun mountain, which they worship, and upon which they place a flag, a few sprigs of trees, and some flowers. The trading classes open new account books on this day, and worship them under the name of "Suruswutee," with all the sixteen acts, excepting that of bathing. They sprinkle the first leaf with the red preparation of turmeric, and head it in some such fashion as the following, making a few fictitious entries, for good luck, of articles used on festive occasions :—

" Praise to Shree Gunesh ! Shree Sârdâjee [2] is true ! Praise to the " floods of the jewel-treasury—the ocean ! Shree Umbâjee mother is " true ! Shree Boucherâjee is true !

" In the year of Vikrum, 1908, on the first day of the light half of " the month Kârteek, being Saturday, in Shree Bhownugger, the chief, " Shree Veejye Singh, is ruling ; his heir apparent is the Prince Shree " Dâjee Râj, and Desâee Soorujrâm is the minister. This book " is the account book of the present writer, Shâ Moteechund " Soorchund."

Dr.	*Cr.*
Turmeric, ½ seer.	Turmeric, ½ seer.
Sugar, 1 seer.	Sugar, 1 seer.
Betel, ¼ seer.	Betel, ¼ seer.
Nutmegs, 7.	Nutmegs, 7.

The third day of the month of Wyeshâk, which, in the language of of Goozerat, is called Ukhâturee, is supposed to be the day on which the storms of the monsoon commence, and the sea becomes unfit for navigation. It is the great day of omens. The Hindoos, on the evening of the 2nd, make, outside the villages, model towns built of corn, and stored with little heaps of various grains. They place therein, also, a copper coin to represent the raja, betel-nut to stand for the minister, a little cotton, some sugar, and other articles. On the morning of the 3rd the villagers examine the model. If the ants

[1] The story may be found at length in the Prem Sâgur, chapters 25 to 28 : *vide* translation of that work by Professor Eastwick. London : James Madden, 8, Leadenhall-street. 1851.

[2] Suruswutee.

have interfered much with any kind of grain during the night time, the people think that the grain will be scarce during the ensuing year. In whatever direction the cotton has been removed, there, they believe, cotton will be in demand that season, and they conclude that the raja or minister will prosper or suffer misfortune, accordingly as the money or the betel-nut has been carried away or allowed to remain unmolested. This custom is said to be still more prevalent in Marwar than it is in Goozerat. Of omens, Krishnâjee, the author of Rutun-mâlâ, has left us a very full enumeration. The following are the inauspicious omens which an army encountered on its way to a field of battle, where it was defeated :—

"First, as they went, a man sneezed when he met them, a dog "howled—an omen not good, a cat passed them on the right hand, a "donkey brayed, and a kite cried terribly. Meeting them, came a "widow and a Sunyâsee, a Brahmin without a teeluk on his forehead, "a person dressed in mourning garments, one who carried a plate of "flour, and a woman with her hair dishevelled." On another occasion, however, the same army rejoiced in a string of good omens :— "They met a learned Brahmin, book in hand; they met a married "woman with her son who had gone out to fetch water; they met a "horseman, a Kshutree, with his arms; they met a gardener who "carried a vase of flowers; they met a cow with her calf, the cow "adorned with red ointment and with garlands."[1]

"In a certain village, on the morning of Ukhâturee," says a modern Goozeratee author, "five men went outside the gate to take "omens. Having listened to the noise of the jackals and other "animals, they turned to proceed homewards. As they went, one "man stopped, and sat down, and the other four stood waiting for "him. At this time they heard a cultivator's wife ask her husband "whether he thought they would be obliged to purchase a bullock "that year or not. The cultivator said, 'There is no fear of those "four that are on their legs, but I have little hope of the one that "cannot stand; it will die this year without a doubt.' The man who

[1] "Sneezing," says Brand, "has been held ominous from times of the most re- "mote antiquity." Eustathius upon Homer has long ago observed that sneezing to the left was unlucky, but that to the right prosperous. The custom of blessing persons when they sneeze has, without doubt, been derived to the Christian world, where it generally prevails, from the time of heathenism.

The same author remarks that the howling of a dog by night, in a neighbourhood, is the presage of death to any that are sick in it; also that omens were drawn from the coming in and going out of strange cats. The omens known in Goozerat may, in short, be paralleled in England and many other countries, which did (or do still) boast of an exclusive civilization.

"sat, hearing this omen, was fully persuaded in his mind that he "would not survive the year. I heard, too, that he fretted himself to "such an extent, that he really did die within the time allotted.

"A ringdove sat upon the roof of an old Koonbee woman's house. "She, hearing it cooing, began to weep and beat her breast. A "Brahmin, having come there at the time, the old woman said to "him, 'O! Muhârâj, this cursed pigeon is after me again. It has "carried off already my husband, my two sons, and my daughter, "and now it has come for me, and sits every day on the top of my "house, crying.' The Brahmin gave her some charmed pebbles, with "which she pelted the pigeon every day for seven days as often as it "came. After that it returned no longer. The old woman thereupon "reverenced the Brahmin as if he had been the Supreme Being.

"In Goozerat, if a pigeon or an owl sit on a housetop constantly, "people believe that the death of some one of the inhabitants of the "house will follow. If, also, a crow[1] alight upon a man, or a spider "fall upon him, they believe that his life will be shortened. To pre- "vent this calamity, the man strips off the clothes he wore at the "time the accident happened, gives them to Brahmins, and goes

[1] The owl and crow have always been held to be birds of ill omen: *vide* Brand's "Popular Antiquities," where the following, among other examples, are quoted:—

"When screech owls croak upon the chimney tops,
"It's certain then you of a corse shall hear."
Reed's Old Plays, VI. 257.

"The boding raven on her cottage sat,
"And, with horse croakings, warn'd us of our fate."
Gay's Pastorals.

"The owl shriek'd at thy birth, an evil sign;
"The night-crow cried, aboding luckless time;
"Dogs howl'd, and hideous tempests shook down trees;
"The raven rook'd her on the chimney's top,
"And chattering pies in dismal discord sung."
Third Part of King Henry VI., Act V. sc. 6.

The boatmen on the Indus will not suffer a crow to alight on their vessels, and consider it to be extremely unlucky. In Sweden, the magpie, like others of the raven or crow family, is a mystic bird, a downright witches' bird, belonging to the devil and the other hidden powers of night. When the witches, on Walpurgi's night, ride to the Blokulle, they turn themselves into magpies. When these birds are moulting in summer, and become bald about the neck, the country people say they have been to the Blokulle, and helped the evil one to get in his hay, and that the yoke had rubbed their feathers off. In Denmark, the crow is a bird of omen, but not necessarily of ill omen. Olaf Tryggvason, although a Christian, observed whether a crow stood on its right or left foot, and predicted good or evil accordingly, whence his enemies nick-named him *krakâbein* (crow-leg). In North Germany it is believed that if ravens fly over a house, making a great croaking, a person will soon die in it.

" away to perform ablution. If such a thing happen to a raja, he " performs sacrifice by fire. Whenever many meteors fall from the " sky, or the earth quakes, or wild animals enter a village, or any " other portent occurs, people have recourse to a section of the Sâm " Ved, in which remedies are prescribed which rajas ought to adopt. " If the raja neglect this duty, people believe that great injury will be " occasioned to the country over which he rules. However, things " happen as they are disposed, be the remedy taken or neglected."

Bânâsoor and his queen, says the " Rape of Okâ," one of the most popular poems in the language of Goozerat, were seated, in the early morning, at a window of their palace of Shoneetpoor, on the coast of the ocean, when an outcaste, who came thither to sweep the road, beheld them, and averted his face from the evil omen. The king and queen called him to them, and demanded the cause of his behaviour. He said, at first, that being of so low a caste he was afraid that if he showed his face to them he should be put to death; but on being pressed to tell the truth, and assured of pardon, he confessed that he had averted his face from them because they were childless persons, and to behold them at that hour was ominous of misfortune. The Rânee was very much distressed, and wept bitterly. She said that her palace, without a child's cradle in it, seemed to her like a Gosâee's monastery or a funeral ground, and she entreated her husband to procure the boon from Shiva. Bânâsoor repaired to Kyelâs and devoted himself to austerities of so great severity that Shiva was driven to seek the advice of Pârwutee as to the means of satisfying this importunate worshipper. The goddess possessed herself but two children, Gunesh and Okâ, and she refused to surrender either. With much entreaty, however, Shiva extorted from her a consent to relinquish Okâ, whom he conveyed, accordingly, to the suppliant monarch, to be brought up as his own daughter.

Bânâsoor some time afterwards having procured great strength from Shiva, became so inflated with pride as to challenge that deity himself to the combat. Shiva cursed him for his arrogance, and predicted that his strength should be reft from him by the grandfather of Okâ's future husband. The king now thought of putting Okâ to death, but, at the suggestion of a counsellor, altered his determination to that of keeping her unmarried. He built a tower by the sea-side, to which he left no means of access, and there he placed Okâ and her maiden confidante, setting a guard around the tower, and ordering that its inmates should be supplied only with such food as they should themselves draw up in a basket by a rope. Okâ, however, from her place of confinement, addressed her prayers for a husband to her mother Pârwutee, or Gowree. She repeated her petitions thrice, and the goddess then made answer that she should marry three husbands. Okâ now prayed that she might not be subjected to the calamity of becoming twice a widow, and Gowree answered, that she should marry once in a dream, a second time in private, and a third time publicly, but that her husband should be one and the same. She married, accordingly, Uneeroodh, the son of Prudyoomnâ, the son of Krishn, and that divinity (though Shiva fought for him) reft his strength from Bânâsoor.

Such, according to the popular version, was the origin of the festival called "the Worship of Gowree," which is held on the twelfth day of the light half of Âshâd, the first month of the monsoon season. In preparation for this day, little girls, between the ages of five and ten years, form an earthen image of Gowree, and dress it up in clothes. On either side, they set a vessel full of earth in which they have sown wheat and jowâree. The morning of the twelfth, as soon as they get up, they go to the river-side to bathe. Returning from thence, they proceed to some place where all the female children of the village or quarter of the town are assembling, and thence the whole proceed together, singing songs in praise of either their deity, Shree Krishn, or their temporal master, the lord of the village, to the house of some Brahmin, to whose care the image of Gowree has been entrusted. They now worship the goddess with the sixteen prescribed ceremonials, making her presents, which fall as perquisites to the Brahmin. The mothers, or elder sisters of the girls, at this time prompt them to ask a boon of the goddess, and the children, one after the other, say, "Gor! Mâ! grant me a good bridegroom." From the Brahmin's house they return home, worshipping on their way a sacred basil-tree, a cow, a well, and, lastly, the threshold of their father's house. The votaries of Gowree are bound by a vow to eat once only during the day, but this rule they comply with in form alone. At four in the afternoon the little girls are again assembled, decked out, each of them, in as brilliant a manner as the means of their parents permit, and they now set forth to worship all the Devs, one after the other. The day is generally concluded by these juvenile holiday-makers at the village tank, beside which they romp until bed-time. One of their great amusements is to strut about in procession, beating their breasts, as female mourners do at a funeral, and crying out, "Alas! Dedâ, alas! alas!" Or, perhaps, for the obnoxious Dedâ, they substitute a chief with whom theirs is at enmity, or some other unpopular person.

Betrothed girls receive, at the time of this festival, presents of clothes and other articles from the house of their intended bridegroom.

There is a verse in common use among the women of Goozerat, to the effect that if rain do not fall in the first five days of Shrâwun, a famine will ensue :—

> If in the first five days of Shrâwun,
> The cloud-king do not begin to scatter his drops,
> Husband, do you go to Malwa,
> I shall go home to my father's house.

When the fall of rain is long delayed the Hindoos think that Indra wishes to lay waste their town or village, and to deprecate his wrath by submission, they quit the place in a body for the day, leaving it "oojud," or waste, and cook their dinner outside. This is called an "Oojânee." In the territories of native chiefs, the raja issues proclamation by beat of drum, the day before the Oojânee is to take place, that a fine will be imposed upon any person who presumes to light a fire within the town.

Another mode of inducing the rain to fall, is to send for one of the persons called Bhoowos, who are supposed to be inspired by a local Devee. The man arrives, and, after certain preliminaries, begins to counterfeit inspiration. The Hindoos then address him as the goddess and say, "Mâtâjee, why is it that the rain does not fall?" The Bhoowo, flinging his limbs about, and rolling his eyes, makes answer, "Why should it fall? you make me no offerings." "We "were wrong, Mâtâjee!" they say, "we are your children, we will "bring offerings whenever you please." He then orders them to present certain kinds of food, which he describes, on the next day which is sacred to the Devee. The offerings must be put in broken earthen vessels, which represent the human skulls out of which the Yogeenee delights to eat; they must be carried outside the eastern door of the city, and then set down in a circle which has been previously sprinkled with water. As each householder has to present an offering, the number of the vessels which are thus set down is sometimes very large. The dogs, or the Dhers, eat the food, and if the rain fall it is believed that the Devee has sent it.

The following is another mode of inducing a fall of rain. The outlet by which water passes off from the basin that the symbol of Shiva is set in must be closed up, and libations made until the ling is immersed. This process should be repeated for eight days, unless rain fall in the meantime.

Koonbee and Bheel women sometimes parade the streets on these occasions, singing songs addressed to the goddess of the rain :—

> The cultivator has abandoned the plough, O ! Meyhoolâ,
> In pity to him do thou rain, therefore, O ! Meyhoolâ,
> The good man has packed off the good woman home, O ! Meyhoolâ,
> Separated from her are her little children, O ! Meyhoolâ,
> The stream is dry in the river's-bed, O ! Meyhoolâ.

* * * * *

A boy accompanies the singers, bearing on his head a basket containing mould, with three sprigs of the limb tree stuck in it. When the party approaches a Hindoo house, the women come forth and pour water over the sprigs, so that the boy is drenched through; they make presents of grain at the same time to the women who form the procession.

On the fifth of the second half of the month of Shrâwun the people of Goozerat prepare a white surface on some wall in the interior of their houses, upon which they paint in black a rude picture of the house of Shesh Nâg, the snake-supporter of the universe. They worship this figure with all the prescribed forms, and address the snake-king, saying, "Sire! be propitious to me," in the hope of securing his favor for the ensuing year. This is the day upon which, according to the Hindoo practice, the royal yearly grants ought to be paid. The festival is called "*Nâg Punchmee.*"

The next day is entitled "*Rândun Chut*," or "Cooking Sixth," and is devoted to the preparation of food for the seventh, the day dedicated to Seetulâ Devee, or the small-pox. The goddess is supposed to wander about on that day among the ovens of the householders, on which account no fire must be lighted there for fear of annoying her. The following account of Seetulâ Devee is from the modern author we have already quoted :—

" In the course of the present year, the daughter of a neighbour of " mine, who was four years old, fell sick of small-pox. When the " disease appeared, as the parents were old and had but one daughter " and two sons, they were very much alarmed that they should lose " their favorite. They brought her bed into the house, put a screen " before it, with branches of the limb tree, and having mixed ass's " dung and cow's urine with limb leaves, put this into an earthern " vessel, into which each of them, as they had occasion to return into " the house, dipped their feet, so as to moisten the big toe of the " right foot. If neighbour or relation or other visitor came, the " same purification had to be gone through. The reason was this, " that whoever attends a person who is sick with small-pox must not "allow the shadow of another person to fall upon himself; but if he "dips his foot as described the ill effect is avoided. The shadow of "a woman at the time of menstruation, or of one cohabiting with "her husband, is also injurious—as is that of a man who is newly "bathed. What objection there can be to this last, I do not under-"stand. Each person belonging to the house keeps beside him a "bunch of limb leaves, to avert the ill effect produced by the shadow "of an unclean person falling on him. All these precautions had "been duly observed by my neighbours. As the days went on the "disease also increased. A learned Brahmin was then called in, "who read the 'Seetulâ Stotra,' which is contained in the 'Roodray-"âmul.' It consists of praises of Seetulâ, among which are these :—"That she is naked, seated on a donkey, wearing a broken winnow-"ing fan on her head, with the pad of a water-vessel in one hand "and a besom in the other, and that she is of the Chundâl caste. "At the end of such equivocal praises as these, the book continues—"'O! great Devee! you are the mother of the world: Brumhâ, "Vishnoo, Muhâ Dev, Indra, and the other gods, worship you con-"tinually. I therefore entreat you to heal this child.' Such praises "they caused to be read, and, to please Seetulâ, they fed a donkey "with grass and cakes of wheat. Notwithstanding all this, the disease "went on increasing. They now had recourse to vows, and promised "that if the child recovered, they would give its weight in coarse "sugar to Brahmins, and also the same weight of dates. Every hour "they made some new vow or other; as, for instance, that they would "take the child to Boucherâjee's; would feed twenty-five Brahmins "at the temple of that Devee, and would shave off the hair of the "child's head there. The mother took a vow that she would not "wear a bodice until the sick child had worshipped at Buleeâ "Devee's, and that she would go thither carrying a lighted brazier "on her head and a shoe in her mouth, which latter should be "smeared with human ordure. She vowed, also, to offer a pair of "silver eyes, a sheet of paper, and two rupees' weight of sugar, with "grapes and other cooling things. She promised, too, a vessel of "cold water. The father vowed to wear no turban until the child "should have worshipped Buleeâ, and to proform the distance of "the last four fields in a series of somersets. The woman suggested "that as he was not well he should reduce the distance to two "fields; but the father declared himself willing to undergo the "annoyance if only his daughter might recover. A whole day they "went on vowing one vow after another to Dev after Dev; but the "child did not get well. Then father and mother, both of them, "began to weep. The visitors tried to encourage them, and told "them to place confidence in Buleeâ. The mother answered, "'Die and be wailed, Buleeâ! You were my enemies in former "birth! Murderess! you are come to take my girl's life.' The "standers-by said, 'Bâee! you should not speak so! As the raja "frightens his minister when he wants to force their spoils from "them, so Buleeâ is frightening you that you may worship her the "more. Do not be alarmed. Some of the children in your house "have been wittingly or unwittingly deriding Buleeâ. You must ask "pardon.' They then repeated a mode of asking pardon, which I "am almost ashamed to write. It is this:—'O Buleeâ! if at any "time wittingly or unwittingly I have derided you, pardon me. I "have committed a fault. I have done wrong. I have eaten your "dung. Be merciful, and preserve my daughter!' Notwithstanding "that the woman said this, the girl died. Then, abusing Buleeâ "very much, the mother beat her breast, crying, 'Ah! murderess! "Ah! sinner!' Such was her wail. She also, with the other women, "wept, continually crying out against Buleeâ. A month afterwards "the same woman's son was attacked with small-pox. Then she be-"took herself to vows as before. The boy recovered, and she per-"formed the vows she had undertaken."

Succeeding "Seetulâ's seventh," is the "Birth-day eighth," the natal day of Shree Krishn. This is a day of fast. The birth of the god is supposed to take place at midnight, on the eighth; and wherever a temple of Krishn exists they perform during that night all the ceremonies usual on the birth of a royal infant. The image of Bâl Krishn is rocked in a cradle; music sounds before him; and gifts are liberally bestowed. At the supposed hour of birth the temple is crowded with worshippers.

The fifteenth of the light half of the month of Shrâwun is called *Bulev*, or Bulee's day, being the anniversary of the contest between the raja of that name and Vishnoo, in the incarnate form of Wâmun. Brahmins upon this festival proceed to the river-side, where they worship the Shâlagrâm stone as an emblem of Vishnoo, and perform the rite called "Bodily purification," which will afterwards be described, for the cleansing of all sins committed during the year, as well as of impurities contracted from the touch of Shoodras, or other unclean persons. They next worship the seven sages, the ancestors of the Brahminical race, and Uroondhutee their consort, to represent whom they make eight figures of sacrificial grass. At this time, also, they change for a new one the junoee, or cord worn by the regenerate classes, which they have used during the year. The new cord has been constructed during the preceding month or two, by themselves or by other Brahmins, and precautions have been taken to make it of great strength. Some Brahmins, who affect much strictness in ritual observances, grow the cotton which is required to form the cord in a pot within their own houses. The Brahmins touch the grass figures with their new cords and put them on. They then break the old cords and throw them into the river. Next they take some sacrificial grass and the new cord into their hands, and make libations of water; after which they recite "the sages' genealogy," and then either cast the grass figures into the river, or carry them home to use them as objects of worship during the year. Libations are made at this time with the view of presenting to the sages (who are supposed to transmit them to the gods) "first-fruits," or offerings of the new water of the river which has fallen from the autumnal clouds.

The preceptor of the Brahmins now binds upon their arms a red or yellow bracelet, made of silk or cotton, with artificial pearls, called *Râkhudee*, which is said to have been originally employed as an amulet against a disease which used to be prevalent at this time of the year. The Brahmins return into the city or village, and bind similar bracelets upon the wrists of their disciples and friends.

The fourth of the light half of Bhâdrapud is called "Gunesh fourth," being the birthday of that divinity. An earthen image of Gunesh, dressed in costly clothes, is worshipped every day from this day until the eleventh, particularly with offerings of sumptuous food, in which the Dev is considered to take especial delight. On the eleventh the image is carried out in great noise and pomp to the river-side. A Brahmin, bearing the image with him, walks into the water until he is nearly out of depth, and then drops it into the stream, and swims to the bank. The rest of the company, who have meanwhile stood or sat at the river-side watching the proceedings, remain silent for a few minutes. They then rise, the banners and scarlet umbrellas are again elevated, muskets are fired, the cavaliers cause their horses to curvet and prance, the elephants swing along at their swift but heavy-seeming trot, the bells suspended from them sounding as they go, and the whole procession retraces its steps into the town.

On the birthday of Gunesh the poorer class prepare a sweet cake, which the Dev is represented as holding in his hand, and of which he is considered to be particularly fond, and, first offering it to himself, break it in pieces, and throw it behind the grain jars and heavy boxes, of which there are always plenty in their houses. The intention is to supply a feast for the rats and mice, which there abound, and which are esteemed to be the attendants of Gunesh.

It is a popular superstition that to behold the moon on the night of "Gunesh fourth" is unlucky, and that whoever does so is sure to get into some disgrace in the course of the year. The evil may, however, be averted by incessant reiteration of a sacred stanza. Some persons take the precaution of shutting themselves up in their houses, and closing all the windows: others, who, for whatever reason, have been compelled to go out of doors and to see the moon, throw stones at a neighbour's door or upon his roof, in order that he may abuse them, and that this harmless fulfilment of the ominous prediction may avert more serious consequences.

The day which follows the "Gunesh fourth" is called the "Sage's "fifth." On this day the people of Goozerat, in commemoration of the sages who are supposed to have lived upon uncultivated grain, use only such vegetable food as springs up spontaneously.

Many of the Jains observe a two-months' fast, which is called "the "Pujoosun," during the monsoon, supposing that greater production of life than is usual then takes place. The fast is one of great severity when strictly observed. Shrâwuks should abstain from ablutions, and from every species of purification, and should take no sustenance but water, which has been boiled and allowed to cool. The greater number of the Jains fast for a certain number of days, and every one is expected to observe at least the last day of the Pujoosun, which falls on the same day as the "Sage's fifth." At the close of the fast the Shrâwuks go round to visit all their friends, a custom derived (as they say) from the necessity of inquiring what persons had perished in consequence of the severity of the fasting which they had undergone. Each Shrâwuk, as he enters his friend's house, takes hold of him by both hands, and repeats the following sacred stanza:—

"Twelve months, twenty-four half months, forty-eight and four "weeks—if during this time I may have said or done anything an- "noying to you, pardon me!"

The ascetics of the Jain religion, and particularly those of the Doondeeâ[1] sect, take at this time occasionally a vow called "sun-

[1] The Doondeeâ sect did not arise, it is said, before Sumwut 1700 (A.D. 1644). The word Doondeeâ means "searcher," and is assumed by these sectaries on the ground of their being reformers of the Jain religion. Their adversaries, the Tupâ sect, however, derive the word from "doond," a husk; and pronounce the Doondeeâs to be the husks of the Shrâwuk grain. The Doondeeâs neither use temples nor worship idols. They abstain from ablutions with the idea of

"thâro," which pledges them to produce their death by abstaining from food. As soon as a jutee has taken this vow, the news is carried to all parts of the country, and large numbers of Jains assemble to pay him worship. For fifteen days, it is said, the monk is sometimes able to maintain a sitting posture; after that time he lies along on the floor. The persons who surround him dab his feverish body with moist cloths, but are careful to prevent his receiving sustenance of any kind.

From the day on which the monk has taken the vow, preparations are commenced for his funeral. A litter is constructed, and ornamented with colored paper and tinsel, upon which the jutee, when his last moments approach, is placed in a sitting posture. Music sounds before him as he is carried out in procession, and women who seek the blessing of a male child strive to secure it by creeping beneath his litter, or by joining in the scramble for fragments of his clothes.

The fourteenth of the light half of Bhâdrupud is called "Ânund "Choudush," or the joyful fourteenth. The name is, however, originally derived from "Ununt," one of the titles of Shesh-Nâg, the supporter of the world. Vows for almost any purpose are made to Ununt. They must be kept for fourteen years; but the observance is not apparently very burdensome, consisting merely in wearing a bracelet of red string, with fourteen knots in it, on the upper part of the right arm. Vishnoo must be worshipped at the

avoiding the destruction of life, and will drink no water but what has been boiled. The Doondeeâ ascetic is a disgusting object. He retains no property, even the convent in which he lives belonging to his followers. He quits his dwelling only for the purpose of procuring food. He carries a fan of goat's hair in his hand, which he employs in removing anything possessing life from the path on which he treads or the ground on which he sits. He wears a screen of cloth, called a moomutee, tied over his mouth, lest he should inhale insects to their destruction. His body and clothes are filthy in the last degree, and covered with vermin.

About fifteen years ago the Doondeeâs and Tupâs came into violent collision at Goondul, in Kâteewâr, where there is a great Shrâwuk temple; and the former, gaining the mastery, destroyed the idols. A similar contest afterwards occurred at Wânkâner, when relations were arrayed against each other in arms. The followers of the Jhâla chieftain interfering to put down the disturbance were furiously attacked by both parties.

The Tupâs, in the province of Kutch, finding themselves in danger of being supplanted by the Doondeeâs, broke up the Shrâwuks into two castes. In the city of Ahmedabad it would seem that the Tupâs and Doondeeâs still eat together, but that they have ceased to intermarry. The greater asceticism of the latter sect has up to the present time gained them more followers than their rivals can secure, and a new and stricter sect, called the Shumbegee, has sprung up among the Tupâs themselves.

time of taking the vow, and an offering must be presented to him of dishes, the names of which are of the masculine gender. The bracelet is changed every year, and on the termination of the fourteenth year the votary performs "Oodyâpun," a ceremony which releases him from the vow, and which consists in performing a fire-sacrifice, and making, of different grains, a mansion for Vishnoo, upon which he places fourteen copper cups containing cocoa-nuts. The Dev is invited into the mansion, and the usual acts of worship are performed. The votary who thus acquires his release presents to persons inclined to receive the vow fourteen bracelets. He also invites the family priest and his wife, and presents to them, after having worshipped them, fourteen complete suits of clothes, under the title of "Oomâ Muheshwur."

"The Book of Ununt," which professes to be a portion of one of the Poorâns, contains several stories, which relate how Krishn recommended the vow to Yoodishteer and the other sons of Pândoo, pronouncing that he himself was Ununt; how a Brahmin's wife, in the golden age, procured wealth for her husband by observing the vow, which melted away on the ignorant removal by her lord of the mystic bracelet from her arm; how the repentant priest on discovering the cause of his misfortunes sought the protection of Ununt, and received from that deity, in addition to the gift of wealth, the promise of *religion* in the present life, and the heaven of Vishnoo in the life to come; and how many other strange and wonderful effects were produced by the worship of "*the Illimitable*,"[1] for the repetition of which we possess, however, too little space in the present volume.

The Nowrâttra, or *Festival of Nine Nights*, occupying the period from the first to the ninth of the moonlight half of Âsho, is consecrated to the Family Goddess, or to Doorgâ, the consort of Shiva. On the first day of the feast the Hindoos having carefully whitened a sufficient surface of wall within their houses, paint upon it, with vermillion, the trident, which is the emblem of the goddess. In front of it they build a model of her dwelling, which, placed as it usually is on the mountain-top, amidst forests, or in other spots equally *difficult of access*,[2] is represented by a heap of earth sown with wheat and barley, and surmounted by a metal water-vessel, containing a cocoa-

[1] Shesh means the remnant of anything, as the unused paper of a manuscript book, and hence is applied also to the void remaining around and "supporting" the world. This is also "Nâg" (motionless) and "Ununt" (illimitable). Shesh-Nâg is further termed "Bhoodhur" (supporter of the earth.)

[2] Hence her name *Doorgâ*, which means "difficult of access."

nut. The goddess is now, by the first of the sixteen acts of worship, "invited" to occupy her temple. An earthen vessel, pierced with numerous holes, and containing a light, is placed near the trident, or perhaps in country places a tree, to which lamps are hung, is erected in some open spot in the village, round which the people walk or dance, clapping their hands and singing songs.[1] A lamp, fed with clarified butter, and placed upon a stand, is kept burning night and day before the goddess during the nine days of the Nowrâttra, and a member of the family, who abstains from eating grain while so employed, watches continually to replenish the lamp, and to worship the sacred emblems. The family priest reads, during the nine days, "the Book of Doorgâ," which contains a description of the achievements of that goddess, and of the prescribed modes of her worship. On the eighth day fire-sacrifice is performed in each private house, and in the temples of the goddess. At the shrine of the Ârâsooree mother, or at the temple of the Choonwâl Devee, Koolees and others at this and similar times offer animals in vicarious sacrifice to the goddess for their sick friends and children. On the ninth day the mound of earth, in which the wheat and barley has by this time sprouted, is raised from its position, and carried out to the side of a river or reservoir of water, to which pure element it is consigned, that it may not be subsequently defiled. The vessel which contained the lamp is placed at the same time in front of a Devee's image.

The Rajpoot chiefs and others, who claim the possession of Kshutreeya blood, offer sacrifices of animals at the Nowrâttra in their private temples for the welfare of themselves and their followers during the year. With them the cannon is the most appropriate emblem of Doorgâ Devee, and they mark her trident therefore upon it, and raising before it the representation of her shrine, surround it with lamps.

The day immediately succeeding the ninth day of the Nowrâttra is the "Dussera," or "tenth day," a festival which commemorates the entrance of the sons of Pândoo into Wyerât Nugger, as well as the destruction by Râm of the giant-king of Ceylon,—events celebrated in the two great epic poems of the Hindoos. As Urjoon and his brothers worshipped the *Shumee* tree,[2] and hung up their arms upon it, so the Hindoos go forth to worship that tree on the festival of the Dussera. They address the tree under the name of Upurâjeetâ, the

[1] The lamp and the tree are called "Gurbo," "Gurbee," and hence the song is also called "Gurbo."

[2] "*Mimosa Suma.*"

"invincible goddess," sprinkle it with five ambrosial liquids,[1] wash it with water, and hang garments upon it. They light lamps and burn incense before the symbol of Upurâjeetâ, make *chândlos* upon the tree, sprinkle it with rose-coloured water, set offerings of food before it, and perform the ceremony of circumambulation, repeating as they walk the following stanzas :—

I.

Shumee pacifies for sins,
Shumee destroys enemies,
Shumee cures diseases,
Shumee procures success in every object.

II.

Holder of the bow of Urjoon !
Exhibitor of his heart's desire to Râm !
Restorer of life to Lukshmun !
Assuager of the grief of Seetâ !

Then, turning themselves round, they worship in succession the ten Dig-Pâls, or protectors of the ten points of Heaven, beginning with Indra, the Deity of the East, whom they thus address :—

In the East, whatever works I have,
To those works cause success :

and proceeding similarly with the other nine. At this time the Hindoos break, and throw from them, the bracelet which they had assumed in the Bulev festival.

The Rajpoot chiefs, on the evening of the Dussera, worship also the *Fort-protectress*, the goddess Gudeychee. On their return from the Shumee worship into the city they join together in bands, brandishing their spears, gallopping their horses, and enacting in other ways the part of an army taking the field. Salutes of cannon are at the same time fired.

Many of the Hindoos, as they return home, take earth from the roots of the Shumee tree, a few of its leaves, some betel-nut, and a stalk of the wheat that has grown up around the model temple of Doorgâ. Of these articles they compound a ball, which they keep about them as an amulet, and carry with them if called upon to perform a journey. The piece of wheat-stalk which remains they fix upright, as an ornament in their turbans.

[1] *Punchâmrit*, a mixture of milk, curds, sugar, clarified butter, and honey.

CHAPTER VII.

MARRIAGES.

MARRIAGES among the Hindoos in Goozerat can take place only between members of the same caste, and if that be permanently subdivided, as, for instance, into right and left hand, of the same subdivision of it. Brahmins refer back to a "gotra," a supposed ancestor of whose period they are not distinctly informed, and they do not permit alliances among his descendants. Other Hindoos, maintaining the same rule, construe it less strictly, as they do not pretend to be possessed of information extending back to so remote a date as that of the Brahmins. The bard, called Wyewunchâ—the genealogist of the caste—can, however, usually trace back to about twenty descents; and the degrees within which marriage is prohibited are regulated by the information supposed to be in his possession. In addition to these rules there exists another, of less authority, but commanding, nevertheless, almost invariable acquiescence, which prescribes that the descendants of the brothers and sisters of a female ancestor within five descents, or of a stepmother within three descents, are not fit persons with whom to contract a marriage. It is further declared that a man may not marry the sister of the wife of his father's brother.

The different *Kools*, or families of the same caste, are not treated with equal consideration. One Kool assumes a superiority to another, founded usually upon benefits conferred on the caste generally by ancestors of the house. It is always an object of solicitude to the parents of a female child that they should procure her marriage with the scion of a more noble family. To wed her to a bridegroom of inferior rank is considered disgraceful, and it is this feeling which has so often urged the Rajpoot or even the Koonbee of Goozerat to practice the dreadful crime of infanticide.[1]

[1] "The reasons why the higher castes of Rajpoots murder their girls are various. "The chief inducement to this crime is the heavy expense to which their customs "expose them on the occasion of a marriage of a daughter. These may be thus "stated :—On the conclusion of a match between the parents a sum of money is "sent to the father of the youth by the father of the girl. This sum is not large, "probably about the tenth of the amount of 'Zuheez,' or dower. This is a sort

In the case of male children, parental anxiety, though scarcely less in amount, is different in the form which it assumes. Careful persons can avoid a large expenditure on occasions of obsequies, though few are so cautious, the usual rule being that they incur debt for the purpose; but, prudent or imprudent, all are compelled to lavish sums altogether inconsistent with the means of the majority in marrying their sons, or, if their father be dead, their younger brothers. To be unmarried is contemptible, ignominious. The man who has not begotten a child, or who has lost his children, is despised as an eunuch; to meet him in the morning is an omen of misfortune; when he dies he becomes a miserable ghost, his spirit haunting his former abode, and enviously beholding the happy enjoyment by some other of those blessings which the curse of sonlessness has rendered nugatory to himself.

Some curious customs which obtain in particular castes may be worth alluding to in this place. The Kuruwâ Koonbees celebrate marriages only under a certain sidereal conjunction, which occurs about once in thirteen years, and hence it is asserted by others, though they themselves deny it, that their unborn children are often contracted in marriage on the chance of their being male and female.[1] A shepherd caste, called "Bhurwâds," fix upon a

"of earnest money, and when the ceremony of 'Tilluk' is completed the father "of the girl cannot recede from the engagement.

"After this comes the 'Luggun,' when half of the dower agreed upon is paid, "and the date for the nuptial procession, called the 'Burat,' is settled. The "Burat, or chief marriage ceremony, to which all the relations and friends are "invited, is the occasion of the most profuse expenditure in feasting them; "the greater the multitude fed, the better satisfied is the pride and vanity of the "father of the girl, who, at the same time, pays the remainder of the dower. "This sum varies according to the rank of the parties, but is generally enough to "throw the father into debt and difficulties. Unless a handsome sum be offered, "a husband of good caste is not to be procured; and, unless the feasting be "profuse, and the invitations to the marriage feast general, then the girl's parents "are held up to public scorn, as stingy or poverty-stricken. This is the chief "reason why the high caste and proud Thakors hate the idea of a daughter "being born to them. Another reason is the blind pride which makes them hate "that any man should call them Sala, or Sussoor—brother-in-law, or father-in-"law. This crime of infanticide is not confined to the Rajpoots; some tribes of "the Aheers are equally guilty. We remember remonstrating with the heads of "an Aheer village, who had ten girls to eighty boys living. They said, 'Sir, "it is all very well for Bunyans and such people to beget girls, but they are very "seldom or ever born to men of our caste.'"—*Article on the Landed Tenures in the North-West Provinces. Benares Magazine for October*, 1850.

[1] In the hills near Râj Muhâl, "It is not uncommon for two neighbours to "agree, when their respective wives are pregnant, that the offspring, in the event

particular year, about once in ten years, for the celebration of their marriages, and they purchase from the Rajpoot chief, or other ruling power, a piece of ground upon which the hymeneal ceremonies are performed. This caste, also, finds itself compelled, for similar reasons, to contract children of the age of two or three months. The ground cannot be employed for marriage rites a second time, but it is retained henceforth in pasture, and never subjected to cultivation. Upon it the shepherds erect an ornamental wooden post, called "a marriage pillar," which is preserved as an indication of the purpose to which the ground has been applied.

The bridegroom is called "wur," and the bride "kunyâ." Proposals of marriage are symbolized by a cocoa-nut, which is sometimes richly studded with gems. They emanate from the house of lesser pretention, and the father of either bride or bridegroom, who seeks to ally his child to the redder blood of a more distinguished Kool, must balance the scales with gold. If the families are considered to be on an equality, the father of the bride makes proposals, and money is not demanded on either side. When the bridegroom is of high rank, so that he is under no difficulty as regards providing himself with a wife, he has frequently many proposals made to him. The family priest, or a relation, is then sent to ascertain, by personal interview, that the young ladies are neither blind, lame, nor afflicted with other bodily defect, and that they are in every respect eligible. The priest (or gor), however, as it is said, invariably fills a purse for himself, and not unfrequently, to increase his gains, behaves treacherously to those who have employed him, by concealing the ladies' defects, or exaggerating their good qualities. There is a Hindoo saying, founded on the mendacity of the priest upon such occasions, which states that sufficient weight of sins to bear him down to hell is accumulated by a king in three months, by the head of a monastery in three days, but by a gor in three hours.

Acceptance of proposals of marriage is followed by a more binding betrothal. The relations of the contracting parties meet at the house of the bridegroom's father, who commences the ceremony by producing a tiny stone or metal image of Gunesh, which he washes with water, with milk, and again with water, in imitation of the washing with "five ambrosial liquids," prescribed by the Shâstras, and marks in the centre of the forehead with the chândlo. He

"of their being a boy and a girl, shall be married to each other."—*Vide Asiat. Res.* iv., p. 63.

worships the Dev, under his title of Vighun Râj, the smoother of difficult paths, and frequently repeats the following verse :—

"O ! thou of the terrible face, thou of the large body,
"Splendid as ten million suns,
"Cause me to be free from obstacles, O ! Dev,
"In all works, at all times."

The bride's father now pays obeisance to his entertainer, marks his feet with a preparation, the red color of which is symbolical of prosperity, and offers him, in his joined hands, betel-nut, turmeric, and flowers, as an earnest that he has betrothed his daughter. He next places the royal teeluk on the forehead of the young bridegroom and presents him with the cocoa-nut, which, if he cannot afford to adorn it with precious stones, he marks with a red spot, upon which he sets a silver coin. The family priest repeats the names of the affianced parties, their parents and ancestors, and when he has exhausted his list pronounces that the ceremony is concluded. The women of the family, assisted by their neighbours, now chant an appropriate song, and entitle themselves to a much-prized dole of sugar and coriander.

The general rule is that betrothal cannot be set aside, but the practice of different castes varies. Among Rajpoots, if the betrothed bridegroom die, the girl who should have been his wife is treated as his widow, and considered incapable of entering into the married state. Some Brahmins, on the other hand, do not consider themselves bound by either betrothal or any other ceremony short of the actual joining of hands in marriage. In most castes a betrothed bride is not treated as a widow on the death of the affianced, and in many she may, with permission of the caste, marry another person even in his lifetime, should he, before the marriage is concluded, become afflicted with any serious disease.

The Kuruwâ Koonbees, when they cannot procure a husband for their daughter, will sometimes marry her to a bunch of flowers. The next day they throw the flowers into a well, and the bridegroom thus disposed of, the widow is eligible for nâtrâ, or second marriage. A similar practice is that of marrying the girl to a person called "a hand-husband." This bridegroom may be any male of the caste who is willing to contract, beforehand, that he will receive a certain sum for a divorce and give his bride a release from her marriage the moment the ceremony has been performed. The wife so divorced may then marry in nâtrâ.

The object of these proceedings is the avoidance of expense. No money need be spent by the bride's father upon a nâtrâ marriage, except such as is required for entertaining the friends who accompany the bridegroom. The lady's trousseau is supplied by her husband. An unmarried woman cannot, however, be given in nâtrâ.

When the bride has attained the age of nine or ten years, an astrologer is called for to point out the day indicated by the stars as propitious for the marriage. Seasons of family mourning are always carefully avoided. The day fixed, letters of invitation, termed kunkotree, are sprinkled with rose-colored water and forwarded to the kindred of both bridegroom and bride. They run in something like the following strain :—

" To the dweller at the auspicious Shree Ahmedabad, the great " and excellent place of residence, to the worship-worthy treasury of " all good qualities, the benefactor of others, the able administrator of " affairs of state, the head-jewel of the clever, who knows the qualities " of the fourteen sciences and is deserving of every epithet;[1] Shet- " jee, Shree, five times repeated, Sâmuldâs Bechurdâs, and Shet Ku- " rumchund Purumchund, may your lives be long! Here from Shree " Mhowâ the sea-port writes Shâ Âtmârâm Bhoodhurdâs. Receive " his salutation of 'Victory to Gopâl!' (Krishn). Further, the fol- " lowing is the cause of writing :—All is well and prosperous here. " Be pleased to write intelligence of your prosperity. Understand " besides, that sister Kunkoo Bâee's marriage-day is appointed to be " Wednesday, the 2nd of the dark half of Chyetra. Therefore do you, " bringing the whole of your family with you, come speedily. By " your coming the work will be adorned."

Then follows the date. Sometimes, if previous invitations have not been treated with sufficient attention, the writer adds—

" You were not able to attend brother Chugun's marriage, but " if you fail to come on the present occasion, you and I will not " be able to drink water together again. I say little, but consider it " much."

About twenty days before the marriage, the houses of the parents are carefully cleansed, and adorned by the wealthy with strings of pearls or handsomely embroidered curtains, and by the poor with garlands of leaves. In front a temporary building, called mundup, is erected, which, in the case of poor persons, is merely a thatched hut, but where the higher classes are concerned, is frequently a very brilliant pantomime-like edifice, lined with mirrors and adorned with lamps, rich curtains, soft

[1] This expression being considered somewhat equivocal, it has of late been usual to insert the qualifying word "good" before epithet.

carpets, and abundance of tinsel. Near one of the corners of the mundup a wooden post, called a "jewel-pillar," is set up, adorned with flowers and other ornaments, and worshipped. Within the mundup the planets, Gunesh, Vighun Râj, and the progenitors are worshipped —the last-mentioned, in order that the household may not, as long as the ceremony lasts, be rendered unclean by the occurrence of a birth or death in the family.

A ceremony, called "Gotruj," is performed within the dwelling-house. A flat surface of wall having been whitened, a pyramid is made upon it of red spots, which increase from one at the apex to seven at the base. Below the base line other seven spots are made with clarified butter, which the heat causes gradually to trickle downwards. The figure, which represents a genealogical tree, becomes the subject of adoration.

The bridegroom, or (in her own house) the bride, is now adorned as splendidly as the resources of the family will permit. If a Rajpoot, the boy wears red silk drawers, which, like the rest of his attire, are embroidered with gold; if a Brahmin or Wâneeo, a long white cloth, with a broad red silk border wrapped round the waist and tucked up between the legs; over this he wears a red or yellow body-coat, a waistband and scarf of the same colors; his turban must be red. The bride's father presents him with a yellow handkerchief called "Ootureeyâ." The bride wears a white silk bodice and a red or yellow silk petticoat, and over these a very long white silk scarf, bordered and spotted with red, which is wrapped round the waist, and then passed over the shoulders and head, of which it forms the only ordinary covering. During her marriage festivities, however, the bride wears above the scarf a triangular head-dress, representing a crown, over which is thrown a large square red scarf, the substitute for a marriage veil. The bride and bridegroom wear each of them on the right wrist a bracelet made of beads, which they remove at the conclusion of the ceremony. Among the poorest classes of Hindoos, the children whose marriage is celebrating are invariably ornamented with, at the least, necklaces of alternate gold and coral beads, which are borrowed, or frequently even hired. The bridegroom now assumes the state and title of "Wur Raja." He is attended by companions of his own age,—"the children of the bride-chamber," and particularly by a friend who bears the title of "Unwur," and must be selected from among his juniors, in order that the bride, to whom he acts as accredited ambassador, may be able to receive him unveiled. He is also the bridegroom's purse-bearer, makes all his purchases, and presents certain marriage gifts, such as those called "the brother-in-

"law's dagger," and "the priest's dress," which are due at the conclusion of the ceremony.

At night, the bridegroom king publicly appears in his newly acquired royal state. Musicians head the procession—singers and dancing girls; following them come the bridegroom's relations, and visitors, mounted on horses or elephants, and surrounded by torch-bearers, cavaliers, and footmen; guns are discharged, rose-colored powder is sprinkled on all sides, the horns scream their loudest, the kettle-drums make a deafening rattle, the flaring torches are rendered nearly invisible by the clouds of dust which rise into the air. Soon the bearers of the silver rods, in their scarlet coats, appear, and, following them, with royal umbrella borne above him and horse-hair fans waving on either side, the Wur Raja, mounted on his white and richly ornamented palfrey, sweeps gaily past, bearing in his hands the jewel-adorned cocoa-nut, the emblem of marriage-festival. Behind him follow the great camel-drums, flaunting in their red drapery, and rolling forth a majestic sound, and troops of women, chanting nuptial hymns, bring up the rear.

In these processions of the bridegroom-king is dimly recalled somewhat of the regal state of former days—of those pageantries which welcomed to Unhilpoor Sidh Râj, the "Victorious Lion," from subjugated Malwa, or hailed the sainted Koomâr Pâl, and his train of white-robed priests returning from some desperate encounter of wits with the "evil-disposed" servants of Shiva.

The friends of the bridegroom's family, as the procession passes their houses, come forth, and present to him a cocoa-nut. Every other cavalcade, even that of the lord of the village, which meets the bridegroom's procession, makes way for it, and if two Wur Rajas meet, each gives up half the road to the other. Thus passing through the village, the bridal train returns to the house from which it set forth, where it is welcomed by the mother of the boy, who performs a ceremony called "Nyoonchun," in which she expresses by significant pantomime the worthlessness in her eyes of even the necessaries of life in comparison with her beloved child. Around his head she waves a cake of bread and then a cup of water, both of which she throws from her; she next takes in her hand the "sumpot," which is composed of two vessels full of rice, fastened together mouth to mouth, and expressing the idea of a hoard of any kind, and lays it at the feet of the Wur Raja. The boy, however, is not behindhand in his part of the drama,—he crushes the "sumpot" indignantly with his foot, and hastens into the house to embrace his mother.

During the days which remain before that appointed for the marriage, the Wur Raja's procession moves forth evening by evening from the house of some hospitable relation, who has previously entertained with feasting the strangers who have been invited to the ceremony.

The proper time having arrived, the bridegroom is conveyed by his friends in similar state to the village in which the bride resides. He usually arrives there late in the day preceding that of the marriage, and halts outside. The father-in-law, attended by his male and female relations, with torch-bearers and music, goes forth at night to the bridegroom's camp, and conducts him from thence to the house which has been prepared for his reception within the village.[1] Over the door of the bride's dwelling there is hung at this time a garland of leaves, which the Wur Raja, if of the warrior class, must break down with his lance, but which in other cases is allowed to remain until it drops from decay.

On the morning of the marriage-day the bride is assisted at her toilet by her mother and her female relations, and is invested with her marriage bracelets, which are made of ivory, and coloured red. The bridegroom is also prepared by his friends, with the sound of music and song, and is conducted in state to the house of his affianced. There he is received by the mother of the bride, who performs the Nyoonchun ceremony. She marks the Wur Raja with the royal teeluk, waves round his head, and then throws from her a bullock-yoke, a pestle, a churning stick, a spindle, the "sumpot," an arrow, a cake of flour and one of ashes, which last expresses her desire to throw dust in the eyes of his enemies.

When the Nyoonchun has been completed, the bridegroom takes his seat in the pavilion, called the "Mundup," and his father-in-law, after having washed his feet and marked the red spot upon his forehead, brings the bride forth, and places her at his side. In remembrance of the old rite of "Gomed," or sacrifice of a cow, one of these animals is at the present time brought forth when the bridegroom takes his seat in the pavilion, and fastened beside it. Grass is thrown before the cow, and she is worshipped by the Wur Raja and his friends. A water hour-glass is placed beside the bridegroom to announce the fortunate hour, or sometimes that time is selected at which half of the

[1] The procession of welcome is not confined to marriages, but is usual whenever a visitor of any importance arrives. See, for instances, the story of Jug Dev Purmâr, pp. 103.—116. It was common in feudal Europe also. The following is an example:—"Jacques de Clèves vint à Eu le 19 août 1563. La noblesse alla à sa rencontre, à cheval, jusqu'à Criel, et, lorsqu'il fut arrivé au château, le maire lui présenta deux barriques d'excellent vin, qui avaient coûté dix écus.—*History of Eu and Tréport.*

disc of the setting sun has become obscured. The auspicious moment arrived: the father of the bride, taking her hand, places it in that of the Wur Raja, presenting him at the same time with a piece of the sacred basil, and saying, "I give a Krishn gift." After the father has joined their hands, the Gor hangs around the necks of the bride and bridegroom the "Wur Mâlâ," or marriage-garland, which is composed of twenty-four threads of red cotton. At the same time the playfellows of the bridegroom throw a red cloth over their joined hands, and under cover of it present them with betel-nut. The pair remain seated in the pavilion for about an hour.

Outside the Mundup is formed the "Choree," or marriage hall. Nine metal or earthernware water-vessels are set up one above the other, at each of the four corners of a square, and are retained in this position by the support of bamboos. A fire-pit is made in the centre, and the bride and bridegroom are seated by its side. The priest performs fire-sacrifice before them, and fastens the boy's scarf to the marriage veil of the girl. The bride's mother brings a plate of food, of which both partake, the girl first helping her husband, and he then presenting food to her. During the whole celebration singing is kept up by the women. Their songs are usually poetical compositions in honour of Seetâ or Rookmunee, the wives of Râm and Krishn, or else ludicrous and not unfrequently obscene stanzas. We quote a few verses from a ballad called "Seetâ's Marriage," by one of the best reputed poets of Goozerat:—

"I touch the feet of the great preceptor,
And to Gunesh I pay obeisance;
I pray for wealth of successful skill,
By which the heart's longing may be satisfied.
I sing the nuptials of Râm.

The Prosody's leaves who has not turned,
Knows not how to frame the verse:
With all my strength I will sing my song;
O! Poets count not its faults.
I sing the nuptials of Râm.

Dusruth King was Uyodhyâ's lord,
His heir was the illustrious Râm;
At Jânporee ruled Junukjee the King,
To whom a Princess Royal, Seetâjee, was born.
I sing the nuptials of Râm;

Vyekoonth's lord was this illustrious Râm;
Seetâ was incarnate Lukshmee;
Assuming human form they wedded:
To sing their praises is destructive of sin.
I sing the nuptials of Râm.

First I relate how Junuk's daughter was born,
Then the story of the marriage,
How where sages dwell on the banks of Ganges,
So great calamity was caused by Râwun.
I sing the nuptials of Râm, &c., &c."

At last the bridegroom and the bride circumambulate the fire-pit four times, and the marriage is complete.

The Wur, if a Rajpoot chief, instead of going himself to be married, frequently sends his sword, which is treated as his representative, the whole ceremony being gone through with it, as if he were present in person, but the concluding circumambulation is in this case performed twice only, and again twice when the bride joins her husband. The practice originated probably in the necessity of secrecy in certain cases,[1] and it has been retained for convenience sake, and especially as a means of avoiding expense.

When the circumambulation is completed, the bride and bridegroom worship the polar star and the seven sages. Their relations, as many as are so disposed, come forward and present offerings to the pair, of which their parents take possession.

The bride and bridegroom now visit the lodging of his family, and his mother performs Nyoonchun to both. They worship the "Gotruj," and play a game of chance with betel-nut, dried dates, and coins—seven of each put in a cup. The women affirm that the mastery in wedded life falls to the victor in this game. The bridegroom's father presents to the guests offerings of clothes, disposed upon a shield or a metal tray, so as to hang down upon all sides.

When the Wur Raja's suite is ready to return home the bride's friends sprinkle their guests with rose-colored water, and mark them back and front with the impression of a hand. They fasten, also, to the carriage of the bridegroom a large vessel full of sweetmeats, and a lamp called "the lantern of Râm," as a sign that they have introduced light into his home through the marriage which has been completed. They take also from the hands of the bride and bridegroom the cocoa-nuts which they have held throughout the ceremony, and place them under the wheels of the carriage that they may be broken. As soon as they have cleared the village, the Wur Raja's relations dismiss the Brahmins, bards, and musicians who have attended them, making them presents. The stragglers are now collected from the village tank, where they have been washing their

[1] See that of Rana Rutna of Mewar.—Tod's Rajasthan, vol. i. p. 308.

hands and faces, and making their final preparations for the journey, and the whole party proceed homewards.

The bride goes home with her husband and remains a month, after which she returns to her father's. When she reaches the age of about twelve years her husband's friends send for her. The girl is usually exceedingly indisposed to leaving home, and weeps as an English child of the same age might do at going to school. Her father and mother persuade her, reminding her that her sisters and her cousins have gone in like manner and returned, and promising that she shall not remain long, and that her aunt or any other relation who happens to be married in the same village shall visit her constantly. They will also address themselves to the husband's father, and say, "You "must take care of our girl; she has never been outside the village "up to this time, nor left her mother for a minute; you must let her "go and visit her aunt, and take care that people don't frighten "her." The father-in-law protests, in reply, that no one is more interested in her than he himself is, and that he will take better care of her than her own father has taken. Other married girls, too, give her courage, and say, "Never mind: I've been and come back, "have'nt I?" The child turns to her father, and says, "Bâpâ! "when will you come for me? Do come quick!" He promises to do so in ten or fifteen days, though perhaps he has no definite intention of going within a year. The girl makes him swear to her, and says, "Mâ! mind you send him: and take care of my dolls and "toys, and don't give them away." At last she goes off with her husband's friends, and from that time she lives for the most part with them, paying only occasional visits to her native village.

Hindoo women neither receive nor expect that attention from the other sex which the customs of European countries allow of, or rather demand. The decided absence of gallantry expressed in a verse of Toolshee-dâs's far-renowned poem, "The story of Râm," would have met with the approbation of the Yankee clockmaker himself. It runs thus:—

"A drum, a fool, a beast, and a woman,
"These, all of them, are subjects for beating."

A padishah, so says the story, once commanded his minister to fetch him the most shameless person and the most modest, the greatest coward and the person least accessible to fear in all his realm. The minister bowed obedience, and soon after re-appeared, leading in a woman. "How," said the padishah, "is this? I asked "for four persons." "The qualities of the four, may it please your

"Majesty," replied the minister, "are concentrated in this one. She "will veil herself in the presence of her elder brother, but if she go "to a marriage she will sing obscene songs, such as a lewd man "would be ashamed of. If her husband ask her to give him water "in the night-time she is afraid, it is so dark; but if she have a "lover to meet, it is light enough for her to clamber over a "mountain."

Disrespect to women, however, crept in in the Mohummedan times. In older days rânees sat beside rajas in the court, and reeshees' wives beside their husbands in the assemblies of sages. To this hour the presence of woman is necessary to the due performance of a fire-sacrifice, and if none be there a figure is made to represent her, and dressed in female vestments. The marriage rite is also sanctified by the necessity which exists for a legitimate son. The Rajpootnee, of whose valour and constancy in days of old so many tales are related, still retains a high reputation even among those who concede but little honour to her "unbusiness-like" lord. "The "wise woman's son," says the trading wâneeo, "is a fool, but the "foolish woman's son" (alluding to his own wife or mother) is "wise."[1] The women's subjection is, however, in any case rather

[1] "While the master of the family," says Captain Macmurdo, in his account of the Province of Kutch (*vide* Transactions of the Literary Society of Bombay, vol. ii., p. 226), "is thus careless and lost to everything that is honorable or "respectable, his wives (for they, the Jhârejas, have often more than one) are "active, jealous, and intriguing. They are the daughters of the Jhâlâ, Wâghela, "Shodâ, or Gohil Rajpoots, who marry the grâs and not the man. These wives "have each their respective establishment of servants, cattle, carriages, &c., and a "village, or more or less, according to the means of the husband. The women of "the Rajpoots are much distinguished from those of any other caste of Hindoos. "They are high-spirited, bold, and enterprising, and are justly celebrated for a "remarkable neatness of person, and anxiety about personal appearance, even "when advanced in life, which is met with in no other native. The Rajpootnee "has her cosmetics and washes, as well as the ladies of Europe, and understands "the method of making an artificial mole or patch on the most favourable spot "to set off the beauty of the skin or countenance; and, next perhaps to the love "of wealth and rank, the improvement of her personal charms is the strongest "passion in this lady's breast.

"They are by no means exempt from the softer passion; but how can they "love their drunken lords? and they have no access to gallantry of the higher "kind. Sorry I am to be obliged to say that scandal loudly asserts that the fair "and interesting Rajpootnee is reduced to intrigue with servants and menials."

The same author adds, that "Rajpoot women seldom or never suckle their "children, for fear of destroying the beauty of their persons." He writes thus in another place:—"Until I came to Kutch, I never heard of females procuring abor-"tions merely to prevent their figures and their breasts being injured in appearance. "This practice is also peculiar to the grâssiâ class, and not frequent; although I

apparent than real, and they are themselves not a little anxious to maintain its appearance, resenting any want of imperiousness in the behaviour of their husbands to them in public, and expressing their astonishment at and contempt for the manners of their European rulers in this respect, by inventing a mythological story to account for that which otherwise would appear to be so wholly unintelligible.

"When Râwun," say they, "carried off Seetâ, the wife of Râm, "he placed her under the care of the demons of Ceylon and their "wives, which latter became her personal attendants. Seetâ received "so much homage, from the latter especially, that she predicted that "the demons should, in the iron age, acquire supreme power "throughout Hindoostan, and enjoined upon them the respectful "treatment of their wives in remembrance of her prophetic boon."

It is hardly necessary to add, that they trace the fulfilment of Seetâ's prediction in the sovereignty of the British, accompanied, as it is, by the well-established supremacy of the ladies.[1]

There is, however, at least one occasion upon which the Hindoo wife becomes the object of unusual solicitude and care. When the young married woman has reached the fourth month of her pregnancy a bracelet is fastened upon her arm, to which is affixed, as an amulet to protect her from the evil eye, a packet of dark coloured cloth, containing scrapings from the image of Hunoomân and dust from the cross-roads. A feast is given on her investiture with this bracelet, and she is released, during the time she wears it, from the performance of any part of the household duties, for in India as in England,

> "Fairies and *nymphs with child* must have the things
> "They long for."

In the sixth or eighth month of her pregnancy the caste are again assembled to a feast, and the family priest performs fire-sacrifice before them. The woman is conveyed to the house of some relation, where she performs ablutions, and dresses herself in handsome clothes and ornaments. She is thence conducted in procession, attended by

"have known a woman who acknowledged to five abortions of this kind in her "own person." *Idem*, pp. 229—234.

[1] Many people in Goozerat believe that Europeans worship Seetâ. An English or a Portuguese clergyman is commonly called "a Seetâ Padre," and Brahmins or Wyerâgees, when asked by Europeans who they are, will frequently, by way of making their position more intelligible to the stranger, tell him that they are "Seetâ Padres." The notion was induced most probably by the Mariolatry of the Romish Church.

musicians and singers, to the house of her husband. Her friends precede her as she walks thither, and strew her path with betel-nut and coins. At home she is received by her father, who has come from his village for the purpose, and who presents her with clothes, jewels, money, and other offerings, not forgetting the symbolical cocoa-nut, disposed together upon a shield. He also binds a new turban upon her husband's head, and presents her mother-in-law with a scarf. The latter receives the young married woman at the threshold with "Nyoonchun," and the fire-sacrifice, called "Gurbh "Sunskâr," is performed. The woman retires with her own family to her father's house.

If a male child be born, letters called "Wudhâmunee," announcing the joyful occurrence, are despatched at once to the father's house. The bearer on his arrival is entertained, and presented with a new turban. If the father be a chief the royal drum is sounded, and prisoners are released. Sometimes, on the letter announcing the birth of a son, the mark of the new-born child's feet is made in a liquid of the auspicious colour. The "Wudhâmunee" is very similar to the letter of invitation to a marriage, which has been already given, but in the principal place runs somewhat as follows :—

"Sister Kunkoobâ has (on such a day and hour) given birth to a "son, a turban-wearer. His horoscope promises well."

If the child be a girl, the expression is "a daughter, a veil-wearer." The reason for this addition is, that in all places originally people wrote (as they now in many places write) only consonants, omitting vowels, so that without the further description, the word *deekuro* (son) might be read *deekuree* (daughter), and *vice versâ.*

Some friend, immediately the birth has taken place, proceeds, bearing a cocoa-nut in his hands, to the astrologer's, who notes down the year, the month, the day of the month, and week, and the hour, also the signs in which the sun and planets stand. From this paper the astrologer subsequently draws out the child's horoscope.

On the sixth day after the birth Brumhâ is worshipped, under the name of Vidhâtâ, the supposition being that he is on that day employed in recording the various incidents of the child's future career by writing them on the forehead of the skull. A piece of blank paper, a pen, and an inkstand, are placed in order for the use of Vidhâtâ, but care is taken that the ink shall be red, not black, that the letters traced by the hand of destiny may be of the auspicious colour. On the same day strings or chains made of silver or gold, and called "Kundoro," are tied round the loins, hands, and feet of the child.

On the thirteenth day after its birth the child acquires a name. The first letter of it is fixed by the astrologer. The names of relations must be avoided, as well as those of ancestors, but Rajpoots sometimes give the names of their own fathers to their children. Under these restrictions the name is determined by the father's sister, who is called Phye. Four women, taking each of them a leaf of the sacred fig-tree in their hands, raise the child in a cloth, which they hold by the corners, and move about, repeating seven times a barbarous rhyme :—

"With this cloth and peepul leaf
"The Phye has fixed the name of ——."

The women and children are then regaled with sweetmeats.

Within a year and a quarter of the birth the relations are once more called together to witness the ceremony called "Unnprâshun," performed on the child's first tasting farinaceous food. Brahmins once more worship the Gotruj, and kindle the sacred sacrificial fire. In order to determine the course of life which the child is to follow, they set before it the insignia of several professions :—

"That which first the child doth touch,
"Vessel, money, weapon, or book,
"The livelihood of the child
"By that same will be procured."

The vessel probably alludes to cooking, if the Goozerat proverb may be taken as a guide, which celebrates the accomplishments of him who can handle

"The pen, *the ladle*, or the spear."

If a child die before the "Unnprâshun" ceremony has been performed it is buried in the ground, instead of being committed to the funeral pile. A similar custom was, it appears, observed among the Greeks, in regard to infants who died before cutting a tooth. The Romans also had the same custom, applied sometimes to children who did not reach their fortieth day, and the observance is particularly mentioned as having obtained in the case of members of the *Gens Cornelia.*

CHAPTER VIII.

FUNERALS.

"All things that we ordained festival
"Turn from their office to black funeral:
"Our instruments to melancholy bells;
"Our wedding cheer to a sad burial feast;
"Our solemn hymns to sullen dirges change;
"Our bridal flowers serve for a buried corse,
"And all things change them to the contrary."

In addition to that of children who have not undergone the "Unnprâshun" ceremony, there is also another exception among the Hindoos of Goozerat to the otherwise universal rule of cremation—that of the Sunyâsee. At the devotee's interment no wailing or expressions of grief are allowed. The corpse, seated in a litter, is borne to the grave preceded by musicians and attended by persons who cast rose-coloured powder into the air, or demonstrate in other modes their joy. It is placed in the earth in a sitting posture, instead of being consumed on the pile. A small platform raised over the spot, and exhibiting the sculptured feet of the deceased, commemorates his sanctity.

When age or infirmities warn a man of the near approach of death, he should (so say the Shâstras) perform, to the best of his ability, "deh shooddh prâyuscheet," or expiatory penances for the purification of his body. To this end the Yujmân, or performer of penance, calls in the assistance of one or more Brahmins skilled in the Veds. He bathes, dresses himself in wet clothes, and, fasting, circumambulates the seated Brahmins, and prostrates himself before them. He is instructed to confess the sins, whatever they may be, which he has committed from his birth up to that hour, "in childhood, in youth, or in old age, be they secret or open, wilfully or unwittingly committed, whether of thought, of speech, or of act, whether great or small." In this category he is directed to include not only those offences which are acknowledged throughout the world as violations of the universal moral law, but also those peculiar crimes which the religion of the Poorâns treats as equally heinous.

He is called upon to confess if he have slaughtered cows, if he have sat in his spiritual preceptor's seat, drank fermented liquor, cut a tree for fire-wood, been the cause of loss of caste to man, or of loss of life to insect,—if he have eaten what was not fit to be eaten, served one who was not fit to be served,—if he have drank water while sitting on a couch,—if he have ridden astride on a cow, a bull, a buffalo, a donkey, or a camel,—if he have reclined in a litter borne by Brahmins,—if, above all, he have disappointed a Brahmin's expectations. The Yujmân entreats the readers of the Veds to point out to him the means of expiating these sins.

"From Brumhâ to the insects,"

he is taught to say,

"The universe is thralled by you;
"The Yukshes, the Râkshuses, the Pisâchs too,
"Devs, Dytes, and men together.

"You know all that relates to religion;
"You are its conservators, O! Brahmins all.
"For my body purity
"Procure, O! good Brahmins.

"By me have been committed very terrible
"Wilful or unwitting sins:
"Show kindness to me!
"Give me good instruction!

"By you, who are worship-worthy, cleansed
"Shall I become, O! best of the regenerate."

Sometimes he is directed to wash the feet of these imperious priests, and, drinking the thus purified water, to acknowledge their supremacy in such language as the following:—

On earth whatever Teerths exist,
Those Teerths into the ocean;[1]
From the ocean all Teerths
Into the twice-born's right foot travel.
Destiny-thralled is all the world;
Charm-thralled are the Devtâs:
Those very charms are Brahmin-thralled;
Therefore Brahmin is Devtâ.

The Brahmins answer, "You shall be cleansed!" They then prescribe fastings and penances, or enjoin ten thousand repetitions of the sacred Gâyutree, or the offering of a thousand fire-sacrifices; or, more usually, that most effectual of all pious actions, the feasting of

[1] "Teerths" are places of pilgrimage. The allusion is to the rivers, whose banks abounded with consecrated spots.

Brahmins. The Yujmân causes himself to be shaved while a Brahmin mutters this charm :—

The various sins,
Brahmin-murder equalling,
In the hair, sheltered, reside ;
Therefore the hair I remove.

A tuft, however, must be allowed to remain on the crown of the head. The Yujmân is directed to bathe in the ten prescribed forms, —with ashes of the sacrificial fire, with dust of the earth, with dust of cow-dung, with urine of the cow, with milk, with curds, with clarified butter, with drugs, with sacrificial grass, and with water. Charms must be muttered suited to each ablution. The penitent dresses himself in clean clothes, and worships Vishnoo in his emblem—the shâlagrâm ; and while the Brahmins offer fire-sacrifice, he must present "ten gifts,"—

A cow, land, sesamum, gold, clarified butter,
Garments, grain, sugar,
Silver, and salt,—these are prescribed
As the "ten gifts," by the learned.

These offerings made, the penitent presents to the Brahmins "the "shadow gift,"—a cup of melted butter, in which he has beheld the reflection of his countenance. He then says to the priests, "This penance of mine must be rendered valid by you." They reply, "It "is rendered valid."

The rites above described are performed also by pilgrims on their arrival at the sacred spot, and by those who seek reinstitution into the caste-privileges of which they have been temporarily deprived. If a man should die leaving the "deh shooddh prâyuscheet" unperformed, it becomes the duty of his successors to perform it in his stead at the time when he celebrates his obsequies ; and if *he* neglect this sacred obligation, both father and son descend to the pits of hell.

On the road to the city in which Yuma, the king who judges the dead, keeps his court, is a river called Vyeturunee, the means of passing which must be provided in this world.[1] "If any one,"—it is Krishn himself who has said it,—"be by his good destiny incited, "while in this world, with the desire of passing Vyeturunee in "comfort, let him when the resolve comes into his heart, or at some "virtuous time, present a good cow as a gift." The vulgar notion is that the animal precedes the deceased, who grasps its tail, and drying

[1] On the subject of gifts made to supply the necessities of the dead, see note at the end of this chapter.

up a passage before him, enables him to cross the river of Hades. If he relax his hold, the stream, it is believed, returns upon him.[1] The cow should have its horns gilt, and its hoofs shod with silver. It should be either black or white. With it must be presented to the Brahmin a copper-brass vessel, to be used in milking it. Black garments must be laid upon it. Clothes, for the use of the departed spirit, should be presented at the same time, shoes, a ring, and an umbrella; also the seven gifts of grain. There must be offered, also, a copper trough, which represents Vyeturunee, which is filled with honey and placed upon a heap of cotton. A gold image of Yuma must be made, and an iron staff placed in its hand. A boat made of sugar-cane must also be prepared. The Brahmin worships the Kings of Hades, and calls him into the image, thus addressing him :—

Rider of the mighty buffalo,
Holder of the staff and chain,
Red-eyed, large-handed,
Dhurum Râj, I praise thee !

These arrangements completed, the cow and the image of Yuma must be worshipped, obeisance paid to the Brahmin, and circumambulation of the whole performed. The gifts are then presented to the priest, the giver holding in his hand the tail of the cow, with some sacrificial grass and a piece of purple basil, and repeating this charm,—

On Yuma's road, the very terrible,
I have heard of Vyeturunee river.
To cross it, I offer this cow ;
O ! twice born, I praise Vyeturunee !

He next addresses the cow thus,—

O ! Dhenoo, wait thou for me
On that great road which leads to Yuma's gate ;
To cross I am desirous, O ! Devee,
To cross Vyeturunee ! praises to thee.

Lastly, turning to the Brahmin, and paying him obeisance, he presents the cow to him, and says,—

Vishnoo-like, O ! Brahmin great !
O earth-Dev ! cleanser of a line of men !
For passage of Vyeturunee
This sable cow to thee I offer !

[1] We have frequently seen in Goozerat cowherds, whose pasture ground was on the opposite side of a river from that on which their village stood, swimming their cattle across the stream, and assisting themselves in the passage by holding on to the tail of one of the animals.

When a Hindoo appears to be at the point of death his friends prepare a place on the ground by smearing it with cow-dung; they strew it with sacrificial grass, with sesamum and barley. The dying man is stripped of his ornaments and of his clothes, with the exception of a single garment. The hair of his head and his moustaches are removed, and his body is washed with water. He is then laid upon the place which has been prepared, with his feet pointing northwards towards Meroo and the abodes of the blessed, and his back turned upon the city of Yuma. A small cup, containing a cake with a silver coin laid upon it, is placed in his hand. Some poor Brahmin is then called in to receive the cup from the hands of the dying man. Rich persons present a cow, gold, or other valuable presents, and they promise their departing relative that they will carry his bones to Benares and cast them into the Ganges, or that they will make pilgrimage (the merit of which shall be his) to Muthoorâ, Dwârkâ, Somnâth, or other celebrated holy ground. They take vows, also, on behalf of the dying man, to fast or to spend money in religious offerings, sealing the promise by presentation of a handful of water. Sometimes they offer gifts of iron to propitiate Yuma, whose weapons are of that metal. These offerings are meritorious alike to the giver and to him on whose behalf they are presented. "The son," it is said, "who presents gifts by the hands of "a dying father, should be honoured as the lamp of his race."

At the same time they set near the dying man a lamp supplied with clarified butter, pour Ganges water into his mouth, and place therein a leaf of the purple basil and a portion of curd.

It has been pronounced that if, even when the life has reached the throat, a man declare that he has abandoned the world, he reaches Vyekoonth after death, and is released from further transmigration. Some persons, therefore, when they believe that their end is approaching, perform the rite of "Âthoor Sunyâs," and, calling for an ascetic, receive at his hands initiation and the tawny garment which proclaims that they have renounced the world and its concerns.[1]

[1] These tardy devotees remind us of some of the earlier proselytes of Christianity, and, in particular, of the great Constantine, whose reluctance to assume the white vestments of the neophyte, and the obligations attendant on a new birth unto righteousness, could only be overcome, as Gibbon mentions, at that latest moment when the stern hand of death was tearing from his shoulders the imperial purple.

"All this year (A.D. 1128)," says the Anglo-Saxon Chronicle, "King Henry "was in Normandy, on account of the war between him and his nephew, the Earl "of Flanders; but the earl was wounded in battle by a servant, and, being so "wounded, he went to the monastery of St. Bertin, and forthwith he was made

The Hindoos have been taught to believe that the agonies of the death-struggle are pangs caused by the tyrannous servants of the King of Hades, who are dragging the unwilling soul from its tenement. Stricken with sorrow and with awe, they vent these mingled emotions by repeatedly calling upon Râm. A few moments pass, and the convulsive throes of the dying man are over—the immortal soul is disengaged from its fleshy host and companion. Whither has it departed?

"Quæ nunc abibit in loca,
"Pallidula, rigida, nudula?"

Before, however, we pursue this interesting inquiry, let us stay awhile to bestow the corse, and observe the mourners until they have "compounded it with dust whereto 'tis kin."

When all is over, the relations and neighbours assemble at the house of the deceased; and, like an *entre-acte* to the tragic drama, commences the humming moan of lamentation. The nearer relatives enter the habitation, exclaiming, "O, father! O, brother!" The women, standing in a circle near the door, bewail the deceased, and sing a funeral dirge, beating their breasts in sad accompaniment to the measure. Young persons are lamented longer and more poignantly than those whose advanced age seems to have pointed them out as the natural victims of the angel of death. The dirge, which usually consists of unconnected exclamations of grief, is sung by one or two women, while the remainder join in chorus. That, of which we proceed to give a part, bewails the death of an early victim—one, it will be observed, who, crowned in former days as a bridegroom-king, is now lamented as a chief and a warrior:—

Alas! alas! without the village the wail resounds,
Voi! the valiant, alas! alas!
Alas! alas! this is Râmjee's anger,
Voi! the valiant, alas! alas!
Alas! alas! with blood the clouds have rained,
Voi! the valiant, alas! alas!
Alas! alas! its bounds the sea has abandoned,
Voi! the valiant, alas! alas!
Alas! alas! the home-leaving bride is plundered,
Voi! the valiant, alas! alas!
Alas! alas! Yum Raja's plunderers have come,
Voi! the valiant, alas! alas!
Alas! alas! they have slain the bridegroom-king,
Voi! the valiant, alas! alas!

"a monk, and lived five days after, and then died, and was buried there—God "rest his soul!"

Alas ! alas ! his mundup has been cast down,
Voi ! the valiant, alas ! alas !
Alas ! alas ! the vessels of his Choree have been broken,
Voi ! the valiant, alas ! alas !
Alas ! alas ! his life has been treacherously stolen,
Voi ! the valiant, alas ! alas !

* * * * *

These utterances of grief are rude, but they are far from unaffecting, even to the stranger—the *sea-dwelling* Englishman ; and, as they alternately rise and fall, their sound, stealing from a distance upon his ear, reminds him of that measured melancholy tone which the breakers of ocean produce on some calm evening, as, by turns, they roll upon and recede from a shingled beach.

This " threnos " finished, the female mourners sit down panting and exhausted ; but still weeping, they cry to each other, and chant forth exclamations such as these : " Ah, son ! who will take care of me " now ? who will light the funeral pile for me ? " " Ah, husband ! " you have deserted me treacherously ; you have left me with my " children unmarried ! " or, " Ah, brother ! who will welcome me " now, when I return home from my husband's ? Ah ! the fig-tree " will grow now in my father's house ! "[1]

While the women are thus engaged, two or three persons are employed in the interior of the house in preparing the corpse for the funeral pile. A litter of bamboos is made, and the corpse is wrapped in a new scarf of the auspicious colour. Lump-offerings of flour and water are prepared, of which two, called " shub " and " pânthuk," are placed, the former on the pallet of sacrificial grass upon which the corpse reclines, and the latter at the threshold of the house.

A married woman returning home from a visit at her father's house is presented with clothes, and anointed with red ointment on the

[1] The lamentation for the dead in use among the Greeks appears to have been originally sung by women, with vehement expressions of grief, but to have been so far systematized, as early even as the time of Homer, that singers by profession stood near the bed where the body was laid out, and began the lament, while the women merely assisted. (See Müller.) The evil effects produced by the custom of beating the breast, still retained by the women of Goozerat, has, we believe, induced some benevolent Hindoos to endeavour to introduce professional mourners, who would exactly occupy the place given by the Grecians to the *ἀοιδοὶ θρήνων ἐξάρχοι*. The prophet Jeremiah is supposed to be repeating part of the usual funeral dirge, when he predicts of Jehoiakim, the son of Josiah, King of Judah, that " They shall not lament for him, saying, Ah, my brother ! or, Ah, sister ! they " shall not lament for him, saying, Ah, Lord ! or, Ah, his glory ! "—*Vide* Jeremiah xxii. v. 18, *and note with references in D'Oyly and Mant.* See also Amos v. 16 ; Ecclesiastes xii. 5, 6.

forehead: the ceremony is called the Sâsur-wâso. If she die at the house of her parents, or in the village where it is situated, her family prepare for the corpse *the last sâsur-wâso.* They anoint its forehead, dress it in new clothes, and adorn it with a marriage scarf.

The corpse prepared, and placed upon the litter, four persons raise it upon their shoulders.[1] They have previously performed ablutions, and dressed themselves in silk garments. The corpse is carried forth feet first; one man precedes it, bearing an earthen vessel which contains fire. The relations and neighbours follow, bareheaded, without shoes, and half naked,[2] running and calling upon their god, the son of Dusruth; or sometimes one man alone cries to the rest as they run—"Call on Râm!" to which they reply in chorus, "Brother! "Râm!" The women follow the funeral procession to the gate of the village, and thence return slowly home.

It is written in the Shâstras that the corpse should be set down at cross-roads within the village, and that the third lump-offering, called "Khechur," should be offered there: this custom has, however, fallen into disuse. The Gurood Poorân prescribes that the inhabitants of a village in which a death has taken place are to abstain from food until the corpse has been carried out; at the present time the occupants of the adjoining houses alone observe this practice,

The funeral company, when they have passed outside the village, make a halt, and lay the corpse upon the earth: some one of them who has preceded the rest, sprinkling water of purification from a vessel which he carries in his hand, sanctifies the ground. Here the third and fourth lump-offerings, of which the latter is called "Bhoot," are offered together, and the bearers of the corpse reverse its position, and carry it henceforth head foremost. Hence they proceed to the place of cremation, which is usually on the bank of a river, and here they erect the funeral pile, which, if their means allow it, they form of sandal and other costly woods, interspersed with cocoa-nuts. The corpse is separated from the litter to which it was attached, and from the scarf which covered it, and both these are cast aside: it is laid upon the pile with its face towards the abodes of the

[1] "The Rajpoot warrior," says Colonel Tod, "is carried to his final abode "armed at all points as when alive, his shield on his back, and brand in his hand; "while his steed, though not sacrificed, is often presented to the deity, and becomes "a perquisite of the priest."—*Vide Rajasthan*, vol. i., p. 73.

[2] So the Jews in their mourning. "Uncover not your heads, neither rend your "clothes."—Leviticus x. 6. "Forbear to cry, make no mourning for the dead, "bind the tire of thine head upon thee, and put on thy shoes upon thy feet."—Ezekiel xxiv. 17.

blessed, and is covered with additional fuel heaped upon it. The fifth and sixth lump-offerings, which are called respectively "Sâdhuk" and "Pret," are here set down. The son, or nearest of kin to the deceased, lights a bundle of dry grass, and passing three times round the pile, places the fire as near as the wind permits him to the head of the corpse. The party of mourners sit down, and await the issue with lamentation; when the corpse is nearly consumed they pour clarified butter upon the pile to feed the fire. As soon as the cremation is finished, the ashes of the dead are collected from the pile and are cast into the river water, or if no stream be at hand they are deposited in a pit dug for the purpose, and sprinkled with water. He who fired the pile collects seven small pieces of bone, and enclosing them in mould commits them to the earth in the place on which the head of the corpse had rested. Over the spot the poor raise a simple mound, and place thereon a water-vessel and a cake of bread, but wealthy persons erect upon the site of the funeral pile a temple, which is consecrated to Muhâ Dev.

The ceremonies above described are intended as a figurative compliance with each of the four modes of disposing of a corpse which are prescribed by the Shâstras,—casting out into the jungle (the type of which is the setting down the corpse outside the village gate), cremation, plunging into water, and interment.

At the funeral of a wealthy person a cow is frequently brought to the pile, and its milk sprinkled on the spot where the body has been consumed: the cow is then given to a Brahmin. The legend of the Sâbhermutee accounts for the name of Doodhesur—a well-known place of cremation on the banks of that river, near the city of Ahmedabad—by asserting that when the corpse of the sage Dudeechee was consumed on the pile at that spot the sovereign and the denizens of Paradise brought thither Kâm Dhenoo, the sacred cow, with whose milk they consecrated the ground.

These ceremonies complied with, the mourners perform ablutions and wash their clothes, and the heir presents an offering of sesamum and water to the deceased "to cool him after the flames."[1] The friends who have attended the corpse to the pile rejoin once more, at the house of the deceased, the women and those who have remained behind, and thence disperse to their own homes.

[1] Our readers will be reminded of the chalice of oblivion in Moore's "Epicurean":—

"Drink of this cup—Osiris sips
The same in his halls below;
And the same he gives *to cool the lips*
Of the Dead who downward go.

A woman, on the death of her husband, breaks the bracelets which were placed on her arms at the time of her marriage. If she be a Brahminee she causes her head to be shaved on the tenth day after the funeral. For a whole year she mourns, seated in a corner of the house; at the end of that time her relations come "to put an end to "her mourning," and take her with them home. If no house be open to receive her she makes a pilgrimage to Boucherâjee's, to Prubhâs, or to the Nerbudda. The widow absents herself from all caste entertainments. At the present day, however, in case she has not attained the age of fifteen years, her marriage bracelets are allowed to remain, and she is not treated as a widow; but when she is thirty years old, the occurrence of a death among her near relations—as, for instance, that of her father, or her brother—is considered as a proper season for her retirement into the state of widowhood. The widow, if she be wealthy, replaces her marriage bracelets with gold ones; if of the Rajpoot blood, she wears black clothes; if of the Brahmin or Wâneeâ castes, she adopts a dress of any sombre colour, unadorned by a figure. The Shâstras, however, prescribe a white dress to the widow, and forbid her to use any ornament.

The time of mourning, as regards others than widows, varies from a month to a year, according to the age of the deceased and the degree of consanguinity. Mourners abstain from festivities and from certain kinds of food, and dress themselves in white or sombre-coloured garments. Absent relations are informed of the death by letters forwarded by the hands of an out-caste, and marked on the outside "strip and read." The object of this inscription is to avoid inconvenience,—the person who has received such intelligence being held to be unclean, and the dress he wears defiled. These letters are called "Krishnâkshuree" (black letters), or by a more common name conveying the idea of impurity. We introduce one of them with the view both of showing their character, and of calling attention to a point upon which we have already remarked,—the reckless extravagance which has become almost compulsory upon Hindoos in performing the obsequies of the dead[1]:—

> "Drink of this cup—the water within
> Is fresh from Lethe's stream;
> 'Twill make the past, with all its sin,
> And all its pain and sorrows, seem
> Like a long-forgotten dream!"

No such happy oblivion would, however, appear to be held out to the hopes of the Hindoo; on the contrary, it would seem to be part of the reward of the virtuous that they should be gifted with reminiscences of a former birth.

[1] See on this subject Tod's "Rajasthan," vol. i., p. 207, for sumptuary edicts

FORM OF KRISHNÂKSHUREE.

To Mehta Kuleeânrow Keshuvrow, and Mehta Jumeeutrâm Nurbherâm (the son-in-law and uncle of the deceased), residing in the city of Ahmedabad, Mehta Bhuwaneerâm Munchârâm (the friend of deceased) writes from Surat. Receive his salutation. Further, the cause of writing is this:—On Wednesday, the second of the current month of Chyetra, at the sixth hour of the night, our good friend, Jâdoorâm Vehemshunkur, became a denizen of Paradise. This has fallen out very ill, but what the illustrious Supreme Lord may do must be assented to. In such a matter no one's strength avails. Up to the third watch of the second Jâdoorâm had no disease, even in the nail of his finger, but was hale and well; however, he was attacked with cholera when two hours of the day remained. We used very many remedies, and made very many vows, but as his allotted term of life had come to a close, no remedy availed. Our relations had all gone on a pilgrimage; on this occasion, therefore, I and Vivekrâm (a neighbour) were the only persons on the spot, and we, too, had gone out to procure medicine. Meanwhile our good friend, Jâdoorâm, fell into the last agonies, but by his good fortune, and on account of the great number of his virtuous actions in his former states of existence and in his present, we both of us immediately arrived, and carefully attending him in his dying moments, caused him to offer virtuous gifts, placed him upon the earth, and poured Ganges water into his mouth. If we had not arrived he would have died on his bed, and we should then have been compelled to perform "pootul veedhân."

Console good mistress Ugunântâ (daughter of deceased and wife of Kuleeânrow), and do not permit her to wail or beat her breast. Do we what we may, we shall never behold his face again; therefore let us be composed, and arrange how we are to entertain the caste according to the respectability of the family. If we should be compelled to spend five or ten rupees over and above, never mind that, because, working and labouring, we will make that up. But our parent's obsequies will not occur again. There is a house worth Rs. 500, and ornaments worth Rs. 200, and vessels, furniture, and other things worth Rs. 100,—in all, property worth Rs. 800. But it will cost Rs. 1100 to feast the caste in Surat for three days, therefore we shall have to borrow Rs. 300 at interest. The boys are young now,

by Muhârânâ Singrâm Singh of Mewar, and the great Jey Singh of Amber. The latter had an ordinance, restricting the number of guests on these occasions to fifty-one, and restraining the less wealthy classes from the use of expensive food.

but when they grow up they will work, and clear off the debt. Entertain no anxiety on this account. It is a proverb that there is no calamity for him who has sons, so, as there are sons, what difficulty is there about borrowing or lending? They will clear all off to-morrow. Therefore, if you are good relations, come to arrange the obsequies. When you have read this letter prepare in the sixth part of a day. Do not wait to drink water. If you do not come, then the blame will be laid on you by the caste. We will have nothing to do with it.

(Signed) BHUWÂNEERÂM MUNCHÂRÂM.

NOTE ON THE SUBJECT OF GIFTS MADE TO SUPPLY THE NECESSITIES OF THE DEAD.

"A man," says a Hebrew fable, "had three friends; two of them he loved ex-"ceedingly; to the third he was indifferent, though he was the most sincere. One "day he was summoned before the justice for a matter of which he was innocent. "'Who among you,' said he, 'will go with me, and witness for me?' The first "of his friends excused himself immediately on the pretence of other business. "The second accompanied him to the door of the tribunal, but there he turned "and went back for fear of the judge. The third, upon whom he had least de-"pended, went in, spoke for him, and witnessed his innocence so cheerfully, that "the judge released him, and made him a present besides. Man has three friends "in this world. How do they behave in the hour of death, when God summons "him before his judgment-seat? Gold, his best friend, leaves him first. His "relations and friends accompany him to the brink of the grave, and return again "to their houses. His good deeds alone accompany him to the throne of the "Judge; they go before, speak of him, and find mercy and favour." So far the fable, of which Mr. Trench remarks (Notes on the Parables, sixth edition, p. 51), that it is ingenious enough, though a notable specimen of Jewish self-righteousness. Grosser conceptions of the truth than this appear, however, to have been popularly entertained even among the children of Israel—the chosen of God. In the contemplation of a future state of happiness, their thoughts still clung to the pleasures, and glories, and occupations of this world, and they were unable to comprehend that the interest of the departed in the affairs of the present life had ceased for ever. Thus, the marital rights acquired on earth, and not voluntarily renounced by bill of divorce, were, in their eyes, valid even after death had separated husband and wife, and it was no strange thing to them that a dead Alexander should claim his forgetful Glaphyra from the incestuous embraces of Archelaus. It is not surprising, then, that we should find in the popular creed of *heathen* nations a constantly recurring idea that the spirits of the dead still retain a share in human concerns, and may be rendered happy or miserable by the forethought or neglect of mortals. The tribes which have remained unconverted to Christianity, whether of ancient or of modern times, whether enlightened or barbarous, appear to have adopted with one consentient voice the idea that the passage of the soul to its destination after death is to be smoothed, and its necessities provided for, by the due performance of funeral rights. The nations of classical antiquity placed in the mouth of the corpse the piece of money which was destined to be Charon's fee for ferrying the soul over the infernal river, and beside it they laid the cake of flour and honey which was designed to appease the fury of Cerberus, the gate-keeper of Hades. The Romans placed in the sepulchres of the dead, to appease their *manes*, the "cœna feralis" of milk, honey, water, wine, and olives. And the heroes of Scandinavia firmly believed in the assurance, which they had received from Odin himself, that the arms, the war-horses, and the servants, which were buried with them in their graves, should avail them in the day on which they were to enter Valhalla, and present themselves before the throne of its warrior god. "The Laplanders to this day provide their dead with a flint, and everything necessary for lighting them along the dark passage they have to traverse after death," and the red woodsman of America buries a rifle with his departed friend, that he may be enabled to pursue the chase in the world of spirits. "The Tartar sovereigns," remarks M. Huc, "are sometimes interred in a manner which appears "the very height of extravagance and barbarism ; the royal corpse is placed in an "edifice of brick, adorned with stone images of men, lions, tigers, elephants, and "divers subjects from the Buddhist mythology. With the illustrious defunct they "inter, in a large vault in the centre of the building, considerable sums in gold and "silver, precious stones, and costly habits.

"These monstrous interments frequently cost, also, the lives of a number of "slaves ; children of both sexes, distinguished for their beauty, are taken and "compelled to swallow mercury until they are suffocated. By this means, it is asserted, the color and freshness of the victims is preserved so well that they appear "alive. They are then ranged standing round the corpse of their master, to serve "him as in life. They hold in their hands the pipe, fan, the little vial of snuff, "and the other numerous baubles of Tartar royalty.

"To guard these buried treasures, there is placed in the vault a kind of bow, constructed to discharge a number of arrows, one after the other. This bow, or "rather these bows, are bound together, and the arrows fixed. This species of "infernal machine is so placed that the act of opening the door of the vault discharges the first arrow, the discharge of the first releases the second, and so on "to the last. The bow-makers keep these murderous machines already prepared, and the Chinese sometimes purchase them to guard their houses in their "absence."

The case of the Sutee, of which we shall presently have to speak, is but another phase of this "*one great delirium*," as it has been justly called. It has its parallel alike in Africa and among the negroes of Polynesia :—"It is the custom here (in "Jenna)," says Mr. Lander, "when a governor dies, for two of his favourite wives "to quit the world on the same day, in order that he may have a little pleasant "social company in a future state ; but the late governor's devoted wives had no "ambition or inclination to follow their venerable husband to the grave, and went "and hid themselves before the funeral ceremonies were performed, and have remained concealed ever since, with the remainder of his women. To-day, how-"ever, one of these unfortunates,—she to whom our house belongs,—was discovered in her hiding-place at the present governor's, and the alternative of a "poisoned chalice, or to have her head broken by the club of the fetish-priest, was "offered her. She has chosen the former mode of dying, as being the less terrible "of the two."—*Journal of an Expedition to Explore the Course and Termination of "the Niger*, vol. i., pp. 92, 93.

"As a chief's wives are strangled for the sake of exemplifying their fidelity, and "accompanying him to the invisible world, so this kind of death is often imposed "upon courtiers and aides-de-camp, and always considered an honour and distinc-"tion. One reason of many, and perhaps the greatest, for strangling the wives of "chiefs who have children surviving him, is that it is taken for a certain proof "that these children are legitimate, and claim their rights as vasus to the places "to which their deceased mothers belonged. If a mother neglected being strangled, "it would leave a doubt in the minds of the people as to her fidelity; and if any "of her children were to go to the places she belonged to, and claim property as "their right, the owners would immediately embrace the opportunity of upbraid-"ing the vasu with his mother being an unchaste woman, and saying that they would "not allow him to carry anything off, because the infidelity of his mother cut off "all his claim and rights as a vasu, and that it was an undeniable proof of her "loving some other man better than his father, that she had not been buried with "him. The whole thirty of Tui Kila-Kila's brother's wives wished to be strangled; "but, being a little wiser than the generality of his countrymen, and not led away "by the customs of his country, Tui Kila-Kila advised all who had borne children "to his brother to be strangled, as a matter of course. On the other hand, he "said that the young women who had borne no children had no occasion to "sacrifice their lives, knowing that they would make himself very good wives, and "add greatly to his advantage—the greatness of a chief being estimated, in a mea-"sure, by the number of his women.

"Fourteen of these women readily acceded to this proposal, and, as far as I "could learn, were extremely happy to escape with their lives, especially in such "a reputable way in the eyes of the world, being backed by the advice and "opinion of such a great prince as Tui Kila-Kila, whose infallibility dared not be "questioned. But one young girl (who made up the fifteen that were to be saved, "and on whose account it was always supposed, more than for any other reason, "he proposed to save the others, so as to come at the object of his desire) dared "to question his opinion of the propriety of living and violating the laws of be-"trothment, and demanded the privilege of being strangled. She asked Tui Kila-"Kila where was the man she cared or was worthy of living for now that his "brother was dead? Tui Kila-Kila was so piqued at this reflection on his inferi-"ority to his deceased brother, that he ordered the two women, whose office it was "to strangle her, to haul tight at each end of the strip of cloth previously placed "round her neck, which they obeyed; and as soon as she began to show symptoms "of agony, he ordered them to slacken it, thinking, as she had tasted partially "the pangs of death, she would repent of her foolishness; but with her it was "different, for she seized the ends, and began hauling tight again, so as to com-"plete what the stranglers had begun; and then the chief was satisfied with her "foolish obstinacy, as he called it, and told the women to settle her quickly. This "young woman was renowned for her beauty, and certainly she must have been "as completely so as possible for a human being to be, except that she was not "white,—if that has anything to do with it,—because, when I pointed out sym-"metrical forms, and asked if she was anything like them, they always said she "was far superior."—*Journal of a Cruize among the Islands of the Western Pacific, including the Feejees and others inhabited by the Polynesian Negro Races, in Her Majesty's Ship Havannah. By John Elphinstone Erskine, Captain R.N. With Maps and Plates. John Murray.*

Those heterodox Hindoos, the Jains, would appear to have, perhaps rather from a spirit of opposition to Brahminic customs than from any other cause, juster ideas than are usual upon this subject. According to the account collected from a priest of the sect at Mudgeri, which is printed in the ninth volume of the Asiatic Researches, " they say, that the foolish people of other tribes, being deficient in sacred know- " ledge, spend money in vain on account of deceased relations: for how can a " dead man feel satisfaction in ceremonies, and in the feeding of others ?—'even a " 'lamp no longer gives light by pouring more oil into it, after its flame is once ex- " 'tinguished,'—therefore it is vain to make feasts and ceremonies for the dead; and " if it be wished to please relations, it is best to do so while they are yet living. " 'What a man drinketh, giveth, and eateth in this world is of advantage to him, " 'but he carrieth nothing with him at his end.'" These Jains might have expressed their ideas in the words of the British poet :—

" For in the silent grave no conversation,
" No joyful tread of friends, no voice of lovers,
" No careful father's counsel,—nothing's heard,
" For nothing is,— but all oblivion,
" Dust, and an endless darkness !"

CHAPTER IX.

THE STATE AFTER DEATH—SHRÂDDH—BHOOTS—OTHER POPULAR BELIEFS.

IT is laid down in the Gurood Poorân and other Hindoo scriptures, that, on the occurrence of a death, the son or other heir of the deceased must offer lump-offerings, and that if he neglect to do so the spirit passes into the state of a goblin. We have described the manner in which the first six of these offerings are made. If, after the fourth lump has been offered, the obsequies proceed no further—if, for example, any cause occur to prevent cremation—the spirit, it is believed, remains a Bhoot. Similarly, if six lumps only be offered, the spirit remains a Pret. For twelve days the soul, it is supposed, is seated on the eaves of the house in which it has parted from the human body. At sunset, therefore, the compassionate relatives place upon the roof for its subsistence a vessel of water and another of milk. Other accounts fix the residence of the soul, during this calamitous period, at the place of the funeral pile, or at cross-roads; and some assert that it dwells alternately in the elements of fire, air, and water, and in the house which was its home.[1]

[1] There is, so to speak, a fresh trodden way between the body and the soul which has just forsaken, and, according to that Jewish legend which may rest on a very deep truth, lingers for a while and hovers near the tabernacle where it has dwelt so long, and to which it knows itself bound by links that even now have not

One lump-offering should be made daily, until the tenth day from the day of decease, for the construction of a new body for the Pret. The body, at the end of that time, attains to the size of the upper joint of a man's thumb. On the tenth day a lump should be offered for the purpose of satisfying the hunger and thirst which the Pret now begins to feel. The common practice in Goozerat, at the present time, is to make the lump-offering ten times on the tenth day.

Shrâddh must be performed on the tenth, eleventh, twelfth or thirteenth day succeeding the decease, and afterwards monthly on the day of the month on which the death occurred, and yearly on its anniversary. The son who neglects to perform shrâddh dies childless, and expiates the sin amid the torments of hell. The gifts which are offered in shrâddh, are for the purpose of supplying the necessities of the Prets in their painful journey to the city of Yuma. They are conveyed by the god of the waters to Krishn, who, in turn, consigns them to the sun—the all-beholding Narâyun—by whom they are delivered to the spirits of the deceased. A bed presented at this time to Brahmins procures for the Pret a litter to ride in ; shoes, umbrellas, and fans, are also acceptable offerings, and lamps should be suspended in the temples of Shiva to light the Pret on his road.

Shrâddh must be performed beside a reservoir or on the banks of a river. The sacrificer shaves his face, and, holding in his hand a copper cup containing water, with sesamum and sacrificial grass, he repeats the names of his progenitors, both paternal and maternal, sprinkling water as he repeats each name. The ceremony, which is called "Turpun," has been already described in detail. The heir now forms an image of the deceased with sacrificial grass, washes it, and strews it with flowers. A similar representation of a Vishwa Dev is also made to witness the performance of the rite. The sacrificer sprinkles these, muttering a charm which has been taught him by his family priest, and which is supposed to call the Dev and the soul of the deceased into the figures. A Shâlagrâm stone is placed beside them to represent Vishnoo, and the three are worshipped with the usual ceremonies. Food is then set before the grass figures and the Shâlagrâm, and the heir, sprinkling them once more, repeats the

been divided for ever. Even science itself has arrived at the conjecture, that the last echoes of life ring in the body much longer than is commonly supposed ; that for a while it is full of the reminiscences of life. Out of this we may explain how it so frequently comes to pass, that all which marked the death-struggle passes presently away, and the true image of the departed, the image it may be of years long before, re-appears in perfect calmness and in almost ideal beauty.—*Trench's "Notes on the Miracles,"* fourth edition, p. 187.

charm which is supposed to dismiss their inhabitants. The grass is thrown before a cow to be eaten. These rites performed, the relations and neighbours of the deceased are entertained, and Brahmins feasted according to the means of the sacrificer.[1]

If a man be sonless he must in his own life-time perform shrâddh, and offer lump-offerings for the repose of his soul; and he whose obsequies have not been performed either remains, as we have seen, a hungry ghost, wandering miserably day and night, or is born again and again in the form of an insect, or is conceived in the womb of a woman, and dies before beholding the light, or is born only to die. In other cases of non-performance or mis-performance of obsequies, the soul, having suffered certain pains in hell, returns to earth in goblin form, to torment those whose neglect has occasioned its misfortunes. It becomes a fever or other disease to afflict them, it causes quarrels among brothers, produces the death of cattle, prevents the birth of male children, excites wicked and murderous thoughts, and destroys men's faith in the sacred writings, in images of Devs, in holy places of pilgrimage, and even in thrice holy Brahmins.[2]

The Gurood Poorân contains the further information, that if at the time of his death a man have had his affections excessively fixed on

[1] It may be noticed that the word "superstitio" (the etymology of which has been so much controverted), has been supposed by some to mean the duty of *survivors*, as such, to their ancestors. Under this supposition the importance attached in the Hindoo law to the worship of Peetrees, or forefathers, throws a light upon the primary sense of that word.—*Vide Morris's Essay towards the Conversion of Hindoos*, p. 196.

[2] The opinion that the happiness of the spirits of deceased persons is affected by the neglect of friends, in regard to the performance of their funeral rites, is not confined to India. Mr. Grose, the antiquary (as quoted by Brand), has the following :—

"Some ghosts of murdered persons, whose bodies have been secretly buried, "cannot be at ease till their bones have been taken up, and deposited in conse- "crated ground, with all the rites of Christian burial. This idea is the remains of "a very old piece of heathen superstition; the ancients believed that Charon was "not permitted to ferry over the ghosts of unburied persons, but that they "wandered up and down the banks of the river Styx for an hundred years, after "which they were admitted to a passage."

Connected with this belief, is the following superstition on the death of great men :—"A superstition prevails among the lower classes of many parts of Wor- "cestershire that, when storms, heavy rains, or other elemental strife takes place "at the death of any great man, the spirit of the storm will not be appeased till "the moment of burial. This superstition gained great strength on the occasion of "the Duke of Wellington's funeral, when, after some weeks of heavy rain, and "one of the highest floods ever known in this country, the skies began to clear, and "both rain and flood abated. The storms which have been noticed to take place "at the time of the death of many great men known to our history, may have had any object of earthly enjoyment, as his son, his wife, or his property, his soul in that case does not readily part from his body, but quits it after a violent struggle, and becomes a Bhoot. The suicide, he who dies of the bite of a snake, or is struck by lightning, or drowned, or crushed by the fall of earth,—he, in fact, who meets with any kind of sudden and miserable death, becomes a Bhoot. He who dies in an upper room or in a bed, instead of being laid out upon the ground, becomes a Bhoot, as does he who after death is defiled by the touch of a Shoodra or any other cause. There are many other modes in which the spirits of deceased men become Bhoots. In the Kurum Kând of the Veds, however, expiatory rites are appointed for such cases, of "death out of season," which if his heir employ, the spirit of the deceased is preserved from passing into the state of a Bhoot.[1]

Before proceeding to consider the state of the souls which pass to the upper or lower loks,—the Devs of Swerga, and the denizens of Pâtâl,—it will be convenient that we should devote a few pages to the Bhoots,—those "perturbed spirits" who wander still in this world of men.

Bhoots and Prets reside, it is said, in the place where funeral piles are erected, in trees which are not used for sacrificial purposes, such as the tamarind and the acacia, in desert places, at the spot were death occurred, or at cross-roads,—for which reason people set at these places food for the use of the Bhoot.[2] He is most at a loss for

"something to do with the formation of this curious notion in the minds of the vulgar. "It was a common observation hereabout in the week before the interment of his "grace, 'Oh, the rain won't give over till the duke is buried.'"—*Notes and Queries*.

The Demauno (or oracular priest) of the Râjmuhâl Hills is an exception to the rule. He must *not* be buried.

"When a Demauno dies, his body is carried into the Jungles, and placed under "the shade of a tree, where it is covered with leaves and branches, and left on the "bedstead in which he died. The objection to interring his remains is a "superstitious idea that he becomes a devil, and that, if buried, he would return "and destroy the inhabitants of the village; whereas, by placing the body under "a tree, he is thus compelled to play the devil in some other."—*Vide Asiatic Researches*, iv., p. 70.

[1] Not only the unburied, but those also who died before their time were, in the opinion of the ancient Greeks, compelled to wander in the state of goblins. "The souls, then," says Bishop Pearson, "of those whose bodies were unburied "were thought to be kept out of Hades till their funerals were performed, and the "souls of those who died an untimely or violent death, were kept from the same "place until the time of their natural death should come."

[2] The Arabian Jinn also frequents cross-roads; and the fairies of the Scottish lowlands carry bows made of the ribs of a man buried *where three lairds' lands meet.* See also "A Midsummer Night's Dream," Act iii. sc. 2:—

"damned spirits all,
"That in cross-ways and floods have burial."

"Desert places," in Goozerat, correspond exactly with the "dry places," (αννδρων τοπων) assigned to the evil spirits in Matthew xii. 43, Luke xi. 24.

water to drink. The pipe of his throat is, it is said, the size of the eye of a needle, and he is continually thirsty enough to drink twelve gallons of water. The watchmen of Wuroon Dev, however, are stationed wherever there is water, to prevent the Bhoots from drinking, and their thirst is therefore as continual as it is intense. The Bhoots feed upon all kinds of refuse. The goblin of the best class, he, that is to say, whose funeral ceremonies have been duly performed, but who has been debarred from liberation by his own intense affection for earthly objects, is called a "Poorwuj Dev," and resides in his own house or in a sacred fig-tree.[1]

The powers which Bhoots and Prets exercise are the following:—They take possession of a corpse, and speak through its mouth; they exhibit themselves in the form which they possessed when living; they enter into a living man, and cause him to speak as they please; sometimes they afflict him with fever, or various other diseases; sometimes they assume the forms of animals, and frighten people by suddenly vanishing in a flash of fire; sometimes, remaining invisible, they speak in whispers. A Bhoot has been known to come to fisticuffs with a man, and to carry a man off and set him down in a distant place. It is even said that women are sometimes found with child by Bhoots.[2]

"In the dialogue of Dives and Pauper, printed by Richard Pynson, in 1493, "among the superstitions then in use at the beginning of the year the following is "mentioned:—'Alle that take hede to dysmal dayes, or use nyce observances in "the newe moone, or in the new yeere, *as setting of mete or drynke by nighte on "the benche to fede alholde or gobelyn.*"—*Vide* Brand.

[1] See note A, at the end of this chapter, for notices of Bhoots in other parts of India. Our remarks upon the subject in the text are derived principally from an essay entitled, "Bhoot Nibundh," or "The Destroyer of Superstitions regarding "Daimons," which was written in the language of Goozerat, by Treewâdee Dul-"putrâm Dâyâ, a Shreemâlee Brahmin, of Jhâlâwâr, and obtained the prize of the "Goozerat Vernacular Society, for A.D. 1849. An English translation, by the "author of the present work, who was then secretary to the society, was published "at Bombay A.D. 1850.

[2] In every age and country, it appears, ladies have been glad to cover a *faux pas* by the assertion of supernatural visitation. "When Demaratus had thus "spoken," says Herodotus, "his mother answered him in this manner:—'Son, "because you so earnestly desire me to speak the truth, I shall conceal nothing "from you. The third night after Ariston had conducted me home to his house, "a phantom, entirely like him in shape, entered my chamber, and having lain "with me, put a crown on my head, and went out again."
Similarly in the Bacchœ of Euripides, the hero says:—

"For that the sisters of my mother (least
"Becomes it them) declared that not from Jove
"I sprung, but pregnant by some mortal's love
"That Semele on Jove had falsely charged
"Her fault, the poor device of Cadmus."

* * * * *

The Jain Shâstras teach a different doctrine in regard to spirits from that which is taught by the Poorâns. They assert that there are eight kinds of Vyuntur Devs, and eight of Wân-Vyuntur Devs, who reside below the earth. Each of these has two Indras, or sovereigns, ruling respectively the northern and southern regions, and who are in colour black, white, or blue. The Vyunter and Wân-Vyuntur Devs appear upon earth, where they possess the bodies of men, exhibit themselves in various shapes, and perform many strange feats, whence their common name of Kootohulee (or surprising) Devs. Below them reside the Bhuwunputee Devs, who also sometimes appear on earth. Below them again are the Nârkina, or infernal spirits. Above this earth, in the atmosphere, five kinds of "Devs of splendour" reside:—the sun, moon, stars and others. Above them, in twelve Dev-Loks, the Devs who ride in chariots dwell; these, sometimes drawn by their own desire, or compelled by charms, appear in the world; but they do harm to no one. Above them are nine classes of Griveks, and five of Unootur Veemânees. They are of great power, and never visit the earth. Men who have lived a life of austerity and righteousness are born again in these classes of upper or lower Devs, but the sinner is not born in them. Of old, a man who had performed the rite of "Uthum" by fasting for three days, acquired the power of calling Devs to him, but now, it is said, these Devs never visit the earth at any one's call.[1]

In British History, Merlin, and Arthur himself, were both the sons of Bhoots. *Vide* Geoffrey's History, book vi. chap. xviii., and book viii. chap. xix., to the former of which cases Spenser thus alludes:—

"And soothe men say that he was not the sonne
"Of mortal sire or other living wighte,
"But wondrously begotten and begonne
"By false illusion of a guileful sprite
"On a faire ladye nun."

For Scotland, see the story of the Lady of Drummelziar and the Spirit of the Tweed.—Note M., Lay of the Last Minstrel. For India, see the case of Sheelâditya, in our own work; those also of Usa and Anirud, and of Kamala Kunweri, in Captain Westmacott's Article on Chardwar in Assam, Journal Bengal Asiatic Society, iv. 187, *et seq.* Butler thus alludes to these stories:—

"Not as the ancient heroes did,
"Who, that their base births might be hid,
"(Knowing that they were of doubtful gender,
"And that they came in at a windore)
"Made Jupiter himself, and others
"O' th' gods, gallants to their own mothers,
"To get on them a race of Champions,
"(Of which old Homer first made lampoons)."

Hudibras, Part I. Canto ii. v. 211—218.

[1] "This first aerial heaven," says Bishop Pearson, "where God setteth up his

The most prominent feature in the popular conception of Bhoots is that which relates to the possession of human beings by spirits, denizens of an invisible world. Upon the extensive and difficult general question of the manner in which spirits have been said, in other countries, and at other times, to possess human beings, or of the degree of power which they have exercised over those subject to their influence, it would be little becoming in us to enter,[1] but it is necessary to caution our readers that in our account of possessions in Goozerat, we rely upon a work written by a person professedly incredulous, with the acknowledged view of teaching his countrymen that there is nothing in the matter but what may be readily accounted for on ordinary grounds.[2]

"If one were to pronounce," says our author, "that no such being "as a Bhoot existed, this would be a contradiction of the Hindoo "scriptures. In the Christian scriptures, and in the Mohummedan, "the existence of such spirits is also admitted: the assertion that "they do exist, therefore, cannot be pronounced to be a falsehood.[3] "Perhaps of ten thousand cases in which possessions by spirits have "been asserted, one case may have been actually true; thus much I "would admit as probable, confiding in the scriptures, but as far as "my personal observation extends, it has never, I am bound to say, "included a single case which could be authenticated.

"pavilion, where 'he maketh the clouds his chariot, and walketh upon the "wings of the wind,' is not so far inferior in place as it is in glory to the next, the "seat of the sun and moon, the two great lights, and stars innumerable far greater "than the one of them. And yet that second heaven is not so far above the first as "beneath the 'third' into which St. Paul was caught. The brightness of the sun "doth not so far surpass the blackness of a wandering cloud, as the glory of that "heaven of presence surmounts the fading beauty of the starry firmament. For in "this great temple of the world, in which the Son of God is the High-Priest, the "heaven which we see is but the veil, and that which is above, the Holy of Holies. "This veil indeed is rich and glorious, but one day to be rent, and then to admit "us into a far greater glory, even to the mercy-seat and cherubim. For this third "heaven is the proper habitation of the blessed angels, which constantly attend upon "the throne."

[1] See, however, for a few authorities on the subject, Note B, at the end of this chapter. For ourselves, we cannot, to use Dr. Johnson's words, account it "more "strange that there should be evil spirits, than evil men: evil unembodied spirits, "than evil embodied spirits;" and we can have no hesitation in believing that possessions have occurred, whether or not they do now occur.

[2] *Vide* Note at p. 648.

[3] *Vide* Bishop Hall's Contemplations:—"That there have been such apparitions "of spirits, both good and evil, hath ever been a truth undoubtedly received of "Pagans, Jews, Christians; although in the blind times of superstition, there was "much collusion mixed with some verities; crafty men and lying spirits agreeing "to abuse the credulous world."

"As far as the Hindoo scriptures are concerned, the following "appears to me to be the truth:—It is stated there that unclean "persons, and those who lie, or are guilty of other sins, die, and after "death become goblins, and suffer many calamities. The object is "merely to give a sanction to the injunction against uncleanness and "sin. Similarly, when it is stated that Bhoots take possession of "persons whose lives are evil. Such I conclude to be the intention "of the composers of the scriptures, but people have become very "superstitious, and great evil has been the result. It seems to me "better, therefore, that the belief in Bhoots should not exist. As it "is said, superstition is the Bhoot, and fear is the Dâkin (witch). If "people understood what this really means, they would be saved "much annoyance."

"When a person," says our author in another place, "gets wind "into his head and loses his spirits, and sits silent and solitary, his "relations and neighbours ask him, 'What is the matter?' He will "say that he does not know what can be the matter with him, but "that he feels inclined to cry. The inquirers will ask the sufferer "where he has been to, and whether he has met with anything start- "ling or alarming. He then begins to consider with himself. Others "come and ask him similar questions, and they worry him until he "begins to blubber in downright earnest. His friends then come to "a decision upon his case, and pronounce him to be possessed by a "Bhoot, and the poor man himself believes that it is so. Presently "he begins to tremble, and at last becomes convulsed to such a "degree that if a person who is not a believer in Bhoots were to try "and tremble like him he would not be able to do it, at any rate "without great practice. The sufferer firmly believes that the Bhoot "which possesses him is causing him to tremble, and that his con- "vulsions are wholly independent of any will of his own.[1]

"A Brahmin, a relation of mine," continues the essayist, "dying, his "spirit, seven months afterwards, possessed his wife, and caused her

[1] The following description of what occurs in Tinnevelly is very similar to this:—"If the person happen to feel the commencement of the shivering fit of an "ague, or the vertigo of a bilious headache, his untutored imagination teaches him "to think himself possessed. He then sways his head from side to side, fixes his "eyes into a stare, puts himself into a posture, and begins the maniac dance; and "the bystanders run for flowers and fruit for an offering, or a cock or goat to "sacrifice to his honour." See "The Tinnevelly Shanars," by the Rev. R. Caldwell, B.A., printed for the Society for the Propagation of the Gospel, in A.D. 1850. Compare with the text that extremely humorous scene in "Twelfth Night," the 4th of the 3rd Act, where Malvolio is accused of being possessed.

"to tremble. The woman was naturally a person of mild temper and "weak frame of body; in her fit, however, she became so violent that "no one dared to answer or oppose her. A friend of the deceased "having visited the house, the woman said to him, 'Ah! brother, "recollect what it was I told you that day when we were alone "together.' He said, 'Yes, I recollect.' A Wâneeo neighbour at "another time came to the house. The woman said to him, 'Wâneeo! "why have you not yet told my wife about the money I gave you?' "The man said, 'Yes! I have got seventy-five rupees and a half "belonging to you; I will pay your wife.' The woman went on thus, "having a fit every day, and people were surprised at her saying such "things as the above. I examined into the matter, and it appeared "that the Brahmin used continually to converse with his friend in "private, and that the woman, aware of this, had spoken at a venture, "but the friend was satisfied that she alluded to a conversation in "which the Brahmin had mentioned his fears, that being sonless he "would not obtain liberation after death, because it was laid down in "the Shâstrâs that—

"The sonless obtains not liberation;
"Paradise is not for him—is not for him."

"Everybody suspected that the Wâneeo had in his possession "money belonging to the deceased, a fact which originated in the "woman's mind the idea of making the demand, and the Wâneeo, "believing that the Bhoot of the Brahmin had entered the body of "his wife, thought it safer to admit the truth at once.[1] When I

His madness is unlike that of the Bhoot-possessed in that he is merry and not sad, but Olivia helps us out of this difficulty when she says,—

"I am mad as he,
"If sad and merry, madness equal be."

[1] "There is a strong disposition in the human breast to carry on an intercourse "with the spirits of the departed. The fulfilment of their last wills, which has "devolved on us; the care of their children, in whom even their features and "characters actually survive; the development of the schemes which they have "left on our hands imperfect; the enjoyment of the blessings they have bequeathed "us—all knit them to us; our very dreams will not permit us, even if we would, "to banish them from our presence; our traditions are peopled with them; the "inscriptions on our tombstones, now gathered about our churches, the scene of "our constant resort—of old ranged along the highway-side, amidst the concourse "of the gate—rude as those inscriptions often are, and the more to my present "purpose for being so, testify the passion there is in the hearts of men to hold "dialogues with the dead; the treatises of the most literary nations, and the "customs and superstitions of the most savage, alike bespeak it."—*Four Sermons preached before the University of Cambridge, in November*, 1849, *by the Rev. J. J. Blunt, B.D., Margaret Professor of Divinity*, p. 2.

" went to the house one day, the people said to me, 'Ask, if you have " any question to put, and you will get a satisfactory answer.' The " woman then addressed me as her husband had been in the habit " of doing. I said, 'There is some mistake in the account between " you and me. I am very glad you have come, as you can set it " right.' The woman, trembling all the time, began to cast up the " account in her head, repeating it aloud. I said to her, 'Here is " the account book, in your own hand-writing. Read me what you " have written.' The woman said, 'I can't read what's written in " account books.' Everybody then began to laugh. I was satisfied " that the idea of a possession was in this case false. The woman " could not give an answer to any of the questions I put to her. " Other people asked her what were the names of her husband's " maternal and paternal uncles, and she answered them glibly; but I " inquired what was the name of the book which I and her husband " had been reading together on such and such a day, and she could " make no reply. I then understood that there was no difficulty in " her answering such questions as those which she had shown herself " able to answer."

It is customary in Goozerat, where people wish to prevent the removal of a jungle tree, that they should paint a trident upon it with vermillion, or, if that be inconvenient, that they should collect a number of stones and throw them down at the root of the tree. Whoever, after this, passes by, is sure to add a stone or two to the heap, believing the place to be the residence of a Bhoot. Some, too, throw without taking heed what they are doing. If the place be one where stones are not easily procurable, a bit of old rag is thrown so as to adhere to the tree, and every one who passes by follows the example once set. They call the spot the "Rag-uncle's." In places where trees are scarce these uncles are very common, and people are much annoyed with the dread of touching them. The name "uncle" is given to the Bhoot by women as a term of respect. Men are less superstitious, but no woman ever thinks of passing one of these places, without adding at least one stone to the heap, or one rag to the Rag-uncle's tree. If no rag be forthcoming, she will pull a few threads out of her dress and use these instead. In case a woman have forgotten to perform this ceremony she will be overcome with fear of the consequences, begin to tremble, and cry out that she is "uncle" and that he has taken possession of her body and is vexing her because she neglected to add a stone to his heap.[1] Similarly, whenever in

[1] Our own sagacious King James accounts for the women being more superstitious, thus—

any place there is a hillock or mound upon which a few stones have been piled one above the other, every passer-by considers himself bound to add a stone to the heap, considering that the spot is some Dev's residence, and that if any one raise a little temple there his house will flourish. Such monuments are also set up in places where a person has been slain or wounded.[1]

" The reason is easy, for as that sex is frailer than man is, so is it easier to be " entrapped in these gross snares of the Divell, as was over well proved to be true " by the serpent's deceiving of Eva at the beginning, which makes him homelier " with that sexe sensine."

Colonel Tod describes a custom similar to this in Harawati :—" Half-way we " passed a roofless shed of loose stones, containing the divinity of the Bheels ; it is " in the midst of a grove of thorny, tangled brushwood, whose boughs were here " and there decorated with shreds of various colored cloth, offerings of the traveller " to the forest divinity for protection against evil spirits, by which I suppose the " Bheels themselves are meant." He adds, in a note, " The same practice is " described by Park as existing in Africa."—*Rajasthan* ii., 662.

[1] " Cairns " of this kind are frequently connected with the dead—

" On many a cairn's grey pyramid,
" Where urns of mighty chiefs lie hid,"

says Scott, *vide* " The Lay of the Last Minstrel," Canto iii., 29, and Note 2, U.

Doorgâwutee, Queen Regent of Gurh Mundela, was killed in action against the troops of Akbar, under Asuf Khan, or rather, as an inscription of her family asserts (*vide* As. Res. xv., p. 437), " Doorgâwutee, who was mounted on an elephant, " severed her own head with a scimitar she held in her hand ; she reached the " supreme spirit ; pierced the sun's orb." " She was interred at the place where " she fell" (says a writer in Ben. As. Soc. Journal, vi., 628), " and on her tomb to " this day the passing stranger thinks it necessary to place, as a votive offering, one " of the fairest he can find of those beautiful specimens of white crystal in which " the hills in this quarter abound. Two rocks lie by her side, which are supposed " by the people to be her drums converted into stone ; and strange stories are " told of their being still occasionally heard to sound in the stillness of the night " by the people of the nearest villages."

" The well-known practice among the Highlanders," says Logan, in his 'Scottish " 'Gael,' ii., 371, " of throwing a stone to a cairn on passing, is connected with " two different feelings. In the one case, it arose from the respect which was " had for the deceased, whose memory they wished to prolong by increasing the " size of his funeral mount, and hence arose a saying intended to gratify a person " while alive that the speaker should not fail to add stones to the cairn. It would " appear that the soul was considered much pleased with this attention, and with " the honour of a great monument, in which respect the old Germans seem to have " differed from the Celts, for they raised sods of earth only above the grave, con- " ceiving that large monuments were grievous to the deceased. The other motive " for throwing stones to augment a cairn was to mark with execration the burial- " place of a criminal, the practice, according to Dr. Smith, having been instituted " by the Druids. It is curious that the same method should be adopted with " views so different ; yet the fact is so, and the author has often, in his youth, " *passed the grave of a suicide, on which, according to custom, he never failed to* " *fling a stone. The true motive, in this case, seems to have been to appease the spirit*

The Poorwuj Dev, like the Etruscan Lar, or the Grecian hero, is regarded as hovering about his former abode, averting dangers from the inhabitants and bestowing blessings upon them. He frequently appears in the character of a serpent, and is then treated with great respect by the inmates of the house near which he resides. It is a common belief in Goozerat that serpents are always to be found wherever a hoard is buried, and that these are the Bhoots of the deceased owners who have remained upon earth from affection to their wealth.

"Two guests," says our author, "came once on a time to the "house of a Shrâwuk Wâneeo. The master of the house was at the "market, and his wife, after she had made her friends sit down, was

"*which, by the Celtic Mythology, was doomed to hover beside the unhallowed "sepulchre.*"

The following occurs in the notes to an Aberdeenshire poem, called "the Don," in reference to the district of Alford :—

"In these bounds are many great cairns, such as that of Lenturk, so much "talked of; they are of enormous size; some people think they have been "beacons to give warning in time of danger, but as many of them are situated in "low places, I suppose they are the tombs of some great men who have been "benefactors to the country where they lived. It is a common saying among the "vulgar people to this day, when any person makes them a gift, 'God I wat, gin "'I live ahint you, I'se add a stane to your cairn,' and to this day many old "people never pass by any of these cairns without throwing a stone to it. Many "think that the spirit hovers about the place where the body is interred, and the "higher the cairn is raised, the spirit is raised the higher from earth to heaven."

Hawke Locker, in his Views in Spain, (quoted in Ellis's edition of Brand's Popular Antiquities), speaking of Grenadilla, says, "We passed two or three "crosses, which marked the spot where some unfortunate wretches had met a "violent death by the way. Some of these probably were killed by accident, "but all were described as so many barbarous murders, and the fluency of the "narrative proved that we were listening to a tale which had been told a "hundred times before. The very ancient custom of casting a stone upon these "untimely graves is still observed throughout Spain. Affection, or superstition, "induces many to offer this tribute, accompanied by a silent prayer for the dead; "but even a mere stranger, exempt from such motives, may find a gratification in "adding a stone to the heap, from that veneration for the dead which seems to be "inherent in our constitution."

In the instance we are about to quote, the stone-throwers were actuated by a very different feeling ; it is from Lepsius's "Letters from Egypt." (*Bohn*, p. 216.)

"Before entering this mountain range (Gebel el Mageqa) we came to a place "covered with heaps of stones, which might be supposed to be barrows, though "no one lies buried beneath them. Whenever the date-merchants come this road, "many of whom we met the following morning with their large round plaited "straw baskets, their camel-drivers at this spot demand a trifle from them. He "who will give nothing has a cenotaph, such as this, erected to him out of the "surrounding stones, as a bad omen for his hard-heartedness. We met with a "similar assemblage of tombs in the desert of Korusko."

" obliged to go away to the well for water. While the guests sat " waiting for the master of the house a large snake made its " appearance. One of them jumped up and pinned it to the ground " with a stick, while the other set to work to find a split bamboo, " which people keep ready in their houses for taking hold of snakes " with. Meanwhile, the woman came back with the water, and " seeing the snake pinned to the ground, cried out, 'Let him go; let " him go; he is our Poorwuj Dev; he used to get into my mother-" in-law's head, and set her a-trembling, and then he would mention " the name of my father-in-law, who died some time ago, and say " that he was he. He said also that his soul had been wrapped up " in his property, on which account he had become a snake and was " going to live in the house. One day he bit a neighbour of ours, " and the Jutee came to cure the man. Poorwuj Dev then set the " neighbour a-trembling, and said that he had bitten him because he " fought with his son, and that he would quit him when he got " security that there should be no more quarrelling. In this way he " quitted him. From that day forth if the snake go to our " neighbours' houses no one molests him. If at any time you were " to set him down at a place twenty miles off he would still come " back to this very spot. He has often touched my foot, but he " never bit me; and if I happen to be gone to draw water, and the " child cries at home, he will rock him in his cradle. This I've seen " him do many a time.' In this way she prevented their interfering " with the snake, and, releasing him, paid him obeisance. The " guest, too, who had seized him, took off his turban, and said, 'O! " father snake, forgive my having pinned you to the earth. I am " your child.' After a short time, a cat having killed the snake, the " people of the house took the pieces of it and burned them on a " pyre, offering, in fire-sacrifice, a cocoa-nut and sandal-wood, with " clarified butter."

" A Brahmin, having purchased premises in the ancient town of " Dholka, set to work to make excavations for a new building, and, in " so doing, came upon a subterranean chamber, which contained a " great deal of property. There was, however, a large snake " stationed there to protect the treasure, which snake appeared to the " Brahmin by night in a dream, and said to him, 'This property is " mine, and I live here for its protection; therefore you must not " injure the chamber nor covet the treasure which it contains. If " you do so, I will cut off all your posterity.' In the morning, the " Brahmin poured a vessel of hot oil into the chamber, so that the " snake died. He then destroyed the chamber, having first removed "the treasure, and burned the body of the snake in due form in the "yard of his house. With the treasure he had thus obtained he "erected splendid buildings, but he never had a son, and his "daughter remained childless, and whoever received any part of the "property, or became his servant, or acted as his agent or as his "family priest, was childless too. These things happened, it is said, "about forty years ago."

Similar stories are very common in Goozerat, and it is, as we have said, the general belief that serpents are always to be found wherever a hoard is buried.[1]

For a description of the modes employed in Goozerat in the exorcism of Bhoots who are supposed to have taken possession of the bodies of living men, whether derived from the Kurum Kând of the Veds, or from Boudhist or Mohummedan sources, we must refer to the Bhoot Nibundh itself. Sometimes the relief of the sufferer is the point principally if not wholly regarded; at other times it is sought further to procure release from his painful wanderings for the "extravagant and erring spirit." One instance of each of these cases we now venture to lay before our readers.

"About thirty years ago," says the essayist, "a Chârun asserted a "claim against the chief of Syelâ, in Kâteewâr, which the chief "refused to liquidate. The bard thereupon, taking forty of his "caste with him, went to Syelâ with the intention of sitting in "'Dhurnâ' at the chief's door, and preventing any one coming out "or going in until the claim should be discharged. However, as "they approached the town, the chief, becoming aware of their "intention, caused the gates to be closed. The bards remained "outside; for three days they abstained from food; on the fourth "day they proceeded to perform 'Trâgâ,' as follows:—Some hacked "their own arms; others decapitated three old women of the party, "and hung their heads up at the gate as a garland. Certain of the "women cut off their own breasts. The bards also pierced the "throats of four of their old men with spikes, and they took two "young girls by the heels, and dashed out their brains against the "town gate. The Chârun, to whom the money was due, dressed "himself in clothes wadded with cotton, which he steeped in oil, and "then set on fire. He thus burned himself to death. But as he "died, he cried out, 'I am now dying; but I will become a headless "ghost (Kuvees) in the palace, and will take the chief's life, and cut

[1] There are several stories of the kind in the "Oriental Memoirs," original edition, ii. 384, et seq.

" off his posterity.' After this sacrifice the rest of the bards returned " home.

" On the third day after the Chârun's death his Bhoot threw the " Rânee down stairs, so that she was very much injured. Many other " persons also beheld the headless phantom in the palace. At last " he entered the chief's head, and set him trembling. At night he " would throw stones at the palace, and he killed a female servant " outright. At length, in consequence of the various acts of op- " pression which he committed, no one dared to approach the chief's " mansion, even in broad day-light. In order to exorcise the Bhoot, " Jogees, Jutees, Fukeers, Brahmins, mendicants of every class were " sent for from many different places: but whatever person attempted " a cure the Bhoot in the chief's body would immediately assail, and " that so furiously that the exorcist's courage failed him. The Bhoot " would also cause the chief to tear the flesh off his arms with his " teeth. Besides this, four or five persons died of injuries received " from the Bhoot; but no one had the power to expel him. At " length a foreign Jutee happening to come to that part of the " country, the chief sent a carriage for him, and brought him with " honor to his town. The Jutee was a person of great reputation for " skill in charms and sorcery, and he was attended by seven followers. " Having procured various articles which he required, he entered the " mansion, and worshipped the Dev. First, he tied all round the " house threads, which he had charged with a charm; then he " sprinkled charmed milk and water all round; then he drove a " charmed iron nail into the ground at each corner of the mansion, " and two at the door. He purified the house, and established a " Dev there, beside whom he placed a drawn sword, a lamp of " clarified butter, and another of oil; he then sat down to mutter his " charms. For forty-one days he continued thus employed, and every " day he went to the funeral ground with many and various sacri- " ficial offerings. The chief lived in a separate room all this time, " and continually fancied himself possessed, at which times he would " say, ' Ah! you shaven[1] fellow, you've come to turn me out have you? " I'm not going though; and what's more, I'll make you pay for it " with your life.' The Jutee sat in a room which was closely fastened " up; but people say that when he was at his mutterings stones " would fall thereupon, and strike the windows. When his pre-

[1] "Peeled" would have been the term in England. *Vide* First Part of Henry VI., Act i., scene 3:—

"Peel'd priest, dost thou command me to be shut out?"

" parations were finished, the Jutee caused his own people to bring " the chief to the upper room which he used, and kept all others out " of hearing distance. He sprinkled grain, and rapped upon a " metal cup, in order to place the chief under the influence of the " possessing spirit. The patient then began to be very violent, but " the Jutee and his people spared no pains in thrashing him, until " they had rendered him quite docile. Then the chief's servants were " recalled, a sacrificial fire-pit was made, and a lime placed between " it and the chief. The Jutee commanded the Bhoot to enter the " lime. The possessed, however, said, 'Who are you? If one of " your Devs were to come I would not quit this person.' Thus they " went on from morning till noon. At last they came down out of " the mansion, and assembled in the open space in front of it, where " they burned various kinds of incense, and sprinkled many charms " until they got the Bhoot out into the lime. When the lime began to " jump about, the whole of the spectators praised the Jutee, crying out, " 'The Bhoot has gone into the lime! The Bhoot has gone into the " lime!' The possessed person himself, when he saw the lime hopping " about, was astonished, and left off trembling, being perfectly satisfied " that the Bhoot had left his body and gone out into the lime. The Jutee " then, in presence of all the people of the town, turned the Bhoot out " by the eastern door. If the lime went off the road the Jutee " would touch it with his stick and put it into the right way again. " Several soldiers, with their swords drawn, followed, and drummers " beating a warlike measure; they took the chief also with them. " On the track of the Bhoot they sprinkled mustard and salt. " When they had conveyed the Bhoot in this fashion to the edge of " the town-lands, they dug a pit, seven cubits deep, and buried the " lime there, throwing into the hole above it mustard and salt, and " over these dust and stones, and filling in the space between the " stones with lead. At each corner, too, the Jutee drove in an iron " nail, two feet long, which he had previously charmed. When the " lime reached the limits of the town, some of the towns-men had " suggested that it would be satisfactory if the Bhoot were buried " outside their bounds; but the people of the neighbouring towns " threatened that a serious quarrel would arise if he were buried " otherwise than on the chief's own ground. The Jutee, too, said " that there was no occasion for alarm, and that the Bhoot could not " escape if he were leaded down; besides, that if he were properly " buried, he would pine away, and die in a few days. The lime " buried, the people returned home, and not one of them ever saw " the Bhoot thereafter. The chief gave the Jutee a handsome "present, and people were convinced that there were few such "powerful exorcists in India; 'but,' says the essayest, "no one "understood what had really been done." According to our author the cure was effected by putting quicksilver into the lime.[1]

"When a man is attacked with fever, or becomes speechless, or "appears to have lock-jaw, his friends conclude, from these indica- "tions, that he is possessed by a Bhoot. They call him by his name, "but he does not answer, and then they think it necessary to send for "a Brahmin who is learned in the Book of Doorgâ. If there is any "delay in this Brahmin's coming, some one suggests that the patient "should be fumigated with pepper, or with the dung of a dog, and "that the spirit possessing him will then speak. When the man has "been thus treated, he will sometimes speak and sometimes not. As "soon as the Brahmin who knows the book has arrived, he takes his "seat on a carpet, cleanly dressed. He places a new red cloth on a "low table, and upon it makes the eight-leaved Yuntra (or charmed "figure) with grains of wheat, writing, in the nine chambers, the nine "names of Doorgâ, as follows:—1. Syelpootree; 2. Brumhâchâreenee; "3. Chundraghuntâ; 4. Kooshmândâ; 5. Skund Mâtâ; 6. Kâtyâyu- "nee; 7. Kalrâttree; 8. Muhâ Gowree; 9. Siddhidâ. In the nine "chambers he makes also nine heaps of wheat, in each of which he "performs the 'invitation' of one of the nine Doorgâs. Upon this "he places a vessel filled with water and a cocoa-nut, or sometimes "merely a cocoa-nut. This he worships. He makes incense of gum- "resin and a lamp of clarified butter. The friends having dressed the "possessed person in clean clothes, seat him opposite. The Brahmin "begins to read the 'book.' He repeats the charm of nine letters, "holding rice or water in his hand, with which, when charmed, he "sprinkles the possessed until he begins to tremble. To make him "tremble well he places a copper or brass dish on an empty vessel, "and raps upon it. He sprinkles the possessed with rice or water "charmed with the nine-letter charm, and summons the Bhoot. The "possessed, in reply, mentions the name of some one of his deceased re- "lations, whom he declares himself to be, and he further states that his "life has clung to his house, or property, or wife, and that he has "therefore become a Bhoot. He tells his friends that they are in "possession of his property, and that if they do not attend to what "he says in regard to the protection of his son he will annoy them.

[1] In Tod's Rajasthan, ii. 688, is a description of the expulsion of "Murree," or the cholera, in a similar manner; and in M. Huc's travels, he relates how the Tartar Lamas expel, much in the same way, the "Tchutgour," or Bhoot of that country.

" He further prescribes to them certain means to be used for his own " recovery. Some of the relations assent, and they swear the Bhoot " to the agreement by causing him to place his hand on the platform " consecrated to Doorgâ, or on the book. The Chundee Pât (or Book " of Doorgâ) is found in the Markundee Poorân. It contains a verse " which states that

> " The Gruh, the Bhoot, the Pishâch, the Yuksh,
> " The Gundhurv, the Râkshus, the Brum-Râkshus,
> " The Vyetâl, the Kooshmând, the Bhyeruv,

" and other unclean spirits fly from the man who is armed with the " Chundee Pât."[1]

When a Bhoot sets a man trembling he will sometimes say, "Take " me to Someshwur Puttun, and procure for me liberation. Every " one belonging to the family must go, and I will travel in the body of " one of you and obtain liberation." He further enjoins that a certain vow be taken, which is to be kept until the party reaches the place appointed. One only of the party takes the vow, which is sometimes to eat only half the usual food, sometimes to abstain from the use of milk or of curds, coarse sugar or spices. The most strict of all vows is that to abstain from clarified butter. Some take a vow to convey their food to their mouths by passing it below their knees. The vows are usually taken by a woman of the family. Another vow is that of eating in a standing position out of a black earthen plate, and with the left hand only. Some men vow to abandon the use of a turban, in which case they substitute a small cloth; others vow to wear no shoes, or to travel on foot to the place of pilgrimage. Women vow to wear no bodice. When the person who has taken the vow finds opportunity he proceeds to the holy place, and absolves himself. If before he set out thither any other member of the family be attacked with sickness, the possessed tells the person who has made the vow that this is because of his nonperformance of it, and that it is he (the Bhoot) who is causing pain to the sufferer. The person bound by the vow will then set forth immediately.

Another practice is as follows :—When a person falls sick, some relation waving a jewel round his head puts it away, and vows not to use it after the recovery of the sick person until he shall have entertained so many Brahmins. A poor man uses a metal cup or other vessel for the same purpose. The ceremony is called "Oocheeto."

Pilgrimages to Prubhâs or Someshwur Puttun generally commence

[1] *Vide* Transactions, Bombay Literary Society, iii. 75.

on the eleventh of the light half of Kârteek, and continue during five days,—those days being dedicated to the "Poorwuj," or ancestral Devs. Generally speaking, the whole family, including the man's brothers and their wives, must go, for if one of the party happen to remain at home the Bhoot will frequently remain also, and not go to Prubhâs with the rest.[1] The party proceed thither on foot, shoeless, without turbans, or in whatever other way their vow may direct. They are received at Prubhâs by a class of Brahmins called "Sompurâ," who, whenever a caravan arrives, select certain of the members of it, whom they claim as their disciples on the ground that the strangers' ancestors (as appears from the Brahmins' books) had, at such and such times, visited the holy place, and appointed the Brahmins their Gors. On the morning of the day following, the pilgrims, having shaved and removed their moustaches, go to the river Suruswutee, and perform "Deh shooddh Prâyuscheet" and "Shrâddh." (ceremonies which have been described), they then bathe in the river under the Gor's directions—husband and wife, if such be the form of their vow, wearing one long garment. The Gor says to the pilgrims, "Advance into the "river, and make obeisance to the Dev of the holy place." While the pilgrim pays his adorations accordingly, the priest repeats this verse:—

> "Ganges, Jumna, Godâveree, Suruswutee,
> "Nerbudda, and sea-going Kâveree, enter into this water."

He then repeats, in Sanscrit, the names of the year, month, day of the month, and day of the week, and continues thus: "I bathe in

[1] "It is very difficult, they say, to get rid of a Nis when one wishes it. (The "Nis is the same being in Scandinavia, which is called Kobold in Germany, "Brownie in Scotland, &c.) A man who lived in a house, in which a Nis carried "his pranks to great lengths, resolved to quit the tenement, and leave him there "alone. Several cart-loads of furniture were already gone, and the man was come "to take away the last, which consisted chiefly of empty tubs, barrels, and things "of that sort. The load was now all ready, and the man had just bidden farewell "to his house and to the Nis, hoping for comfort in his new habitation, when hap- "pening, from some cause or other, to go to the back of the cart, there he saw the "Nis sitting in one of the tubs in the cart, plainly with the intention of going along "with him wherever he went. The good man was surprised and disconcerted be- "yond measure at seeing that all his labour was to no purpose; but the Nis began "to laugh heartily, popped his head up out of the tub, and cried to the bewildered "farmer, 'Ha! we're moving to-day, you see.'

"This story is current in Germany, England, and Ireland. In the German "story, the farmer set fire to his barn, to burn the Kobold in it. As he was driv- "ing off, he turned round to look at the blaze, and, to his no small mortification, "saw the Kobold behind him in the cart, crying 'It was time for us to come out! it "was time for us to come out!'"—*Vide Keightley's Fairy Mythology.*

" this place of pilgrimage for the purpose of removing whatever sins " I may have committed of thought, word, or deed; of obtaining the " favor of the Supreme Lord; of purifying my body; of procuring " liberation for the ancestral Devs." He then says to the bather, " Now complete your bathing." In this manner he causes the whole party to bathe, one after the other. As the pilgrims ascend out of the water after bathing they are beset by a crowd of mendicants, commonly Brahmins, among whom they distribute what money they have. There is a sacred fig-tree there, which people suppose to be of the time of Shree Krishn. The pilgrims worship this tree, and pour water upon its roots, under the idea that the Poorwuj Devs drink water so poured. They then circumambulate the tree. When the possessed person beholds this tree he becomes immediately under the influence of the Bhoot, and begins to tremble and roll his eyes. The Gor addresses him, and says, "Now, do you remain here, and whatever " virtuous actions you may prescribe shall be performed for you." If the Bhoot assent, he will direct that one hundred and eight Brahmin's be entertained, or that a bullock and heifer be married. In the latter case, the relations go through the whole marriage ceremonial as if for human beings, and at the close one man takes in his hand the tails of the two animals, and the family perform the rite called "Turpun," using for the occasion water, milk, and oil of sesamum. The whole of these ceremonies are described in the Kurum Kând of the Veds, of which the following is a verse:—

" Those of my ancestors who have become Bhoots, those who have "become Prets,—may they all be relieved of their thirst by my perform- " ing *Turpun* over the tails of the bullock and heifer!"

There are about one hundred and twenty verses of this kind, more or less of which are muttered by the person performing the ceremonial. The family also mention the names of their ancestors, or as many of them as they can recollect, and they make in the same place one hundred and eight lump oblations, and assign them to different Poorwuj Devs, and for those which remain unassigned they repeat a verse of the Kurum Kândsuch as the following:—

" They who have been struck dead by lightning, or by the hands of " thieves, or by the tooth or horn of an animal—these are they for whose " release I offer this lump oblation."

Perhaps, however, the Bhoot will say, "This place does not please " me; I shall go home and live in my own house, so you must make a " sacred place for me there." Then the Gor falls to coaxing the Bhoot very much, and says: "Would you desert such a delightful " place of pilgrimage as this, a place on the very banks of Suruswutee-

"jee? No! no! you will remain here, surely." Some Bhoots notwithstanding, insist upon returning home. If the Bhoot be pleased to remain the party perform "virtuous actions," such as he may order, at Prubhâs.

In the evening the pilgrims, of whom thousands are collected, worship the Suruswutee, after which ceremony they make lamps of clarified butter in leaf vessels, and set them afloat in the stream, so that the whole surface of the river is brilliantly illuminated.[1]

The pilgrimage is now complete, and the party returns home.

In cases where the possessing Bhoot is supposed to be of low caste the most successful exorcists are persons called Bhoowos, who are considered to be favourites of some one or other of the "Shoodra "Devees,"—the local goddesses, such as Boucherâjee, Khodeeâr, Gudeychee, Sheekotur, Melâdee, and others. The Bhoowo is of all castes, from the Brahmin downwards. The Devee to whom he is devoted has an altar in his house, at which her pleasure is consulted before he ventures on an act of exorcism. If the answer be in the affirmative, the Bhoowo proceeds to the residence of the patient, attended by drummers, who beat their instruments and chant a song of the Devee, as—

Mother of the Mânsurowur,
Dweller in the Mid-Choonwâl,
Steadfast Boucherâjee, come!
Thou whose chamber faces the east!

* * * * * *

OR,

True Devee Khodeeâr,
Who dwellest among the hills,
Who when invoked exhibitest thy truth,
Come, swift-speeding mother!

* * * * * *

The Bhoowo, who has seated himself opposite to the possessed person, as soon as he hears the music, assumes the character of one inspired by the Devee, and begins to employ different means of terrifying the Bhoot. The operation lasts sometimes for five or six days; at length the possessed cries out (in the character of the Bhoot), "I'm "off! I'm off!" and having been duly sworn to expend a certain sum of money in the Devee's service is admitted to be convalescent.[2]

[1] This is no doubt derived from the expiation of Chânukya, for which see note, p. 52.

[2] "Satan, the common ape of the Almighty, imitates him also in this point," is an observation made by Bishop Hall in reference to faith, which we might con-

Many Koolees and shepherds in the wild hill-country have altars in their houses consecrated to these "Mâtâs," Melâdee, Sheekotur and others. The altar is called "deroo" and usually takes the form

tinually employ in reference to other subjects. It is recorded of Elisha, 2 Kings iii. 15, that he called for a minstrel, "And it came to pass, when the minstrel played, "that the hand of the Lord came upon him." "It was not for their ears, it was "for his own bosom," says the above-mentioned author, "that Elisha called for "musick, that his spirits, after their zealous agitation, might be sweetly composed, "and put into a meet temper for receiving the calm visions of God."

The "damsel possessed with a spirit of divination," or "of Python," mentioned in Acts xvi. 16, seems to have some points of resemblance to the Devee-possessed person we are describing.

The proceedings of a Bhoowo of low caste appear to have given rise to the following action at law, which is reported in the 1st volume of Selected Cases decided by the Sudder Dewanee Adawlut of Bombay, at p. 91, as follows:—

"Peetâmbur Nurotum, *Appellant*,
versus
"Mukundâs Koober, and Râeejee Mukun, *Respondents*.

"AHMEDABAD.

"This was an action brought by Appellant against Respondents for defamation of "character; damages were laid at rupees 995.

"The parties were Dushâ Dishâwul Wâneeâs, and the Appellant set forth in his "plaint that one Eeshwur Mooljee of their caste went, about the 8th Kârtik Shood, "1880 (4th Nov., 1829), to the Nât-Gor (priest of the caste), Nânâbhâee Vishnoo-"râm, to obtain permission, according to custom, to give a caste dinner; that "leave was accorded, when Respondents told Eeshwur that if he would leave out "Appellants family they would dine with him; that upon inquiring the cause, they "assigned as a reason *that some one was ill in Appellant's house when he got a Bun-"geeâ (or out-caste), to beat a tom-tom*" (a ceremony of exorcism, says the reporter in a note, when an evil spirit is suspected of disturbing a family), "*by which he lost "caste;* that the priest and others tried to persuade them that the mere act of having "a tom-tom beaten did not cause loss of caste" (a *tom-tom*, it may be explained, is a drum, so called because used by criers, who beat 'tâm-tâm' first at one place, then at another, 'tâm' meaning 'place'), "but Respondents would not listen to them, "and consequently Eeshwur Mooljee did not give his caste-dinner, nor did others "who had intended to have done so, and consequently Appellant brought this ac-"tion for defamation.

"The Respondents denied ever having defamed Appellant, and further that not "being putels or leading people of the caste, even if they had said what was as-"serted, it would not have had any effect, and that the Appellant had, since the "day mentioned in the plaint, received invitations to caste dinners: moreover, they "accused Eeshwur Mooljee and Appellant of having brought this charge against "them through enmity.

"Appellant replied and Respondent rejoined when the case was brought on for "hearing before the second Assistant Judge, who took the evidence of Eeshwur "Mooljee and the Nât Gor, Nânâbâee Vishnoorâm, to prove the slander by "Respondents, and that, in consequence of that report, caste-dinners which had "been proposed had not taken place, as stated in the plaint, and dismissed

of a small terrace in the interior of the house, which supports a little wooden image painted red, and is covered with a canopy. These persons, when at enmity with any one, frequently threaten to send their "deroo" to his house. Even if no threat be employed, it is commonly believed that the Mâtâ of a person who owns a "deroo" is sure to take vengeance upon his enemies. The house to which a "deroo" has been sent rocks as if shaken with an earthquake, the tiles clatter, the stalled beasts tremble, and the householder himself is violently agitated by the Devee. Something of this kind then follows. The bystanders ask the possessed who he is? he, convulsed, and throwing his limbs wildly about, cries out, "I am Sheekotur, and have been "sent here by Bechureeo Koolee—if amends be made to Bechureeo, "and he call me back, I will go, otherwise I will take the lives of all "the people in the house and destroy all the cattle." Bechureeo is sent for, and told to demand whatever he will, but to call off the "deroo." Bechureeo now begins to be possessed himself; he lights a piece of rag, saturated with oil, and waves it over the heads of the people of the house and of their cattle, he then thrusts it two or three times into his mouth, and takes it out again lighted to show that he has taken back the "deroo" into his own body. The lookers-on are astonished at this performance. Sometimes the friends of the afflicted person post off to complain to the chief of the village. The Thâkor, somewhat unwillingly, sends for Bechureeo, and, assuming as well as he can an air of unconcern and authority, orders him to remove the "deroo"—he is, however, desperately afraid all the time lest the "deroo" should be sent to his own house. Bechureeo, on the other hand, thinks that it may not be safe to trifle too far with the chief, so he promises to take away his Mâtâ.

"fourteen other witnesses to the same point, whose evidence was not required by "him, these two having, in his opinion, proved the point. Appellant further called "four other witnesses to prove *that the Bungeeâ who beat the tom-tom did not come "into the house but beat it outside and never threw water on his (Appellant's) wife, "who was the sick person so that the house could not have been polluted.* The Assistant "Judge considered this evidence sufficient to this point, he therefore, dismissed the "other two witnesses which Appellant had in attendance, and gave judgment, that "Appellant had proved the defamation of his character, and, further, that there were "no grounds for such defamation, as no act of exorcism alone was sufficient to occa-"sion estrangement from caste; he, therefore, in consideration of the defamation "and Appellant's loss of dinner, awarded rupees 99 damages with all costs, and "dismissed the witnesses which Respondents had summoned to prove the nega-"tive of the plaint, as the Court considered them unnecessary."

This decree of the Assistant Judge was reversed by the Judge, but, in substance, ultimately upheld by the Court of Appeal, which (A.D. 1832) awarded the Plaintiff one rupee damages and all costs.

Sometimes, however, the Thâkor has a "deroo" of his own. A chief of our acquaintance had a very valuable possession in the person of one "Kesur Bâee Mâtâ." When his cultivators showed a disposition to leave his village, he frightened them into remaining by hinting that the Mâtâ might follow them. It is said, too, that he sometimes met the demands of his creditors in a similar manner.

Bhoowos are occasionally employed to relieve persons who are annoyed by a "deroo."

It is believed that a woman who is born upon one of a list of days laid down in the astrological books is a "poison-daughter," or gifted with the evil-eye. Such a person is called a Dâkin, or witch, and it is supposed that they on whom she casts her eyes suffer as if they were possessed by a Bhoot. Some persons, when they feel unwell, think that the effect is produced by a witch having set her Dev at them. Witches are most commonly of the Chârun, or Wâghuree castes. Many precautions are employed to avert the effects of the evil-eye; the best preservatives are iron articles, marks made with black colour, charms, or amulets.

There are six descriptions of charms, or "muntras," known in Goozerat, which are described in a series of works forming the scriptures on the subject, or "Muntra Shâstras." A charm called "Mârun Muntra" has the power of taking away life; "Mohun Muntra" produces ocular or auricular illusions; "Sthumbhun Muntra" stops what is in motion; "Âkurshun Muntra" calls or makes present anything; "Wusheekurun Muntra" has the power of enthralling; and "Oochâtun Muntra" of causing bodily injury short of death.

Dâdbâ, the eldest son of Wujey Singh, Râwul of Bhownugger, died at Seehore in A.D. 1845. About that time Nâroobâ, his younger half-brother, had employed five-and-twenty Brahmins at Bhownugger in the performance of certain religious ceremonies. Dâdbâ also had visited Bhownugger, shortly before his death, to be present at the annual ceremony of the Râwul's worshipping the sea, and it was there that he was taken ill. The people of Seehore, putting these facts together, came to the conclusion that Nâroobâ had employed the Brahmins to take away his brother's life by charms, and that Nâneebâ, the mother of Nâroobâ, had put vetches, charmed for the purpose, among the flowers which were scattered upon the young chief during the celebration. Dâdbâ's mother collected a crowd of persons, strangers, and people of the country, Brahmins, Jutees, and Fukeers, who were supposed to be possessed of skill in charms, and offered them any sum of money she possessed to save the life of her son. The essayist, from whom our account of these popular beliefs is mostly derived, was one of the Brahmins thus called in by the rânee. They were altogether about a hundred in number. The Brahmins sprinkled an image of Muhâ Dev, muttering a charm, called "the conqueror "of death;" some of them worshipped "the Crane-faced Devee," and other goddesses. A Wâneeo, from Calcutta, who was present, distinguished himself by the variety of his resources. Prince Dâdbâ, however, died, notwithstanding all the means employed to prolong his life. It was then currently reported that Nâroobâ had made a fire-sacrifice, in which he had offered goats with their mouths stuffed full of rice in the husk, and that the Brahmins whom he had employed had washed themselves in oil and blood. The principal of these Brahmins, a person named Geerjâ Shunker, was so apprehensive that the friends of the deceased prince would put him to death, that he procured five soldiers from Nâroobâ to remain continually with him for his protection. He is, to this day, pointed at by people as the Brahmin who destroyed Prince Dâdbâ by his charms.

Many similar instances of the employment of "Mârun Muntra" are believed to have happened—in fact, whenever a person dies a sudden death, it is supposed that he has been destroyed by this charm. It is also believed that "Mârun Muntras" have the power of causing trees to wither or rocks to split, and of producing many other effects which it would be an endless task to describe.

"Mohun Muntras" are described in the Shâstras, but the people of Goozerat, it would appear, have much more knowledge of the matter at the present time than the writers of these works were possessed of. Those who are skilled in the use of this charm will throw a jewel into a well, and reproduce it again from another place, and will mention the names of persons whom, it might be supposed, they had never heard of. They will also burn clothes to rags, and produce them again entire; they will cause a mango tree to spring up in a moment create a snake out of a piece of leather, change pebbles into silver coins, produce various articles from an empty hand, and perform many other achievements of the like nature which the spectators believe impossible without the assistance of a Dev.

By the "Stumbhun Muntra," it is said, an advancing army may be stopped, the voice may be taken away from an instrument of music, the skill of an opposing disputant snatched from him, the course of running water arrested, a flying thief compelled to stand.

The following story is commonly told in regard to the "Âkurshun Muntra":—A certain rânee had sent her maid into the market to purchase some scented oil. The maid, as she returned, met a Jutee, who asked permission to dip a straw into the oil: and on her allowing him to do so stirred the oil, muttering the Âkurshun Muntra all the while. The maid, unaware of what had been done, carried the oil to her mistress; but the latter, having taken it into her hand, observed that the oil revolved in the vessel, and inquired of the maid who had met her on the road. The maid said that Gooroojee had dipped a straw into the oil, but that she had met no one but him. The rânee threw the oil upon a large stone, which in the night, owing to the power of the charm, travelled away to the Jutee's convent. When the raja was made aware of what had happened, he put the monk to death.

It was by this charm, as we have seen, that Umur Singh Shewuro, the adviser of Bheem Dev II., "drew to himself men, women, and "Devs." His master also was accused of dealing in charms.[1]

A certain raja, it is said, had two rânees. A Brahmin, gave to each of them a Wusheekurun note, in which he had written, "If the elder "queen be preferred, it is all right, and if the younger be preferred "then, too, it is all right." Both rânees were satisfied that they had obtained what they desired. The raja having got scent of the matter had the notes taken out of the lockets, and the contents of them read when they afforded matter for laughter. Similarly, persons pretending to occult science when consulted by women who were desirous of giving birth to sons, have been known to present them with charmed notes, which were not to be opened until the child was born. In these notes they wrote "*pootra nuheen pootree*," which may be read, "not a son but a daughter," or vice versâ. Sometimes the wise man tells the father, under a pledge of secrecy, that his child will be a son, and the mother, under a similar pledge, that it will be a daughter. When the event occurs the disappointed party is informed that he or she had not faith, and that the coming event was on that account concealed from them.[2]

[1] *Vide* pp. 161-62.

[2] Andrews, in his continuation of Dr. Henry's History of Great Britain, p. 383, quoting Scot's Discovery of Witchcraft, says: "The stories which our facetious author relates of ridiculous charms, which, by help of credulity operated wonders, are extremely laughable. In one of them a poor woman is commemorated who cured all diseases by muttering a certain form of words over the party afflicted; for which service she always received one penny and a loaf of bread. At length, terrified by menaces of flames, both in this world and the next, she owned that her whole conjuration consisted in these potent lines, which she always repeated in a low voice near the head of her patient:—

"Thy loaf in my hand,
"And thy penny in my purse,
"Thou art never the better—
"And I—am never the worse."

The reader will recollect the use made of these lines in one of the closing scenes

We may describe one more charm, which is very commonly used in exorcising Bhoots : it is a Boudhist charm, and is called that of Ghuntâ Kurun Veer, or "the bell-eared spirit." The rites employed in the construction of this charm must be commenced in the light or the dark half of the month, according as the result sought to be obtained is innocent or noxious. The magician takes his place in a garden, a temple, or some well purified place in a house: he must be quite private. He first washes his body, repeating this muntra :—

Hring, Hring, Kling—praise to the water of Ganges !

Then he proceeds to dress himself in clean clothes muttering another muntra :

Om, Hring, Kling, praise to Ânund Dev !

Next he worships the ground, saying :

Om, Hring, Shring, praise to the earth and the other Devs !

He now seats himself and burns incense, lights lamps of oil and clarified butter, reflects upon Ghuntâ Kurun Veer, and draws upon paper or palmyra leaf a portrait of him with bells in his ears, around which he writes the following charm, which he repeats :

" Om ! I praise Ghuntâ Kurun, the great Veer, the destroyer of all " diseases. If eruptions on the body cause alarm, save us, save us, " mighty one ! From where thou standest, O Dev ! pictured amid

of the " Bride of Lammermoor." See also an oracular answer of this kind in Sir George Head's translation of " Apuleius."

It is told of the first of the English architects, that when he had completed the building of Windsor Castle, he caused these words to be inscribed on one of the walls :—

" This made Wykeham."

His enemies endeavoured to represent this as a proof of his arrogance, but Wykeham adroitly explained his meaning to be, not that he had made the castle, but that the castle had been the making of him.

The answer given to Crœsus when he marched against Cyrus is well known : " Crœsus, by passing the Halys, will overthrow a great kingdom !" Crœsus supposed by this that he should overthrow the power of the enemy, but, in reality, he overthrew his own power. In either event the oracle would have appeared true.

So also in Shakspeare :—

" 'The Duke yet lives, that Henry shall depose ;
But him outlive, and die a violent death.'
Why, this is just,
Aio te, Æacida, Romanos vincere posse."

Second Part of King Henry VI., Act I. *sc.* 4.

"lines of letters, thence fly diseases of breath, bile, or phlegm. There "dread of the raja exists not. He whose ear receives the sound "of thy charms, in him Shâkeenee, Bhoot, Vyetâl, or Râkshus finds "no place to dwell—no unseasonable death is there for him; no snake "bites him; fire and thieves cause him no alarm. Hring! O Ghuntâ "Kurun, I worship thee! Tah, tah, tah, Swâhâ!"

This muntra must be repeated thirty-three thousand times in forty-two days. Fire sacrifice is then performed, and the virtue of the charm is complete. The Ghuntâ Kurun charm, if worn in a locket, protects the wearer from all tyranny on the part of Bhoots, Prets, or mortal oppressors: it procures a man wisdom; brings his enemy into subjection to him; or even (which is sometimes a more difficult matter) subdues to him his own wife. It is sometimes posted against the wall of a house for the purpose of excluding snakes, rats, and other vermin, as well as Bhoots.[1]

[1] Plutarch mentions the *Bulla*, which was suspended from the necks of the more noble Roman boys, as a *phylactery*, or "*preservative* of good order, and as it were a bridle on incontinence." But it is not improbable that some of the Jews in our Saviour's time, as they certainly did afterwards, regarded their phylacteries as amulets or charms, which would keep or *preserve* them from evil. There is a remarkable passage in a rabbinical Targum, written about 500 years after Christ, which may both serve to illustrate what our Lord says, Matt. xxiii. 5, and to shew what was the notion of the more modern Jews concerning their phylacteries. It runs thus:—"The congregation of Israel hath said, I am chosen above all people, "because I bind the *phylacteries* on my left hand and on my head, and the *scroll* "is fixed on the right side of my door, the third part of which is opposite to my "bed-chamber, *that the evil spirits may not have power to hurt me.*"—See Parkhurst's Greek Lexicon; also Bishop Patrick, and Calmet, quoted by D'Oyly and Mant, in a note on the passage in St. Matthew.

Many houses in Edinburgh, built previously to the Reformation, have legends over the door, such as "*In thee, O Lord is all my traist;*" "*In Deo est honor et* "*gloria;*" "*Blissit be ye Lord in al his giftis.*" They are said to have been placed there as charms or talismans, with a view to exclude evil spirits from the houses, and this tradition appears to receive confirmation from the circumstance that the name of the Deity is always introduced.—See Chambers's Traditions of Edinburgh.

"The early Christians," observes St. Ephrem, "marked their very doors with "the precious and life-giving cross," as the Jews before them had been in the habit of striking the lintel and the two side posts with the blood of the paschal lamb. We have ourselves frequently seen, in a Mohummedan house, scraps of the Koran pasted near the door to keep out the cholera.

In their expedition in search of the sources of the Niger, the Landers stopping at a village called Moussa, occupied a large round hut, which they thus describe (vol. i., p. 217):—"In the centre of it is the trunk of a large tree, which supports the "roof; it has two apertures for doors, which are opposite each other; and directly "over them, suspended from the wall, are a couple of charms, written in the "Arabic character on bits of paper, *which are to preserve the premises from being destroyed by fire.*"—See also vol. ii. of the same work, pp. 231—2.

The apparently meaningless and unconnected jargon of which these muntras are composed is, notwithstanding, said to be constructed and used according to a system possessing almost scientific regularity. Our author asserts that Bhoots are less numerous in the present day than they were formerly. One of the causes which are popularly supposed to have produced this effect is sufficiently amusing. "Some ignorant people suppose that Bhoots fled away from the "noise of the English drum, because on one side of it there is cow-"skin (at the sound of which the Hindoo Devtâs took to flight), "and on the other side pigskin (which frightened away the Mo-"hummedan divinities); and this, they say, is the reason that Bhoots "have diminished in number and muntras proved false." Similarly, Claudius Buchanan, in his journal of visits to certain churches of the St. Thome Christians, tells us that he observed that the bells of most of their churches were placed within the building and not in a tower: "the reason, they said was this: when a Hindoo temple "happens to be near a church, the Hindoos do not like the bell to "sound loud; for they say it frightens their god."[1]

In Russia a still more practical use is made of a similar religious charm. "The "tradesmen in many instances, particularly those of the public bazaars, do not "reside at their business premises (Hindoo-like), which are thus left without pro-"tection, but though availing themselves of all the precautions of bolts and bars, "they trust less to them than to the superstition of their countrymen. They affix "seals to their doors and window shutters; and as St. Nicholas, the national "saint, is supposed to be peculiarly the protector of such securities, no thief would "venture to commit the sacrilege of breaking them, while bars and chains would "offer no impediment of his violence." * * * "In the days of paganism the "worship of Mercury would have been analogous."—Russia, by Thompson: Smith, Elder, and Co., 1848.

[1] Hindoos will sometimes stop their ears when they hear the Muezzin's call to prayers. The Sikh government positively prohibited its being pronounced aloud. *Vide* Shore's Notes on Indian Affairs, vol. ii. p. 412.

When, in the middle of the ninth century, the Christian church secured, through the instrumentality of St. Anschar, complete toleration in Jutland, "it obtained, "amongst other privileges, the free use of bells, which the heathen, in dread of "sorcery, would never before permit." The soul-bell in England, which was rung while the corpse was conducted to the church, and during the bringing it out of the church to the grave, was supposed to scare away the devils.—*Vide* Brand's Popular Antiquities. The Trolls have been almost all driven out of Scandinavia by the ringing of the bells in the church steeples, and the Korrigans of Brittany seem to have been rendered very insecure in their position from the same cause.—*Vide* Keightley's Fairy Mythology.

NOTE A.

The following remarks upon the Bhoot Nibundh are from an article on "Daimoniac Possession, Oracles, and Medical Thaumaturgy in India," published in the first number of the Bombay Quarterly Magazine and Review, in October, 1850 :—

"Previously to the appearance of the *Bhoot Nibundh*, a series of papers was commenced in the *Dublin University Magazine*, and has since been continued, though unfortunately at intervals too wide apart[1] for the unity of the subject, on WAREN, a term used among the Mahrattas to comprehend the whole field of pneumatology—*Waren* literally corresponding with *πνεῦμα*—under the spiritual machinery of a dual possession, possession malignant and demoniac, possession beneficent and divine; though this apparent duality the writer maintains to be merely on the surface, and to indicate rather two stages of human culture; whether these different stages succeed each other at different periods, as regards the whole mass of society, or co-exist in its various component parts at one time, producing on the mass at different epochs, or on different classes of men at one and the same epoch, two very divergent spiritual impressions, from the same physical and psychological phenomena. The *Bhoot Nibundh* affords ample confirmation of the facts alleged in these papers on *Waren*, which were at first received with some degree of surprise, if not of incredulity, among European readers living far alike from the scene of such occurrences, and from that epoch of civilization in which alone they could have place, and who, from education, had been accustomed to a view of daimoniac possessions not perhaps in its inmost significance materially different from that taken by the writer, but extremely so as to the mode, the order, and the immediate instruments of the spiritual agency or influence,—(the dominion of that murderer from the beginning, who hath the power of death, and goeth about *sicut leo rugiens*, scourging and oppressing man under *every* form of permitted physical evil)—which all alike acknowledge to be exerted in these manifestations.

"Among the Cingalese the same beliefs and nearly the same processes obtain as among the Mahrattas and the people of Goozerat. An English clergyman, resident in Ceylon, who had long observed, with wonder and interest, the prevalence and influence of these singular ideas among the surrounding population, recognised in the descriptions of Waren the very phenomena which had so often attracted his attention in his own locality, and bore testimony to a traveller, whose letter is now before us, to the identity of the two systems.

"They are not, however, even at this day, wholly limited to India. The performances of the fasting chiefs of the Native American tribes, and of the Siberian magicians, as described by recent travellers, bear a considerable resemblance to those attributed to the Bhukts who court and attain to *Waren*.

"But perhaps the most singular and complete analogy to the Hindoo system of Bhoots is to be found in a quarter where we should have been little prepared to meet it in the nineteenth century. In the course of last year, two or three long papers appeared in the *Dublin University Magazine*, on the Popular Superstitions of the Irish; and the details there given regarding the class of fairies called SIDDS, or earth-deities, and their power over human bodies, exhibit a wonderful correspondence, not only in the general train of popular thought, but sometimes even in the most minute and singular particulars,—especially the possession of women, alienated consciousness, fevers, and other obstinate or anomalous kinds of

[1] Ranging from March, 1848, to April, 1850.

disease,—with those described in the *Waren* papers and the *Bhoot Nibundh.* It is both curious and satisfactory to see the facts stated in the first attempt to portray the daimonology of India, many of them of a very singular character, confirmed by parallelisms in places so remote from each other. We might indeed have expected *à priori,* that the daimonological creed, and manifestations witnessed in the villages of the Dekkan and Konkun, should have their correlatives in those of Brahminical Goozerat, and even in Buddhistical Ceylon; we might not have been violently surprised to discover analogous effects produced by violent religious, or rather fanatical excitement, among the sublime forests and cataracts which are the home of the Indian savage, or on the dreary steppes of Siberia, among races whom no ray of divine knowledge, or diviner love, has ever visited; but it is truly astonishing to find the very same beliefs prevailing, though under a supernatural drapery slightly different, in a Christian island so remote from Hindoostan,

'—— partita del mundo, ultima Irlanda.' "

The original meaning of the word "Bhoot" is "an element." Bhoots are not, in Goozerat at least, regarded as "devils," (the idea of a spiritual arch-enemy of God and man having there no existence), but rather as *daimons,* "spirits of men or "women deceased,—human ghosts in fact,—still unhappily entangled in human "passions, desires, or anxieties:—

'Alas! poor ghost!'

"and seeking to inflict pain, to practice delusion, or to enjoy pleasure, through "the instrumentality of a living human body, of which they take temporary "possession."

In other parts of India they are known under different forms. "The worship "of demons," says the Abbé Dubois, speaking of the Hindoos of Mysore, "is "universally established and practised among them. They call them *Bhuta,* "which also signifies *element;* as if the elements were, in fact, nothing else but "wicked spirits personified, from whose wrath and fury all the disturbances of "nature arise. Malign spirits are also called by the generic names of *Pisacha* and "*Daitya.*

"In many parts we meet with temples specially devoted to the worship of "wicked spirits. There are districts also in which it almost exclusively pre-"dominates. Such is that long chain of mountains which extend on the west of "the Mysore, where the greater part of the inhabitants practice no other worship "than that of the devil. Every house and each family has its own particular "Bhuta, who stands for its tutelary god; and to whom, daily, prayers and pro-"pitiatory sacrifices are offered, not only to incline him to withhold his own "machinations, but to defend them from the evils which the Bhutas of their "neighbours or enemies might inflict. In those parts the image of the demon is "everywhere seen, represented in a hideous form, and often by a shapeless stone. "Each of these fiends has his particular name, and some who are more powerful "and atrocious than others, are preferred in the same proportion.

"All evil demons love bloody offerings; and, therefore, their ardent wor-"shippers sacrifice living victims, such as buffaloes, hogs, rams, cocks, and the "like. When rice is offered, it must be tinged with blood; and they are also "soothed with inebriating drinks. In offerings of flowers, the red only are "presented to them.

"The worship of the Bhutas, and the manner of conducting it, are explained "in the fourth Veda of the Hindoos, called Atharwana Veda, and it is on this "account very carefully concealed by the Brahmins.

"I have very generally found that the direct worship of demons is most "prevalent in deserts, solitary places, and mountainous tracts; the reason of "which is, that in such parts the people are less civilized than those of the plains, "more ignorant and timid, and therefore more prone to superstition. They are "therefore more easily led to attribute all their misadventures and afflictions to "the displeasure of their demon.

"Many hordes of savages, who are scattered among the forests on the coast of "Malabar, and in the woods and mountains of Kadu, Kuruberu, Soligueru, and "Iruler, acknowledge no other deity but the Bhutas."

The following occurs in the tenth report of the German Evangelical Mission, in the same part of the country, printed at Bangalore in 1850:—

"At Uchilla, a village thirty miles to the north of Bangalore, a small congregation "has been gathered within the last year, and a large piece of waste land was "kindly granted to the Mission some time ago. Corajea Pujari, one of the great "men of that neighbourhood, has given up his idolatry, destroyed his *Bhuta* "temple, and come over to the side of the Gospel." Then follows the case of "Fakire, a Billavur," of the village of Bolma, who, after long deliberation, "at "last felt love for the Gospel, but for another year kept perfect silence, until three "weeks ago, when his parents desired him to worship the house *Bhuta*, by "submitting himself to be possessed according to the custom. Then, at once, he "declared that he would no longer so degrade himself,—that all this worship was "a lie and a sin."

The Rev. Mr. Caldwell, in his most interesting account of the Shanars of Tinnevelly (a country still further south than Mysore, and adjacent to Cape Comorin) seems to distinguish between "demons" of two classes, the latter of which (though he still calls them "devils") almost exactly correspond with the Bhoots of Goozerat. The former, he says, are forms of Kâlee, and particularly of Bhudra of Kâlee, and are known by the name of "Ammen," or mother; their worship is marked by some distinctive peculiarities, and probably resembles that of the *Mâtâs*, or local goddesses, the Boucherâjee, the Khodeeâr, &c. of Goozerat; "a large majority, however, of the devils are of purely Shanar or Tamil origin, "and totally unconnected with Brahminism in any of its phases or modifications," and of these he gives the following description:—

"The majority of the devils are supposed to have been originally human beings; "and the class of persons most frequently supposed to have been transformed "into devils are those who have met with a sudden or violent death, especially "if they had made themselves dreaded in their lifetime." See the case of Sooruj-mul of Chândunee, p. 460.) "Devils may in consequence be either male "or female, of low or high caste, of Hindoo or foreign lineage. Their character "and mode of life seem to be little, if at all, modified by differences of this "nature. All are powerful, malicious, and interfering; and all are desirous of "bloody sacrifices and frantic dances. The only differences apparent are in the "structure of the temple or image built to their honor, the insignia worn by their "priests, the minutiæ of the ceremonies observed in their worship, the preference "of the sacrifice of a goat by one, a hog by another, and a cock by a third, or in "the addition of libations of ardent spirits, for which Pariar demons stipulate. "As for their abode, the majority of the devils are supposed to dwell in trees; "some wander to and fro, and go up and down in uninhabited wastes, some skulk "in shady retreats. Sometimes they take up their abode in the rude temples "erected to their honor, or in houses; and it often happens that a devil will "take a fancy to dispossess the soul and inhabit the body of one of his votaries; "in which case the personal consciousness of the possessed party ceases, and the "screaming, gesticulating, and pythonizing, are supposed to be the demon's acts."

Bhoots are to be met with it would appear, also, in northern Hindoostan:—"Besides these drawbacks to the holding office in Chota Nagpore," says a writer on the north-western provinces in India, "there was another, and to some minds, "a much greater evil to be incurred. The belief in spells, incantations, and "magic, is rife throughout all India; nor are the most educated free from this "delusion. It is universally credited in the more civilized parts of the country "that the people of the south are powerful in spells, and that among the hills and "forests, ghosts or 'bhoots,' a kind of mischievous devils, abound."[1]

Bishop Gobat, in his "Journal of a Residence in Abyssinia," alludes to the belief, prevalent in that country, in a race of "Sorcerers" (as he terms them), called by the natives "Boudas."

It is supposed that these Boudas "render themselves invisible at pleasure; that "when any one kills an ox, &c., he often finds an empty part in it, or full of "water, which ought to have been filled with flesh—it is the Boudas who have "eaten it; that men, without illness, and with a good appetite, become like "skeletons—they are internally devoured by the Boudas; and, especially, "that hyænas are often killed whose ears are pierced, sometimes even they have "earrings." The Abyssinians believe that the greater part of the hyænas are Boudas metamorphosed, and that persons, under the influence of Boudas, utter cries resembling the howling of the hyæna. They believe, also, that all the Falashas (a tribe of Jews), many Mussulmans, and even some Christians are Boudas. Dr. Gobat relates that, when he was suffering from a violent attack of fever, he was supposed by the persons who attended him to be under the influence of these sorcerers. It appears that the Bishop was successful in persuading the people about him that there were really no *human* beings who could make themselves invisible, or assume the form of hyænas to prey upon their fellow men, but that he was unable to persuade them that Boudas did not exist, or that they had not the power of occasioning diseases. Dr. Gobat was, perhaps, by no means curious in examining what the theory of these Abyssinians really was, but, from the replies which he has reported to his arguments, it appears probable that the people believed in other Boudas besides these human ones, and identified them with the dæmons or evil spirits of the New Testament. The similarity between Bhoots and Boudas, in both name and character, suggests the inquiry whether both may not have had a common origin in the days of the now almost forgotten traffic between the shores of India and the once powerful Abyssinian empire.

Dr. Gobat remarks (and it is an illustration of the practical effect of superstition in rendering people unhappy) that the Abyssinians are usually of a sprightly character, "but when they are indisposed they are doubly miserable from, the "idea that they are under the influence of sorcerers and evil spirits."

Nathaniel Pearce, in his "Small but true Account of the Ways and Manners "of the Abyssinians," published in vol. iii. of the Transactions of the Literary Society of Bombay, has the following on the same subject:—

"There are various kinds of complaints in Abyssinia, which, they say, are caused "by the devil, one of which I shall give a true account of. One, called *buder* in "Tegri, and *tubbih* in Ammerrer, I think myself is only convulsions, similar to "people I have seen troubled with fits in my own country; but they say to the con-"trary, and will have it that the complaint is caught from the people who work in "iron, such as make knives, spears, ploughshares, &c., and those who work in

[1] Benares Magazine, vol. iii., p. 340—Article, "Recollections of an official visit "to the Ramgurh District."

"making earthenware. Those people all go by the name of *buder* and *tubb:h*, and "are hated worse than Mussulmen, and, though they profess the Christian religion, "they are not allowed to receive the Sacrament."

Pearce then goes on to describe the *tegretier*, another complaint in regard to which he admits that he thinks "the devil must have some hand in it." It may be noted that *tubbihs* and *buders* are probably transpositions merely of the same word.

On the subject of Fetish possessions in Africa, *vide* "Lander's Travels," vol. ii., pp. 120, 123—126, 231.

The following contains an account of Bhoots in Tonquin :—

"*Tay-bou* (in *Tonquin*, in the *Indies*, towards *China*), the name of one of the two "great magicians, who makes the people believe that he can foretell things to come; "so that, when they desire to marry their children, to buy any land, or undertake "any considerable business, they consult him as an oracle.

"He keeps a book filled with the figures of men, beasts, circles and triangles, "and three pieces of brass, with some characters on one side only : these he puts "into three cups, and, having shaken them, throws them out upon the ground, "and, if the characters lie uppermost, he cries out that the person will be the hap-"piest person in the world ; but if, on the contrary, they lie undermost, it is ac-"counted as a very bad omen.

"If one or two of the characters lie uppermost, then he consults his book, and "tells what he thinks ; he also pretends to know the causes of distempers, when "they that consult him are sent to him by the *Tay-Bau* (*Phou?*) ; and pretends to "call the souls of the dead out of the bodies to which they are troublesome.

"*Tay-Phou-Thony* (at *Tonquin*), the name of the other *magician*, to whom they "have recourse in their sickness ; if he says the devil is the occasion of the distem-"per, then he orders them to sacrifice, offering him a table well furnished with rice "and meat, which the *magician* knows how to make use of ; if, after this, the sick "does not recover, all the friends and kindred of the sick person, with several sol-"diers, surround the house, and discharge their muskets thrice to frighten the evil "spirit away.

"The *magician* makes the patient (especially if a seaman or fisherman lies sick) "sometimes foolishly believe that he is troubled by the god of water, then he or-"ders that tapestries be spread and huts built, and good tables kept for three days, "at certain distances from the sick man's house to the next river, to induce this "dæmon to retire and see him safe into his dominions again.

"But, the better to know the cause of these distempers, this *magician* sends "them very often to the *Tay-Bou*, who answers that they are the souls of the "dead that cause the sickness, and promises that he will use his art to draw off "these troublesome ghosts to himself and make them pass into his own body (for "they believe the transmigration of souls), and when he catches that ghost that "did the mischief he shuts it up in a bottle of water, until the person is cured ; if "the person recovers, the *magician* breaks the bottle and sets the ghost at liberty "to go whither it will. And if the person dies, after the *magician* has enjoined the "ghost to do no more harm, he sends it away."—*N. Bailey's English Dictionary*, by Mr. Buchanan, fifth edition. London : W. Johnston, Ludgate-street, 1760.

As Bailey's work is not now very common, we take the present opportunity of quoting from it the following curious and interesting article on the transmigration of souls, which contains much that is to our purpose :—

"Metempsychosis—the transmission of souls from one body to another ; what-"ever the modern Jews may say of it, it is not taught in any place either of the "Old or New Testament.

"There is great probability that the Jews imbibed this notion in Chaldea, during "their long captivity in Babylon, or from that intercourse they had with the Greeks, "who themselves had borrowed it from the Orientals. It is certain that at the "time of Jesus Christ this opinion was very common among the Jews. This "appears plain from their saying that some thought Jesus Christ to be John the "Baptist, others Elias, others Jeremias or some of the old prophets. And when "Herod the tetrarch heard speak of the miracles of Jesus Christ, he said that John "the Baptist, whom he had beheaded, was risen again.

"Josephus and Philo, who are the most ancient and the most knowing of all "the Jews, next to the sacred authors, now extant, speak of the metempsychosis "as an opinion that was very common in their nation. The Pharisees held, "according to Josephus, that the souls of good men might easily return into "another body after the death of that they had forsaken. He says elsewhere "that the souls of wicked men sometimes enter into the bodies of living men, "whom they possess and torment. Philo says that the souls that descended out "of the air into the bodies which they animate return again into the air after the "death of those bodies; that some of them always retain a great abhorence for "matter, and dread to be plunged again into bodies; but that others return with "inclination, and follow the natural desire of which they are influenced. The "Jewish doctors wrap this doctrine up in obscure and mysterious terms. They "believe that God has determined for all souls a degree of perfection to which they "cannot attain in the course of one life only; that they are therefore obliged to "return several times upon the earth, and to animate several bodies successively, "that they may fulfil all righteousness, and practice the commandments, both "negative and affirmative, without which they cannot arrive at the state to "which God intends they should come. Whence is it, they say, that we see "some people die in the most vigorous time of their youth? It is because they "have already acquired their degree of perfection, and have nothing remaining to "be done in a frail and mortal body. Others, like Moses, they say, die with "reluctance, because they have not yet accomplished all their duties. Others, on "the contrary, like Daniel, die with satisfaction, aud even desire death, because "nothing remains for them to do in this world.

"The Metempsychosis, or revolution of souls, is performed after two manners. "The first is when a soul comes into a body already animated—thus it was that "Herod the tetrarch imagined that the soul of John the Baptist was entered into "the body of Jesus Christ in order to work miracles. At other times they say "souls enter into other bodies already animated, there to acquire some new degree "of perfection which they wanted; thus they said the soul of Moses to be united "to that of the Messiah, &c. The second manner of transmigration is when a "soul enters into a body newly formed, either to expiate some crime it had "committed in another body, or to acquire a greater degree of sanctity. The Jews "think this revolution is performed at least three or four times. They say that "some souls of a more exalted nature have a great contempt for matter, and do "not return to animate bodies but with great reluctance. Others, that are more "gross and carnal, always preserve an inclination towards the body, and return "thither often without any reason but to gratify this desire. They even extend "this transmigration to brute beasts and to inanimate things: and the number is "not small of those that maintain this opinion. The most famous of the Jewish "doctors have held it, and pretend that Pythagoras, Plato, and Virgil, and the "ancient philosophers that espoused it, had derived it from the writings of their "prophets.

"This notion is very ancient in the East. The Chinese teach that Xekiah, an "Indian philosopher, who was born about 1000 years before Jesus Christ, was "the first broacher of this doctrine in the Indies; that from thence it spread into "China, in the 56th year after Jesus Christ. The Chinese pretend that Xekiah "was born 8000 times, and that at his last birth he appeared in the form of a "white elephant. It is upon this principle that the Indians and Chinese are so "little scrupulous of putting themselves to death, and that they so often kill their "children when they find themselves under any difficulty of maintaining them. It "is related that a king of this country having had the smallpox, and seeing his face "to be much disfigured, could not endure any longer to live under such a frightful "figure, but ordered his brother's son to cut his throat, who afterwards was burnt. "The story of the Indian philosopher, Calanus, is well known, who burned himself "in the time of Alexander the Great. The Indians look upon death with much in-"difference, being persuaded of the metempsychosis, which passes among them as a "thing not to be doubted. Hence it is that they abstain from killing any living "creature, for fear of violating the souls of their fathers, or of some near relation in-"habiting those animals. They do not so much as defend themselves against wild "beasts, and charitably redeem animals out of the hands of strangers who are "about to kill them."

NOTE B.

As a witness in favour of the philosophic and incredulous view, we may call Bentham. "If, says that author, we go deeper into the human breast, we shall "find in it a secret disposition to believe the marvellous as if it extended our "power and gave us the command of supernatural means. Besides, when these "beings of pure creation are the subject, reason is not sufficiently unbiassed to "scrutinize the testimony. Fear comes in the way; doubt appears dangerous; we "are afraid lest we offend these invisible agents; and there are numerous stories "in the public mouth of the vengeance which they have taken on unbelievers. "These are the causes which have established the belief in spectres, ghosts, "*possessed persons*, devils, vampires, magicians, sorcerers,—all those frightful beings "who have ceased to play a part in courts, but still appear in the cottage."

The effects to which a perverted belief in supernatural agencies may lead has been described by Heber, in his usual mellow and musical tones; but he is far from recommending on that account an incredulity which is opposed to the highest of all authority:—

"A belief in evil spirits, whether true or false, is one of a gloomy and disquieting "character. It is one which may produce the worst results when indiscreetly and "too curiously contemplated: it has drawn some into the most loathsome guilt, and "plunged others into the acutest suffering; it has been the usual source of religious "and magical imposture; and its abuses may be traced through innumerable shades "of human misery, from the fears of childhood to the ravings of frenzy. * * *

"But," continues the same author, "if in the history of the supposed demoniac "of Gadara, we apprehend no other person to be concerned but our Lord and His "distracted patient; if it were no more than the diseased imagination of the "sufferer which answered in the demon's name; and if it were the ravings of "frenzy only which desired that his tormentor might take shelter in the swine, can "we suppose that our Lord, not content with simple acquiescence, not content with "conforming his speech to the hallucination of the frantic man, would, by afflicting "the herd with a like disease, have miraculously confirmed the delusion."

"In this reasoning age," says Bishop Horsley, "we are little agreed about "the cause of the disorder to which this name, possession, belongs. If we may "be guided by the letter of holy writ, it was a tyranny of hellish fiends over the "imagination and the sensory of the patient. For my own part, I find no great "difficulty of believing that this was really the case. I hold those philosophizing "believers but weak in faith, and not strong in reason, who measure the pro- "babilities of past events by the experience of the present age, in opposition to the "evidence of the historians of the times. I am inclined to think that the power "of the infernal spirits over the bodies as well as the minds of men suffered a "capital abridgement, an earnest of the final putting down of Satan to be trampled "under foot of men, when the Son of God had achieved His great undertaking; that "before that event men were subject to a sensible tyranny of the hellish crew, "from which they have been ever since emancipated. As much as this appears to "be implied in that remarkable saying of our Lord, when the seventy returned to "him expressing their joy that they had found the devils subject to themselves "through His name. He said unto them, 'I beheld Satan as lightning fall from "heaven.' Our Lord *saw* him fall from the heaven of his power: what wonder "then that the effects should no longer be perceived of a power which he hath "lost? Upon these general principles, without any particular inquiry into the "subject, I am contented to rest, and exhort you all to rest, in the belief, which "in the primitive Church was universal, that possession really was what the name "imports. Be that as it may, whatever the disorder was, its effects are undis- "puted,—a complication of epilepsy and madness, sometimes accompanied with a "paralytic affection of one or more of the organs of the senses; the madness, in "the worst cases, of the frantic and mischievous kind."

"There is one objection to this view of the matter which may still be urged," says a more modern author,[1] "namely, that if this possession is anything more "than insanity in its different forms, how comes it to pass that there are no "demoniacs now? that they have wholly disappeared from the world? But the "assumption that there are none, is itself one demanding to be proved. * * *

"Certainly in many cases of mania and epilepsy there is a condition very "analagous to that of the demoniacs, though the sufferer, and commonly the "physician, apprehend it differently."

Our next extract brings the matter very nearly home:—

"Moreover, we cannot doubt that the might of hell has been greatly broken by "the coming of the Son of God in the flesh; and with this a restraint set on the "grosser manifestations of its power: 'I beheld Satan as lightning fall from "heaven.' His rage and violence are continually hemmed in, and hindered by "the preaching of the Word, and ministration of the Sacraments. *It were another "thing even now in a heathen land*, especially in one where Satan was not left in "undisturbed possession, but wherein the great crisis of the conflict between light "and darkness was finding place through the first incoming there of the Gospel "of Christ. There we should expect very much to find, whether or not in such "great intensity, yet manifestations analogous to these. In a very interesting com- "munication from India, Rhenius, the Lutheran missionary, gives this as exactly "his own experience there,—namely, that among the native Christians, even "though many of them walk not as children of light, yet there is not this falling "under Satanic influence in soul and body which he traces frequently in the "heathen around him; and he shows by a remarkable example, and one in which "he is himself the witness throughout, how the assault in the name of Jesus on the "kingdom of darkness, as it brings out all forms of devilish opposition into

[1] Trench on the Miracles, in his chapter on "The Demoniacs in the country of "the Gadarenes," to which we must refer our readers for a full account of the matter.

"fiercest activity, so it calls out the endeavour to counterwork the truth through "men who have been made direct organs of the devilish will."

"These possessions," says, however, another authority,[1] "are not restricted to "professed heathens. I have met with several cases amongst persons who had "recently placed themselves under Christian instruction, and a few amongst native "Christians of longer standing, in which all the ordinary symptoms of possession, "as recognised by Shanars, were developed. This corresponds, I believe, with the "experience of most of the missionaries in Tinnevelly. The relatives in such cases "do not think themselves at liberty to attempt to exorcise the demon in the usual "way. Accordingly, the missionaries have sometimes been sent for to try the "effect of European remedies, and when they have interfered have generally suc-"ceeded, to the people's satisfaction as well as their own. Some of the posses-"sions yield by degrees to moral influences and alternatives; but in the majority "of cases the most effectual exorcism is—tartar-emetic.

"I do not contend that real demoniacal possessions never occur in heathen "countries. Where Satan rules without opposition, and where belief in the reality "and frequency in the possessions is so general, it is natural to suppose that "there must be some foundation for the belief. Popular delusions generally in-"clude a fact. My mind is open to receive evidence on the subject; and consider-"ing the number of astonishing cases that almost every native says he has been "told of by those who have seen them, I had hoped some day to witness something "of the kind myself. But I have not yet had an opportunity of being present "where preternatural symptons were exhibited, though I have sought for such an "opportunity for nearly twelve years, the greater part of the time in a devil-"worshipping community. This is the experience, as far as I have heard, of all "British and American missionaries, with the exception of one dubious case. Our "German brethren seem to have been more fortunate."

Mr. Caldwell and his friends, we may add, perhaps sought for too much evidence.

CHAPTER X.

THE STATE AFTER DEATH—HADES—PARADISE—FINAL EMANCIPATION.

THE mourners assemble on the evening of the funeral at the house of the deceased, where a Brahmin reads to them the Gurood Poorân; they come together every succeeding evening until this scripture has been read through. Therein Krishn has revealed to Gurood many tests by which the destination of the spirit after death may be infallibly ascertained. Some souls, as the deity has declared, pass at once to Paradise, others attain less perishable joys in the company of the finally emancipated. Of these highly favored beings we shall shortly have to speak, but we turn, for the present, to those more numerous

[1] The Rev. R. Caldwell, B.A., in his Sketch of the Tinnevelly Shanars.

spirits who tread the frequented pathway which leads to the gate of Yuma.

The souls of those who have not secured for themselves an unquestioned right of admission to either of the upper worlds are fated to pass through the valley of the shadow of death, and to appear before the judgment-seat of the sovereign of Hades. According to the predominance of their good deeds, or their crimes, they travel, it would seem, along roads of comparative comfort, or of various degrees of torment. The authors of the Poorân, being apparently of opinion that the human mind is more easily acted upon through its fears than through its hopes, have confined themselves almost exclusively to the description of the latter.

On the thirteenth day after decease the Pret, or newly-embodied spirit, is compelled by the emissaries of Hades to set forth on its journey towards Yumpoor. Its attendants aggravate the miseries of the wicked soul by their threats and upbraidings. They cry to the Pret, "Come quick, evil one! We will carry you to Yuma's door; we "will cast you into Koombheepâk, or some other hell!" Amidst such terrible omens the Pret, groaning "Alas! alas!" pursues its melancholy route, straining its ear to catch the lamentations of its friends, to which it clings, as to the last bond connecting it with earth, until increasing distance renders the mournful sound inaudible.

The city of Yuma is to the south, below the earth, and eighty-six thousand yojuns[1] from it. The roads by which the souls of the wicked are conducted thither are strewed with thorns, which lacerate the feet, or paved as if with heated copper. Along these painful ways, where no tree offers its shade to the weary traveller by day, and where no kindly hand guides him during the hours of darkness, the Pret is urged without any repose. He cries, "Alas! alas! O my son!" and reflects upon his crimes *in having made no gifts to Brahmins.* The servants of Yuma heap upon him annoyance, dragging him along as a harsh keeper drags a monkey. He groans within himself, "I have given nothing to Brahmins; I have offered no fire-"sacrifice; I have performed no penances; I have neglected the "worship of the Devs; I have paid no respect to Gungâ's streams, "which give liberation! Now, O body, suffer the recompense of "your deeds." And again: I have constructed no place of water, "where there was need of it, for men, birds, or animals; I have pre-"pared no pasturage for cattle; I have given no ordinary gifts; no

[1] The yojun is a measure of distance which different authorities make equal to four miles and a half, or to nine miles.

"gifts to cows; I have presented no one with the Veds or with the "Shâstras. Even the virtuous actions which I performed have not "remained in my possession!"

On the eighteenth day of its journey, the Pret arrives at Oograpoor, the first of the sixteen cities which stud the road to Hades. It is inhabited entirely by Prets. There is a river there called Pooshp Bhudrâ, and a large fig-tree beneath, where the servants of Yuma halt a day. Here the Pret receives such offerings as its relatives have presented in Shrâddh, or, if less fortunate, sits solitary, lamenting and upbraiding itself with its neglect in having failed to provide for this sad journey through a land where nothing can be purchased, and where there is no one who gives.

Another fortnight brings the Pret to Soureepoor, where Raja Jungum rules, who is as terrible as the Angel of Death. The trembling Pret makes here another halt, and receives the benefits of the Shrâddh performed that day upon earth. From this place, passing in its way the cities called Wurendra, Gundhurv, Siddhâgum, Kroor, and Krounch, the Pret proceeds to Vichitrâ-nugger, travelling day and night through a thick jungle, sometimes annoyed by a rain of stones, at other times oppressed with blows struck by invisible hands. Vichitrâ Raja, who is the brother of Yuma, rules in this city. When the Pret has left Vichitrâ-nugger it encounters the most appalling part of its journey—

"Hinc via, Tartarei quæ fert Acherontis ad undas."

It now takes the road to Vyeturunee, and it has also to endure the horrors of the Ushee-puttra Wun, a forest whose ever-falling leaves are long and sharp as sword-blades.

"The description of the mighty river, Vyeturunee, is," says Krishn, "a thing terrible to hear." The Pret, arriving at its banks, shrieks with agony when it beholds a river one hundred yojuns broad, whose sands are formed of the flesh of men and whose fetid streams, flowing with human blood and the filthy matter which exudes from ulcers, simmer as butter melting on the fire. In the river's bed, pools and rocks alternate; its depth is prodigious, and buoyancy deserts its floods when they are invited to sustain the sinner. Worms and lice abound therein, alligators and all monsters which infest the waters. The sky glows like a furnace, and for the unprotected sinner no shade is there but such as is to be derived from the out-stretched wings of carrion birds which sail in the air, and vultures whose beaks are iron. "O Gurood!" has Krishn exclaimed, himself apparently trembling at the horrors of the scene, "O Gurood! twelve suns pour forth, in that "fearful place, a heat such as shall be that of the conflagration of the "world."

Amidst these scenes of horror certain sinners, and in particular those who have neglected to employ any means for securing their passage across Vyeturunee, remain for ever. Those who are less miserable are received into the boats of a thousand Kyewurtts, who ferry them across the stream.

The cities which remain to be visited by the Pret, who has escaped the horrors of Vyeturunee are named Buhwâpud, Dookhud, Nânâkrund, Sootupt, Roudra, Pâyowurshun, Sheetâdya, and Bâhoo-Bheetee. In this latter it arrives at the end of a year's journey. Here, by the virtue of the sixteen shrâddhs, it obtains a new body, which is as high as from the elbow of a man to the tip of his finger, and at the same time the old body, which has been so far the travelling companion of the soul, vanishes, "as the divinity passed from Purshoo-"râm when he crossed weapons with Râm."

At this time the Supindee Shrâddh should be performed, which, in some cases, appears to produce actual emancipation. The soul rests in Bâhoo-Bheetee, and obtains a cessation of misery in proportion to the value of the religious gifts which it had presented while on earth.

One more stage, and the soul beholds spread before it the huge city of Yuma, extending to a length of one thousand yojuns. At the entrance thereof, surrounded by an iron wall, towers the mansion of Chitragoopt. On a magnificent throne, studded with pearls, sits this first of the servants of Yuma,—like Azrael the Arabian angel of death, counting the time which is allotted to human life, and recording the good deeds and the crimes of mortals. Around the residence of their chief dwell the ministers of human suffering, Jwur, Lootâ, Vishphotuk, the spirits of fever, leprosy, small-pox, and all the other diseases which afflict mankind, as of old they dwelt in the realms of the long-since dethroned sovereign of Erebus,—

> "Vestibulum ante ipsum, primisque in faucibus Orci
> "Luctus et ultrices posuere cubilia curæ;
> "Pallentesque habitant Morbi, tristisque Senectus,
> "Et Metus, et malesuada Fames, ac turpis Egestas,
> "Terribiles visu formæ."

These, all of them, are the satellites of Chitragoopt, and the messengers who, at his bidding, beckon the soul to Hades.

Yuma's city contains a celestial colony of Gundhurvs and Upsurâs. Thirteen Shruwuns, sons of Brumhâ, keep its gates. Their privilege it is to travel, Hecate-like, through heaven, earth, and hell; and upon them distance has no power in regard of either sight or sound. Such are the sentinels of Chitragoopt, who keep him informed of the actions of mortals. Their wives are of equal power with themselves. The Shruwuns, however,—for the mind which formed the Poorâns can conceive no being, reach he to whatever height of majesty, to be superior to such allurements,—are described as capable of being conciliated by certain gifts. One of them in particular, who bears the illustrious name of Dhurum-dwuj, or "Banner of Justice," is represented as speaking on behalf of the souls by whom he has been propitiated with gifts of the seven kinds of grain.

The palace of Yuma is fifty yojuns long, and twenty yojuns high. It is covered with jewels; the sweet sound of bells echoes through its courts; garlands of flowers ornament its doors; and flags wave over its battlements. Within, seated on a massive throne, the monarch of Pâtâl receives the souls, who are marshalled before his judgment-seat to the sound of the warlike conch-shell. The good behold in him a majestic sovereign; but to the eyes of the wicked, who tremble at the sight, he appears as a hideous fiend. Rising from his throne, he welcomes the former with respect, and soon dismisses them to the regions of Paradise; but, frowning upon the latter, he delivers them to his ministers, that they may cast them into the pits of hell, and there confine them,

> " to fast in fires
> " Till the foul crimes, done in their days of nature,
> " Are burnt and purged away."

The pits of hell are eighty-four hundred thousand in number; the principal hells are twenty-one, whose names are Rouruv, Muhâbheiruv, Tâmeesur, Undhtâmeesur, Koombheepâk, and others. The spirits having there suffered certain punishments, obtain bodies of four classes, each class of twenty-one hundred thousand kinds,[1] such as "Induj," or bodies born of eggs; "Oodbhij," which grow as vegetables; "Sweduj," which are generated of fluids; "Jurâyooj," which are produced by the conjunction of male and female.

Of the spirits whom Yuma dismisses to the upper worlds, some pass to Swerga or Dev-Lok; others, who have little virtue, remain among the unclean Devs, of which class are the Yukshes, Bheiruvs, Vyetâls, the Bhoots[2] which follow Shiva, and others. Female souls

[1] That is to say, perhaps, four classes of one hundred thousand apiece, in each of the twenty-one principal hells.

[2] Not to be confounded with the Bhoot which has been already described, and which is a far inferior spirit.

of little virture become Yuksheenees, Shâkeenees who follow Doorgâ, and other unclean Devees. The residence of the unclean spirits is Bhoowur-Lok, which is immediately above the earth.[1] Above Bhoowur-Lok again is Swerga, the Paradise of Indra, which requires a more particular description.

The author of "Curiosities of Literature" has placed among apparently ridiculous titles of honor bestowed on princes that of the Kandyan sovereign of "Dewo" (Dev), or, as he interprets it, "God." When Mr. D'Israeli saw something absurd in the application of this title to a king, he no doubt understood it in none of its less important meanings, but in that of the Supreme Being, the Sovereign of the universe.

The word Dev has not usually this exalted meaning. It is applied, as we have seen, to other sovereigns than the Kandyan, in much the same sense in which the title of Divus was applied to Julius or to Augustus, by the Romans, and indifferently to those monarchs whose names, like that of Koomâr Pâl, are cherished by their countrymen, and to those who have, like his bloody successor, after a reign of oppression and violence, "departed without being desired." The meaning, however, which is usually conveyed to the mind of a Hindoo by the word "Dev," is, first, indefinitely a dweller in any one of the upper worlds, and, secondly, more particularly an inhabitant of Swerga.

It is to Shiva or Vishnoo alone that prayers are made for that release from the continuing round of transmigration which is called "Moksh," or emancipation. In former days these divinities were not

[1] See Manu ii. 76. Also, "Prince of the power of the air," "Rulers of the "darkness of this world." St. Paul to the Ephesians, ii. 2, and vi. 12. On the latter passage, Mr. Valpy has the following :—

"It was a Jewish and popular opinion, which, as Mr. Mede observes, St. Paul "was disposed to approve, and Scripture seems to countenance, that the air or "sub-celestial regions were inhabited by the evil spirits."

Milton alludes to this in Paradise Lost, book x., 182, 190 :—

"So spake this oracle, then verified,
"When Jesus, son of Mary, second Eve,
"Saw Satan fall, like lightning, down from heaven,
"Prince of the air ; then, rising from his grave,
"Spoil'd principalities and powers, triumph'd
"In open show ; and, with ascension bright,
"Captivity led captive through *the air*,
"*The realm itself of Satan, long usurp'd ;*
"Whom he shall tread at last under our feet."

opposed to each other. "The poet," says Chund Bhârot, at the commencement of his epic,

> "has celebrated the praises of Huree ;
> "In the same strain he has also extrolled Hur.
> "Who pronounces Eesh and Shâm to be distinct,
> "That man will depart to Hell.
> "Higher than the high is the great splendor[1]
> "Which pertains to Nârâyun.
> "Never shall he approach it
> "Who reviles Muheshwur !"

But in the present day no individual addresses himself to both of these divinities. He must hold to the one and reject the other into a subordinate position. Thus it is practically the case that no Hindoo can apply the word Dev, in its sense of God, to more than one being.

Three hundred and thirty millions of Devs are, however, spoken of in the Hindoo scriptures. These are the occupants, at one particular point of time, of Swerga, the Paradise over which Indra rules—they are so far, however, from being gods that they are represented as envying those who precede them in the attainment of emancipation,[2] and it is only by straining the term that the title of King of Immortals can be applied to Indra. "These," saith the Geeta, "having through virtue reached the mansion of the King of the "Soors, feast on the exquisite heavenly food of the gods (Devs); *they "who have enjoyed this lofty region of Swerga, but whose virtue is ex-"hausted, revisit the habitation of mortals.*"[3] They are among those transient things of the poet's—

> "whose flow'ring pride, so fading and so fickle,
> "Short Time doth soon cut down with his consuming sickle."

They are not irrevocably stationed in Paradise, nor exempted from the necessity of being again born into this mortal world, and of undergoing, perhaps, repeated transmigrations. Their tenure of Swerga exhausted, they descend to earth, and their character of Dev is again clothed upon with that of mortal man. Hence, when the Hindoos behold a meteor falling from heaven, they believe that it is a Dev who has enjoyed the happiness which was the reward of his virtuous life in a former birth, and is now returning, with, alas! but feeble reminiscence of his more blessed state, to be reborn upon this earth.

[1] Moksh, that is, higher than Swerga.
[2] *Vide* p. 169.
[3] *Vide* Sir William Jones's Works, vol. xiii., p. 295.

Indra himself reigns only for a season, and then gives place to some other whom a hundred Ushwameds have fitted to fill the throne of heaven. He is, notwithstanding, during the duration of his power, a sublime sovereign ; the arch of Iris is his bow, the lightning is the glitter of his brandished weapons, and the deep-voiced thunder the rolling of his royal drum.

In the endeavour to realize the idea of a future state of happiness, human conception has never risen beyond the assembling into one place of the objects which men hold most dear in the present world. "Instead of using these merely as analogies, which might help them "to some vague conception of those, they take them for specific "earnests of the others."[1] The Hindoo conception of Swerga does not violate the general rule, although its inadequacy seems to have been perceived by its authors. The second of the four means of attaining perfection, indicated by the Vedânt-sâr, is the cultivation of "a distaste of all sensual pleasures, and even of the happiness enjoyed by the gods (Devs)."[2] In the city of Umurâwutee, the capital of Swerga, grows the tree of desire, which confers upon the denizens of Paradise the power of obtaining for themselves or others whatever, in that or the lower Loks, they seek to possess, and thus procures for them such honors as are derivable from the prayers of mortals for objects of terrestrial enjoyment. It is for these only that the Devs of Swerga are worshipped.

The Devs obtain, during their allotted term, bodies ever youthful and incapable of pain. Their food is umrut or ambrosia. Kâmdhenoo supplies them in perfection with all those products of the cow,

[1] *Vide* Sermons, chiefly expository, by Richard Edmond Tyrwhitt, M.A., Oxford: J. H. Parker, 1847. Vol. i., pp. 537—540.

Perhaps as good an illustration as can be readly selected of the truth of this remark is furnished by the following passage from "the Desatir," an apochryphal work, purporting to be "Sacred Writings of the Ancient Persian Prophets." Though the work be a forgery, the conception of heaven will be admitted to be eminently Persian :—

"In the heavens there is pleasure such as none but those who enjoy it can conceive. The lowest degree of enjoyment in heaven is such as is felt by the poorest "of men when he receives a gift equal to this whole lower world. Moreover, the "pleasures that arise in it, from the beauty of wives, and handmaids, and slaves, "from eating and drinking, from dress, and *fine carpets*, and commodious seats, is "such as cannot be comprehended in this lower world. To the celestials, the bounty "of the Most High Mezdam hath vouchsafed a body which admitteth not of "separation, which doth not wax old, and is susceptible of neither pain nor "defilement.—In the name of Lareng !"

[2] *Vide* Ward's Hindoos, vol. i., Introduction, p. v.

which are so indispensably necessary to Hindoo happiness. The Gundhurvs entertain them with celestial music. Nor are they deprived of the pleasures of love. As the Arabian Paradise has its Howris, and the Hall of Odin its Valkyriors, so the more ancient heaven of Indra boasts of its Upsurâs. Like the virgins of Valhalla, the choosers of the slain, the Upsurâs continually hover above the field of battle, ready to convey to Swerga the warriors who pass to heaven through its carnage. Nor is the zeal of the Rajpoot chieftains less sustained by faith than that of the soldiers of the crescent, who—

> "Risk a life with little loss,
> "Secure in Paradise to be,
> "By Howris loved immortally."

It is not, however, the death of the soldier[1] alone, which entitles to canonization as a Dev. He who dies at Broach, Prubhâs, Sidhpoor, or Aboo, attains to the heaven of Indra.[2] It is, however, the faithful only to whom these promises apply. *The wicked slaughterer of fish*, it is said, *daily beholds in vain the sanctifying streams of the Nerbudda*. He who settles annual grants upon priests carries with him to Paradise his father and mother, and the progenitors of both.

[1] The following is extracted from an account given at the time by a French party who humanely employed themselves in relieving wounded Russian soldiers as they lay on the field of Inkermann:—"A Pole, belonging to the Foreign "Legion, who happened to be present, asked some questions of the poor men. "They informed him that their popes and their officers had assured them that the "pagan enemies of the Holy Church of the Autocrat caused the Russian prisoners "to be put to the most frightful torture, and that such of the children of the Czar "as died in the sacred war would mount straight to Paradise, unless they were in "a state of sin, and in which case they would be again born in their own country."

[2] "The most renowned site of these Mongol sepulchres is in the province of "Chan-Si, by the famous Lama convent of the Five Towers; the ground is said "to be so holy, that those who are interred there are sure to effect an excellent "transmigration. This marvellous sanctity is attributed to the presence of old "Buddha, who has had his abode there, within the centre of a mountain, for some "ages. In 1842, Tokowra, of whom we have already spoken, transported thither "the bones of his father and mother, and had, according to his own account, the "happiness of viewing Buddha face to face, through a hole not larger than the mouth "of a pipe. He is seated in the heart of the mountain, cross-legged, and doing "nothing, surrounded by Lamas of all countries engaged in continual prostrations.

"In the deserts of Tartary, Mongols are frequently met with carrying on their "shoulders the bones of their kindred, and journeying in caravans to the Five "Towers, there to purchase, almost at its weight in gold, a few feet of earth "whereon to erect a mausoleum. Some of them undertake a journey of a whole "year's duration, and of excessive hardship, to reach this holy spot."—*Huc's Travels*.

The giver of "bride-gift" to Brahmins obtains the joy of the Soors' dwelling for his paternal ancestors; he who has constructed a wâv, a well, a reservoir, a garden, or a house of Devs, or who repairs these, is admitted to Umurpoor, and the giver to Brahmins of mango trees or daily gifts is borne to that abode of happiness in a splendid chariot, upon which four servants sit to fan him with châmurs. They also attain to Swerga who offer their heads to Shiva in the lotus-worship, who take "the terrible leap" from the summit of some consecrated cliff, who drown themselves in the holy waters of the Ganges, or commit suicide in any of those other modes which the Hindoo scriptures have invested with the character of meritoriousness. Of such self-sacrifices that of the Sutee is the most remarkable, as it has also been the most common. The wife who burns with the corpse of her lord lives with her husband as his consort in Paradise; she procures admission also to that sacred abode for seven generations of her own and his progenitors, even though these should have been consigned, for the punishment of their own misdeeds, to the abodes of torture over which Yuma presides. "While the pile is preparing," is the exclamation of the Brumh Poorân, "tell the faithful wife of the greatest "duty of woman; she is loyal and pure who burns herself with her "husband's corpse." And the Gurood Poorân declares that the Sutee lives with her husband in the unbroken felicity of Swerga for thirty-three millions of years, at the end of which period she is re-born in a noble family, and re-united to the same well-beloved lord.

Sometimes, instead of joining in the ring of mourners, the wife of the deceased sits awhile silent and stern. Presently, with wildly rolling eye and frantic gesture, she bursts forth into exclamations of "Victory to Umbâ! Victory to Runchor!" It is believed that "Sut has come upon her," that she is inspired, or rather has already assumed the nature of those who dwell in Swerga. The hands of the new Devee are impressed in vermillion upon the wall of her house as an omen of prosperity; the same hands are imposed also upon the heads of her children. Her family and friends seek her benediction, and question her of the future; her enemies strive, by submission, to avert her anger, or, trembling, hide themselves from her curse. The raja and his chiefs approach her presence with offerings of cocoa-nuts and bridal vestments, she is set upon horseback, and, preceded by music, goes forth to accompany her husband to the pyre. Dressed in her most splendid garments, in procession such as that of marriage, she passes through the town, the people bending before her, and pressing to touch her feet. She cries, "Quick! quick! my lord will chide my delay, he is already getting "to a distance from me!" She is eager "to join her lord through "the flame." "Victory to Umbâ! Victory to Runchor!" is still her cry, and it is taken up by those around her. When she reaches the gate of the town, she makes the auspicious impression of her hands with vermillion upon its doors.

The pile of the Sutee is unusually large; heavy cart-wheels are placed upon it, to which her limbs are bound, or sometimes a canopy of massive logs is raised above it to crush her by its fall. She seats herself with her husband's head reclining in her lap, and undismayed by all the paraphernalia of torment and of death, herself sets fire to the pile. It is a fatal omen to hear the sound of the Sutee's groan; as, therefore, the fire springs up from the pile, there rises simultaneously with it a deafening shout of "Victory to Umbâ! Victory "to Runchor!" and the screaming horn and the hard rattling drum sound their loudest until the sacrifice is consummated.

These spectacles, so full of horror, are now, it is true, but rarely witnessed: they still, however, occur sometimes.[1] The rite was compulsory only in the case of Rajpoots; by some castes of Hindoos,—as, for instance, by the Nâgur Brahmins,—it was never practised at all.

Goozerat is covered with monuments, more or less permanent, pointing out the spots whence mortals have departed to Swerga. These are sometimes merely unhewn stones, smeared with red-lead, or heaps, such as we have described, loosely thrown together, but more usually engraved head-stones, either standing alone, or covered by the pavilions called Chutrees, and not unfrequently temples of greater or less size, which enclose an image of the Dev. The sculptured monuments are called "pâleeyos." They bear a rude representation of the deceased warrior mounted upon his war-horse, or driving his chariot, according to the circumstances which may have attended his fall. The pâleeyo of the Sutee is distinguished by a woman's arm adorned with marriage bracelets. A dagger piercing the heart or throat of a man often shows the spot where a Bhât has slain himself in Trâgâ. Beneath the sculptured bas-relief is written the name of the deceased, the date of the death, and usually an account of the circumstances which preceded it. These funeral monuments, frequently in great numbers, fringe the reservoirs of water, or cluster around the gateways of the towns. At each pâleeyo the relations of

[1] On the 1st of October, 1853, the wife of the Wâghela chief of Âloowâ became a Sutee at that village, in the Guikowâr's district of Kuree.

the deceased worship once a year, either on the anniversary of the peath, or on some other day appointed for festival, and when a marriage takes place in the family thither the bride and bridegroom repair, to pay obeisance to their beatified ancestor.

Some of these monuments attain insensibly to a high degree of sanctity. If a person who has made a vow at one of them chance to obtain the object which he had in view, his gratitude leads him to spend money in entertaining Brahmins at the pâleeyo, or even in erecting a temple there. In either case the fame of the Dev is spread by those who are interested in maintaining it, and others are attracted to the now general worship.

The temple of the Devee Boucherâjee, as we have seen, grew up out of a rude stone placed to commemorate the death of a Chârun woman. Another much worshipped shrine in the Runn of Kutch, on the road from Hulwud to Âreesur, marks the place where Wurnâjee Purmâr, a Rajpoot chieftain, was slain in the garments of his hardly-celebrated marriage, when pursuing a band of predatory Koolees who had carried off the cattle of his town. One of the most interesting, probably, of the later cases of canonization, is that of Sudoobâ the Bhâtun, which we now propose to describe to our readers.

In the year succeeding that in which the victor of Assaye had crushed the power of Napoleon, the city of Ahmed still owed a divided duty to the Peshwah and the Guikowâr, whose representatives held their respective courts in the two citadels called the Budder and the Huwelee. At this time a set of men of bad character, called Chârdeeâs, followed in the city the trade of common informers. The Chârdeeâs were a source of revenue, and as the governments of that day had but one idea—that of filling their coffers by any and every means—they were esteemed by their rulers in proportion to the gain which was acquired through their agency. A common mode of extorting money, pursued by the Chârdeeâs, was that of accusing respectable women of loose behaviour. They sometimes also procured females of blemished character to name as their paramours men of wealth, from whom the Hindoo rulers, on the ground of their immorality, exacted fines. Of these the Chârdeeâs retained a fixed share, but they also took care to secure perquisites of their own appointment.

The most notorious of these informers was a Wâneeo named Ootum, who lived in the division of the city called Shahpoor, near which is the Bhâtwârâ. This Chârdeeâ, it is said, attempted, without success, the virtue of Sudoobâ, the wife of a Bhât named Huree Singh. In revenge of his repulse, he brought against her a false accusation of adultery, and having procured officers from the Peshwah's governor, proceeded one night to arrest her. The Bhâtun made many protestations of innocence, and ineffectually appealed to the mercy of the Chârdeeâ. He refused to forego his gain and his revenge. The officers were dragging her away, when the terrified woman cried to her husband to preserve her honour by those dreadful means which the Bhâts well knew how to employ. Huree Singh, thus adjured, brought from his house his infant child, and killing it, hung it up in its cradle to the branch of a mango tree, which stands in the centre of Bhâtwârâ. Notwithstanding this sacrifice, Ootum remained inflexible, and repeatedly ordered the officers to drag her along. Sudoobâ, driven to desperation, at last implored her husband to turn his sword upon herself. The fanatical Bhât, without hesitation, struck her head from her body.

The news spread as the night wore away, and the Bhâts and others who were accustomed to practice Trâgâ, assembled at the spot where the tragedy had been acted. They considered their own honour tarnished by the ill success of Huree Singh's first resort to that peculiar means of compelling acquiescence with demands which they themselves might be next day forced to employ, and the sight of the corpses of Sudoobâ and her child excited them to fury. Seizing whatever weapons first presented themselves, they ran to destroy the Chârdeeâs. By the time that morning broke a crowd of Bhâts was collected around the reservoir in front of the college of Azim Khân, and the once royal entrance to the Budder. Râmchunder Molelkur, the Peshwah's officer, became alarmed at the mass of people which had collected, and the heavy gates of the Budder were already swinging on their hinges, when Ootum, watching his opportunity, rushed into the citadel, and threw himself on the protection of the governor. Another celebrated Chârdeeâ, named Jeewun Joweyree, escaped, also, and found shelter in the Guikowâr's Huwelee. The whole of that day the Bhâts, fasting and thirsty, pursued the Chârdeeâs. Some they beat, others they wounded, and a few they put to death. It is mentioned in a ballad which commemorates the event, that one Chârdeeâ, who had concealed himself in a well, was drawn up by the mob and torn to pieces.

The next day the Bhâts assembled at the Guikowâr's Huwelee, and shouted for the blood of Jeewun Joweyree. The commandant, who was a popular officer, remonstrated with them, entreating them not to dishonour his government by compelling him to surrender the Chârdeeâ, and promising that he would himself expel Jeewun Joweyree in a disgraceful manner from the city. In earnest of this he exhibited the Chârdeeâ to them bound, and with his face blackened. The Bhâts were appeased by the exhibition, and withdrew.

They were not, however, so easily induced to retire from the Budder, and the Peshwah's governor was compelled to seat Ootum on a donkey, and cause him to be conveyed, under the protection of a guard of soldiers, to the Kâlâpoor gate, from whence he was to be expelled the city. The mob followed the procession in silence until it had passed beyond the gate. They then pressed forward, and warned the Mahratta officers that it was high time they should secure their own retreat. The hint was not thrown away: the guard hurriedly retired, and the mob had now their victim in their hands. They cast him from off the animal on which he rode, and stoned him to death, continuing to pile missile upon missile, until they had raised a heap above his corpse. Their work of vengeance thus completed, they dispersed to their own homes.

In July of the year following, as is recorded on a marble slab on the left hand of the entrance, a small temple rose upon the spot where the Bhâtun was sacrificed, and an image of Devee Sudoobâ was installed therein. The sacred basil-tree was planted before the shrine of the new denizen of Paradise, and she who on earth was found incapable of protecting her reputation otherwise than by sacrificing her life, has become, through the virtues of the tree of Swerga, a dispenser of all earthly benefits to those who, with incense, burning of lamps, and offerings of scarlet garments, may be enabled to propitiate the favour of a protectress so powerful.

The souls of those whose virtues in their mortal existence have been of a higher character than such as entitle to the position of a Dev of Swerga, attain to Mooktee or emancipation. Indra's Paradise, it would seem, bears to this higher heaven, a relation such as that which Valhalla bears to the Scandinavian Gimli,—the palace covered with gold, where, after the renovation of all things, the just enjoy delights for ever. Among those who pass to the habitation of the Mookt, Krishn has enumerated in the Gurood Poorân those who sacrifice their lives in defence of a Brahmin, a cow, a woman, or a child. He has further thus declared :—

Uyodhyâ, Muthoorâ, Mâyâ,
Kâshee, Kântee, Uwunteekâ,
Dwârâ-mutee-pooree, understand
The whole seven as moksh-procurers.

Where the Shâlagrâm stone is found,
Where a stone of Dwârâ-mutee,
Where both of these meet,
There is Mooktee, without doubt.

All living things, it is believed, possess three kinds of bodies—those called "sthul," "sookshum," and "kârun,"—as well as the "âtmâ" or soul. Of these bodies we can give our readers but a general description. The "sthul," is the tangible body gifted with ten "indreeyâs," five of which are known to us as the five senses: it possesses also four "untuhkuruns" or inner powers,—those of instinctive desire, perception, reflection, and self-perception or egotism "uhunkâr." The "sookshum" body possesses the five senses, and the "four untuhkuruns." In the "kârun" there are three "goons" or qualities—"râjus," "tâmus," and "sâtwa,"—which find their highest developments in the natures of Brumhâ, Shiva, and Vishnoo. The soul which has attained to separation from these three bodies reaches the state of the Mookt.

The Mookt themselves are divided into four classes,—those who have attained to "sâmeepya," or residence in the habitation of the divinity; "sânniddhya," or access to his presence; "sâroopya," or equality with, and "sâyoojya," or absolute incorporation in, the Supreme. The Mookt of the first three classes are no longer subject to transmigration, no longer amenable to the punishment of their sins, nor desirous of sensual pleasures as the reward of their virtue: they are, henceforth, incapable of sin. It is said, however, that they still retain some remnant of "uhunkâr," and that egotistic pride exposes them sometimes to the curse of the Supreme, which they expiate by residence for a limited term upon earth.

The Vedântee believes that the soul of the Mookt is in corporated with Pur-Brumh; the Shaivite, or Vaishnavite, that it dwells in Kyelâs or in Vyekoonth.[1]

[1] There are eighteen Poorâns, of which ten are Shaivite and eight Vaishnavite; their doctrines are, of course, not always consistent with each other. The followers of Shiva regard Vishnoo as merely the first of his servants, and the votaries of Vishnoo similarly regard Shiva. The Hindoo sects may, for popular purposes, be reduced to these two, for the Vedântees have no great hold on the public mind, and the followers of the Shuktees, or female associates of the two great members of the triad, fall under the head of the disciples of either one or other of these. Both sects, it would seem, believe in Swerga, in Kyelâs, and in Vyekoonth, but the Shaivite regards Vyekoonth, and the Vaishnavite regards Kyelâs as merely a second Swerga. Each sect believes that the heaven of their opponents passes away with Indra's Paradise at the Muhâ Prulây, but that their own heaven is not so much destroyed as re-created—Kyelâs merging into Muhâ Kyelâs and Vyekoonth being elevated into Go Lok.

Brumhâ dwells in Sutya Lok, surrounded by Reeshees and by minor gods. He is employed in creating men, and in recording human destiny. Vyekoonth is the seat of Vishnoo—the heaven which he quitted to assume the incarnate form of Râm. There sits the preserver of the world, enthroned with his consort Lukshmee, attended by Hunoomân, Gurood, and all the other beings whose names crowd his mythic story, and watched by Droov, the north star, the keeper of his royal gate. In Kyelâs dwells Shiva—his bride, the mysterious Doorgâ, by his side – and broods upon his endless task of world-destroying. Before him, habited like himself in ashes, their hair matted upon their heads, Gunesh and his goblin crew lead the frantic dance, and with mad orgies move the gloomy deity to smile.

When the four ages—of gold, of silver, of copper, and of iron—have each passed over one and seventy times, a reign of Indra is complete, and a new sovereign rules in Paradise. When fourteen Indras have ruled, a day of Brumhâ is at an end, and, as the night draws on, Swerga, Mrityoo-Lok, and Pâtâl vanish, to re-appear in the morning. When the deity has lived one hundred years, then rages the Muhâ-Prulây—the great fire deluge which envelopes the universe in one crash of ruin.

As the smoke of this scene of awful tumult clears away, the imagination of the Hindoo sees arising beyond it the form of a new heaven, presided over by the God in whom he has centred his faith. The follower of the Preserver beholds a vision of Go-Lok, where Vishnoo in undisturbed sovereignty dwells—a four-armed deity. Thence it was that the greatest of incarnate gods, the divine Krishn, descended upon earth, and there, in the form of the shepherds and shepherdesses of Vruj, his votaries are now assembled to dance for ever in the henceforth uninterrupted circle of Vrindâbun. The worshipper of the Destroyer, on the other hand, realizes to himself the eternal rest of Muhâ Kyelâs, as yet but symbolized by the un-

The Hindoos, we may here remark, do not discompose themselves at the names of God, or Ullah, because they consider these expressions synonymous with Purumeshwur—the Supreme Being, that is to say, the Purumâtmâ, or Supreme Spirit of the Vedântee, the Shiva of the Shaivite, the Vishnoo of the Vaishnavite. This exalted being, they consider, does not interfere immediately in the affairs of men—no question of scripture is necessarily brought forward by the introduction of his name. But when the names of Jesus Christ or Mohummed are employed, the case is different; the Hindoos understand these to refer to some man who appeared on this earth, whom Mlech believe to be of similar nature with Râm or Krishn, and the belief in whom is necessarily inconsistent with the belief in their own scriptures.

utterable silence of loftiest Himalaya, where, freed from the bonds of a troubled and too often recurring mortal life—a life which yet, in reminiscence, seems to him to have been but momentary—his soul is to find peace in amalgamation with the Being from whom it proceeded, as the reflexion of the moon appearing for a while upon the rippling surface of a lake is suddenly withdrawn to heaven, or as a bubble for a moment is distinguishable, and then bursts upon the ocean-bosom of the One Supreme.

INDEX.

* We have placed the conclusion of the reign of Bheem Dev II. in A.D. 1215 on the authority of the Prubundh Chintâmunee and Rutun Mâlâ. But one of the Aboo inscriptions, translated by Mr. Wilson, and dated A.D. 1231, mentions Bheem Dev as Muha Râj Adheerâj at that date (see p. 211). This inscription is not, however, given in full, and there may be some inaccuracy in Mr. Wilson's statement, the difficulty to which we allude not having been, at the time, under his consideration. It is remarkable that in the sister inscription, No. XVIII., though the authors, Tej Pâl and Wustoo Pâl, speak of Veer Dhuwul as existing, and of their own subserviency to him they say nothing of Bheem Dev. When the disorganisation of the latter part of the reign of Bheem Dev II. is considered, it need not surprise us that the time at which his authority ceased should not be fixed without dispute.

THE END.